MW00445481

Combat Biplanes
of World War II

Aviation titles by the same author:

Aichi D3A1/2 Val
Air Combat Manoeuvres
Avro Lancaster
Close Air Support
Curtiss SB2C Helldiver
Dive Bomber!
Dive Bombers in Action
Douglas AD Skyraider
Douglas SBD Dauntless
Fairchild-Republic A-10 Thunderbolt-II
Fist from Sky
Impact! the Dive Bomber Pilots Speak
Into the Assault
Junkers Ju87 Stuka
Kamikaze!
Lockheed Martin C-130 Hercules
Luftwaffe Colours – Stuka Volume 1
Luftwaffe Colours – Stuka Volume 2
North American T-6
Petlyakov Pe-2 Peshka
Royal Air Force Squadron Badges
Ship Strike!
Skua! The Royal Navy's Dive Bomber
Straight Down!
Stuka at War
Stukas over the Mediterranean
Stukas over the Steppe
Stuka Spearhead
Stuka Squadron
T6 – A Pictorial History
The Sea Eagles
The Stuka at War
Torpedo Bombers
Vengeance!
Zero!

Combat Biplanes
of World War II

A Personal Selection

Peter C Smith

Pen & Sword
AVIATION

First published in Great Britain in 2015 by
Pen & Sword Aviation
an imprint of
Pen & Sword Books Ltd
47 Church Street
Barnsley
South Yorkshire
S70 2AS

ISBN 978 1 78340 054 6

See all Peter C. Smith's books at www.dive-bombers.co.uk

A CIP catalogue record for this book is available from the British Library

Typeset in Minion Pro by
Mac Style Ltd, Bridlington, East Yorkshire
Printed and bound in the UK by CPI Group (UK) Ltd,
Croydon, CRO 4YY

Pen & Sword Books Ltd incorporates the imprints of Pen & Sword
Archaeology, Atlas, Aviation, Battleground, Discovery, Family History,
History, Maritime, Military, Naval, Politics, Railways, Select, Transport,
True Crime, and Fiction, Frontline Books, Leo Cooper, Praetorian Press,
Seaforth Publishing and Wharncliffe.

For a complete list of Pen & Sword titles please contact
PEN & SWORD BOOKS LIMITED
47 Church Street, Barnsley, South Yorkshire, S70 2AS, England
E-mail: enquiries@pen-and-sword.co.uk
Website: www.pen-and-sword.co.uk

Contents

List of Illustrations

1. Avia B-534s lined up on a Czech airfield. The product of a small national aircraft industry, she nonetheless saw a surprising amount of action.
2. An Avia B-534 of the *12 Letka*, Slovakian Air Force. They served on the Eastern Front against the Soviets from 1941, but later briefly operated for Stalin's cause when the tide eventually turned.
3. Fairey TSR Swordfish with floats, of No. 700 NAS, being hoisted back aboard the battleship HMS *Malaya* in October 1941. Although showing but marginal improvement over British torpedo-bombers like the Cuckoo of 1918, the Swordfish had an incredible war record.
4. Fairey Swordfish wearing D-Day 'Invasion Stripes' for her anti-U-boat, anti-*S-boot* and anti-midget submarine operations of 1944–45.
5. The Fairey Albacore, showing how her wings folded back for stowage in aircraft carrier hangars. Fairey submitted much more modern designs originally, but the Air Ministry rejected them all, and even at one point in 1940, stated they considered her to be the equivalent of the Junkers Ju.88!
6. The Fairey Albacore. Introduced as a replacement for the Swordfish, she did introduce a few, minor, improvements, but she was obviously obsolete before she ever joined the Fleet, and half the output went straight to reserve units and was never employed. Her performance proved so indifferent that her predecessor far outlived her in service.
7. Fiat CR.32 fighter planes of the *Baleari Gruppo* with Spanish Civil War markings. This lithe little aircraft fostered the myth in Italy that there was still a major place for the biplane in the front line, a myth that the war in the Mediterranean soon terminated.
8. The Fiat CR.32 was popular with her pilots, and proved highly agile in the air. She earned herself a great reputation pre-war, but was soon phased out of service after 1940 when her limitations were shown.
9. The Fiat CR.42 *Falco* was the Italian equivalent of the British Gloster Gladiator, and in some ways a superior aircraft, especially in manoeuvrability. She was produced late and, due to hold-ups in monoplane developments in Italy, was still the mainstay of their fighter force in 1940 when most other major air forces were converting to the monoplane. The CR.42 suffered accordingly, although in combat with the likes of the Fairey Fulmar, she frequently emerged the victor.
10. A captured Fiat CR.42 *Falco* overpainted in British markings, parked at a snowy RAF Duxford. In duels in the Mediterranean and North Africa, the CR.42 proved able to out-turn both the Fairey Fulmar and the Hawker Hurricane, while being

an even match for the Gloster Gladiator. In her brief appearance at the tail end of the Battle of Britain, however, she was completely out of her depth.

11. The Gloster Gauntlet had left front-line service in the RAF by the outbreak of war. Nonetheless she was pressed back into service in North Africa in 1940 as the RAF's 'Answer to the Stuka!' This is an early prototype machine.

12. The Gloster Gladiator earned fame pre-war for her aerobatics at air shows in the UK and overseas, including many European capitals. Here a flight from No. 87 Squadron RAF performs its famous routine, linked together in 1937.

13. The Gloster Gladiator, although totally outclassed by aircraft like the Messerschmitt Bf.109 and 110, still served in some front-line units of the RAF and FAA in 1940 and 1941. She also served with a wide variety of air forces on combat missions from the Nordic countries to Portugal, Greece and South Africa, and both Nazi Germany and the Soviet Union made some use of the ubiquitous Gladiator.

14. A Gloster Gladiator at Malta, known to the Maltese as *Faith*, serial number N5520. It was one of very few operational Gladiator fighter aircraft able to dispute the air space over the Island with the *Regia Aeronautica* in June 1940. The fuselage of *Faith* still survives to this day at the Malta War Museum, at Fort St.Elmo.

15. The Hawker Audax Army Co-operation aircraft. It was one of a highly successful string of 1930s light bombers from the same manufacturer, which included the Hart, Hind, Hector, Hardy, Hartebeest, Nimrod and Nisr. The Audax variant saw combat in British's 'Colonial' episodes of World War II – including the rebellion in Iraq, the pro-Nazi insurrection in Iran, and operations in Somalia and Ethiopia against the Italians.

16. Hawker Audax Army Co-operation bomber. The Audax saw widespread usage on the fringes of Empire in the Middle East and East Africa. This machine belonged to No. 16 Squadron, RAF, in the late 1930s, and features the gold and black cross keys, symbolizing unlocking enemy secrets by day and by night.

17. Hawker Fury fighters of No. 15 Squadron, RAF, stacked up. This delicate little aircraft was the first RAF fighter to fly at more than 200mph (320km/h). Although outdated by 1939, she saw service with several foreign air forces during WWII.

18. The lone Norwegian Air Force Hawker Fury. Norway took delivery of just one machine in 1933 for evaluation, but, after trials, plans to home-produce the type under licence were abandoned in 1936 in favour of the Gladiator.

19. The Heinkel He.50. The first purpose-built dive-bomber for the Luftwaffe, this is an early example, D-IMAA, in her pre-war guise. Rapidly replaced in operational units, first by the Henschel Hs.123 and then the Junkers Ju.87 Stuka, the He.50 still had a meaningful combat role in World War II as a close-support aircraft.

20. The Heinkel He.50, another early model, D-IMOE. The type was a development of an Imperial Japanese Navy order from the Heinkel GmbH, which went on to become the first Aichi D1A naval dive-bomber in Japan. The He.50 itself went on to serve on the Eastern Front in World War II.

21. The Heinkel He.59. Among her many roles was that of air-sea rescue (*Seenot*) duty, which began in the Baltic and later extended to the North Sea, the English Channel

and the Mediterranean. These aircraft also rescued many Allied aircrew as well as German, but Churchill ordered that they all be shot down and many were.

22. A Finnish Heinkel He.59. Heavy, solid and reliable, the He.59 was a stalwart, especially in the Luftwaffe's float-plane armoury, despite her mundane performance. Her missions included mine-laying, special operations transport during the invasion of Holland, and reconnaissance over the Arctic. The Finnish Air Force operated four of them in the period 1943–44.

23. The Henschel Hs.123. She wears the Luftwaffe's 'splinter' camouflage pattern. During the Polish campaign she was highly regarded as a ground-attack aircraft and continued on front-line service for many years on the Eastern Front.

24. The Henschel Hs.123. This is the first prototype, V01, D-ILUA (Werke No. 265), which first flew on 8 May 1935. Indifferent as a dive-bomber, she proved so successful as a ground-attack machine in the Polish campaign and on the Eastern Front that a new production run was called for, but, by that time, all the jigs had been destroyed.

25. A Nakajima E8N *Dave*, being hoisted aboard a Japanese cruiser in April 1939. Photo from the US National Archives, showing the return of the body of the Japanese Ambassador Hirosi Saito to Japan aboard the US heavy cruiser *Astoria* after his demise, via www.ussastoria.org.

26. The Nakajima E8N *Dave*. She proved an agile and nimble fighter aircraft, despite her floats, but was outclassed by US Navy carrier types at Guadalcanal and beyond.

27. The Polikarpov I-15 *Chaika* (Seagull), so named because of her central upper wing form. Despite her tubby appearance she was highly regarded in the late 1930s, but by World War II had become totally outclassed.

28. The Polikarpov I-15 *Chaika* on a forward airstrip. Those that survived the initial Luftwaffe onslaught of June 1941 were pressed into service in the ground-attack role.

29. The Polikarpov Po-2. This little crop-sprayer turned out to be a hidden gem, her very obsolescence being turned into a multi-role versatile combat aircraft and all-rounder, including air ambulance, liaison machine and night harassment unit. She belied all rational ideas by proving to be one of the longest-serving of all combat biplanes.

30. The Polikarpov Po-2, Derided as the *Mule* by incredulous NATO experts, this seemingly unpretentious aircraft was to prove a thorn in the side of the United States during the Korean war. Too slow for jet aircraft to shoot down without stalling themselves, her fragile frame was also almost radar proof. In essence she could be said in some ways to have been the first 'stealth' bomber!

31. Supermarine Walrus coasting along in pre-war livery. This aircraft belonged to the New Zealand manned light cruiser *Leander* and was lost in an accident in July 1939. This official photograph was taken by the late Allan C Greene (1878–1954).

32. A Supermarine Walrus being catapulted from the light cruiser *Bermuda* in 1943. By this period of the war, the widespread introduction of escort carriers was making such cumbersome shipborne aircraft redundant, save for ASR work in the East.

(N.B. All the above images were originally created prior to 1 August 1989; none are engravings; all are photographs and therefore in the Public Domain. Of those taken by representatives of the United Kingdom Government and taken prior to 1 June 1957 HMSO has declared that the expiry of Crown Copyrights applies worldwide.)

Introduction

The biplane age is principally associated with the Great War (along with the triplane) and its immediate aftermath. Images of the Red Baron and other fearless aces duelling in almost medieval aerial aerobatics over the stagnant Western Front are the images that first come to mind. Or whirling battles with vividly coloured aircraft enmeshed in swirling dances of death in a circus of swarming aircraft. In truth the chivalry associated with these first air warfare combats was never that widespread while the carnage and slaughter inflicted was, *pro rata*, on the same ghastly scale as the rest of that hideous conflict. Over the years, in the 1920s 'barnstorming' era of the biplane the image changes from dedicated one-on-one legalized murder to derring-do of a different calibre with crazy and fearless men (and women too) dicing with death in aerial gyrations of a different nature, and daring flights around the world in machines composed of flimsy wires and struts, much as in the pioneering days of aviation.

By the time the Second World War broke out in 1939, the biplane in most countries' national air forces was a relic of that past age. The monoplane dominated both the fighter and the bomber arms, whether it be the British Hurricane and Spitfire, or the German Messerschmitt Bf.109 and 110 in the Battle of Britain; the British Blenheim and Wellington or the German Junkers Ju88, the Heinkel He111 and the Dornier Do.17, or even the crank-winged Junkers Ju87 – it was monoplanes that opened the war in the air and even Poland offered combat with the parasol-winged PZL P7 and P11 fighters and ground attack units equipped with the PZL 23 *Kara* and the 37 *Los*.

In Italy, it was the mass ranks of the Caproni, Fiat and Savoia-Marchetti monoplanes that Mussolini promised would dominate the skies over the Mediterranean. In the Soviet Union it was the same with the Rata fighter cutting her teeth in the Spanish Civil War and against the Japanese in the Far East in a couple of little undeclared 'incidents', while the Japanese themselves were drubbing the Chinese with the Mitsubishi Type 96 monoplane, and were soon to introduce the world-beating Mitsubishi *Rai-sen*, soon to earn fame as the Zero fighter, but still employed the Nakajima E8N floatplane aboard their heavy warships in the early stages of the Pacific War. In the United States the Curtiss Company was replacing its biplane Hawks with monoplane types, the Lockheed P-38 Lightning and Bell P-39 Airacobra, while the little Boeing P-26 Peashooter had been in service many years.

However, some biplanes *did* linger on in front-line service in many nations. It is to the shame of British politicians of this era that the majority of them were in RAF or RN service, showing just how neglected our defences had become. Indeed, in 1940, Britain was still designing warplanes of the biplane type, *viz* – the Fairey Albacore! But if the

British led the way in retaining obsolete machines, other nations also contributed to the total, surprisingly, the Luftwaffe of Nazi Germany and the Soviet Air Force as well. Even the Americans were still flying biplanes (the Curtiss Hawk) in 1939 and 1940, although these were replaced before she herself was forced into the war in December 1941, whereas the British continued to use such aircraft until 1945 and beyond.

Just as remarkable as their continued employment and longevity in combat roles was their resilience. Totally outclassed they might have been, but somehow biplanes continued to be of value, and some, like the Walrus, continued to be employed into the immediate post-war years.

It should also be stressed that this book does not pretend to list *each* and *every* biplane that took part in World War II; even the most fanatical rivet-counter among the critics would be hard-pressed to do that. I am well aware that the RAF still flew the Hawker Hind with No. 609 Squadron at Yeadon and the Hawker Hardy was still serving with No. 6 Squadron in Transjordan, the Blackburn Shark was with No. 4 AA Co-Operation Unit in Singapore as late as 1942, and with the Royal Canadian Navy until 1944, and that the Hawker Hart still flew in some services' air forces. The old Saunders-Roe London biplane flying boats served at Gibraltar in 1940 as did No. 240 Squadron, which also used some Supermarine Stranraers. Another seaplane survivor was the Supermarine Sea Otter, which was still in production in January 1946, a true survivor. Antique Fairey Gordons of No. 4 FTS helped rout the Iraqi Army at Habbaniya in May 1941. Also that the Fairey Fox was operational in May 1940 with the Belgians and others, that the French Breguet Bizerta flying boats were used by both their owners and requisitioned for operational use by the Luftwaffe during the Battle of Britain and that the Luftwaffe also used the Heinkel He.60 float-plane in Norwegian waters in 1941–2; also that the Dutch in the Netherlands East Indies still had the Koolhoven FK-51, and even that the Philippine Air Force was still flying the Keystone B-3 in 1942. One could go on, but the aircraft in these pages are the ones I have selected as meriting fuller descriptions and lack of space meant the line had to be drawn somewhere.

This book is a tribute to these dinosaurs of the skies and a memory of the brave men who flew them against all odds.

Peter C. Smith
Riseley, Bedford, April 2014

Acknowlegements

I would wish to gratefully acknowledge the enormous help I have received in researching this book. Many contributors wish to remain anonymous, but their invaluable assistance is appreciated very much. Among a great many kind and knowledgeable people who have given me their input are:

Tinus le Roux; Torben Jorgensen, Danish Aviation Historical Society; Kirk Kiñnear, South African Air Force Museum; J. N. Houteman; Susan H. Dunn, Senior Archive Officer, Fort Queenscliff, Victoria; Mirek Wawrzyński; Geoffrey Negus; Rudolf Höfling and Dean Wingrin.

Last, but by no means least, I would like to thank my helpful editor, Ting Baker, who steered the work though with the usual patience and skill.

Chapter One

Avia B-534

One of the most advanced and civilized nations in Europe in the period known as 'between the wars', Czechoslovakia was established from the wreckage of the Austro-Hungarian Empire in 1918 as a democracy and remained one at a time when most European nations were turning into dictatorships. The nation thrived and one of the industries that blossomed was that of aviation, with firms that embraced the new technology and brought to it fresh ideas and designs and would, in the end, produce one of the most advanced and successful biplane fighters of all time. One of these firms was the *Avia Aksiova Spolecnost Pro prumysi letecký* (Avia Aksiova Aircraft Industry Company), which was originally established in 1919 by a quartet of engineers, designers and businessmen,[1] and produced a string of successful civilian and military aircraft, including the BH-3, a monoplane fighter, in 1921; the BH-6, a biplane fighter, in 1923; the BH-17, a biplane fighter, in 1924; and the BH-33, another, in 1927.

This innovative company attracted the attention of, and was subsequently absorbed by, the Škoda armaments giant in 1928. The original plant became the largest aircraft manufacturer in the country and the site was moved to Letňany, Prague, as it expanded. Fresh biplane fighter designs continued to flow, with the BH-34 of 1932 and the B-234 in 1932. Prague looked to France and Moscow for her protection, but continued to develop her own defences, and the culmination of these fighting aircraft came in 1933 with the outstanding B-534.

In the autumn of 1938 the Czech nation itself was sacrificed by its French ally and the British Government during the shameful period of appeasement at the Munich 'Agreement',[2] and the rump states that remained lost their final vestiges as an independent nation when Bohemia and Moravia were absorbed by Germany in the spring of 1939, without protest from either Paris or London, and Slovakia itself became an independent state. However, during the two brief decades of existence, the little country had led the way in biplane design, with the apex of its achievement being the Avia B-534.

Having hardly progressed much beyond the Great War stage, it had been decided by the Avia Board of Directors in 1931 to originate a more radical approach to fighter aircraft. The chief designer, František Novotyný, had had previous experience with the Military Aircraft Factory and Hawker in England, where he absorbed the techniques of steel and aluminium alloy construction that they were employing. When Avia's chief designer, Pavel Benes, left the company the year before Novotyný had been offered the vacant position and accepted it. He and the company decided on a multi-project approach to the problem. He brought this fresh thinking to the commercially orientated company, and this contrasted with the Czech nation's own Ministry of National Defence, whose obsession was with wooden aircraft, seemingly more concerned with keeping the state-owned Air Races unit in production, rather than providing modern fighter planes.

The B-34 made her maiden flight on 2 February 1932 with the 850hp (625.17kW) 12-cylinder VK-105 engine, an updated version of the Hispano-Suiza HS-12Ydrs but she was just the basis, the original genus, of Avia's myriad-approach pattern, the others being five more projected designs, the B-134, BH-234, BH-334, BH-435 and BH-534, all of which incorporated different engines, structural solutions and ideas. Comparison tests were done against the Praga E-44 (BH-44) and the Letov Š-231, both home-produced biplanes. The Letov, of which twenty-two only were built, was adopted by the Czech Air Force but quickly sold off to Spain as being inadequate; the E-44 was designed by Novotyný's predecessor, Benes, but did not come up to par.

Two prototypes were constructed, B-534 and B-534-1-2, which adopted the Hispano-Suiza 12 engine of the B-34.

From these sprang the B-534 Series I, which featured an open cockpit, with four machine-guns in two pairs mounted either side of the engine line on the upper wing. It had a metal instead of a wooden propeller. The initial contract was promulgated by the Ministry of National Defence on 17 July 1934 for forty-six machines and the orders that followed took the total to one hundred of this model. They received the serials B-534.2 to B-534.101 inclusive. The first machine of the initial contracts for 147 was delivered to the air force in autumn 1935. Further orders quickly followed and as the war clouds gathered a third in 1936, a fourth in 1937 and, when on the brink of extinction, a fifth in August 1938 for sixty-eight more aircraft, bringing the total on order to 445.

The Series II, was as before but with the machine-guns grouped in pairs either side of the engine in blister fairings; they also had under-wing racks for small bombs. Forty-six machines of this version were built and they were allocated serials B-534.102 to B-534.147 inclusive.

The Series III was similar but with an improved front engine air intake with greater streamlining with the air intake forward. The wheels were now fitted with factory-equipped mud-spats; forty-six were ordered, twenty were foreign orders. Only twenty-five Czech machines of this variant were completed and they received the serial numbers B-534.148 to B-534.173 inclusive.

The Series IV featured a fully enclosed cockpit, with the rear-sliding pilot's canopy extending along the raised after fuselage. An initial order was received for 134 of this variant, but eventually Avia produced a total of 252 in several separate batches as the tension with Nazi Germany ratcheted up, a second batch of fifty being followed by a third for another 87 in August 1938. They were allotted the serial numbers B-534.174 to B-534.445 inclusive, but not all were completed by the time the Germans took over.

With the designed Bk-534 (the k was for *kannonen*), it was planned to incorporate the 20mm FFS Oerlikon cannon firing through a hollow propeller boss. However, this weapon was never fitted due to supply shortage for this very popular weapon, and instead the machine was armed with three 7.92mm machine-guns with one fitted to starboard and two to port. Initially the Government issued a contract in 1937 for fifty machines, with a supplementary order for four additional aircraft, and these were allocated serials Bk-534.501 to Bk.554 inclusive. Just prior to the Munich conference a second full order for a further sixty-six was placed in 1938 and they received serial numbers Bk-534.555 to Bk.534.620. By the time production began almost all of these went straight to the Luftwaffe. Some of these featured a castored tail-wheel in place of the normal tailskid.

The Avia was a staggered-wing, single-bay biplane fighter with the upper wing supported by N-shaped sloping struts by the lower wing and upper fuselage. The wings were of trapezoidal form cross-form, built from Dvuhlonzheronnoe[3] riveted steel with fabric covering and with ailerons on upper and lower wings. The bonded fuselage frame was likewise riveted and bolted, with removable metal panels forward and fabric covering abaft the cockpit area, as was the tail assembly, which had supporting ventral struts to the after fuselage. A deep radiator and intake was straddled by the fixed undercarriage struts, with oleo-springing and wide-bodied tyres and streamlined 'half-spatting', lacking on the early prototype, introduced. The second prototype introduced an enclosed cockpit, had a larger rudder and modified undercarriage fairings.

The Avia had an overall length of 26ft 10.75in (8.20m), a height of 10ft 2in (3.10m) and a wingspan of 30ft 10in (9.40m). The wing area was 253.61 ft^2 (25.56m^2). The Series I had an empty weight of 3,053.40lb (1,385kg) and a fully laden weight of 4,217.44lb (1,913kg). The power-plant was the 850hp (625.17kW) inline Avia (ČKD) HS 12Y drs (the in-house, licence-built Hispano-Suiza HS12Y drs). The Series I achieved a maximum speed of 219.34 mph (353 km/h), with a climbing speed of 16,404 ft (5,000m) in 5.3 mins. She had a surface ceiling of 32,808ft (10,000m) and a range of 360 miles (580km). The Series IV had a maximum speed of 236.12 mph (380 km/h) and a ceiling of 34,777ft (10,600m). The armament of four 0.303in (7.92mm) calibre ×57 Vz.30 (MG.30(t) fixed machine-guns, with 250rpg, two of which were affixed to both sides of the pilot's cabin and the other pair, with 400rpg, also fixed, were emplaced in fairings on the upper wing, close to the Karman connections. There were six small *Pantof* racks under the lower wings, each of which could hold a 44lb (20kg) bomb. The Series II, III and IV differed from this in that the four guns, of the same type, were positioned either side of the cockpit, with 300rpg on the upper and 250rpg on the lower mountings.

Czechoslovakia

The prototype B-534 made her maiden flight on 25 May 1933 with an Hispano-Suiza HS-12Ybrs, imported from France. The intended power-plant, the licensed, Czech-built HS-12Ydrs, was not yet available. When it was, trials and tests followed through to August 1933 with the second prototype piloted by Vaclav Koci. The new fighter was proudly put on exhibition on 10 September at the Army Air Day and drew much admiration for her clean lines. She established the Czech national speed record on

18 April 1934, attaining a speed of 277.26mph (365.74km/h). Unfortunately, both prototypes were damaged by crashes in 1934, but although this caused hold-ups it did not affect the air force's decision to continue to production with the type. The majority of Czech warplanes still flew on the BiBoLi fuel, a mixture of Romanian oil (50%), alcohol (30%) and Benzol (20%), at a time when others were switching to high-octane. The ability to obtain supplies of this mixture proved more and more difficult once the war got underway and helped reduced operational availability in the end.

There was a year's delay between production and the first delivery to the Czech Air Force. The first batch was received by 4 Air Regiment at Kbely airfield, Prague, in October 1935. A second unit, 52 Air Regiment, began equipping at Avia on 14 January 1936 while six machines were posted to the Air Force Training Establishment. Negotiations with the Spanish Government for a contract for a number of these aircraft probably contributed to the delay, but thereafter the Czechs got better service, and 145 machines had been delivered by January 1937 with a further 130 the year afterwards, the 2 Air Regiment changing over that year.

Comparative, if unofficial, tests were conducted against the Luftwaffe's latest fighter aircraft prototypes at the Zurich Air Show in 1937, being measured against the Bf.109 V-8 and V-13, which outshone it, although the Avia outperformed the Henschel Hs.123 V-5. However, as production flowed the B-534 eventually equipped no fewer than twenty-one front-line Czech fighter squadrons, she never got the opportunity to fight for her country of origin, but only for other nations.

There was constant tension with Hungary over disputed territory in Ruthenia that almost led to war and this continued when Slovakia split away.

Germany service

Once they had been taken over by the Germans, all production of the Avia assembly line was halted on 15 March 1939, with 443 aircraft having been completed from the total orders for 534, seventy-two remaining incomplete. B-534 serial numbers allocated were in the range 501 to 620. The Avia aircraft joined other Czech warplanes at Merseburg, Erding, near Munich where they were assigned to Luftwaffe units or to Germany's allies and were organized on the *Avia Lehrganag* (conversion course) at *Deutsche Fliegershule* at Herzogenaurach (Herzaura), Bavaria, for selected German pilots to train on the new acquisitions. In order to provide a steady flow of spare parts the Kunovice airfield plant near Uherské Hradiště was geared up and stocks were held at Olomuc (Holomóc), Moravia, Luftwaffe air depot.

The Luftwaffe incorporated some of these as training aircraft, notably with Theo Osterkamp's I/JG.51 at Bad Aibling from July 1939. Some were re-built with all-round vision cockpits, and served with the *Flugzeugführerschule A/B 115* (FFS A/B 114) under *Kommandeur* Major Otto von Laghmaier, at Wels, Austria and at the *Flugzeugführerschule A/B 114* (FFS A/B 114) under *Kommandeur Oberst* Bruno Wentscher, at Zwölfaxing.

Some Avia B-534s were utilized as improvised *Nachtjagdwaffe* (Night Fighter) aircraft when these '*Wild Sau*' units were first being established in a hurry and being filled with whatever was available. In July 1940 both the 3/JG 70 and the 3/JG 71 at Friedrichshafen (*Bodenee*) by Lake Constance, commanded by *Staffelkapitän Oberleutnant* Heinz Schumann, employed the B-534s briefly before they were replaced with Bf.109Ds early in 1940.

Other B-534s were used as glider tugs with the *Luftlandergeschwader 1* (*LLG.10*) under *Oberstleutnant* Gustav Wilke, and were fitted with a strong hook and associated towing gear for the large type DFS-230A (DFS = *Deutsche Forschunganstalt für Segelflug* – German Research Institute for Sailplane Flight) troop and cargo carrying glider, proving especially useful when they were employed in supplying the German ground forces encircled in the Demyansk Pocket ('*Festung Demjansk*') on the Eastern Front south of Leningrad (St Petersburg) in the awful winter of 1942. The German troops were cut off on 9 February but the DFS-230s with their one-ton cargoes of food and supplies, helped maintain them until they were relieved on 5 May.

Ironically, for being built by a nation 'without sea' during 1940–41 two Avia Bk-534s were employed during catapult trials by the OKL for the *Fleugzeusträger* (aircraft carrier) *Graf Zeppelin* then under construction for the *Kriegsmarine*. Serial No. 594, with German registration D-IWNF, was used from 10 August 1939 by the unit under *FF Dipl-Ing* Sebastian Reccius for rope-restricted landing tests; the second, serial No. 534, with registration D-IUIG, was used from 4 October 1939, to test the cable restriction test landings. Both aircraft were fitted with carrier-type folding tail-hooks for these trials at *Erpobungsstelle See* (*E-Stelle*) at Tavemünde on the Baltic Coast.

During the making of the propaganda film *Kampfgeschwader Lützow* a few B-534s were painted up as imaginary Polish PZL-11c biplane fighter planes complete with mock unit insignia.

Bulgaria

Although Bulgaria was one of many countries that were legally bound by the Versailles Treaty not to operate military air forces, once Adolf Hitler had shrugged that off with the creation of the Luftwaffe, and been allowed to get away with it, the smaller nations lost no time in following suit. In 1937 the official formation of the *Bulgarski Voennovazdushni Sili* (BVVS – Bulgarian Air Force) was announced. When it was decided to add a second fighter unit, the *2 orlyak Istrebitelen* (2 Fighter Regiment) was formed, and seventy-eight Avia B-534s, Series IV, were purchased via the *Wirschaftsgruppe die Luftfahrtindustrie* in Berlin. Of this group, sixty equipped the 2 *Isrebitelen orlyak* (2 Fighter Regiment) with the 212, 312, 412 and 512 *Yato* (squadrons) at Karlovo airfield, near Apriltsi, six formed a staff unit and the remaining twelve went to the training unit at the same base. The Bulgarian pilots nicknamed the B-534 *Dogan* (Hawk). In 1940 2 Regiment was transferred over to Bozhurishte, Sofia, to try and stop reconnaissance flights by Yugoslav Dornier Do.17s.

In March 1942, the *6 Orlyak* under the command of General Avia Kjustenil was formed as a mixed unit, with both B-534s and Bf.109Es, the biplanes being allocated to the 612 *Yato* at Vrazhdebna, Sofia, and 622 *Yato* at Bozhurishte. Their main mission from that summer was the interception of US Army Air Force Consolidated B-24 Liberator four-engined bombers who were making determined attacks on the vital oil installations at Ploiesti in Romania. On 1 August 1943 six B-534s from 612 *Yato* and four from 622 *Yato* were scrambled at 1225 to intercept a large bomber force, part of the 'Tidal Wave' assault that took very heavy losses, but only two of the B-534s, with *Podporuchyks* (Ensigns) Daskalov and Vaptzarov as pilots, managed to close even within sighting distance of the high-flying B-24s over the River Danube and even they could not get close enough to attack. The Avias were just too slow. Nonetheless they were scrambled again at 1500 to meet the same bomber formations making their way back to their bases. Four B-534s from 612 *Yato* and seven from 622 *Yato* intercepted between Vratza (Vratsa) and Ferdinand (now Montana) in north-west Bulgaria, at an altitude of 9,845ft (3,000m) but again they took a long time to close and attack and heavy defensive fire was met, causing several Avias so much damage that they crash-landed and were destroyed after running out of fuel in the effort. Conversely, the thick hides of the B-24s seemed impervious to the B-534s' machine-guns even when hits were scored.

Clearly outclassed, the Avias of the 622 and 623 *Yato* were replaced by Bf.109G2s and G6s and Dewoitine D520 fighters and, finally, the 612 *Yato* as ground-attack machines and were also employed against the communist-backed partisans, until the surviving aircraft were sent to reinforce the 2/2 *Shturmovy orlyak* (Ground-Attack) Regiment. By 30 August 1944, there were still nineteen Avias on establishment, only nine of which were operational. Many of these were destroyed on the ground in the period July–August.

On 7 September 1944, under the young Tsar Simeon II, the Bulgarian Government pulled out of co-operating with the Axis and the B-534s were turned against their former allies. Between 10 September and 12 November the Avias flew 211 combat sorties, mainly ground-attack missions during which they claimed to have destroyed twenty-four heavy guns, fifty-two trucks and four tanks. They also flew sixty-two fighter escort missions, mainly protecting Bulgarian Ju.87 dive-bomber missions. They operated to the last in the area of Tzurkvitza village near Kyustendil, on the Serbian border, but lost serial 62 on 15 September, serial 19 on 18 September and serial 58 on 24 September. On 10 November a final air-to-air encounter between six B-534s and six German Bf.109s left one damaged aircraft from each side. By 1 January 1945 2 Regiment was operating in Hungary with just six operational Avias while some rejoined 2 *Istrebitelen orlyak* (2 Fighter Regiment). The B-534 was not finally pensioned off until the summer of 1945 with the end of the war in Europe.

Greece

Greece was a poor nation and surrounded by potential enemies, especially Turkey to the east and Bulgaria to the north, while Italy, which occupied the Dodecanese

Islands and Rhodes in the Aegean, outflanked her to the south. She could spread her limited resources as best she could but fortunately a few of her richest sons were also fierce patriots. One such was Giorgos Koutarellis, a millionaire expatriate businessman living in Egypt, who purchased outright two Series II Avia B-534s, serial numbers 534.1001 and 534.1002, which he presented as a gift to the Greek Government at a ceremony held at Dakeleia airfield on 18 August 1936. They joined four existing Avia BH.33s already on hand in the *Polemiki Aeroporia* (Hellenic Air Force). They were known as the 'Donation of Koutarellis' and received the serial numbers ΔK1 (1001) and ΔK2 (1002). They were based at Sedes, Thessaloniki, with 1 Flight of 20 *Mira Dioxes* (Fighter Squadron).

During their early service careers these two machines were used to train up new pilots and were not finally called into operational service until 9 December 1940, when they joined 24 *Mira Dioxes* (Fighter Squadron). On 24 January 1941 ΔK1 made a forced landing and suffered very heavy damage. The wreck was transported to the *Κρατικό Εργοστάσιο Αεροπλάνων* (KEA – State Aircraft Factory) to be repaired and restored to service, but she never flew again. Her sister, ΔK2, survived her until 19 April 1941, when she was caught sitting on the ground at Amfikleia, Phthiotis, air base by strafing attacks by Messerschmitt Bf.109Es and, along with many other 24 *Mira* machines, was totally burnt out.

Hungary

During the brief 'war' between Slovakia and Hungary over the disputed territory of Carpathian-Ruthenia in March 1939, one Slovak B-534, that piloted by Joseph Zachar, was damaged by AA fire and had to crash-land in a Hungarian-occupied area. This machine was relatively intact, hauled back to a workshop and restored to full working condition, which included a strengthened wing structure and the fitting of stabilizers. The Hungarians allocated the serial number G.192 to this aircraft and conducted a series of tests and air trials with her against the Italian-supplied CR.32 and CR.42s of their own air force. They concluded that, overall, the Avia was an inferior aircraft, particularly in respect of maximum speed and climb rate. Once these comparative tests had been completed the Hungarian air force had no further interest in her, and, in 1943 they discarded her, handing her over to the Gliding and Aero Club at Győr (Ráb) airfield in north-west Hungary, as a glider-towing aircraft with the civilian registration HA-VAB. When the Soviet army overran Győr in May 1945, she was among the aircraft destroyed in the chaos.

Slovakia

The *Slovenské Vzdusné Zbrane* (SVC – Co-Belligérante Slovak Air Force) was formed when Slovakia broke away from Czechoslovakia on 14 March 1939. They took over seventy-nine Avia B-534s and eleven Avia Bk534s, which formerly belonged to 3 Regiment, and formed three fighter squadrons with them with 11 and 12 *Letka* at

Piešťany, Trnava, and 13 *Letka* at Vajnory, in north-eastern Bratislava. They were soon called to action with the border dispute with Hungary that broke out immediately, but Hitler intervened and imposed a settlement that favoured the latter.

Hungary occupied disputed Ruthenia on 23 March 1939. Next day twenty B-534s, ten each from 12 and 13, were pitted against *Magyar Királyi Honvéd Légierö* (Royal Hungarian Air Force) units that included Fiat CR.32s from the I/1 *Ijász* from 23 March for the next four days. The Avia pilots had been instructed never to open fire first, even when Hungarian aircraft overflew their territory on reconnaissance missions pending an invasion. However, this restraint was not applied by Hungarian dissidents in the region, who, on 23 March, claimed two B-534s shot down by ground fire. That of Joseph Zachar crash-landed and was captured by Hungarian troops.

On 24 March three B-534s from Slovakian 49 *Letka,* commanded by *Porucik* (Lieutenant) Ján Prhácek, engaged three Hungarian CR.32s of 1/1 *Vadászszázad* above Szobránc (now Sobrance). In the ensuing melee *Föhadnagy* (Lieutenant) Aladá Negró shot down Prhácek and *Örmester* (Sergeant) Sandor Szojak shot down *Desiatnik* (Corporal) C. Martis near Lúcky, Kösice, while the third B-534 escaped unharmed. That same afternoon further aerial clashes occurred, two further B-534s being shot down by CR.32s, *Rotmajster* (Sergeant) Ján Hergott close to Bánovce nad Ondavou, Trenčin, and František Hanovec at Szojak, Senné. A third, piloted by *Desiatnik* Martin Danihel of 45 *Letka*, was badly damaged and crash-landed near Brezovice nad Torysa, Trenčin.

After four days' fighting, during which a total of seven B-534s were lost in action, the Germans stepped in and imposed a cease-fire and the 'Border Treaty' of 28 March, the First Vienna Award.

During the German invasion of Poland in September, the Slovakian Avias carried out fighter escort missions on a few Junkers Ju.87 combat sorties. They claimed to have destroyed one Polish fighter but lost two B-534s to Polish anti-aircraft fire.

After this brief taste of action the surviving Avias were relegated to second-line duties, chiefly reconnaissance patrolling and pilot training duties. This period of calm vanished when the Panzers rolled into Soviet-occupied territory in June 1941 with Slovakia as a willing ally. On 6 June the 12 and 13 *Letka*, each with eleven Avias, flew across the mountains into the Ukraine where they came under the control of *Luftflotte* 4 (4 Air Fleet), commanded by *Generaloberst* Alexander Löhr, and were again assigned escort duties for the Junkers Ju.87 along with another Luftwaffe biplane, the Henschel Hs.126, working with the *Aufklärungsgruppes* (Reconnaissance Groups) 3.(H)/Aufkl. Gr 32 and the 32 (H) 4/ LufAufkl, Gr.32. Here they undertook a variety of missions, but mainly acted in the ground-attack role as well as fighter patrolling.

The Slovak B-534s performed commendably within their limitations, and between June and 16 October 1941, they flew 1,119 combat sorties, which broke down into ninety-one fighter escort missions, mainly escorting Slovakian Junkers Ju.88 bombers; plus fourteen ground-attack and fourteen dive-bombing attacks. The Avias were involved in fifty-eight air-to-air fights during which they claimed to have destroyed four Soviet fighters. The first of these kills was claimed by Josef Pallenicek.

At the end of this period the Slovak Avias returned home and were gradually replaced by Bf.109s. The B-534s continued to find useful employment in back-area missions, such as anti-partisan patrols, which steadily increased in intensity.

When the tide turned and the Red Army began to remorselessly roll westward after the Kursk battles in the summer of 1943, Germany's allies on the Eastern Front began to nervously re-adjudge their position. On 31 August 1944 there was a Communist-inspired uprising in Slovakia and fighting lasted throughout September. Colonel Viliam Antoniov Talský's part in it ensured that the Czech air force was deeply involved.[4] Many Avia pilots went over to the Russians, while a few of the remainder tried to hold together as a cohesive force but switched allegiance and began to attack their former allies. They took control of four B-534s and a single BK-534 from the *Letecká skola Slovenských vzdusnych zbraní* (Slovakian Air Training School), commanded by Major Ondrej Ďumbala, at Trenčin, for this purpose.

During this confused period, with neither friend nor ally being completely certain of how things stood, the last biplane victory was claimed by Slovak pilot František Cyprich. He was conducting a test flight with a B-534 (serial 217) that had no radio fitted, at Tri Duby (now Silač), on 2 September and, while landing, was informed a hostile aircraft was approaching. It turned out to be a Hungarian-crewed Junkers Ju.52 3m transport, piloted by *Föhadnagy* (Lieutenant) György Gáchi, *en route* to Krakow, who, seeing the yellow markings that signified Axis aircraft, and knowing nothing of the Slovak change of sides, naturally assuming the B-534 to be friendly, was taken by surprise when it made two attacks on her. Badly damaged, and with two of the crew killed and two badly wounded, the Ju.52 was forced to crash-land near Banská Bystrica, the surviving air crew and their seven passengers, including two high-ranking officers, managing to join up with Hungarian troops. František Cyprich later made several more claims of kills, but all these were in monoplane fighters. German land forces arrived at the airfield in October and overran it, but not before the two surviving B-534s were burned by their crews and destroyed.

Soviet Union

It is claimed that as many as eight B-534s were acquired by the NKVD's clandestein spy squadron and used to monitor Luftwaffe aircraft over the frontier area during the build-up to Barbarossa in 1941.[5]

Preserved aircraft

1. A mainly replica aircraft, but with several original parts, is preserved at Košice Airport, Slovakia.
2. Another replica is exhibited at Prague Military Museum at Kbely airfield.

Chapter Two

Fairey Swordfish

Between the years 1918 and 1940 British naval torpedo-bombers had hardly improved in any way for more than two decades. The tale was a dismal one. With the Sopwith T1 Cuckoo under the driving force of visionaries such as Murray Fraser Sueter,[1] the Royal Navy had led the world in the development of this form of sea warfare. The Cuckoo was a single-seater biplane powered by a single 200hp (149.13kW) Sunbeam Arab engine, and she had a top speed of 103mph (165.76km/h) at an altitude of 2,000ft (609.6m). The Cuckoo could carry a 1,086lb (492.60kg) Mk.IX 18-inch torpedo externally and she first entered service in July 1918, a total of ninety being delivered by the time of the Armistice. The Admiralty had plans to attack the German High Seas Fleet, which had been skulking in its home ports since the Battle of Jutland and refusing to fight, by sending in a striking force of 120 of these machines from five aircraft carriers. This would have been a spectacular attack, pre-dating and far exceeding both Taranto and Pearl Harbor by more than two decades, but the war ended before it could be implemented. The last of the Cuckoo type were not finally retired until 1923 and served aboard the carrier *Argus*.

Even before the war terminated the Admiralty was actively seeking a torpedo-bomber that could carry a much more powerful weapon, the 1,423lb (645.46kg) Mk.III torpedo, which carried a 50 per cent larger warhead and should have proven a far more lethal ship killer. The result was two further torpedo-bombers. The Blackburn Aeroplane & Motor Company, at Brough, Yorkshire, came up with the Blackburd, which had a top speed of 91mph (146 km/h), while Short Brothers, designers of a series of successful torpedo-launching seaplanes, produced the N.1B Shirl, which had a top speed of 92mph (148 km/h). In July 1918 these were trialled against each other with torpedo drops in the River Humber. Only three Blackburds were ever built, but the Shirl, coming out on top, had an Admiralty order for 100 placed. However, this was later cancelled and production was concentrated on further Cuckoo orders.

Meanwhile, the Blackburn Company developed the T1 Swift as a private venture in 1919. The Swift, designed by Major Frank Arnold Bumpus, appeared in 1920 and underwent trials at Gosport and then engaged in deck trials aboard the *Argus* piloted by Flight Lieutenant Gerald Boyce. It was innovative, having a split undercarriage to facilitate torpedo dropping and a self-sealing fuel tank, one of the earliest examples. She attracted much attention, being sold to Brazil, two being bought by Japan, three by Spain and even the United States purchased a couple. An improved version of the Swift was the Blackburn T2 Dart, which had the same 450hp (335.56kW) Napier Lion engine and a maximum speed of 110mph (177km/h) at sea level. She had a range of 410 miles (660km) and 118 were built, including one prototype. Again, trials aboard the carrier *Argus* in 1921 led to her adoption as the standard British carrier-borne torpedo-bomber and orders for 117 resulted, serving with the fleet aboard both *Argus* and the newly converted *Furious* between 1923 and 1933. They showed their potential when, during combined fleet exercises off the Isle of Wight on 9 September 1930, fifteen Darts from Lee-on-Solent, achieved eight direct hits with dummy torpedoes on the fleet, including the new battleships *Nelson* and *Rodney*. This was a far greater potential threat that the much-touted and farcical bombing 'tests' of Billy Mitchell in the States, but received almost no publicity whatsoever.

The Royal Naval Air Service (RNAS) had become part of the RAF in 1918 and the Air Ministry operated all aircraft from the fleet's carriers; in consequence, the development of naval aircraft underwent a dramatic decline. It was regarded as a backwater by the RAF hierarchy, and was granted minimal funding.[2] One Air Marshal, appointed head of Coastal Command, expressed the view that he could not see the sense of approaching a ship target at 200mph (321.86 km/h) and then attacking it with a weapon that could only run at a speed of 40mph (64.37 km/h)[3] The potential power of the torpedo-bomber totally passed him by. Little wonder then, with such attitudes, that Great Britain's commanding lead in this field was allowed to wither and die.

The next stage of development was the Blackburn Velos, developed from the Dart and powered by the 450hp (335.56kW) Napier Lion V engine, as a floatplane. She was a three-seater with twin floats and had a top speed of 107mph (172km/h). Sixteen of these machines were sold to the Greek Navy as coast defence aircraft but she was not adopted by the British. Blackburn continued to develop the torpedo-bomber at this stage, with the elegant Ripon, which became the Dart's replacement. The Ripon was powered by a 750hp (560 kW) Napier Lion XIA engine and had a maximum speed of 126mph (202km/h) but had exactly the same range as the Dart. She first entered service in August 1929 proving most popular with her aircrews, but only ninety-four were ever built, including two prototypes, between 1928 and December 1933, a fair indication of the lack of effort devoted to the Fleet Air Arm. She remained the mainstay of the fleet between 1930 and 1935.

The Blackburn Baffin followed and she was powered by the 565hp (421.32kW) Bristol Pegasus engine, achieving a top speed of 136mph (218.87km/h). Her maiden flight was in June 1933 with Flight Lieutenant Arthur Mitchell William Blake at the controls.

The termination of the Blackburn domination of the British torpedo-bomber concepts came with another biplane design, this one from the design team at Fairey Aviation. However, far from being a breakthrough in design, she was yet another biplane, wire-and-struts aircraft that simply followed in the long line of British types that plodded on down the decades adding 10mph (16 km/h) or so to each succeeding model. She was different, however, in that she was to earn fame and renown, not for innovation or design, but for the longevity of her service and her truly outstanding war record. This was the famous and beloved Fairey Swordfish.

Design and development

The Torpedo-Spotter-Reconnaissance (TSR) concept that had dominated inter-war naval air thinking as defined by the Air Ministry, probably reached its apex with the Swordfish, but the concept itself was flawed, the three roles hardly being compatible. It was more a case of restricted funding forcing service thinking into producing 'maids-of-all-work' designs to spread what limited cash there was as widely as possible. Unfortunately, as with the Skua (a dive-bomber expected to act as a fighter aircraft – and wrongly judged as such by posterity) and the Fulmar (made-over light bomber design into a second-rate fighter), such aircraft usually proved 'masters of none'. Certainly they suffered in comparison with their equivalents in the Imperial Japanese Navy and United States Navy, where the sailors retained control of their aircraft and built specialist machines for specific tasks, machines that were a decade in advance of British naval aircraft types.

The origins of the Swordfish can be traced back to an enquiry from Greece for the *Polemikó Naftikó* (Hellenic Navy) to be provided with a coastal torpedo-bomber to replace the existing Fairey IIIF still in service in the early 1930s. This being so they turned naturally to the Fairey Aviation Company at North Hyde Road, Hayes, London, and their chief-designer, Marcel Lobelle, a former Belgian army officer, who was in process of working on two carrier-type aircraft projects, both incorporating the orthodox single-engined, steel-strip-and-tubing with fabric-covering, biplane technology of their day. The enquiry engendered a Private Venture (PV) design adaptable either for a two-seater torpedo-bomber or a three-seater spotter-reconnaissance machine, the TSR II, and which became colloquially known in-house as 'The Greek Machine'.

The Fairey PV was initially powered by the 638hp (478kW) Armstrong-Siddeley 14-cylinder, twin-row, air-cooled Panther VI radial engine, and made her debut flight from the Fairey-owned Harmondsworth field,[4] on 21 March 1933 piloted by Chief Test Pilot Flight Lieutenant Chris Staniland.[5] In July 1933 the TSR II. was re-engined with Roy Fedden's 635hp (474kW) 9-cylinder, air-cooled, Bristol Pegasus IIM, and re-designated as the TSR II. Meanwhile, the Air Ministry had issued their S.15/33 specification, which called for a 'Naval Carrier-Borne Torpedo/Spotter/ Reconnaissance' aircraft, which Fairey's design seemed a viable contender for.

Before things developed along those lines, however, on 11 September 1933, the TSR I. went into an uncontrollable spin and Staniland used up yet another of his nine lives by baling out just in time. This crash was in some ways providential for Fairey because it enabled them to come back with an amended design more attuned to the Air Ministry's requirements and Lobelle, aided by Horace Frank Chaplin, had come up with a re-jigged design, the TSR II. Fairey had eventually submitted not one, but ten differing schemes to meet the earlier Air Ministry S. 9/30, seven of them being conventional biplanes, while three of them were monoplanes. The latter pair, schemes 9 and 10, would have had enormous advantages over the TSR II, for they featured an all-enclosed cockpit, (a most-desirable feature, which was not to appear on the Swordfish until the very last variant, some 110 Mk. II and Mk. IIIs being retro-fitted with enclosed cabins for use by the Canadians, not introduced until ten years later), fixed spatted undercarriage (akin to the earlier Junkers Ju.87 and civilian racing types), telescopic sight, radio and aerials, a smaller, sloping tail-plane, with the entire forward fuselage being metal, with composite structure aft like the Hurricane. They were to offer them up again as alternatives to what later became the Albacore. Sadly, these all proved too visionary for the Air Ministry.

The TSR II machine had an additional fuselage bay and because the centre of gravity (CG) had been suspected as a major contributory factor to the accident with the original, the upper wings were given a 4 per cent sweep to restore the balance. She had her maiden flight on 17 April 1934 and she was submitted to the Air Ministry. There followed a rigorous testing programme at Martlesham Heath, which engendered criticism of stalling potential and a large number of minor modifications. In the interim trials with float-equipped TSR IIs were commenced in November 1934 and were followed by test catapult launchings and sea recovery conducted with the battle-cruiser *Repulse*. On the successful conclusion of these experiments the floats were removed and wheels refitted. Competitors for the new specification included the Blackburn T9 (later to become the short-lived Shark) and the far more visually pleasing Gloster TSR 38, with an in-line engine, but the latter fell out of the reckoning being marred by slow development. The upshot was an order for eighty-six aircraft being awarded to Fairey on 23 April 1935, followed, rather tardily, by an order (contract No. 402278/35 to specification 38/34) for three pre-production (development) aircraft in August, the first being airborne on 31 December 1935. K5661 served at the Technical Development Unit (TDU) at Gosport between November 1938 and May 1942.

The Fairey Swordfish (serial K5936), as she had now been christened, made her debut in July 1936, when she joined No. 825 Squadron aboard the carrier *Glorious* as No. 978. In November of the same year the first Mk. I (serial K8360, coded G3C), went aboard the *Glorious* with No. 812 Squadron and later served in No. 825 Squadron between 1937 and 1938. These were followed by 150 further Mk.Is ordered under contract No. 534297/36 to specification 38/34. The steady flow of Swordfish that followed saw the replacement of both the Fairey Seal and the Blackburn Baffin by combining their mission sets, while the Blackburn Shark, also ordered into production, barely lasted a twelve-month period in active service.[6]

While all around her aircraft design was moving forward at an unheard of pace and technological advances were altering the face of military aviation almost daily, in the world of the Fairey Swordfish construction methods had not advanced much in two decades. What she *did* have, however, was an all-metal basic structure mainly of steel tubing, which was overlaid with fabric. Her three-man aircrew (pilot, observer (optional) and telegraphist/air gunner –TAG), were exposed to all the elements in open cockpits with the barest minimum of shielding, which in operations that mainly centred the North Atlantic and the Arctic, would have been risible if it were not so unnecessary. The straight empennage was braced by a single tail-wheel and had an uncompromising vertical fin with no flair. The wing assemblies featured parallel strutting, with single bays and cabling, and while the re-aligned upper wing had a mild dihedral the lower remained level. For restricted carrier hangar stowage, both wings were hinged at the roots for folding backward. The majority of surfaces were rounded off and contoured where possible.

A comparison with her contemporaries, the Japanese Nakajima 'Kate' and the United States Navy's Douglas TBD-1 Devastator, are revealing of the gulf between them and the Fleet Air Arm.

Aircraft	Type	Crew	Cockpit	Top speed	Normal range	Power plant
Douglas TBD-1	Monoplane	3	Enclosed	206mph (331km/h)	435 miles (700km)	1 × 900hp (672kW)
Nakajima B5N-1	Monoplane	3	Enclosed	235mph (378km/h)	1,237 miles (1,990.75km)	1 × 1,100hp (750kW)
Fairey Swordfish	Biplane	2/3	Open	139mph (224km/h)	576 miles (878km)	1 × 775hp (578kW)

Undoubted anachronism that she was, the 'Stringbag' was to outlive both her rivals in front-line service and was also to see off her immediate successor!

The Fairey Swordfish in classic form featured the 775hp (578kW) Bristol Pegasus IIIM3, 9-cylinder, radial air-cooled, supercharged engine as its power plant, apparently attached to the fuselage in the words of one wit, '...as an afterthought...' The later models of the Mk.II introduced the upgraded 750hp (560kW) Pegasus 30 engine. This engine drove a three-bladed, fixed-pitch Fairey-Reed metal propeller, which had replaced the TSR II's two-bladed prop. This combination gave her a speed of 139mph (224km/h) at an altitude of 4,750ft (1,450m), an advance over the Cuckoo of twenty years earlier of 26mph (41.84 km/h)! Certainly, at encounters like the Battle of Spartivento, against a head wind and trying to get into position against fast Italian heavy cruisers fleeing at 33 or 34 knots flat out, it was a long, long haul under constant fire to get a Swordfish into any kind of attacking position. During the war as the ordnance loadings grew and changed, and additional equipment was incorporated into that antique body, with a 1.5m wavelength Air-to-Surface-Vessel (ASV-II) Mk. X centimetric radar pod strapped between her legs, ASR equipment, and such, even the upgrading of the main engine to the Pegasus 30 proved inadequate to easily assist the burdened-down old lady airborne and with the Mk.III, she was equipped with the RAE's Rocket Assisted Take-Off Gear (RATOG). With this assistance, a pair of solid-fuel rockets on each side of the fuselage, slanting inboard for maximum effect and the rocket exhausts positioned under and astern of the lower main-plane, an initial normal take-off run of 100ft (30m) ensured sufficient forward momentum for the pilot to depress the rocket ignition button on the control column and power her off within 270ft (82m) of firing.

She had a wingspan of 45ft 6in (13.87m), with the lower main-plane being 43ft 9in (13.34m), and a wing-folded width of 17ft 3in (5.26m). She had an overall length of 36ft 4in (11.07m) and a height of 13ft 5.75in (4.11m). The gross wing area was 607ft^2 (56.39m^2). The empty weight for the Mk.I was 4,700lb (2,132kg), while the loaded weight was 8,100lb (3,674kg). The fuel capacity of the Swordfish was a main fuselage-

mounted tank with 155 Imperial gallons (705 litres), with a gravity tank containing a
further 12.5 Imperial gallons (57.1 litres). In addition, a 60-Imperial gallon (273.1-litre)
auxiliary tank could be carried by omitting the observer from the aircrew; or it was
possible to ship a 69-Imperial gallon (314.1-litre) auxiliary tank in lieu of the torpedo
armament. Normal range with a torpedo up was 576 miles (878km), but this could be
extended to a maximum of 1,030 miles (1,658km) with all tanks and just two crew. She
had a service ceiling of 10,700ft (3,260m).

Defensive armament varied, but was usually a single fixed, forward-firing 0.303in
(7.7mm) Vickers machine-gun, housed in the starboard fuselage and with either
another 0.303in (7.7mm) Vickers 'K'/VGO (Vickers Gas Operated) machine-gun or
a 0.303in (7.7mm) Lewis gun with 600 rpg, mounted on a Fairey flexible mounting
located in the rear-cockpit. As a conventional torpedo-bomber the Swordfish carried
a single 1,610lb (730kg) 18-inch (45.7cm) Mk.XII aerial torpedo beneath the forward
fuselage. This weapon had a dual speed setting for 43 or 48mph, (69.20 or 77.24km/h),
a range of 3,500 yards (3,200.4m), and a 388lb (156kg) warhead, with dual contact/
magnetic influence detonator settings.

Alternative offensive loads were legion, but the chief weapons were, as a bomber or
anti-submarine aircraft – two 500lb (226.8kg) bombs under the fuselage and two 250lb
(113.4kg) bombs under the wings with alternative loadings of a single 500lb (226.8kg)
bomb beneath the fuselage and two more under either lower wing or combinations of
up to eight 100lb (45.35kg) anti-submarine bombs, or two to four 450lb (220kg) depth-
charges; as a minelayer, a single 1,500lb (680kg) sea mine. Later in the war the Mk.II
Swordfish was strengthened with metal under-skinning to carry eight 60lb (27kg)
rocket projectiles or 25lb (11.34kg) solid-head armour-piercing (AP) projectiles with
600 yards (549m) effective range against submarines caught on the surface or small
surface warships such as minesweepers, R-boats and S-boats.

The Swordfish, when she first appeared, with her tangle of wires, struts, colossal
appendage of fixed undercarriage and bracing wires, 'tacked on' engine and great
planks of wings, certainly did not inspire any aesthetic feelings among onlookers. In
truth, it was easy to understand why she became, almost inevitably, known and loved
by her more normal *epithet* – 'Stringbag'. That affectionate, if derisory, name, indicating
a random jumble of objects loosely held together, fitted her appearance perfectly but,
thanks to her young aircrew, she was to turn that label into a source of pride and
renown in the years ahead.[7]

What the Swordfish did have going for her, as a weapon of war, was not just her
adaptability (she was designed as a torpedo plane but was often used as a makeshift
dive-bomber down to as low as 200ft above sea level, her frail structure holding together
simply because the assembly of wires and struts kept her vertical air-speed to around
200 knots), ability to absorb punishment (as the *Bismarck* episode showed, explosive
AA shells went *through* her rather than *into* her more often than not), short take-off
distance which proved so vital for escort-carrier operations, (she could leave their short
flight decks and be pulled into a climbing turn at just 63mph (101 km/h) with ease)

and simplicity of construction in the over-stretched British aircraft manufacturing industry, but, in common with most of the biplanes featured in these pages, an agility and durability in service that was second to none. Thus she proved to be the last British biplane in active combat service.

Mk.I

The first batch of 104 were produced from 1936 onward (serial numbers K8346 to K8449 inclusive), the lead aircraft first joining No.812 Squadron aboard the carrier *Glorious*. Seventy-eight of these machines remained on charge in September 1939.

A second batch of twenty-seven (serials K8860 to K8886 inclusive) appeared from April 1937, and soon joined the FAA, of which the first (serial K8873) arrived at Gosport Torpedo Training Unit (TTU) in April.

Some 150 Swordfish Mk.Is were ordered against contract No. 534297/36 to specification 38/34. Serial numbers L2717 to L2866 inclusive began arriving in November when L2717 arrived at Heathrow. Of these, 150 were still on charge in September 1939. A further sixty-two Swordfish were ordered against contract 6712134/37 to specification 38/34 and received the serials L7632 to L7701 inclusive, the first (serial L7651), arriving at the TTU, Gosport, in March 1938. By September 1939 just fifty-two remained on charge.

Orders continued to be placed at regular intervals, and contract 743308/38 to specification 38/34 called for another fifty-two Mk.Is, which had serials L9714 to L9785 assigned to them. Serial 9767 went to No.701 Squadron and, equipped with floats, joined the battleship *Warspite* in December 1938. All fifty-two were still on charge in September 1939. The next contract issued was No. 9363679/38 to the same specification, and these were given the serials in the range of P3991 to P4279 inclusive. In June 1939 P4010 joined No. 810 Squadron's 'A' Flight; in August P4409 joined her and in September P3992 joined No. 825 Squadron aboard *Glorious*. Of this group, 176 had been received on charge as at September 1939.

Blackburn sub-contracted the next batch, ordered against contract B31192/39, and started building them at Sherburn from 1940, with the aircraft receiving the serials in the range V4288 to V4719. Of this batch V4288 was delivered on 1 December 1940, followed by V4289 on 29 December, the rest following during 1941 when float-fitted V4289 went to No. 700 Squadron and served aboard the battle-cruiser *Repulse* from February. The final order for the Mk.I, again, was awarded to Blackburn under contract B31192/39, and received the serials in the range W5836 to W5995. The first twenty-seven from this order arrived at 82 MU in October 1941.

Mk.II

The Mk.II omitted the provision for floats, and later there was little requirement for these once the escort carrier programme got underway. Contract B31192/39 went to Blackburn, the batch receiving serials in the range DK670 to DK792. They were delivered between November 1941 and April 1942, DK674 being taken into No. 786 Squadron in February 1942, DK696 by No. 823 Squadron the same month, DK673 into No. 833 Squadron in May and DK670 by No. 811 Squadron in June of that year.

These were followed, under contract B311923/39, by a further batch, which received serial allocations in the range HS154 to HS678, and deliveries commenced in May 1942. Of these twenty went to HMS *Korongo*, the Royal Navy Aircraft Repair Yard (RNARY) at Athi Plains, four miles south-east of Eastleigh airfield, south of Nairobi, Kenya, which was first commissioned in September 1942.[8] From that distribution centre, HS164 went to No. 810 Squadron and HS161 to No. 811 Squadron, while HS154 joined No. 833 Squadron at Gibraltar in November 1942. Many RNARY-stocked Swordfish survived and were still serving many years after the war.

The next contract awarded to Blackburn was B31192/39 and these Swordfish were delivered from May 1943 onward and were allocated serials LS151 to LS461, of which LS153 joined No. 819 Squadron in June 1943. These were followed by serials in the range NE858 to NF414. They were distributed out to the squadrons from December 1943, when NE861 joined No. 735 Squadron, NE858 joined No. 835 Squadron and NE863 joined No. 811 Squadron, both in January 1944. The Royal Canadian Navy (RCN) received a large quantity of this order, taking serials NF338 to NF413 inclusive, which equipped Nos 119 and 415 Squadrons.

Mk.III

This mark featured the ASV Mk.XI radome. They also came under contract B31192/39. They had serials in the range NR857 to NS484 but NS204 was the final one of one hundred that were actually completed before the contract was terminated. Delivery was from July 1944 onward with NR859 going to No. 835 Squadron at Worthy Down that month. Likewise, the entire batch allocated serials in the range RL435 to RL933 was cancelled in its entirety.

Mk.IV

There was officially no such beast, but the fitting of canopies to Mk.II and Mk.IIIs for Canadian service led to the unofficial term being widely used.

By the war's end, production from the Blackburn Aircraft plant at Sherburn-in-Elmet, Selby, North Yorkshire, numbered 1,699 of the total 2,391 Swordfish produced. Inevitably, the Swordfish built by Blackburn became known in the fleet as 'Blackfish'.

FAA Squadrons

No. 810 NAS had its Blackburn Sharks replaced by Swordfish in September 1939, and twelve of them joined the carrier *Ark Royal*. They served in the Atlantic and then took part in the Norwegian campaign, bombing Værnes airfield, Trondheim, on 25 April

1940. They accompanied the *Ark Royal* to Gibraltar with Force 'H' and at the Mers-el-Kebir operation attacked the Vichy-French battle-cruiser *Strasbourg*, but failed. At Dakar, Senegal, the Vichy-French battleship *Richelieu* was attacked, but again without success. The Swordfish carried out raids against Cagliari airfield, Sardinia, took part in the naval battle of Spartivento, attacked the Tirso Hydro-Electric Dam, Sardinia, on 2 February 1941, but only three out of eight aircraft were able to launch their torpedoes due to intense flak, and they failed to bust it. The fourteen Swordfish also attacked the Azienda Oil Refinery at Leghorn and Pisa airfield on 9 February, while others laid mines off Spezia for the loss of one aircraft, while the battle-fleet bombarded Genoa. They transferred to the carrier *Illustrious* in March 1941, going out to the Indian Ocean with her and attacking the Vichy-French at Diego Suarez, Madagascar, before returning to *Ark Royal* via Durban. There followed Malta convoys, the blockade of Brest and the hunt for the *Bismarck*, and the unit left Ark *Royal* prior to her loss and served at Jamaica until April 1943 when No. 810 NAS finally became a Fairey Barracuda unit.

No. 811 NAS on the outbreak of war was aboard *Courageous*. When she was lost, survivors helped form No. 815 NAS. No. 811 reformed at HMS *Daedelus*, RNAS-on-Solent in July 1941 but with the Vought SB2U Vindicator dive bomber (known as the Chesapeake in the Fleet Air Arm). However, they were converted to Swordfish in November 1941. They were then based at RAF Bircham Newton, Norfolk, conducting coastal, anti-shipping sorties and minelaying under RAF Coastal Command in 1942. On 21 February 1943 they embarked aboard the escort carrier *Biter*, but when she was damaged they went to HMS *Nightjar*, RNAS Inskip, not re-embarking on *Biter* again until 12 January 1944 and here they covered UK to Gibraltar convoys until August 1944. They resumed duties with Coastal Command from RAF Limavady (Aghanloo), Londonderry, Northern Ireland, for a period then re-embarked yet again for final convoy escort work until October, before disbanding in December 1944.

No. 812 NAS equipped with the Swordfish in 1936, replacing the Blackburn Baffin aboard the carrier *Glorious*. In 1940 the unit was transferred to RAF Coastal Command for minelaying and bombing operations until March. She embarked aboard the carrier *Furious* for Mediterranean operations and the farcical attack on Petsamo, Liinahamari, Finland, Operation 'EF', on 30 July 1941, where the harbour was found to be almost bare of shipping and the Germans ready and waiting for them. The squadron lost no Swordfish and transferred to *Ark Royal*, taking part in Malta convoy operations and returning to the UK in April 1942, again under RAF Coastal Command, working over the Channel. On 18 December 1942 No. 812 NAS merged with No. 811 NAS, and then converted to the Fairey Barracuda.

No. 813 NAS was embarked aboard the carrier *Illustrious* and took part in numerous Mediterranean convoy operations and sank the destroyer *Zeffiro* and the 3,955-ton freighter *Manzoni* at Tobruk, badly damaging the destroyer *Euro* and two other freighters in this attack on 5 July. They also took part in the Taranto attack in November 1940. From July 1943 the unit worked out of North Front airfield, Gibraltar. The unit lost Swordfish WS843 when she landed in Spanish Morocco in error and her aircrew were interred. A Flight was detached to Tafaraoui airfield, Algeria, and later took part in the invasion of Sicily (Operation *Husky*) with the Northwest African Coastal Air Force (NACAF) in July 1943. The squadron was then embarked aboard the escort carrier *Campania* for Russian convoy work. Their high point was the destruction of the *U-365* in the Arctic.

No. 814 NAS spent most of the early war period embarked aboard the carrier *Hermes*, hunting German raiders in the Caribbean, South Atlantic and Indian Oceans, and attacking the Vichy French battleship *Richelieu* at Dakar and supporting the suppression of the Iran uprising before joining the Eastern Fleet in March 1942. Assigned to the Madagascar operation, 814 NAS was landed from the *Hermes* at China Bay in order to arm them with torpedoes as a reserve air striking force against the Japanese carrier force known to be approaching Ceylon in April. In the event they were not so sacrificed, although several were destroyed when China Bay airfield was bombed. In December 1942 the squadron was formally disbanded at HMS *Ukussa*, RNAS Katukurunda, Ceylon.

No. 815 NAS formed on 15 October 1939 at Worthy Down from survivors of Nos 811 and No. 812 NAS Swordfish from the sunken carrier *Courageous* and operated from there until May 1940. In May 1940 they covered the Dunkirk evacuations and then were embarked aboard the carrier *Illustrious*, serving at all her famous Mediterranean battles including minelaying missions off Benghazi, and attacks on Rhodes and Tobruk and the Taranto raid, until the carrier was damaged by Stukas off Malta in January 1941. The squadron then served from shore bases at Eleusis, near Athens, Greece and Maleme, Crete and in North Africa and also was engaged in the Syrian campaign, where an excellent result was obtained on 16 June when five TSRs of No. 815 NAS sank the large Vichy-French destroyer *Chevalier Paul* off Sidon. The squadron was then assigned to No. 201 (Naval Co-Operation) Squadron RAF, at Malta, from where they took part in the invasion of Sicily from 10 July 1943. After Operation *Husky* they squadron was disbanded, being reformed later with the Fairey Barracuda.

No. 816 NAS was based at RAF Perranporth, on Cligga Cliffs, north Cornwall, and conducted anti-submarine patrols in conjunction with RAF Coastal Command. The unit was reinforced during the D-Day operations in the summer of 1944 to counter increased U-boat activity trying to enter the English Channel.

No. 818 NAS was formed at HMS *Fieldfare*, RNAS Evanton, Ross and Cromarty, in August 1939. With nine Swordfish they embarked aboard the carrier *Ark Royal* for hunting operations off Norway and then transferred to the carrier *Furious* in time for the Norwegian campaign, her sixteen Swordfish unsuccessfully attacking three German destroyers, *Paul Jacobi*, *Theodor Riedel* and *Hermann Künne*, at Trondheim on 11 April 1940. Disembarked, the unit moved to Thorney Island and RAF Carew, Cheriton, under RAF Coastal Command control for operations over the Channel. The squadron then embarked aboard the carrier *Ark Royal* and with her went to Gibraltar taking part in the Mers-el-Kebir operation and the abortive attack on the Vichy-French battle-cruiser *Strasbourg*. There followed Malta convoys, operations against Spezia, the hunt for the *Bismarck*, where No. 818's Swordfish scored the torpedo hit that delivered that ship up to the British battleships *King George V* and *Rodney,* and, in 1942, the unit converted to the Fairey Albacore.

No. 819 NAS was formed at HMS *Peregrine,* RNAS Ford, Sussex, in January 1940, with twelve Swordfish. The unit moved to the No. 4 RAF Bombing School at West Freugh, Wigtownshire, and then back to Ford. Embarked aboard the carrier *Furious* they took part in the Norwegian campaign, an early loss being U3L piloted by Sub-Lieutenant Sidney George John Appleby and Leading Airman Ernest Tapping, which was shot down in Ofotfiord on 12 April, the two aircrew being rescued by the destroyer *Grenade,* both injured. A detachment of six Swordfish was sent to RAF Detling in May from where it conducted searches for U-boats suspected of attacking the Dunkirk evacuation ships. The squadron was then embarked aboard the carrier *Illustrious* at Bermuda and went out to the Mediterranean with her, working from HMS *Grebe,* RNAS Dekheila, Alexandria, Egypt, from August. In September No. 819 Swordfish dive-bombed the Italian airfield of Calato on the island of Rhodes and the squadron also took part in the Taranto attack in November. When *Illustrious* was crippled by many bomb hits from Junkers Ju.87 dive-bombers off Malta in January, many of the squadron's aircrews were killed and aircraft destroyed in her hangars. The few surviving Swordfish were amalgamated into No. 815 NAS and No. 819 was disbanded.

In October 1941, No. 819 was reformed at HMS *Daedalus,* RNAS Lee-on-Solent, with nine Swordfish. These went aboard the escort carrier *Avenger* for deck landing training in June 1942. During July the squadron served under RAF Coastal Command flying patrols in the North Sea before embarking on the escort carrier *Archer* for convoy work, No. 818 NAS Swordfish sinking the *U-572* with rocket projectiles among the first successes with this weapon. In August 1943 the squadron went aboard the escort carrier *Activity* and with her another submarine, *U-288,* was destroyed. In April 1944 more Coastal Command work was undertaken flying night patrols over the North Sea and from June the unit was based first on the South Coast of the UK, and then moved over to the Belgian airfields at St Croix, Maldeghem and Knocke-le-Zoute from October onward where they operated under No. 155 and then No. 157 Wing, RAF. In February 1945 No. 819 NAS moved to Bircham Newton, Norfolk, where it was disbanded the following month.

No. 820 NAS had their existing Blackburn Sharks replaced by Swordfish in the autumn of 1937 aboard the carrier *Courageous.* In November 1938 the unit moved to the carrier *Ark Royal* until June 1941, serving in her famous exploits in the Mediterranean and the Atlantic until they were transferred to the carrier *Victorious.* The Swordfish went ashore in Iceland in November and were replaced by the Fairey Albacore.

No. 821 NAS had replaced their Blackburn Sharks with the Swordfish in September 1937, and in November 1938 were transferred to the carrier *Ark Royal.* After operating in the North and South Atlantic on anti-submarine and then German raider hunting operations, April saw them involved in the Norwegian operations. On 21 June attempts were made to attack the German battle-cruiser *Scharnhorst* which was returning to Kiel from Norway with an escort of four destroyers and four torpedo boats. Six Swordfish located this powerful force off the Utsire Light (Utsira, Rogaland) and duly attacked, but no hits were made and two of the six Swordfish were shot down.

The squadron was reorganized at Detling in July 1941 and conducted anti-submarine operations in the Orkney Islands before going out to the Mediterranean in November. Here, No. 821 NAS was re-equipped with the Fairey Albacore.

No. 822 NAS was converted from the Blackburn Shark to the Fairey Swordfish aboard the carrier *Furious* in August 1937. By February 1939 the squadron was embarked in *Courageous* but was disbanded when that ship was sunk. The squadron was reformed in October 1941 with Swordfish but in March 1942 converted over to the Fairey Albacore.

No. 823 NAS had the Swordfish from 1937 and served aboard the carrier *Glorious* in the Red Sea and Indian Ocean during the early months of the war. The squadron served at Norway and five Swordfish went down with *Glorious* when she was sunk; the remainder were at RNAS Hatston with No. 821 NAS. On 14 April 1940 they attacked the two German destroyers *Bruno Heinemann* and *Friedrich Eckoldt* returning home from Trondheim, Norway, but without success. The unit was disbanded in December 1940 but was reformed at Crail in November 1941 with Swordfish embarking aboard *Furious* but shortly afterward converting to the Fairey Albacore.

No. 824 NAS serving ashore from the carrier *Eagle*, six Swordfish made a classic torpedo attack in the Gulf of Bomba, Tobruk, on 20 July 1940, sinking the destroyers *Nembo* and *Ostra* and the 2,332-ton freighter *Sereno*.

No. 825 NAS was serving at Dekheila and joined the carrier *Glorious* in September 1939, seeing raider hunting and convoy duties in the Red Sea and Indian Ocean before the vessel was recalled home in April 1940 to take part in the Norwegian campaign where she was sunk. Some Swordfish were ashore at RAF Hal Far, Malta, while the rest returned home with the carrier and were disembarked at HMS *Gannet*, RNAS Prestwick. They were transferred south via Worthy Down to Detling and Thorney Island airfields during the Dunkirk evacuation period under Lieutenant-Commander James Brian Buckley. Losses were heavy – eight of the twelve Swordfish, five on a single day on 29 May. Reinforced by spare aircraft and crews the squadron then embarked aboard the carrier *Furious* from her made night attacks on the ports of Trondheim and Tromsø in September. By February 1941 the unit was still aboard *Furious* off the Gold Coast, escorting troop convoys to the Middle East via the Cape, but she was recalled home in May 1941 to help with the hunt for the *Bismarck*.

On 22 May No. 825 NAS joined the carrier *Ark Royal* and took part in Malta convoy operations and raids on Sardinia until the carrier was sunk off Gibraltar in November. Those Swordfish that were not lost with the *Ark Royal* were assembled at Gibraltar but the squadron was disbanded. In January 1942 the unit was being reassembled at Lee-on-Solent under Lieutenant-Commander Eugene Esmonde when the Channel Dash episode, Operation *Cerberus*, took place between 11 and 13 February. The German battle-cruisers *Gneisenau* and *Scharnhorst* and heavy cruiser *Prinz Eugen*, steamed up the English Channel escorted by destroyers and protected by standing patrols of fighters overhead. Six of 825's Swordfish were flown to RAF Manston from where they flew their forlorn hope mission. Their Spitfire escorts failed to protect them and the Swordfish were massacred by defending Luftwaffe fighter aircraft making attacks with their flaps fully extended to prevent overshooting their target, without the Swordfish being able to score any hits on the German warships. Esmonde received a posthumous Victoria Cross; only five of the aircrew survived.

The squadron continued re-forming at Lee-on-Solent and then joined the escort carrier *Avenger*, from which ship they fought through to Russia on convoy PQ18. They then worked under 16 Group Coastal Command from Thorney Island and Exeter airfields. In March 1943 the squadron embarked aboard the carrier *Furious* and carried out missions from Iceland and off Norway. With twelve Swordfish-IIIs they flew aboard the escort carrier *Vindex* and conducted further Arctic convoy work, the Swordfish sinking, or assisting in sinking, the *U-563* and *U-765* in March and June 1944. In August the twelve Swordfish rejoined *Vindex* and resumed Russia convoy escorting, and assisted in sinking the *U-354* on 22 August, *U-344* on 24 August and *U-394* on 2 September. The squadron then switched to the escort carrier *Campania* for further Russian convoy missions before their Swordfish were merged into No. 815 NAS.

No. 826 NAS first formed as a Fairey Albacore squadron at RNAS Ford, Sussex, in March 1940 and by 1941 was in the Mediterranean with the carrier *Formidable*, where some Swordfish-Is joined on 1 July 1940. The squadron, commanded by Lieutenant-Commander Wilfred Henry Gerald Saunt DSO, took part in the Battle of Cape Matapan in March 1941, damaging the battleship *Vittorio Veneto*, and later took part in the Mediterranean Fleet operations against Tripoli and Bardia. They attacked Luftwaffe bases at Scarpanto Island and when *Formidable* was badly damaged by return Stuka attacks, the squadron operated ashore from Dekheila, Egypt, and then in the North African campaign from Fuka and Ma'aten Bagush Camp, near Mersa Matruh, Egypt, in the desert. During the Syrian campaign in July 1941, the squadron operated from Nicosia, Cyprus, against Vichy French naval units working from Beirut. The last Swordfish left the squadron at the end of September 1941.

No. 828 NAS was another Fairey Albacore unit formed at Lee-on-Solent in September 1940. The squadron was transferred to Malta via the carriers *Argus* and *Ark Royal*, where they had some Swordfish-Is added to their strength at Hal Far airfield, under the command of Lieutenant-Commander David Erskine Langmore, the Swordfish operating from October to November against Axis supply convoys attempting to reinforce North Africa, but losses and accidents soon reduced the number of operational aircraft.

No. 829 NAS was yet another Fairey Albacore squadron, formed at Ford, Sussex, in June 1940. They took part in the Syrian campaign operating from Nicosia, Cyprus, with 815 and 826 NAS and between 31 May and 13 July 1941 these units flew 139 sorties. The squadron successfully attacked the Vichy supply ship *St Didier*, putting two torpedoes into her in Adalia (Antalya) harbour after she had earlier evaded patrols by disguising herself as a Turkish vessel. In August 1941 they had their Albacores replaced by ASV-equipped Swordfish and they embarked aboard the carrier *Illustrious*.

No. 830 NAS was formed from the Swordfish-I of No. 767 NAS detachment at Hal Far, Malta, in July 1940. They made their combat debut with a bombing attack on the port of Syracruse, on 30 June 1940 and attacked Axis shipping targets off Libya and dive-bombed an oil storage facility in Sicily.[9] In January 1942 the Swordfish-Is were replaced with Swordfish-IIs but, by March 1942, losses from varying causes had reduced the operational strength of the squadron to just three aircraft and it merged with No. 828 NAS, becoming Naval Air Squadron, Malta, as a flare-dropping unit. The combined unit was credited with the destruction of about thirty Axis ships with damage to fifty more, but, by March 1943, numbers again became so reduced that the squadron was disbanded, being reformed as a Fairey Barracuda unit in May 1943

No. 833 NAS was formed with Swordfish-Is at HMS *Daedelus,* RNAS Lee-on-Solent, on 8 December 1941, and commanded by Lieutenant-Commander Robert John Hilary Stephens. Swordfish-IIs were added to the strength from January 1942 onward. In January 1944 the squadron amalgamated with No. 808 NAS, being reformed in April 1944, under Lieutenant-Commander (A) Jack Gordon Large, again as a Swordfish-II outfit and operated over the Channel and North Sea sporting D-Day 'Invasion Stripes' for rocket attacks, but was disbanded in September 1944 at HMS *Gannet,* RNAS Eglinton.

No. 834 NAS was formed at HMS *Buzzard,* RNAS Palisadoes, Jamaica, in December 1941, operating Swordfish-Is under the command of Lieutenant-Commander Lionel Charles Brian Ashburner and Lieutenant Leslie George Wilson from the escort carrier *Archer* from USNAS Floyd Bennett Field, New York, and sailed for South Africa. They escorted transatlantic and Gibraltar convoys before being subordinated to 19 Group, Coastal Command, and flew patrols over the English Channel.

In July 1942 Swordfish-IIs joined the squadron and the unit was embarked aboard the escort carrier *Hunter* working in the Western Atlantic area on convoy protection and down to Gibraltar. A Flight was later transferred to the escort carrier *Battler* and with her took part in the Salerno landings in September 1943. The unit embarked aboard the escort carrier *Battler* for Aden and the Indian Ocean and flew anti-submarine patrols with Swordfish-IIs from Bombay, including the search for the German tanker *Brake* and three U-boats refuelling from her. After working from HMS *Ukussa,* RNAS Katukurunda, Ceylon, the squadron re-embarked aboard *Battler* between August and September 1944. The unit was finally disbanded, minus its Swordfish, back in the UK in December 1944.

No. 835 NAS was originally established at HMS *Raven,* Eastleigh, in February 1942 and then moved to HMS *Buzzard,* RNAS Palisadoes, Jamaica, on 17 January 1943. On 12 March the squadron moved to USNAS Norfolk, Virginia, and then joined the carrier *Furious,* leaving Norfolk on 3 April and disembarking at HMS *Daedelus,* RNAS Lee-on-Solent on 15 April. In June the squadron was at HMS *Sparrowhawk,* RNAS Hatston, and then moved to HMS *Blackcap,* RNAS Stretton, near Warrington on 22 September.

The unit was continually on the move, first to HMS *Landrail,* RNAS Machrihanish, on 29 January 1943, then conducted deck-landing trials and then escort duties aboard the escort carrier *Battler* from RAF Kirkistown, County Down, NI, before, on 7 May, returning again to Machrihanish once more for rocket projectile training. On 7 April 1943 No. 835 NAS again embarked aboard the escort carrier *Battler* for a short period before going ashore once more to HMS *Sealion*, RNAS Ballykelly, County Londonderry, on 15 May, moving to HMS *Gannet*, RNAS Eglinton, on 22 May. In June 1943 the squadron was at HMS *Wagtail*, RNAS Ayr. Next base was HMS *Gannet*, RNAS Abbotsinch, before finally joining the escort carrier *Ravager* in September and October 1943, with some Swordfish aboard the carrier *Argus*. The next move via RNAS Eglinton, was to the escort carrier *Chaser* for a three-week spell and then ashore once more to HMS *Sanderling*, RNAS Abbotsinch. On the last day of 1943 the squadron was transferred by the escort carrier *Nairana*, to RNAS Hatson and then RNAS Machrihanish.[10]

The squadron, with fourteen Swordfish-IIIs, under the command of Lieutenant-Commander Val Jones, finally went afloat once more aboard the escort carrier *Nairana*, working in the North Atlantic and protecting the convoys to and from Gibraltar across the Bay of Biscay and then moved to Russia convoy duties through to January 1945. Their final combat duties were sorties against enemy shipping off the coast of Norway in February and March and the squadron was disbanded on 1 April 1945.

No. 836 NAS was unique among FAA Swordfish squadrons flying the Swordfish-II in March 1942, at HMS *Raven*, RNAS Eastleigh, and was then embarked aboard the escort carrier *Biter* in June for the UK where it briefly operated from RAF Thorney Island over the English Channel, commanded from July 1942, by Lieutenant-Commander Ransford Slater, operating under RAF Coastal Command. They then moved to RNAS Machrihanish and were transported aboard the *Biter* to Northern Island where on 15 May 1943 they became the feeder unit for the newly formed MAC ships working from HMS *Shrike*, RNAS Maydown, near Lough Foyle, and crewed by RNVR personnel.

Because of the unusual nature of the MAC ships (they remained fully independent mercantile vessels and the Swordfish aircrew and maintenance teams were the only Royal Navy personnel aboard) several unique solutions (which did not always meet with official approval) had to be adopted to ensure the smooth-running of operations. Thanks to Slater's tact and aplomb this was mainly achieved. Slater himself led by example, making the initial touchdown with a Swordfish on the *Empire MacAlpine* on 7 May 1943; on one occasion he landed on board with two depth-charges still affixed to his aircraft, despite the fact that his tailhook had become detached, for which he received the OBE.[11]

Eventually, like Topsy, No. 836 grew and grew, absorbing over time both Nos 838 and 840 NAS as well as the former 700 Flight and also had elements of Nos. 833 and 834 NAS among its aircraft. From an original establishment of twenty-seven, at its peak some ninety-one Swordfish were on the strength of No. 836 making it easily the largest squadron in the FAA, more so when No. 860 was also added from December 1943. This latter unit was a Royal Netherland Navy squadron that had originally been formed to operate from converted Dutch cargo ships. The combined unit subsequently became a Merchant Aircraft Carrier (MAC-ship) Wing. Originally No. 744 NAS provided training for the crews but this task was later passed onto the unit once sufficient spare Flights became available. The Swordfish themselves were painted overall white, and some wags replaced the standard 'Royal Navy' title under the tail with 'Merchant Navy', which certainly did not sit well either. The MAC-ship scheme was very popular and proved so successful that ultimately there was a total of nineteen commissioned, and No. 836 organized a Flight of either three or four Swordfish for each one (the Flight letters 'I', 'O' and 'S' were omitted from the roster to prevent confusion with numerals). The Flights would embark from HMS *Shrike*, RNAS Maydown at the start of each Atlantic crossing and disembark on termination of the round-trip. No. 836 NAS was finally dissolved on 21 May 1945 and No. 860 on 1 August 1945.

No. 837 NAS was formed in May 1942, at HMS *Buzzard*, RNAS Palisadoes, Jamaica. Commanded by Lieutenant-Commander Alexander Stephen Whitworth, they flew Swordfish-I and II. Four of the squadron's Swordfish-Is of 'D' Flight embarked aboard the escort carrier *Dasher* for deck landing and flight training, and then the whole unit was carried by her across the Atlantic, and disembarked at HMS *Landrail*, RNAS Machrihanish, Campeltown. Re-equipped with Swordfish-IIs from September 1942, the squadron was split into two separate Flights in January 1943. 'A' Flight went aboard the carrier *Argus* and escorted convoys to Gibraltar; the other Flight was again taken aboard *Dasher* to Iceland and served on convoy escort work. The whole squadron reassembled at HMS *Jackdaw-II*, RNAS Dunino, Kingsbarns, Fife, at the end of March before the unit was disbanded in June 1943. They later reformed in September 1944 as a Fairey Barracuda squadron.

No. 838 NAS was formed at Dartmouth, Halifax, Nova Scotia, in May 1942 under the command of Lieutenant-Commander John Ramsay Corson Callandar, flying Swordfish-I aircraft until April 1943 when they were replaced by Swordfish-II and IIIs, which remained until February 1945. The squadron initially flew to USNAS Alameda Island, San Francisco, in July 1942, where it even conducted anti-submarine patrols until September, before it embarked aboard the escort carrier *Avenger* in December for passage to USNAS Quonset Point, Rhode Island, via the Panama Canal. They re-embarked and carried out convoy escort duties to Curacao in the Dutch West Indies before transferring across the Atlantic to RNAS Machrihanish, being involved in MAC ship training aboard the carrier *Argus* and escort carrier *Activity*, embarking aboard the MAC-ship *Rapana* in August 1943.

The squadron was amalgamated as 'L' Flight of No. 836 NAS but was reformed at Belfast in November the same year under Lieutenant-Commander Peter Snow, with four Swordfish-II and carried out deck landing and flight trials aboard the escort carrier *Nairana*. The unit was then subordinated to No. 156 Wing, Coastal Command, at RAF Harrowbeer, Yelverton, Devon, and conducted operations in the English Channel for the D-Day operations, moving to RAF Fraserburgh, Aberdeenshire, in October. The squadron moved south again the following month and finally disbanded in February 1945 at RAF Thorney Island.

No. 840 NAS was reformed at HMS *Buzzard,* RNAS Palisadoes, Jamaica, under Lieutenant (A) Lawerence Ryder 'Tan' Tivy, on 1 June 1942 and later Lieutenant (A) Christopher Maurice Tytler Hallewell. The unit was equipped with Swordfish-I and from September, with Swordfish-II aircraft, and, after working up at USNAS Miami, Opa-locka, Florida, was, along with Nos 790, 892 and 894 NAS, transferred aboard the escort carrier *Battler* to USNAS Quonset Point, Rhode Island, between 12 and 26 December. The squadron conducted training with the escort carrier *Attacker* from Quonset and then embarked for the passage to Willemstad, Curacoa, along with No. 838 NAS, the *Attacker* transporting them across to the Clyde between 20 March and 1 April. Both squadrons disembarked at RNAS Machrihanish on 2 April. The squadron prepared for MAC-ship work, and went to sea aboard *Empire MacAndrew* in July but, after one Atlantic crossing; the unit became 'M' Flight of No. 836 NAS on 13 August 1943.

No. 841 NAS was a special night-operations unit established on 1 July 1942 at HMS *Daedelus,* RNAS Lee-on-Solent, with black-painted Fairey Albacores. In 1943 the unit was merged with No. 823 NAS and the combined squadron had sixteen Albacore and three Swordfish-I and II on its strength, flying the latter between January and April 1943. It was disbanded on 1 December at RAF Manston, and the mission handed over to No. 415 Squadron, RCAF. The unit was later re-established as a Fairey Barracuda unit.

No. 842 NAS was established in March 1943 at HMS *Daedelus,* RNAS Lee-on-Solent, in March 1943 as an anti-submarine and attack squadron, under Lieutenant-Commander Charles Bentall Lamb and then Lieutenant-Commander Lawrence Ryder Tivy. In July the squadron embarked aboard the escort carrier *Fencer* to cover the occupation of the Azores, and then conducted a series of convoy escort operations on the Gibraltar route. The *Fencer* then escorted convoys to Russia, the Swordfish sinking the *U-666* on 10 February 1944, and *U-277, U-874* and *U-959* between 1 and 3 May 1945. The squadron also took part in strikes against the German battleship *Tirpitz* (Operations *Tungsten* and *Mascot)* at Kaa Fjord, Norway, during April and July 1944, when she provided the anti-submarine patrols for the attack carriers, working from the carriers *Furious* and *Indefatigable,* before rejoining *Fencer* for Gibraltar convoy escort duties. In September 1944 the Swordfish-IIs were loaned to Coastal Command and based at RAF Benbecula, North Uist, Hebrides, before moving to Thorney Island in November. The unit was finally disbanded in January 1945.

No. 860 NAS was formed in June 1943 at HMS *Merlin,* RNAS Donibristle, as a Royal Netherlands Navy outfit commanded by Lieutenant Jan van der Tooren, and equipped with six Swordfish-Is. The squadron was manned by Dutch personnel and moved to HMS *Shrike,* RNAS Maydown, in November 1943 with twelve Swordfish-II. Here they trained for MAC-ship operations working from Dutch MAC-conversions *Acavus* and *Gadila,* and also later aboard *Macoma,* in conjunction with No. 836 NAS. The squadron was split into two Flights, equipped with Swordfish-IIIs from March 1945 onward, one working from Maydown the other from Dartmouth. When these were subsequently disbanded, the unit became a Fairey Barracuda squadron aboard the escort carrier *Nairana.*

No. 886 NAS was a fighter unit established at HMS *Merlin,* RNAS Donibristle, in March 1942. They flew the Fairey Fulmar and then the Supermarine Seafire. In June 1943 a Flight of Swordfish was added to the unit at RAF Turnhouse, between Edinburgh and Glasgow, and they embarked aboard the escort carrier *Attacker,* from which ship they took part in the Salerno landings in Italy in September. The squadron was split with one detachment at Paestrum airfield, Salerno, and the Swordfish were put ashore at North Front, Gibraltar, and these were later disbanded while the fighters joined 3 Naval Fighter Wing at HMS *Ringtail,* RNAS Burscough, Lancs.

The final Swordfish squadron was established as late as June 1943 and manned by Dutch naval personnel in exile in Britain.

Second line units

Numerous Fleet Air Arm ancillary squadrons were formed during World War II as the air complement expanded vastly. Some were specialized units, while others operated a wide range of types according to the needs of the area and the theatre of war. Many had Swordfish aircraft on their strengths at various times; others just had the odd one or two added for brief periods. They are too numerous to list them all; here is a selection.

When the decision was made to concentrate the bulk of Royal Navy aircraft procurement from the United States so the British aviation industry could concentrate on the RAF, HMS *Saker* was opened in Washington DC on 1 October 1941 with an operational base at Lewiston, Maine. Swordfish units were frequently worked up in the USA and then embarked on American-built escort carriers. Their obvious obsolescence was the comment of much mirth, mitigated by the Taranto and *Bismarck* achievements and later tempered by the US Navy's own enormous torpedo bomber losses at Midway in June 1942.

No. 700 NAS was formed at HMS *Sparrowhawk,* RNAS Hatson, in the Orkney Islands, from 700 and 701 Flights, to centralize the aircraft, Walrus, Sea Fox and float-equipped Swordfish, serving on the capital ships and cruisers of the fleet. Swordfish served briefly aboard the battleships *Barham, Resolution* (who had her Swordfish stop her 'X' turret damaged by 15-inch gun blast fire during Operation *Menace* at Dakar in September 1940), *Rodney* (who also carried them on a catapult on her 'X' turret in July 1939) and *Valiant,* before being replaced by Walrus aircraft. Two Swordfish served aboard the battleship *Warspite* and two aboard the battleship *Malaya* with the main Mediterranean Fleet. Casualties from war operations thinned these latter machines down, one being lost off Bardia on 2 June 1940 when caught by Fiat CR.42s of *80 Grupp°*; and one aboard *Warspite* was damaged beyond repair. She was replaced by fitting floats to one of *Eagle's* Swordfish (K8389) and transferring her across. One of *Malaya's* machines was also transferred to *Warspite* and lost while on a reconnaissance sortie on 19 July 1941.

With the abundance of flight decks from 1942 onward these float Swordfish were phased out, one on 22 August 1942, one on 6 July 1943 and one on 1 November 1943. No. 700 NAS itself became redundant and was finally disbanded in 1944.

No. 701 (Catapult) Flight was formed on 15 July from No. 444 (Fleet Reconnaissance) Flight at RAF Kalafrana, Malta, but was mainly a Walrus unit.

No. 702 NAS was formed as a Flight on 15 July 1936 to provide catapult aircraft for the battleships of the Second Battle Squadron working from RAF Mount Batten, mainly using the Fairey Seafox and Supermarine Walrus amphibians, which the float-equipped Swordfish replaced. The unit was briefly awarded Squadron status before being disbanded in 1940. Later it was resurrected to supply the Seafox to Armed Merchant Cruisers (AMCs) as they converted from liners.

No. 703 NAS was formed at HMS *Daedalus*, Lee-on-Solent, on 3 March 1942 as a long-range catapult squadron for equipping Armed Merchant Cruisers (AMC) with the Supermarine Walrus and Vought OS2U Kingfisher types. Some Swordfish were also carried on this unit's establishment for a while. The unit was disbanded on 1 May 1944.

No. 705 NAS was formed in June 1936 from No. 447 Flight, RAF, and employed float-fitted, catapult-launched Swordfish aboard the battle-cruiser *Repulse*. In 1936 *Repulse* had been fitted with two seaplane hangars abaft her rear funnel, along with two 7-ton cranes for hauling them out of the water and a D(II)H launching catapult athwart-ships. She initially carried the Blackburn Shark floatplane but replaced these with float-equipped Swordfish in 1939. Later they were, in their turn, replaced by the Walrus. Her sister ship, *Renown*, was completely rebuilt between 1936 and 1939, replacing her catapult with a hangar, but never embarked on the Swordfish.

Early in the war the *Repulse* was involved in hunting German raiders in the North Atlantic and the unit was awarded squadron status briefly before being disembarked at RNAS Lee-on-Solent in December 1939, and it was disbanded early in 1940.

No. 707 NAS was formed at HMS *Ringtail*, RNAS Burscough, Lancashire, as a torpedo-fighter and radar training establishment, an offshoot of HMS *Kestrel* at RNAS Worthy Down, and had a few Swordfish on its strength initially and worked with those from No. 825 NAS.

No. 710 NAS was formed in August 1939 at RNAS *Daedalus*, RNAS Lee-on-Solent, and operated Swordfish as well as Fulmar, Anson, Oxford and Walrus aircraft, some of the latter of which flew from HMAS *Albatross*.

No. 722 NAS was a Fleet Requirement Unit formed at HMS *Valluru*, RNAMY Tambaran, Madras, India, on 1 September 1944, with Miles Martinet target tugs, Supermarine Walrus aircraft plus a few Grumman F4F Wildcat and Swordfish aircraft on establishment, serving until March 1945.

No. 726 NAS was a Fleet Requirement unit, established in South Africa.

No. 727 NAS was established on 26 May 1943 as a Fleet Requirements unit at Gibraltar, supplying the French North African area from Algiers to Bizerta. The unit had Boulton Paul Defiant target tugs, Hawker Hurricane 1Cs and Swordfish on its establishment. It was disbanded on 7 December 1944.

No. 728 NAS was a Fleet Requirements squadron, based at Malta.

No. 731 NAS the Deck Landing Control ('batsmen') had a special training squadron established at the Deck Landing Training School at HMS *Peewit*, RNAS East Haven,

Angus, once the idea introduced by *Illustrious* had become adopted throughout the FAA. The Swordfish ran continuous circuits and landings ('clockwork mice') aboard dedicated or available escort carriers assigned to them while working up. The batsmen were all experienced pilots re-training for this very different, but equally dangerous job, as Charles Lamb's experience aboard *Implacable* clearly demonstrated.

No. 740 NAS was part of No. 2 Observer School at HMS *Condor*, RNAS Arbroath, whose aircraft included the Percival Proctor, Supermarine Walrus, Blackburn Shark, Fairey Sea Fox and Vought OS2U Kingfisher as well as the Swordfish.

No. 741 NAS was also part of No. 2 Observer School at HMS *Condor*, RNAS Arbroath, whose aircraft included the Percival Proctor, Supermarine Walrus, Blackburn Shark, Fairey Sea Fox and Vought OS2U Kingfisher as well as the Swordfish.

No. 742 NAS was a Squadron Air Transport squadron at HMS *Garuda*, Royal Navy Aircraft Maintenance Yard (RNAMY) Coimbatore, Tamil Nadu, India, from 21 September 1944 to 1 February 1945. They flew Beech Expeditors and Miles Martinet target tugs as well as the Swordfish.

No. 743 NAS was a Fleet Replenishment squadron established at HMS *Seaborn*, RCAF Dartmouth, Nova Scotia, to store and maintain Swordfish as a pool for MAC-ships.

No. 745 NAS was set up to provide aircraft for the training of Naval TAGs at RCAF Yarmouth, Nova Scotia, under the British Commonwealth Air Training Scheme (BCATS).

No. 753 NAS was part of No. 2 Observer School at HMS *Condor*, RNAS Arbroath, whose aircraft included the Percival Proctor, Supermarine Walrus, Blackburn Shark, Fairey Sea Fox and Vought OS2U Kingfisher as well as the Swordfish.

No. 754 NAS was part of No. 2 Observer School at HMS *Condor*, RNAS Arbroath, whose aircraft included the Percival Proctor, Supermarine Walrus, Blackburn Shark, Fairey Sea Fox, Vought OS2U Kingfisher and even Westland Lysanders used as target tugs, as well as the Swordfish.

No. 755 NAS formed in 1939 and was part of No. 1 Air Gunners' School, which provided wireless operating at HMS *Ariel*, and air gunner training for TAGs, carried out at HMS *Kestrel*, RNAS Worthy Down. They flew Blackburn Shark, Hawker Osprey, Westland Lysander and Curtiss SO3C Seamew aircraft in addition to the Swordfish.

No. 756 NAS was a Squadron Deck Landing Training unit and worked from RNAS Worthy Down between 1939 and 1943.

No. 763 (FAA Pool) NAS worked from RNAS Worthy Down between February and July 1941.

No. 765 NAS was a Squadron Communications unit.

No. 766 NAS included Swordfish on its strength at HMS *Condor*, RNAS Arbroath, East Angus, in 1944/1945, serving for brief periods aboard the escort carrier *Ranee*.

No. 767 NAS served as the Advance Training unit from November 1939 to June 1940, operating from the carrier *Argus* based in the south of France. The unit was dispersed in July and those based at Hal Far formed the nucleus of No. 830 NAS, which operated from there until disbanded. The squadron was subsequently reformed and was based at HMS *Peewit*, RNAS East Haven, Angus, for deck landing training, serving briefly aboard the escort carrier *Rajah* between 12 and 14 August 1944, and the escort carrier *Smiter* for periods between 21 December 1944 and 25 May 1945.

No. 768 NAS, which included some Swordfish on its establishment, was variously based at RNAS Arbroath, at HMS *Wagtail*, RNAS Ayr, South Ayrshire, and also at HMS *Sanderling*, RNAS Abbotsinch, Renfrewshire[12] for deck landing training, serving briefly aboard the escort carrier *Rajah* between 31 July and 14 August, the escort carrier *Empress* for night deck landing trials between 30 August and November 1944; the escort carrier *Speaker* for periods between 16 October and 29 November 1944, the escort carrier *Smiter* for periods between 21 December 1944 to 25 May 1945.

No. 769 NAS, which included some Swordfish on its establishment, was based at HMS *Peewit*, RNAS East Haven, Angus, for deck landing training, serving briefly aboard the escort carrier *Rajah* during 7–12 August 1944, and escort carrier *Smiter* for periods between 21 December 1944 and 25 May 1945.

No. 771 NAS was formed on 24 May 1939 at HMS *Daedelus*, RNAS Lee-on-Solent, as a Fleet Requirement squadron and was equipped with fourteen Swordfish. These acted with the fleet in AA practice, target-towing and similar duties. Split into 'X' and 'Y' Flights, the former became No. 772 NAS on 28 September 1939 while 'Y' was based at HMS *Sparrowhawk*, Hatston, with a wide range of aircraft for the rest of the war.

No. 772 NAS was formed by 'X' Flight, No. 771 NAS, on 28 September 1939, at HMS *Daedelus*, RNAS Lee-on-Solent, as a southern area Fleet Requirement unit and flew Swordfish floatplanes as target tugs and on other related duties. Based at HMS *Osprey*, RNAS Portland, the unit was moved north to RNAS Campeltown in July 1940.

No. 774 NAS provided the advanced element of the TAG gunnery courses, at HMS *Vulture*, RNAS St Merryn, Cornwall, which featured live firing. Air-to-ground bombing was conducted at nearby HMS *Vulture II*, Trieligga airfield.

No. 775 NAS was a Fleet Requirements squadron, based in Egypt.

No. 779 NAS was a Fleet Requirements unit, based at Gibraltar.

No. 788 NAS was a Fleet Requirements unit and was transferred to Ceylon (now called Sri Lanka) where it was utilized in a combat role during the crisis of April 1942 in lieu of anything more potent. The intent was to build up the squadron as a fully operational outfit, to be designated as No. 839 NAS. They were working up at China Bay when the five carriers of the Japanese Admiral Chūichi Nagumo's *Kido Butai* arrived in the Indian Ocean, and, on Sunday 5 April, were ordered to clear out to HMS *Seruwa*, RNAS Ratmalana, out of harm's way. Unfortunately for them, while *en route* in two three-plane flights, led by Lieutenant Cyril Longsdon and Lieutenant Cyril Pountney respectively, and, while over Colombo at 0732, they ran slap into the Mitsubishi A6M Zero fighters of Lieutenant-Commander Shigeru Itaya's thirty-six plane escort force, who probably could not believe their eyes at these examples of the British Empire's armed might!

Whatever surprise the Japanese fighter pilots felt at the sight of these flying antiques, the Fleet Air Arm pilots were caught even more unawares, Lieutenant Pountney reporting that he was being attacked by '...a Hurricane with a large red dot painted on the wings and fuselage...', a description that probably says everything there needs to be said about the state of British awareness of their enemy, even after five months of war! In a matter of minutes all six Swordfish had been professionally butchered by the Zeros who then sought slightly more taxing opposition.[13]

No. 789 NAS was a Fleet Requirements squadron, based in South Africa.

No. 797 NAS was a Squadron Fleet Requirements unit.

No. 1700 NAS was a Squadron Air-Sea Rescue unit, based in Ceylon.

Other second line units with Swordfish on their establishments were Nos 730, 732, 733, 735, 737, 739, 744, 747, 759, 764, 770, 773, 776, 777, 778, 780, 781, 783, 785, 787, 791, 794 and 796 NAS.

Fleet and light carriers

Argus – she was mainly employed as a training carrier in the western Mediterranean from November 1939 and frequently embarked or operated Swordfish of No. 767 NAS from Hyères de la Palyvestre, Toulon (nowadays Aéroport de Toulon-Hyères) for advanced training. When Italy finally declared war on 10 June 1940, nine of the squadron's instructors carried out a bombing raid against Genoa on 13 June. When *Argus* was recalled for her own safety shortly afterward, the bulk of No. 767's aircraft moved over to Bône, Tunisa, although six soon joined the aircraft complement of *Ark Royal* at Gibraltar and the others went to Hal Far airfield, Malta, where they were to form No. 830 NAS under Lieutenant-Commander Francis Deschamps Howie.

In the desperate days of 1942 with few alternatives available, she was used on Malta aircraft ferry operations but also deployed as part of Force 'H' on occasions and at such times she embarked a detachment of four Swordfish from No. 824 NAS.

Ark Royal – in September 1939 she carried twelve Swordfish of Nos 810 and nine Swordfish of 820 NAS aboard when she was mistakenly used to hunt U-boats. After her narrow escape she went to the South Atlantic hunting groups searching for the pocket battleships. On returning home during Operation 'DX', she had aboard twelve Swordfish of No. 810 NAS and nine Swordfish of No. 820 NAS. Off Norway between 7 May and 13 June there were a total of twenty-one Swordfish operational from these two units. She went out to Gibraltar to become one of the mainstays of Force 'H' in the western Mediterranean taking part in the attack on the Vichy French fleet at Mers-el-Kebir, the battle of Spartivento and the bombardment of Genoa, as well as frequent Malta convoy operations and the flying off of aircraft to Malta in the period from July 1940 to her loss in November 1941. She also conducted patrols in the Bay of Biscay during the watch on the French ports and the *Bismarck* operation when she had twelve Swordfish of No. 810 NAS, nine Swordfish of No. 818 NAS and nine Swordfish of No. 820 NAS among her complement. She was finally torpedoed by the *U-81* east of Gibraltar on 13 November 1941 and sank the following day despite efforts at salvage.

Courageous – in September 1939 she had twelve Swordfish of No. 811 NAS and twelve Swordfish of No. 822 NAS embarked, and all went down with her when she was torpedoed and sunk by the *U-155* off the Irish coast on 17 September 1939.[14]

Eagle – was on the China Station on outbreak of war but was called back to the East Indies and Indian Ocean to hunt raiders and escort Australian troop convoys soon after. She had embarked nine Swordfish of No. 813 NAS and nine Swordfish of No. 824 NAS. She next served in the Mediterranean joining via the Suez Canal in May 1940, and with these aircraft she went to war in earnest from June 1940 onward. During occasions when she was immobilized, many of her Swordfish served ashore in North Africa and, in the period May to September 1941, both Greece and Crete. With continuing problems with her engines, *Eagle* had nine Swordfish from each of No. 813 and No. 824 NAS embarked but contributed some to *Illustrious* for the attack on Taranto. After refitting back in the UK, *Eagle* was used in several Malta aircraft ferry operations and Malta convoys, and she had embarked nine Swordfish of No. 813 NAS and nine Swordfish of No. 824 NAS, although the latter were put ashore to enable extra Hawker Sea Hurricanes to be embarked for big Mediterranean operations like *Harpoon*. On the *Pedestal* Malta relief operation of August 1942, she had mainly fighter aircraft aboard when she was torpedoed and sunk by the *U-73* in the western Mediterranean.

Furious – in September 1939 she had nine Swordfish of No. 816 NAS and nine of No. 818 NAS embarked. Between 8 and 25 April 1940 she was serving with the Home Fleet with these same units, but in order to ferry Sea Gladiator fighters to Norway in May, No. 818 was put ashore. During the period September to October 1940 she conducted strikes off the Norwegian coast, and as well as No. 816 NAS, she had aboard the nine Swordfish of No. 825 NAS. She contributed to the disastrous failure of the strikes on Petsamo and Kirkenes in 1941, for which she deployed nine Swordfish of No. 812 NAS. During her later period with the Home Fleet during 1943–44 *Furious* operated nine Swordfish of No. 825 NAS from July 1943 onward. During the massive FAA attacks on the battleship *Tirpitz*, Operation *Tungsten*, on 3 April 1944, *Furious* had embarked twelve Swordfish-IIs from No. 842 NAS and three Swordfish of this squadron were still aboard her for the repeat attack, Operation *Mascot*, on 17 July 1944.

Glorious – remained in the East Indies and Indian Ocean between October 1939 and January 1940 with three Swordfish units embarked, twelve each from Nos 812, 823 and 825 NAS. She then returned to the Mediterranean. She was recalled to home waters. At the time of her loss from 3 June to 8 June when she was surprised and sunk by the German battle-cruisers *Gneisenau* and *Scharnhorst* off Norway, she had aboard nine Swordfish of No. 823 NAS as well as Sea Gladiators and the RAF Gladiators and Hawker Hurricanes, which had landed aboard. But, amazingly, not a single aircraft was in the air at all on the day of her loss.

Hermes – had twelve Swordfish of No. 814 NAS transferred to her from *Ark Royal* on 4 September 1939 and this unit constituted her main air strength for almost the rest of her life. The *Hermes* was too small and too slow to be considered for any type of fleet work for most of her wartime career; even when new she had only been good for twenty-five knots and that was two decades earlier. She was therefore despatched to where she might do the most good for the least risk and joined Force 'N' searching for German surface raiders in the Caribbean with the French battle-cruiser *Strasbourg* and from there she moved via Africa to the Indian Ocean during November and December 1939, and by May was providing air protection to ANZAC troop convoy US3. On relief by the *Argus,* another doughty old veteran, she became immersed in the operations against the Vichy-French fleet, by launching a six-Swordfish torpedo strike, led by Lieutenant-Commander David Richard Luard, against the new French battleship *Richelieu* at Dakar, Senegal, on 8 July 1940. One torpedo struck the battleship on her port side aft in this attack, causing severe damage, and she was still undergoing repairs in September when the ill-fated Operation *Menace* by the Free French against the Vichy-French, took place.

Hermes continued anti-raider patrols in the South Atlantic for the rest of 1940 and then in the Indian Ocean from January 1941 onward, interspersed with attacks on Italian targets at Mogadishu and Kismayu in February, and operations in the Persian Gulf during the Iran uprising in April. After refitting at Durban she was with the battleship *Prince of Wales* at Cape Town in November, but was rejected from Force 'Z' due to her slow speed. In March *Hermes* joined Admiral Sir James Somerville's Eastern Fleet and was earmarked to take part in the occupation of Vichy-French Madagascar, but was sunk by the Aichi D3A1 'Val' dive-bombers off Ceylon on 9 April, and went down after forty or more bomb hits, sinking with only a single, inoperational, Swordfish aboard her.

Illustrious – operated a wide variety of Swordfish squadrons during her early career. Between June and December 1940 she had No. 819 NAS embarked and between June 1940 and January 1941 when she was crippled off Malta by Stuka attack, had No. 815 NAS aboard. For special operations in the Eastern Mediterranean she also occasionally embarked Swordfish-Is from the *Eagle* when she was incapacitated, having a detachment from No. 813 NAS aboard in September 1940, a detachment from No. 824 NAS in November and a second deployment from No. 813 NAS the same month. She also operated Swordfish-Is from both No. 810 and No. 829 NAS in December 1941 for the voyage to the USA to repair.

After extensive repairs in American dockyards and recommencing her career, in March 1942 *Illustrious* embarked Swordfish-IIs of No. 829 NAS fitted with AV radar, which she had aboard until September 1942, and Swordfish of No. 810 NAS, which she operated as late as April 1943.

Unicorn was built as a FAA aircraft maintenance carrier, but was several times pressed into active combat service due to lack of other flight decks, notably at Salerno in July 1943 when she had four Swordfish of No. 818 NAS and nine Swordfish of No. 824 NAS embarked.

Victorious – during the hunt for the *Bismarck* in May 1941, and before she or her squadrons were properly worked up, she had embarked nine Swordfish of No. 825 NAS, but otherwise mainly operated the Fairey Albacore.

Escort carriers

A total of forty-four British escort-carriers operated the Swordfish at one period or another, some only for training. These carriers were – *Activity, Ameer, Arbiter, Archer, Attacker, Audacity, Avenger, Battler, Begum, Biter, Campania, Charger, Chaser, Dasher, Emperor, Empress, Fencer, Hunter, Khedive, Nabob, Nairana, Patroller, Premier, Pretoria Castle, Puncher, Pursuer, Queen, Rajah, Ranee, Ravager, Reaper, Ruler, Searcher, Shah, Slinger, Smiter, Speaker, Stalker, Striker, Thane, Tracker, Trouncer, Trumpeter* and *Vindex.*

Activity was a British conversion to an escort carrier, and embarked Swordfish from HMS *Landrail* of No. 835 NAS for deck landing training between 27 October and 3 November 1942. She also conducted extensive DLT with No. 768 NAS's various aircraft types including Swordfish between November 1942 and June 1943. In July four Swordfish from No. 838 NAS joined from HMS *Shrike*, RNAS Maydown, NI, and on 30 August nine Swordfish of No. 819 NAS, from the out of operation escort carrier *Archer*, were embarked, these being offloaded at HMS *Nightjar*, RNAS Inskip, Lancashire, on 27 September to be fitted with AV Type X radar. Seven of these aircraft were re-embarked on 12 January 1944, but were later reduced to five machines aboard.

Activity joined Western Approaches Command and took part in ten convoy operations, working also with the escort carrier *Nairana* and 3 Escort Group. She also covered Russia convoys JW58 and RA58 with the escort carrier *Tracker* and this proved her most fruitful period of operations. On 3 April 1944 Swordfish 'C' piloted by the aptly named Lieutenant Stanley Brilliant, sank the *U-288* off Bear Island and 819 also assisted in the destruction of *U-355* and caused damaged to *U-362, U-673* and *U-990* in this period. On return to the UK No. 819 NAS was disembarked at HMS *Sparrowhawk*, RNAS Hatson, on 13 April.

These Swordfish were replaced by three others, the former 'F' Flight of No. 836 NAS, which flew aboard on 17 April and *Activity* sailed with the escort carrier *Fencer* to conduct Operation *EZ*, losing two Swordfish to accidents in the process. On 1 and 2 May 1944, Swordfish LS280 attacked two separate U-boats. *Activity* then conducted a series of sweeps in the Bay of Biscay with the escort carriers *Tracker* and *Vindex*, designed to intercept U-boats heading for the Normandy invasion beaches in June. When these operations were completed in August *Activity* returned for modifications in dockyard hands and put her final Swordfish ashore at RNAS Maydown, before becoming a ferry carrier and going out to the East Indies and the re-taking of Singapore.

Archer was one of the first American converted escort carriers and, as became commonplace, suffered from numerous engine and other defects. She finally embarked eleven Grumman F4F Wildcat fighters (Martlets as they were termed in the FAA at this period of the war) at Norfolk, Virginia, on 12 January 1942 and sailed for Kingston, Jamaica, to embark four Swordfish of No. 834 NAS from HMS *Buzzard*, RNAS Palisadoes, but a Peruvian merchant ship rammed her and she had to return to dockyard hands until March when her programme was resumed, with the Swordfish flying over to Norfolk to embark.

After more engine problems she reached Freetown, Sierra Leone, with convoy AS2 on 3 April where her engines again broke down. She did not sail again until 15 May and then more engine problems aborted her intended ferry trip to the Mediterranean via Mombasa and instead she was routed back to New York for repairs and modifications. One of her Swordfish, piloted by Lieutenant Eric Dixon-Child, made the first ever landing at Georgetown, Ascension Island, on 15 June. A bomb explosion aboard caused more havoc and then her engines broke down again, leaving her adrift mid-Atlantic and, while at Hamilton, Bermuda, a flu outbreak aboard caused yet further problems, only one man from 834 Squadron being fit to fly patrols, and she did not reach New York until 15 July. Repairs at Hoboken took until October and in November *Archer* carried a deck cargo of USAAF fighter aircraft with convoy UGF2 to Morocco, which mission was beset by yet more problems and when she finally arrived in the UK it was to undergo further conversions and modifications that were not completed until February 1943.

On 28 February 1943 No. 819 NAS with nine RP armed Swordfish were flown aboard from HMS *Landrail*, Machrihanish, Argyll, to join West Approaches Command. They damaged two Swordfish during trials with the escort carrier *Biter*, but she had to have still further dockyard work and finally re-embarked 819's Swordfish again from Belfast at the end of the month. She then sailed to Iceland and with 4 Escort Group, commanded by the destroyer *Faulknor*, left Hvalfjörôur on 7 May escorting ONS.6. Next day a Swordfish piloted by Sub-Lieutenant John Harrison Lamb had a landing accident and smashed up four other Swordfish, two of them having to be ditched overboard as irreparable. Later the same day another Swordfish piloted by Sub-Lieutenant Ronald Edgar Martin crashed over the side while landing aboard.

After escorting ONS6 *Archer* was detached to Argentina, Newfoundland, and then escorted ON184 making an abortive U-boat attack on 22 May and a more successful one the following day, which damaged their target. Later that day they were finally rewarded when Swordfish 'B' piloted by Sub-Lieutenant Harry Horrocks DSC sank the *U-752* with four rocket salvoes of two per attack. On 23 May another Swordfish, 'K', was lost due to engine failure but the aircrew were rescued. The surviving Swordfish were disembarked the following day and more dockyard work followed.

Archer then re-embarked No. 819 NAS and carried out Operation *Regulation*, hunting German blockade-runners in the Bay of Biscay during July 1943 working from Plymouth as well as escorting troop convoys destined for the invasion of Sicily, Operation *Husky*. Further Bay of Biscay anti-submarine sweeps followed Operations *Musketry* and *Seaslug*, damaging two more Swordfish in the process. Then yet more engine repairs and 819 NAS was flown ashore to RNAS Machrihanish. This time her repairs required so much work that the Admiralty decided enough was enough and withdrew her from active service, and she served out the war as an accommodation hulk, and finally as the aircraft ferry transport *Empire Lagan*.

Attacker was of the original US-built escort carriers and on 12 November 1942 she embarked four Swordfish of No. 838 NAS from USNAS Alameda Island, San Francisco, and conveyed them to USNAS Quonset Point, Rhode Island, where they disembarked on 1 January 1943. Swordfish from both 838 and 840 NAS visited the ship from

Quonset during February and she then embarked six Swordfish from 840 NAS from that base, for the Atlantic crossing, putting those of Nos 838 and 840 NAS ashore at HMS *Landrail*, RNAS Machrihanish. Between 19 and 21 June 1943 Swordfish from No. 886 NAS flew aboard for training on 12 July, with six Swordfish and nine Seafire fighters. She conveyed them to Gibraltar, where the Swordfish were disembarked to work from RAF North Front until 1 October when they rejoined *Attacker* briefly before being finally disembarked on 6 October.

Avenger commenced a flight deck landing training programme with four Swordfish from No. 816 NAS but this was curtailed due to the carrier's engines breaking down. After repairs she then joined transatlantic convoy AT17 on 30 April and in bad weather on 4 May two 813 Swordfish and their crews were lost as the carrier had not been fitted with a homing beacon. *Avenger* was modified in the Clyde during May and June 1942, and like most US escort carriers, had an extra 42ft (12.80m) added to her flight deck in order to accommodate the Swordfish and other essential upgrades. She then embarked three Swordfish-IIs and five aircrew from No. 825 NAS from RNAS Hatston on 22 July. From 3 September she provided air cover for Russia convoy PQ18, losing one machine in an accident. On 14 September one Swordfish assisted the destroyer *Onslow* in sinking *U-589*. On returning home with QP14 the Swordfish were used on anti-submarine patrols whenever the weather permitted, but the CO reported that they were unable to take off the flight deck with a torpedo or full equipment.[15] On return the Swordfish were disembarked to HMS *Sparrowhawk* again.

Avenger embarked three Swordfish-IIs of 'B' Flight No. 833 NAS from RNAS Machrihanish at Loch Ewe on 16 October and sailed to take part in the North African landings, Operation *Torch*, with *Victorious* and *Biter* in company. On arrival at Gibraltar the Swordfish were disembarked at RAF North Front fortunately for them as *Avenger* was sunk by the *U-29* with heavy loss of life on 15 November.

Battler was commissioned on 15 November 1942 and embarked the Swordfish-I/IIs of No. 840 NAS from USNAS Miami on 12 December; these being later disembarked at USNAS Quonset Point on 21 December. She crossed the Atlantic and was modified up to Royal Navy standards and then embarked six Swordfish-IIs of No. 835 NAS on 10 April 1943, disembarking them at RAF Ballykelly, Londonderry, Northern Island, on 14 April. On 5 June five Swordfish-IIs of No. 835 NAS joined her from HMS *Gannet*, RNAS Eglinton, Londonderry. The *Battler* took part in Operation *Avalanche*, the invasion of Salerno, Italy, in September, having taken aboard three Swordfish-IIs from No. 834 NAS from the escort carrier *Hunter* earlier. Six Swordfish of No. 834 NAS were at RAF North Front, Gibraltar, working as 'Z' Flight between 9 September and 1 October when they re-embarked. *Battler* arrived at Aden where her disembarked Swordfish operated ashore between 3 and 17 October before she sailed into the Indian Ocean and gave air cover for convoys, including AB18A, AB20, AB24A and AB27.

On joining the Eastern Fleet the CO, Admiral Sir James Somerville, inspected *Battler* and her aircrew. He noted, 'I was surprised to learn from the pilots that many of them preferred her flight deck to that of a fleet carrier. Apparently freedom from side obstructions was the advantage. I noted with interest the RP (Rocket Projectiles) fittings on the Swordfish.'[16] The Swordfish subsequently carried out prolonged anti-submarine sweeps off Madagascar before offloading No. 844 NAS to HMS *Kongoni*, RNAS Stamford Hill, Durban, between 4 and 13 February 1944. She undertook the search for the German U-boat supply tanker *Brake* in March, and she was located by one of the Swordfish with two U-boats alongside and a third astern on 12 March, one of which the Swordfish damaged by rocket attack. Eventually the destroyer *Roebuck* intercepted and sank *Brake* 100 miles south-east of Mauritius.

No. 834 NAS was again disembarked at Stamford Hill from 21 March to 24 June 1944, helping to escort convoys CM53 and KR11, and was ashore once more at HMS *Garuda*, RNAS Coimbatore, in southern India, between 19 and 28 September and then moved to HMS *Kalugu*, RNAS Cochin. The squadron re-embarked on 7 October to 9 November when they landed ashore at the Military Harbour at Adabiya in the Gulf of Suez, disbanding on 21 November 1944.

Biter was completed in May 1942 at New York but suffered repeated engine breakdown and failures, which dogged the first year of her life. She embarked six Swordfish-Is of No. 833 NAS from RNAS Machrihanish on 2 September, but these had to be disembarked again on 30 September. On 9 October 'A' Flight, No. 833 NAS, with Swordfish-Is, joined here and she sailed south with *Victorious* and *Avenger* for the North African landings. The Swordfish were put ashore at North Front, Gibraltar, on 7 November.

Six Swordfish-IIs of N. 811 NAS, under Lieutenant-Commander Anthony Jex-Blake Forde, were embarked on 21 March and she commenced work with 5 Escort Group, escorting ONS4, and the Swordfish assisted in the destruction of *U-203* by the destroyer *Pathfinder*. During the passage of returning convoy HX237 several of her Swordfish and their aircrew were lost attempting to battle it out with surfaced U-boats and in the end were ordered only to fly in pairs. However, on 3 May 1943 the Swordfish had assisted the destroyer *Broadway* and frigate *Lagan* in the sinking of *U-89*. Ordered to join convoy SC129, *Biter* found that due to hardly any wind over the flight deck, and the inability of the Swordfish to use the launch rail, they were restricted to the ineffective bomb load of just two 40lb (18kg) bombs, which proved totally inadequate to harm a U-boat's tough hide. After this experience it became the practice to fit escort carriers with the Type 237 Blind Approach System, and also fit them with aircraft homing beacons.

A continuous period of Atlantic convoy work followed, escorting HX244 and SC134 and many more throughout 1943, with 7 Support Group. While escorting convoy HX 265, with six Swordfish of 811 NAS embarked, *Biter* was damaged on 16 November when a Swordfish ditched with engine failure and her *Fido/Oscar* homing torpedo[17] locked on to the carrier's screw noise. The resulting detonation crippled her steering, tore away two-thirds of her rudder assembly and breached the hull beneath the waterline. *Biter* got home, but repairs took a month to effect.

On 13 January 1944 *Biter* re-embarked No. 811 NAS from HMS *Nightjar*, RNAS Inskip, Lancs, and with eleven Swordfish-IIIs embarked, joined the escort carrier *Tracker* and the 7 and 8 Escort Groups. They patrolled the Bay of Biscay and covered convoys ONS29 and OS68 between 26 February and 2 March 1944, before offloading 811's Swordfish at North Front, Gibraltar, for a short period re-embarking them for continual convoy duties with SL150 and MKS42 in March and SC136 in April and continuing to protect convoys to Gibraltar and West Africa in May and June. The decision was made to convert *Biter* into a ferry carrier[18] and she returned home for conversion in August, finally offloading No. 811 NAS in August.

Campania was the last British conversion and benefitted by having an Action Information Centre (AIC) suite installed along with a superior Type 277 radar. In April 1944 she embarked twelve Swordfish of 813 NAS. Her first operation was escorting convoys OS79 and MKS53 down to Gibraltar and she also covered SL160 and MS51 back home. During June and July she continued the same pattern taking OS82 and KMS56 out and bringing SL163 and MKS54 back to the UK. Her Swordfish were disembarked in September but when she sailed to escort convoy RA60 back from Russia on 30 September it was still with that squadron aboard. On 30 September the Swordfish sank the *U-921* off Bear Island. She again re-embarked twelve of 813's Swordfish-IIIs on 27 October, to cover convoy RA61A and in December joined with *Nairana* in covering JW62. Another victory followed when the Swordfish sank the *U-365* on 13 December while covering the returning RA62.

Russian convoys continued with JW64 in February, followed by special operations of the Norwegian coast and No. 813 NAS were disembarked on 27 February. In March 1945 she embarked twelve Swordfish-IIIs of No. 825 NAS and with the escort carrier *Trumpeter* provided air cover for Russia convoys JW65 and RA65. Following these operations she was selected to carry out trooping duties and the Swordfish were put ashore for the last time.[19]

Chaser embarked No. 835 NAS's nine Swordfish on 6 November 1943, and took aboard a further three from HMS *Gannet*, RNAS Eglinton, Northern Ireland on her way north to replace three lost in training accidents between 26 and 28 of the month. On 19 January 1944 she embarked the eleven Swordfish of No. 816 NAS from HMS *Merlin*, RNAS Donibristle, and provided air protection for Russia convoys JW57 and RA57. While with the latter the Swordfish assisted in the destruction of *U-472* on 4 February, and they themselves used their rocket projectiles to destroy *U-366* the following day and *U-973* on 6 February, a superb achievement. Unfortunately this success was marred when, on returning to the UK, she was badly damaged when she dragged her anchor and collided with the escort carrier *Attacker*. Swordfish were ashore and after languishing in dockyard hands between April and December 1944, she went out to the British Pacific Fleet with Supermarine Seafires embarked.

Dasher was handed over in the USA on 2 July and embarked four Swordfish of No. 837 NAS on 25 July 1942 for deck landing training and, on conclusion of their programme, then conveyed the unit across the Atlantic to HMS *Landrail*, RNAS Machrihanish, near Campeltown, where she put them ashore on 10 September. In November she participated in the North African landings, Operation *Torch*, with the escort carrier *Biter* as a fighter carrier. After returning to the UK and having an extra 42ft (12.8m) added to her flight deck, in mid-January 1943 she re-embarked three Swordfish of 'D' Flight, No. 837 NAS and sailed to escort Russia convoy JW53. This accomplished, she took aboard six Swordfish of No. 815 NAS on 16 February but was forced to turn back with engine problems. On 24 March 1943 she embarked six Swordfish of No. 816 NAS in readiness for her next convoy operation. On 27 March 1943 the *Dasher* blew up in the Clyde after a huge fuel detonation, and sank with enormous loss of life.[20]

Empress operated some Swordfish from No. 768 NAS from 30 August to November 1944, conducting night deck landing training.

Fencer was completed as a carrier on 27 February 1943 and after trials and crossing the Atlantic she embarked nine Swordfish of No. 842 NAS on 5 August. Her first wartime operation was conveying in top secret No. 247 Group of RAF wireless and signals operatives to set up a base in the 'neutral' Azores. She added a further four Swordfish from 'W' Flight, No. 700 NAS, to her complement, along with a solitary Walrus amphibian, for operations, briefly disembarking them at RNAS Machrihanish between missions.

The first Swordfish success working from *Fencer* was the destruction of *U-666* to the west of Ireland on 10 February 1944. *Fencer* became part of the Home Fleet carrier strikes against the German battleship *Tirpitz* holed up in her Norwegian fiord from 3 April, Operation *Tungsten*. No. 842 NAS was utilizing twelve Swordfish-IIs at this date and she subsequently gave cover for Russia convoys. While covering the returning convoy RA59 the Swordfish excelled themselves, sinking the *U-277* on 1 May, *U-674* on 2 May and *U-959* on 3 May. During the remainder of the year *Fencer* was engaged with air strikes off the Norwegian coast interspersed with convoy protection work covering OS85, KMS57 and SC164 and NS55 and conducted minelaying operations off Norway on 15/16 July, before she underwent a refit and went out to the British Pacific Fleet.

Hunter was commissioned in January 1943, and worked up in West Indies, before crossing the Atlantic from Norfolk, Virginia. After unloading stores at Casablanca, she called at Gibraltar and embarked Swordfish from No. 813 Squadron from North Front airfield for a period of anti-submarine patrolling. They were then disembarked and she sailed for the Clyde where she was modified up to Royal Navy standards. She embarked nine Swordfish of No. 834 NAS on 29 August 1943, from RNAS Machrihanish, but several were damaged during bad weather when one broke loose. She called into the Clyde and embarked replacement Swordfish and then proceeded down to the Mediterranean, offloading Swordfish ashore at North Front, Gibraltar, where they operated as part of 'Z' Squadron until 1 October. Three Swordfish remained aboard for passage to Malta on 5 September and then transferred over to the escort carrier *Battler* on 7 September.

Hunter subsequently took part in Operation *Avalanche*, the Salerno landings in Italy, as a Seafire carrier. Just a solitary Swordfish remained aboard *Hunter* when she took part in Operation *Dragoon*, the landings in the South of France, in August before sailing for the East Indies Station.

Nairana was a British conversion to an escort carrier and commissioned on 26 November 1943. After sea trials she embarked twelve Swordfish of No. 838 NAS for a short period. On 25 January she embarked nine Swordfish-IIIs of No. 835 NAS and took part in the escort of convoys OS66 and KMS70. During February and June she escorted frequent convoys across the Bay of Biscay to Gibraltar and back as well as conducting anti-submarine sweeps in the eastern Atlantic. In October 1944 she refitted and began to escort Russia convoys, embarking fourteen Swordfish of No. 835 NAS to cover JW61 and RA61 and JW62 and RA62, the latter in company with the escort carriers *Tracker* and *Vindex*.

During January 1945 she conducted sweeps off Norway and also covered Russia convoys JW64 and RA64. Russian convoy work continued through to March 1945 when the Swordfish-IIIs were finally exchanged for Fairey Barracuda aircraft.

Pretoria Castle was a British conversion; the reason she retained her mercantile name for naval service is not known other than she had previously been commissioned under it as an armed merchant cruiser. She was not a success as a carrier, being employed mainly for trials and training with new aircraft types. She did embark fifteen Swordfish-IIIs of No. 825 NAS in October 1943 and provided for troop convoy DS46 to Iceland but was involved in several collisions in her brief career as a carrier and saw no other combat service.

Rajah operated some Swordfish from Nos 767, 768 and 769 NASs for deck landing training, for short periods between 31 July and 14 August 1944.

Ranee, operated some Swordfish from No. 768 NAS off Rosyth and Methil, for periods from 23 November 1944 to January 1945. On 15 December 1944, Sub-Lieutenant Frederick Sumner RNVR from No. 766 NAS was killed attempting a night landing in Swordfish NF315, when she bounced, went over the bows of the carrier and sank.

Smiter operated a few Swordfish as part of Nos. 767, 768 and 769 NAS deck landing training programmes off Methil between 21 December 1944 and 25 May 1945.

Speaker operated a few Swordfish from No. 768 NAS deck landing training programmes off Methil between 16 October and 29 November 1944.

Striker was first commissioned in the spring of 1943 and on 28 April embarked nine Swordfish-IIs of No. 824 Squadron NAS, which she operated for a period on the Gibraltar convoy route covering nine convoys and in anti-submarine sweeps in the Bay of Biscay. Her Swordfish were put ashore at HMS *Robin*, RNAS Grimsetter, Kirkwall, Orkney Islands, on 12 April 1944. She then embarked them with three extra Swordfish for the Home Fleet air attacks on the battleship *Tirpitz*, operating with *Vindex*. On conclusion of these sorties she escorted two Russian convoys before No. 824's Swordfish were finally disembarked at HMS *Sanderling*, RNAS Abbotsinch, Glasgow, on 16 October 1944. After a refit *Striker* went out to the British Pacific Fleet.

Tracker first commissioned on the American west coast in January 1943 and, after sea trials, conveyed cargo to Casablanca before entering the Clyde. She finally embarked her air group of Supermarine Seafires and Swordfish of No. 816 NAS in August 1943. During this period Swordfish DK683 was lost with two of her aircrew during night deck landings. *Tracker* was a most successful escort carrier, escorting several Atlantic, Russian and Gibraltar convoys and not finally disembarking No. 816 NAS until 28 December, when they were replaced by No. 846 NAS flying the Grumman Avenger type.

Trouncer operated a few Swordfish from various Deck Landing Training Squadrons off Methil between 2 November and 5 December 1944.

Vindex was one of the British conversions and was completed in January 1943; she first embarked Swordfish with No. 816 NAS in August. The unit did not have an auspicious beginning, losing Swordfish DK683 with two of her crew during a night deck landing on 26 August. Due to a variety of technical glitches her operational losses were very high, but she nonetheless in her career escorted twelve convoys across the Atlantic, through the Arctic and down to Gibraltar between September 1943 and November 1944.

No. 816 NAS was disembarked and its place taken by No. 825 NAS, which flew aboard off the Cumbrae Light on 18 December 1943 and from January she commenced working with mainly Canadian escort groups. On 14 March she suffered the first of many Swordfish losses due to the contamination of their fuel when she was forced to ditch, the crew being rescued by Canadian frigate *Outremont*. Despite the fact that Swordfish attacked three German U-boats they all escaped due to the faulty factory assembly of the untested modified depth-charges that they carried, scandalously only two out of 127 dropped actually detonated! This setback was then compounded when between 23 and 26 May, three Swordfish were lost to accidents and three more were damaged during periods of operating in terrible weather conditions. Flying was suspended but, when it was resumed the losses continued, one ditching on 17 April, another with petrol failure on 29 April, a third for the same reason on 6 May and yet another on 11 May, when all her crew were lost.

On 3 June the first Swordfish-III equipped with ASV radar, RATOG take-off boost and four depth-charges landed aboard. During further operations two more Swordfish were lost to accidents on 12 July. At this period she was escorting convoy JW69 to Russia with *Striker* and during the return voyage with convoy RA59A, on 22 August 825 Swordfish assisted escorts in sinking the *U-344* and on 2 September assisted in the sinking of *U-394* also. On return to port No. 825 NAS was disembarked.

The next phase commenced on 10 October when *Vindex* embarked No. 811 NAS and sailed to escort Russia convoy JW61 and return with RA 61. Again the Swordfish were beset by a series of mishaps; on 28 October one crashed at sea and her crew were lost, and on 3 November another crashed, one crew member being lost, while on 7 November the RATOG system failed during launch but the crew were rescued. On 8 November No. 811 NAS was disembarked as it was considered that its aircrew required further training, and No. 825 NAS was re-embarked for Russia convoy JW63. In January No. 825 NAS went ashore once more and No. 813 NAS took part in Russia convoys JW66 and RA66, the *Vindex* working with *Premier* on this occasion, which was the last in which Swordfish were employed aboard her.

Carrier summary

The greatest operational losses suffered by the Fairey Swordfish were sustained during the Channel Dash fiasco and off Colombo, both in 1942. However, the greatest numerical losses occurred when their carriers were sunk, *Courageous, Glorious, Ark Royal, Eagle, Avenger* and *Dasher,* while just one disassembled Swordfish went down with the *Hermes,* the only aircraft she had aboard!

Merchant Aircraft Carriers (MAC ships)

MAC ships were converted oil tankers and grain ships with a basic flight deck affixed atop their hulls, but with minimal servicing facilities. It was thought that, having only low speeds, twelve knots or so, flying operations would have been impossible, but, with the incredible Swordfish if with no other aircraft, it proved a practicable proposition. Originally bulk grain carrying ships were converted, following a suggestion from Sir James Lithgow, who was the Director of Merchant Shipping in the wartime Cabinet. He offered to put his idea to a practical test by converting two ships at the family shipyard with the strict proviso that the Admiralty did not interfere, the old mercantile marine antagonism toward their protectors being ever present. The first two converted were the *Empire MacAlpine* and *Empire MacAndrew* and other grain ships followed. They were successful.

Strong reservations about doing similar conversions to tankers remained but, after considerable debate, due to natural safety fears about operating aircraft from such vessels, oil tankers were also adopted and later flying-off operations actually continued while the tankers were oiling other vessels.

The 8,000-ton *Empire* Class grain carriers *did* have hangars, *Empire MacAlpine, Empire MacAndrew, Empire MacCallum, Empire MacDermott, Empire MacKendrick* and *Empire MacRae,* but no launch catapults and only four arrestor wires added. But of course the later oil tanker conversions, the 9,000-ton *Empire MacCabe, Empire MacColl, Empire MacKay* and *Empire MacMahon,* and the 8,000-ton *Acavus, Adula, Alexia, Amastra, Ancylus, Gadila, Macoma, Miralda* and *Rapana,* could not have hangers for obvious reasons and their Swordfish aircraft were exposed on deck to whatever the North Atlantic weather cared to throw at them, including snow, ice and gales. Each Air Party aboard comprised a Lieutenant-Commander as Air Staff Officer, the Swordfish aircrew, a doctor, a landing control officer (batsman), ten AA gunners, four signalmen and four able seamen.

In total, the MAC-ships with their Swordfish escorted 323 transatlantic convoys and, while only losing six pilots, five observers and eight TAGS during their many flying operations in all weathers, never lost a ship from the convoys they were attached to.

The larger vessels could carry four Swordfish against three on the earlier ships, all such Flights being from No. 836 NAS at HMS *Shrike,* RNAS Maydown to which a Dutch unit, No. 860 NAS, was added working from Netherlands-flagged vessels, but whereas the British ships remained strictly mercantile, the Dutch operated two under the *Marine-Luchtvaartidienst* (MLD – Naval Aviation Service) and so were, officially, naval vessels.

The Swordfish operated from nineteen such vessels, details being: *Acavus* converted in October 1943, operated three Swordfish-IIs of No. 860 NAS between 1943 and 1944; *Adula* converted in February 1944, operated three Swordfish of 'M' Flight among others, including protecting convoys ONF286 and SC170 between 21 February and 31 March 1945; *Alexia* converted in December 1943, operated three Swordfish-IIs in 1944 escorting SC168, SC175 and HX301; *Amastra* converted in September 1943, operated Swordfish-IIs on five round trips from Liverpool to Halifax Nova Scotia up to September 1944, before becoming a ferry carrier in 1944; *Ancylus* converted October 1943, operated three Swordfish-IIs of 'G' Flight from November 1943 to May 1944, 'D' Flight between August and October 1944, and 'O' Flight, before becoming a ferry carrier in 1944.

Empire MacAlpine converted in April 1943, saw the first tanker deck landing by Lieutenant-Commander Ransford Ward Slater on 7 May 1943; *Empire Mac Andrew* converted in July 1943, operated four Swordfish-II in the Atlantic; *Empire MacCabe* converted in December 1943 operated three Swordfish-IIs in the North Atlantic; *Empire MacCallum* converted in December 1943, operated four Swordfish of 'K' Flight; *Empire MacColl* completed in November 1943 operated three Swordfish in the Atlantic, losing Swordfish HS609 on 11 December 1944 when she was knocked off the flight deck and into the sea by another Swordfish which joined her in the drink – fortunately she was unmanned at the time and NE865, which did the deed, was safely rescued by a destroyer; *Empire MacDermott* completed in March 1944, operated four Swordfish in the Atlantic; *Empire MacKay* completed in October 1943, operated three Swordfish in the Atlantic; *Empire MacKendrick* converted in December 1943, operated four Swordfish in the Atlantic; *Empire MacMahon*, completed 1943 operated three Swordfish-IIs on a North Atlantic run and *Empire MacRae* converted in September 1943, operated four Swordfish in the Atlantic.

Gadila operated three Swordfish of 'S' Flight, No. 860 NAS; *Macoma* operated three Swordfish of 'O' and then 'F' Flight, No. 860 NAS; *Miralda* converted in January 1944, operated three Swordfish of 'O' and 'F' Flights and *Rapana*, converted in July 1943, operated Swordfish-II of 'L' Flight, No. 836 NAS.

At the Canadian end of the convoys a facility was set up, No. 743 Fleet Repair Unit, at HMS *Seaborn*, Dartmouth, Nova Scotia, where customized Swordfish were stored and maintained to take the places of any damaged on the crossings.

RAF units

No. 119 Squadron was a Coastal Command unit equipped with long-range flying boats like the Consolidated Catalina and Short Sunderland for most of the war, but with the Battle of the Atlantic won, it had been disbanded. However, with the focus of the European sea war moving to the English Channel and along the Dutch coast, the squadron was re-constituted by re-designating a Flight from No. 415 Squadron at RAF Manston, Kent, and flying the Fairey Albacore from RAF Bircham Newton, Norfolk, from July 1944 and attacking enemy E-boats (*Schnellboot* or S-boot, the equivalent of

Royal Navy MTBs). When the Germans started deploying midget submarines (*Biber, Marder, Molch* and *Seehund* types) against the Allied fleets, these in turn became 119's main targets

As if this transition was revolutionary in January 1945 they were then re-equipped with the Swordfish-III with ASV radar and painted overall night black. These were deployed to hunt German midget submarines operating off the coast of Holland, with detachments of Maldeghem (B.64), St Croix (B.63) and Knocke-Le Zoute (B.83). This task remained their prime duty, and three confirmed victories being claimed, until the final sorties conducted on 8 May 1945.[21]

No. 202 Squadron was based at Gibraltar and mainly conducted anti-submarine patrols with a variety of seaplanes, including eleven Saro London biplane flying machines. They also utilized 3 AACU's three float-equipped Swordfish, as Captain Thomas Quintus Horner explained to this author:

> No. 3 AACU operated three Swordfish floatplanes from Gunport Wharf, where there was a crane big enough to lift the aircraft into and out of the water. The main object of the unit was anti-aircraft co-operation with the Army land-based AA batteries. When the need arose, we used them for short-range patrols.[22]

No. 209 Squadron was a long-range flying boat unit for most of the war, serving world-wide, but had a few Swordfish attached at periods.

3 Anti-Aircraft Co-Operation Unit (3 AACU) served at Gibraltar and Malta while 4 AACU was at Seletar, Singapore, with Swordfish serials P4026 to P4030 inclusive having originally been assigned from August 1939 as part of 'B' Spotter Unit.

No. 9 (Pilot) Advanced Flying Unit at RAF Hullavington, near Chippenham, Wiltshire, was formed from No. 9 Service Flying Training School and later moved to Tealing, Dundee, between August 1944 and June 1945.

War service

Home waters

By the end of 1938, the Swordfish had eclipsed all other carrier-borne torpedo-bombers in the Fleet Air Arm and, upon the outbreak of war on 3 September 1939 there were no fewer than thirteen squadrons that had the Swordfish, and twelve of them formed the principal air complements of the six front-line operational aircraft carriers *Ark Royal, Courageous, Eagle, Furious, Glorious* and *Hermes*.[23] There were also three Flights of float-equipped Swordfish mainly embarked aboard some of the fleets' catapult-equipped heavy ships. Shore-based aircraft included the Mk I serial L9770 detached to 3 AACU at Gibraltar in March 1939 and attached to 'B' Flight No. 202 Squadron RAF from 27 October 1940. A further five Mk.Is (serials P4026 to P4030 inclusive) were based at RAF Seletar, Singapore, from August 1939 with 'B' Flight Spotter Unit from 1 October 1939, being transferred to 4 AACU at the same base up to March 1941.

Narvik and Norway

The German invasion of Norway in April 1940 saw the vital iron ore port of Narvik in the far north of the country seized by German forces landed from ten destroyers and supported from the air. At the 1st Battle of Narvik on 9 April, a flotilla of five British destroyers attacked and destroyed two of these destroyers, plus many transport ships, for the loss of two of their own. The British returned in greater force on 13 April, with the battleship *Warspite* leading a flotilla of nine destroyers. At 1152, when five miles west of Baroy Island at the entrance to Ofotfiord, *Warspite* catapulted off her float-fitted Swordfish to search ahead of the squadron for enemy ambushes. The Swordfish, L9767, was piloted by Petty Officer Frederick Charles 'Ben' Rice DFC, the observer was Lieutenant-Commander Walter Leslie Mortimer Brown and the TAG was Leading Airman Maurice George Pacey.

The cloud cover was low and the steep-sided fiord was hemmed in like a tunnel, through which the Swordfish flew. A U-boat was seen fifty yards off the Bjerkvik jetty and the Swordfish immediately made a dive-bombing attack on her, down to 300 feet (91.44m) before release, scoring a direct hit with one bomb and a near miss with the second; the TAG also sprayed the submarine's conning tower with machine-gun fire. The submarine's return fire damaged the tail of the Swordfish but she kept in action, while the submarine, the *U-64*, then sank within 30 seconds.

At 1240 a German destroyer was sighted by Brown, lurking in a side bay and this ship was engaged by British destroyers and finished off by *Warspite*. Brown then spotted five torpedo tracks heading for the squadron in time for them to be avoided. A second enemy destroyer was sunk in Narvik harbour while the other four fled up Rombaks Fiord. At 1500 Brown reported two destroyers at the head of the fiord, one of which was engaged and ran aground. The Swordfish still had one bomb left to her and she duly dropped this on the destroyer, adding to her discomfiture and she was finished off by shellfire. This left three enemy ships in the inner fiord but on the approach of the British destroyers two were scuttled by their crews and one was torpedoed, making a clean sweep of all eight. The Swordfish was finally recovered by *Warspite* after a continuous four hours airborne, and an outstanding performance during which she had sunk a U-boat, reported enemy torpedoes, bombed a destroyer, taken photographs and sent in a stream of detailed reports of enemy movements. The British commander, Vice-Admiral Sir William Jock Whitworth, was fulsome in his praise, writing in his official report:

The enemy reports made by *Warspite's* aircraft were invaluable. I doubt if ever a ship-borne aircraft has been used to such good purpose as it was in this operation.

Dunkirk

In May, Swordfish went on loan to Coastal Command and carried out patrols over the English Channel interspersed with minelaying the ports of the Low Countries as they fell to the Germans in rapid succession. They were based at Detling, Manston, North

Coates and Thorney Island RAF stations and continued through to October when the threat of invasion waned.

Eleven Swordfish of No. 812 Squadron each armed with a 250lb (113kg) bomb, carried out dive-bombing attacks on a German gun battery and concentrations of Panzers seen near Gravelines, south-west of Dunkirk, on 25 May 1940. They claimed to have destroyed three German tanks for the loss of one of the Swordfish. The following day six RAF Hawker Hector light bombers accompanied by nine of the No. 812 Swordfish, dive-bombed the same target while No. 825 NAS provided spotter Swordfish for the light cruiser *Galatea* to bombard the same target with her 6-inch guns, destroying two artillery pieces.

Mers-el-Kebir – 3 July 1940.

The French Government set up at Vichy refused offers to disarm their ships and the British determined to put them out of commission in case they either 'collaborated' with Hitler or were seized by the Germans and Italians. After considerable delay Force 'H' under Admiral Sir James Somerville with the battleships *Resolution* and *Valiant* and battle-cruiser *Renown*, opened fire on the French squadron at the naval harbour of Mers-el-Kebir, near Oran, Algeria, (Operation *Catapult*) sinking the battleship *Bretagne* and damaging the battleship *Provence,* battle-cruiser *Dunkerque,* and destroyer *Mogador.* The undamaged battle-cruiser *Strasbourg* with an escort of five destroyers, managed to escape Somerville's attention and got free at high speed. By the time it was realized they were off only a strike by six Swordfish armed with 250lb SAP bombs remained between them and safely, and this was launched at 1825 and claimed to have scored one hit, but, in truth, no hits were scored and two of the Swordfish were shot down, their crews being rescued by the destroyer *Wrestler*.

A further sortie by six Swordfish, this time with torpedoes, was launched at 1950 and attacked at 2055, some twenty minutes after sunset. The aircraft approached from the land side of the battle-cruiser thus having her silhouetted against afterglow and once more a hit was claimed, but, once more, none was obtained and *Strasbourg* escaped unscathed.

On 6 July three further Swordfish attacks were launched from *Ark Royal* in an attempt to finish off the damaged *Dunkerque* (Operation *Lever*), which had been run aground at St André. The first consisted of six Swordfish and achieved complete surprise; they claimed to have scored four hits on the stationery vessel on her starboard side amidships. The second attack was by a flight of three Swordfish and met heavy AA fire, they claimed to have scored two 'possible' hits on her starboard side. The third Swordfish attack was by a further three-aircraft flight and was opposed by Vichy French Dewoitine D520 fighter aircraft, and although all returned safely to *Ark Royal*, they failed to score any hits. Despite all these claims only one torpedo actually hit the *Dunkerque*; a second destroyed the patrol vessel *Terre-Neuve* alongside her, and detonated her fourteen depth-charges and 3,086lb (1,400kg) of TNT tore a large hole in her side.[24]

Calabria – 9 July 1940

The main Italian fleet with two battleships, six heavy and eight light cruisers and numerous destroyers was at sea covering a convoy from Naples to Benghazi. The Mediterranean Fleet, which included the carrier *Eagle*, intercepted this huge force on 9 July and launched two-bomber attacks with her Swordfish. An air striking force of nine of No. 813 NAS's Swordfish, was launched at 1145. The enemy was about ninety miles distant but at their best speed of 100mph it took them a while to close the gap, arriving at 1252. They missed the main target, the two battleships, and, instead, attacked the 8-inch cruisers *Trento*, *Fiume*, *Zara* and *Pola* in error, attacking between 1315 and 1326 at a height of 80ft and launching at ranges of around 3,000ft. Heavy fire was met from the cruisers and their destroyer screen, but no Swordfish were hit. Likewise, the Italians ships escaped totally unscathed.

On landing back aboard the Swordfish were re-armed for a second attempt, and meanwhile the heavy ships duelled, Admiral Andrew Browne Cunningham's flagship, the battleship *Warspite*, scoring a 15-inch shell hit on the enemy battleship *Giulio Cesare*, upon which the Italians turned and ran for home. The only hope of bringing them to book was for them to be slowed down.

The second Swordfish attack comprised nine aircraft, which attacked at 1545, but again, instead of attacking the two battleships, they concentrated on the heavy cruisers when they arrived. The Swordfish attacked in three waves of three aircraft apiece between 1610 and 1615, making their drops from ahead of their targets, which proved to be the Italian 3 Division, led by *Bolzano*. The young pilots claimed to have scored at least one hit on this 8-inch cruiser, while the Italians, in their turn, claimed to have shot down at least one Swordfish. Both were totally mistaken and no hits were made by either side. Once again, warships steaming at speed and throwing up a heavy defensive fire had proved elusive targets. Pre-war exercises did not resemble actual combat. One Swordfish pilot, Commander John Bruce Murray, told this author:

> Looking back, it does seem that we failed miserably, but it was the first time that we had experienced anything quite like it. A Swordfish is a slow aeroplane and is not an ideal aircraft for daylight attacks on very heavily defended targets, for one is within range of opposition for a very long time up to the point of dropping the torpedoes, and also a very long time is spent getting out of range afterwards. The heavy gun barrage was also most disturbing. Our aim was not good and we failed in our objective.[25]

Operations off Norway – September/October 1940

The carrier *Furious* mounted two air attacks against Norwegian targets in September 1940 in which what remained of No. 825 NAS participated. At 0800 on 6 September, Operation 'DF' saw *Furious*, escorted by the battleship *Nelson*, light cruisers *Bonaventure* and *Naiad* and destroyers *Ashanti*, *Bedouin*, *Eskimo*, *Matabele*, *Punjabi*, *Somali* and *Tartar*, leave Scapa Flow. By 0500 the next day the force reached 62° 00' North, 01° 00 East, where the air striking force was flown off.

The target, Tromsø harbour, was found to be almost barren of suitable targets but two small vessels were attacked and left in 'a sinking condition'. In actuality the Norwegian steamer *Tellus*, one of the targets, was not damaged at all, while the other, the Danish steamer *Sejrø*, was only slightly damaged and, although her crew abandoned her in panic, the German auxiliary *Schiff-47* forced them to re-board their vessel and she was stopped from drifting ashore. After the raid the squadron was back in Scapa Flow by 2000 the same day.

This was followed on 22 September by Operation 'DT', which saw *Furious* escorted by the heavy cruiser *Berwick* and destroyers *Eskimo*, *Matabele* and *Somali* mount a similar Swordfish air strike on shipping at night against Trondheim. Again targets were scarce and although attacks were made on the *NT-13 Adler* and some freighters, very little damage was inflicted on any of them. For this meagre outcome No. 816 NAS had lost two Swordfish and No. 825 NAS three, including one that crash-landed in Sweden and was interned along with her crew.

On 16 October yet another attempt was made to attack Tromsø, Operation 'DU' and for this *Furious* had embarked nine Swordfish from No. 816 NAS and nine of No. 825 NAS. This was to be the first night torpedo attack mounted in squadron strength and the aircraft were despatched in two waves of six Swordfish apiece, from each Swordfish squadron, each wave being escorted by three Blackburn Skua-II dive-bombers from No. 801 NAS. Again results were mediocre, one freighter was attacked in Tromsø harbour, while the Skuas dive-bombed oil tanks at Ramfjordnes and the seaplane based of Skattoia. Thankfully this time no Swordfish were lost, but one Skua force-landed in Sweden.

Taranto – 11/12 November 1940

Operation *Judgement* had been long in the planning. The main Italian fleet base, 'secure' within the heel of Italy and surrounded by numerous *Regia Aeronautica* airfields, it had an extensive 87-strong balloon barrage, 2.6 miles (4.2km) of anti-torpedo nets, 22 searchlights, and anti-aircraft batteries with 101 heavy weapons and 193 machine-guns, plus the numerous guns of the fleet itself, consisting of six battleships, seven heavy and two light cruisers and many destroyers. There was no radar of course, only 22 listening devices. The harbour could only be approached from the open central Mediterranean, far from the British fleet anchorage at Alexandria, Egypt, and, in theory, the Italians would have ample time to prepare for any such approach. Little wonder Benito Mussolini would boast from his balcony at the Palazzo Venezia that it was '*Invulnerabile*' (invulnerable).

Quietly, a number of senior British naval officers had been thinking quite the reverse. As early as the Abyssinian crisis of 1935 plans had been drawn up to convert the planned torpedo bomber attack on the German Fleet at Kiel in 1918, into an updated version to take out the equally battle reluctant Italian fleet at Taranto. Under the pre-war command of Admiral Sir Dudley Pound, this plan was again dusted off in 1938 and Captain Arthur Lumley St George Lyster, captain of the Mediterranean Fleet's only carrier, the *Glorious*, informed him that such an attack was indeed viable and had been trained for. Two years later Pound was the First Sea Lord, while Lyster commanded the two carriers, *Illustrious* and *Eagle,* in Admiral Sir Andrew Cunningham's Mediterranean Fleet and Britain and Italy were at war. The plan was put into effect.[26]

The plan was to use both carriers, but the old *Eagle* was having constant problems with her equipment and suffered first a fire, which consumed three Swordfish aboard her, and then her fuel system broke down. Five of her Swordfish were therefore transferred over to *Illustrious* and she carried them into battle, having aircraft from Nos 813, 815, 819 and 824 aboard, and escorted by the heavy cruisers *Berwick* and *York,* light cruisers *Glasgow* and *Gloucester* and destroyers *Hasty, Havock, Hyperion* and *Ilex.* Of the twenty-four aircraft assigned to the attack, twelve only carried duplex magnetic/contact torpedoes, the other twelve were divided into bombing aircraft and flare droppers. The water of the harbour was very shallow at 39ft (12m) and it was feared that the torpedoes would 'bottom out' if dropped from too great a height or at too great a speed. The missiles were duly modified with wood stability fins added.

The attack aircraft were flown off in two waves of twelve aircraft apiece. The initial attack was led by Lieutenant-Commander Kenneth 'Hooch' Williamson of No. 815 NAS and flew off at 2100 on 11 November. The second wave flew off at 2230, one aborting the mission and another twenty minutes late. The leading section attacked at 2258 dropping flares and then dive-bombing oil storage tanks. Three torpedo-armed aircraft then attacked the battleship *Conte di Cavour* scoring a direct hit, which blew a 39ft × 26 ft (12m × 8m) hole in her and she sank. Although she was later salvaged she was never operational again. Williamson himself was shot down by AA fire, his observer, Lieutenant Norman Scarlett, recalling, 'We put a wing tip in the water.' Fortunately they were both rescued. Their other target, the battleship *Andrea Doria,* was unharmed. Three more torpedo droppers followed and launched at the two new battleships *Littorio* and *Vittorio Veneto,* hitting the former twice but missing the latter. The rest of this wave were bombers that attacked both cruiser and destroyer targets from 1,500ft (460m).

The second wave was commanded by Lieutenant-Commander John William Hale of No. 819 NAS and around midnight they began dropping flares. They again targeted *Littorio,* scoring one more hit, and again missed the *Vittorio Veneto,* while another scored a torpedo hit on the battleship *Caio Duilio* and knocked a 36ft × 23 ft (11m × 7m) hole in her, which caused her forward magazine to flood and she had to be run aground to prevent her sinking. Again this wave suffered one casualty, Lieutenant Gerald Wentworth Loscombe Abingdon Bayly being destroyed by the heavy cruiser *Gorizia.* The final attack was a dive-bombing run against a cruiser by the tardy aircraft that arrived a quarter-of-an hour behind the others, but survived. The *Littorio* had two hits on her starboard hull, with one 49ft × 33 ft (15m × 10m) hole and one 39ft × 30ft (12m × 9m) hole; and one on her port hull, with a 23ft × 4ft 11in (7m × 1.5m) hole, and also had to be run aground with her bows under water and 32 of her crew killed. The heavy cruiser *Trento* was hit by one bomb that failed to explode, as was the destroyer *Libeccio,* while the destroyer *Pessagno* was near-missed and damaged.

Such a success deserved pressing home and plans were made for a repeat strike the following night with fifteen more Swordfish, but this had to be aborted due to deteriorating weather.[27]

The Swordfish had lost two of their number and one aircrew, a remarkably light casualty list considering the Italians had fired off 13,489 shells from their shore guns and many more from the warships themselves, while, as for the balloon barrage, '... nobody noticed it...'[28] Cunningham's verdict was, 'Admirably planned and most gallantly executed in the face of intense anti-aircraft fire, Operation *Judgement* was a great success.' Mussolini's opinion was remarkably sanguine, his son-in-law Count Galeazzo Ciano, Italian Foreign Minister, recording in his diary:

> A black day. The British, without warning [sic], have attacked the Italian fleet at anchor in Taranto, and have sunk the battleship *Cavour* and seriously damaged the battleships *Littorio* and *Duilio*. These ships will remain out of the fight for many months. I thought I would find the Duce downhearted. Instead, he took the blow quite well and does not, at the moment, seem to have fully realized its gravity.[29]

Spartivento – 27 November 1940

Force 'H' from Gibraltar, under Admiral Somerville, was charged with escorting a convoy through the western Mediterranean (Operation *White*) and meeting a detached force from Alexandria. The British had the battle-cruiser *Renown*, the carrier *Ark Royal*, four light cruisers (two with RAF personnel as passengers) and eight destroyers. The battleship *Ramillies*, accompanied by one heavy, one light and one AA cruiser, with four destroyers were to rendezvous west of the Sicilian Narrows. The Italians sent an intercepting force comprising two battleships, *Vittorio Veneto* and *Giulio Cesare*, six heavy cruisers and fourteen destroyers, to intercept before the two British groups could join forces. In the event that plan failed and the British had united when the fleets met on 27 November. The Italian Admiral Inigo Campioni therefore, having considered that, 'A state of affairs was thus created which, taking into consideration all the information at my disposal, was unfavourable to us numerically and qualitatively,' decided to run for home again. He signalled his ships at 1220, 'Do not, repeat, not, engage in battle.' But to get safely away his units had to pass across the front of the British squadron, which was actively seeking battle with him. He had the same number of battleships but they were faster ships; if *Ark Royal*'s Swordfish could slow them down, prospects looked good.

Accordingly, *Ark Royal*, operating separately and astern, launched eleven of her Swordfish from No. 810 NAS led by Lieutenant-Commander Mervyn Johnstone; their slow speed meant that the two fleets were fully engaged in a gunnery action by the time they arrived over the enemy. The Swordfish concentrated their attacks on the two enemy battleships, launching at ranges from between 700 and 800 yards (640 and 731m) through heavy flak, some even machine-gunning the bridges of their targets as they flew over. They claimed to have scored a torpedo hit on *Vittorio Veneto*, but this was not the case and once more every torpedo missed its target. No Swordfish were hit either and on return to the carrier they prepared for a second strike, although it was now late in the afternoon and prospects were not good.

At 1410 *Ark Royal* flew off seven Swordfish and these made an attack out of the sun against a squadron of heavy cruisers led by the *Pola*. Surprise was achieved, and torpedo hits were again claimed on both the leading and rear cruiser of the column, but again, this was not the case and the Italians were unharmed. Two Swordfish were hit by AA fire, but all seven managed to return to the *Ark Royal*. With the Italian ships far ahead and increasing the gap as they fled homeward, and with the convoy needing his support, Somerville gave up the chase and turned back and the battle was over.

Cape Matapan – March 1941

Promised ample Luftwaffe air support, the Italian Fleet sortied out on 26 March with the battleship *Vittorio Veneto* with six heavy and two light cruisers and seventeen destroyers, to attack convoys running to Greece through the Mediterranean, but they were intercepted by the Mediterranean Fleet under Admiral Cunningham who had been forewarned by the breaking of the Italian codes. Aboard the carrier *Formidable* were Nos. 826 and 829 NAS with a total of ten Fairey Albacores and four Swordfish, while ashore at Maleme, Crete, were five more Swordfish from No. 815 NAS. Five catapult seaplanes from No. 700 NAS were aboard the battleships *Warspite*, *Valiant* and *Barham* of Cunningham's fleet.

Initially a torpedo-bomber strike at 1127 by No. 826 failed to score any hits but a second attack, led by Lieutenant-Commander John Dalyell-Stead of No. 829 NAS, mounted at 1520, did obtain a hit aft on the *Vittorio Veneto*, which opened her up to 4,000 tons of sea water and reduced her speed to 19 knots. This persuaded the Italians to head for home, although they remained unaware that the British had battleships at sea. Sterling work by one of the float Swordfish embarked aboard *Warspite*, piloted by Petty Officer Ben Rice, in the air for a record five hours and nearing the end of her endurance. Forced to land alongside her parent ship with just 15 minutes' flying fuel left, this aircraft was recovered at 18 knots, swung inboard without a hitch, refuelled and sent off a second time and in touch with the enemy until sunset, established sighting of the Italian fleet withdrawing slowly and this aircraft maintained a close watch on her, directing in further strike forces until forced to make for Suda Bay as fuel again ran low.

A third attack was mounted by six Albacores and two Swordfish from No. 829 NAS, led by Lieutenant-Commander Gerald Saunt, from *Formidable*, to which two of No. 815 NAS Swordfish contributed from Crete. One of these Swordfish pilots, Lieutenant-Commander Michael Torrens-Spence of No. 815 NAS, watched the Albacore attack fail, but was able to observe a gap in the Italian smoke-screen, through which he launched against the heavy cruiser *Pola*, scoring a hit, which reduced her speed to just six knots. The Captain of the *Pola*, later rescued, stated, 'Either that pilot was mad or he is the bravest man in the world.'

The hit was decisive for at 2015 the Italian Admiral Angelo Iachino ordered her two sister cruisers, *Zara* and *Fiume*, with destroyers *Alfieri* and *Carducci*, to return and stand by her, and in a night action they were all destroyed by Cunningham's battleships and destroyers in short order. *Vittorio Veneto*, unfortunately, eluded all pursuit and escaped.

Bismarck action

When the new German battleship *Bismarck*, accompanied by the heavy cruiser *Prinz Eugen*, sailed from the Baltic on 18 May 1941 on Operation *Rheinübung* to attack Atlantic convoys, the new carrier *Victorious* was with the Home Fleet but still in the process of working up her squadrons, one of which was No. 825 NAS with nine Swordfish, some of which were fitted with the new ASV radar. The veteran carrier *Ark Royal* was with Force 'H' at Gibraltar having just escorted a troop convoy through the Mediterranean. After sinking the battle-cruiser *Hood*, the *Bismarck* escaped but on the night of 24–25 May nine Swordfish from No. 825 NAS aboard *Victorious*, in three sub-flights led by Lieutenant-Commander Eugene Esmonde, Lieutenant Philip David 'Percy' Gick and Lieutenant (A) Henry Charles Mitchel Pollard respectively, made a torpedo attack and scored one direct hit. The Swordfish survived and even survived landing back aboard the *Victorious* with her deck rising and falling by 60ft (18.2m) each thirty seconds in the appalling conditions, and only one of them was damaged.

On 26 May *Ark Royal* joined the hunt and made two attacks. The first around midday mistakenly attacked their own escorting light cruiser, *Sheffield*, but failed to hit her.[30] A second wave of fifteen Swordfish from Nos 810, 818 and 828 NAS led by Lieutenant-Commander Trevensen Penrose Coode, made a series of attacks that same evening between 2055 and 2125 through heavy AA fire. One 18-inch torpedo, released by Swordfish L9726, piloted by Temporary Sub-Lieutenant John William Charlton Moffat, with Temporary-Lieutenant John D Miller and Leading Airman Albert J Hayman, hit aft on the port stern of the ship, crippling the battleship's steering gear. One Swordfish had aborted her attack due to heavy flak and five were damaged, one crashing aboard the *Ark Royal* on returning. But that one hit had been crucial, allowing the battleships *King George V* and *Rodney* to close with her and pound her to a wreck, which was then sunk by torpedoes from the heavy cruiser *Dorsetshire*.

North Africa and Malta strike forces

While the carriers *Eagle* and *Illustrious* were operational in the western Mediterranean, they made their presence felt on a regular basis. A few of the choice operations they conducted against Axis merchant shipping are included here. From time to time they disembarked and operated from land bases, and, when these two carriers were finally withdrawn due to damage, this became a regular feature of their work.

On 5 July No. 813 NAS flying from a shore airfield, made a dusk attack on Tobruk harbour sinking the destroyer *Zeffiro*, blowing the bows off the destroyer *Euro*, sinking the 3,955-ton freighter *Manzoni* and forcing two more to be run aground. Five days later No. 813 NAS attacked Augusta harbour, Sicily, sinking the destroyer *Leone Pancaldo*. On the night of 20 July six Swordfish from No. 824 NAS, working out of Sidi Barrani, sank the destroyers *Nembo* and *Ostra* and the 2,333-ton freighter *Sereno* in the Gulf of Bomba.

Between 22 and 24 August 1940, three Swordfish from No. 824 NAS, commanded by Captain Oliver Patch, RM, with Lieutenant Neville Cheesman and Lieutenant John Welham, had been readied at Maaten Bagush landing field with extra fuel tanks and flown up to Sidi Barani to attack an Italian force reported anchored in the Gulf of Bomba, near Tobruk. Here they duly arrived at 1230 and flew line abreast at 200 yards apart. Patch sank the Italian submarine *Iride* offshore while the other two sank the 1,976- ton depot ship *Monte Gargano*. It transpired that these vessels were part of a force attempting to convey *Maiali* (Pig) slow running torpedoes manned by frogmen, to attack the British fleet anchorage at Alexandria and this success delayed that operation for a year. Claims that '...four ships were sunk by three torpedoes...', although still bandied about even today by some authorities who should know better (including the Fleet Air Arm Museum), have long been known to be false – the torpedo boat *Calipso* was unharmed and helped with rescue work, and there never was a second submarine present, as frequently claimed.

No. 815 NAS from *Illustrious* sank the freighters *Gloria Stella* and *Maria Eugenia* on the night of 16/17 September at Benghazi. On the night of 24/25 October, however, fourteen Swordfish from Nos 815, 819 and 824 NAS made an attack on Tobruk, with four of No. 824's Swordfish working from the Fuka Landing Ground dropping bombs to distract the enemy while the twelve other aircraft dropped mines off the entrance to the harbour. In essence, the two Swordfish squadrons aboard *Eagle* had searched 1,851,586 square miles of ocean, consumed 166,732 gallons of aviation fuel, the pilots had clocked up 8,000 flying hours, and the Swordfish had made 1,979 deck landings, made nineteen torpedo hits for the loss of four of their number, all between 4 August 1939 and 4 August 1940.[31]

The *Illustrious* launched a raid on Port Laki, Leros, in the Aegean on 26 November, with fifteen Swordfish from Nos 815 and 819 NAS. After the carrier was badly damaged her surviving aircraft worked out of Malta. On 21 December nine Swordfish from *Illustrious* attacked two Italian convoys off Kerkkenah Islands, Tunisia, *en route* to Tripoli, sinking two transports of 7,437 tons.

The establishment of a Swordfish striking force based on Malta was an early development and in July No. 830 NAS was formed from the Swordfish-I of No. 767 NAS detachment at Hal Far, Malta, that had been earlier training with the carrier *Argus* in the South of France. They were later replaced by Swordfish-IIs. They later merged with No. 828 NAS, to form Naval Air Squadron, Malta, as a flare-dropping unit.

Like the fighter aircraft on the island, but with far less publicity, the Swordfish required continual reinforcements and during Operation *Excess*, the *Ark Royal* embarked six Swordfish-IIs for the island, one of which became inoperational, the other five being successfully flown off on 9 January. During Operation *Railway-I*, on 27 June, the carrier *Furious* flew off another nine Swordfish-IIs, which all arrived safely. During the large Operation *Substance* convoy six more Swordfish-IIs were flown off on 25 July 1941 and finally, on 16 October, Operation *Callboy* saw the *Argus* with No. 828 NAS embarked fly off Albacores plus two Swordfish, but one was lost *en route*.

Between January 1941 and November 1942, in only one single month, November 1941, were there ever more than ten to twelve serviceable Swordfish active from Malta, but despite their tiny number they made the hours of darkness in the central Mediterranean a place of fear for Axis troop and supply convoys. Lieutenant-Commander Charles Lamb took over the squadron and recorded that during July the unit was able to sink an average of 50,000 tons of Rommel's supply ships with an average hit rate of 75 per cent. It was during this time that the ASV (Anti- Surface-Vessel) radar began to be fitted, which made them even deadlier and in August they sank 100,000 tons. One of these was a 6,338-ton vessel put down on 3 September, while on the night of the 12/13 September they sank a further three transports totalling 15,538 tons, part of a convoy from Naples to Tripoli.

During the brief and unhappy Greek adventure, No. 815 NAS from *Illustrious,* was disembarked at Eleusis airfield, Athens, and moved up to Paramythia, Albania, for a five-week period where they were joined by No. 819 NAS. Operating in bitter weather conditions and flying across mountain ranges, these Swordfish were credited with the destruction of five Italian transport ships, including the spectacular destruction of an ammunition ship, in the Adriatic and damage to five others, making their final foray on 1 April 1941. The German invasion marked a long withdrawal back via Eleusis, Maleme, Crete and finally Dekheila, Egypt.

Those Swordfish operating in the desert eventually came under control of No. 201 Naval Co-operation Group at Alexandria, under Air Commodore Leonard Horatio Slatter. Admiral Cunningham was full of enthusiasm for these operations (contrary to some more recent allegations) writing:

> Apropos of the Fleet Air Arm, we had had Swordfish and Albacores operating in the Western Desert for some time. Because of their specialised sea training in navigation they had made quite a name for themselves as accurate flare-droppers, circling the bombing area with flares after which the Wellingtons made their attacks with bombs. I believe the Germans reported that the British had some helicopters in the Western Desert which were very accurate bombers. These were probably the old Swordfish going up wind.[32]

Channel dash

Following their foray into the North Atlantic during 1941, the German battle-cruisers *Gneisenau* and *Scharnhorst* had taken refuge in Brest, where they were later joined by the heavy cruiser *Prinz Eugen*, the latter having narrowly missed sinking the carrier *Furious* with a convoy bound for Gibraltar. The three ships were subjected to sustained bombing attacks over a period of months, while British warships blockaded the port in the Bay of Biscay in case they put to sea once more. The Germans decided that it was too risky to face the Royal Navy, but that with boldness they could surprise the British by taking the shortest and most direct route home, via the English Channel. Hitler reasoned, quite correctly, that British reaction would be slow and fragmented and that, escorted by destroyers and minesweepers, and guarded overhead by continuous fighter patrols, a high-speed dash had an excellent chance of success. Thus Operation *Cerberus*, was mounted between 11 and 13 February 1942.

The operation worked even better than the Germans had hoped; their ships were well into the Straits of Dover by 1100 on 12 February without detection despite the British mounting Operation *Fuller* with continuous Coastal Command patrols. The RAF despatched over 242 bombers to destroy the enemy ships, something they had been saying for two decades they could achieve with ease, but of these, most failed to even find the enemy ships at all, while others attacked a flotilla of British destroyers heading for the scene instead. No hits were made on any target. As a last resort a scratch force from No. 825 NAS at Lee-on-Solent, and still commanded by Lieutenant-Commander Eugene Esmonde, was assembled. The squadron was being rebuilt after the loss of *Ark Royal* and just six of the Swordfish deemed ready had been moved over to RAF Manston to make a night attack on the German squadron. Instead, they were sent off in broad daylight having been promised an escort of five squadrons of Supermarine Spitfires.

In the event only a single squadron of Spitfires, just ten fighters, met them at the rendezvous and this proved insufficient to protect them from the hordes of Luftwaffe fighters over the German fleet. In the ensuing one-sided action all six of the Swordfish were shot down by fighters and flak, and only five of the eighteen aircrew survived this forlorn hope.

North Atlantic and Arctic convoys

The Swordfish was credited with the destruction, or of assisting in the destruction, of twenty U-boats. Most notably, Swordfish from the escort carrier *Vindex* sank four U-boats during the passage of one Arctic convoy. In her aggressor role the Swordfish was said to have destroyed in excess of 300,000 tons of Axis shipping.

The ASV Mk.XI radar in a radome mounted under the chin of the Swordfish, had a range of about 25 miles (40km) against surface ships, and even surfaced U-boats in certain weather conditions, but with the introduction of the *Schnorkel* breathing apparatus to Admiral Karl Doenitz's underwater fleet, this shrank to less than 5 miles (8km) in the calmest of waters.

Night patrols were conducted, ranging out ahead of the convoy to distances of 25 miles (40km) to 90 miles (145 km). Once radar contact was established flares were dropped and attacks made, while escorting destroyers were vectored out to known last positions of the enemy.

Foreign use

Australia

Six crated Swordfish-Is arrived unannounced at Bullsbrook railway sidings, Freemantle, on 17 March 1942. These were assembled on the orders of Group Captain Paddy Hefferman at RAAF Pearce and 'unofficially' added to the establishment of the Pearce Station Headquarters (V4685, V4692, V4694) as station hacks; by No. 14 (V4693, V4694) on communications duty; and No. 25 Squadron RAAF (V4688, V4689, V4693), these latter flying anti-submarine patrols in the Rottnest island and Gage Roads area of the Port of Freemantle. These were subsequently re-crated in April and May and returned to RNARY Nairobi, Kenya.[33]

Yet a seventh Swordfish-I came into Australian hands when K8849 from the battleship *Warspite* visited Sydney, NSW, in February–March 1942. Six of these float planes were en route to 151 MU at Singapore as reserves for the battleship *Prince of Wales* and the battle-cruiser *Repulse*, but they were sunk and re-allocated to the fleet reserve at Ceylon instead. They arrived at Freemantle with the floats in crates. K8849 joined the Seaplane Training Flight at RAAF Rathmines, NSW, where it was subsequently written off.

Canada

From 1943 onward the Swordfish was used by the Naval Gunnery School, Yarmouth, and also at the Royal Navy Station, Dartmouth, both in Nova Scotia. They had sliding hoods fitted to their open cockpits during the winter months. As late as 1946 the Royal Canadian Navy's Fleet Requirement Unit had Swordfish on its establishment and as a training aircraft the last recorded flight by the RCN was on 12 July 1947. The Royal Canadian Air Force also employed the Swordfish.

Germany

During an attack on German ground positions near Dunkirk by No. 825 NAS, led by Lieutenant-Commander James Brian Buckley, on 29 May 1940, five Swordfish were destroyed. One of these Swordfish, coded '5B', was captured relatively intact.

On 15 November, Swordfish L9724 from No. 812 NAS, operating from RAF North Coates, was hit by AA fire while attacking Barley airfield near Dunkirk. The aircraft ended up on her back but the crew survived and were made PoWs.

Italy

The *Regia Aeronautica* came into possession of at least three Swordfish.

On 2 August 1940, the *Ark Royal* launched an attack on Cagliari, in Sardinia. One Swordfish, P4127, was hit by flak and force-landed at Elmas airfield; the aircraft was almost intact and the aircrew were made PoWs. This machine was restored to full working condition by the local offshoot of the *Società Italiana Caproni* aircraft company, who replaced the Pegasus engine with a more available and familiar 650hp (485kW) Alfa Romeo 125 engine, itself a derivative of the Bristol Jupiter. She was then transported to *Stabilimento Costruzioni Aeronautiche* (Aircraft Construction Plant) at Guidonia, near Rome, on 27 February 1941 and remained there as late as 6 April 1942.

On 9 September 1940, the *Eagle* launched an attack on Maritza airfield, Rhodes, but the aircraft were intercepted by Fiat CR.32 and Cr.42 fighters alerted by an earlier attack from the carrier *Illustrious*, and four Swordfish were shot down. K8422 was one of those hit and forced to crash land. Eventually this machine was also transported to Guidonia. She was returned to serviceable condition on into 1941 being cannibalised to maintain P4127.

The *Regia Aeronautica* captured one of the Swordfish used in the Taranto attack, 'L4A' piloted by Lieutenant-Commander Kenneth Williamson of No. 815 Squadron, which went into the harbour from a height of only 20ft (6.09m), but she was certainly non-operational after salvage.

Netherlands

The Dutch converted two of their merchant vessels, the *Acavus* and *Gadila,* into MAC-ships as full *Marine-Luchtvaartidienst* (MLD – Naval Aviation Service) warships and to fly from them, in June 1943, formed No. 860 NAS at HMS *Merlin,* RNAS Donibristle. They had six Swordfish-Is on establishment under Lieutenant Jan van der Tooren. They were transferred to HMS *Shrike,* RNAS Maydown, in November 1943, and having built up to a strength of twelve Swordfish-IIs commenced operations. They also later operated from the *Macoma,* in conjunction with No. 836 NAS. The squadron was later again re-equipped with Swordfish-IIIs from March 1945 onward, and operated in two sections, one based at Maydown the other at Dartmouth. They ended their days as a Fairey Barracuda squadron aboard the escort carrier *Nairana,* which post-war became the Netherlands carrier *Karel Doorman.*

Spain

While shadowing the German battle-cruisers *Gneisenau* and *Scharnhorst* on 8 March 1942, the Swordfish floatplane P4073, of No. 700 NAS, operating from the battleship *Malaya,* ran out of fuel. The two German warships had approached convoy SL.67 off West Africa but, on seeing that it was protected by a battleship, along with the destroyers *Faulknor* and *Forester,* the German Admiral turned away but *Malaya's* floatplane followed to ensure they did not return. They pressed their tailing too far and their aircraft was forced to make a landing in the Spanish territory of the Canary Islands, where both Swordfish and aircrew were interned. The Spanish found that the aircraft was otherwise in perfect condition and they impressed her into service with the Spanish air force with the 54 *Escuadrilla* based at Puerto de la Cruz, Tenerife, assigning to her serial HR6-1 on 6 December 1943. They utilized her for patrol work and did not finally pension her off until March 1945.

Strangely, a similar incident followed a month later. On 30 April 1942, Swordfish W5843 of No. 813 NAS working from North Front, Gibraltar, was carrying out an anti-submarine patrol over the Gibraltar Strait. Somehow the aircrew became disorientated and, running out of fuel, had to make a force-landing in Spanish Morocco, coming down in the area of Ras el Farea and Pota Pescadores. The Spanish interred the aircrew and took into custody the Swordfish, of which no more was heard.

Sweden
On 22 September 1940 No. 825 NAS was part of the force that attacked Trondheim and Swordfish L2860, made a force-landing at Jamtland, near Lake Krycktjarn, in neutral Sweden. The crew survived and were interred.

Vichy-France
During an attack on an Italian convoy Swordfish L7689 (coded 'B') made a forced-landing on the beach at Hammamet, Tunisia, and the aircrew, Petty Officer Charles Herbert Wines DCM, RNVR and Leading Airman Leslie M Edwards, were interred.

Finale

The last ever Swordfish was delivered as late as August 1944. The final Fleet Air Arm usage of the Swordfish was with No. 836 Squadron, which did not finally disband until 21 May 1945. Even then a few Swordfish continued operating in training squadrons until the summer of 1946. The two longest-serving Swordfish were HS255 at RNARY disposed of in 1952 and HS255, which survived at Youngsfield airport, at Cape Town, RSA, until the following year.

Production had ceased in 1944 with 2,396 Swordfish being built, 898 Mk.Is, 1080 Mk.IIs and 327 Mk.IIIs. It was the final end of the military biplane age.

Preserved aircraft

1–3. Three aircraft, Swordfish Mk.I serial W5856, formerly of the Strathallan Collection; Swordfish Mk.II serial LS326 with a newly rebuilt engine; and Swordfish Mk.III serial NF389, are part of the Royal Navy Historic Flight based at HMS *Heron*, RNAS Yeovilton, Somerset. W5856 and LS326 are in flying condition, while NF389 is being restored to airworthy condition by the Flight.

4. Swordfish Mk.II, serial HS618, is on permanent display at the Fleet Air Arm Museum, also at HMS *Heron*, RNAS Yeovilton, Ilchester, Somerset.

5. Swordfish Mk.II (for some reason bestowed with the false serial number of NS122 due to its original serial number being lost after years of neglect), is with Vintage Wings at the Canada Aviation and Space Museum, Ottawa/Rockcliffe Airport, Ottawa, Ontario, Canada.

6. Swordfish Mk.III, serial NF370, is a display item at the Imperial War Museum site at Duxford, Cambridgeshire. She is painted overall black to represent her time with No. 145 Squadron, RAF, at Bircham Newton, Norfolk, from January 1945 onward.

7. Swordfish Mk.III, construction number F/B 3527A, is in flying condition and carries the civilian registration C-GEVS. It is operated by Vintage Wings of Canada, at Gatineau, Quebec, Canada.

8. Swordfish Mk.IV, serial HS469, is a Mk.II, but presented as a Mk.IV, although there was no such thing. She is a display aircraft at the Shearwater Aviation Museum, located at Canadian Forces Base (CFB) Shearwater, Nova Scotia. She is a former No. 841 NAS machine, that later served with No 743 Fleet Replenishment Squadron from HMS *Seaborn* at RCAF Dartmouth, Nova Scotia. She was later in No. 745 NAS, which supplied aircraft to No. 1 Naval Telegraphist and Air Gunners' Training unit under the British Commonwealth Air Training Scheme (BCATR) being later transferred to the Royal Canadian Navy on 2 August 1945. After surviving for many years post-war she was saved and restored to airworthy condition, flying again in 1992.

9. Swordfish-II serial HS491, part of the collection of the Malta Aviation Museum, Ta' Qali, Malta, is currently awaiting restoration.

10: Swordfish-II, serial unknown, is held by the Aero Space Museum Association of Calgary (Canada), awaiting restoration.

11. Swordfish-II, coded '4C', a former No. 813 NAS aircraft, is at the Museum of Transport and Technology, New Zealand. One aircraft DK791, piloted by Lieutenant (A), William Dickson Winterbottom, which crashed aboard the escort carrier *Archer* on 3 August 1942, has her remains stored there also.

12. Swordfish-II, serial HS498, served with No. 745 NAS from 1943 and was delivered to RCAF Mount Hope in 1946. It is currently owned by Karl Enholder, Vancouver, British Columbia.

13. Swordfish-II serial HS554 has the civilian registration C-GEVS. HS554 is owned by Robert Spence, Bob Spence's farm, Muirkirk, Ontario, Canada, Spence Vintage Airworks, Kent County. It is a former No. 745 NAS aircraft with the RT Flight at Yarmouth, Ontario from 1943 to 1944. Restored from parts of various aircraft and first flew on 17 August 1992.

14. A Swordfish-II static display is at National Air & Space Museum, Washington, DC. The history and serial are unknown.

15. There is a Swordfish – type, history and serial unknown –static display at Bristol Heritage Collection, Nashville, Tennessee.

Chapter Three

Fairey Albacore

On 14 December 1940, a meeting took place in Room 5002, Thames House South, in order to analyse detailed reports from the Royal Aircraft Establishment at South Farnborough into the methods employed so very successfully in dive-bombing with the Junkers Ju.87 and Junkers Ju.88 aircraft. Their accuracy far exceeded anything remotely obtained by the RAF bombers and it was felt that, despite twenty years of resistance, there might possibly be some merit in the tactic! It was concluded that the method, '…demands an aeroplane which can dive at approximately a constant speed at an angle in the region of from 40 degrees to 70 degrees from the horizontal'. After some discussion of available British types the aircraft selected to pioneer the British response to the Ju.88 was, the Fairey Albacore! The reasoning was that, 'As dive bombing is one of its operational duties, the Fleet Air Arm would be able to take immediate advantage of the method.' One person at the Air Ministry ventured the opinion that to use such an obsolete biplane of antiquated design and performance was farcical, they were immediately slapped down. The Albacore, he was informed, '… was of the same vintage as the Vickers Wellington' (one of which was being used by the RAF for dive-bombing experiments at this time, unbelievably), and was therefore '…quite suitable'.[1]

This total lack of realism, even at this stage of the war, reflected the wider thinking behind the concept of the Fairey Albacore throughout its short career. For it is a fact that the successor to the slow and obsolete Fairey Swordfish biplane was yet another slow and obsolete biplane and one that, moreover, lacked the manoeuvrability of its predecessor, a quality many considered its saving grace. Such thinking extended back many years; indeed when consideration was first given to a replacement for the Swordfish the Air Ministry came up with not one, but two specifications, one for a Torpedo Spotter Reconnaissance machine as before (M.7/36) and another for a dive-bomber (O.8/36). The two requirements could hardly be more different, one requiring a low-level approach, specifically the ability to cruise at 210mph with a torpedo mounted and a stall speed of just 66mph; the other a near-vertical attack scenario with a bomb. Perhaps unsurprisingly, both these specifications were quickly cancelled. But they had not helped clarify what exactly was being looked for.

The Fairey company design team began work on meeting the M.7/36 specification, but without coming anywhere close to what was a challenging commitment. But although some of the offerings they put forward were radical, and might have resulted in a decent warplane by the standards of the day, these were passed by and instead their more basic and conventional response served to fulfil the needs of the moment and thus Specification 41/36 was introduced, largely based on Fairey's design. So it was more a case of the Air Ministry altering its requirement to fit Fairey's offering than the conventional way of doing things. This, perhaps, answered many questions on why such a pedestrian aircraft ever came into being despite it clearly being obsolescent even while still on the drawing board. Fairey went along with it, presumably on the basis that '...the customer is always right!' despite the fact that only a marginal speed improvement to 161mph resulted, about half that of contemporary RAF fighter designs!

In other words, the generally accepted acceptance of second-rate aircraft for the Fleet Air Arm had, at a time of rapid development, slithered into adopting third-rate machines. Many felt that high-performance aircraft were incapable of making good carrier aircraft, despite the examples of Japan and the USA, whose new torpedo-bombers were capable of twice the speed and range, and this myth was very slow to die, even in wartime, as the above quoted exchanges show.

Therefore the Air Ministry specification S.41/36 became the basis for this 'new' design. In fairness, the Fairey team did provide a few rudimentary improvements. They came up with a single-engined, three-seater, all-metal monocoque construction fuselage, with an enclosed, heated crew cabin, complete with a windscreen wiper. For all that it was still a painfully slow, biplane, with the wire-braced and fabric-covered wings of a bygone era. The aircrew nicknamed their new mount the 'Applecore' and thought it undemanding to fly and forgiving in operation. But these were hardly qualities that were really paramount in November 1940 when the Albacore first went to war. It *did* feature stressing to give it a limited dive-bombing capability having automatic leading-edge slats on the upper wings, and hydraulically operated lower wing flaps. She also boasted a 1,065hp Bristol Taurus II engine.

Fairey built two prototypes, the first of which, serial L7074, made her maiden flight on 12 December 1938. The second prototype, serial L7075 followed, and was delivered to A&AEE at Boscombe Down in June 1939. Under contract No. 625954/37, the Hayes plant produced a further ninety-eight machines, serials L7076 to 7173 inclusive. The first production aircraft of this batch, L7076, joined No. 767 NAS, a special trials unit for the Albacore to help her into service, at HMS *Merlin*, RNAS Donibristle in September 1939. The first operational squadron to receive the Albacore (serial L7081) was No. 826 NAS at HMS *Peregrine*, RNAS Ford, Sussex, on 15 March 1940.

The initial one hundred aircraft were followed by a further order, made under the same contract number, for three hundred more, which were to be built at Hayes, to which serials N4152 to N4554 inclusive were allocated. However, serials N4426 to N4525 inclusive were subsequently cancelled from this batch and only two hundred were ever completed. The first of these, serial N4152, arrived at 38 MU in August 1940, and No. 825 NAS received serial N4154 the same month, while serial N4153 went to No.828 NAS at HMS *Daedelus*, RNAS Lee-on-Solent, in September, both Nos 827 and No. 828 NAS receiving the first bulk deliveries.

A third order followed under contract B35944/39 for one hundred machines to be built at Hayes, and these were in three batches, the first forty-five receiving serial allocations T9175 to T9131 inclusive; the following twenty-five were given serials

T9191 to T9215 inclusive; and the third batch of thirty machines were allocated serials T9231 to T9260 inclusive. Of these, serial T9131 was delivered to 82 MU in April 1941, and No. 826 NAS took delivery of T9149 in January 1942.

Another order under the same contract number was placed for a further 250 Albacore-Is, again to be built at Hayes. They were allocated serials in six batches, forty-five received serials X8940 to X8984 inclusive; fifty received serials X9010 to X9059 inclusive; forty-five received serials X9073 to X9117 inclusive; fifty received serials X9137 to X9186 inclusive; twenty received serials X9214 to X9233 inclusive and forty received serials X9251 to 9290 inclusive. The first of these, serial X8940, went to 82 MU in August 1941, and No. 827 NAS received X8944 in September 1941 with the bulk being delivered to East Africa, the Middle East and Aden in 1942 and some as late as 1944.

Yet another order, for a further 150 Albacore-Is, was placed under this same contract, again Hayes built. These were allocated serials in four groups: thirty-five received serials BF584 to BF618 inclusive; fifty received serials BF631 to BF680 inclusive; forty-five received serials BF695 to BF739 inclusive and twenty received serials BF758 to BF777 inclusive. The first of these went to 76 MU in March 1942, with No. 823 NAS receiving serial BF590 in May 1942, while others went to HMS *Seahawk*, RNAS Wingfield; Hal Far, Malta; HMS *Tana*, RNAS Tanga; HMS *Garuda*, RNAS Coimbatore; HMS *Goshawk*, Piarco Savannah, Trinidad; and HMS *Korongo*, RNARY Nairobi.

The total number of Albacores built was therefore 800.[2]

The power plant for later Albacores became the single 1,130hp (843kW) twin-row, 14-cylinder, sleeve-valve radial Taurus XII, and this drove a three-bladed de Havilland variable-pitch propeller. This lent itself to an improved take-off procedure and smoother running, but the maximum speed did not improve very much, being 195mph (256km/h) and, additionally, in the field it was found that the Taurus was much more temperamental and unreliable than the noisy but rugged Pegasus. Famous naval test pilot Captain Eric 'Winkle' Brown, described the Taurus as having, '…sewing machine-like qualities…' that, '…after the raucous bellowing of the Pegasus of the "Stringbag", reminded me of the purr of a contented cat'.[3]

The Fleet Air Arm pilots operating the Albacore in combat from their dusty, makeshift, forward landing strips in North Africa had a rather different take on her power plant. The following piece of doggerel, sung to the tune of the Scottish folk song 'My Bonnie Lies over the Ocean', expressed their views about their new mount perfectly.

> The Swordfish relies on her Peggy,
> The modified Taurus ain't sound
> So the Swordfish flies off on her missions
> And the Albacore stays on the ground
> Bring back, bring back,
> Oh bring back my Stringbag to me, to me
> Bring back, bring back.
> Oh bring back my Stringbag to me!

And, eventually, they did!

The fuel capacity was 193 Imperial gallons (877 litres) in an internal tank meaning that the maximum range of the Albacore was reduced from that of the Swordfish, being just 932 miles (1,500km) against a maximum of 1,030 miles (1,657.62km) in the 'Stringbag' and was the source of some gripe, restricting operations and making her more of a coastal than an ocean aircraft. The Albacore had a service ceiling of 20,700ft (6,310m).

The wings were equi-span, twin-bay and fitted with hydraulically actuated flaps. They had a span of 50ft (15.24m), and a wing area of 607ft^2 (57.88m^2). The Albacore's overall length was 40ft (12/14m) with a height of 12.5ft (4.32m). Her empty weight was 7,250lb (3289kg) with a maximum weight of 12,500lb (5670 kg). She was a bigger aeroplane, a less manoeuvrable aeroplane, and a bigger target but docile and easy to handle. Her deck landing speed was 86.37mph (139km/h)

Offensive ordnance was the standard 1,610lb (730kg) 18-inch (45.70cm) torpedo or, as a dive-bomber, either three 500lb (226.8kg) General-Purpose or Armour-Piercing bombs or six 250lb (113.4kg) bombs with mixtures of four 20lb (9kg) loadings. For dive-bombing the Albacore's designed Indicated Air Speed (IAS) with flaps extended was 248.5mph (400km/h). Defensive armament was still primitive, a single, fixed, forward-firing Vickers .303-machine gun mounted in the starboard wing and two Vickers 'K' machine-guns on flexible mounting in the rear cockpit. The aircraft had other innovations, including, of all things, a dingy-launching device that activated automatically on contact with the sea.

The first production Albacore joined the fleet on 15 March 1940.

Replacement of the Swordfish was swift and, by 1942, no fewer than fifteen NAS featured the Albacore. But her reign was destined to be very brief; she was not popular with many Swordfish aircrew and the appearance of the Fairey Barracuda and the Grumman TBF/TBM Avenger totally eclipsed her in all areas.

Some four hundred Albacores were still being built with no front-line usage for them, so they were supplied in numbers to a great many second-line units far from the front, so the naval Albacore appeared in numbers with the Royal Canadian Navy, from May 1943 onward, and the Royal Canadian Air Force, which had six Albacores operational between 1943 and 1949. Others appeared at Aden and Khormaksar, Tanganyika and Kenya, in South Africa, Coimbatore and Trinidad. Others went to equip specialized RAF units and some for civilian duties such as mosquito spraying from Juba and Nairobi.

Operational squadrons

No. 810 NAS had flown Fairey Swordfish-IIs in battle, but on return to the UK the unit had these replaced by Albacores on 1 January 1943. No new CO was appointed until March when Lieutenant-Commander (A) Anthony Jex-Blake Forde took over. Within four short months, the Albacore herself had been replaced by the Fairey Barracuda-II in April, before the unit went back to sea again.

No. 815 NAS was a Swordfish-equipped squadron that was re-equipped at RNAS Dekheila, Alexandria, from August 1941 with twelve Albacores and two ASV-equipped Swordfish under the command of Lieutenant-Commander Trevenen Penrose Coode. The unit moved up to Maaten Bagush, in October to assist the British 8th Army during the North African campaigns working from advance landing grounds in Egypt and Libya. Lieutenant-Commander Philip David Gick took over the squadron in September 1942. A special Flight was formed with some of the Albacores to form a Fleet Bombardment Spotting unit. On 19 February 1943, the Albacores assisted a Vickers Wellington of No. 38 Squadron, RAF and the destroyers *Hursley* and *Isis*, in sinking the German submarine *U-652* when she tried to attack convoy XT.3. The final commander was Lieutenant-Commander John Walter George Welham, who remained until with the unit, which was by then sub-ordinated to No. 201 (Naval Co-Operation) Group, RAF, for Operation *Husky,* the invasion of Sicily. Its work done, the squadron was disbanded at Mersa Matruh, Egypt, on 10 July 1943. The unit was later re-formed at home as a Fairey Barracuda-II squadron.

No. 817 NAS formed at Crail under Lieutenant-Commander Dennis Sandersen, receiving the Albacore on 15 March 1941 and operating them until September 1943. In July they were embarked aboard the carrier *Furious*, transferring the following month to the carrier *Victorious*. They served on Home Fleet duties covering Arctic convoys from Scapa Flow and Reykjavik, Iceland, and making strikes against targets in occupied Norway, while all the time seeking the opportunity to torpedo the battleship *Tirpitz* when she ventured forth from her lair in Kaa Fjord, Kavvatn, north Norway. They eventually launched the attack in March 1942, but failed to hit her. They took part in the invasion of Vichy-French North Africa (Operation *Torch*) from November 1942 onward operating over Algiers and the Western Mediterranean. Lieutenant-Commander Peter Goldthorne Sugden had taken over command in February 1942 and on his death was succeeded by Lieutenant-Commander Leigh Edward Delves Walthall from June.

On 12 February 1943 the squadron transferred back to the carrier *Furious* once more until March when they joined the carrier *Indomitable*. With her they went out to the Mediterranean covering Operation *Husky*, the invasion of Sicily, but on the night of 16 July, while six of her Albacores were away on night submarine hunting missions, a lone Junkers Ju.88 hit the *Indomitable* with a single torpedo at 0025. Not a shot was fired in defence as the Albacores were due back aboard. The carrier was badly damaged, taking on a list of more than 12° and at one point seemed lost. She was saved but had to withdraw and the Albacores were therefore put ashore at Gibraltar until September, when they returned home to RNAS Lee-on-Solent, where the Albacores were replaced by Fairey Barracuda-IIs.

No. 818 NAS was a pre-war squadron flying Swordfish when it was re-equipped with nine Albacores in November 1941 and taken on board the carrier *Argus*. On 4 February 1942 the squadron, under the command of Lieutenant-Commander Terence Waters Brown Shaw, DSC, RNR, joined the carrier *Formidable* and sailed with her with Admiral Sir James Somerville aboard, to establish the Eastern Fleet in the Indian Ocean. After narrowly avoiding a showdown with the *Kido Butai's* five-carrier task force the squadron was put ashore in Ceylon where it was subsequently disbanded. The squadron was re-formed at Lee-on-Solent on 19 October under Lieutenant-Commander Arthur Humpries Abrams as a mixed squadron and in March 1943 joined the carrier *Unicorn* seeing service at the Salerno landings in Sicily in July.

No. 820 NAS, under the command of Lieutenant-Commander William Elliott, took delivery of the Albacore in July 1941 and operated them during the invasion of Madagascar and later Vichy-French North Africa (Operation *Torch*) from November 1942 onward, when they assisted in the sinking of the *U-33* on 17 November 1942. Embarked aboard the carrier *Formidable* the unit took part in Operation *Husky*, the invasion of Sicily, and the Salerno landings (Operation *Avalanche*) on the Italian mainland. Under the command of Lieutenant-Commander John Charles Nicholls Shrubsole, the squadron was the last carrier-born unit to fly the Albacore and disbanded in November 1943. It reformed as a Fairey Barracuda unit in January 1944.

No. 821 NAS was formed at Dekheila, Egypt, in March 1942 with six Albacores and commanded by Major Alan Charles Newson, RM. Their first mission was to bomb airfields on the island of Rhodes. The squadron operated in the North African desert from Ma'aten Bagush, near Marsa Matruh, Egypt; Gambut (Kambut), Libya; and El Daba (Landing Ground 105) from then until November 1942, apart from a short period working from Cyprus during April 1942. In November they were based at Hal Far, Malta, where they remained until June 1943, command of the unit changing to Lieutenant-Commander Charles Howard Colomb O'Rourke in March. The squadron transferred a detachment of four Albacores to Castel Benito, near Tripoli, in March. They flew anti-submarine patrols in Tunisian waters until the squadron was disbanded on 10 October 1943. It later was reformed with the Fairey Barracuda.

No. 822 NAS converted from a Swordfish-II squadron to an Albacore squadron with the arrival of nine machines in March 1942 and embarked aboard the carrier *Furious* in July. The squadron took part in the invasion of Vichy-French North Africa (Operation *Torch)* from November 1942 onboard the *Furious* and *Argus* being part of the British Central Task Force. The squadron attacked Es Sénia airfield, near Oran, with eight Albacores on 11 November 1942, and delivered six 250lb GP bombs into the hangars containing forty aircraft, and claimed a total of forty-seven enemy machines destroyed on the ground. The raid was opposed by Vichy-French Dewoitine 520 fighters and No. 822 NAS lost four Albacores, including one piloted by Lieutenant (A) John George Alastair McIntire Nares, the unit's commanding officer, which was shot down and his crew, Lieutenant (A) John Vernon Hartley and Leading Airman Gordon Dixon, were killed.

The squadron regrouped ashore at Gibraltar under the command of Lieutenant Hugh Alan Leigh Tibbetts, RCNVR, and continued operations along the coast of Algeria and the western Mediterranean in December and January, before re-embarking in *Furious* in February 1943 and, under the command of Lieutenant John William Colletts, returned home to the UK. Initially based in the Clyde, keeping watch on the German battle-cruiser *Scharnhorst* between March and May 1943, she then was part of a force that covered the reinforcement of the garrison at Spitzbergen (Operation 'FH'). The squadron continued working in the Arctic and in July the *Furious,* with the battleships *Anson, Duke of York* and *Malaya* and escorts, made a sweep off the Norwegian coast (Operation *Governor*) to divert attention from the Allied landings in Sicily.

The *Furious* was then docked and the squadron went ashore where it was re-equipped with the Fairey Barracuda-II and was attached to 45 Naval Wing, for transfer to India.

No. 823 NAS was a Fairey Swordfish squadron but in August 1942, under the command of Lieutenant-Commander John William Colletts, was re-equipped with nine Albacores and briefly served aboard the carrier *Furious* until September then carried out convoy protection work and anti-submarine patrolling under 16 Group Coastal Command until June 1943 commanded from November 1942 by Lieutenant-Commander Ronal William Spackman and from March 1943 by Lieutenant-Commander George Douglas DFC, RNR. They were based at RAF Tangmere and Manston and conducted anti-submarine sorties over the English Channel and southern North Sea. In June 1943 the Albacores were replaced by Fairey Barracudas.

No. 826 NAS received their first batch of Albacores on 15 March 1940. The unit was based at HMS *Peregrine*, RNAS Ford, Sussex, under Lieutenant-Commander Frank Henry Edward Hopkins and subsequently, from April, under Lieutenant-Commander Charles John Thomson Stephens. The squadron operated from RAF Detling under the command of Lieutenant-Commander (Squadron Leader) Wilfred Henry Gerard Saunt from May during the Dunkirk period, working off the Dutch Coast, with anti-S-boot patrols, dive-bombing attacks on targets of opportunity at Westende, Belgium, and similar work. The Squadron moved up to RAF Bircham Newton, Norfolk, to work under Coastal Command, where they were involved in nocturnal minelaying (214 mines were dropped by the Albacores), bombing operations (56 tons deposited) and convoy escort patrols (92 escorted). Four Albacores were lost in this period. The squadron embarked aboard the carrier *Formidable* on 26 November 1940. The carrier proceeded around the Cape to replace the damaged carrier *Illustrious,* but was delayed when the Luftwaffe mined the Suez Canal. On 29 March the squadron took part in the preliminaries to the Battle of Cape Matapan. During the Greece and Crete campaign they were constantly in action, and on 25 May dive-bombed the German Stuka airfield on the island of Scarpanto, inflicting little damage but stirring up a hornet's nest with the result that *Formidable* was badly damaged by the Ju.87s and had to imitate the *Illustrious* and retire to the USA for prolonged repairs.

The surviving aircraft of No. 826 were disembarked and deployed forward to the Ma'aten Bagush base on coastal patrol work before embarking on a period of nocturnal dive-bombing and flare dropping in support of the British 8th Army. From January 1942 the commander was Lieutenant-Commander Charles Warwick Bowman Smith from March 1942 until August when he was shot down and killed, whereupon Lieutenant Paul Walter Compton led the unit. When the British were forced back to Egypt by General Irwin Rommel's *Afrika Korps* with the fall of Tobruk in the summer of 1942, No. 826 mounted a daring attack on a vital Axis supply convoy in the central

Mediterranean by staging through a landing strip 250 miles (400km) behind German lines and being refuelled by RAF Bristol Bombay transport aircraft of No. 216 Squadron RAF.

In December 1942 part of the squadron moved to Malta to assist No. 821 NAS in attacks on Axis sea communications and the squadron regrouped at Dekheila in January 1943, before moving back to Malta in June to cover the landings in Sicily, Operation *Husky*. On completion of this the squadron was disbanded. It was to be reformed at RNAS Lee-on-Solent in December 1943 as a Fairey Barracuda squadron.

No. 827 NAS equipped with the Albacore in September 1940 at RNAS Yeovilton, under the command of Lieutenant-Commander William George Cortlandt Stokes, before moving the Torpedo Training School, HMS *Jackdaw*, RNAS Crail. From March 1941 they operated under No. 18 (Reconnaissance) Group, Coastal Command at RAF Stornaway, Isle of Lewis. In May 1941 they moved south to Thorney Island and then St Eval, Cornwall, where they conducted aerial-minelaying operations off the ports of Brest and Cherbourg in an attempt to keep the German battle-cruisers *Gneisenau* and *Scharnhorst* bottled up.

In July 1941, now commanded by Lieutenant-Commander James Andrew Stewart-Moore, the unit embarked aboard the carrier *Victorious* and from her took part in the attack on Kirkenes, where, for the claim of one Junkers Ju.87 dive-bomber destroyed, the squadron lost twelve Albacores. The few survivors were put ashore at RNAS Hatston, in the Orkneys to reform. In October, commanded by Lieutenant-Commander Patrick George Osric Sydney-Turner, they took passage aboard the carrier *Indomitable* to Jamaica, rejoining her at Norfolk and then voyaging via Cape Town to the Indian Ocean and, after a sojourn ashore at Port Sudan while the carrier made two ferry trips taking Hurricanes to Java, took part in the Madagascar operation. The squadron remained aboard *Indomitable* and, from May, and commanded by Lieutenant-Commander David Kennedy Buchanan-Dunlop, operated anti-submarine patrols during Operation *Pedestal*, the biggest Malta relief convoy. The *Indomitable* suffered both direct hits and near-misses from a very accurate and fierce Junkers Ju.87 Stuka dive-bomber attack on 12 August 1942. One 550lb (250kg) bomb detonated in the air just five feet from her port side and the shrapnel and bomb fragments penetrated her hull plating in the area of the wardroom where most of the off-duty officers, pilots and observers, from her Albacore aircrew were relaxing. Every man there was a casualty, with six killed outright and the rest badly wounded, the latter including the Squadron Commander, although he later survived and went on to a long career, which terminated as Commanding Officer of the Greenwich Naval College. The unit later reformed as a Fairey Barracuda unit in January 1943.

No. 828 NAS was formed at HMS *Daedelus*, RNAS Lee-on-Solent, on 1 September 1940, under Lieutenant Eric Arthur Grenwood, with the Albacore, and they remained with the squadron through to September 1943. Lieutenant-Commander (A) Leonard Arthur Cubitt assumed command in September and they initially moved up to Scotland where they operated under Coastal Command until May. The squadron, now commanded by Lieutenant-Commander David Erskine Langmore from May to December, embarked aboard the carrier *Victorious* in July and from her took part in the disastrous Kirkenes raid, where they lost five Albacores achieving very little. What remained of the unit embarked aboard the carrier *Argus* in September for passage to Gibraltar and then transferred to the carrier *Ark Royal* for passage through the Western Mediterranean and were flown off to Hal Far, Malta.

They flew numerous anti-shipping missions from Malta between September 1941 and March 1942, Lieutenant-Commander Gerald Mellor Haynes DSO, RAN assuming command in December 1941 and Lieutenant-Commander Martin Ernest Lashmore in November 1942. But heavy attrition steadily reduced their numbers and 828 and 830 NAS merged to form Naval Air Squadron Malta, and continue the good work. Between them the combined squadrons were credited with the destruction of thirty Axis supply ships and with causing damage to another fifty. Lieutenant-Commander (A), Mackenzie Jesse Gregory assumed command in February 1943, but once more, by December, only two Albacores remained operational and all were absorbed into 826 NAS and the remains of 860 NAS. In May and June 1943, commanded by Lieutenant-Commander (A) John Frayne Turner, the unit flew anti-shipping missions with 821 NAS and provided flare illuminations for the bombardment of the island garrisons of Pantelleria and Lampedusa by several British cruiser and destroyer forces until they surrendered. The combined squadron was based at Monastir, Tunisia, for a period before being disbanded in September 1943 as there were no more enemy shipping targets left for them!

No. 829 NAS formed at Ford, Sussex, in June 1940 with nine Albacores, and, after working up, moved to RAF St Eval from where they attacked the harbour of Brest, losing their commanding officer Lieutenant-Commander Owen Sanbach Stevinson as a PoW on 9 October; he was replaced as CO by Lieutenant-Commander John Dalyell-Stead. The squadron was embarked aboard the carrier *Formidable* on 26 November 1940 and conducted anti-submarine operations escorting a convoy south while on her way to join the Mediterranean Fleet via Freetown and the Cape. The German pocket battleship *Admiral Scheer* sank the refrigerator ship *Duquesa,* but air searches flown by the squadron's Albacores subsequently failed to find the enemy, so no attack was made on her.

On passing up the Red Sea in February 1941, the opportunity was taken to fly air strikes against the Italian strongholds of Mogadishu and Massawa. The Germans had mined the Suez Canal and *Formidable* was delayed reaching Alexandria. The squadron played a prominent part in the preliminary air operations that led to the Battle of Cape Matapan, when commanding officer Lieutenant-Commander Lionel Charles Brian Ashburner, who had just taken over the squadron, was shot down. During the battle for Crete the Albacores attacked German Stuka bases on the island of Scarpanto but many were lost in that attack and the Ju.87 attack that crippled *Formidable* on 26 May.

When *Formidable* was waiting to be sailed to the USA for repairs, the squadron was based ashore at Lydda (Lod), Palestine, south-east of Tel Aviv. From here they took part in attacks on Vichy-French forces during the Syrian campaign. The Albacores were left ashore in Cyprus when *Formidable* finally sailed to the States, ceasing to be carried on the squadron books in August, and the unit later became an ASV-equipped Swordfish-based squadron aboard the carrier *Illustrious*.

No. 830 NAS was flying the Blackburn Skua-II dive-bomber in September 1940 when it was re-equipped with the Albacore and Captain Keith Langler Ford took over command. From July 1941 ASV-equipped aircraft arrived in the unit to assist in the continuing night sorties.

In September 1941 Lieutenant-Commander John Gunthorpe Hunt briefly took over the squadron, being replaced by Lieutenant-Commander Frank Henry Edward Hopkins in December. They were at full stretch attacking Axis convoys attempting to reach Tripoli and Benghazi during the to and fro of the North African campaign, and were highly successful. They also conducted strikes against targets in both Libya and Sicily and harried enemy submarines in the central Mediterranean.

By March 1942 lack of remaining operational aircraft forced Nos 828 and 830 NAS, with just three Albacore serviceable, to amalgamate as Naval Air Squadron Malta. Between them they sank thirty Axis supply ships and damaged fifty more, as well as operating as flare droppers.

In July 1942 the unit had once more used up most of its Albacores and ceased to exist. It was later reformed at RNAS Lee-on-Solent as a Fairey Barracuda unit in May 1943.

No. 831 NAS was formed on 1 April 1941 as an Albacore squadron under the command of Lieutenant-Commander Peter Lawrence Mortimer, RAN. The squadron joined the carrier *Indomitable* in Jamaica in October 1941 and she sailed to Aden, where the Albacores were offloaded and RAF Hurricanes embarked for ferry operations from Port Sudan to Singapore (Operation *Opponent)*. The destination of these fighters was changed and when, after refuelling from the RFA *Appleleaf,* she flew them off on 12 August they went to Batavia. A second ferry run from Port Sudan was conducted and then the Albacores were re-embarked. They served aboard her in the Indian Ocean and were at the occupation of Diego Suarez in May 1942 and the take-over of Vichy-French Madagascar before the Japanese could become established, making attacks on airfields and spotting for heavy naval guns. The *Indomitable* was brought back to take part in the Malta relief convoy, Operation *Pedestal,* in August 1942, under the command of Lieutenant-Commander Andrew Gurney Leatham. There were casualties when the carrier was badly damaged by Stuka attack on 12 August.

When the *Victorious* was sent to repair in the USA, the squadron was put ashore at HMS *Jackdaw*, RNAS Crail. In December 1942 the first Fairey Barracudas arrived in the unit and it had become a full Barracuda squadron by May 1943.

No. 832 NAS formed with the Albacore on 1 April 1941 and continued using them until December 1942. The first commanding officer was Lieutenant-Commander Arther James Philson Plugge. They embarked aboard the carrier *Victorious* in August and took part in air attacks against the Lofoten Islands and Tromsø on 3 and 7 September. On 14 September the Albacores again made air strikes on Tromsø and Vestfjorden, sinking the 2,000-ton supply ship *Barøy* and setting an aluminium works on fire and bombing an electric power station; they suffered no losses. On 7 October enemy shipping off Bodø was attacked.

In February the squadron CO was lost in bad weather off the Norwegian coast while searching for enemy shipping, being replaced by Lieutenant-Commander William John Lucas. They covered Arctic convoys and took part in the abortive attack on *Tirpitz*. In August they took part in the Operation *Pedestal* convoy to Malta, and in October were back in the Mediterranean for the North African landings (Operation *Torch*) in November working from the carrier and Algiers. They went to the USA and while there the squadron converted to the Grumman TBM/TBF Avenger torpedo-bomber in readiness to act with American task forces in the South Pacific.

No. 841 NAS was formed with just two Albacores in July 1942 at HMS *Daedelus*, RNAS Lee-on-Solent, commissioned under Lieutenant Richard Lawson Williamson for 'Special Duties'. The unit was attached to RAF Fighter Command, Middle Wallop, and later served at RAF stations Manston, Kent, and Coltishall, Norfolk. When Lieutenant Williamson was lost Lieutenant-Commander (A) Lancelot John Kiggell assumed command in October 1942 until December when Lieutenant-Commander (A) Sidney Michael Patrick Walsh DSO, DSC, RNVR succeeded him. The Albacores expanded in numbers and during this period carried out ninety-nine separate attacks on enemy shipping and *S-boots* in the English Channel and southern North Sea.

By May 1943 the squadron had detachments at both RAF Tangmere and Exeter working under 16 Group RAF Coastal Command and making sorties and patrols up and down the whole English Channel, by this period with strength of sixteen Albacores working with three ASV-equipped Swordfish. The squadron was disbanded at Manston in December 1943, when its aircraft and duties were handed over to No 413 Squadron, RCAF. It later reformed as a Fairey Barracuda squadron.

Second line squadrons

Like the Swordfish before her, the Albacore was supplied to a large number of training establishments and storage facilities around the world, and usually the same ones as already listed. Those squadrons known to have featured Albacores on their establishments at one period or another are: Nos 700, 733, 747, 750, 753, 754, 756, 763, 766, 767, 768, 769, 771, 774, 775, 778, 781, 782, 783, 785, 786, 787, 788, 789, 791, 793, 796, 797 and 799.

RAF units

When Japan attacked Pearl Harbor and Malaya on 7 December 1941, the only Albacores in the Far East were five in storage with the Fleet Requirements unit at Seletar, near Singapore. On 12 December these five were brought out of storage and handed over to the RAF to form 'B' Flight of No. 36 Squadron, commanded by Squadron Leader Arthur William Darley Miller, and later Squadron Leader Richard Markham, operating the

Vickers Vildebeest torpedo-bomber and they were manned by spare aircrew including several RAAF and RNZAF personnel.

On 30 January 1942, two of these Albacores attacked Japanese positions in the region of Bandar Maharani (Muar), Johor and Gemas, Negeri Sembilan, where the final battle of the Malayan campaign was raging, escorted by six Brewster Buffalo fighters and next afternoon two Albacores were sent from Seletar to Japanese-manned craft[4] off Batu Pahat, south of Muar, again with a six Buffalo escort. Next day two Albacores were despatched against a Japanese troop column reported pouring across the Parit Sulong bridge, this pair being led by T9135 crewed by Flight Lieutenant Bernard Bruce Wilmott and Sergeant Keith Minton, along with an ancient Blackburn Shark from 'A' Flight, 4 AACU with four 250lb (113kg) bombs apiece, which they duly delivered in single dive-bombing runs before running for cover. All returned safely.

No. 36 Squadron continued to attack the advancing Japanese when it could. On 25 January three Albacores accompanied the Vildebeests attacked Batu Pahat itself without loss. After making night attack on Japanese forces in the area of Batu Pahat and Muar, the only three serviceable Albacores of No. 36 Squadron at Seletar were sent off at 1615 on 26 January 1942, each armed with six 250lb bombs, and led by Squadron Leader Richard Frederic Cyprian Markham, to attack a Japanese invasion fleet reported off Endau, south-eastern Malaya. The aircrews were: X9106 – Squadron-Leader Richard Frederic Cyprian Markham RAFVR, Flight Sergeant Humphrey Frank Hicks and Flight Sergeant John Binning Seaton; T9184 – Flight Sergeant George Bryan William Peck RNZAF, Flight Sergeant Cecil Harry Lockwood RNZAP and Sergeant Alexander Kelly; and T9135 Flight Lieutenant George Edward Richardson, Flight Sergeant Bernard Vernon Harris and Sergeant Joseph Lockhart.

They were met with clear blue skies over the target and by ten Nakajima Ki.27 *Nate* fighters of the 1 *Sentai* and two Japanese Army Nakajima Ki.44 *Tojo* fighters of 47 *Chutai*, who proceeded to shoot them to pieces. Markham made a dive-bombing attack against the troopship *Kanbera Maru*, but was brought down in the sea with the loss of all aircrew. Fleming's Albacore, was also heavily hit, and crashed in shallow water to the north of Teloksari, with no survivors. Bizarrely, Flight Sergeant's Peck's two crew members baled out while he was making evasive manoeuvres to throw off the Japanese fighters. With the petrol tank holed by cannon fire and spewing fuel, the defensive Vickers knocked off its mount and disabled and the intercom dead, and with Peck putting the aircraft in a steep dive, they thought she was done for, but Peck safely evaded the enemy and brought his aircraft safely home to Seletar. No Japanese ships were harmed.

Two Albacores remained and they were evacuated to Kemajoran airfield, Batavia, Java, on 31 January 1942, but only one remained operational when the unit moved to Tjilkampek in February and carried out an attack on a Japanese invasion convoy five miles off Rembang, in company with six Vildebeest. The Albacore, piloted by Pilot Officer Frank Elwood Cummins, RAAF, made her attack alone and survived, Cummins later reaching the safety of Australia.[5]

No. 119 Squadron was formed from No. 415 Squadron, RCAF, in July 1944 and flew black-painted Albacores from RAF Bircham Newton, Norfolk, against German small naval units in the English Channel from there and from liberated Belgian airfields until the end of the year, before the Albacores were replaced by ASV and R/P equipped Swordfish in January 1945.

Naval war service

Channel and North Sea coastal operations

No. 826 NAS based at RAF Bircham Newton in Norfolk, was early in action with attacks on the Dutch targets of *Mariteiem Viegkamp De Kooy* airfield (De Kooy Naval Air Base) and the nearby Den Helder naval base, which were occupied by the Germans. The Albacore took its first war loss here on the night of 21/22 June when Albacore L7081 was destroyed by Messerschmitt Bf109s when attacking a German convoy near the island of Texel Waddensea, crashing on the beach at Dechavij Iinsel and her aircrew, Sub-Lieutenant Victor John Dyke, Lieutenant William Shorrocks Butterworth and Leading Airman Robert Joseph Jackson became PoWs, Dyke dying of his wounds and Jackson dying in captivity in 1945.

On the night of 23/24 May 1944, a German torpedo boat[6] flotilla, *Falke, Greif, Kondor* and *Möwe,* attempted to reach Le Havre from Cherbourg in order to attack the D-Day landing transports. They were attacked by Albacores. The *Greif* and *Kondor* collided; the *Greif* was damaged, taken in tow and later sank.

Petsamo and Kirkenes 1941

As a 'gesture' of solidarity to the new-found Soviet ally, an attack was made against what had been reported as a heavy concentration of German shipping at the northern ports of Petsamo, Finland, and Kirkenes, Norway. It was yet another of Premier Winston Churchill's hare-brained politically motivated notions that so bedevilled the war at sea. The carrier *Victorious* had embarked twelve Albacores of No. 827 NAS and nine Albacores of No. 828 NAS, while the *Furious* had aboard the nine Albacores of No. 817 NAS and nine Fairey Swordfish of No. 812 NAS. Very little appeared to have been learnt from previous strikes in Norway (like the disastrous Blackburn Skua attack on the *Scharnhorst* in June 1940), the same long and difficult approach made over difficult terrain, with ample warning for the defences to prepare featured, with the inevitable result of high losses for little gain. The attack was supposed to have been a 'surprise' one, but with perpetual daylight in the Arctic this was blatantly impossible, more so when the whole fleet was sighted by German Dornier Do.18 reconnaissance aircraft even before the air strike had been launched! The intelligence on which the attack was based proved totally without foundation, with only a few small vessels actually being present and the whole operation was a costly fiasco.

Furious conducted the strike on Petsamo with nine Albacores and nine Swordfish escorted by six Fairey Fulmar fighters. They found the harbour virtually empty, with just a few small coastal vessels not worth expenditure of ammunition, which they duly bombed and claimed to have sunk. For lack of any other target the majority dropped their bombs on the jetties in the harbour. The defensive flak was intense and one

Albacore, N4250, with Lieutenant Leslie Horace Lee, Sub-Lieutenant George Gorrie and Leading Airman N F Train, was shot down by a Messerschmitt Bf.109, the three aircrew surviving and eventually joining the Russians.

Petsamo was futile; Kirkenes was a disaster. Here at least were a few worthwhile targets; the Gunnery Training Cruiser *Bremse* was in port with just three other ships. Here, once more, the Germans were ready and waiting, the flak was intense and worse, the Messerschmitt Bf.109E and Bf.110 fighters of Major Hennig Strümpell's *Jagdgruppe zur Besonderen Verwendung (z.b.V.)* were already airborne.[7] The result was called 'A humiliating defeat' and a 'disaster' by the Fleet Air Arm Archive and this indeed it was. *Victorious* had despatched twelve of No. 827 NAS Albacores and eight from No. 828, with a nine-Fulmar escort. They claimed to have sunk a 2,000-ton freighter and another set on fire, and also to have destroyed two Bf.109s and one Bf.110. The Germans later reported only 'slight damage' to two ships and no sinkings at all, while their fighters had a field day.

No fewer than eleven Albacores (six from No. 827 and five from No. 828) and two Fulmars were destroyed, and eight other Albacores shot up and damaged with twenty aircrew becoming PoWs while twelve were killed. No. 827 was just about wiped out in this one brief encounter. *Victorious* operated with nine Albacores of No. 817 NAS, twelve of No. 832 NAS thereafter, with No. 820 NAS relieving No. 832 between November 1941 and February 1942.

As a footnote to this debacle, one No. 828 NAS Albacore, serial N4172, lost over Kirkenes, was recovered by a Royal Navy team many years after the war and, with the help of parts from another machine, it was restored. It is the only preserved Albacore in the world and is on display at the Fleet Air Arm Museum, at RNAS Yeovilton, Somerset.

Malta and North Africa – 1941–2

Flare-dropping, which the Swordfish had pioneered, became the Albacore's forte in the desert war. No. 767, the carrier training squadron previously operating with the *Argus* in the South of France, was the first squadron to arrive at Malta in June 1940 but the Swordfish that followed were eventually supplemented by supplies of Albacores and with the amalgamation of various squadrons these assisted in carrying out the thirty-nine anti-shipping strikes, which sank thirteen Axis supply ships and shared in the destruction of four more; they made eight attacks against ships in enemy harbours and six attacks on defended ports mainly in Libya and Sicily; carried out twenty-two minelaying missions, again mainly against Tripoli, which was the main feeder for the Axis armies in North Africa.

Singapore 1941

The Albacore served with No. 36 Squadron's Vickers Vildebeeste torpedo-bombers at RAF Seletar and carried out numerous attacks against Japanese maritime and land targets in the battle for Malaya and the few survivors fought on in Java until all were expended.

Attack on Tirpitz *– 9 March 1942*

The only time this German battleship, sister ship of the *Bismarck*, was ever taken under attack at sea, was during Russia Convoy operation PQ12/QP8. The outgoing convoy sailed from Reykjavik, Iceland on 1 March while the returning convoy left Kola Inlet on the same date. The Home Fleet was to provide cover for both and all were mindful of Churchill's admonishment of 25 January that: 'The destruction or even crippling of this ship is the greatest event at sea at the present time. No other target is comparable to it.' Thus, when on the evening of 6 March, the submarine *Seawolf* sent in a sighting report of an enemy heavy ship 55 miles north-east of Trondheim steering north-east, everyone was animated. When it was confirmed that this was indeed the *Tirpitz* making a rare combat sortie, it seemed the opportunity had arisen to deal with her as they had her sister. *Tirpitz*, with an escort of four destroyers, narrowly missed convoy QP8, even finding one of them straggling, the Soviet *Izhora*, which one of the destroyers quickly sank.

The covering fleet at this time consisted of the battleship *Duke of York*, battle-cruiser *Renown*, carrier *Victorious*, one heavy and a light cruiser and twelve destroyers. The *Victorious* had embarked aboard her the Albacores of Nos 817 and 832 NAS. At 0640 on 9 March 1942 the Commander-in-Chief Admiral Sir John Tovey ordered *Victorious* to fly off a reconnaissance force of six Albacores on a diverging search between 105° and 155° to a depth of 150 miles. Then, some fifty minutes later the carrier flew off her strike force, which consisted of twelve more Albacores commanded by Lieutenant-Commander William John Lucas, they being ordered to steer 135° and to act on any intercepted enemy reports. At 0802 Albacore 'F' sighted *Tirpitz*, escorted by one of her destroyers, *Friedrich Ihn*, in company and duly reported her position. Initially four of 832's scouting Albacores made an attack out of thick cloud, which was avoided, and one of the aircraft was hit, wounding the observer, Sub-Lieutenant Geoffrey Dunworth RNVR, although she managed to return to the carrier.

At 0917 the main strike force arrived overhead, the *Tirpitz* being some eighty miles west of the Lofoten islands, and also attacked. The attack was well pushed home through heavy flak. There was some confusion on the bridge of the *Tirpitz* while manoeuvring to avoid the torpedoes, Admiral Otto Ciliax, the C-in-C of the squadron, at one point ordering hard left, an order that Captain Karl Topp, as the captain of the ship, countermanded and he ordered hard right! In the event all the torpedo tracks were evaded and the battleship escaped scot-free being last observed heading at high speed for the safety of Vestifiord. There was much heartache in Downing Street, the contrast between the ease at which *Prince of Wales* and *Repulse*, with no air cover, had been despatched by the Japanese Navy flyers, and the escape of the *Tirpitz* from the Fleet Air Arm in the same circumstances evermore tainting the Premier's attitude to the service. But, in truth, circumstances were very different, both in the weather conditions and the fact that twelve Albacores would never be able to do the damage that eighty-two Mitsubishi aircraft were capable of inflicting. Two of the Albacores were shot down by AA fire. A return attack against *Victorious*, mounted by three Junkers Ju.88s, also failed.

Indian Ocean 1942

Admiral Sir James Somerville took over command of the British Eastern Fleet in January 1942, in the aftermath of Churchill's disastrous policy of reinforcing the Soviet Union at the expense of Malaya in air power, and of sending an ill-balanced and quite inadequate naval force (one brand-new battleship, one old and unmodernized battle-cruiser and four destroyers, two of which had to be docked immediately on arrival!), which quickly succumbed to Japanese strength, which he always vastly underestimated. From the debris of the shambles of Singapore Somerville was given an equally hastily assembled heterogeneous collection of mainly obsolete warships with which to make a fleet from, and included among them were the carriers *Formidable*, *Indomitable* and *Hermes*, the first fresh from USA shipyards that had repaired the Stuka damage she had suffered in the Mediterranean earlier, the latter hopelessly inadequate in speed and capacity and quickly disposed of when separated from the rest of the fleet. The crews of the two fleet carriers were therefore not fresh, nor were their aircrews, being mainly fresh out of training schools, while their aircraft, Fairey Fulmars and Albacores, with a few Grumman Wildcats (Martlets), were totally out-ranged, out-sped, out-classed and outnumbered by the 350 modern aircraft embarked on Admiral Chūichi Nagumo's five big carriers. With this force Somerville actively sought combat in April, blithely ignorant (*exactly* like Admiral Tom Philips, whom he had much criticized, before him), of just what exactly he was going up against.

Fortunately the Japanese search planes failed to find the Eastern Fleet, but on 6 April they came awfully close to it, just thirteen miles. *Formidable* had embarked both Nos 818 and 820 NAS, while *Indomitable* had aboard Nos. 827 and 831 NAS with a detachment from No. 796. All of these units were equipped with the Albacore-I. Modern American internet heroes maintain that Somerville stood a good chance of defeating Nagumo by making night torpedo-bomber attacks with their ASV radar. The British admirals on the spot had rather more realistic views on that topic. On the Albacores Somerville wrote in his diary '…I find the observers and pilots are terribly green and inexperienced', adding, 'They certainly want a good shake up.' He commented:

> What is more annoying is that another Albacore crashed on landing and is a complete write-off. I'm beginning to be seriously disturbed by the lack of skill and pep in this party here. They are all quite complacent and think they are the cat's whiskers and in my opinion they are quite bum.

Despite objection from Captain Arthur William La Touche Bisset, Somerville insisted on Albacore pilots doing deck landing training, '…which they evidently needed sorely'. He wrote to the First Sea Lord on 2 March:

> After we had crashed 3 Albacores and lost one on a very moderate recco I realised we had to start from scratch and therefore ordered a series of deck landing and other elementary practices, which were continued daily during our passage here.

I don't think anyone on board here quite realised how bad they were, it was not only the flying but D/F, W/T, RDF, in fact everything as rusty as it could be. I hope that by the time we get to Colombo the ship will be in proper order, but she's got a long way to go yet.[8]

It was with aircrew in this state that the Eastern Fleet was expected to take on the *Kido Butai* and (in hindsight on the internet nowadays) win! Fortunately it was not put to the test.

After the scare was over and Nagumo had retired to the Pacific once more Somerville wrote to the Admiralty on 8 April, that it had shown the need for, 'A better performance aircraft than the Albacore for search and shadowing. Against Japanese aircraft these are not effective. When will Barracuda replace Albacore and Firefly the Fulmar?'

Madagascar – May 1942

The carrier *Indomitable* had both No. 827 NAS and No. 831 NAS embarked aboard her, each with twelve Albacores on strength, when she joined with *Illustrious* with her Swordfish for this operation. The Vichy-French made their airfields in Indo-China available to the Japanese earlier, thus enabling them to sink the *Prince of Wales* and *Repulse* with their shore-based naval bombers, and the French had openly cheered this British humiliation at the time. Now there were Intelligence indications that they were equally welcoming of Japanese submarines establishing themselves at Diego Suarez, in the French colony of Madagascar off the east coast of Africa, and setting up refuelling bases for them and German surface raiders on the main route from the UK to the Middle East via the Cape.[9]

On 5 May the British Task Force with the two carriers, the battleship *Ramillies*, one heavy and one light cruiser and eleven destroyers covered the landing force at Cap d'Ambre the northern tip of the island. The Albacores attacked the French airfields where the French fighters were based, while the French auxiliary cruiser *Bougainveille-II* was sunk by aerial torpedo attack. The Vichy submarine *Beveziers* attempted to attack the force but was sunk by Swordfish from *Illustrious*; on 7 May they also eliminated another Vichy submarine, *Le Héros*, which had sunk the Norwegian freighter *Thode Faselund* off South Africa earlier. The sloop *D'Entrecasteaux* was dive-bombed by the Albacores, badly damaged, and finished off by the destroyer *Laforey*. The same day Diego Suarez (now called Antsiranana) surrendered. On 8 May a third Vichy submarine, *Monge*, attacked the *Indomitable*, but her torpedoes were narrowly avoided, and she was quickly sunk by the destroyers *Active* and *Panther*. On 30 May the Japanese midget submarines torpedoed the *Ramillies*, damaging her, and sank the tanker *British Loyalty*.

Collaboration on this scale could not be tolerated and Operation *Ironclad* was mounted to eliminate the threat.

Operation *Pedestal* – August 1942

This was the largest of the Malta relief convoys and the Admiralty committed strong forces to fight it through. The *Victorious* had embarked twelve Albacores of No. 832 NAS and two from No. 817 NAS (nine others were detached), the *Indomitable* had embarked twenty-four Albacores, twelve each from Nos 827 and 831 NAS, while *Furious*, operating as a ferry carrier with thirty-eight Spitfires bound for Malta, had a detachment of four Albacores from No. 822 NAS aboard her as an anti-submarine patrol.

The Italian Navy sortied out and the Albacores might have been required to mount a torpedo striking force to aid the two British battleships *Nelson* and *Rodney* contain them, but the Italian ships were later recalled and it was mainly on the fighter aircraft that the air fighting was conducted. *Indomitable* was badly damaged by Stukas and many of her aircraft destroyed. The Albacores were therefore confined to flying anti-submarine patrols.

Operation *Torch* – Invasion of French North Africa – November 1942

Four British carriers and three escort carriers provided air cover for these landings in Algeria against the Vichy French but only three provided Albacores. The *Formidable* had embarked twelve Albacores from No. 820 NAS; *Victorious* had nine Albacores of No. 817 NAS and nine from No. 832 NAS, with the 'B' Flight being disembarked; while *Furious* provided eight Albacores from No. 882 NAS, which had their 'C' Flight disembarked.

Home Fleet Operations 1943

Various carriers moved in and out of the Home Fleet during this year but the mainstay was the old *Furious* which, from the end of February, had embarked nine Albacores from No. 822 NAS, and nine Swordfish of No 825 NAS, but from October both units had replaced these with the Fairey Barracuda.

English Channel Operations 1944

In July 1944 No. 415 Squadron, RCAF, was re-designated as No. 119 Squadron, RAF. The transferred Albacores were painted black overall and for the next six months were employed from airfields both in southern England and in newly-liberated Belgium, in hunting down small units of the *Kriegsmarine* (German Navy), both surface craft such as R-boots and S-boots and the many varieties of midget submarines attempting the disrupt the masses of Allied shipping off Normandy and off Antwerp. In January 1942, these operations were taken over by radar and rocket-equipped Swordfish, an ironic twist of fate that Fairey's designers could never have predicted!

Foreign operators

Canada

The Royal Canadian Air Force used Albacores with No. 415 Squadron, a unit initially equipped with the Vickers Wellington XIII fitted with ASV, with which they detected the U-boats and then directed the Albacores in to make the attacks. They continued in a similar role against German small craft through to July 1944, being the very last biplane to see operational use by the RCAF.

The final naval Albacores

The Albacore was being produced long after its usefulness, limited at best, had expired. Of the eight hundred churned out, half had no real purpose, but because they were so widespread, they lingered on in the service. In April 1945 one of the original batch, serial L7165, was sent to the Store, Servicing and Flight-Testing satellite of HMS *Daedelus* at Lee-on-Solent, RNAS Cowdray Park, South Ambersham, Midhurst, West Sussex. No. 750 NAS, the Basic Observer Training unit, still had serials T9139 and T9171 on strength at HMS *Goshawk*, Piarco Savannah, Trinidad, in August 1945, she being Signed Off Charge (SOC) on 9 May 1946; and Albacores X9259 and X9287 were still being delivered to Aden CF in February 1946; while No. 700 NAS at Worthy Down also had Albacores on establishment in February 1946.

Preserved Albacore

Only a solitary Albacore currently survives, this being on display at the Fleet Air Arm Museum, RNAS Yeovilton, Ilchester. This aircraft is a composite reconstruction from serials N4389 and N4172 respectively. N4389 was one of the lost aircraft ('4M') from No. 827 NAS, shot down in the Kirkenes attack, which was married up with N4172, a machine that crashed at A'Mhoine, Whiten Head, Sutherland, on 1 April 1941 after getting lost in a blizzard on an anti-submarine patrol from RNAS Hatston. The wreck was recovered in 1974 and sent to the Museum.

Chapter Four

Fiat CR.32

This agile little biplane fighter was designed by Celestino Rosatelli,[1] and built by Fiat Aviazione Italia (Fiat Italy Aviation) of Turin, a company that had grown out of the Società Italiana Aviazione in 1918 and that had consolidated several other manufacturers into itself in the immediate post-World War I period. With the advent of Benito Mussolini, the self-proclaimed Il Duce ('The Leader' – analogous Der Fuehrer in Germany) and his Fascisti one-party state, with the King as merely a titular figurehead, the expansion of Italy's armed forces proceeded apace in line with their leaders' towering ambitions to re-instate the Roman Empire in the Mediterranean and Africa. The build-up of the Regia Aeronautica (Royal Air Force) followed and the massive expansion that followed included many fighter squadrons, despite the doctrine expounded by Italian General Giulio Douhet that '…the bomber would always get through', a tenet also adopted by the British Lord Trenchard and the American Billy Mitchell and eagerly embraced by politicians in those two countries anxious to avoid military expenditure during the same period.

Rosatelli's earlier design, the CR.30, had proven itself most successful and the CR.32 was essentially a logical progression of this aircraft. Design work commenced in 1932 and maintained the CR.30's sesquiplane layout with the lower wing being not more than half the area of the upper but D H R White offered an alternative definition after careful study that of '…having a lower wing of distinctly less area than the upper ones'. The advantage of this layout, with less chord, over the normal biplane included the reduction of drag, increased downward visibility, less weight, and a higher climb rate. The first such military application had been by the French with the Nieuport 11-27 series designed by Gustave Delage in 1914, which ended the ascendancy of the Fokker and was copied by the Germans, with Robert Thelen's Albatross DIII fighter, which appeared in 1917. The first British machine that applied this technique was the Armstrong-Whitworth Siskin, an all-metal fighter with great aerobatic performance developed from the Siddeley-Seasy SR2, but that was not until December 1918 when the war had finished.

Developed immediately from the CR.30 but with pared-down dimensions to save weight and enhanced performance, the dimensions for the CR.32 were a wingspan of 31ft 2.25in (9.5m), 39 inches less than the CR.30, and her overall length was reduced by more than twenty inches to 24ft 6in (7.47m), and a height of 7ft 9in (2.36m). She had a wing area of 237.88 ft^2 (22.1m^2). Weights came out at 2,921lb (1,325kg) empty; with a 4,079lb (1850.20kg) take-off weight. Her maximum speed was just 206.30mph (332km/h) at sea level, 224mph (360km/h) at 3,000m, which was disappointingly only marginally faster than the CR.30. She had a service ceiling of 28,870ft (8,800m) with a 1,822ft/min (9m/s) climb rate, and she had a maximum operation range of just over 466 miles (750km).

The prototype CR.32 (MM.201 – MM = *Matricola Militare* = Military Serial Number) first took to the air on 28 April 1933 from the Fiat field at Turin. A single-seater biplane fighter, she was powered by a single 12-cylinder 600hp (447kW) 60-degree V12 Fiat A30 R.A. in-line, water-cooled engine, (the same power plant utilized by the CR.30 and the *Industrie Meccaniche Aeronautiche Meridonali* (IMAM) Ro.37 *Lince* (Lynx) two-seater reconnaissance biplane) whose design owed much to Arthur Nutt's Schneider Trophy piston engine the Curtiss D-12 rated at 2,600rpm, which drove a 9ft 3$^{3/32}$ in (2.82m) two-bladed metal *passo variabile* (variable-pitch) propeller. This latter was only ground adjustable and used 94 Octane fuel (55 per cent gasoline, 22 benzine and 23 per cent alcohol). The prominent radiator was retained in the same ventral 'chin' position as her predecessor. There were two fuel tanks; the main 71.49 gallon (325-litre) fuel capacity one was positioned inbetween the engine and the cockpit, and the secondary 5.5 gallon (25-litre) emergency reserve tank was located in the centre of the upper wing. These had been re-positioned from the CR.30 and this improved distribution of weight improved her performance slightly. She was of composite construction throughout. The fuselage was constructed from aluminium tubing and steel, sheathed in duralumin up to the pilot's open and wind-shielded cockpit and along the rear section, beneath the tail, with canvas covering for the remainder. The wings kept the rounded tips of the CR.30 and were composed of similar duralumin spars and ribs and canvas covering. Ailerons were fitted to the upper wings along with bench-type 'boost' ailerons above their upper surface. Bracings were rigid tubular-shaped, W-type, Warren truss diagonal inter-plane struts, these uprights being of the Savoia-Verduzio-Ansaldo (SVA) type with steel tie rods.[2] The ailerons were the same but only on the upper wing. The fixed, wide-track, undercarriage was fitted with hydraulic shock absorbers and pneumatic brakes and the wheels were of the spatted 'sports' type.

Armament for the CR.32 and CR.32 *quater* (the fighter-bomber variant fitted with racks for light bombs) was initially Breda-SAFAT (*Società Anonima Fabbrica Armi Torino*) 0.303-inch (7.7mm) machine-guns, with synchronized firing through the propeller arc, but the design for the CR.32*bis* was for an extra two 0.5-inch (12.7mm) machine-guns, each with 350rpg, mounted in blisters above the lower wing. An onboard camera could be fitted, the *Cinefotomitragliatric* OMI FM.62, synchronized with these guns. Pilot instrumentation was basic, a 03 *Ottico Meccanica Italiana* (OMI) compass, anemometer to 460km/h, tachometer, altimeter, telescopic sight. There was provision for fitting an RA80-1 transmitter/receiver radio, powered by an electric generator mounted on a fairing in the centre of the upper wing. Racks for light bombs were carried. The CR.32*bis* also had the improved Fiat A.30 RA*bis* engine but even so, the additional weights dramatically affected performance and the extra guns were frequently removed in combat units.

The CR.32*ter* variant abandoned the wing guns, featured a gun-sight, had the undercarriage strengthened and modified for rough terrain operations and improvements to the engine. The C R.32 *quater* further modified this model to cut down on the overall weight to compensate for the introduction of the radio and racks for light bombs.

The original CR.32 was introduced to the *Regia Aeronautica* after intensive trials. The first operational units to receive the nimble little fighter were 1⁰, 3⁰ and 4⁰ *Stormi* (Wings).

Production continued between March 1933 and February 1939 with a total of 1,212 being finally built plus 100 of the variant built later in Spain. The variants in Italy produced were:

CR.32, built between March 1934 and February 1936 – 383
CR.32*bis* built between April 1936 and July 1937 – 328
CR.32*ter*, built between July 1937 and December 1937 – 103
CR.32*quater*, built between January 1938 and May 1939 – 395

During the war twenty-three older aircraft were rebuilt by the *Società Construzioni Aeronautiche* (SCA) and their Guidonia plant, Rome.

The Gorizia (Merna) based 4⁰ *Stormo* (Wing) formed one of the 'unofficial' *Pattuglie Acrobatiche* (Acrobatic Patrol) teams utilizing ten of these aircraft extensively to give aerobatic displays from which she became famous for her manoeuvrability, they being the 'Red Arrows' of their day. They also performed throughout Europe in 1936, from the Vatican to Berlin, and widely in South America in 1937, earning substantial orders for Fiat's latest product.

During the Italian intervention in the Spanish Civil War on the side of General Francisco Franco y Bahamonde's (another 'Leader', the Falange's *Caudillo*) Nationalist forces, the CR.32 saw considerable combat action where its sturdiness and versatility enhanced her reputation when flown by Italian 'volunteers' serving with the *Legionaria Aviazione*.[3] The first batch of twelve CR.32s was shipped to Melilla, the Spanish enclave on the North African coast adjacent to Morocco, arriving on 14 August 1936. These were fitted with two 12.7mm cowling-mounted machine-guns. Their first recorded aerial victory was achieved on 21 August when a Nieuport 52 was destroyed. Their first casualty soon followed when ten days later, a Hawker Fury destroyed a CR.32 in combat. They established the *Cucaracha Squadriglia* at Cáceres, Extremadua Region, in central western Spain; later shipments included three CR.32s sent to Palma de Mallorca Majorca aboard the Italian freighter *Emilio Morandi* on 27 August (which became the *Squadriglia Mussolini*, and later the 1300 *Squadriglia* of the *Aviazione delle Baleari*) and nine to Vigo de Garlicia, arriving aboard the freighter *Aniene* (an Italian name for the Spanish ship *Ebro*), on 7 April 1937, formed the X *Gruppo Baleari* and also the *Chirri Gruppo*. In total some 407 CRs were sent of which 377 saw service until the end of hostilities in March 1939. This was in addition to those piloted by Spanish Nationalist pilots while some units had mixed Spanish and Italian pilots.

They were soon in action, Carestiato single-handedly destroying three Republican *Società Idrovolanti Alta Italia* (SIAI) S.62 observation seaplanes of 5 Squadron at Cala

Morlanda on 28 August. Further actions followed against the *Aviación Aéreas de la República Española* with forty-eight confirmed victories over the fast Soviet Tupolev SB bombers, (four by *Capitán* Manuel Vázquez Sagastizábal alone), almost three hundred Polikarpov I-15 and I-16 fighters for the loss of 175 CR.32s from all causes. The Spanish pilots who flew the CR.32 included Joaquin Garcia Morato y Castaño who claimed three dozen enemy aircraft destroyed with his machine coded 3-51. Capitan ace was the Spanish flyer Manuel Vasquez Sagaztizabal, who claimed twenty-one victories in the CR.32 while flying with *Grupo*-2-G-3 before he was killed on 23 January 1939, while Miguel Guerrero Garcia shot down a trio of SB-2s and an I-16 in one day, 2 September 1938.

Six CR.32s were captured intact by Republican forces.[4] One of these captured CR.32s was sent to Russia after being flight-tested by a Soviet pilot at Los Alcazares airfield, Murcia, in south-east Spain. On comparative trials against Russian types it was found that while the I-15 had a better armament and the I-16 some 60mph excess of speed over the CR.32, the CR.32 could outpace the Soviet I-15 *Chato* (Spanish – Pug-Nose) in level flight, and that also it was more heavily armed and more manoeuvrable, with a superior turning circle and diving rate than the Russian I-16 *Mosca* (Spanish – Midge). The initial combat in November 1936 had seen the experienced Soviet pilots use their qualities to overpower the CR.32 but with experience the tables came to be turned. The Italian pilots made claims to have destroyed three hundred Nationalist machines for the loss of 132 of their own fighters, seventy-three in combat, and a large portion of both the killers and the killed were CR.32s.

By the outbreak of the Second World War in June 1940 the CR.32 was outdated, but still equipped the larger majority of Italian fighter units, although it was in the process of being replaced in its turn by the Fiat CR.42. However, around three hundred still remained with front-line units, mainly at colonial air bases and some of these saw combat service in Albania, Rhodes, Greece, Libya and East Africa. A few CR.32s were converted for use as night fighters (*Caccia Notturna*) by the 71[0] *Squadriglia* of the 17[0] *Gruppo* of 1[0] *Stormo* in 1940. This involved elongated gas exhausts that stretched externally right down the side of the fuselage from the engine to behind the cockpit. However, the aircraft's performance by this time precluded any actual operational use. Other CR.32s were employed as makeshift dive-bombers and carried up to 220lb (99.79kg) of light bombs into battle, but mainly they became relegated to training duties and miscellaneous duties as 'hacks' and message carriers.

War service

This was brief as the CR.32 was already obsolete by June 1940 and had been totally withdrawn from front-line combat service a year later.

The 1[0] *Gruppo*, with 150[a], 151[a] and 152[a] *Squadriglia*, 6[0] *Stormo Autonomo*, were based at Grottaglie, Puglia, on 1 June and engaged in fighter patrols over the Ionian Sea until November. During this period they saw no combat and the CR.32s were slowly phased out and replaced by Fiat G.50 fighters.

The 3⁰ *Gruppo*, with 153ᵃ, 154ᵃ and 155ᵃ *Squadriglia*, 6⁰ *Stormo*, were based at Monserrato, Sardinia, but only briefly operated their CR.32s, along with CR.42s, but these had not all been replaced until April 1941.

The 8⁰ *Gruppo*, with 92ᵃ, 93ᵃ and 94ᵃ *Squadriglia*, 2⁰ *Stormo*, likewise had some CR.32s still on hand at the Tobruk, Libya, T2 airfield on 3 June, but these had all been replaced by CR.42s by 2 July.

The 12⁰ *Gruppo*'s, 160ᵃ *Squadriglia*,[5] 50⁰ *Stormo*, were the most heavily involved units, and were used in the mainly ground-attack role. Their bases followed the fluctuating fortunes of the Italian ground forces in North Africa, being based at Soman on 10 June and moving to El Adem by the end of that month. They were based at Tobruk T2 in September and were at Benina by 1 December, but back at Derna by 7 January 1941 flying the last mission with the CR.32 on the 28th, before moving to Zuara, Libya, in February and re-equipping with the Fiat G.50.

The 13⁰ *Gruppo*, with 77ᵃ, 78ᵃ and 82ᵃ *Squadriglia*, 2⁰ *Stormo*, was also in the process of replacing their CR.32s with the CR.42. They were based at Castelbinito, Tripoli on 10 June 1940 but by the end of the month had fully re-equipped and their CR.32s were transferred over to 50⁰ *Stormo*.

The 16⁰ *Gruppo*'s 167ᵃ *Squadriglia*,[6] 50⁰ *Stormo*, also utilized their CR.32s as ground-attack aircraft until fully converted over to the Macchi MC.200 fighter by the end of January 1941. Their bases also shifted with the ebb and flow of the first North African campaign, being at Soman on 10 June and Tobruk T2 by the 30th, moving to Bir el Cuasc in October and back at Derna by December. On the 16th of that month they were at Benina N1 field and then were at El Adem ending their CR.32 service at Benghazi K1 in January 1941.

The CR.32 served just a brief wartime period with 17⁰ *Gruppo*'s 71ᵃ, 72ᵃ and 80ᵃ *Squadriglia*, 1⁰ *Stormo* at Boccadifalco, Sicily. They transferred their Macchi MC.200 fighters to 6⁰ *Gruppo* in May 1940 just prior to the outbreak of the war, but by September these had been again replaced by MC.200s.

The 20⁰ *Gruppo*, with 351ᵃ, 352ᵃ and 353ᵃ *Squadriglia*, 51⁰ *Stormo*, were a home defence unit, based at Ciampino *Sud*, and operating temporarily as *ad hoc* night fighters for the defence of Rome. This unit was selected to participate in the Blitz on London in September 1940, for which the CR.32 was patently not suitable and they were discarded.

The 21⁰ *Gruppo*, with 354ᵃ and 355ᵃ *Squadriglia*, 51⁰ *Stormo*, were also utilized in the night defence role for a brief period at Ciamapino *Sud* before moving to Guidonia and then to Capodichino where 356ᵃ *Squadriglia* joined them as 52⁰ *Stormo* on 11 September with Fiat G.50 aircraft, to which three CR.32 quarters were added as night fighters on 7 November. For the disastrous Greek campaign from 28 October the 354ᵃ and 355ᵃ *Squadriglia* became *Autonomos* and moved to Albania. The 21⁰ *Gruppo* had fully converted to the Macchi MC.200 by April 1941 and the Yugoslavian operation.

When the two *Gruppo* had originally been formed into the 51⁰ *Stormo* under the command of *Tenente* Umberto Fonda at Ciampino, on 1 October 1939, they also had some IMAM. Ro.41 trainer aircraft and both Caproni Ca.111 and Ca.133 transport aircraft on the unit's strength.

The 24⁰ *Gruppo*, with 361ᵃ and 362ᵃ *Squadriglia*, 51⁰ *Stormo*, was based at Sarzana, Liguria, on 10 June 1940, and in October became an *Autonomo* and converted to the Fiat G.50 before moving to Albania for the Greek campaign.

The 260⁰ *Gruppo*, with 393ᵃ and 394ᵃ *Squadriglia*, was at Tirana, Albania, on 10 June 1940, and as *Autonomo* moved to Drenova and Devoli, respectively, on the 28 and 29th. They were a mixed unit with eight CR.32s and eight CR.42s initially but full conversion to the latter was completed by February 1941.

The 163ᵃ *Autonomo Squadriglia* was also converting to the CR.42 on 10 June 1940 and was based in the Aegean, at Marizza, Rhodes. After the German conquest of the Greek island of Crete in May 1941 the CR.32s were reduced to a training role only with 161⁰ *Gruppo*.

In Ethiopia (Abyssinia), conquered by Italy in 1935–6, 410ᵃ *Squadriglia* was based at Dire Daua with the CR.32 and moved to Giggiga in July. By March they were based at Addis Ababa and on 5 April were at Gimma, but with only two operational CR.42s on their strength. The unit disbanded at Gonda on 5 June. Likewise the 411ᵃ *Autonomo Squadriglia* began the war at Addis Ababa and worked out of Javello (Yavello), Oroma, from the 20th. The unit then operated from Dire Daua in the north-east close to Djibouti, Asmara, Dessie, Gimma, and Gondar in the north, before expanding their final CR.32s and disbanding.

The first CR.32s to engage in combat operations during World War II was 94ᵃ *Squadriglia* of 8⁰ *Gruppo*, which was initially based at Castel Benito, Libya, but which moved up to Tobruk airfield just prior to the Italian commencement of hostilities on 10 June 1940. Mussolini was counting on the fact that France, Belgium and the Low Countries had just about been knocked out of the war by Nazi Germany and that he would have easy pickings with the minimal effort, as he expected Great Britain to negotiate a truce. When this did not happen, the *Regia Aeronautica* found itself fully engaged against the Royal Navy fleets in the Mediterranean and the fortress island of Malta, and against a small British army and air force in Egypt and other African colonies. The first fighter mission flown by the CR.32 was on 11 June and six of them achieved the destruction of two RAF Bristol Blenheims and two damaged in air fighting over El Adem, Tobruk, without loss in return. On 14 June the first CR.32 was destroyed by a British Gloster Gladiator. On 4 August *Capitano* Duilio Sergio Fanali, who had achieved several victories in Spain destroyed a Gloster Gladiator (K7908) piloted by Sergeant Kenneth Rew. During General Rodolfo Graziani's offensive into Egypt (the much-heralded 'March on Alexandria'), which began on 14 September, the CR.32 was frequently used as a light bomber, as well as fighter escort for bombers attacking the Suez Canal Zone, but during the British counter-offensive from 10 December, many were destroyed or abandoned during the rapid Italian retreat. Count Ciano noted in his diary on 26 July, 'Our air losses during the first month of the war amount to two hundred and fifty planes; we are producing the same amount. The question of pilots is more difficult. Their losses cannot be easily replaced.' And again, on 3 October, he wrote:

Biseo [General Attilio], a man who really understands aviation, has painted a black picture of our Air Force in North Africa. Our planning is bad, and we are short of fighter planes. Although the English are numerically inferior, they cause us plenty of trouble.[7]

In East Africa both the 410ᵃ and the 411ᵃ *Squadriglia* were equipped with the CR.32 and they saw much fighting, *Tenente* Aldo Meoli and Flaminio Bossi claiming one Junkers Ju.86 bomber of No. 12 SAAF and one Hawker Hurricane of No. 1 SAAF Squadron destroyed when they intercepted an attack on Wavello airfield. Later they claimed victories over both types and other Allied aircraft, for a total of fourteen British machines shot down, but by the end of April only a single CR.32 remained in flyable condition.

Foreign service

This little fighter was widely adopted overseas and served for many years in the following air forces.

Austria – 45 CR.32bis
As they arrived in Austria they equipped *Jagdgeschwader II* based at Weiner Neustadt. Of these, thirty-eight of them were subsequently absorbed into the Luftwaffe after the *Anschluss*[8] on 12 March 1938, becoming *I. Gruppel Jagdgeschwader 138*. However, they did not fit into the German organization and were soon sold on to the Hungarian Air Force.

China
The Republic of China Air Force was formed in April 1931 with the threat from Japan first becoming menacing. The *Kuomintang* Government of Chiang Kai-Shek set about seriously building up its strength from zero at the best speed it could. An Italian Military Mission under Generale Roberto Lordi, comprising pilots, technicians, engineers and trainers arrived in China and Lordi became Chief of the Chinese Air Staff. His position and influence helped Italy secure some military aviation contracts, one of which was the placing, in 1933 by the Chinese Nationalist Air Force an order for sixteen of the initial batch of CR.32s, being the first nation to do so. These machines were to be equipped with the Vickers 7.7mm machine gun in lieu of the Breda-SAFAT as supplies already existed, and they were to be fitted with radios, electric lamps for night landings and other minor modifications. However, lethargy in Rome precluded any further orders and Lordi was recalled home under a cloud and resigned his commission.

To fly these fighters sixteen aviation students were sent to Italy to train. On arrival at Shanghai fifteen of these CR.32s formed the 8 *Tutai* (Pursuit Squadron) in August 1937. Those CR.32s that were unloaded at Shanghai operated from nearby Nangahang airfield. By May 1936 only six remained in an operational condition due to accidents. Difficulties were found in obtaining the correct aviation fuel, thus limiting their effectiveness and shortage of spares further depleted their numbers apart from combat losses. The 8 *Tutai* was led by Commander Chen Yau-Wei. During the Shanghai incident and again during the Japanese offensive against Nanking the following year, these aircraft were based at Chu Yung airfield. These Fiats were flown against the Japanese with mixed success and by the end of the year nearly all had been expended.

There were many actions, one of the most spectacular being when five CR.32s engaged twenty Mitsubishi G3M bombers of the *Kisarazu Ku*, on 15 August 1937, destroying three of them, with Yau-Wei and Huang Chu-Ku sharing one kill and Flight Leader Shen Tse-Liu and Liu Chi-Wei claiming another near Lui Shui. Subsequently the unit was heavily engaged and suffered severe losses, Chen Yau-Wei and all the other pilots of the unit were either killed or wounded. By autumn 1937 just one CR.32, No. 806, remained operational and was flown by Captain Shen Tse-Liu, until he was shot in the face by a Mitsubishi A5M on 22 September. No. 806 was then transferred to 25 *Tutai* and used in the defence of the capital, Nanking, the last recorded action being conducted in this machine by Captain Chow Tin-Fong of the 25 *Tutai*, who attacked three Japanese Navy Mitsubishi A5M monoplane fighters on 4 January 1938 and survived the encounter. This aircraft was finally pensioned off on 25 January and, along with the unit's surviving Curtiss Hawk 75s, was re-equipped with Soviet supplied Polikarpov I-15*bis* fighters at Sianxi, Shansi Province, from August 1937 onward.

Hungary

The Royal Hungarian Air Force placed two orders of twenty-six aircraft each, totalling fifty-two CR.32s, following the Rome Protocol between Austria, Hungary and Italy of 12 July 1934, which facilitated trade and increased co-operation between the three nations. The Italians agreed to help build up the *Magyar Légügyi Hivatal* (Hungarian Aviation Department, the air arm of the Hungarian Army). These fighters were armed with the Hungarian-manufactured 7.92mm GKH (*Gebauer Kényszermeghattású Motorgéppuska* – Positive-Driven Motor-Machinegun) machine-guns[9] and reached Hungary in batches in the period 23 April to 2 December 1936. These CR.32s formed the 1/1 *Ilász* (Archer) *Vadászszázad* (Fighter Squadron), the 1/2 *Ludas Matyi* (Mattie Goose Boy – from Hungarian folklore) *Vadászszázad* and the 1/3 *Puma* (Mountain Lion) *Vadászszázad* of the 1 *Mérésügyi Csoport* ('Metrological' Group). This subterfuge had to be resorted to as Hungary was official forbidden to re-arm after World War I, but, as always, a way was found around the problem. Following the 22 August 1938 Bled, Yugoslavia, agreement, the way was cleared for the formation of an 'official' air force, the *Magyar Királyi Honvéd Légierö* (Royal Hungarian Air Force).

As noted above a further thirty-six former Austrian machines were obtained from Germany as being surplus to Luftwaffe requirements with some further Hispano-built CR.32*quater* received during the war. One Hungarian CR.32 was experimentally fitted with a 750hp (559.5kW) Gnome-Rhône 14M *Mars* engine. This machine achieved a top speed of 261mph (420km/h) at an altitude of 13,123ft (4,000m) As a result it was proposed to re-equip the rest of the fleet with this power plant, but problems with supply caused the project to be abandoned.

The Hungarian CR.32s were mobilized during the period of the dismembering of Czech-Slovakia during the Munich Crisis of September 1938, when the Slovaks declared their independence. The Hungarian army on the border remained ready to invade the rump Slovakian state and the situation was very tense. One incident on 25 October saw a Czech Letov Š-328 fighter from 10 Squadron shot down by a CR.32 piloted by Föhadnagy László over Hodzovo. The Czech observer was killed and the pilot wounded. The Germans and Italians forced the so-termed Arbitration of Vienna on 2 November when some territory was ceded to Hungary. Even so border clashes continued and the situation remained fragile. In March 1939 Hitler annexed Bohemia and Moravia and Hungary took the opportunity to seize Ruthenia on the 23rd. When Mukačevo was attacked the Slovak air force struck at the advancing columns and on 24 March the Hungarian CR.32s retaliated in kind. There were aerial dog-fights involving the 1/1 and 1/2 *Vadászszázads* against Slovak Avia B-534s over Szobranc during which two B-534s were claimed as destroyed and damage was inflicted upon a third machine. The same afternoon they claimed two more and also a brace of Letov aircraft. The Hungarian troops, supported from the air by one regiment of CR.32s, counter-attacked toward Orhegyalja and then Pongrácz, finally pushing on to the Polish border and the CR.32s from 1/2 *Vadászszázad* also provided escort for Hungarian Junkers Ju.86K-2 bombers that struck at Spisska Nova Ves' airfield. Further combat followed and the CR.32s claimed a total of ten enemy machines destroyed and one damaged in total. The fighting ended with the Hungarian and Slovaks signing a Border Treaty on 28 March. Much of the territory occupied was formally ceded to Hungary by the Budapest Treaty of 4 April.

By the end of that year the CR.32 was replaced in the 1/3 *Vadászszázad* and became the 2/2 *Vadászszázad* while 1/1 *Vadászszázad* retained its Fiats. These were not involved in combat again until 6 April 1941, when Germany invaded Yugoslavia from Hungarian territory and when Hungarian troops moved into the northern part of that country a week later the 1/1's and 1/2's CR.32s provided air cover. The Yugoslav air force resisted briefly and two CR.32s were lost and a third damaged before hostilities ceased on 13 April. As one of Germany's allies again, Hungary was forced to mobilize all available units when the Soviet Union was attacked on 22 June 1941. Both CR.32 units were readied for defensive duties guarding Diósgyör and Miskolc, 1/1 *Vadászszázad* being based at Ungvár (now known as Ushgorod) and 1/2 *Vadászszázad* at Felsöábrány (now known as Kosice). On 26 June three Soviet bombers attacked Kassa (now known as Kosice) and the CR.32s tried to intercept but lacked the speed. They were clearly obsolete and although the 1/1 *Vadászszázad* took their CR.32s to Miskole on 4 July they were soon all relegated to training duties.

Paraguay

Since the bitter little Chaco War of 1933, relations between South American neighbours Bolivia and Paraguay, which had been the first conflict on that continent to involve military aircraft, had remained strained. The Bolivian Army Air Corps was larger by far, and concentrated at Villa Montes and Muñoz, but because of the construction of the forward landing-strip at Isla Poí, the *Fuerezas Aéreas del Ejército Nacional del Paraguay*, was able to deploy its machines closer to the front. The FAP had already used Fiat CR.20 fighters during that combat to good effect and in 1937 they wished to update their fleet.

The Paraguay Government of Colonel Rafael Franco approached the Italian Legation at Asuncion in 1936 and placed an order for ten CR.32*bis* fighters. A League of Nations arms embargo did not prevent both sides building up their air strengths by purchases abroad, but the abrupt overthrow of Franco saw his successor cut the order by half and, in the end, the FAP only received five aircraft. These were allocated the serials 1-1, 1-3, 1-5, 1-7 and 1-9 and joined to the *Primo Escuadrilla de Caza* (1st Fighter Squadron) based at Ñu-Guazú airfield, Asunción, between 1939 and 1941 before being retired.

South Africa

In April 1941 a CR.32 was captured intact at Addis Ababa (serial number MM4191). It was made flyable and Major Edward A. Biden of No. 41 Squadron, South African Air Force, flew her down to Nairobi, Kenya on 2 August. On arrival at Zwartkop Air Station, Gauteng, a week later, this aircraft was given the SAAF serial 21 and on 4 September was taken onto the strength of No. 42 Squadron, who sent her on a public tour. In April 1942 she was on the establishment of No. 6 Squadron based at Durban and used for AA practice and as a communications hack. She had to make a force-landing due to engine failure on 18 July, and although she only had slight damage this ended her flying days. On 6 November she was handed over to Natal University Air Training Squadron (ATS) where she remained until 1945, when she was discarded.

Spain

The Spanish authorities sought and were granted permission to licence-build the CR.32 in 1938. The Spanish company *Hispano Aviación*, located in the Nationalist-held area at Tablada, Seville, was selected and, between 1939 and 1942, eventually produced one hundred and twenty-six aircraft as the HA-132-L *Chirri*. These were serials 3-51 to 3-177. Later the Italians supplied a further batch totalling 114 surplus CR.32s , which were refurbished by the Spanish to the same standard at Park Tablada in the period 1940–41, these being serials 3-178 to 3-292.

Finally, when the Civil War ended in March 1939, the parent Hispano-Suiza company refurbished two batches of fifty CR.32s, these being given serials 3-293 to 3-392.

Thirty-one HA-132-L aircraft converted to two-seater trainers, and modified by *Hispano Aviacion* in Seville, went to the General Air Academy at Morón airbase, *Fázquez Sagastiz á Bal,* in southern Spain and were flown by pilots from the *Academia General del Aire* (General Air Academy) at San Javier, Murcia, and some continued to serve there as the C.1 aerobatic training aircraft, until as late as 1953.

Venezuela

In 1938 the *Fuerza Aérea Venezolana* (Venezuelan Air Force), placed orders for nine CR.32s, which were modified with larger radiators to cope for tropical conditions, and which were delivered to Maracay during the period 1938–39. In 1939 these formed 9 *Grupo de Caza* (9 Fighter Group) of No. 1 *Regimiento de Aviación Militar de Venezuela* (1 Aviation Regiment). A further order for six more CR.32s was pending when Italy joined World War II and the British blockade frustrated completion of this, and the order was cancelled. Two FAV Fiats were lost in separate accidents in 1940 and two more were also lost in accidents in 1941. The final five CR.32s were discarded in 1943.

Preserved aircraft

A Fiat licence-built HA-132-L (C.1-328/3-52) is held at the Museum of Aeronautics & Astronautics, Four Winds, Spain.

Chapter Five

Fiat CR.42 *Falco*

Successful and popular as the CR.32 was it created a dangerous frame of mind in the *Regia Aeronautica* for it fostered a belief that the biplane was still capable of outpacing the latest monoplane fighter aircraft then on the verge of being introduced into most of the world's major air forces. This belief saw Celestino Rosatelli and the Fiat design team continue to develop the CR.32 concept through the three prototype CR. 33s that were powered by the Fiat V supercharged engine in 1936/37, the single CR.40, which had a Bristol Mercury IV radial developing 585hp (331kW) engine, the solitary Cr. 40*bis* with the Fiat A59R of 700hp and the only CR.41, which had the Gnome-Rhone 900hp (662kW) engine, in a steady progression until they arrived at the CR.42.

The CR.42 was the culmination of Rosatelli's ideals and with her he created a superlative biplane fighter that was acclaimed as a versatile, immediately responsive and sturdy but light little aircraft that pilots loved to fly. She made her maiden test flight in May 1938, and the first orders were placed even before this aircraft had completed her trials. There is some evidence that the Italian higher authorities were not so naïve as to believe that the biplane still had a place in modern warfare, and indeed the Fiat G.50 *Freccia* (Arrow) and Macchi MC.200 *Saetta* (Lightning) monoplanes were on the stocks following a replacement specification issued as early as 1936, although heavily delayed by problems. The G.50 did not enter service until 1939, the G50*bis* in December 1940 and the MC.200 in October 1939; few of either type were with combat units on 10 June 1940. One reason for the bulk ordering of the CR.42 might have been the need for *Generale* Giuseppe Valle, Under-Secretary of Aviation and Chief of the Air Staff, to get as many aircraft on the stocks as he could, if only to have the numbers in fact to match the much exaggerated figures he was constantly feeding to Mussolini. Ciano recorded that Valle, '…on too many occasions, has made assertions and promises which are either untrue or impracticable'. However, Valle himself is said to have all along regarded the CR.42 as a 'Transition' aircraft, a fighter to fill the gap until the first monoplanes arrived. Nonetheless, it remains a fact that the Italians were introducing the CR.42 biplane into service at a time when every other major air force had switched, or were switching, over to the monoplane fighter.[1]

Nonetheless, the CR.42 was ordered in bulk and by the time Italy entered the Second World War in June 1940, she was in production to replace the CR.32 in the front-line. She not only captivated the hearts of Italian pilots but those of Belgium, Germany, Hungary and Sweden as well. About 1,781 *Falco* aircraft were eventually built in various guises and served as far apart as the UK, the Baltic and East Africa. Although an outdated machine she made her mark in war and her manoeuvrability saw her best some Allied monoplane fighters, like the Fleet Air Arm's Fairey Fulmar, with considerable ease. Her day as a front-line fighter over, she soldiered on in various roles, night attack and trainer among them. Purely as a delightful aircraft to fly she proved the best of the biplanes and was widely liked by her pilots of all nations.

The CR.42 in her original form was a single-seater fighter powered by a single Fiat A.74 RC 38, 14-cylinder radial, air-cooled, engine which rated at 840hp (617.82kW). She had fixed, spatted, landing gear and an open cockpit with a small windshield. She had a wingspan of 31ft 10in (9.70m), a length of 27ft 3in (8.30m) and a height of 10ft 10in (3.30m). The fully loaded weight was 5,060lb (2,295kg). She had a maximum speed of 273mph (440km/h) at 19,685ft (6,000m) and an absolute ceiling of 34,450ft (10,500m). Her range was 490 miles (785km). Her main armament comprised 2×12.7mm SAFAT machine-guns synchronized to fire through the propeller arc; and she was able to carry 2×220.5lb (100kg) bombs on under-wing racks.

The CR.42 equipped the following *Regia Aeronautica* units:

3^0 *Gruppo*, with 153ª, 154ª and 155ª *Squadriglie*, 6^0 *Stormo*, were based at Soman in Tripolitania, moving to Ara Fileni in December and El Merduma by January and then moving into Egypt, being at Sidi Omar, by the end of that month, where their existing CR.32s began to be replaced by the CR.42, and this was completed by April. The unit was back at Benghazi K2 by May and later at Martuba, Cyrenaica.

7^0 *Gruppo* with 76ª, 86ª, and 98ª *Squadriglie*, 5^0 *Stormo*, were based at Araxos, Greece and during the summer of 1942 had some CR.42CNs on their strength.

8^0 *Gruppo*, with 92ª, 93ª and 94ª *Squadriglie*, 5^0 *Stormo*, were at Tobruk on 3 June 1940, moving to Berka, Cyrenaica, by the end of July, and then Derna a month later. By September 1940 they were at El Adem, then Uadi el Menastir and were based at Berka once more by mid-December. The unit had withdrawn to Mirafiori on the mainland by the end of December and were at Torino Caselle at the end of January 1941. They started converting to the MC.200 in February 1941 and were concentrated at Oria Manduria by April and once again at Tornio Caselle by May.

9^0 *Gruppo*, with 73ª, 96ª and 97ª *Squadriglie*, 4^0 *Stormo*, was at Goriza on outbreak of war and then Torino Mirafiori, moving to Comiso, Sicily on 1 July. They had the new MC.200 fighter but because the pilots much preferred flying the CR.42 they exchanged their aircraft with those of 1^0 *Stormo*, flying from Berka in North Africa by 11 July, then Benghazi in August and the following month they were at El Adem. They could not postpone the inevitable, however, and by the end of the year had converted once more to the MC.200.

10^0 *Gruppo*, with 84ª, 90ª and 91ª *Squadriglie*, 4^0 *Stormo*, had been flying the CR.42 from September 1939 onward and, like 9^0 *Stormo*, arranged to have their new MC.200s transferred to the 1^0 *Stormo* so they could continue flying the *Falco*. They were based at Tobruk T2 on 10 June 1940 when the war began, moving to Benina and then Berka and by August were working out of Bir el Gobi, reaching El Adem in September and then back at Berka the same month. In January 1941 they finally accepted the MC.200 and the CR.42 was phased out.

12⁰ *Gruppo* with 159ª and 160ª *Squadriglie,* 50⁰ *Stormo* was based at Castelvetrano in May 1943 and had an unspecified number of CR.42s on their strength.

13⁰ *Gruppo,* with 77ª, 78ª and 82ª *Squadriglie,* 2⁰ *Stormo,* was a mixed CR.32 and CR.42 outfit and at the beginning of hostilities was at Castelbenio, moving up to Tobruk T2 by 19 June and then to Berka in August, Gambut by mid-September, then Tmimi, also in Cyrenaica. They were pulled back to Jesse, Italy, by February 1941, and transferred up to Genova by June for local defence duties. From October 1941 their *Falcos* were replaced by the MC.200.

16⁰ *Gruppo,* with 167, 168 and 169 *Squadriglie,* 54⁰ *Stormo,* was flying MC.200s and MC.202s in mid-1942 but were registered as having some CR.42s still on their operational strength at Crotone at this period.

18⁰ *Gruppo* had the most interesting change of venue. Its 83ª, 85ª and 95ª *Squadriglie* of the 3⁰ *Stormo* were flying the CR.42 at Novi Ligure on the mainland on the outbreak of war and a month later were at Mirafiori and was at Monaco on 6 October. The unit was selected to represent the *Regia Aeronautica*'s contribution to the blitz on Britain and moved to its new battle zone via Darmstadt, Germany (17 October) to Ursel in Belgium where they arrived on the 19th. They flew missions against England until early in the New Year, then returned home via Frankfurt (10 January 1941) to Pisa where they arrived on the 13th. The unit was then transferred south to Sorman and Mellaha, Tripoli, by the 29/30th. By mid-February they were based at Tamet and moved to Benghazi K2 field by 7 April but were back at Tamet and Sorman in August 1941 where they converted to the MC.200.

23⁰ *Gruppo* with 70ª, 74ª and 75ª *Squadriglie,* 3⁰ *Stormo,* were flying the CR.42 from Cervere when war commenced on 10 June 1940 and were later at Torino Mirafiori Vilanova, and Campiglia the following month when they became an *Autonomo* and moved down to Regio Calabria before commencing escorting the bombing attacks against Malta from Comiso, Sicily, from 11 July. On the conclusion of this period the unit moved to North Africa reaching Castelbenito on 16 December and moving via Ain el Gazala to Derna by the 20th to Ain el Gazala once more by 1 January 1941. In that month the CR.42s flew from Derna, Berka and Benghazi and were working from Tamet and Sorman by early February. They returned to Comiso on 1 March and were based on the island of Pantelleria the following month. By the end of June they were at Boccadifalco, Sicily, and then returned to Castelbenito and Misurata, Tripoli, where they began to gradually receive replacement MC.200 monoplane fighters towards the end of the year before returning to Trapani Milo, Sicily, but did not fully complete the full conversion until early in 1942.

24⁰ *Gruppo,* comprising the 254ª, 355ª, 361ª, 370ª and 395ª *Autonomo Squadriglie* was established at Monserrato, on the island of Sardinia in July 1941 with the Fiat G.50 fighter, but utilized the CR.42 on occasions against the British Force 'H' and convoys from Gibraltar to Malta, where they scored some successes. They remained in Sardinia for a year but shed the 361ª and 395ª *Squadriglie* and became a totally G.50-equipped outfit.

46⁰ *Gruppo*, with 20ᵃ and 21ᵃ *Squadriglie*, 15⁰ *Stormo*, converted from a bomber unit to the CR.42-equipped unit at Vicenza in May 1942 and moved to Benghazi at the end of August. During Rommel's canter up to El Alamein and back they were various based at El Adem, Bu Amud in September, but were back at Tamet, Tripoli, by mid-November and, with the fall of Tunis, evacuating to Vicenza in January 1943. They moved over to Capoterra, Sardinia, in May when it was expected the Allies were going to invade there, but returned to Pontederea in July and spent their final operational days at Firenze Peretola.

Likewise, the 47⁰ *Gruppo*, a bomber unit, with 53ᵃ and 54ᵃ *Squadriglie*, switched to the *Assalto* role at Vicenza in May 1942 and also became part of the 15⁰ *Stormo*. Their movements were similar to their sister *Gruppo*, moving to Benghazi at the end of August and operating out of Bu Amud, Barce and Agedabia between September and November of that year. By November they were back at Tamet and then Sorman and Zuara before being pulled out to Vicenza in January 1943. They also moved to Sardinia, being based at Oristano in May but returned to the mainland when no invasion materialized there to end their days at Firenze Peretola before the Italian armistice.

Another bomber-to-ground-attack conversion was 59⁰ *Gruppo*, with 232ᵃ and 233ᵃ *Squadriglie*, initially with 41⁰ *Stormo* at Treviso. This unit, however, converted to the night-fighter mission with a variety of aircraft, which included the CR.42CN. They were at Torino Caselle in January and by May had moved to Metato. In June 1943 the *Gruppo* became *Autonomo* and were based at Ciampino, switching to first Littoria in mid-July, Lagnasco by the end of that month and finally Venegono by early August.

A similar conversion was undertaken by 60⁰ *Gruppo* with 208ᵃ and 209ᵃ *Squadriglie*, which up to then had been operating as a *Tuffo* (dive-bombing) outfit with the German-built Junkers Ju.87 Stuka. Owing to heavy losses in the summer of 1942 when a whole unit went astray in the desert, the Fiat CR.42 was drafted in from 27 April. In June they were at Ciampino *Sud* and the following month at Capodichino on the mainland, but moved to Gerbini *Nord* airfield in Sicily and then to the island of Pantelleria from 15 July 1942. Their next move was to North Africa where they arrived at Tamet late in July and worked from Benghazi and Derna and were as far forward as Abu Nimeir, Egypt, at the end of August. During the final Axis push in October they were based at Abu Smeit at the end of that month, but had been bundled back to Bu Amud, Agedabia and then En Nofilia, Tripoli, by mid-November with the British counter-offensive. They spent the first few days of December at Buerat and then Misurata but by the 8th they had been withdrawn to Gerbini and the *Falco* aircraft were replaced by Fiat G.50s.

150⁰ *Gruppo*, with 363ᵃ, 364ᵃ and 365ᵃ *Squadriglie* of 53⁰ *Stormo* had been equipped with the CR.42 as early as May 1939 and on the outbreak of hostilities were at Torino Caselle. Moving to Valona in Albania at the start of the Greek campaign they became an *Autonomo* on 23 October 1940 and re-equipped with the MC.200.

The very first *Gruppo* to receive the CR.42 *Falco* had been 151⁰ with 366ᵃ, 367ᵃ and 368ᵃ *Squadriglie* of 53⁰ *Stormo* in March 1939. On 10 June they were at Casabianca but by early September had moved to North Africa and were working out of El Adem. On

23 October 1940 they became *Autonomo* and by December 1941 were operating from Agedabia in Cyrenaica while by the end of September they were at Ara Fileni, Tripoli and then Sorman. They then re-equipped with the Fiat G.50*bis* from January 1942 onward.

153⁰ *Gruppo*, with 372ᵃ, 373ᵃ and 374ᵃ *Squadriglie, Autonomo,* was a Macchi MC.202 fighter unit but nine CR.42s supplemented its strength during the brief campaign in Yugoslavia in April 1941. By November they were working out of Brindisi and 372ᵃ *Squadriglia* took its *Falco* aircraft across to North Africa as a mainly *Assalto* unit before returning to Torino Caselle in December. The remaining aircraft all converted over to the MC.200 and MC.202 early in 1942.

156⁰ *Gruppo* with 379ᵃ and 380ᵃ *Squadriglie* only briefly operated as an *Autonomo* from Comiso, Sicily, between January and April 1941 before being disbanded.

Equally brief was the tenure of 157⁰ *Gruppo*'s time with the *Falco*, 384ᵃ, 385ᵃ and 386ᵃ of 1⁰ *Gruppo* being at Trapani Milo on Sicily on 10 June and becoming *Autonomo* by August. By as early as 9 December all their CR.42s had been replaced by the MC.200.

158⁰ *Gruppo*, with 387ᵃ and 388ᵃ *Squadriglie,* had the distinction of being the last *Regia Aeronautica* unit to operate the CR.42. This *Assalto* unit was not formed until December 1941 at Sorman, Tripoli, and was joined by the 236ᵃ *Squadriglie* a month later. They were based at Aviano on the mainland in early May 1942 but left for North Africa and were at Benghazi K3 by the 13th of that month. The unit followed the same pattern of Rommel's advance to El Alamein, his defeat there and the Axis withdrawal, working respectively from El Ftehja, Cyrenaica at the end of May, Deran in June and reaching Sidi Barrani and then Abu Nimeir in Egypt at the end of June. By late October they were back at Martuba, then Benghazi once more by mid-November and rapidly were at Ara Fileni, and then Buerat before withdrawing to Aviano by 7 December. In May 1943 they were based at Osoppo, Italy, and then subsequently converted to the Fiat G.50*bis*.

159⁰ *Gruppo*, with 389ᵃ, 390ᵃ and 391ᵃ *Squadriglie* came late to the CR.42, equipping in early May while at Aviano. By 25 May they had shifted to Castelbenito in North Africa and then moved to El Ftehja and then Derna by June. At the end of that month they were based at El Aden before advancing to Egypt working first from Sidi Barrani and then Abu Nimeir. By mid-September they were recuperating at Benghazi before returning to the front in September but in the general withdrawal they found themselves back at Martuba by the end of October and then Benghazi once more and Ara Fileni, Buerat, Misurata, Gars Garabulli and then Zuara by January. With the end in Tunisia, the remnants were back pulled back to Aviano where they re-equipped fully with the Fiat G.50*bis*.

160⁰ *Gruppo*, with 393ᵃ and 394ᵃ *Autonomo*, were based at Tirana, Albania, on the outbreak of war, and for the Greek campaign moved to Drenova and then Devoli at the end of October. Following the winter campaign the unit was back at Osopo, Italy, in February 1941, where they were joined by 375ᵃ *Squadriglia*. The whole CR. 42 complement had been expended by September and replaced by the Fiat G.50. With this aircraft the *Gruppo* took part in the final North Africa campaigns and was withdrawn to the mainland. In March, replacement *Falcos* reached the unit and they were based at Ajaccio, on the island of Sardinia. By the time of the Italian Armistice in September 1943 all save two of these CR.42s had also been written off.

An early conversion to the CR.42 was done by 161⁰ *Gruppo*, with 162ª, 163ª and 164ª *Squadriglie Autonomo*, which were based at Rodi Marizza on the island of Rhodes in the Aegean in June 1940. They operated their *Falcos* through the first two years of the war from here and were not withdrawn back to Italy until early in 1943. While at Palermo, Sicily, the unit received replacement Fiat G.50*bis* and Macchi MC.200 fighters but still retained a few CR.42CNs for night-fighting operations at this time.

By contrast the 167⁰ *Gruppo*, with 300ª and 303ª *Squadriglie Autonomo*, did not receive the CR.42CN night-fighter until May 1942, along with a very mixed bag of aircraft of all such types while at Ciampino. They worked out of Grottaglie as well but were back at Ciampino Sud in June 1943 where the last CR.42s were retired, being replaced exclusively by Reggiane RE.2001CNs.

The first CR.42 *Caccia Notturna* (Night-Fighter) unit formed was 171⁰ *Gruppo*, which briefly operated the CR.42CN with 301ª and 302ª *Squadriglie Autonomo* at Gela, Sicily, from October 1941 but a month later they were disbanded and the airfield taken over by the Luftwaffe.

A special unit was hastily formed in July 1942 at Hon, Tripoli, and named the *Battaglione Aviazione Sahariana* (Sahara Aerial Battalion) with 36ª and 99ª *Squadriglie* flying the CR.42. Their mission was to provide fighter protection for the vital oasis of southern Libya during the advance into Egypt. Their last CR.42 had been expended by January 1943, by which time with the Axis land forces driven back to Tunis, they had no role left to perform and were redundant.

There were also many Autonomous (*Autonomo*) *Squadriglia* that used the CR.42 for varying periods. 110ª *Squadriglia* operated the *Industrie Meccaniche Aeronautiche Meridonali* (IMAM) Ro37*bis Lince* (Lynx) reconnaissance biplane, from Dire Daua, Ethiopia, and on 17 January was allocated a quartet of *Falcos* to reinforce its strength. They worked from Gimma from 24 March onward but by 5 June, when forced to evacuate by the British offensive, all four had been expended.

161⁰ *Squadriglia* was operating the IMAM Ro.43 and Ro.44 maritime floatplanes from Rhodes but these proved totally inadequate aircraft in practice and were replaced by the CR.42 in June 1941. They operated for eighteen months until replaced in their turn by Fiat G.50s and Macchi MC.200s.

163⁰ *Squadriglia* was likewise based on Rhodes, at Marizza and then Gadurra in June 1940 but on 11 June 1941 it became part of 161⁰ *Gruppo*.

236⁰ *Squadriglia* was a dive-bomber unit equipped with the Junkers Ju.87R ('Richard' or long-range *Tuffo*) and worked through the early North African campaigns with some success. While at Agedabia on 3 November 1941, the unit replaced these with the CR.42AS[2] They operated from Agedabia in November 1941 and a month later were at Sorman, Tripoli, and then Ara Fileni. By mid-January 1942 these CR.42s were at El Merduma, Agheila, and then Agedabia again by the end of the month and finally worked from K2 field at Benghazi from 9 February.

300ª *Squadriglia* first formed at Guidonia from the *Sezione Caccia Noturne* (Night Fighter Section) to provide Rome with night-fighter defence and worked out of Ciampino. Between January and May 1942 they were operated under the auspices of 51^0 *Stomo* and subsequently joined 167^0 *Gruppo*.

375^0 *Squadriglia* was hastily formed at Tirana, Albania, on 1 February 1941, and subsequently took part in the Axis invasion of Yugoslavia. They transferred to North Africa being based at Agedabia by December and in January 1942 were at En Nofilia, Tripoli, where they joined 160^0 *Gruppo*.

376^0 was not formed with the *Falco* until 29 April 1941 at Torino Caselle and then Ciampino. By the end of May they had transferred to Castelbenito, Tripoli, and in August were working out of Ain el Gazala, reaching Bir Hacheim by mid-November. They were recalled home that month and the CR.42s were replaced by the MC.200 at Naples that same month.

Another night-fighting and anti-submarine (two seemingly diametrically-opposite missions) outfit was 377^0 *Squadriglia*, which was based at Sciacca, Sicily, from September 1942 where some CR.42s supplemented the existing Macchi MC.200 and Reggiane Re.2000 fighter complement until February 1943.

Also very late to the *Falco* was 392^0 *Squadriglia*, a component part of the *Caccia Terrestre* (Territorial Fighters), which was a mixed-complement unit with Fiat G.50*bis*, Macchi MC.200s and IMAM Ro.41s, which briefly operated from 1 March from Tirana, Albania.

Isolated in East Africa the 412^0 *Squadriglia* was based at Massaua on the outbreak of war. The CR.42s fought a steadily debilitating campaign with little or no hope of relief or reinforcement in both Eritrea, (operating successively from Agordat, Asmara, Gura, Barentu and Gura), and Ethiopia (Abyssinia) from Dessie, Alomata, Gimma and Gondar, throughout 1940 and into 1941. The final CR.42 carried out her last mission, a ground-attack run against Allied forces near Kulkakber, on 22 November and was burnt to prevent it falling into British hands on 26 November.

Similarly the companion unit, 413^0 *Squadriglia*, fought the same lonely war exclusively in Ethiopia between 10 June 1940 and July 1941, being based respectively at Assab, Dire Daua, Gondar, Adi Ugri, Dessie, Addis Ababa, Sciasciamanna and Gimma, with the final attack being mounted on 9 July 1941.

The final East African CR.42 unit was 414^0 *Squadriglia* based at Gura, Eritrea, when the war began. The combat career of their CR. 42s was extremely brief, for after moving to Assab in Ethiopia on 28 of that month, all the remaining six *Falco*s were destroyed there on 10 July and the unit was disbanded.

War service

The CR.42s that served in North Africa were fitted with a large sand filter under the nose, some sported new, enlarged, spinners to assist in the desert atmosphere, and most had their wheel spats removed.

The attack on Malta, and also the attacks mounted against the Royal Navy squadrons based at Gibraltar in the west and Alexandria, Egypt, in the east and the various troop and supply convoys they escorted between 1940 and 1942, saw the CR.42 frequently called into action. Their opponents were usually Hawker Hurricanes based on Malta (the use of the six Gloster Gladiators there, which would have been the closest examples of like duelling with like, had almost ceased by the time the *Falcos* started to be used, as described elsewhere) and also against the Royal Navy's Blackburn Skua, Fairey Fulmar (invariably described by the Italians as Hurricanes or Supermarine Spitfires) and Gloster Sea Gladiator fighters, of which never more than a handful were available on each carrier at any one time until Operation *Pedestal* in 1942. The *Falcos* usually outnumbered these opponents many times over and had the support of the MC.200s as well, but the CR.42s performed well in their own right against all these types and their manoeuvrability and agility enabled them to frequently score successes against the slow and clumsy Fleet Air Arm types during the early years. A few examples must suffice of both combat operations.

The first CR.42 sortie over Malta took place on 2 July 1940 and was mounted by eleven machines from 9⁰ *Gruppo*, 4⁰ *Stormo* with 73ᵃ, 96ᵃ and 97ᵃ *Squadriglia*. Mainly the sorties involved escort missions for the Savoia Marchetti Sm.79 *Sparviero* (Sparrowhawk) and Cant Z1007*bis Alcione* (Kingfisher) three-engined bombers and later Italian-flown Junkers Ju.87 Stuka dive-bombers, and fighter sweeps were also conducted, but even single aircraft sorties occurred from time to time almost as a throwback to the man-to-man duelling of the Western Front days with similar mutual respect, although this did not long survive the arrival of the Luftwaffe in Sicily in January 1941.[3]

The first victory achieved by the CR.42 over Malta occurred the following day, when nine fighters, three from each of the three *Squadriglia* under *Maggiore* Ernesto Botto, badly damaged a Hawker Hurricane, piloted by Flying Officer John Waters, that had just itself destroyed a Sm.79 over Kalafran, causing the British fighter to be wrecked when it crash-landed. This was followed on 4 July by a mass fighter sweep by two dozen CR.42s, again led by Botto, which strafed Har Far airfield damaging two Fairey Swordfish on the ground, but having two of their own number damaged by flak. On 16 July twelve CR.42s from 23⁰ *Gruppo* scored another success over the Hurricane by destroying that of Flight Lieutenant Peter Keeble, which crashed and exploded by Wied il-Ghajn; the CR.42s also lost one from 74ᵃ *Squadriglia* in the same encounter.

The long-expected clash of the biplanes came on 31 July, when nine CR.42s of 23⁰ *Gruppo* escorting a reconnaissance flight were intercepted by three Gladiators. One Gloster, piloted by Flying Officer Peter Hartley, was hit in the fuel tank, which exploded and crashed off Ras il-Fenek, the pilot surviving but with severe burns. In return a CR.42 piloted by *Capitano* Antonio Chiodi of 75ᵃ *Squadriglia*, was also destroyed. On 15 August the CR.42s claimed their third Hurricane scalp when eighteen from 17⁰ *Gruppo* and one from 23⁰ *Gruppo* tangled with No. 261 Squadron and shot down Sergeant Roy O'Donnell without loss to themselves. A fourth Hurricane was destroyed on 24 August when seventeen CR.42s on a bomber escort mission were intercepted by four Hawkers. The mount of Flight Lieutenant George Burgess was badly damaged by *Tenente* Mario Rigatti of 75ª *Squadriglia* and wrecked when it crash-landed. In return one CR.42 was shot down and another damaged.

On 17 September twelve Italian Stukas attacked Luqa (Mikabba) airfield destroying two bombers on the ground. Their fighter escorts included twenty-one CR.42s of 23⁰ *Gruppo* who clashed with four Hurricanes and lost one of their number when *Sottotente* Francesco Cavalli of 70ª *Squadriglia* had his oil feed pipe rupture and baled out. Another attack was made on Luqa on 24 November, when six CR.42s of 23 *Gruppo* based at Comiso under *Maggiore* Tito Falconi, strafed at dusk, destroying two Vickers Wellington bombers. The CR.42s lost one aircraft to fuel starvation on the return leg but *Tenente* Ezio Monti baled out and survived.

When the carrier *Illustrious* was severely damaged off Malta by six heavy bombs from two German *Stukagruppen*, she sought sanctuary in the dockyard to repair her damage and this led to repeated attacks by the Luftwaffe to finish her off. The bulk of 23⁰ *Gruppo* had departed for North Africa but a *Nueclo* remained at Comiso, which became the 156⁰ *Gruppo Autonomo* led by *Capitano* Luigi Filippi with nine CR.42s of 379ª and 380ª *Squadriglia*, and they joined in the escorts of these violent assaults, losing two of their number in the process before the *Illustrious* slipped away to Alexandria a few days later.

The 23⁰ *Gruppo* returned to Comiso in mid-March and re-absorbed 156⁰ *Gruppo Autonomo* and on the 18th a force of fifteen CR.42s clashed with Hurricanes of No. 261 Squadron off Malta, losing one machine. Another was lost on 20 April above Valetta, *Sergente* Giuseppe Sanguettoli of 74ª *Squadriglia* being killed. When the bulk of the Luftwaffe moved north for the invasion of Russia in May 1941, the CR.42s returned to the Sicilian airfields with 1⁰ *Stormo* consisting of 6⁰ *Gruppo* with six *Falcos*, 17⁰ *Gruppo* with seven, the 23⁰ *Gruppo Autonomo*, which had fifteen, and the *Reparto Volocaccia* with one.

The first night-fighter unit, 171⁰ *Gruppo Caccia Notturno Autonomo*, commanded by *Maggiore* (Major) Giovanni Buffa, with 301ª and 302ª *Squadriglia*, reached Gela airfield on Sicily on 1 October 1941.They were equipped with CR.42 'Serie XIII' *Caccia Nottura* (CN) night-fighters with long exhaust flame dampers and machine-gun flame dampers but they lacked suitable instrumentation and within a month they were disbanded as the Luftwaffe returned to open the second Blitz on Malta.

The *Falco* continued to be deployed on convoy protection missions and on 22 February 1942 when the British submarine *P-38* was depth-charged by the torpedo-boat *Circe* and the destroyer *Antoniotto Usodimare* in position 32⁰ 48'N, 14⁰ 58' E, east of Tripoli, a CR.42 assisted by bombing and strafing the surfacing submarine, which was destroyed with all hands.

Fleet and convoy actions included the attack on Rhodes by Fleet Air Arm aircraft from the carriers *Eagle* and *Illustrious* on 4 September 1940. The Italians lost one CR.42, which collided with a CR.32 while scrambling to intercept, writing off both aircraft, but four Fairey Swordfish were shot down in return. At the Battle of Spartivento on

27 November, off Italy's west coast, Admiral Sir James Somerville's Force 'H', although outnumbered, chased an Italian fleet back to its bases. The carrier *Ark Royal* with Blackburn Skua dive-bombers and Fairey Swordfish torpedo-bombers, attempted to hit and slow down the enemy battleships and heavy cruisers but failed to score any hits. The CR.42s of 32⁰ *Gruppo Automo* were heavily involved in interceptions and escort duties. One Skua was claimed shot down by three CR.42s of 154ª *Squadriglia* but this was not so,[4] five CR.42s of 153ª *Squadriglia* clashed with seven Fairey Fulmars of No. 807 Squadron FAA, shooting down one of them, while a CR.42 ran out of fuel and was also lost. The troopships that Force 'H' was escorting through to Malta and Suez were met by Admiral Sir Andrew Cunningham's main fleet the next day and Italian air attacks were directed both at Valetta harbour and the fleet south of Malta. Eight CR. 42s of 23⁰ *Gruppo* scouted Malta, losing one of their number to AA damage, and later six Italian Ju.87s, with an escort of sixteen CR.42s, attacked the light cruiser *Glasgow* without result. The *Falcos* tangled with Fairey Fulmars of No. 806 Squadron FAA from the carrier *Illustrious* who claimed to have destroyed four CR.42s but none were in fact lost; in return one Fulmar was badly damaged.

The convoy taking tanks to North Africa via Gibraltar, Operation *Tiger*, was mounted in May 1941 and protected by Force 'H' and was not spotted by the Axis until 8 May when it was assailed for four consecutive days. The only CR.42 involvement was an escort mission by fifteen machines from the 3⁰ *Gruppo*, which tangled with four Fairey Fulmars of No.808 Squadron FAA, during which they destroyed one and damaged the other three. In July a similar convoy, Operation *Substance*, was in train and on the 21st 23⁰ *Gruppo* escorting SM79 torpedo-bombers to attack this formation and destroyed one Beaufighter of 272 Squadron. On 30 August a Vickers Wellington bomber was also destroyed off Pantelleria by 23⁰ *Gruppo*. Another success by this unit was the destruction of two Bristol Blenheim bombers of No. 105 Squadron on 12 September and damage to third. Yet another Malta convoy, Operation *Halberd*, took place at the end of September and eight CR.42s from 23⁰ *Gruppo* provided escorts to Italian bombers. *Sergente* Luigi Valotti bravely conducted elaborate aerial manoeuvres over the convoy to divert the ships AA fire from the bombers, but paid the ultimate sacrifice. Thomas Woodrooffe, a war correspondent aboard the light cruiser *Edinburgh* described it thus: 'A destroyer, who was not impressed, hit him at the top of a loop.'[5]

Operation *Harpoon* was a disastrous Malta relief convoy undertaken from Gibraltar in June 1942. 24 *Gruppo* joined in the heavy air attacks on this force, which included the old carriers *Argus* and *Eagle* with Hawker Sea Hurricane and Fairy Fulmar fighters embarked. In early attacks on the 14th nineteen *Falcos* from Elmas in Sardinia joined the assault and shot down one Sea Hurricane and two Fulmars for the loss of one of their own.

The last big convoy operation was mounted in August 1942, with three carriers *Eagle*, *Indomitable* and *Victorious*, providing the air cover. Sixteen CR.42s of 160⁰ *Gruppo* from Ajaccio took part in the very heavy and continuous air attacks on this force in the fighter-bomber role on the 11th. Eight *Falcos* were despatched but were intercepted by Grumman Martlets (Wildcats) from No. 806 Squadron FAA, who broke up their formation. Three continued in and made mast-head height bombing and strafing attacks, but their only success was a near-miss on the destroyer *Lightning*, which did no damage.[6]

The contribution of the *Corpo Aero Italiano* (CIA – Italian Air Corps) to the Battle of Britain[7] was, in reality, more of a symbolic gesture of Axis solidarity, with Air Commanding (AOC) being *Generale sa* (Air Marshal) Rino Corso-Fougier. Its establishment was largely cosmetic, the Luftwaffe did not really need them, the OKW did not want them at all, but, for propaganda purposes at home Mussolini insisted upon it. The Corps was therefore duly established on 10 September. Its strength was two *Stormi* of bombers, 13⁰ and 43⁰, a reconnaissance unit, 179ª *Squadriglia* with Cant Z.1007*bis* bombers and, as fighter escorts, the 56⁰ *Stormo*, which as well as 20⁰ *Gruppo* with the Fiat G.50*bis*, included 18⁰ *Gruppo* under the command of *Maggiore* Ferruccio Vosilla, with the 83ª, 85ª and 95ª *Squadriglia* with a total of forty-five C.42 *Falcos*. These were based at a Luftwaffe auxiliary airfield close to the coast, Ursel, south-west of Eeklo in East Flanders where they came under the operational control of 2 *Fliegerkorps*, the *Gruppo* receiving the Luftwaffe identity 18/JG.56. Neither the facilities, nor the miserable Flanders October weather, appealed to the Italian air and ground crews.[8] The armaments of the CR.42s had been reduced to just two machine-guns, a single 12.7mm and a single 7.7mm in order to save weight, which, it was stated, would increase their already superior manoeuvrability over the Hawker Hurricane and extend their range across the cold waters of the North Sea. Again, it did neither.

Among the notable CR.42 pilots at this time were *Capitano* (Captain) Giulio Anelli, *Sottotente* (Sub-Lieutenant) Franco Bordoni-Bisleri, *Sergente Maggiore* (Sergeant-Major) Francesro Campanile, *Sergente* Cassano, *Sergente* Gualtiero Lolli, *Tenente* (Lieutenant) Guido Mazza, *Sergente* Pietro Melano, *Capitano* Edoardo Molinari, *Sergente* Enzo Panicchi, *Maresciallo* (Marshal) Mario Sandini, *Maresciallo* Felice Sozi and *Tenente* Pietro Tacchini of 83ª *Squadriglia; Sergente* Otello Bonelli, *Sergente* Carlo Cavallari, *Tenente* Giulio Cesare Giuntella, *Sergente Maggiore* Luigi Gorrini, *Sergente* Antonio Lazzari, *Tenente* Armido Pilatone, *Sottotenente* Peppo Re, *Maresciallo* Giuseppe Ruzzin and *Sergente* Felice Squazzini of 85ª *Squadriglia;* and *Tenente* Vittorio Bariletta, *Maresciallo* Giovanni Ferrari, *Sergente Maggiore* Guido Fibbia, *Sergente Maggiore* Giacomo Grillo, *Capitano* Gino Lodi, *Maresciallo* Felice Longhi, *Tenente* Vittorio Morellato, *Sergente* Pietro Salvadori, *Tenente* Eugenio Salvi and *Sottotenente* Giorgio Solaroli of 95ª *Squadriglia.*

The first attack involving the CR.42 was against the harbour area of Ramsgate, Kent, on 29 October. Fifteen Fiat BR.20M bombers were given a strong fighter escort, which included thirty-nine *Falcos* , practically the whole of the operational strength of 18⁰ *Gruppo. En route* two bombers aborted and one crash-landed, the remaining twelve dropped seventy-five bombs at low-level and five bombers were damaged by flak, but the *Falcos* were not involved. On 1 November a low-level fighter sweep was conducted by thirty-nine CR.42s in the area of Ramsgate and Dover, venturing as far inland at Canterbury, without being challenged by the RAF.

On 11 November ten BR.20Ms attacked the port and naval base of Harwich, Essex, with an enormous fighter escort comprising both Luftwaffe and Italian machines and including forty-two CR.42s. Despite being the only biplanes in the force, when poor weather forced the Messerschmitt Bf.109s and Fiat G.50s to abort the mission, the *Falcos* continued. The Italian force was picked up by radar and intercepted by three RAF Hawker Hurricane from Nos. 17, 46 and 257 Squadrons and the Supermarine Spitfires of No. 41 Squadron. The Hurricanes attacked the bombers and when the Spitfires arrived they were, in turn, attacked by the CR.42s and a fierce whirling melee broke out above Orfordness. Claims by both sides were wildly exaggerated but in the final accounting the Italians lost three CR.42s while nineteen others made forced landings, one crashing in an Amsterdam square and eight were damaged as a result. The Italians also lost three BR.20Ms, with four others making crash-landings back in Belgium. In return two RAF fighters were damaged. The three *Falco* casualties were *Sergente* Antonio Lazzari (MM6976) of 85ª *Squadriglia*, who crashed by the rail station at Corton and was made prisoner; *Sergente* Enzio Panicchi (MM6978) of 83ª *Squadriglia* who was shot into the sea and killed; and *Sergente* Pietro Salvodori (MM5701) of 95ª *Squadriglie*. The latter crash-landed near the lighthouse at Orfordness, the pilot was made a PoW and the aircraft restored and used by the RAF in tests with the registration BT474, and still survives to this day. All-in-all a disastrous day for the Italian contingent.[9]

On 18 November a pair of *Falcos*, piloted by *Maresciallo* Giuseppe Ruzzin and *Tenente* Guslielmo Specker, were detached for night-fighter duties at Vlissingen in Holland.[10] On 23 November another large fighter sweep was made by 18⁰ *Gruppo* under *Maggiore* Ferruccio Vosilla with a force of twenty-nine CR.42s, backed by two-dozen G.50s. This force left the Belgian coast over Dunkirk and flew along the Kent coast from Margate, via Eastchurch to Folkestone, returning via Calais. While nearing the end of this offensive arc twelve Spitfires of No. 603 caught up with them and made a surprise attack, shooting two of them, *Tenente* Guido Mazza (MM5694) of 83ª *Squadriglia* and *Sergente Maggiore* Giacomo Grillo (MM5665) of 95ª *Squadriglie*, into the sea. Four other CR.42s were damaged and two pilots wounded. In return one Spitfire was damaged. (Both sides made the usual outrageous claims of course, seven CR.42s 'certain' and two more 'probables' against five Spitfires destroyed.) The result did not deter the Italian airmen for on 25 November a similar operation was mounted with twenty-five *Falcos*, which conducted the operation in reverse, but, after crossing Margate the force encountered bad weather over Eastchurch and the sweep was aborted without any contact being made. A similar negative result followed a sweep by two dozen CR.42s with accompanying G.50s and Bf.109s, made three days later.

This marked the end of the CR.42's war against the British mainland for, although a few small bombing raids were conducted against Harwich by the BR.20Ms, the bulk of the Italian aircraft, including the *Falcos*, returned to Italy in January, leaving just the G.50 contingent to conduct patrols along the eastern coast of the English Channel. In truth, open cockpits, no heating, little or no navigational training and weakened armaments all contributed to make the operation a fiasco for the CR.42.

Post-war a few served with the Lecce Flying School in overall silver finish.

Foreign service

Belgium

Belgium adopted an almost suicidal policy of neutrality on the outbreak of World War II, despite the bitter lessons of the Great War. A policy of appeasement prompted by fear meant that all attempts by the British and French to co-ordinate defences prior to the German invasion of May 1940, were ignored and not until the Panzers had crossed her borders did Brussels appeal for Allied assistance. Nonetheless, efforts had been made by the Belgians to shore up their air defences and, surprisingly enough, it was to Hitler's Axis partner, Italy, that the *Aéronautique Militaire* (Belgian Air Force) turned in September 1939. Equally surprisingly, the Italians agreed,[11] although they made certain that the Belgian Government, desperate for early deliveries, paid a high price for each machine.

The purchasing mission arrived at Fiat's plant in Milan tasked with obtaining forty CR.42s to replace the obsolete Fairey Firefly fighters that equipped the IIème *Group de Chasse* (Fighter Group), commanded by Major Jacques Lamarche, and based at Nivelles, Walloon, airfield south of Brussels. The unit comprised the 3ème and 4ème *Escadrilles* with an establishment strength of fifteen aircraft apiece. The urgent requirement was for a delivery within a period of three months. Permission was finally granted and Contract 39/581 was signed in December for forty CR.42s and eight spare engines existing machines at a cost of US$2,640.000, all to be made available as soon as possible.

On 6 March 1940, the first deliveries were made, being received at the *Établissements Généraux de l'Aéronautique Militaire* (*AéM*), at Evere, Brussels, where they were assembled, re-painted in Belgian markings and assigned serials in the range R-1 to R-30. Ten machines were assigned as spare aircraft to replace accident losses.

On 10 May 1940 twenty-four of the imported CR.42s had joined their units, with the 3ème *Escadrille* (Red Cocotte) being at full strength, and the 4ème *Escadrille* (White Cocotte) having received just nine machines.[12] The pilots of these two dozen fighters had only just begun to familiarize themselves with their new mounts when they had action thrust upon them. The IIème took off early to transfer up to their assigned frontline war base, which was Field 22 at Brustem (Sint-Truiden known to the Germans as St Trond) airfield. The Luftwaffe attack began just as twenty-three of the CR.42s led by Major Jacques Lamarche were taking off to make this shift. The Junkers Ju.87 Stuka dive-bombers of the *I/St.G.2* destroyed two CR.42s still on the ground, and another was lost on landing at Sint-Truiden and another was lost on landing at Sint-Truiden but claimed one Junkers Ju.52/3m above Tongres. Clashes with Messerschmitt Bf.109s that morning cost a fourth CR.42 but one Bf.109 was destroyed in return. Another sortie claimed two Dornier Do.17s damaged while strafing Bf.109s destroyed two more CR.42s on the ground. Then the Stukas of *I/St.G.2* re-appeared and destroyed the Belgian force, their precision dive-bombing attack that same afternoon destroying fourteen of the remaining twenty-two CR.42s in a single concentrated blow, wiping out 3ème *Escadrille* on day one of the battle.

A total of thirty-four CR.42s were ordered for the *Aéronautique Militaire* in 1938. The plan was to re-equip two *Escadrilles* of fifteen aircraft each, with a reserve quartet to replace accidental losses. The first batch of these machines reached Belgium on 6 March 1940 and were allocated to 2 *Escadrille*, who commenced transition training in April. But time was running out and although Mussolini did his utmost to fulfil the order by the eve of the *Blitzkrieg* on 10 May, only twenty-five had been accepted by the Belgians. Allocations were fifteen to the *3/II/2* and nine to the *4/11/2*, at Nivelles, south of Brussels, one of which was actually being delivered the day the Germans poured across the border! All of these except one *3/II/2* machine (R-27 which had a propeller vibration problem) were operational on that day. They were in the process of moving to their wartime base at Brustem (St Truiden, known to the Germans as St Trond, ALG A-92) early that same day.

The Luftwaffe had hit St Truiden hard, the strafing attack by Messerschmitt Bf.109s being followed up by a full-blown Stuka assault and losses among the CR.42s included R-1, R-3, R-4, R-6, R-7, R-8, R-11, R-14, R-16, R-17, R-18, R-19, R-20 and R-43 (formerly R-13, her superstitious change of number not proving lucky at all). Another, R-9, had already been lost that morning in a training accident, and R-30 overturned while landing and was written off; while damaged machines were R-2, R-21, R-27 and R-30, which were all capable of repair but nonetheless also given up as lost. The same fate awaited R-21, which was being serviced at Nivelles and was damaged in an attack there the same day, and abandoned. A total of twenty-one CR.42s were destroyed in a matter of hours on Day One without firing a shot!

4ème *Escadrille*, with just seven surviving aircraft, moved via Grimbergen to a new base, Nieuwkerke-Waas (Sint-Niklaas), East Flanders. From here they were involved in a aerial battle over Fleurus on 14 May when they clashed with the Bf.109s of 8./ JG.3 but without decisive result while the following day one CR.42 was lost and one Bf.109 were destroyed in the same area. Two days later the six surviving CR.42s were pulled back to Chartres, Loire, France, along with eight Fireflies, and here they were joined by the last three Fiats.[13] Of the few survivors few lasted much longer. R-26 was bombed and destroyed at Chatres on 19 May, R-23 and R-28 were both bombed and destroyed on 3 June. Five more CR.42s had reached Bordeaux Merignac airfield (R-24, R-29, R-31, R-32, R-33) and, as the Germans closed in, were abandoned. The final four CR.42s of the order, R-15, R-22, R-25, R-34, never ever made it and were held on the border and eventually re-absorbed back into the *Regia Aeronautica*.

The Belgian CR.42s made further sorties as the Allied front crumbled and lost another CR.42 but on 11 June they all withdrew to Merignac once more. The surviving airworthy five (R-24, R-29, R-31, R-32 and R-33) were subsequently flown over to Montpellier airfield in the south of France, where they were deliberately wrecked by their own ground crew to prevent any further operations. The Belgian Government sued for peace on 28 June and on 27 August these five aircraft were confiscated by the French Armistice Commission who, in turn, handed them over to the Germans on 28 November. A few were used as training machines for a while by *JG.107* based at Toul, Moselle, France, where they received the sobriquet *Die Pressluftorgel* (Pneumatic

Organ).[14] This was by no means the last service the CR.42 performed for the Luftwaffe, however.

French

One CR.42 that for a very brief period was under the ownership of the French authorities was one of a batch of five that were discovered at Sabha (*Fortezza Margherita*), Fezzan, along with six other totally or partially destroyed aircraft deliberately wrecked when the Italians abandoned that airfield during the British offensive from El Alamein. A Free French force, part of General Philippe de Hauteclocque Leclerc's Free French attached column moving up into Libya from Chad, liberated this site in December 1942. A more detailed examination of these orphans by Chief Sergeant Paul Kersaho and Alphonse Leroy on 12 January 1943, revealed that one of the CR.42s was still in excellent condition, only having a flat battery.

By 20 January the French had managed to get the engine fired up once more and on the 21st they conducted a series of ground tests that satisfied them she was salvable and on the 30th a tentative test flight was conducted by Captain Marcel Finance of the *Rennes Escadrille*, part of the *Bretagne* Group under Lieutenant-Colonel Saint-Pierre Tassin Péreuse. Péreuse himself, while conducting a reconnaissance mission earlier in a Westland Lysander, one of eight allocated to his force by the British, had been attacked by a CR.42, which had set his aircraft on fire and reported him shot down. However, his aircraft was only slightly damaged and he survived intact. Finding his attackers thus must have been very satisfying to him. Having safely air tested for himself, the Captain initiated a rolling programme for every pilot in his unit to fly the CR.42 in turn. This programme continued until 4 February and only ceased when the supply of suitable fuel ran out.[15]

The *Bretagne* Group moved on to the west in March, abandoning the Fiat once more, leaving her intact in a surviving hangar. Her serial number, like her subsequent fate, is unfortunately unrecorded.

Germany

The Luftwaffe's major involvement with the CR.42 started when, to meet the increasing needs of the *Nachtschlacht* (NSGr – Night Ground Attack) units, which was becoming an increasingly necessary arm as the Germany armies retreated on all fronts and Allied air power swamped the daylight skies. When the Italian Government sued for peace and obtained an armistice on 8 September 1943, the areas of the country under the control of Germany continued to support the Fascists, now reduced to the status of a puppet state. All Italian aircraft production in the north was immediately placed under German control, being operated by the Luftwaffe's *Rüstungs-und-Kriegsproduktion Stab* (Reich Ministry for Armaments and War Production), headed up by Karl Saur. Their availability meant another resource for the increasingly pressurized Reich and an order was placed for 200 CR.42LWs,[16] which were to be used as night harassment aircraft, with flame dampers on their engine exhausts, special German radio equipment, and ultra-violet lightning for the instrument panels. Other specialized equipment included two ETC50 electrically-operated bomb racks under each lower wing capable of carrying two SC50 50kg bombs each and they carried either two 12.7mm BREDA SAFAT machine-guns or alternatively the German 13mm MG131. They had an armour-plated bulkhead installed behind the pilot seat, dust filters fitted to the engine air intakes, and cut-back wheel fairings for bad terrain operations, the intention being that they would also be capable of conducting anti-partisan operations around Istria and Croatia in the Balkans and the southern Alpine area of Italy, another growing concern at this period.

The Fiat works at Turin was bombed by the American Boeing B-17s of the 15th Air Force and a large number of incomplete CR.42LWs were destroyed on the production line and this reduced the number of the type actually completed to around 150, of which only 112 were finally accepted into the Luftwaffe.

On 7 February 1944 the *NSGr.9* at Caselle, Turin, which had been flight testing the Caproni Ca.314 in the anti-partisan role, and finding it unsatisfactory, established a 2. *Staffel* with the CR.42LW straight from the production line and the 1. *Staffel* also began to convert to this aircraft when it moved to Caselle from Udine the same month. *Hauptmann* Rupert Frost was appointed *Gruppekommandeure* and authorized to combat test the CR.42LW against the Allied beachhead at Anzio, Lazio, on the north-west coast of Italy 35 miles (56km) south of Rome. A small detachment of seven CR.42LWs was sent to Rome's Centocelle airfield in February and early the following month six arrived at another Rome airfield, Viterbo, for night-time operations and started flying night sorties at period of bright moonlight as they lacked the full night operational equipment. Missions were flown against Allied supply columns caught on the move and known ammunition dumps and dispersal areas in the southern Lazio region. Isolated missions were also conducted over Allied lines at Monte Cassino where the Germans were also holding out strongly against repeated attacks until May.

Both *Staffeln* were briefly based at Bolsena, Viterbo and Diavolo, Blera, northern Lazio, during this period and on occasions, utilized the civilian airport at Rieti (G. Giuffelli airport) north of Rome, as a dispersal option. It was here that the unit lost five CR.42LWs when the field was strafed by Republic P-47 Thunderbolt fighter-bombers of the 12th Air Force on 21 April. Another loss was the 2. *Staffelkapitän, Oberleutnant* Rolf Martini, who died when his aircraft crashed during a training exercise with Fiat Test Pilot Valentino Cus at Casselle on 22 May. In essence, the CR.42LW only operated with NSGr.9 in combat for about five months. One German pilot who trained on the CR.42 at Turin-Caselle (*Unteroffizier* Herbert Fietz) recorded that this aircraft was '...unfit in action...' and he re-trained on the Junkers Ju.87 at Gross-Stein. However, most German pilots praised the CR.42's flying qualities. Pilots of the NSGr.7 thought that it was superior to the Henschel Hs.126 and the Heinkel He.46 in many respects. From April onward the unit began to again re-convert, this time to the modified Stuka and the CR.42LWs started to be phased out.[17]

By mid-April 1. *Staffel* was re-deploying to Tuscania, with detachments at Casa Marcigliana, in May and at Fabrica di Roma, north of Rome in June, from where they carried out an attack against the Allied transports and bombardment warship fleet off Anzio on the night of 1/2 June, although what exactly their light bombs were hoped to achieve against such targets is hard to understand. The operation cost one CR.42LW to prowling Bristol Beaufighter IV night-fighters, when *Feldwebel* Horst Gressler was forced to crash-land back at base after heavy damage from a Beaufighter VIF of No. 600 Squadron from Marcianise over Lago di Vico.[18]

2. *Staffel* moved to Foiano-della-Chiana, Tuscany, with fifteen serviceable CR.42LWs from an establishment strength of eighteen. By 8 June the unit was predominantly flying the Ju.87 but still had some operational on its strength and was working from Bologna. One of the last missions these German Fiats were involved in was on the night of 13/4 June when a mixed force of nine aircraft attacked Allied troops in the vicinity of Orbetello, Grosseto, Tuscany.

The second unit to use the CR.42LW was *Nachschlachtgruppe 7*, which was originally formed under Major Theodor Blaich from the *Nahaufklärungsstaffel Kroatien* (Close Cleansing Squadron Croatia). A new 3. *Staffel* was formed at Agram (Zagreb-Lučko) on 7 March and equipped with the CR.42LW from April onward. 3. *Staffel* shifted base to Pleso, Croatia on 2 June 1944 and was joined there by 2. *Staffel* with twenty-six CR.42LWs on its establishment strength. 1. *Staffel* also re-equipped with the CR.42LW and moved to Graz-Thalerhof, Austria from October 1944.

The *Stab* (Staff) and 2. *Staffel* with ten Fiats undertook a major anti-partisan mission on 8 February 1945, initially being assigned to targets at Grabovia, Karlovac, but this was changed and concentrations of resistance forces concentrated around their base in the Brezovica Forest, an area north-west of Sisak in central Croatia.[19] *En route* to this target the formation was intercepted by Lockheed P-38 Lightning twin-engined fighters of the USAAF's 37th Fighter Squadron, who destroyed three of them, while a fourth was shot down by AA fire. In return two P-38s were destroyed, according to American records by ground fire, but according to historian Csaba Becze one at least was shot down by a CR.42LW. If the claim is correct this would appear to have been the last combat victory ever achieved by a biplane.

On the German surrender in May the Stab, 2. and 3. *Staffeln* at Zagreb-Gorico (Goriza), mustered about two dozen CR.42LWs serviceable plus those with 1. *Staffel*.

One other Luftwaffe unit, the *NSGr.20*, commanded by Major Kurt Dahlmann, which was formed from the *III./KG.51* at Bonn-Hangelar on 31 October 1944, was known to have some CR.42AS on its establishment. They were flying ground-attack missions with the Focke Wulf FW.190F/G and were based at Germersheim from January to March 1945, moving to their combat base Twente, Zwolle, in Holland in March and April and ending the war at Delmenhorst, Hagenow.

Hungary

As early as 1938 the *Magyar Királyi Honvéd Légierö* (MKHL – Royal Hungarian Air Arm) had ordered eighteen CR.42 fighters from Fiat. As with many foreign orders, although the *Falco* had already established a good reputation as a pilot's plane, it was the fact that the Turin company was willing and able to supply them quickly, at a time of endless crisis in Europe and the Balkans, that swung the deal when it was known faster and more powerfully armed monoplane fighter aircraft were being developed. Delivery was indeed fast, and the CR.42s reached Hungary between 16 June and 20 November of the following year. The first Hungarian unit to be equipped with the new machine was the 1 *Vadász Ezred* (1 Fighter Regiment) whose 1/3 *Kőrász Vadászszázad* (Ace of Hearts Squadron) at Mátyásföld air base near Budapest, commenced familiarization flying with the type early on. On 4 October 1939 V.207 was lost along with the pilot, *Szakaszvezető* Béla Simon, in a crash.

A second order was placed with Turin that same November, this time for fifty aircraft and these were even more promptly delivered between 10 February and 30 June 1940. By the time of the German attack on Yugoslavia these CR.42s had been divided between the 1. /II *Osztály* (Fighter Group) at Mátyásföld and the 2/II *Osztály* at Kolozsvár-Szamosfalva (Cluj-Napoca). This brief campaign saw the baptism of fire for the Hungarian *Falcos* although they proved incapable of intercepting Yugoslav Bristol Blenheims over Pécs, Baranya, and the airfield and marshalling yards at Szeged (Csongrád), although they ensured no bombs hit the former city.[20]

When Germany invaded the Soviet Union in June 1941 Hungary was a benevolent bystander, and although a member of the Axis, did not initially participate in Operation *Barbarossa*. However, that changed when Soviet bombers bombed the city of Košice (Kassa) on 27 June. This unprovoked attack provoked Hungary's declaration of war the same day and they sent an Army Corps to aid the German and Rumanian forces on the Carpathian Front. Air cover was provided by a hastily assembled Air Brigade, of which the twelve CR.42s of 1/3 *Kőrász Vadászszázad* of 1./II *Osztály* were the spearhead. The first mission actually conducted was by nine CR.42s of the 2/3 *Ricsi Vadászszázad* of 2./II *Osztály*, commanded by *Százados Vitéz* Aladár Szobránczy, who provided fighter escort for thirty Junkers Ju.86 bombers in a revenge raid on Stanislav (Ivano-Frankovsk) south of Lviv. Two CR.42s were lost by forced landings but their pilots survived. Similarly, on 29 June a second bomber strike was made against Striy, Lviv, and another CR.42 also force-landed but the pilot escaped. In compensation two Soviet Tupolev ANT-10 (Tupolev SB = *Skorostnoi Bombardirovschik* – High-Speed Bomber) were shot down over Csap (Chop), Ukraine.

In July both Hungarian CR.42 units were engaged almost continuously against retreating Soviet columns and duelling with Soviet fighter types like the I-15 and I-16 that the *Falco* had already mastered in Spain. The 2/3 *Vadászszázad* moved from their advance Ukrainian airfield at Bustyaháza (Bushtyno) via Kolomea (Kolomyia) to Yezierzany by 12 July. The 2/3 *Vadászszázad* lost three Cr.42s (V.253, V.254 and V.255) on 8 July in bad weather over the Carpathians, one pilot being killed, while on the 10th an I-16 was destroyed and on 12 July another five were claimed shot down over Zwanczyk, north of Khotyn, although two CR.42s were lost, one in a mid-air collision with an I-16. The unit returned to Hungary on 15 July. In the same period the 1/3 *Vadászszázad* had operated several missions before moving base to Bar, Ukraine, on 20 July. During strafing runs on retreating Russian columns many CR/42s received damaging hits, due to the lack of armour, but no pilots were lost. Progress of the Axis armies was rapid and the unit had to frequently shift base to keep up with the advance through the Ukraine, moving through Sutyska, Annopol-Rachów to Berschad and were working from Pervomaysk by 8 August. During the Battle of the Uman Pocket six CR.42s shot up a Russian transport full of VIPs at Podvysokoye on 5 August, but lost two of their number in the process, one pilot being lost. The only escape route out of the trap was across the Nikolayev Bridge over the River Bug and a bombing attack was mounted against this target on 11 August. The CR.42s were engaged by Soviet I-16,s four of which were destroyed.

The same pattern followed throughout the rest of August and September, with the *Falcos* moving bases into Russia proper using the airfield of Krivoy Rog and conducting patrols and attacks over the Dniepropetrovsk bridgehead, claiming five further I-16s on the 26th and five on the 27th, and by 10 October they were operating from Dniepropetrovsk airfield with one forward section at Golubovka, Russia, and another at the important rail junction of Losovaya, south of Kharkov. With the onset of the severe Russian winter weather the unit was ordered to return to Hungary on 15 November the last aircraft crossing the Carpathians on 26 November. In total they had claimed to have destroyed seventeen Polikarpov I-16s, seven low-wing monoplane fighters,[21] three ANT-10s, one R-5 and three other unidentified Soviet types. On their return to Mátyósfáld air base all the CR.42s of both 1. /II and 2.II *Osztály* were retired from front-line duties and assigned training duties.[22]

South Africa

Two CR.42s were captured intact by the South African Air Force with the fall of Addis Ababa to General Alan Cunningham's army moving up from Kenya via Mogadishu and Harar on 6 April 1941. Two machines were eventually made airworthy by No. 3 Squadron SAAF by May. One of them being test flown on 12 May by Major Servas van Breda Theorn DSO, DFC, AFC. Unfortunately, when coming in to land he overshot the landing field and the aircraft ended up in a ditch, a total wreck. The second CR.42 (serial 14274) had rather better luck and on 2 August she was flown from Addis Ababa to Nairobi by Major Ed A Biden of No. 41 Squadron SAAF. From there she was flown south to Zwartkop Air Station arriving on 9 August where she was given the SAAF serial '22'. A month later she was added to the charge of No. 42 Squadron and used on the 'Air Command' tour of captured Italian aircraft. By May 1942 she was still flyable and was allocated to No. 6 Squadron for AA practice where she was worn out. When the unit disbanded in July 1943 the airframe arrived at No.69AS for ground training and was eventually scrapped.

Sweden

When Marshal Stalin cynically ordered the invasion of Finland early in 1940 he expected an easy 'walk-over', after all his millions were up against a sparsely populated little country with very few friends other than her Nordic neighbours. Germany might be sympathetic to the Finns but Hitler had a pact with the Soviet Union, which he had to keep for the time being, while the Western Allies were helpless and the United States strongly isolationist. Unexpectedly, the initially exchanges went the way of the Finns who defeated the first invasion. The 'Winter-War' could only end one way of course, but while Finland resisted, her Swedish neighbour, while announcing a policy of 'non-belligerency', turned a blind eye to 'volunteers' going across the border to give what aid they could and among them was the Air Wing *Flottiljer-19*. The Swedish pilots were flying the British Gloster Gladiator biplane fighter and using them as both fighters and makeshift dive-bombers. However, it was deemed essential that a more potent aircraft be obtained against the latest Soviet machines.

Starting in February 1940 a funding appeal was set up under the auspices of Swedish rector Isaac Been who had declared, 'What Finland really needs are fighters!' Sufficient money was raised by 15 February to enable the purchase of five CR.42s and, such was the fervour, for a second contract for another seven *Falcos* on 24 February, both for delivery and entry into service by April. Long before that time the Finns had been forced to cede a large and vital area of their nation to the Soviets and the war came to an end on 13 March. The Finns, having no urgent need for the CR. 42s any more, told the Swedes they no longer required them, so the *Flygvapnet* (Swedish Air Force), having already placed the orders, decided to accept their delivery anyway and to take them into their establishment to equip their own F3 Wing at Malmen Air Base, Linköping, Östergötland. When most of many American-built fighters also ordered by Sweden for themselves failed to materialize due to the US Government embargo, it was decided to top up this dozen *Falcos* with a further sixty CR.42s, making a total order for seventy-two machines. These were fitted with the Fiat 870hp (640kW) A74R.1C.38 14-cylinder two-row, radial engine and given the *Flygvapnet* designation of J.11.

Deliveries commenced in April and continued in small batches through to September 1941 with the initial dozen being shipped out in February and March. These first CR.42s were allocated to F3 and replaced their licence-built Fokker C.V.E (S6) reconnaissance planes. Subsequent allotments of five and three machines arrived crated up from the Fiat works and were delivered to the *Centrala Flygverkstäderna Malmslätt* (Central Air Workshops, Malmslätt – CVM) where they were assembled, tested and modified before being despatched to their units. The subsequent Swedish modifications included the addition of 20mm armour plating inserted behind the pilot's seat, radio and some aircraft were fitted with ski attachments. The J.11s were given serials in the range 2501 through to 2572.

The principal recipient of the J.11s, the last of which joined in November 1941, was the *Flottiljer9* based at the newly constructed Air Base of Säve, Hisingen Island, near Gothenburg (now the City Airport). During the German-Soviet conflict, which erupted in June 1941, the Swedes placed their forces on high alert and maintained a constant readiness in case the war spilt over onto their territory. While the 2 and 3 Squadrons were retained in the Gothenburg area, 1 Squadron was briefly transferred north to Kiruna, Lapland, the most northerly air base in Sweden, between March and April 1942 to cover the vital rail link with Norway. German offensives to take Archangel and

Murmansk all failed but there was considerable tension in the area as Swedish iron ore was shipped south to be sold to Germany, at which the Soviets protested, while Germany wanted to ship supplies and troops to Norway, which was refused, although clandestine operations did take place. Sweden managed to walk the tightrope until the war ended. Occasionally the Fiats were scrambled when either Soviet or German aircraft violated their air space but no shooting instances took place. The Fiats often proved unable to catch the newer German and Russian types and began to show their limitations. Additionally, the harsher operating conditions in Sweden revealed that the *Falco*, although still loved as a superb little aircraft to fly, was not really fit for purpose. Accidents reduced their numbers, other were transferred to F13 and increasingly they began to be replaced by the indigenously built *Kungliga Flygförvaltningens Flygvekstad I Stockholm* (Royal Air Administration Aircraft Factory in Stockholm – FFVS) J.22 monoplane fighter from October 1943 onward.

By 15 March just fifteen J11s remained, with six reserve machines, and these were sold out as obsolete. A private firm, *AB Svensk Flygtjänst* bought them all for target-towing operations, and their military serials were exchanged for the following civil registrations – 2503 became SE-AOH, 2506 became SE-AON, 2514 became SE-AOR, 2520 became SE-AOI, 2521 became SE-AOL, 2525 became SE-AOM, 2528 became SE-AOO, 2531 became SE-AOS, 2539 became SE-AOP, 2545 became SE-AOW, 2548 became SE-AOK, 2563 became SE-AOU and 2569 became SE-AOX. They only had short lives in this role, being scrapped between 1946 and 1948.

Preserved aircraft

1. CR.42 with RAF serial BT474, (MM701), which crash-landed at Orfordness on 11 November 1940, was salvaged and restored at nearby Martlesham Heath and when airworthy, evaluated at the RAE Farnborough. It was subsequently placed in storage at RAF Stafford in December 1943 and not until June 1973 was it restored at RAF St Athans. When completed it was presented to the RAF Museum, Hendon, London, in 1978 and has been on display there ever since.
2. Several parts of scrapped CR.42s were re-assembled together by AREA at Venegono, Varese, northern Italy as a whole machine in the colours of 162ª *Squadriglia*. Serial 917 (MM4653, FU2539, SE-AP. This is on display at the *Museo Storico, della Aeronautica Militare*, Vigna di Valle Air Force Museum.
3. A J.11 is on display at the *Flygvapenmuseum*, Malmslätt. This was Serial No. 2543 (c/n 921) which flew with the *Kungliga Göta Flygflottilj* F9 from Säve Air Base, Gothenburg, between 1941 and 1942.
4. Another AREA assembly, Serial Number 920, FV2542, G-CBLS is being restored at the Fighter Collection, IWM, Duxford, Cambridgeshire, UK.

Chapter Six

Gloster Gauntlet

The British Air Ministry issued requirements F.9/26 and F.20/27 for a new day-and-night single-seater, high-altitude fighter aircraft to replace the Gloster Gamecock and Armstrong-Whitworth Siskin types, which proved unable to match the speed of the Fairey Fox light day bomber.[1] A heavier gun armament was thought to be essential so that in the brief period of contact with enemy bombers of a similar type, enough damage could be inflicted to bring them down.

At Gloster designer Henry Philip Folland honed his skills to produce a series of fighters to meet the requirement. His plans for what was essentially an improved Goldfinch, an all-metal construction fighter, were beset by problems in finding a suitable power plant and the delays held up development considerably. Meanwhile, the Air Ministry had issued the even more challenging F.7/30 specification, which called for a minimum of four machine-guns and a speed of 402km/h.

The maiden flight of the Gloster S.S.18A (serial no. J.9125) was in January 1929. This aircraft initially flew with the 480hp (353.04kW) Jupiter VIIf engine, while a second aircraft, the S.S.18B, was fitted with the 560hp (411.88kW) Armstrong-Siddeley 14-cylinder Panther III as her power plant. Despite the increase in power the latter was not a success and the weight badly affected performance and was quickly dropped and development continued with the Jupiter with a Townsend ring surrounding the cylinder heads. At a trial held at Martlesham Heath in 1933 the S.S.19B attained 346km/h, which impressed. The armament was increased to six machine-guns, with two Vickers one each side of the fuselage and synchronized to fire through the propeller, and four Lewis guns mounted along the lower surface of the upper wing. In this configuration the S.S. 18A was re-designated as the S.S.19. The fixed undercarriage had half-spatted wheels when first employed but this was later changed to whole-spatting and the tail-skid on the original was changed to a wheel. As such the aircraft was once more re-designated as the S.S.19A.

The Gloster S.S.19B was a biplane fighter prototype, subsequently re-engined in 1932 with the 645hp (474.4kW) Bristol Mercury VIS2 air-cooled radial engine, which had a centrifugal compressor that was driven from the engine shaft and she first flew with that power plant in February 1933. She logged a top speed of 163mph (262.32km/h) at sea level and 210mph (337.96 km/h) at an altitude of 14,000ft (4267.2m). In the subsequent competition this machine lost out to what was to become the Hawker Fury but despite this the Air Ministry was impressed enough to place an order for twenty-four of the type in September 1933, under their Specification 24/33 and assigned the name Gauntlet.

For construction Gloster used a welded light alloy structure, which was sheathed in canvas fabric in its construction, but when Hawker-Siddeley took over Gloster in 1934 they introduced a simplified construction method to both the fuselage carcass and the wing spars and these, with other modifications, became the Gauntlet-II. The Air Ministry eventually ordered 204 of this revised mark.

The Gauntlet had an open cockpit, the last such fighter to be used in RAF service. The forward section of the fuselage from the cockpit was replaced with removable dural panels. She had a two-bladed wooden propeller. The equi-size wings were double-span braced with parallel strutting, while the after horizontal stabilizer was also braced. She initially had a Wyatt two-bladed propeller but later the three-bladed Fairey Reed was fitted with a coned spinner.

The Gloster S.S.19B was designed to mount a powerful armament, for its day, of six machine-guns, four Lewis guns carried in the wings and two each side of the fuselage. This was widely advertised around the world at the time, and a great deal of nonsense was generated,[2] but, despite all the hype, the Gauntlet when she entered service was eventually equipped with just two fixed, forward-firing 0.303in (7.7mm) machine-guns on the sides of the fuselage, with 600rpg, and the wing-mounted Lewis guns were omitted. Wingspan was 32ft 10in (9.99m), overall length was 26ft 5in (8.05m) and height was 10ft 3in (3.12m). Maximum speed was 230mph (370km/h) at an altitude of 15,800ft (4,815m), with a cruising speed of 205mph (329.99km/h). The initial climb speed was 2,310fpm and they took nine minutes to climb to 20,000ft (6,100 m). Their service ceiling was 33,500ft (10,210m). Empty weight was 2,769lb (1,256kg), and gross weight 3,972lb (1,800kg). They had a range of 460 miles (740km). They could land at 49.71mph (80km/h) within a distance of 443ft (134 m).

Development of the type was continued at Gloster in order to meet an advanced Air Ministry specification F.14/35, and the S.S.37 took to the air on 12 September 1934. She was to become the famous Gloster Gladiator.

RAF service

The first unit to take delivery of the Gauntlet-I was No. 19 Squadron at Duxford, Cambridgeshire, in May 1936. The new aircraft replaced the Bristol Bulldog and had an excess of 56mph (90km/h) over that machine, which made it very popular. Indeed, the Gauntlet was the fastest aircraft in service with the RAF between 1935 and 1937. The Gauntlet-Is received the serial numbers K4081 to K4104 inclusive, and the Gauntlet-IIs had serials K7792 to K7891 inclusive.

The Gauntlet-II began to join the RAF shortly afterward, equipping both No. 56 Squadron and No. 111 Squadron in May 1936 and by the end of that year had re-equipped six more squadrons. By 1937 a total of fourteen RAF squadrons were flying the Gauntlet. One notable event was the participation of three Gauntlets of No. 32 Squadron when they were ground-directed in the interception of a civilian airliner by the RDF (Radio Direction Finding – Radar) installed at Bawdsey Manor, Suffolk, as early as November 1937. As front-line fighter squadrons re-equipped the

Gauntlets were handed on, and, in total, some twenty-six RAF Squadrons featured her on their establishments at one time or another, these being Nos. 6, 17, 19, 32, 33, 46, 47, 54, 56, 65, 66, 73, 74, 79, 80, 111, 112, 151, 213, 234, 237, 504, 601, 602, 615 and 616.

Peacetime usage always involved attrition and the Gauntlet was no exception. On 3 August 1938 a Gauntlet-II (serial K7809) with No.66 Squadron at RAF Duxford, piloted by Australian Pilot Officer Richard Maurice Power, struck an obstacle while taking off and was a total write-off. Between 8 November 1935 and 17 July 1939 accidents wrote off no fewer than fifty-seven Gauntlets. The worst offenders were No. 66 Squadron who lost nine; while No. 46 Squadron lost seven; No. 19 Squadron lost six; No. 32 Squadron lost five and No. 213 Squadron lost four. No.17 Squadron lost three in a single day on 23 November 1937 over Farthing Down, near Coulsdon, Surrey (serials K5349, 5348 and 5344). Two of these victims were taking part in a night-flying exercise from RAF Kenley and collided. One pilot was incinerated in his machine while the other parachuted out, but was caught in a tree that tore off his leg and he later died. The third plane was in an earlier accident and the pilot survived.

Three Gauntlet squadrons went out to the Middle East where the Italian invasion of Abyssinia and the subsequent sanctions applied at one time appeared to threaten war between Britain and Italy, but, with appeasement being the policy of the government of the day, they were never called into action. However, in this area of the Empire they remained in front-line service long after their UK-based sisters had been reduced to second-line duties. No.6 Squadron used its Gauntlets to maintain internal order during 1940 until the last one was withdrawn at Helwan on 7 June 1940 when she joined No. 112 Squadron and five were still on that squadron's establishment on 10 June. No. 9 Squadron in British-mandated Palestine remained a Gauntlet outfit until April 1940.

At home, other late examples included No. 616 Squadron, which was still operating Gauntlets after the outbreak of war in September 1939, while No. 70 Squadron did not fully convert to Spitfire-Is until June 1940, although, officially, it had done so as early as February 1939! The Aldergrove Meteorological Flight made its last sortie with a Gauntlet (serial no K5280) on 6 December 1939. For the majority, however, by 1938 the brief hey-day of the Gauntlet already appeared to be over with the introduction into service of the Gloster Gladiator and subsequently the monoplane fighters, the Hawker Hurricane, Supermarine Spitfire and Boulton Paul Defiant, of the immediate pre-war years, but as these types replaced them in the front-line squadrons, the Gauntlets were passed on and used to familiarize the new intakes of pilots as advanced trainers. No. 616 Squadron, based at Finningley as part of No. 12 Group, still had fourteen Gauntlets on its strength at the outbreak of war in September 1939, six of them in reserve and No. 6 Squadron, at Ramleh and Haifa in Palestine was operating six Gauntlets at this period, thus ensuring they performed a vital and essential function right up to the eve of the war, and beyond.

War service

No. 3 Squadron RAAF was still using the Gauntlet-II with one of its Deployment Flights. The squadron had received six of them, spares from Nos. 33 and No. 112 Squadrons, as late as October 1940 some months *after* Italy had declared war on Britain. Another one of these (serial K5331) was written off by the squadron on 2 July and two others were out of commission through lack of spares with No. 208 Squadron at Sanyet el Quasaba, but five of these old warriors were at Kasaba, Mpulungu, and forward deployed to Advanced Landing Ground 74, (ALG.74) on 9 December, for a ten-day period while still under attachment to No. 208 Squadron. They were thrown into the early desert campaigns in North Africa, Operation *Compass,* operating as ground-attack aircraft and as make-shift dive-bombers, their pilots jocularly dubbing them as, '...the RAF's answer to the Stuka'.

Their operational debut was made the same day, when they were despatched at 1235 to attack an Italian army transport column to the north-west of Sofafi, Libya. One machine aborted the mission but the others succeeded and all returned to base. The same five were sent off at first light to similarly dive-bomb Italian forces reported to be retreating through 'Halfway House' near the Halfaya ('Hellfire') Pass but failed to locate any targets. However, a second sortie by four Gauntlets returned later that morning and this time found some two hundred motor vehicles packed with troops in the same area and carried out both dive-bombing and machine-gun attacks with satisfying results. They repeated the operation that same afternoon even though they were briefly reduced to four flyable machines, piloted by Flight Lieutenant Blake Pelley, and Flying Officers Allan Rawlinson, Lyndsey Knowles and Wilfred 'Woof' Arthur, with Flight Lieutenant Gordon Steege and Pilot Officer Alan Davidson as back-up pilots,[3] the unit continued its combat missions.

On 12 December the same area was again re-visited in the morning by all five Gauntlets and again dive-bombing was carried out. After this brief period in the front-line, lack of spare parts eventually saw them finally withdrawn on 13 November when the personnel all returned to No. 3 Squadron at Gerawla, Libya, by 15 December without any losses. The following day two Gauntlets (serials K7843 and K7825) flew over from Bagush (ALG-14) to act as escorts for three Westland Lysanders that were ferrying General Sir Archibald Wavell and his Staff to ALG 75, and duty done, returned to Gerawla.

No. 33 Squadron boasted six Gauntlets[4] at Mersa Matruh in February 1940 and continued to utilize them after 10 June. These were all gradually transferred as above, or replaced and retired. Those that remained in the Middle East were all lost to accidents, as opposite:

Date	Serial No.	Unit	Location
17-2-39	K7885	102 MU	2 miles south-east of Abu Sueir
24-5-40	K5273	No. 33 Squadron	Fuka
26-6-40	K7891	PRRP	Ismailia
26-6-40	K5299	PRRP	Ismailia
2-7-40	K5331	No. 3 Squadron	?
29-8-40	K5316	PRRP	Ismailia
7-11-40	K5337	TURP	Ismailia
8-2-41	K5265	No. 430 Flight	Gedaref
15-3-41	K7859	AD	Aboukir
13-10-41	K7852	SF Lydda	South of El Arien, Palestine

In a similar manner 'D' Flight No. 47 Squadron, (which later became No. 430 Flight) was still based in the Sudan in June 1940. In July six Gauntlets were flown down from Egypt to form this unit, from No. 1 South African Squadron at Abu Sueir (ALG-205). One aircraft, serial K7885, force-landed some two miles from its start point with a burnt-out exhaust ring and was a write-off. The other five, with three RAF pilots and two SAAF pilots, arrived safely. They joined 'A' Section on 16 August but one was damaged in a gale on the 20/21 August. The remaining trio operated out of Gedaref (Al Qadarif, Sudan) from 21 August and became immediately engaged with Italian forces which had crossed the Eritrean border earlier.

On 24 August a pair of Gauntlets, along with two Vincent bombers from 'B' Section, bombed Fort Galabat, near Metemma, with good results. They then moved forward to Azzoza landing ground, now at a strength of four Gauntlets, and on 7 September made a dive-bombing attack on Metemma airfield with each plane carrying eight 25lb (11.33kg) incendiaries. During the operation a tri-motor Caproni Ca.133 transport aircraft appeared and, oblivious to the Gauntlets, began a parachute supply drop. This machine was immediately engaged in a head-on attack by Flight Lieutenant Arthur Brewerton Mitchell in K5355 and the Italian machine crashed nose-first into the ground. Mitchell made several attempts to finish the job by dropping his incendiaries and then machine-gunning the wreck, to little obvious effect. This Caproni was the only recorded Gauntlet kill of the war.[5]

This quartet of Gauntlets served in a combat profile at the beginning of the East African campaign and were credited with the destruction of an Italian Caproni Ca.133 bomber. The Tessenei (Teseney) airfield was attacked again on 20 September and five days later Mitchell repeated his tactics at Metemma, strafing three Ca.133s parked there and claiming to have damaged one of them. A follow-up attack was made by the Gauntlets that same afternoon. A repeat bombing attack was also mounted against Fort Galabat by two Gauntlets carrying 20lb (9.07kg) bomblets. This was the last such attack by the unit, which in 1941 was re-designated as No. 1430 flying just Vincent bombers.

At home, four Gauntlets were still operational as late as 1943 flying meteorological sorties with No. 1414 Met Flight based at Eastleigh.

Foreign service

Denmark

The Danish Government negotiated a deal with the Air Ministry on 23 October 1934, under which the original RAF Gauntlet (serial K4081), without engine or armament, was purchased outright as a pattern aircraft for the manufacture of this fighter. This machine (serial FV-86, J-21) was shipped to Denmark in April 1935 but, inexplicably, was not able to make her first flight in Danish colours, piloted by *Kaptajn* Hans Ludvig Valdemar Bjarkov until as late as April 1936.

Seventeen licence-built Gauntlet-IIJs were built between 1936 and 1938 at the *Haerens Flyvertroppers Vaerksteder* (Danish Army Air Force Workshops) at the Kløvermarken, Copenhagen. Assembly was at a leisurely pace, the Danes complaining that the Gauntlet had 56,000 individual parts and required 3,200 technical drawings, being far more complicated that anything they had attempted before. In the event two were completed in 1936 (serials J-22 and J-23), fourteen in 1937 (serials FV086 to FV-101, J-24 to J-37) and the final machine (serial FV-102, J-38) in 1938. These aircraft were all fitted with the two-bladed Heine propeller.

The Gauntlets went to equip the *1 Eskadrille* of the Danish Army Aviation and flew neutrality patrols from Oksbøl (Oksboel) airfield along the west Jutland coast. These were reduced to thirteen operational machines, serials J-26, J-27, J-31, J-33 and J-35, all being lost due to accidents, and the survivors were based at Vaerløse, Copenhagen, airfield when the Germans invaded on 9 April 1940, the majority of them being shot up on the ground by the strafing attacks of the *Gruppenstab* and *1. Staffel* of *Zerstörergeschwader 1*'s Messerschmitt Bf.110s led by *Hauptmann* (Captain) Wolfgang Falck. The J-32 was destroyed and J-25, J-28, J-29, J-30 and J-38 were all damaged in varying degrees. However, all these damaged machines were later repaired. The Gauntlets were all moved to Kløvermarken where they were placed in storage. When the Danish Government attempted to end their co-operation in the summer of 1943, the Germans initiated *Unternehmen Safari* (Operation Safari) on 29 August 1943, during which the German army quickly occupied all Danish military installations and disarmed all the personnel. The stored Gauntlets were among the aircraft seized in this take over, after which they appear to have all been destroyed.

Finland

The twenty-nine ex-RAF Gauntlets from those awaiting shipment to the South African Air Force were presented as gifts by the South African Government to the Finns. They were shipped to Gothenburg, Sweden, from the UK classed as 'Imported Machinery' and then flown from Sweden to Finland, but only twenty-five finally arrived in batches between March and May 1940, too late for the war, and only twenty-four were made operational. The Gauntlets were assembled at *Centrala Flygverkstaden*, Malmslätt, Linköping, and here they were allocated GT-codes and used as advanced trainers being fitted with three-bladed propellers. The Finnish pilots of the *Suomen imavoimat* dubbed them *Kotletti* (Cutlet).[6] When the 'Continuation War' started, with the Finns adopting a 'Parallel War' with Germany in order to recover some of their lost lands, the Gauntlets were thrown into the war effort and the training of many new pilots took a heavy toll on them. Ten were total write-offs and almost every one was damaged to some extent. A few served as ski-fitted aircraft until 1945.The last one to fly was GT-396 on 18 February 1945.

Greece

Following the Axis defeat of Greece in April 1941 and the occupation of Crete the following month surviving Greek Army and Air Force personnel who managed to escape were assembled in the Middle East and, on 23 June, the 1 Greek Brigade was formed in Palestine. Included in this was the establishment of No. 335 Squadron at Akir (Aqir), Ramla airfield (currently the Israeli AFB Tel Nof.) on 10 October and to assist in training a flight of Gauntlets was made available, which became the 'Greek Flight'.

This unit operated into 1942 and during the course of that year was destroyed by accidents, K7861 being lost on 17 February, K5318 on 13 April and K7838 on 16 July all in the Gaza area.

South Africa

In 1940 No. 6 Squadron SAAF was disbanded at Air Base Waterkloof, Pretoria, and immediately re-formed under Major Niblack Stuart as No. 1 Squadron. They were equipped with Hawker Hurricanes and Hawker Fury fighters, but also had a Flight of four Gauntlets which were used by the squadron as training aircraft.

Further batches of Gauntlets were in the UK awaiting shipment to South Africa after being purchased as trainers to build up the SAAF on the outbreak of war. Unable to assist the Finns when they were suddenly attacked by the Soviet Union at the start of the 'Winter War', the South African Government, donated twenty-five of them to Finland instead. The residue of No. 430 Flight, three Gauntlets, ultimately joined No. 2 Squadron in lieu of the Finnish ones and they were employed in the East African campaign in subsidiary duties. Wear and tear had reduced this trio to two aircraft by the end of the year.

South Rhodesia

Three Gauntlets were purchased from Britain, along with six Hawker Harts and six Hawker Audax bombers, in September 1938. They joined two Hawker Harts and some de Havilland Tiger Moth trainers, which had hitherto equipped the Southern Rhodesia Air Unit (SRAU) commanded by Flight Lieutenant Jimmy Powell, and which was administered by the Rhodesia Regiment. The Gauntlets were based at Cranbourne, near Salisbury (now Harare). This force became No. 1 Squadron, Southern Rhodesia Air Force on 6 September 1939.

The longest-serving Commonwealth Gauntlets appear to have been this flight of three South Rhodesian machines, which were not finally stood down until 1944.

Preserved aircraft

1. Gloster Gauntlet Mk.II, (RAF serial K5271), Finnish serial GT-400, civilian registration OH-XGT, is thought to be the only surviving Gauntlet. On 13 February 1945 this aircraft was retired with 133 hours on the clock and sold out for civilian use. It was purchased by a farmer at Alpo Hinktikka, Kuorevesi, who stripped all useful parts from her. The remains were recovered in November 1975 and she was restored at the *Lentotekniikan Kiltary, Halli AB* (Air Force Technical Guild, Halli) between 1976 and 1982. From 21 June she was based at the Hallinportti Aviation Museum, at Halli Airport, Kuorevesi, Jämsä, Finland. She was frequently flown by Test Pilot Jyrki Laukkanen.

Chapter Seven

Gloster Gladiator

Much has been written on the Gladiator. As the last biplane fighter built for the RAF it was perhaps inevitable that, having been delivered as late as 1939, this aircraft would earn a special niche in aviation history. That she should become the legend she did was due to a combination of the superb way she fought against the odds, and the British fixation to luxuriate in being the underdog and wearing her invariably obsolete weaponry as a kind of badge of honour. The Gladiator also found fame in no fewer than ten foreign air forces before she was finally put out to grass.

As the private venture S.S.37, the G.37 prototype (serial K5200) designed by the team under Henry Philip Folland and Howard Preston in 1933, was basically a development of the same company's Gauntlet (it used the same fuselage) but one that approached Air Ministry Specification F.7/30 issued in 1931, for a day and night interceptor, armed with four machine-guns and capable of a speed of 250mph (402km/h). Although the RAF stated that the Rolls-Royce V-12 steam-cooled Goshawk was its engine of choice to obtain the 40-knot increase in speed desired, this proved difficult to achieve and delayed the selection process by a year. There were seven contenders and Gloster's example featured an open, single-seat cockpit, single-leg cantilever landing gear, with two Vickers machine-guns in the nose and two Lewis guns mounted on the lower wings and a 485hp (361.66kW) Bristol Mercury IV driving a Watts two-bladed, fixed-pitch wooden propeller, single-bay wing with hydraulically controlled landing flaps on upper and lower wings, with a large, internally sprung, Dowty landing gear. The take-over of Gloster by Hawkers had meanwhile taken place and she first took to the air on 12 September 1934.

As the design came closest to fitting their interim demands the RAF took over S.S. 37 on 3 April 1935, allocating her the serial K5200 and began flight testing her at Martlesham Heath and this resulted in her being announced as the winner of the original specification. Gloster now offered a Hawker-type build, with the tail re-designed, the cockpit now a fully enclosed type and with the 840hp (625kW) Mercury X as a power plant. Both the Watts fixed two-blade wood propeller and the Fairey Reed fixed three-bladed metal propeller were tested with this engine. This machine was offered up for a production run and this resulted in the RAF ordering her under the revised Specification F.14/35. On 1 July they allocated the name Gladiator to her and placed an order for twenty-three machines, followed in September 1935 by another, this time for 180 aircraft.

Thus, as the Gladiator, the first production machines first flew in January 1937 and she began entering service on 23 February with No 72 Squadron based at Tangmere.

The initial batch of Gladiator-Is (serials K6129 to K6151 inclusive), which featured the Watts two-bladed propeller, were built in 1936–37 for the RAF but foreign orders followed. The Gladiator was on the strength of eight RAF squadrons by that September.

The second production run appeared in 1937 and carried serials K7892 to K8055 (twenty-three aircraft) inclusive and L7608 to L7623 (sixteen aircraft) inclusive.

A batch of twenty-five replacement aircraft, as a follow-on order of September 1935, were also completed in 1937 and had the serials L8005 to L8032 inclusive. Of these latter L8005 and L8012 to L8028 inclusive, eighteen machines, were sold to the Egyptian Government, and were delivered in April 1939.

The Watts propeller was not found to be a suitable companion for the Mercury engine and Gloster put forward an alternative pairing, the Mercury VIII engine driving an all-metal, three-bladed Fairey-Reed propeller. This gave rise to the Gladiator Mk.II and the first Air Ministry order followed in 1938.[1]

The Gloster Gladiator-II first appeared in 1938 being a modified Mk.I powered by the 825hp (615.20kW) Mercury VIIIA or VIII AS and tropicalized. An initial batch of fifty aircraft received the serials N2265-N2314 produced under Air Ministry Specification F.36/37. Large production batches followed the same year and on into 1939, receiving serials N5500–N5549 inclusive; N5565 to N5594 inclusive; N5620 to N5649 inclusive; N5680 to N5729 inclusive; N5750 to N5789 inclusive; N5810 to N5859 inclusive and N5875 to N5924 inclusive for a total of 284 aircraft. Some 490 served in the RAF, with sixty more in the Royal Navy, while 216 were exported to no fewer than thirteen nations.

The total number was 768, comprising one prototype, 378 Mk.Is, 311 Mk.IIs, 60 fully navalized (unofficially known as Sea Gladiators) and 18 modified Mk.IIs for Sweden with the NOHAB Mercury VIIIS.3 engine, known as the J8A.

Technical details for the Mk.II were a wingspan of 9.83m; an overall length of 8.36m; and a height of 3.58m. Her total wing area was 323ft^2 (30.01m^2). Compared with earlier designs she had a high wing loading, which was to catch out the unwary. The power plant was the 840hp (626.38kW) Bristol Mercury VIIIAS nine-cylinder air-cooled engine, with automatic mixture control, Hobson control box, cockpit controlled electric starter and the Vokes air cleaner and sand excluder. This plant drove a three-bladed Fairey metal propeller and gave her a maximum speed of 257mph (413km/h) at a height of 14,600ft (4,449m). Her empty weight was 3,448.62lb (1,562kg) and her gross weight was 4,864lb (2,206kg). The time to climb to 10,000ft (3,050m) was 4.5 minutes. She had a 64-gallon (291-litre) main tank and a 20-gallon (90-litre) gravity fuel tank. She had a service ceiling of 33,500ft (11,570m) and a range of 444 miles (715km) and a maximum ceiling of 32,800ft (10,000m). She was armed with the two Vickers and two remote-controlled Brownings in under-wing blisters, but the notorious tendency of the Vickers to jam soon led to its abandonment. From the seventy-first production aircraft all machine-guns were factory-installed 0.314in (8mm) Browning machine-guns and earlier machines were retro-fitted as soon as possible.[2] Equipment included a Sperry directional gyro operated by a vacuum pump, artificial horizon, and Reid and Sigrist turn-and-bank indicator, airspeed indicator, Hughes rate-of-climb indicator and Kollsman altimeter.[3] The construction comprised an all-metal Warren-girder incorporating steel tube and internal bracing wires. Wings were two-spar steel strips with steel compression ribbing and dural lattice ribbing, and were fabric-covered. The aircraft had a prominent cantilever main undercarriage.

The Gloster Gladiator served with twenty-seven RAF squadrons:

No. 1 Squadron had its 'B' Flight removed in 1937 to form No. 72 Squadron equipped with the Gloster Gladiator.

No.3 Squadron operated the Gladiator-I from May 1937 onwards and lost K7896 near Warlingham, Surrey, on 23 November 1937 and also lost K6150 on 24 January 1938 at Hove, Sussex. In May 1939 the Gladiator gave way to the Supermarine Spitfire.

No. 6 Squadron was a mixed unit flying army co-operation and police-co-operation operations based at Ramleh, Palestine pre-war during the tense confrontations between Jews and Arabs that built up in the Mandated territory. It was first joined by a batch of Gladiators, serials N5820, N5821, N5822, N5830 and N5851, in August 1941 and they operated until January 1942, flying tactical reconnaissance missions over the Western Desert.

Although a bomber squadron flying the Vickers Wellesley aircraft in the Middle East, No. 14 Squadron moved to Port Sudan in June 1940 and commenced operations against the Italians in Eritrea and had a flight of Gladiators attached when it re-equipped with Bristol Blenheims. These continued serving with the squadron for the course of the campaign and remained when it moved back to the Middle East once more during 1941.

No. 25 Squadron was flying the Hawker Demon as a night fighter unit from Hawkinge and began receiving the Gloster Gladiator in April 1938, taking the machines from No. 56 Squadron. The Gladiators were used for night flying training for the next eight months and, just prior to the outbreak of war, the squadron was equipped with Bristol Blenheims for the same role.

No. 33 Squadron was a Middle East light bomber squadron flying Hawker Harts when, on 1 March 1938, they were replaced by the Gloster Gladiator. They continued supporting British forces in Palestine until the outbreak of war with Italy. The squadron lost K8050 on 19 May 1938 north of Ismailia, and loaned a Gladiator (K7897) to Iraq on 12 October 1940. The Gladiators saw action at Fort Capuzzo on 14 June, destroying a Caproni Ca.310 and a Fiat CR.42, while on 19 June they lost a Gladiator but destroyed two CR.42s. Their highlight was on 6 August when thirteen of the squadron's Gladiators took on twenty-seven CR. 42s and claimed to have destroyed nine for the loss of two Gladiators. Hawker Hurricanes replaced the Gladiators during September 1940.

No. 46 Squadron re-formed at Filton on 20 October 1939, with Gladiator-Is from No. 605 Squadron. They familiarized themselves with these machines and became operational by the turn of the year. The Gladiator-Is were replaced by twenty-two Gladiator-IIs and they made their first combat foray on 12 January, without result. They took part in the Norwegian campaign where they were wiped out.

No. 54 Squadron was a Gauntlet fighter squadron based at Hornchurch, east of London, until April 1937 when the Gloster Gladiator arrived. The unit had K7933 go into the sea off Leysdown, Kent, on 16 June 1938, and the first Supermarine Spitfires arrived in March 1939. The Gladiator lingered on in a secondary role until as late as February 1941 in the squadron but saw no combat.

No. 56 Squadron, in a similar manner, was a Gauntlet squadron based at North Weald, Essex, until July 1937, when the Gladiator briefly replaced her. Two Gladiators were accidently lost, K7993 at North Weald on 26 July 1937, and K7994 on 28 April in same place. The squadron was re-equipped with the Hawker Hurricane from May 1938 onward.

No. 65 Squadron was also a Gauntlet outfit but these were replaced by the Gladiator from June 1937 onward. The squadron lost both K8014 and K7940 in a collision over Uckfield, Sussex, on 17 January 1938, and again had both K8002 and K7942 destroyed on 11 February 1938 at North Weald airfield. They also lost K7941 at Hornchurch on 10 October 1938. In March 1939 the Gladiators were replaced by Supermarine Spitfires.

No. 72 (Basutoland) Squadron was reformed from 'B' Flight of No. 1 Squadron on 22 February 1937 with the Gloster Gladiator and worked from Church Fenton, North Yorkshire. The squadron lost several Gladiators in accidents and in April 1939 they were replaced by Supermarine Spitfires.

No. 73 Squadron was a Fury-II squadron but converted to the Gladiator in June 1937, receiving direct from the Gloster works, serials K7952 to K7963 inclusive and K7965, K7984, K7985, K7986, K8023, K8024, K8025, K8031 and K8032 between June and September 1937. The squadron lost K7953 near Debden, Essex, on 3 July 1937 when her wings folded up on her while performing aerobatics, Pilot Officer J A Thomas baling out. Further accidents included K7955, damaged on 14 October 1937; K7958 and K7959, both of which overshot the flare-path at Digby on 21 March 1938, and K7963, which was in a ground collision with K6145 from No. 56 Squadron on 11 June 1938, at Sutton Bridge. Replacement aircraft, serials K6151 and K7893, were received on a temporary loan from No. 3 Squadron. In July 1938 the Squadron, which had moved to Digby, converted to the Hawker Hurricane.

No. 80 Squadron briefly flew Gauntlets but they were replaced within two months when in March 1937 the first Gladiators arrived at Kenley. The squadron lost K7906 at Debden, Essex, on 29 November 1937. In April 1938 the squadron moved to Egypt as an Air Defence Unit for the Suez Canal. On 12 September 1938 they lost K7909 at Zaweda, Palestine. When war broke out with Italy in June 1940 the squadron moved up to Amriya, Alexandria, where it formed an all-Gladiator Wing with No. 33 Squadron. Between August and November the Gladiators worked from Sidi Haneish South. Joined by some Hawker Hurricanes the squadron moved over to Trikkala, Greece, in November, and then subsequently flew from Larissa, Iannina, Eleusis and finally Argos, but when the British were bundled out following German intervention the following spring the survivors returned to North Africa. The squadron had meanwhile transferred a Gladiator (K8011) to Iraq in April 1941 when it became fully converted to the Hurricane.

No. 85 Squadron was re-formed with the Gloster Gladiator at Debden, Essex, from 'A' Flight of No. 87 Squadron on 1 June 1938. Under the command of Flight Lieutenant Donald Eric Turner the squadron only operated Gladiators for a few months before, from 4 September, they were replaced by the Hawker Hurricane.

No. 87 Squadron was flying the Hawker Fury at Tangmere in June 1937 when she was replaced by the Gladiator. The unit then moved to Debden, Essex, and here it lost K7975 on 21 October 1937, K7966 on 23 March 1938 and K8028 on 8 June 1938. In July 1938 conversion to the Hawker Hurricane took place.

No. 94 Squadron was formed with Gladiator I and IIs at Khormaksar, Aden, on 26 March 1939. Between May 1939 and April 1940 their main base was Sheikh Othman, Aden. On the outbreak of war with Italy in June 1940 the squadron had sixteen Gladiators on strength, but half were in reserve. The unit flew various defensive patrols and clashed with intruders, claiming to have destroyed or damaged a Savoia-Marchetti Sm.79 and Sm.81 as well as several Fiat CR.42s. The Gladiators provided cover during the capture of the Italian submarine *Galilei Galileo* by the anti-submarine trawler *Moonstone* in the Red Sea on 18 June. During the Italian invasion of British Somalia a detachment was based at Berbera, but took heavy losses in the ensuing retreat. On 20 November the final victory was shooting down another Sm.81. The squadron then moved from Aden to Ismailia, Egypt, in readiness to convert to the Hawker Hurricane but the revolt in Iraq saw this delayed as a detachment of Gladiators had to be rushed out to Habbaniya to reinforce the garrison at that airfield. In operations against a small Luftwaffe contingent one Gladiator was shot down by a Heinkel He.111 bomber, while in return the Gladiators claimed two Messerschmitt Bf.110s. From May 1941 the conversion to the Hurricane continued and the Gladiators were handed over to the SAAF.

No. 112 – On 16 May 1939, No. 112 Squadron had reformed with twenty-two crated Gladiator-Is (serials K6130, K6134, K6135, K6136, K6138, K6140, K6141, K7892, K7893, K7895, K7897, K7899, K6142, K6143, K7574, K7604, K7608, K7612, K7615, K7904, K7907 and K7914), mainly former No. 72 Squadron machines, aboard the aircraft carrier *Argus* at Southampton under the command of Squadron Leader Donald Macdonald Somerville, for transportation to the Middle East, arriving at Helwan, Egypt, ten days later. Gladiators were received in June and when Italy joined the war a year later the squadron flew fighter patrols over the Western Desert.

The Squadron suffered several losses due to accidents at this period, including K8024, which had flow from the carrier *Argus* but ditched some twenty miles east of Helwan, Egypt, on 15 April, 1940; they also lost K6136 on 18 June in a crash at Erkowit and while K6130 flew into a hill at Qaret el Naga on 18 July 1940 and K6134 crashed into the Red Sea fifteen miles south of Suakin on 23 December. In January 1941 No. 112 Squadron moved to Greece to provide air defence and fly offensive patrols over Albania. When the Germans invaded Greece the squadron provided fighter cover for the Athens area until the surviving pair (serials K6138 and N5825) were evacuated first to Crete and then back to Egypt. In July 1941 No. 112 Squadron was re-equipped with Curtiss Tomahawks.

No. 117 Squadron was formed at Khartoum, Sudan, on 30 April 1941 and had a rag-bag miscellany of aircraft to perform its communications and transport functions, including the Gladiator-I along with Percival Proctor-Is, Vickers Wellesley bombers, and even captured Italian machines like the Caproni Ca.148 and some Savoia-Marchetti Sm.79s. Most of these were left behind when the unit moved to Egypt in November 1941 and became a transport squadron.

No. 123 Squadron had its personnel moved from Turnhouse, Scotland, to Egypt, in June 1942, leaving its Spitfires behind it. No aircraft were received until October when a Flight of Gladiator-IIs was formed at Abadan, Iran, to protect the vital oilfields. They only served for a few weeks in this role before being replaced by the Hawker Hurricane at the end of November.

No. 127 Squadron was formed on 29 June 1941 with four Gladiator-IIs and four Hawker Hurricane-Is, which were based at Haditha, Iraq. They briefly flew reconnaissance and fighter missions during the Syrian Campaign but had no contact with the enemy. After just two weeks' operations, the unit was re-designated as No. 261 Squadron.

No. 141 Squadron was reformed at Turnhouse, Scotland, on 4 October 1939. It was due to be a Boulton Paul Defiant I unit, but these aircraft were delayed and the squadron conducted training operations with some Gladiator-Is and IIs, later joined by some Bristol Blenheim IFs, as a temporary measure. The Defiants finally arrived in April 1940.

No. 152 'Hyberabad' Squadron was reformed at Acklington, Northumberland, on 1 October 1939. While awaiting the arrival of the Supermarine Spitfire, which did not begin to reach them until January, the unit was equipped with Gladiator-IIs and they served as training and operational machines through until February 1940.

No. 237 'Rhodesian' Squadron was formed on 22 January 1940 by re-designating No. 1 Squadron Southern Rhodesian Air Force and was based at Nairobi. It flew a mix of obsolete aircraft during the East African campaign, Audax, Hardy, Hart and finally the Westland Lysander I and II. In March some Gladiator-IIs joined the squadron at Barentu and in April it moved to Umritsar and then to Asmara, all in Eritrea, until June. The unit moved to North Africa being based at Wadi Halfa, Sudan, in August, when the Gladiators were handed over to No. 6 Squadron and replaced by Hawker Hurricanes.

No. 247 Squadron was formed from the Shetland Fighter Flight at Roborough near Plymouth on 1 August 1940, with the Gladiator. The squadron was assigned to fighter protection of the Plymouth Navy Base and the mercantile shipping port of nearby Falmouth.

No. 261 Squadron formed on 2 August 1940 from the Malta Fighter Flight and had both navalized Gladiator-Is and with Hawker Hurricane-I aircraft flown in from the carrier *Argus*. This squadron was based at the airfields of Luqa, Hal Far and Ta' Qali, Malta, and faced almost the whole of the *Regia Aeronautica* alone and then a whole Luftwaffe *Fliegerkorps* and saw continuous action until disbanded on 21 May 1941.

The squadron was reformed on 12 July 1941, by the simple process of re-numbering No. 127 Squadron at Habbaniya, Iraq, which initially had just four Gladiator-IIs and four Hawker Hurricane-Is on its strength. The squadron served at Shaibah (Az Zubayr), Iraq, and then at Mosul in Iran, Haifa and St. Jean near Acre, in Palestine patrolling over the Levant and Cyprus. The unit later became a wholly Hurricane unit and transferred Gladiator K6147 to Iraq.

No. 263 Squadron was reformed at Filton, near Bristol, on 2 October 1939 under Squadron Leader John William Donaldson. On 10 October six Gladiator-Is were collected from No. 695 Squadron at Tangmere and on 11 October a further four were collected from the same squadron. Training commenced for the pilots and twenty-two new Gladiator-IIs were received from No. 6 MU at Little Rissington: six on 26 October, five on 27 October, five on 28 October and six on 6 November. On 14 November the existing armament was changed with the Browning .303-inch (7.7mm) machine-gun being fitted to all aircraft, two in the nose and two more beneath the lower wing.

Four former Auxiliary Squadrons flew the Gladiator.

No. 603 (City of Edinburgh) Squadron at Turnhouse, was flying the Hawker Hind when it was re-designated as a fighter unit and it received the Gladiator in March 1939. It was part of the defence of the Rosyth naval base early in the war but began converting to the Supermarine Spitfire-I in October.

No. 605 (County of Warwick) Squadron, was another Hind-equipped unit, based at Castle Bromwich, but from February 1939 received the Gladiator when it converted to a fighter operator. In August 1939 it moved south to Tangmere and on the outbreak of the war had ten Gladiators and six Hawker Hurricane-Is on strength. By October all the Gladiators had all been replaced.

No. 607 (County of Durham) Squadron was based at Usworth, near Sunderland, flying the Hawker Demon when it converted over to the Gladiator in December 1938. Early in the war the unit moved up to Drem, East Lothian, to protect the naval base at Rosyth, but returned to Usworth before being assigned as part of the air component of the BEF in France in November being initially based at Merville, Pas de Calais. In December the squadron moved to Vitry-en-Artois, close to the Belgian border, but by April 1940 was at Abbeville in Picardy and busy converting to the Hawker Hurricane.

No. 615 Squadron was based at Kenley, London, and was equipped with Gloster Gauntlets in May 1939 when it converted over to the Gladiator. In August 1938 the squadron re-located to Old Sarum but was back at Kenley again in September, moving to Croydon airfield shortly afterward. In November the squadron moved to France, first to Merville and in December to Vitry-en-Artois. In April the unit was at Poix-en-Picardie, north-west of Paris. Conversion to the Hawker Hurricane had commenced and was not quite completed when the Blitzkreig rolled over them, and in May they were at Moorseele, Wevelgem, Belgium. Within ten days the squadron was back in the UK leaving what remained of their Gladiators behind them.

The Gladiator's misfortune was to be the last of her kind and that she arrived at the same time as a new era was beginning with the eight-gunned monoplane fighters totally outclassing her. Thus she was usually the bridesmaid and seldom the bride, and rarely served for very long with any one squadron, although there were exceptions.

Nonetheless, perforce of sufficient numbers of monoplane fighters in the first year of the war, she gave sterling service and then soldiered on in secondary duties until the end of hostilities.

Fleet Air Arm

At the time of Munich in 1938, a wake-up call for the complaisant Governments of Britain and France, fears were raised again about the lack of any high-performance fighter aircraft in the fleet, which only had the Hawker Nimrod for aerial defence. The Royal Navy was always constrained by the fact that the RAF controlled both the ordering, specifications and production of all aircraft, and did not understand (or care much) for the specialized needs of naval aircraft. It was the Gloster company itself that put forward a proposal that, until a more suitable monoplane fighter might eventually appear, a modified Gladiator might just fit the bill as an interim fleet fighter in what limited time remained before the shooting started.[4]

The naval requirements were for an arrester hook for deck landings, hard points for catapult launchings, and fairings for a collapsible dinghy in case of ditching at sea. Other maritime equipment included a new brake lever, new air speed indicators (ASI) calibrated in knots and similar amendments from RAF standards. The TR.9D Marine Radio equipment with a Type R.1120 receiver had an air-to-ship range of only thirty-five miles and an air-to-air range of five miles, and was an AM set with an electro-mechanical controller in the pilot's cockpit using Teleflex cables. Widespread VHF usage didn't come in until 1940.

Of these aircraft the Royal Navy obtained two batches modified for carrier use; the first batch being interim conversions and comprising the following serials – N2265, N2267 to N2277 inclusive; N2281 to N2282 inclusive; N2296 to N2299 inclusive and N2300 to N2302 inclusive. These nineteen machines were transferred to the Admiralty between 24 May 1939 and 22 August 1940. All were fitted with tail-hooks for carrier landings but none of them went to sea. Thirteen of these went to the Naval Air Station HMS *Kestrel* at Worthy Down, near Winchester, for training, these being serials N2265 to N2277 inclusive, later joined by serials N2281 and N2301. Of these, N2265, N2266, N2272, N2274, N2275, N2276 and N2281 were transferred to the Admiralty on 24 May 1939 when the Fleet Air Arm was finally officially transferred from the RAF. The remainder were spread out to other NAS, to HMS *Merlin* at Donibristle, Fife; HMS *Raven* at Eastleigh, Hampshire; HMS *Sparrowhawk* at Hatson in the Orkney Islands; and to RAF Khormaksar at Aden, from where they were to work with (rather than on) the Eastern Fleet's sole carrier (*Eagle*) in the Indian Ocean.

The second batch of sixty machines were full conversions with catapult spools, arrestor hooks and additional maritime equipment including stowage between the undercarriage legs for a dinghy, and comprised N5500 to N5529 inclusive (fifty-one aircraft); N5565 to N5574 inclusive (nine aircraft). They joined the Navy in 1939–40, the first going to sea aboard the carrier *Courageous* with No. 801 Squadron in February 1939.

The 'navalized' Gladiator (so-called 'Sea Gladiator' – an unofficial term) served with twenty-three Naval Air Squadrons (NAS) but many only briefly or as unit 'hacks'.

No. 759 NAS was formed on 1 November 1939 at HMS *Raven*, RNAS Eastleigh, Southampton, as a fighter training squadron and aircraft pool and four Sea Gladiators were on its strength, which was mainly Blackburn Skuas and Rocs. These machines were K8039 (transferred from the AAEE), N2298 (from 5 MU), N2301 (from Worthy Down) and N2302 (from 5 MU). After a month the squadron absorbed No. 769 NAS and became the Fleet Fighter School. Two of these aircraft were lost in accidents: N2301 was destroyed along with her pilot Lieutenant Victor Carmichael Marryat near Wilton, Salisbury, on 24 April 1940; and N2302, piloted by Sub-Lieutenant Peter Mittell, crashed at Portswall Farm, Camelford on 23 March 1941, killing the pilot. K8039 flew from July 1940 to July 1941 and was then grounded before being transferred to No. 771 Squadron in July 1942. N2298 was transferred to No. 791 Squadron in March 1942.

No. 760 NAS was a fighter training squadron based at HMS *Heron*, RNAS Yeovilton, Somerset.

No. 767 NAS was formed in March 1940 at HMS *Condor*, RNAS Arbroath, as a flight deck-operations unit and conducted carrier landings and take-offs from the old carrier *Argus* in the Mediterranean working from Toulon. Later, the squadron worked from HMS *Merganser*, RNAS Rattray, Crimond, Aberdeen, training telegraphist air gunners and torpedo-bomber reconnaissance aircrew.

No. 769 NAS was a training unit formed at HMS *Merlin*, Donibristle, in 1939 from No. 801 NAS, and later was based at HMS *Condor*, Arbroath, and HMS *Peewit* (Hatton Farm, Easthaven, Tayside). The squadron's Sea Gladiator complement was sixteen aircraft (serials N2298 [from No 791 Squadron], N2299 [from No. 880 Squadron], N5500 to N5511 inclusive, N5537 and N5539). In April 1944 N2299 was transferred to No. 771 Squadron.

No. 770 NAS worked from HMS *Jackdaw*, RNAS Crail, Fife, which was a torpedo training establishment between 1939 and 1945.

No. 771 NAS was a training unit at HMS *Tern*, at Twatt, Orkney Islands, from 1941 and included two Gladiators on its strength, K8039 received from No. 759 Squadron in July 1942 and N2299 received from No. 769 Squadron in April 1944, but this latter was discarded on 17 May.

No. 774 NAS worked from HMS *Vulture*, the Observer and Carrier Flight Manoeuvres training establishment at St Merryn, north Cornwall, between 1937 and 1945.

No. 775 NAS was the Alexandria Fleet Requirement (Training) Squadron in Egypt. The eight Gladiators included on its complement were serials N5503, N5505, N5506, N5509, N5510, N5543, N5547 and N5549. The unit was based at Dekheila airfield as HMS *Grebe* from 16 September 1940. Two Gladiators were written off in accidents here, N5547 on 4 August 1942 and N5506 on 7 November 1942.

No. 776 NAS served at HMS *Ringtail*, RNAS Burscough, near Ormskirk, Lancashire, which was the Night and Torpedo Fighter Squadron training establishment from 1943 onward.

No. 778 NAS served at HMS *Condor, Jackdaw* and between 1940 and 1943 at HMS *Landrail*, RNAS Machrihanish, Campeltown, Argyll and Bute, the torpedo-bomber training school.

No. 787 NAS served at HMS *Heron*, RNAS Yeovilton and HMS *Condor*, RNAS Arbroath, on training duties.

No. 791 NAS served at HMS *Condor*, Arbroath, on deck-landing training from 1938 onward.

No. 792 NAS was formed in August 1939 at HMS *Vulture*, RNAS St Merryn as an Air Target Unit, and initially equipped with six Blackburn Skuas. It disbanded in 1945.

No. 800 NAS was a carrier-based squadron but during a period 1937/38 was ashore at Gosport and utilized two Gladiator aircraft to conduct service trials. Serial K6129 was the machine used by Glosters as the test-bed for the navalized Gladiator, and arrived at Gosport on 14 June 1938 to conduct development trials. On 24 June she was returned to Gloster to have the Mercury VIII engine fitted, returning to Gosport on 7 July. On 26 August she went to No. 800 Squadron and returned to Gloster on 17 November. She was finally transferred to the Aeroplane & Armament Experimental Establishment (AAEE) at Martlesham Heath, Suffolk, on 24 January 1939. K8039 arrived from 1 ASU in January 1938 and was also used on Sea Gladiator comparative trials, returning to Gloster on 25 April 1938 for specialized naval equipment to be installed. She went to No. 800 Squadron on 26 August, then had a new propeller fitted by Gloster on 25 November, finally departing for the AAEE on 2 January 1939. The squadron itself re-equipped with the Blackburn Skua dive-bomber from October 1938 onward.

No. 801 NAS at Donibristle re-equipped from Osprey and Nimrod aircraft in 1939 when she received twelve Sea Gladiators on 8 February 1940 (serials N5500 to N5511 inclusive) and a further six (serials N5512 to N5517) on 21 March. The Gladiators only served briefly, from February to May and were gradually replaced by Blackburn Skua-IIs. The squadron disbanded and became No. 769 Squadron tasked with conversion training. The second batch of Gladiators, now surplus to requirements, was sent out to Egypt with those destined for No. 802 Squadron via 36 MU. All twenty-four arrived at Malta aboard the carrier *Glorious* in 1939, and there they were unceremoniously dumped ashore by her captain when the ship left for the Red Sea. One returned home, and two were lost in accidents, six were put into storage at Alexandria, seven remained in store at Malta and nine returned home when *Glorious* was later recalled in the spring of 1940.

No. 802 NAS embarked some of the eighteen Gladiators (serials N5518 to N5535 inclusive) that 36 MU had delivered to Egypt earlier, aboard the carrier *Glorious* in the Mediterranean and her aircraft when ashore were based at HMS *Glebe*, Dekhelia. Two Gladiators were lost in accidents: serial N5534 crashed into the Mediterranean on 19 May 1939 and N5528 was lost when she crashed into a lake on a training flight on 11 October 1939. In the spring of 1940 *Glorious* was called home to participate in the Norwegian campaign re-embarking twelve Gladiators (serials N5518, N5519, N5521, N5525, N5526, N5527, N5530, N5532, N5533, N5535, N5537 and N5539) on 11 April. The remaining machines were transferred to the storage site at Kalafrana, on the south-eastern tip of Malta including serials N5520, N5529, N5531, where they later became the Hal Far Fighter Flight on 19 April 1940.

No. 804 NAS was formed in November 1939 from No.769 Squadron's twelve Sea Gladiators (serials N2266, N2272 to N2276 inclusive, N2300, N5509, N5510, N5532, N5533, N5535 and N5538), which were detached to Hatston in the Orkney Islands to provide some fighter defence for the Scapa Flow Naval Base at which the Home Fleet was based. In April 1940 they were embarked aboard the carrier *Glorious* to bolster her fighter patrol capability during missions to ferry RAF aircraft to Norway. Early in May 1940 they transferred to the carrier *Furious* at Campletown, then disembarked again to continue working from HMS *Sparrowhawk* at Hatston. Officially she then became one of only two Fleet Air Arm squadrons operating with the RAF during the Battle of Britain (the other was No. 806 NAS), although of course many naval pilots were drafted in as losses mounted. During the period June to October detachments of Gladiators served aboard *Furious* for periods but, by November the unit had converted to the Grumman Martlet (as the F4F Wildcat was initially named in the FAA). The surviving Gladiators were then shipped out to the Mediterranean where they went into store at Alexandria as spares.

No. 805 NAS was a waif, being formed and re-formed several times and ending up post-war as a Royal Australian Navy unit. In May 1940 the unit briefly operated with the Blackburn Roc, and in January 1941 it was re-formed at HMS *Nile-II*, Aboukir, nominally with the Fairey Fulmar in readiness for a planned invasion of Rhodes that never took place. Some Gladiators served from March 1941 onward, these being N5517 and N5567 from the *Eagle* Fighter Flight received on 23 March, N5509 and N5538 received on 27 March, N5538 and N5568 received on 17 April, and N5513 from No. 806 Squadron. Some of these were sent out to Maleme airfield, Crete, along with Brewster Buffalo fighters, and during the German invasion in May N5513 was lost, while N5517 which made an escape attempt on 15 May, was also destroyed.

No. 806 NAS was formed at Worthy Down in February 1940 initially with the Blackburn Skua and Roc, and then with the Fairey Fulmar. In October 1940 the new carrier *Illustrious* had finished working up in Bermuda and joined the Mediterranean Fleet at Alexandria, where she embarked two Sea Gladiators as additional fighters, serial N5513 from the *Eagle* Fighter Flight, and N5509. When *Illustrious* was badly damaged by Stuka attack south of Malta in January 1941, the squadron's surviving aircraft served ashore in Egypt and were assigned to the carrier *Formidable* until she, in her turn, was 'Stuka'd' off Crete in May 1941. N5513 was transferred to No. 805 Squadron.

No. 813 NAS was a Fairey Swordfish unit embarked aboard the carrier *Eagle* on the China Station. She served in the Indian Ocean and had joined the Mediterranean Fleet at Alexandria by June 1940 when Italy declared war. Five of the stored and crated Sea Gladiators stored ashore (serials N5512, N5513, N5517, N5523 and N5567) were hastily embarked to join the squadron forming the *Eagle* Fighter Flight on 16 June 1940, and four volunteer Swordfish pilots, led by the Commander (Flying) Commander Charles Lindsey Keighley-Peach, were given training in fighter tactics to fly them. The Gladiators proved a morale-booster for the fleet, which was bombed continuously by high altitude formations of the *Regia Aeronautica* when at sea, fortunately without much success. The Gladiators needed a great deal of advance notice in order to claw their way slowly up to sufficient altitudes to engage, and encounters were rare, but kills were made. They served in this makeshift role until March 1941, when the *Eagle* left the Mediterranean to return home to have her tired old engines refitted and the Gladiators were disembarked again.

No. 880 NAS was formed at Arbroath under Lieutenant-Commander Francis Elton Christopher 'Butch' Judd, RN, in January 1941 as a Fleet Fighter unit with three Grumman Martlet-Is and was intended as the fighter complement of the new carrier *Indomitable*. In February 1941 three Sea Gladiators on loan from RNAS Donibristle and nine Sea Hurricane Ia aircraft were added and these served as stop-gap aircraft until June 1941 when sufficient Sea Hurricane-Ib machines were received. One Sea Gladiator (serial N2299) was not returned to No. 769 Squadron until as late as July 1942.

No. 885 NAS was formed at Dekheila, Egypt, as a Fleet Fighter unit in March 1941, equipped with six Sea Gladiators and three Brewster Buffalo fighters. Two days after forming the squadron embarked aboard the carrier *Eagle* but, after just one week at sea, disembarked again at Dekheila. The squadron was disbanded in May 1941.

Meteorological flights

The fully enclosed cockpit of the Gladiator made her suitable for conducting meteorological flights and many of the surplus aircraft were converted to this duty. All armament was taken out and replaced by a thermometer between the wings, attached to the rear, port strut and a cockpit headlamp for illumination. These machines also had added a second aerial, used to measure air humidity. Apart from that little was altered and there was no special pressurization for the pilots engaged on high altitude flights other than two pairs of socks and an extra layer of clothing! When the first of these new units were formed on 1 March 1941, the Gladiator joined No. 401 Squadron. In this capacity the Gladiator's role rapidly increased with the expansion of the requirement and these units were re-configured in the 1400 sequence soon afterward. The Gladiator subsequently served with the following Met. flights:

RAF Meteorological Flight, Mildenhall, had five Gladiators on strength, serials N2307, N5583, N5594, N5620 and N5621 in 1938 and became No. 401 (Met) Flight on 4 February 1941. The Air Ministry Meteorological Flight at Aldergrove, near Belfast, had four Gladiators on strength, serials N5590 to N5593 inclusive, and on 15 January became 402 (Met) Flight.

No. 401, which in turn became No. 1401 (Met) Flight (coded TE) in March, had Gladiator N5897 added from No. 247 Squadron to replace N5620, which was destroyed in a night-landing accident on 13 February 1941, and was based at Mildenhall in Suffolk until October 1941 when it transferred to Bircham Newton, Norfolk, and was joined by modified Hurricanes and later Spitfire IIA and 5s. Two Gladiators, serials N5583 on 21 March 1942 and N5594 on 1 August 1943, were written off but replacements machines, serials K8043, from 2 AACU, N2309 from No. 18 Squadron, and N2310 from No. 53 Squadron were added. In June 1942 this unit merged with No. 1403 to become No. 521 (Met) Squadron on 22 July 1942. No. 402 (Met) Flight, which became No. 1402 (Met) Flight on 1 March, was based at Ballyhalbert near Belfast, and remained there for the duration. Additional Gladiators were received at intervals, serials N5576 from 2 AACU and N5576 from No 247 Squadron, N5637 from No. 263 Squadron, N5703 from 1401 Flight, N5900 from No. 18 Squadron and N5902 from the Northolt Flight, and K7918 and K7927 both on 18 May 1943. Attrition was also high; Gladiator N5576 was damaged beyond repair in a night landing, N5590 similarly destroyed at Langford Lodge on 13 May 1941, N35592 crashed in County Antrim on 6 September 1941, N45593 crashed on 3 January 1942 and N5637 crashed on 19 January 1943. The Gladiator was gradually replaced by Hurricanes and Spitfires but a two (serials N5900 and N5902) still remained active with No. 521 Squadron as late as 1945. 1403 was reformed at Gibraltar in May 1943, working from North Front, and featured Gladiator N5630 from No. 263 Squadron and when the unit was again disbanded she went to No. 520 Squadron.

The Meteorological Flight at Heliopolis on 1 January 1942 became No. 1411 (Met) Flight, which was initially nominally a North African unit, attached to RAF Middle East HQ, but piloted and maintained by Egyptian personnel and with Egyptian markings. The Gladiators were of diverse origins, none came from the same unit originally, they being serials K6138, K7893 (which was shot down on 20 July 1942), K7925, K7943, K7961, K7963, K8003, K8008 (which force-landed near El Adem on 26 January 1942 and was written off), K5825 and K5830. They conducted flights over the Suez Canal and Red Sea areas. The Gladiators were gradually replaced by Hurricanes, one, K7961, being transferred to the Iraqis as late as June 1944. Similarly, the Meteorological Flight at Khartoum, which was established on 21 September 1941, and which had five Gladiators on establishment at various dates, serials K6140, K7951, N5756, N5831 and N5833, of which N5756 was written off in a landing accident on 21 October 1941. This unit also disbanded on 1 January 1942 to change into No. 1412 (Met) Flight in the Sudan, initially under No. 203 Group but later with Middle East HQ. Equipment included Gladiators K6140, K7951, K8001, K5828, N5829, N5831, N5833 and N5851, the last three being destroyed in accidents on 10 March 1943, 27 April 1942 and 30 September 1942 respectively. Gladiators were still on hand in March 1942 when K6147 was received from the Iraqis, but were soon likewise later replaced by Hurricanes.

Finally, the Meteorological Flight at Ramleh, Palestine, formed on 21 September 1941, featured four Gladiators, serials K7919, K7924, K7949 and K7999. Again, from 1 January 1942 it became No. 1413 (Met) Flight working over the Levant, Palestine, Syria and the Eastern Mediterranean littoral. Equipment included Gladiators K1341,

K7914 and K7978 all transferred from 'X' Flight, K7926 from 5 OTU, K7932 and K7988 both from Greece and K7983 from 8 OTU. The flight at Ramleh, Palestine, lost K7924 on 20 January 1942. This long-serving unit finally transferred its last Gladiator to Iraq in 1944:

No. 1414 (Met) Flight was formed in December 1941 at Eastleigh, Kenya, and covered the Red Sea and Sudan regions. She flew two former Egyptian Gladiators, K1340 and K1344, along with a former SAAF machine, K7913, K8037 from No. 112 Squadron and N5821 from No. 6 Squadron, the latter of which was destroyed when she ran out of fuel and crashed into the sea off Mogadishu on 25 October 1943.

No. 1415 (Met) Flight was established at Habbaniya, Iraq, and received one ex-Iraqi Gladiator (K6147) in March 1942, but she was later destroyed in a landing incident on 18 October 1943. The unit by this time was operating the Westland Lysander and Avro Anson aircraft.

No. 1560 (Met) Flight was formed at Maiduguri, Nigeria, on 6 December 1942 and was equipped with four Gladiators, N5622, N5625, N5631 and N5682, the first three being transferred to No. 1562 (Met) Flight. No. 1561 (Met) Flight (coded VM) was also set up at Ikeja, Nigeria, on 1 May 1943 with three Gladiators, N5593, N5648, which was destroyed in a landing accident on 28 March 1944, and N5703, the two survivors later transferring to No. 1562 Flight also.

No. 1562 (Met) Flight (coded B9) was another West African Flight formed at Waterloo, Sierra Leone, on 3 February 1943 and was not disbanded until 17 December 1945. Seven Gladiators served with this unit, five from 1560 and 1561 Flights, together with N5684 from No. 247 Squadron and N5702 from Andover Station Flight. Two machines were lost in accidents at Waterloo, N5625 on 6 June 1944 and N5684 on 17 December 1944. No. 1563 (Met) Flight was set up on 22 December 1942 from a 1411 detachment and based at Helwan, Egypt, operating flights over Libya and Tunisia. She had two Gladiators on strength; K8003 donated by 1411 Flight and K8027 from 6 OTU. The final Gladiator Meteorological outfit was No. 1565 (Met) Flight, formed at Nicosia, Cyprus, from a detachment from 1413 Flight. Three Gladiators flew with this unit, K7914, K7932 and K7988, but the former suffered engine failure and crashed near Beirut on 25 March 1943.

There were short-lived UK-based units, like No. 1563(Met) Flight, which was formed from No. 1411 (Met) Flight at Helwan on 22 December 1942 with just K8003 plus K8027 from No 6 OTU. They became part of No. 212 Group Middle East in 1942, by which time the Gladiators had been replaced by Spitfire 5Bs and 8sl.

Flying Training Schools

With the arrival of the Hawker Hurricane, the Supermarine Spitfire and the Boulton & Paul Defiant, the Gladiators were soon being shuttled off from active Home squadrons to the advance fighter pilot training role. A few Gladiators appeared very briefly on the lists of the following RAF Flying Training Schools (FTS):

No. 2 FTS at Brize Norton, Oxfordshire, received Gladiator K8040 from 1 ASU on 13 June 1938 but the following month she was transferred to No. 7FTS.

No. 3 FTS, based at South Cerney, Gloucestershire, received Gladiator K8052 from No. 5 FTS on 15 August but she was transferred out to 1 ASU on 21 October of the same year.

No. 4 FTS was formed from 4 Service Flying Training School in September 1939. The unit's 'C' Flight received Gladiator K7907 from No. 112 Squadron in October 1940 and transferred her to No. 127 Squadron on 29 June 1941 after the action at Habbaniyah.

No. 5 FTS flying from Shotwick, Chester, received Gladiator K8052 from No. 6 FTS on 13 July 1938 and passed her on to No. 3. FTS on 15 August.

No. 6 FTS at Ternhill, Shropshire, received Gladiator K8040 from 1 ASU on 13 June 1938 but the following month she went to No. 5 FTS.

No. 7 FTS was formed on 2 December 1935 and had Gladiator K8040 delivered from No. 2 FTS on 13 June 1938, but transferred her to No. 10 FTS on 9 August.

No. 9 FTS from Thornaby, near Stockton-on-Tees, received Gladiator K613 from No. 72 Squadron as a wrecked machine, which was never repaired.

No. 10 FTS at Shawbury, Shropshire, received Gladiator K8040 from No. 7 FTS on 9 August 1938 and despatched her to 1 ASU on 9 September. On 29 November she went to Glosters for the fitting of a Rotol propeller[5] and joined No. 65 Squadron on 1 March 1939.

Operational Training Units

Other training duties were performed by the Gladiator with the following RAF Operational Training Units (OTUs):

No. 5 was formed at Aston Down, Minchinhampton, Gloucester, on 6 March 1940, with the re-designation of 12 Group Aircraft Pool. The unit was supplied with eight Gladiators, serials K7943, K7944, K7945, K7951, K7970, K8001, K8015 and K8052 on 6 March; three more from No. 141 Squadron, serials K7926, K7928 and K7990 arrived on 4 April; while K8033 was received from No. 65 Squadron on 6 April. Several machines (K7926, K7943, K7951, K7990, K8033) were later modified at Marshalls, Cambridge airfield; and others were transferred to the Middle East (K7926, K7928, K7943, K7944, K7951, K7990), while K8033 went to the Royal Hellenic Air Force on 11 March 1941. K7928 was transferred to No. 261 Squadron in July 1941 and K7926 and K7943 joined 1411 (Met) Flight.

No. 6 OTU was formed under Squadron Leader Philip Pinkham in March 1940 and was based at Sutton Bridge, Lincolnshire. The unit received two Gladiators (serials K8020 and K8027) from No. 263 Squadron on 14 April, a third on 17 May and a fourth on 28 May, both from 5 OTU. The unit became 56 OTU in November 1940, and K8015 and K8052 transferred to 2 Anti-Aircraft Co-Operation Unit (AACU) in October and K8020 and K8027 went to 27 MU in August.

No. 8 OTU formed at Fraserburgh on 18 Mary 1942 to train Spitfire photo-reconnaissance pilots. One Gladiator was assigned to the unit from the Gosport

Station Flight on 13 August 1940, but was despatched to 8 MU on 11 October. Another Gladiator joined from 2 AACU after being modified at Marshalls Flying Services, Teversham, Cambridge, arriving on 1 May 1944.

No. 41 OTU was formed at Old Sarum on 20 September 1941 to train Tactical Reconnaissance pilots. The unit received Gladiator N5636 from 1 SAC, which remained until 28 November 1946.

No. 60 OTU formed at Leconfield, Yorkshire, on 28 April 1941 to train night-fighter pilots. It received two Gladiators, serials K8044 and K8045. The unit was disbanded on 24 November 1942.

No. 61 OTU was formed at Heston on 9 June 1941 but moved to Rednal, Worcestershire, where the Gladiators became the 'stars' of a wartime propaganda film depicting heroic 'against the odds' action during the German conquest of Greece in 1941. The Flight consisted of ten aircraft, nine Gladiators and one Wellington (Gladiator serials K6149, K7898, K7927, K8004, K8042, K8044, K8045, K8046, L8032). Another machine, N5903, was also received (from No. 141 Squadron) and still exists today. Two of the Gladiators (serials K7927 and K8045) were destroyed in a mid-air collision over Penrhos, Audlem, Cheshire, during the making of the film.

No. 71 OTU was formed at Ismailia, Egypt, on 1 June 1941 from 'B' Flight 70 OTU to train aircrew in desert acclimatization. The unit received ex SAAF-1341 on its strength.

No. 72 OTU was formed on 10 November 1941, at Cathargo, Sudan, from part of No. 211 Squadron to train aircrew in desert and tropical conditions. The unit received Gladiator K8037 from 1414 (Met) Flight on 3 December 1942 but she was damaged in a landing accident on 2 January 1943.

Accidental losses

As always, some attrition was suffered through accidents but the Gladiator was notorious when she first appeared, suffering a higher than average loss rate, with frequent 'spin-ins' contributing. In 1937 seven Gladiators were lost, in 1938 this more than doubled to twenty, in 1939 eleven were written off, in 1940 forty-one and in 1941 fourteen were lost. The squadrons who suffered most pre-war were No. 33 Squadron, which lost seven Gladiators, serial no. K8050 on 19 May 1938, near Ismailia, K8034 on 2 August 1938, near Ismailia, L7610 on 17 October 1938 south of Qantara, K8055 on 28 January 1939 at Haifa, Palestine, L7613 on 1 March 1939 at Mersah Matruh, K8053 on 31 May at Ismailia and L7618 on 23 September 1939 at Mersa Matruh; then follows No. 65 with five losses, including two collisions on 17 January when K8014 and K7940 were lost near Uckfield, Sussex, and on 11 February when K8002 and K7942 collided over North Weald airfield in Essex. No 72 Squadron (Basutoland) Squadron lost five Gladiators between 23 July 1937 and 1 December 1938; while No. 87 Squadron lost three Gladiators between 21 October 1937 and 8 June 1938. Interestingly Gloster's themselves wrote off the first one, K7976, at Brockworth, Gloucestershire on 24 June 1937.

Wartime RAF and Royal Navy operations

When war was declared on 3 September 1939 only Auxiliary Squadrons No. 603 at Turnhouse, with sixteen Gladiators, No. 605 at Tangmere with ten Gladiators, No. 607 Squadron at Usworth with sixteen Gladiators and No. 615 Squadron at Kenley, with sixteen Gladiators, featured the type in front-line service. At overseas bases No. 33 Squadron at Qasaba, with fourteen Gladiators, No. 80 Squadron at Amriya with fourteen Gladiators and No. 112 Squadron at Helwan, with sixteen Gladiators, all in Egypt; and No 94 Squadron at Sheik Othman, Aden, with twelve Gladiators, also carried the type in front-line service.

Incredibly the Gladiator *still* featured on the strength of Nos. 607 and 615 Squadrons when they went to the Continent as part of the Advanced Air Striking Force (AASF) to support the British Expeditionary Force (BEF) in November 1939, but took heavy losses from modern Luftwaffe types and had to withdraw to England to replace them. Both squadrons had largely re-equipped with the Hurricane by July 1940. They were also still serving with Nos. 603 and 605 Squadrons on the outbreak of war. In the Royal Navy, strangely enough the only Sea Gladiators afloat on the outbreak of war were the twelve from No. 802 Squadron allocated to the carrier *Glorious* in the Mediterranean, while No. 801 Squadron was allocated the carrier *Courageous*; none of the Navy's six other aircraft carriers had any embarked.

Home

The Shetland Fighter Flight consisted of ten Gloster Gladiators based at RAF Sumburgh, twenty-five miles south of Lerwick, also known as the Sumburgh Fighter Flight. They operated from the field's grass strips for a while, but suffered heavily from accidents; N5701 stalled and crashed on Sumburgh beach on 22 December 1939; N5643, crashed on landing at Sumburgh on 20 March 1940; N5716 had engine failure and crashed on the beach at Haroldswick, Unst; N2266 crashed on take-off on 6 July 1940 and N5642 suffered engine failure and crashed on Samphrey island. The survivors, N5622, N5644, N5682, N5702 and N5901 were relocated south to Plymouth in the summer of 1940.

No. 804 Squadron, based in Scotland, saw considerable service with patrols off the north-eastern coast on Fleet and convoy protection duties. They had several notable encounters with the Luftwaffe; on 10 April 1940 Heinkel He.111s were claimed destroyed by Lieutenant Richard Michael Smeeton, Sub-Lieutenant Michael Frampton Fell and Petty Officer (Air) Albert William Sabey while on 27 April, Lieutenant Smeeton claimed another. No. 607 Squadron was credited with one confirmed Dornier Do.18 on 17 October, shot down into the Firth of Forth, this being among the first RAF aerial victories of World War II. On 1 May Lieutenant Commander John Clayton Cockburn DSC, claimed a Junkers Ju.87. Two Gladiators were lost, N2275 crashing in the Pentland Firth in June 1940, while on 9 December N2300 was badly damaged at on the ground at Skara Brae, Orkneys, and written off. N5533 went afloat aboard the carrier *Glorious* on 11 April for a brief period with No. 802 Squadron and later that month flew ashore to Donisbristle, rejoining No. 804 Squadron in September.

Norway

From 9 April 1940 onward, both RAF and Royal Navy Gladiators saw action in the disastrous Norway debacle. No. 46 Squadron was ordered out and on 20 April, flew via Sealand to Scapa Flow naval base where the pilots embarked and the Gladiators were flown by FAA pilots aboard the carrier *Furious*. Eighteen Gladiators were flown ashore in Norway, where they set up base on Lake Lesjaskogsvatnet, Oppland, in central southern Norway. No. 263 Squadron was also despatched aboard the carrier *Glorious* and operated from the same lake in lieu of a better alternative, but when the Luftwaffe took the simple step of bombing the ice and wiping out the Gladiators on the 25 and 26 April, No. 263 had to withdraw north to Narvik where they received replacement Gladiators. No. 46 was also withdrawn, refitted with all Hawker Hurricanes, and returned to Bardufoss, near Narvik. No. 263 Gladiators flew off the carrier *Furious* on 21 May and while *en route* ran into snow and fog, losing two aircraft (serials N5697 and N5693) as well as the guiding Fairey Swordfish aircraft, on Mount Høystakktind.

From Bardufoss, both squadrons continued in action until 7 June flying 249 sorties and claiming a total of twenty-six victories. On 24 May two Gladiators, piloted by Flying Officer Herman Francis Grant Ede and Flight Lieutenant William Riley, shot down a Heinkel He.111 bomber over Fjordbotneidet, Gratangen, and on 26 May two more Gladiators, flown by Flight Lieutenant Alvin Thomas Williams and Sergeant George Stanley Milligan, destroyed a Dornier Do.17F bomber over Skaanland landing field. The successes continued with Milligan claiming an Heinkel He.111 over Narvik on 27 May and the same afternoon two Gladiators, flown by Flight Lieutenant Tony Lydekker and Flight Lieutenant Caesar Barrand Hull, intercepted three Junkers Ju.87R Stukas that were busy demolishing the Bodøsjøen radio masts, shooting down one of them, but, in return, their Messerschmitt Bf.109 escorts nailed N5635, killing Hull. The same German pilot, *Leutnant* Helmut Lent, destroyed a second Gladiator, (serial N5914 flown by Pilot Officer James Leon Wilkie) on 2 June near Rombaksfjorden. Next day, a Gladiator piloted by Williams so damaged another He.111 that it was written off in a forced landing at Gjømmervann, Bodø, and this led to the loss of a second He.111 when it tried to land to rescue the crew but was wrecked in the process. Yet another He.111 was destroyed on 29 May by Milligan and its crew made PoWs. Eventually, due to sustained pressure from the German advance northward and competing demands of the Blitzkrieg in the Low Countries, Narvik, and Norway, were abandoned by the Allies.

On 8 June five Fairey Swordfish TSRs led the ten Gladiators of No. 263 Squadron that were still flyable, along with the Hurricanes of No. 46 Squadron, from Bardufoss back to sea, where they landed back aboard the aircraft carrier *Glorious,* first the Gladiators, then the Swordfish and, once the carrier's own Sea Gladiators of No. 802 Squadron and Swordfish of No. 823 Squadron had been struck down below, finally the seven Hurricanes. This was all splendidly carried out, but this magnificent achievement was all for naught for the carrier herself was caught by surprise (incredibly, she had no aircraft aloft to keep watch at the time) and quickly sunk, along with her escorting destroyers *Acasta* and *Ardent,* by the German battle-cruisers *Gneisenau* and *Scharnhorst* on 10 June.[6]

France

Although Nos. 607 and 615 Squadrons in France nominally had Gladiators on their strengths they saw little fighting, the only recorded incident being an unsuccessful Heinkel He.111 interception by Flight Lieutenant James Sanders of No. 615 Squadron on 29 December 1939. Things remained static until the Germans attacked on 10 May 1940, by which time both squadrons had just about switched over to the Hawker Hurricane. No. 615, which received its first Hurricane on 12 April, was fully operational with the new aircraft on the very day the Panzers rolled forward. While the Hurricanes battled vainly to stem the tide, the Gladiators were retained for base defence and Flying Officer Lewin Freidman tried to attack another Heinkel He.111 but lacked the speed. On 11 May two Gladiator reconnaissance missions were flown to check out suitable forward landing fields in Belgium but the tide of battle swept both squadrons away and within ten days the remnants of both were back in England. Here a Flight of four Gladiators (serials K7928, K7970, K8001 and K8033) known as 'G' Flight, commanded by Flight Lieutenant James Sanders of No. 615 Squadron, were based at Manston, Kent, between 23 and 30 May, again as local defence aircraft, during the period of the Dunkirk evacuation.

Battle of Britain

The Gladiator served with No. 247 Squadron during this period, being based at Roborough and tasked to defend the Navy dockyard at Devonport, Plymouth. They patrolled extensively but, perhaps fortunately, never encountered the enemy. The closest they came to action was on 25 September 1940, when two dozen Dornier Do.17 bombers escorted by twelve Messerschmitt Bf.110 twin-engined fighters approached over Start Point to target Plymouth Naval Base. Four Gladiators tried to intercept but were too slow. During subsequent night attacks the Gladiators attempted radar-directed interceptions, making visual contact on occasions but not having the speed to get into an attacking position. On Christmas Eve 1940 the squadron's Gladiators were finally replaced by Hawker Hurricanes.

Malta

Despite what famous test pilot Eric 'Winkle' Brown implied, the Gladiator *did* combat the Fiat CR.42, and on many occasions, but only once did they clash over Malta.

When Italy threatened to join the war on the side of Hitler, the main fleet base of the Royal Navy in the Mediterranean, Valletta, Malta, was disgracefully exposed to attack. Despite the precedent set during the Abyssinian crisis five years earlier and warnings since, British Government inertia had ensured that little had been done; there were no bomb-proof shelters for the submarines based there, little in the way of AA gunnery, and no fighter defences. The Sea Gladiators put ashore by the carrier *Glorious* earlier, had been stored at Kalafrana where they were hastily re-assembled as Mussolini's threats increased and on 19 April they became the Hal Far Fighter Flight.

Three Gladiators from the store, and four from Hal Far Fighter Unit (serials N5520, N5521, N5525, N5527, N5530, N5533 and N5535) were re-embarked aboard the *Glorious* on 11 April when she left the station for Norway.

Those at Hal Far were organized under Wing-Commander Garth Richard O'Sullivan into the Station Flight, and manned by volunteers. They operated between March and June 1940 and journalistic hyperbole soon hyped up their indisputably heroic defence to 'star' status as 'Faith', 'Hope' and 'Charity', three Gladiators that saved the islands, and that deserved, but inaccurate, portrayal, that has continued ever since.

The Gladiators thus immortalized then, and in post-war accounts also, were N5520 ('Faith'), N5531 ('Hope') and N5519 ('Charity'). However, contrary to popular myth, they were not the only Gladiators to defend Malta in this period. On 10 June when Italy declared war, there were five Sea Gladiators at Hal Far and two at Luqa, a total of seven machines, N5519, N5522, N5524 and N5529 being the other four aircraft. Initially five, and eventually nine, pilots gained sufficient flight experience to participate in fighter defence operations, these being Squadron Leader Alan Cresswell Martin, Flying Officer John Waters, Flying Officer William Joseph 'Timber' Woods, Flight Lieutenant George Burges, Flying Officer Peter Bruce Alexander, Flying Officer Peter Hartley, Flying Officer Roger Atherstone Hilton-Barber, Flying Officer Frederick Frank Taylor and Flying Officer John Walters. Some of these Gladiators received Hamilton-Standard/de Havilland two-position three-bladed propellers, taken from Bristol Blenheim-Is, between 11 and 12 May 1940.

Interestingly another twelve Gladiators were intended for the Mediterranean via 36 MU, but six of these (serials N5565, N5566, N5570 to N5574 inclusive) were retained in the UK; and two were retained at Gibraltar (serials N5548 and N5549) for a while. Those that reached Alexandria were serials N5567 to N5569 inclusive and the former was lost at Crete in May 1941.

They were in action from 11 June onward, three of them damaging one Sm.79 that day. However, on 21 June two Gladiators were damaged in accidents during scrambles, both N5522 and N5524 being declared as write-offs. Fortunately the ever-resourceful Squadron Leader Arthur Edward Louks, Command Engineering Officer, and his team managed to cobble together the two wrecks into one flyable aircraft, and N5524 survived to carry on fighting. Next day two Gladiators flown by Burges and Woods destroyed a Sm.79 over the island and on 23 June Burges came out on top in a dogfight with a Macchi MC.200, shooting it down into the sea off Sliema. Meanwhile reinforcements in the form of some Hawker Hurricanes flown off carriers started to arrive on the island, but these were quickly expended so the Gladiators continued to operate until more could be flown in from the carrier *Argus*.

On 31 July Sea Gladiator N5519, flown by Hartley, was blown up over the sea by a CR.42, the remains falling off Ras-il-Fenek, while, in return, Woods destroyed one CR.42. By 1 January 1941 just four operational Gladiators remained at Malta. From the end of January the few surviving Gladiators were transferred into No. 806 Squadron where they were employed mainly on the meteorological mission but even so managed to get in some final actions. Sub-Lieutenant Jack Sewell for example, was attacked by a Junkers Ju.88 from the 4./L.G.1 over Hal Far and managed to get into a position to shoot it into the sea on 24 January 1941, a magnificent victory over a much faster aircraft. On 4 February the roles were reversed and a Gladiator (serial N5531 – 'Hope') was burnt out at Hal Far during an evening raid by the Luftwaffe. The last Gladiator continued to fly meteorological sorties when No. 806 Squadron was withdrawn to Egypt following the earlier severe damage to *Illustrious*, to await the arrival of the carrier *Formidable* as her replacement.

HMS *Eagle* in action

The five Gladiators aboard the carrier *Eagle* were the sole aerial defence at sea for Admiral Sir Andrew Cunningham's Mediterranean Fleet based at Alexandria, Egypt. The fleet was aggressively handled and took the fight to the Italian Navy, whom they defeated time and time again. The *Regia Aeronautica* used their Savoia-Marchetti S81 and Sm.79 bombers flying in tight formations and high altitudes to bomb the fleet, in accordance with Air Force doctrine of the 1930s but, despite the prophecies of the likes of Giulio Douhet, Billy Mitchell and Lord Trenchard, few, if any, hits were ever achieved against moving warships at sea by this method.[7] Nonetheless the continual bombing, to which the ships were unable to effectively reply, was a morale-sapping experience and even the occasional success by the *Eagle*'s pitifully few Gladiators was a welcome relief.

On 11 July 1940 two Sea Gladiators flown by Charles Lindsey Keighly-Peach and Lieutenant (A) Kenneth Lloyd Keith DSC, shot down an Sm.79 over the fleet and the same pair nailed another two Sm.79s plus a Sm.81, all on 13 July. Again, on 29 July, two Sea Gladiators, piloted by Keith and Lieutenant (A) Patrick Wilfred Villers Massey, intercepted a force of Sm.79s and destroyed one of them. Unfortunately Massey's Gladiator (N5512) ran out of fuel and had to ditch, Massey being rescued by the Australian destroyer *Stuart*. On return to port this aircraft was replaced by another Sea Gladiator (N5523). While in harbour the three Sea Gladiators operated ashore from Sidi Barrani, Libya, alongside Gladiators of No. 112 Squadron, giving air cover while the battleships bombarded the Italian supply port of Bardia on 17 August. Between them they destroyed four Sm.79s without loss to themselves.

Eagle was at sea again with the fleet on 31 August during another convoy operation, and Keighly-Peach and Lieutenant (A) Ralph Henry Hood Laurence Oliphant were scrambled away, surprising a Cant Z.506B off Kythera Island, which they shot into the sea. The new carrier *Illustrious* joined the fleet in August and a combined raid launched against the Rhodes airfields by both carriers was mounted on 4 September.

On 8 September to cover more Malta convoys, and in addition to some of her Swordfish, two of *Eagle*'s Sea Gladiators (serials N5513 and N5523) were embarked aboard the carrier *Illustrious*. That day two of *Eagle*'s Sea Gladiators, shot down a Cant Z.501 caught snooping at the fleet. In December, with the engines unreliable, *Eagle* mainly remained at Alexandria, only being used to cover essential convoy operations, or cover transport heading for Suda Bay, Crete, which was being built up as a British base for the Greek operations; but when not at sea herself her aircraft were flown ashore and continued to operate successfully against the enemy. In January two Blackburn Skua aircraft were embarked for one such mission, MC6 (Malta Convoy 6), to reinforce her Gladiators but they met no opposition. Fairey Fulmars were also tried as well as the American Brewster Buffalo, but the latter proved unsuitable to operate from the carrier and were sent ashore at Crete to bolster the defence from Maleme airfield.

The surviving trio from *Eagle*, K7928, K7970 and K8033, were returned to 5 OTU on 29 May after the carrier had sailed for home to refit.[8]

Greece and Crete 1941

The successful British operation to clear North Africa of the Italians was halted by Churchill and among the many units taken away and sent to Greece was No. 80 Squadron, which reached Trikkala on 19 November 1940. Several encounters with the Italian Fiat CR.42s followed with results fairly even. No. 112 Squadron arrived on 3 December bringing more Gladiators into the combat arena and they too were heavily involved. Pilot Officer William Vale of No. 80 Squadron destroyed both a Fiat G.50 fighter and a Sm.79 while flying N5829 from Himare. Conversion to the Hawker Hurricane proceeded even as these battles were being fought and by February 1941, all of No. 80's remaining Gladiators were transferred to No. 112 Squadron. The intervention of the Luftwaffe on 5 April soon reversed that trend and the RAF and the British troops were quickly bundled out of Greece, and later from the island of Crete where they had hoped to hold out. Heavy losses were suffered by the surviving Gladiators who were soon withdrawn to Egypt once more.

North Africa

Between 28 August 1941 and 12 January 1942, a detachment from No. 6 Squadron, normally working out of Wadi Halfa, and including several Gladiators, was sent to the isolated Kufra Oasis, each on the back of a truck. Here they operated until 12 January 1942. On 26 September the base was attacked by a Savoia-Marchetti Sm.79 three-engined bomber and this aircraft was chased and caught by Sergeant Ron Walker in Gladiator N5851. After a very long stern chase Walker finally got within 400 yards and fired away, and finally his target was said to have crash-landed. This little action is thought to have been the final claimed 'kill' obtained by an RAF Gladiator, although the Italian records show no damage was done.

Iraq

During the Rashid Ali rebellion the pro-Nazi group of the Iraqi Army overthrew the Government in April 1941. No. 4 FTS at Habbaniya had four Gladiators on its establishment and these became part of the Air Striking Force hastily assembled by

Group Captain Walter Archer Bourchier Savile, the School's CO, when an Iraqi force of nine thousand men and twenty-eight guns surrounded the base on the 30th. On 29 May Italian aid reached the Iraqis and when the Audax bombers carried out an attack on Iraqi army columns that day, they were intercepted by Caproni CR.42s and one bomber was destroyed. In return the Gladiators, who were providing fighter escort for the mission, drove off the rest, damaging one CR.42 near Khan Nuqta in the process. That marked the sum total of Italian intervention.

Meanwhile, two Iraqi Gladiators had carried out a daring attack near Baghdad on 1 Battalion, Essex Regiment on 30 May. This proved their swan-song but it had an effect. Even after the Iraqi rebels had been forced to flee, along with their Axis friends and advisers, 4 FTS at Habbaniya formed a nucleus of a fighter squadron with twelve Gladiators and six Hurricanes, which was designated as 'X' Flight and commanded by Flying Officer Kenneth Henry Osborne Young. This unit flew to Amman, Transjordan, on 7 June 1941 to protect the British Relief Column en route to Baghdad against any more surprises.

Syria

The Vichy-French regime in Syria had been aiding the rebels and the Axis in every way possible and Operation *Exporter* was mounted to crush their hold on Syria. The Gladiators were based at Mafraq landing ground and flew six-plane patrols at dawn each day. In one of the earliest dogfights on 15 June, a patrol was over Kissoué at 8,000ft (2,438.4m) when they were surprised by a force of modern monoplane Dewoitine D.520 fighters from the Vichy *Groupe de Chasse III/6*. Immediately the Gladiator of Flying Officer John Norman Craigie (serial K7947) was hit and crashed killing the pilot. A second Gladiator (serial K7914) flown by John Maxwell Watson, was damaged but managed to reach Amman. The Gladiators then got stuck in and in reply two of the D.520s were so badly damaged that they crash-landed on return to base and were write-offs. Three days later the roles were reversed and this time it was the French who were taken by surprise. Five Gladiators, led by Kenneth Henry Osborne Young, surprised seven D.520s of the same unit over Kissoué at 0952 on 18 June and destroyed two of them, one falling to the guns of Flight Lieutenant Arthur Frederick Appleby, before the rest fled.

With the fighting over in Syria Flight 'X' flew back to Habbaniya and disbanded, their Gladiators being absorbed into No. 261 Squadron

Sudan

With the battle for Italy's African colonial empire under way, 'B' Flight of No. 112 Squadron at Summit airfield, sixty miles west of Port Sudan, was re-designated as 'K' Flight on 1 September 1940. No. 112 had been based there since June, and the field was also used by Bristol Blenheims and Vickers Wellesley-1s in mid-1940. Gladiators were assigned, serials K6134, K6135, K6143, K7948, K7969, K7974, K7977 and K7986; later they were joined by three from No. 33 Squadron, serials L7612, L7614 and L7619; two former SAAF Gladiators, N5815 and N5828, and also another five machines, N5629, N5833, N5895, N5896 and N5917.

The former South African Gladiators clamed two 'kills' on 22 February 1941 Flight Lieutenant John Scoular destroyed a Savoia-Marchetti Sm79 bomber and on 26 February Pilot Officer Stanley Wells claimed a Fiat CR.42. However, losses were high, some were war casualties – on 6 November Fiat CR. 42s accounted for three Gladiators, K7969 was shot down near Gallabat, L7614 was shot down near Metemma and L7612 was damaged in the same action and crash-landed at Hawaton; and three were lost in accidents – K7986 crashed on take-off from Port Sudan on 15 September 1940, K7974 crashed and burnt on take-off at Port Sudan on 22 December 1940 and K6134 ran out of fuel and ditched off Suakin the following day.

Foreign operators

Australia

Just a single RAAF Squadron equipped with the Gladiator, this being No. 3 commanded by Squadron Leader Ian Douglas McLachlan, DFC RAAF, which on the outbreak of war had been flying Hawker Demons on Army Co-operation work. The squadron sailed for Egypt on 24 July 1940, and were based at Helwan, near Cairo, where they were assigned two flights of Gladiators and one of Westland Lysanders. The initial combat mission was on 19 November 1940 when the two Gladiator flights, conducting a reconnaissance sortie, were jumped by two groups of nine Fiat CR.42's each. The more experienced Italian pilots shot down Squadron Leader Peter Heath without loss to themselves. Their chief opponents were these Fiat CR.42's and they suffered heavily at their hands, losing N5752 , N5765 and N5766 over Sollum in one encounter on 13 December 1940.

Accidental losses included K6142, which was badly damaged when she crashed on take-off at Ikingi, Maryut, on 31 December and was sent to 51 RSU as irreparable; K7901, which was damaged landing at Tmimi and was also a write-off; K8009, which had two crashes on 8 February and 30 March; L7615, which crashed-landed with engine problems; N5763, which was damaged at Tobruk on 5 January; N5769, which made a forced landing at Helwan on 5 October; and N5799, which ground-looped at Bir Mella near Fort Nibeiwa, on 13 December.

The missions that followed were diverse and included strafing and dive-bombing sorties around Sofafi, and offensive patrolling at Sidi Barrani and Halfaya where the Italian land advance had stalled. No. 3 Squadron was then moved forward, first to Sidi Barrani and then to Sollum, Egypt, close to the Libyan border supporting 6 Australian Division. The counter-offensive by General Archibald Wavell kicked off early in January 1941 putting the Italians to flight, and No. 6 Squadron followed the rout, moving to Gambut airfield on 8 January and, once Tobruk had fallen, on across Cyrenaica. The Gladiators were constantly renewed from other units to keep the unit up to strength, and, in the meantime, the first of the Hawker Hurricanes that were to replace them, began to arrive in February. By 7 February, further moves had taken place and No. 6 was based at Benina, close to Benghazi where they remained for six weeks, and the Hurricanes had fully taken over.

The Australians also received a large number of Gladiators, most of which never saw combat. Those used, and their fates when known, are as follows:

Transferred from No. 30 Squadron – K7947, which was later transferred to 'X' Flight at Amman, Transjordan. Transferred from No. 33 Squadron – K7947, later transferred to 'X' Flight at Amman, Transjordan. N5752 was the mount of Flying Officer Alan Boyd who claimed to have destroyed four Fiat CR.42s with her, three on 19 November 1940 east of Rabia, Egypt, and a fourth north-west of Bir Sofafi on 12 December during Operation *Compass*. In turn he was shot down by CR.42s near Sollum on 13 December 1940. N5753, piloted by Flight Lieutenant Blake Pelly, was damaged in aerial combat east of Rabia on 19 November 1940 and crash-landed at Minqar Qaim, Egypt, and was later written off. N5756 was later transferred to the Metrological Flight at Khartoum, Sudan. N5764 was struck off on 16 December 1940; N5765 was shot down on 13 December 1940 with the loss of Flight Lieutenant Charles Burton Gaben RAAF; N5766 was shot down by Fiat CR.42s at Sollum, Libya, 13 December 1940; N5768 was struck off on 31 May 1941; N5769 crashed on 3 October 1940 by Helwan, Egypt; N5776 was later transferred to No. 80 Squadron; N5777 was later transferred to 'X' Flight at Amman, Transjordan; N5780 was transferred to No. 94 Squadron on 1 June 1943; N5782 was later transferred to No. 112 Squadron.

Transferred from No. 80 Squadron were serials K7901, which was written off after a crash-landing at Tmimi, Libya, on 24 January 1941; K7913, which was later transferred to No. 1411 Flight; K8008, later transferred to the Meteorological Flight at El Adem and crash-landed there on 26 January 1943; K8009, later transferred to No. 51 Repair and Salvage Unit (RSU); K8022, while being flown at 2,000ft by Flying Officer James Chippindale Campbell in a flight of five, as air cover for 19 Australian Brigade, was bounced by five Fiat G.50*bis*. Three Fiats were damaged and four Gladiators, while Campbell was killed, the last Gladiator loss suffered by No. 3 Squadron; N5763 was disposed of at Gerawla, Libya, on 5 January 1941.

Transferred from No. 94 Squadron was N5889, later transferred to No. 33 Squadron. Transferred from No. 112 Squadron were serials K6142 which crashed during take-off at Ikingi, Maryut, near Alexandria, Egypt, on 31 December 1940; L7893, which later transferred to No. 1411 Flight and was lost on 20 July 1942; K7922, later transferred to the SAAF; K7963, which on 25 January 1941 piloted by Flight Lieutenant Allan Rawlinson damaged two Fiat G.50*bis* fighters, later transferred to No. 1411 Flight; K8048 later transferred to No. 127 Squadron; L7615, which was struck off charge on 21 April 1941; L7616, later transferred to the Wadi Halfa Flight and then to the Iraqi Conversion Flight; N5857, later transferred to No. 123 Squadron. Transferred from No. 274 Squadron were serials N5750, which was destroyed by Fiat CR42s east of Rabia, Libya, with the loss of Squadron Leader P R Heath; N5786, later transferred to No. 80 Squadron; N5810, later transferred to No. 112 Squadron.

Other Gladiator serials that served with No. 3 Squadron were L7617, L8008, which was struck off in January 1941; L8009, later transferred to No. 80 Squadron; L8022, which was shot down in combat with the Fiat G.50*bis* aircraft from *20 Gruppo CaT* on 25 January 1941 with the loss of Pilot Officer Campbell; and N5878.[9]

Belgium

The Belgians ordered twenty-two Gloster Gladiator-I aircraft for *l'Aviation Militaire* on 27 September 1936 to be powered by the 825hp (615.20kW) Bristol Mercury IX engine, and these began to be delivered as early as September, fifteen direct from Gloster while it was also hoped to produce the remaining seven at the *Sociétés Anonyme Belge de Constructions Aéronautques* (SABCA) Brussels plant, under licence in Belgium. The whole order was to be completed by the end of the year. However, no satisfactory resolution was reached on this, although talks were not finally abandoned until May 1938.

The Gladiators therefore arrived in Belgian in fits and starts, the first batch of six machines being delivered in June 1937 and the first of the second assignment of nine arrived in September of the same year. They were given the registrations G5-1 to G5-15. SABCA-assembled machines first appeared at the end of March 1938, receiving the serials G-17 to G-38. The Belgians soon became familiar with the new fighter and the public also was shown its potential in a series of air shows flown prominently by *Captaine* Pierre Arend (G-343), *Adjutant* Jacques Jean Edouard Wegria (G-27) and *Sergents* Paul-Marie Janssens (G-21), Nathalie Delorme (G-31) and Denys Rolin (G-24).

Several of these machines were lost in accidents before the war; on 18 March 1938, G-35 went into an uncontrollable spin and crashed into the North Sea off Wenduine, although on this occasion the pilot was saved, while G-17 was lost on 9 December 1939 because the oxygen equipment failed and she crashed at Wevelgem (Ingelmuster), killing her pilot, *Sergent* Hubert Dopagne. G-35, piloted by *Sergent* Carlos Pipart, made a terminal descent at Seene airfield, Ostend, on 11 March 1940, possibly for the same reasons. On 14 March G-20 and G-23 collided at Schaffen, and on 18 March G-35 was lost off Ostende. A further five were out of service when war suddenly came upon them, including G-18, an unarmed aircraft belonging to *Général* Paul Hiernaux, the Commander-in-Chief of *Aéronautique Militaire Belge (AéMI)*, which had been allocated to the unit at Diest.

On 10 May 1940, there was an establishment strength of fifteen Gladiators, fourteen being with the *1ére Escadrille de Chasse*, of I*éme* Group of 2 Regiment (*1/I/2 Aé*) and lined up at Schaffen-Diest airfield along with about 50 per cent of Belgium air power. Even though they had been on General Alert for the previous three days, they had all been stood down at 1030 on 9 May thinking it was yet another false alarm and the majority of the pilots had gone for R&R in Diest itself. The alarms sounded at 0300 on 10 May and by 0400 the majority of the aircraft (Hawker Hurricanes, Gloster Gladiators and Fairy Fox bombers) had been quietly readied and, on the orders of Major Arro Hendricks[10] remained in orderly lines before their hangars awaiting events. They were not long in coming.

Shortly afterwards heavy formations of aircraft were seen overhead flying west, and the feeling was that the British and Germans were duelling over the English Channel. Few at the base appeared to think there was anything to worry about! One would think that with the fates of Denmark and Norway starkly before them the shield of neutrality might have appeared rather fragile, but this seems not to have been the case. The Gladiators were told to take off by *Capitaine* Max Guisgand, CO of 1/I/2, against orders, to prevent being caught flat-footed, and by 0420 had started to do so. Before they were all airborne, a *kette* of *KG 77*'s low-flying Dornier Do.17 bombers appeared and began strafing. One Gladiator, piloted by Lieutenant Marcel Wilmots, was hit on the runway, and skidded into a Hawker Hurricane, being so badly damaged she was written off. The Germans turned their attention to the orderly lines and were soon reinforced by wave after wave. At 0442 another German attack commenced with Do.17s bombing from an altitude of 6,000ft (1,828.80m) and Bf.110s strafing, finishing off Wilmots' aircraft and destroying a second Gladiator that had failed to get off the ground. At 0530 a third wave hit. After they had departed the Belgian machines had been reduced to blazing hulks; just two Hawker Hurricanes and three Gloster Gladiators survived the carnage on the ground. Meanwhile, while over Tirlemont, the airborne Gladiators ran into ten of *3./JG 27*'s Bf.109s at 0955 and these claimed to have destroyed two of the Belgians, while, at 1033, *9./JG 54* with more Bf.109s hit them again above Tongeren, and claimed another three destroyed. Twelve Gladiators managed to land at Beauvechain.

The next day six Gladiators, led by *Capitaine* Guisgand (G-27), with *Sergents* André Pirlot (G-19), A. Vanden Broeck (G-31), Denys Rolin (G-22), Henry Wiand (G-32) and Henri Clinquart (G-34), were assigned to escort nine Fairey Battle light bombers making suicidal attacks against bridges over the Albert Canal, which were in German hands. Again they found the *1./JG 21* ready and waiting and in the ensuing *mêlée* four more Gladiators, G-19, G-22, G-27, G-34, were shot down. *Sergents* André Pirlot and Henri Clinquart were both killed, *Sergent* Denys Roslin baled out and was made a PoW, while *Capitaine* Max Guisgand crash-landed at Waremme. Both of the remaining pair of Gladiators were damaged but not beyond repair. Three further aircraft were damaged in the battle but returned and were deemed capable of repair, however all these, including G-31, G-31 and G-38, were caught on the ground at Le Culot (Beauvcechain), by twelve fighters from the *I./JG 1*, strafed and destroyed.

That same afternoon a further seven Gladiators were shot down by Bf.109s and another was destroyed by a Heinkel He.111 bomber. The damaged machines were simply abandoned during the following night when the unit evacuated to Belsele.

China

Throughout the 1930s China was pillaged by Japanese incursion from the north and east, and by the ongoing civil war between the Nationalist *Kuomintang* (KMT) and the Communists under Mao Tse-tung, backed by the Soviet Union, and these campaigns grew fiercer and more costly as the decade progressed. The government of Chiang Kai Shek did everything it could to obtain modern military aircraft from any source it could, but they increasingly found that placing orders was one thing, but that actually obtaining the aircraft themselves was another. Japan was by far and away the dominant power and could exert influence with threats and cohesion not only on its natural allies, Germany and Italy (although they found ways around it) but also on Great Britain, increasingly estranged from its old ally Japan, and distracted by events in Europe. As most of the aircraft destined for China passed through British Hong Kong, this made for a frustrating scenario as is recorded elsewhere in these pages.

The Chinese Government ordered a total of thirty-six Gladiator-I aircraft in 1937, originally to have been armed with the Mk.V Vickers machine-guns, for delivery in December, but the American-built Browning was preferred due to the high availability of the .30-6 Springfield ammunition in general Chinese use. The aircraft duly arrived by sea at Hong Kong in January 1938, and were joined by a party of Gloster mechanics and test pilots to oversee their assembly and testing at the RAF's Kai Tak airfield before they flew up-country. This plan fell through because of intense Japanese diplomatic pressure on Britain, which forced the abandonment of any technical assistance of that nature. Instead the Gladiators had to be sent from Kowloon to Guangzhou by rail and then laboriously transferred to Pearl River junks, which took them on to their destination. The actual assembly of the first twenty machines was carried out at Shougouling airfield, Tienhe, but others were put together at a variety of locations to avoid destruction by the Japanese air forces. The second batch of sixteen were likewise kept in reserve to replace losses. Even when assembled successfully these machines were flown to dispersal landing fields until sufficient pilots had familiarized themselves with the type. Even this proved problematical and several were written off during training.

These aircraft served with 5 Fighter Group, the No. 17 Pursuit Squadron, commanded by Captain John Wong, and received four aircraft (serials 1701 to 1704 inclusive), which they used along with Russian I-15s, working over the Chuyung Pass, Nanking; Xi'an, Shaanxi; Hankow (Hanchou) and Xinyang, Henan Province. No. 28 Pursuit Squadron, commanded by Captain Chan Kee-Wong, (serials 2801 to 2814 inclusive) received fourteen, and No. 29 Pursuit Squadron (serials 2901 to 2917 inclusive) received seventeen Gladiators, which they flew from Canton (now Gunzhou); Hengyang, Hunan; Changsha, Hunan; and Nanchang, Jiangxi Province, while, in 1938, No. 32 Pursuit Squadron (serials 3201 to 3209 inclusive and 5723 and 5732) received eleven machines and were led by Squadron-Leader Captain Zhu Jia-Xon.

By February the first Gladiators were ready for combat but their first sortie was inauspicious; eleven Gladiators from 28 Pursuit Squadron from Heng Yang, Hunan, were guided to Nanchang, Jiangxi, by Commander Wong Pan-yang, CO 5 Group. Their mission turned to disaster when they flew into a snowstorm *en route*. Wong, flying a Vought V-92C, turned back but the Gladiators pressed on only for two machines, Major 'Arthur' Chin Shui-Tin (serial no. 2801) and Chou Yung-Shu, to crash while a third, Chou Ling-Hsu (serial 2810) had to make a forced landing. A victory was achieved on 24 February when Captain John Wong Sun-Shui, destroyed a Mitsubishi A5M near Nanking. Their next encounter was on 31 May, when they engaged nine

Nakajima E8N Navy fighters from the seaplane carrier *Kamikawa Maru* over Hukou, destroying two and damaging a third.

On 16 June while working out of Xiawei eight Gladiators located six Mitsubishi Ki-21 Type 97 ('Sally') heavy bombers over Xixin, Fujian, and attacked with the advantage of height and surprise, shooting down three and damaging five of them, but in the process they lost two Gladiators, Kwan Yensum (serial no. 2811) and Shen Mu-Hsiu (serial no. 2814). On 3 August eleven Gladiators, working with 4 Pursuit Group, joined a force of more than fifty Chinese fighters, which engaged a force of eighteen G3Ms protected by seventy fighters *en route* to Hankow. They destroyed three Mitsubishi A-5Ms, one by Chin Shui-Tin a ramming attack that he survived but lost three of their Gladiators. No. 28 Pursuit Squadron was moved over to the 3 Pursuit group on 1 October 1938 and sent by rail to Lanchou for re-training on the Polikarpov I-15*bis*, while their surviving Gladiators were despatched to Liu-Chow (Liuzhou) to be refitted.

Attrition was high both from combat, ten aircraft (serials 2803, 3811, 2812, 2184, 2902, 2905, 3909, 2910, 3206 and 5723) and accident, six aircraft (serials 2801, 2805, 2808, 2809, 2905 and 2907) with a further five damaged (serials 2810, 2901, 2907, 2908 and 2917) and thus, by September 1938, the majority of the Gladiators had been written off or were inoperational, with only a remote chance of receiving spare parts due to the embargo. The surviving Gladiators continued in a combat profile under the leadership of Major Chin Shui-Tin, including Fan Hsin-Min (serial No. 2805), Shen Mushiu (serial no. 2804) and Louie Yim-Qun (serial 5732), during the so-called 'Guerrilla Campaign' of August to December 1939, flying out of Kwangsi.

Not until the summer of 1939 were the refitted Gladiators collected in batches from Liu-Chow and taken back to Lanchou. On 1 August Chin Shui-Tin had just collected one such batch of refreshed Gladiators from Liu-chow and had flown them back to Lanchou, just in time for the next day the Japanese launched an attack on Kwangsi, Guangxi. On 2 November the Gladiators damaged a Mitsubishi C5M, Type 98 ('Babs') reconnaissance aircraft over Wuming, Nanning, airfield, and in December Chin Shui-Tin claimed to have destroyed a bomber above Kwangsi. His final Gladiator mission took place on 27 December 1939 when two of them, along with a No. 32 Pursuit Squadron Polikarpov I-15*bis,* flew escorts for three Soviet 'Volunteer' Tupolev SB bombers but were ambushed by Japanese Mitsubishi A5M's from the 14 *Kokutai* under Ensign Kazu-o Muranaka. The CO of 32 Pursuit Squadron, Wei Yi-Ging in a Gladiator, was shot down and killed, the I-15*bis* crashed-landed and Chin himself was hit, his aircraft turning into a blazing torch, which he steered back over Chinese lines at Nanning and baled out, suffering bad burns.

Three Gladiators ended their brief flying careers as fighter trainers and the last known Chinese Gladiator was destroyed in December 1939.[11]

Egypt
The Anglo-Egyptian Treaty of 22 August 1936 contained a Defence Agreement that promised British help to modernize the Royal Egyptian Air Force, which had been formed in 1930 as part of the Army and became an independent air arm in its own

right in 1937. As a result the Egyptian Government purchased eighteen later-series Gladiator-Is from the last production batch of that type (RAF serials L8005 and L8012 to L8028 inclusive). These aircraft were all modified up to Mark II standard and tropicalized at the RAF's No. 27 Maintenance Unit (MU) at Shawbury, near Shrewsbury, from January 1939 onward prior to being delivered in April 1939. They were re-assigned the Egyptian Serials K1331 to K1348 inclusive. These machines equipped No. 2 at Almaza and No. 5 Royal Egyptian Air Force squadrons at Suez commanded by Flight Lieutenant Mohammed Abou Zaid.

In 1940 it was decided to purchase an additional batch of eighteen Gladiators from the RAF surplus stock and serials N5875 to N5892 were transferred, receiving Egyptian serials L9020 to L9047 inclusive. As the war progressed further Gladiators were transferred to and fro, including N5755, N5758, N5760, N5762, N5767 and N5771 from the RAF to Egypt on 23 January 1941 and K8016, which was transferred on 1 March 1944. An ambiguous unit was the RAF's No. 1411 (Meteorological) Flight, which was attached to Headquarters RAF Middle East, but was a wholly Egyptian piloted and maintained unit, with REAF markings

Gladiator movements in the other direction: K1340 and K1344 were returned back to the RAF for use with No. 1414 (Meteorological) Flight at Eastleigh, Kenya, and K1341 to No. 1413 (Meteorological) Flight in the Levant. Four further Egyptian machines, N5887, N5889, N5890 and N5892, were taken over by No. 94 Squadron for a period, before returning to Egyptian service in May 1941; likewise two more, N5755 and N5891, were taken over by No. 33 Squadron, N5876 by No. 80 Squadron and N5760 by No. 112 Squadron and N5888, which was also taken over by the RAF and destroyed in combat by CR.42s at Sollum on 19 June 1941.

Both Egyptian Gladiator squadrons remained intact until 1943 when the main dangers had long passed, and were gradually replaced by Hawker Hurricanes, before being finally downgraded to subsidiary duties from 1945 onward.

Finland

The unwarranted Soviet invasion of Finland on 30 November 1939 by the Soviet Union after Stalin's demands for concessions (which became known as 'The Winter War') had been rejected led to world-wide sympathy for that little nation set upon by the rapacious communist state[12] and even though the British and French had been at war with Germany for some time, help was immediately sent. On 12 December 1939 thirty Gladiator-IIs, serial nos. N5584, N5683, N5686, N5687, N5688, N5689, N5691, N5692, N5694, N5688, N5689, N5691, N5692, N5694, N5696, N5700, N5704, N5706, N5707, N5708, N5709, N5710, N5711, N5712, N5713, N5715, N5718, N5721, N5722, N5724, N5726, N5727, N5728, and N5729, were purchased, of which ten were outright donations to the Finns.

These aircraft were partially assembled and shipped over to Sweden where they were completed at the *Centrala Flgverkstaden* at Malmslätt and then flown up to the Swedish airfield at Barkarby *Flygstation* near Akalia, north of Stockholm. This airfield was the base of Sweden's F8 fighter unit and they oversaw the transfer of the Gladiators

1. Avia B-534s lined up on a Czech airfield. The product of a small national aircraft industry, she nonetheless saw a surprising amount of action.

2. An Avia B-534 of the 12 *Letka*, Slovakian Air Force. They served on the Eastern Front against the Soviets from 1941, but later briefly operated for Stalin's cause when the tide eventually turned.

3. Fairey TSR Swordfish with floats, of No. 700 NAS, being hoisted back aboard the battleship HMS *Malaya* in October 1941. Although showing but marginal improvement over British torpedo-bombers like the Cuckoo of 1918, the Swordfish had an incredible war record.

4. Fairey Swordfish wearing D-Day 'Invasion Stripes' for her anti-U-boat, anti-*S-boot* and anti-midget submarine operations of 1944–45.

5. The Fairey Albacore, showing how her wings folded back for stowage in aircraft carrier hangars. Fairey submitted much more modern designs originally, but the Air Ministry rejected them all, and even at one point in 1940, stated they considered her to be the equivalent of the Junkers Ju.88!

6. The Fairey Albacore. Introduced as a replacement for the Swordfish, she did introduce a few, minor, improvements, but she was obviously obsolete before she ever joined the Fleet, and half the output went straight to reserve units and was never employed. Her performance proved so indifferent that her predecessor far outlived her in service.

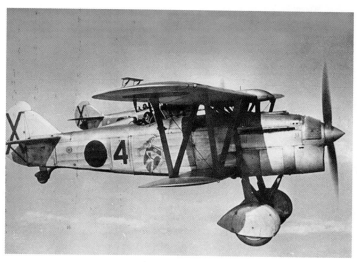

7. Fiat CR.32 fighter planes of the *Baleari Gruppo* with Spanish Civil War markings. This lithe little aircraft fostered the myth in Italy that there was still a major place for the biplane in the front line, a myth that the war in the Mediterranean soon terminated.

8. The Fiat CR.32 was popular with her pilots, and proved highly agile in the air. She earned herself a great reputation pre-war, but was soon phased out of service after 1940 when her limitations were shown.

9. The Fiat CR.42 *Falco* was the Italian equivalent of the British Gloster Gladiator, and in some ways a superior aircraft, especially in manoeuvrability. She was produced late and, due to hold-ups in monoplane developments in Italy, was still the mainstay of their fighter force in 1940 when most other major air forces were converting to the monoplane. The CR.42 suffered accordingly, although in combat with the likes of the Fairey Fulmar, she frequently emerged the victor.

10. A captured Fiat CR.42 *Falco* overpainted in British markings, parked at a snowy RAF Duxford. In duels in the Mediterranean and North Africa, the CR.42 proved able to out-turn both the Fairey Fulmar and the Hawker Hurricane, while being an even match for the Gloster Gladiator. In her brief appearance at the tail end of the Battle of Britain, however, she was completely out of her depth.

11. The Gloster Gauntlet had left front-line service in the RAF by the outbreak of war. Nonetheless she was pressed back into service in North Africa in 1940 as the RAF's 'Answer to the Stuka!' This is an early prototype machine.

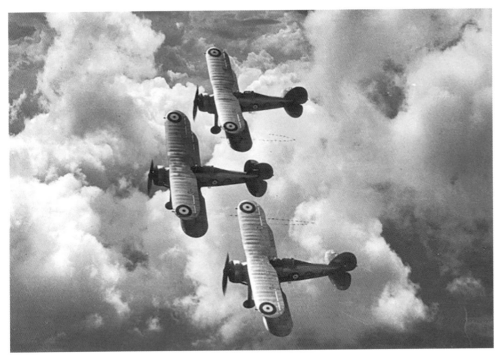

12. The Gloster Gladiator earned fame pre-war for her aerobatics at air shows in the UK and overseas, including many European capitals. Here a flight from No. 87 Squadron RAF performs its famous routine, linked together in 1937.

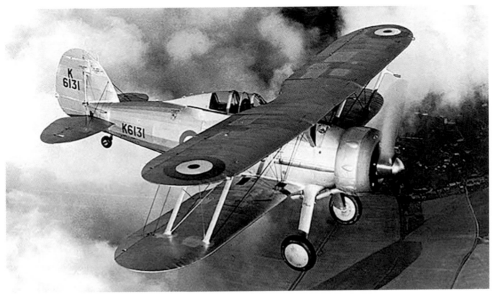

13. The Gloster Gladiator, although totally outclassed by aircraft like the Messerschmitt Bf.109 and 110, still served in some front-line units of the RAF and FAA in 1940 and 1941. She also served with a wide variety of air forces on combat missions from the Nordic countries to Portugal, Greece and South Africa, and both Nazi Germany and the Soviet Union made some use of the ubiquitous Gladiator.

14. A Gloster Gladiator at Malta, known to the Maltese as *Faith*, serial number N5520. It was one of very few operational Gladiator fighter aircraft able to dispute the air space over the Island with the *Regia Aeronautica* in June 1940. The fuselage of *Faith* still survives to this day at the Malta War Museum, at Fort St.Elmo.

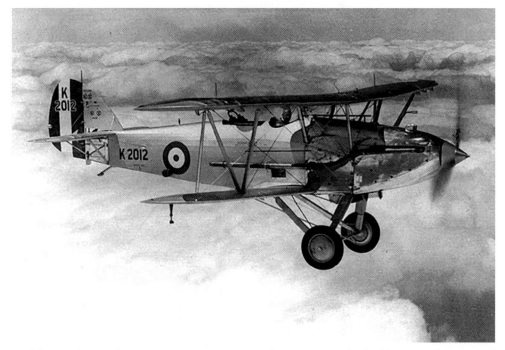

15. The Hawker Audax Army Co-operation aircraft. It was one of a highly successful string of 1930s light bombers from the same manufacturer, which included the Hart, Hind, Hector, Hardy, Hartebeest, Nimrod and Nisr. The Audax variant saw combat in British's 'Colonial' episodes of World War II – including the rebellion in Iraq, the pro-Nazi insurrection in Iran, and operations in Somalia and Ethiopia against the Italians.

16. Hawker Audax Army Co-operation bomber. The Audax saw widespread usage on the fringes of Empire in the Middle East and East Africa. This machine belonged to No. 16 Squadron, RAF, in the late 1930s, and features the gold and black cross keys, symbolizing unlocking enemy secrets by day and by night.

17. Hawker Fury fighters of No. 15 Squadron, RAF, stacked up. This delicate little aircraft was the first RAF fighter to fly at more than 200mph (320km/h). Although outdated by 1939, she saw service with several foreign air forces during WWII.

18. The lone Norwegian Air Force Hawker Fury. Norway took delivery of just one machine in 1933 for evaluation, but, after trials, plans to home-produce the type under licence were abandoned in 1936 in favour of the Gladiator.

19. The Heinkel He.50. The first purpose-built dive-bomber for the Luftwaffe, this is an early example, D-IMAA, in her pre-war guise. Rapidly replaced in operational units, first by the Henschel Hs.123 and then the Junkers Ju.87 Stuka, the He.50 still had a meaningful combat role in World War II as a close-support aircraft.

20. The Heinkel He.50, another early model, D-IMOE. The type was a development of an Imperial Japanese Navy order from the Heinkel GmbH, which went on to become the first Aichi D1A naval dive-bomber in Japan. The He.50 itself went on to serve on the Eastern Front in World War II.

21. The Heinkel He.59. Among her many roles was that of air-sea rescue (*Seenot*) duty, which began in the Baltic and later extended to the North Sea, the English Channel and the Mediterranean. These aircraft rescued more Allied aircrew than German, but Churchill ordered that they all be shot down and many were.

22. A Finnish Heinkel He.59. Heavy, solid and reliable, the He.59 was a stalwart, especially in the Luftwaffe's float-plane armoury, despite her mundane performance. Her missions included mine-laying, special operations transport during the invasion of Holland, and reconnaissance over the Arctic. The Finnish Air Force operated four of them in the period 1943–44.

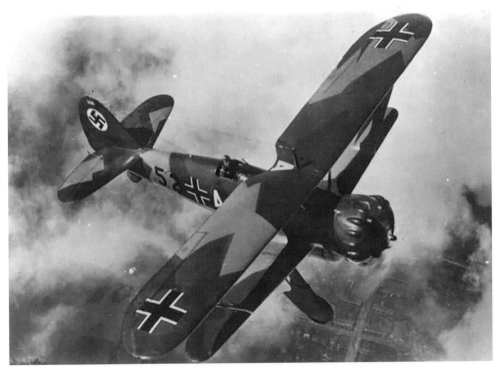

23. The Henschel Hs.123. She wears the Luftwaffe's 'splinter' camouflage pattern. During the Polish campaign she was highly regarded as a ground-attack aircraft and continued on front-line service for many years on the Eastern Front.

24. The Henschel Hs.123. This is the first prototype, V01, D-ILUA (*Werke No.* 265), which first flew on 8 May 1935. Indifferent as a dive-bomber, she proved so successful as a ground-attack machine in the Polish campaign and on the Eastern Front that a new production run was called for, but, by that time, all the jigs had been destroyed.

25. A Nakajima E8N *Dave*, being hoisted aboard a Japanese cruiser in April 1939. Photo from the US National Archives, showing the return of the body of the Japanese Ambassador Hirosi Saito to Japan aboard the US heavy cruiser *Astoria* after his demise, via www.ussastoria.org.

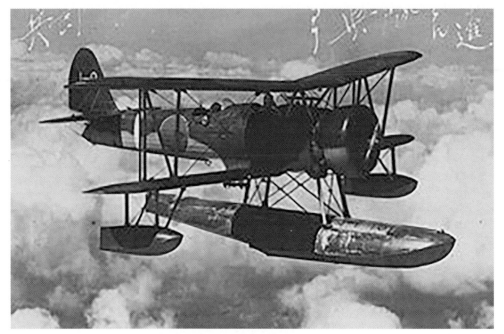

26. The Nakajima E8N *Dave*. She proved an agile and nimble fighter aircraft, despite her floats, but was outclassed by US Navy carrier types at Guadalcanal and beyond.

27. The Polikarpov I-15 *Chaika* (Seagull), so named because of her central upper wing form. Despite her tubby appearance she was highly regarded in the late 1930s, but by World War II had become totally outclassed.

28. The Polikarpov I-15 *Chaika* on a forward airstrip. Those that survived the initial Luftwaffe onslaught of June 1941 were pressed into service in the ground-attack role.

29. The Polikarpov Po-2. This little crop-sprayer turned out to be a hidden gem, her very obsolescence being turned into a multi-role versatile combat aircraft and all-rounder, including air ambulance, liaison machine and night harassment unit. She belied all rational ideas by proving to be one of the longest-serving of all combat biplanes.

30. The Polikarpov Po-2, Derided as the *Mule* by incredulous NATO experts, this seemingly unpretentious aircraft was to prove a thorn in the side of the United States during the Korean war. Too slow for jet aircraft to shoot down without stalling themselves, her fragile frame was also almost radar proof. In essence she could be said in some ways to have been the first 'stealth' bomber!

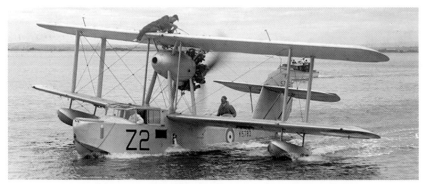

31. Supermarine Walrus coasting along in pre-war livery. This aircraft belonged to the New Zealand manned light cruiser *Leander* and was lost in an accident in July 1939. This official photograph was taken by the late Allan C Greene (1878–1954).

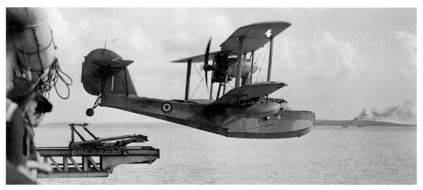

32. A Supermarine Walrus being catapulted from the light cruiser *Bermuda* in 1943. By this period of the war, the widespread introduction of escort carriers was making such cumbersome shipborne aircraft redundant, save for ASR work in the East.

33. The Vickers Vildebeest torpedo-bomber – the RAF's defender of Singapore. This lumbering anachronism contrasted starkly with the Imperial Japanese Navy's land-based Mitsubishi G3M and G4M long-range bombers that so quickly dispatched the battleship *Prince of Wales* and the battle-cruiser *Repulse*. In fact, the Vildebeest only saw limited action and then never in her designed role but with small bombs.

34. A Vickers Vildebeest dropping a practice torpedo. The design, as appears obvious, dated back to 1926, but the British Government still expected them to defend the Singapore naval base from Japanese attack in December 1941.

35. A Walrus on her catapult aboard the New Zealand-manned light cruiser *Achilles* at Suva, Fiji Islands, in February 1942.

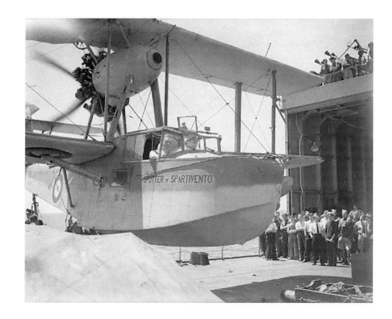

36. Another Walrus, named after an earlier battle, being winched back aboard the light cruiser *Sheffield*.

across the border to Finland in batches between 18 January and 16 February 1940 secretly in order not to compromise Swedish neutrality.[13]

These Gladiators, which were given the Finnish serials GL-251 to GL-280 inclusive, were readied from January 1940 onward and were assigned to the *LentoLaivue* (*LeLv* – Air Squadron), eventually serving with *LeLv12*, *LeLv14*, *LeLv16* and *LeLv26*. The latter unit, commanded by *Majuri* (Major) Jean William Raoul Harju-Jeanty, part of the *Lentorykmentti 2* (Air Regiment 2) commanded by *Kapteeni* (Captain) Erkki Heinillä, based at Heinjoki with Bristol Bulldog IVAs, was the first to fly them, receiving the first batch of thirteen Gladiators on 18 January and a second delivery of seventeen in February. By 1 February the operational base of Utti, Kouvola, had 1 *Lentue,* under *Luutantti* (Lieutenant) Pekka Siiriäinen with four Gladiators on strength and 2 *Lentue* under *Luutantti* Ensio Kivinen with seven. They were fitted with ski undercarriages and operated from frozen lakes most successfully. Their first brush with the enemy occurred on 2 February when *Luutnantti* Paavo Berg, flying from Littoinen, Turku, engaged six Polikarpov I-153s over Hangö Stad (Hanko) and destroyed one of them. In total *LeLv 26* flew over six hundred combat sorties and destroyed thirty-four Soviet aircraft, for the lost of thirteen, with six pilots killed. With the arrival of the G-50s the unit distributed its Gladiators to *LeLv 12* and *LeLv 16*.

LentoLaivue 12, commanded by *Majuri* Oskar Holm, began to receive Gladiators from *LeLv 26* from 12 February onward. Two *Lentue* were equipped with this little fighter, 1 *Lentue* operating GL-270, 271, 272, 275 and 277, while 2 *Lentue* used GL-253, 255, 256 and 264. They mainly used their Gladiators for aerial reconnaissance work, monitoring the advance of the overwhelming Soviet land forces across the Suurjoki River and over the Gulf of Vyborg, which was frozen solid. Later they operated in the same manner off the Bay of Viipuri and the Karelian Isthmus acting as fighter cover for the slower Fokker C.X. machines and also carrying out staffing missions. In total the Gladiators carried out sixty-seven operational sorties before the war ended with the signing of the dictated 'Peace of Moscow' in March. However, it was not until 4 July that the unit gave up its Gladiators and replaced them with the export version of the Curtiss P-36 Hawk monoplane fighter, the Curtiss H-75.

The *LentoLaivue 14,* commanded by *Kapteeni* Jaakko Moilanen, was part of *Lentorykmentti 1,* and took delivery of its first Gladiator on 13 February. With six Gladiators on strength they began patrols over the eastern Karelian Isthmus. Fitted with a pair of 110lb (50kg) bombs, three 55lb (25kg) bombs and six 7.7lb (3.5kg) bombs, the Gladiators attacked and strafed the heads of the Soviet columns pushing up from their beachhead at Vilaniemi Bay on 5 March. That same day they claimed their first kill, *ylikersantti* (Staff Sergeant) Martti Perälä, destroying a Polikarpov I-153 at Äyräpää, (Pölläkkälä), whose crash was confirmed by the enemy. Another success was scored on 7 March, *Luutnantti* Tauno Ollikainen flying GL-279 led six Gladiators GL-273, GL-274, GL-276, GL-278 and GL-279, covering Finnish troops at Tienhaara, north of Vipuri, and shot down at least one I-153. The unit flew a total of thirty-four combat sorties during the war, until, on 9 July, they exchanged their Gladiators for Curtiss H-75A monoplane fighters.

The other post-Winter War Gladiator-equipped unit was *Lentolaivue 16,* commanded by *Kapteeni* Vilhelm Viherto but they saw no combat until Operation *Barbarossa* got underway in June 1941.

In addition to these thirty aircraft, twelve extra Gladiator-Is were made available by Sweden later as well as a Swedish Volunteer unit. Again F8 at Barkaby was given the responsibility for setting the clandestine *Flygflottilj 19* (F19 squadron of the Swedish Volunteer Corps) to aid their Finnish cousins. This unit comprised twelve Gloster Gladiators, five Hawker Hart light bombers and three transport machines, which the Swedish Government allowed the Finns to fly. These machines remained Swedish property but wore the Finnish nationality markings. The serials and codes of the F19 Gladiators were: 268/F8-38; 271/F8-41; 274/F8-44; 275/F8-45; 276/F-8-46; 278/F8-48; 279/ F8-49; 281/F8-51; 282 /F-8-52; 283-/F8—53; 284/F8-54 and 285/F8-55. Of these Swedish Gladiators, serial 274 was destroyed during a test flight on 10 March 1940 and *ingenjörlöjtant* (Engineering-Lieutenant) Åke Hildinger was killed, while serials 281 and 282 were both lost in Finland on 23 January and 20 February 1940.

A second group of Swedish Gladiator was later formed at Barkaby but the war ended in March 1940, before they could be deployed in combat.

The Continuation War

In June 1941, in what became known as 'The Continuation War' whereby the Finns joined in Germany's assault on Russia in order to regain their lost territories, the Gladiators also saw combat service once more with *Lentolaivue 16,* whose command by this date had passed to *Majuri* Risto Pajari at Kuopio *Lentokentta* (airfield), Rissala. Their initial assignment was providing fighter cover, reconnaissance, aerial photography and ground-attack missions for the Finnish Army of Karelia. Here the 1 *Lentue* had six Gloster Gladiators commanded by *Kapteeni* Harri Pursiainen. They transferred base to Joensuu, Lipen, and worked from the hard beach of Lake Höytiäinen, north Karelia. They operated over the old Tolvajärvi battlefield of the Winter War and clashed with I-153s once more, without loss, but Soviet flak gunners nailed GL-267 at Suvilahdessa on 17 July. By August the five surviving Gladiators were flying from Uomaa, Russia, north of Lake Ladoga. Here they took further losses, *vänrikki* (2nd Lieutenant) Toivo Purhonen being shot down by MiG-3s on 18 September, before moving base again far to the north at Solomanni, Äänislinna (Petrozanodsk or Petroskoi) at Lake Onega on 9 October 1941.

By 6 December the unit had a new commander, *Kapteeni* Kyösti Kurimo, but only two Gladiators remained and one of these was destroyed in a bad weather accident on 19 January 1942. *LLv 12* and *LeLv16* combined forces in the Maaselkä command at the end of February and with their combined few remaining Gladiators continued reconnaissance missions near frozen-over Lake Onega. By May the six Gladiators formed just one *Lentue* of the 1/*LeLv 16* and on 9 May they made bombing and staffing attacks on Soviet supply barges at Ustjenkylä on the Vodla River dropping seven 220lb (100kg), sixteen 33lb (15kg) incendiaries and fourteen 27lb (12.5kg) bomblets. More Gladiators arrived and enabled the formation of a 2 *Lentue* with three aircraft led by *Luutnantti* Mikael Somppi, and these were based in the south, at Hirvas west of Helsinki.

Losses continued: *2/LeLv 16* had GL-264 destroyed by AA fire near Särkijärvi on 9 July, and *1/LeLv 16* had another destroyed by accident on 2 September. Nonetheless the survivors carried on throughout the rest of the year and by January 1943, 1 *Lentue* moved to Viiksjäarvi and 2 *Lentue* to Kumsjärvi where they both flew missions over the Maaselkä Isthmus. But *Luutnantti* Hålam Strömberg was lost to suspected ground fire on 7 April and a second, GL-265, was lost in an engine failure on take-off from Vitska, Karhumäki on 21 June 1943. Combat was rare on this front throughout that year but Gladiators were still flying under the new commander, *Majuri* Oskar Holm, on 14 February when the unit became *TLeLv 16*.

Remarkably the Gladiators saw yet further action, losing GL-252 at Vitska on 11 June 1944 and having *Luttnantti* Aulis Kurki's GL-253 damaged in aerial fighting eight days later. 1 *Lentue* traded in its last three Gladiators for Polikarpov I-153s on 19 June 1944, while the last Finnish Gladiator combat sortie took place on 31 July 1944, before they were replaced, finally, by the home-designed and built *Valtion Lentokonetehdas* (VL) *Myrsky* ('Storm') monoplane reconnaissance/fighter. They had lost ten machines in total, and three pilots while achieving just one aerial victory.[14]

France

Although the Government of France conducted an armistice with the Germans and based itself at Vichy in the unoccupied area of their country, headed by collaborators and dupes like Marshal Henri Philippe Pétain and Pierre Laval, many Frenchmen chose to fight on. Some joined *Generale* Charles de Gaulle's 'Free-French' forces and others, not enamoured by either of these choices, joined British units to fight on for the liberation of their country. One such *Forces aériennes françaises libres* (Free-French squadron) was *Groupe de Chasse n° Alsace*, which was a Hawker Hurricane outfit, but in 1942 it featured six former No. 237 Squadron Gladiators on its establishment as advanced trainers. That squadron had one Flight equipped with Gladiator-IIs in March while in Sudan and used them for tactical reconnaissance, along with Westland Lysanders but on moving to the desert they had become surplus.

The Frenchmen had these painted up with the Cross of Lorraine and they subsequently served through until 1 May 1943. Among the known serials are K7937, a former No. 80 Squadron machine, which made a crash landing at Assuit, Egypt, on 26 June 1942 and spent months under repair at 58 RSU; N5824 and N5856.

The unit had abandoned these Gladiators earlier when it was reformed at RAF Turnhouse as No. 341 Squadron (*Groupe de Chasse n° 3/2 'Alsace'*), on 15 January 1943.

Germany

Former Latvian and Lithuanian Gladiators featured briefly on the strength of the Luftwaffe along with the odd captured machine from other sources. The Germans recorded that by 1 September 1941 they had acquired thirteen Gladiators of which eleven were fully airworthy or had suffered very little damage (*'Zustland I/II'*) with two more damaged, but capable of being fully restored at unit level (*'Kustland III'*). Many of these were the Latvian Gladiators overpainted with the Soviet Red Star and they arrived in a dismantled state at Langendiebach, Hanau. Whether any of the captured Norwegian or British Gladiators retrieved in Norway were considered worthy of shipment back to the Fatherland is possible, but doubtful. Mainly they appear to have been Mark Is fitted with fixed-pitch wooden propellers.

Ten of these machines were stripped down and repainted in Luftwaffe livery, and assigned new codes (NJ and later 1E) and also Luftwaffe serial numbers on transfer into the *Erganszungsgruppe (S)* (S = *Schlepp* – Towed) I unit. The *Erg. Gr. (S) 1* was based at Langendiebach between 1941 and 1943 and was a primary and operational training unit for Assault Glider pilots assigned to the DFS230. The 'Gloster's' role was that of glider tug and based at German training establishments along with an assortment of other types. Four were listed by the Quartermaster-General as being lost in this period, *Werke No.* 45829 crash-landed on 15 April 1942 receiving 45 per cent damage; *Werke No.* 45710 crash-landed on 13 June 1942, with 80 per cent damage; *Werke No.* 45717 crashed in March 1943 and *Werke No.* 45826 crashed near Babenhausen on 27 April 1943.

On 16 March 1943 those that survived were authorized for scrapping by the Luftwaffe authorities.[15]

Greece

Two Gladiator-Is were purchased directly from the Gloster Company by M. Zaparkis Hoimogenos (at a cost of £9,200) and presented as a gift to the Greek Government. They carried the serials Δ1 and Δ2. They served in the *Elleniki Vassiliki Aeroporia* (Royal Hellenic Air Force) in 1938 but were not operational when Italy invaded Greece from Albania on 28 October 1940. Not surprisingly Greece turned to Great Britain for assistance and on 2 December sixteen Egyptian-based RAF Gladiators sold to Greece were flown across the Mediterranean. These Gladiators were K8031, K8054, L7609, L7611 and L7623 from No. 112 Squadron, K8018, L7620 and L7621 from No. 33 Squadron, and K7892, K7923, K7971, K7973, K8013, K8017, K8047 and L8011 from No. 80 Squadron, which were handed over to the Greeks and the pilots returned to Egypt.

These Gladiators were assigned to *21 Mira,* based at Eleusis airfield, and commanded by *Sminagos* (Captain) Ioanis Kellas, who had previously been flying the PZL. P.24 fighter. Once the Greek pilots had familiarized themselves with their new aircraft they transferred to Yanina air base on 23 December. Further batches of Gladiators followed in a similar manner in 1941, with K6135 from 'K' Flight being transferred to Greece on 13 April, K7961 the following day being taken from No. 5 MU, K7988 and K7989 on 10 March and K7984, K7990 and K8033 on 14 March, with K7893 on 30 March, all these being provided by No. 52 MU. A final transfer was K8019, a former No. 112 Squadron aircraft, which went over on 13 April.[16]

The early arrivals soon began to make their presence felt and claimed to have destroyed ten and probably destroyed another three Axis aircraft in the period

8 January to 2 April 1941, but not all these were confirmed. Their own losses were four, *Hiposminagos* (Lieutenant) Anonios Papaioannou having his aircraft damaged beyond repair over Kakaβiá on the Albanian border on 9 February; *Anthiposminagos* (2nd Lieutenant) Anastasios Bardivilias being shot down by a CR.42 from 150° *Gruppo* at Katsika airfield, near Agrinio, Greece, on 11 February; *Episminias* (Master Sergeant) Konstantinos Chrizopoulos being shot down by a Fiat G.50*bis* on 23 February in the Këlcyrë – Rrethi I Devolit region of eastern Albania, and *Sminagos* (Captain) Ioanis Kellas being shot down by a Bf.109 from the *4./JG27* west of Tβíkaλa on 15 April.

Another four Gladiators joined these machines and all these former RAF aircraft retained their British serial numbers. The *21 Mira* moved to Paramythia airfield and subsequently worked from Kalambaka, Vassiliki, and by 16 April were operating from Amphiklia, Lodi, with eight Gladiators still operational with a very mixed group of aircraft. On 19 April the Greeks were surprised by an attacking force of Messerschmitt Bf.109Es. Just three survived and reached Eleusis but here two of those were shot up the following day by *II/JG 27*. By 30 April the whole of Greece was under Axis occupation and what remained of Greek air power had been evacuated.[17]

Iraq

Under their late 1930s modernization programme the *Al Quwwa al Jawwiya al Iraqiya* (Iraqi Air Force) 'acquired' fifteen Gladiator Is between 1937 and 1938 from surplus RAF stocks and allocated to them the serials 80 to 94 inclusive. The Iraqi air force based these at Mosul and Raschid airfields and later nine Gladiators were based at Kirkuk with the 2 (Fighter) Squadron. The British Aircraft Depot at RAF Habbaniyah provided necessary maintenance facilities. The RAF later resumed ownership of a few of these machines including K6141, K6147 and K7954.

Despite this, the Iraqis had no hesitation in turning them against the British at that base in May 1941, No. 2 Squadron claiming to have destroyed one British aircraft in the subsequent fighting. At the time No 2 Squadron had nine Gladiators operational at Kirkuk air base. Six of these made a strafing attack on Habbaniya runway on 2 May destroying two RAF Hawker Audax and one Airspeed Oxford on the ground. This was followed up by a bombing attack mounted by four Iraqi Savoia-Marchetti Sm.79B bombers, which were intercepted by a single RAF Gladiator piloted by Flying Officer Richard Cleaver. In another raid by Iraqi Breda Ba65's a second RAF Gladiator flown by Flying Officer John Norman Craigie, inflicted damage on one raider. When RAF Vickers Wellingtons of No. 70 Squadron attacked the enemy positions that same afternoon they were intercepted by two Iraqi Gladiators, without damage to either side.

Further Iraqi air attacks followed the next day; the S.79s returned and were again met by the Gladiator of Flying Officer Cleaver who claimed to have hit one and left her smoking and losing height. A similar result was obtained by another RAF Gladiator pilot, Flight Lieutenant Robert May, who tacked some Iraqi Northrop 84-4 ground-attack aircraft and again damaged one of them.

The Iraqi Gladiators scored a success on 4 May, when they intercepted an attack by eight Vickers Wellingtons against Raschid, destroying one of the bombers and damaging a second. An Iraqi Gladiator was destroyed on the ground at Baghdad the same day and another was damaged at Raschid on 5 May. Next day Habbaniya was attacked by a Northrop 84-4, which was damaged by a RAF Gladiator. On 7 May finally came a Gladiator-versus-Gladiator duel over Ba'quba and the RAF fighter, flown by Pilot Officer John Maxwell Watson, came out the victor.

Subsequently a further twenty-nine Gladiators of various types entered Iraqi service between 1942 and 1944. 'X' Flight turned over three Gladiators, K7907 on 6 December 1942, N5780 on 1 June 1943 and N5857 on 1 March 1944. The Iraqi Government used these aircraft internally, mainly to keep the ever-restive Kurdish tribesmen under control. Another three former RAF Gladiator-IIs were turned over to the Iraqis on 1 March 1944 that had been stored at Habbaniyah, N5825, N5828 and N5830; two of these latter aircraft remained in service at Mosul as late as 1949, one of them surviving until 1951.

Ireland

The Republic of Ireland (Eire) ordered four Gladiator-Is for the *an tAerchór* (Irish Air Corps) in 1937. When delivered the following year they were allocated the serials 23 to 26 inclusive and these were allocated to 'B' Flight of 1 Army Co-Operation Squadron, based at Baldonnel (Casemate) airfield in south-west Dublin. They served here between 1938 and 1940, becoming No. 1 Fighter Squadron in 1939. One of this quartet, serial 23, was damaged early on in a landing accident and never subsequently flew again.

A further order for another four was placed, but due to the requirements of the RAF and Royal Navy, these were never delivered.[18] Later, via the British Air Attaché in Dublin, a further four were ordered but at this time an arms embargo was in place and these never arrived either.[19]

During the war the Luftwaffe frequently overflew Eire, which had adopted a strict policy of neutrality despite all provocation and on several occasions German bombs were dropped and Irish citizens killed. On occasion the Gladiators were sent to try and intercept such intrusions by daylight, but never ever managed any sightings. Even when the Luftwaffe dropped bombs on North Strand, Dublin, on 31 May 1941, killing twenty-eight civilians, and admitted doing so, it occasioned no reaction other than diplomatic protest as this was a night flight error.

Later the arms restrictions were lifted, but by that time the requirement was for more modern aircraft and Hawker Hurricanes were made available, these replacing the surviving trio of Gladiators from 1943 onward. Serial 25 was retired in August 1943, 26 by the end of that same year and 24 remained until January 1944, when she crashed and was totally destroyed.

Latvia

In 1935 a new identification coding system was adopted, under which the Gladiators of the *Latvijas Gaisa spēki* (Latvian Air Force) were later assigned Type D4. A series of Aviation Festivals were held in the country that helped raise sufficient funds to purchase new aircraft, the balance being obtained from the sale of eleven Bristol Bulldogs to the Spanish Nationalists. With sufficient money secured, *Kapitan* Jānis Balodis (the Latvian Defence Minister) and *Kapitan* Augusts Graudins were sent to England specifically to purchase the Gloster Gladiator. They familiarized themselves with English aircraft controls on an Avro Tudor and then each flew more than thirty hours in the Gladiator, including periods of blind/night flight training. This resulted in Latvian Government orders in May 1937, which totalled twenty-six Gladiator-Is to replace the Bristol Bulldogs currently in service. The Latvian machines were powered by the 840hp (626kW) Bristol Mercury Mk IX and were to be armed with the 0.303in (7.7mm) Vickers machine-gun.

On 11 September the first four Latvian Gladiator-Is were crated up and embarked aboard the freighter *Balttraffic* in the port of London, for shipment to Riga, and these were followed by nine more on 25 September and in November. Once disembarked the crated machines were transported to Spilve where they were re-assembled and test flown by British test pilots before being officially transferred to Latvia. Although built with an open cockpit the Latvians quickly ordered glass canopies for their Gladiators as a separate order.[20]

This first order was followed by a second for another thirteen Gladiators, and these arrived in two batches in April and May 1938. On 21 August, during the Spilve Aviation Festival, the Aviation Regiment ceremonially accepted twenty-six new Gladiators. The Gladiators were assigned to two units, 1 Fighter Squadron, established in April 1938 and commanded by *Kapitan* Nikolajs Balodis, which received serials 114, 115, 116, 117, 118, 119, 120, 121, 122, 123, 124, 125 and 126, while 2 Squadron, established in October 1938 under *Kapitan* Janis Balodis, received serials 163, 164, 165, 166, 167, 168, 169, 170, 171, 172, 173, 174 and 175. In September 1939, four of these were transferred to the newly established 3 Squadron, by which time accidents had reduced 1 Squadron to nine operational aircraft and 2 Squadron to twelve. Gladiators thus lost were serial 121, which was totally destroyed in a landing accident in 1938; serial No. 167, piloted by Lieutenant Evalds Karklins, which was badly damaged in a crash in 1939; serial No. 171, flown by Zanis Tomsons, who was performing unauthorized aerobatics over his parents' house near Bildene, Kurzeme, on 19 July 1939, when it crashed and was totally destroyed; and serial No 175, piloted by Teodors Abrams, which crash-landed at Daugavpils, the pilot surviving.

During the Soviet-Finnish 'Winter War', Soviet bombers frequently violated Latvian air space, which increased tension and led to increased training activity to counter this. However, the fate of Latvia had already been decided in a shabby deal between Nazi Germany and the Soviet Union, dignified by the title of the German-Soviet Boundary and Friendship Treaty, signed on 28 September 1939, in which Hitler had sacrificed Latvia, Lithuania and Estonia to the Soviet area of influence. In June 1940 Stalin cashed that particular cheque in and sent his troops to occupy all three little states.

Lithuania

The Lithuanian *Karo Aviacija* (Military Aviation) had originally been founded in August 1920, but it was not until 1938 that the Sauliai (National Guard) formed an aviation unit to provide air training for reserve officers. Like most European nations the late 1930s saw frantic attempts to re-arm and under *Brigadier-Generolas* Antanas Gustaitis, the Lithuanian air force was no exception. In May 1937, the Lithuanian Government purchased fourteen Gladiator-Is and followed their Latvian neighbours in having them armed with the Vickers Mk VM machine-gun. These were shipped out to the Baltic and arrived in October and November of the same year, and were assigned to 5 *Eskadrilia, II Nailintuva Grupe* (Figher Group) based at Vilnius and Kaunas. They were give serial numbers G-701 to G-714 inclusive. Later the unit, commanded by Major Juozas Nauseda, moved to Shiauliai airfield.[21]

Two machines had been lost in flying accidents and two were under repair but they were seized by the Soviets in the June 1941 invasion.

Norway

The Norwegian Government negotiated directly with Gloster over the purchase of the Gladiator for the *Jagevingen* (Fighter Wing) of the *Haerens Flygevåpen* (Norwegian Army Air Service) and this resulted in an order being placed in June 1937. Twelve aircraft were originally requested, to be equipped with Colt 0.303-in (7.7mm) machine-guns and six Mark Is were delivered to Oslo in August of that year. With the upgraded Mark II appearing it was decided to upgrade the second batch of six to this standard and that these would arrive during 1938. This plan was thwarted by the delayed entry of the Supermarine Spitfire into RAF service, which in turn meant that that service took priority for the Gladiators arriving off the assembly line to tide them over. Finally, the last six Gladiator-IIs to be built, with Air Ministry serials N5919 to N5924 inclusive, were allocated to Norway and finally delivered in 1939. They received the Norwegian serial numbers 413, 415, 417, 419, 421, 423, 435, 427, 431, 433 and 435 respectively.

By April 1940 ten Gladiators remained on strength, four Mark Is and six Mark IIs, which were based at Fornebu, near Oslo, to defend the capital, under the command of *Kaptein* (Captain) Erling Munthe Dahl. Of these ten it appears that only five were actually in operational condition, but another two were urgently made ready for a total of seven aircraft, (serials 413, 419, 423, 425, 427, 429 and 433.) The remaining three were inoperational due to lack of spark plugs, and had to be concealed. Just ten pilots were available to fly these machines, with three of them still under instruction.

The Luftwaffe was early astir on the morning of 9 April and two Gladiators, 433 piloted by *Fenrik* (2nd Lieutenant) Finn Thorsage, and 425 piloted by *Løytnant* (Lieutenant) Arve Braathen, were scrambled away around 0500 in a vain attempt to intercept a Bf.110 observed over the airfield. Despite several attacks this machine eluded them. A second sortie mounted at 0600 by three aircraft, *Løytnant* Dag Krohn (423), *Sersjant* (Sergeant) Kristian Fredrik Schye (427) and *Sersjant* Per Waaler (429) was also fruitless.

The German Navy (*Kreigsmarine*) had meanwhile attempted to storm the Oslo defences with *Generaladmiral* Oskar Kummetz leading the pocket battleship *Lützow,* heavy cruiser *Blücher*, light cruiser *Emden*, three torpedo-boats and various smaller warships but alert Norwegian defences in the Dröbak Narrows in Oslofjord had torpedoed and sunk the *Blücher*. Meanwhile, a massive air invasion commenced with troops being flown in by the Junkers Ju.52/3m transport aircraft of *II/KGzbV 1* and *KGrzbV 103* with heavy fighter escort. Five Gladiators were airborne around 0700 with 429 piloted by *Løytnant* Rolf Thorbjørn Tradin, 423, 433, 425 and 427 flown by *Sersjant* Kristian Fredrik Schye. They were followed by 413, piloted by *Løytnant* Arve Braathen and 419 flown by *Sersjant* Oskar Albert Lüken, although the latter had to abort almost immediately due to engine failure.[22] The Gladiators engaged the mass of German aircraft, having the advantage of height, Tradin destroying one Ju.52/3m along with its crew and the twelve soldier passengers; Krohn destroyed a Bf.110 and Schye got another before himself being shot down. The *1./ZG 76* under *Oberleutnant* Werner Hansen, quickly rallied after these unexpected losses and in strafing attacks torched two Gladiators refuelling at Fornebu, while damaging three others so badly that they had to make emergency landings and were written off. Two made it to Tyrisfjord and then on to frozen Lake Mjösa, Hamar, where one went through the ice and was abandoned. The sole survivor, flown by Krohn, flew to Brummunddal (Hamar), but here his aircraft was drained of its fuel and left. This machine, 423, was later retrieved and became part of Group 'R' at Vangsmjösa. This aircraft conducted her final sortie on 21 April, piloted by Sergeant Per Waaler, but on approaching Gardemoen airfield, engine problems caused him to hit treetops and, although he managed to coax his machine back to base with the tree embedded, the Gladiator was another write-off.

Portugal

The sole fighter defence of Portugal in 1937 was three Hawker Fury aircraft and to rectify this lamentable situation three new *Lutadopr Vôo* (Fighter Flights) were authorized, which, it was planned, would be based at Ota, north of Lisbon, Portela, at Lisbon and Tancos, north-east of Lisbon, respectively. As 'Britain's Oldest Ally'[23] it was natural that it was to her she would look, and in July 1938 a Purchasing Delegation, headed up by *Tenente-Colonel* (Lieutenant-Colonel) Braamchamp Matos Vilardeboo, arrived in the UK with authority to purchase the best of what was available. The delegation's choice fell upon Gloster and, after inspections, the Gladiator-II was deemed to be most suitable for Portugal's requirements. This was a strange decision in some ways, for advance pilot training had already been put in place for future Portuguese fighter pilots, in both Britain and in Germany, and the latter were flying the Messerschmitt Bf.109, a far superior machine.

Nonetheless the Portuguese Government duly placed an order for fifteen Gladiator-IIs in 1938. These machines were assembled by the *Oficinas Geriais de Material Aeronáutico* (OGMA) at Alverca do Ribatejo, north of Lisbon, in September 1938, and received the serial numbers 450 to 464 inclusive. They were allocated to the *Escadrrihla de Caca* at Ota under the command of Lieutenant-Colonel Jose Pedro

Pinheiro Correia. By this time it was clear that the Gladiator did not represent the most modern technology and, for a second order, attempts were made by the Portuguese to obtain fifteen Supermarine Spitfires. This was doomed to failure, for with the British Government's belated attempts to rectify twenty years of neglect of defence, every available Spitfire was required for the RAF. Consideration was given to equivalent Italian and German types, but for much the same reason, nothing was forthcoming by this late date and so a second order was placed for a further fifteen Gladiators. These were readily available, a block being taken from the existing Air Ministry Contract No. 773235/38. These were sent out to Portugal, and they received the serial numbers 465 to 479 inclusive, and were allocated to the *Escadrrihla de Caca BA3*, based at Tanco. When airworthy an air display was held with the Gladiators making attacks on German-supplied bombers, the Junkers Ju.52s and Ju.86s.

By 1941, with Great Britain and the Commonwealth fighting alone against both Germany and Italy, and with the USA a neutral onlooker, fears were expressed that one of these powers might seize the Portugal Atlantic Azores Islands as a base.[24]

Faced with this unenviable situation the Salazar Government decided to reinforce the Azores as best they could to withstand any such take-over and a special fighter unit was established in June 1941, *Escadrrihla de Caca Expedicionara No. 1 dos Acores,* with fifteen Gladiators on its strength. These aircraft were to be based on San Miguel island at the Rabo de Peixe airfield (*Base Aerea* (BA) 5). A second unit, *Escadrihla de Caca Expedicionara No. 2 dos Acores,* also with Gladiators, was set up, and was based on Terceira Island at Teja airfield, Lajes (*Base Aerea 5*). Implementation of these plans commenced on 4 June when the first batch of Gladiators was shipped from Lisbon aboard the freighter *Miarandela* for Ponta Delgada, where fifteen machines were landed, and she then moved on to Terceira where the remaining fifteen were discharged. The two fighter units each had a front-line allotment of ten machines with a reserve of five. Over time two Gladiators were lost in the Azores, *Sergento* Alvaro Guimaraes of *1. EEC,* crashed at Pico da Vara on 10 October 1941, but survived, and *Sergento* Manuel Cardaso crashed on 17 May 1943, killing the pilot.

From 1942 onward, these Gladiators began to be used to cover Allied convoys and flew both fighter patrols, vain interception missions against the four-engined Focke-Wulf Fw. 200C-4s *Kondor* bombers of *Fliegerfüher Atlantik*, and meteorological flights. Portugal further compromised her neutrality in 1943 when, realizing that she could not really stop any potential aggression should it come to it, permitted both the British and the Americans to establish the right to use bases in the Azores to protect Atlantic convoys, Lajes becoming RAF Lajes for this purpose. In return Britain re-equipped Portugal's air force and supplied her with surplus Curtiss P-36 Mohawk fighters, which eventually took over the Gladiator's role and they became trainers and liaison machines.

With the post-war era, there was no longer need for their presence and in 1946 the surviving Gladiators were returned to Ota, serving at BA2, before being handed on to *Esquarão de Lutador 3 Escadrrihla de Caca BA3*, being based at Tancos with the Hurricane. However, two years later, the Gladiator was back in the Azores once more, with the *Esquarão de Lutador 3 Escadrrihla de Caca* back at Lejas. Wear and tear and accidents had reduced the Gladiator strength to a mere seven aircraft by 1950, which found serials 459, 461, 466, 469, 476 and 477 back at Tancos carrying out pilot training duties. Three years later the Portuguese Army and Navy air forces merged and the Gladiators were all scrapped.[25]

Romania
It is alleged in many sources that Romania used the Gladiator but none show up on any Romanian Aircraft Registration Lists, either military or civilian, of the period.

Singapore
No Gladiator ever served in the defence of Malaya against the Japanese in 1941–42 of course, but, such was the dearth of fighter protection for those vital colonies that, in the summer of 1941, the Chief-of-the-Air Staff signalled the Air Officer Commanding, Singapore, Air Vice Marshal Conway Walter Heath Pulford, CB, OBE, AFC, that he could make available twenty-one Gladiators, drawn from various Middle Eastern units, including the Free French, Metrological and Communications Flights. Not surprisingly, this offer was rejected. The British were incredibly naïve about the power of the Japanese Navy and Army Air Forces but even they knew that Gladiators would not be up to the job. In the event the Brewster Buffalos and Hawker Hurricanes that were eventually sent out proved totally unable to cope with the Mitsubishi aircraft.

South Africa
The South African Air Force acquired twelve Gladiator-Is and eleven Gladiator-IIs, all from the RAF. The first batch was received by 1 SAAF at the advance bases of Wajir, Kenya, where they were to replace the existing Hawker Fury aircraft. On 7 August Lieutenant Hendriks Johannes Burger tested his usual Hawker Fury fighter against one of the newly arrived Gladiator replacements for climb rate, and the Fury came out best. Nonetheless the Gladiators ultimately replaced the Fury in No. 1 Squadron, commanded by Major Noel Gray Niblock-Stuart, and when No. 2 SAAF Squadron was formed on 30 September 1940 from two Flights of No. 1 Squadron, there were nine Gladiators among the mixed batch of Furry and Hurricane fighters in its make-up and they also joined No. 3 Squadron SAAF.

On 13 May 1940 the unit moved north to Egypt and received a total of nineteen Gladiators, mainly from No. 6 and No. 80 Squadrons, these being serials N5788, N5789, N5813, N5815, N5818, N5820, N5821, N5822, N5824, N5826, N5828, N5830, N5831, N5850, N5851, N5852, N5383, N5855 and N556 ('Lulu Belle').[26] In January 1941 No. 1 Squadron's detachment at Azzoza, Abyssinia, had six Gladiators (N5853 ('A' Flight); N5820 and N5831 ('B' Flight) and N5821 and N5824 ('C' Flight) plus N5789 which moved to 2 Squadron). These remaining Gladiators worked with the Hawker Hurricanes in Abyssinia and Sudan before moving to Egypt in April 1941.

The Gladiators were heavily engaged in the East African campaigns that saw Mussolini's colonies and conquests picked off one-by-one by incredibly small British and Commonwealth forces. Led by Captain Schalk van Schalkwyk nine Gladiators were deployed to Khartoum from Egypt on 5 August 1940 for the defence of Sudan. Their first engagement was on 18 September over Kassala when two CR.42s were claimed as destroyed, 2nd Lieutenants John Coetzer and John Hewison sharing one and Major Schalk van Schalkkwyk claiming the other. On 18 October 1940 three Gladiators bombed Barentu, Eritrea, and claimed to have hit three CR.42s about to take off, as well as six bombers. On 1 November, Captain Robin Fraser Pare DFC, while on an escort mission, destroyed a Caproni Ca133. A disastrous day was 6 November when ten Gladiators, from 1 SAAF Squadron and 'K' Flight, were caught flat-footed at low level over Gallabat Fort by the Fiat CR.42s of 412ª *Squadriglia*, and destroyed four of them (L7614, piloted by Flight Lieutenant Kenneth Savage; K7969, Pilot Officer Henry Bell Kirk; L7612, Pilot Officer Jack Hamlyn; and N5855, Major Schalk van Schalkwyk). Captain Brian Boyle went to their aid in N5852, but was himself badly shot up and crash-landed. The destruction of five Gladiators in a single day was accomplished without loss to the Italians. That same day another five Gladiators from both units again were caught by surprise by the Fiat CR.42s, losing Flying Officer Jack Maurice Haywood in K7977 but claiming two Caproni Ca. 133 bombers. On 4 November three Gladiators tangled with four CR.42s and Lieutenant Leonard LeClues Theron shot down one as did Captain Brian Boyle. On 27 January 1941 six Gladiators were part of a mixed fighter strike on the Eritrean airfields of Gura and Adi Ugri (now Mendefera), claiming seven Italian aircraft badly damaged.

On 3 February six Gladiators forward deployed to the 'Pretoria' landing strip to refuel before strafing a landing strip close to Azzozo, claiming five Caproni Ca.133s and a Savoia-Marchetti Sm.81 hit. Engaged by defending Fiat CR.42s the Gladiators shot one down.

Other known and confirmed 'kills' registered to the South African Gladiators were a Fiat CR.42 claimed by 2nd Lieutenant John Hewitson over Kassala, Sudan, on 18 September 1940; a Fiat CR.42 was shot down by Captain Serevaas de Kock Viljoen and another claimed destroyed by Captain Brian Boyle but not verified, on 4 October 1940; a second Fiat CR.42 was claimed by Captain Boyle on 4 November; a Caproni Ca.133 was destroyed by Captain Andrew Duncan on 6 November 1940; a Fiat CR.42 by Lieutenant Thomas Condon flying serial N5789 on 27 December 1940 east of Gedaref airfield; a Fiat CR.42 claimed by Captain Brian Boyle near Khartoum on 3 February 1941, while on 5 February 1941 Lieutenant John Coetzer claimed another CR.42 in the vicinity of Asmara.

Losses were N5852 and N5855 both destroyed by CR.42s near Gallabat, Sudan, on 6 November 1940; N5850, which crashed at Al Qadarif, Sudan, on 24 November 1940 killing Lieutenant William Harry Morris; N5851, flown by Lieutenant Edward Arthur Jarvis, which crash-landed at Heston on 14 December 1940; and N5822, piloted by Lieutenant James Sydney Robert Warren, destroyed by a Fiat CR.42 near Aroma, north of Kassala, on 12 January 1941.

By mid-February 1941 the unit had converted fully to the Hawker Hurricane.[27]

One South African fighter pilot will always be associated with the Gloster Gladiator of course and that was Marmaduke Thomas St John Pattle, who claimed no fewer than fifteen Italian scalps in this aircraft flying with No. 80 Squadron in North Africa and Greece in 1940/41, during his tragically brief but illustrious career.[28]

Soviet Union

When Stalin's Soviet Union cynically and callously crushed the small and briefly independent states of Latvia and Lithuania in July 1940, it absorbed into its capacious maw the Gladiators of both nations. The twenty Latvian aircraft had five of their number in storage at Krustpils, in south-eastern Latvia, the other fifteen being located at several different locations. Those based at Spilve were given instructions to secretly fly away after dusk to new bases. No. 1 Squadron was assigned to Rumbuli (Jumpravmuiza), 2 Squadron to Koknese and the three operational Gladiators with 3 Squadron were sent to the Latvian University Farm complex at Ramava. Despite these precautions, with the Soviet occupation the majority of these were seized and concentrated at Krustpils, escorted by Russian fighter aircraft ('for their own protection!') disarmed and used as training aircraft by the VVS, painted in Soviet colours and markings. Others were disassembled, crated up and sent to Germany, still at that point, Germany's firm ally. A trio of the Gladiators that remained in flyable condition took part in a 'United' Air Festival staged by the Soviets at Spilve on 17 August 1940, their final participation and humiliation. Those that remained were mainly destroyed by the Luftwaffe attacks in June 1941.

The twelve Lithuanian Gladiators of the *Karo Aviacija* were likewise taken into Soviet control, although two of them were found damaged. Their new masters formed the *Tautine Eskadrilia* at Pluonija, Ukmerge, commanded by Major J. Kowas, as an air section of the Red Army's 29 Territorial Army Corps and some of the Gladiators were employed in this unit.

Only a few of these Gladiators survived the initial Luftwaffe onslaught in June 1941, most being strafed and burnt on the ground. Those at Krustpils suffered a similar fate but those that survived, along with some intact machines captured at Schaulen (Šiauliai) airfield, were, in their turn, taken over by their liberators and shipped off to Germany.

Sweden

Like many small countries, even traditionally neutral ones, Sweden grew increasingly alarmed during the 1930s as aggression spread across the globe. The Japanese in China, Italy in Abyssinia and, closer to home for the Swedes, Germany's take-over of Austria and Czechoslovakia, all of which had been unopposed by the democracies, boded ill for all small nations. The Swedes began to look to their defences and found them sadly lacking. With regard to their air defences, these were lamentably tiny and a mission was despatched under the Head of the *Flygvapnet* (Air Force) *Generallöjtnant* (Lieutenant-General) Torsten Friis, to examine what British warplanes might best suit their needs.

The Swedish Government imported thirty-seven Gladiator-Is (which were designated as the *Jaktplan*-8 (J-8 – Fighter Type 8) powered by the 645hp (481kW) Nydqvist & Holm AB (NOHAB)[29] licence-built Bristol Mercury VIIIS.2 engine, for the *Flygvapnet*, which were built in 1937–38. These were deemed sufficient to equip two squadrons that were formed at Barkarby.

For the third planned squadron, to complete the *Flottilj* (Wing), which was tasked with defending Stockholm, a further order was made for eighteen Gladiator-IIs (J-8A) powered by the 840hp (5626kW) Bristol Mercury VIIIS3 engine, which gave a top speed of 254.76mph (410km/h) and a maximum ceiling of 35,100ft (10,700m). They were built in 1938. As well as Swedish instrumentation, both types had the wooden double-bladed Watts propeller when supplied but the Mark IIs had their engines fitted with an automatic mixture control, electric starter and the Swedish Volkes-Air air filter in the carburettor intake and they carried the Colt-Browning machine-gun armament in the fuselage and wing positions in lieu of the four 8mm (0.314in) *Kulspota m/37* (Browning).

On arrival with the F1 at Västerås in 1937, the first three were greeted with some strong reservations about the purchase of the Gladiator. She was no longer modern technology, being four years old at a time when progress was speeding up and the world was moving rapidly to the monoplane fighter. While her manoeuvrability was pretty good, it did not match the CR.42 in the biplane bracket, while her top speed was relatively poor. Nonetheless the Swedes (and the Finns) saw her as an available stop-gap and utilized her both as a short-range reconnaissance aircraft *and* a fighter plane until more modern types became available.[30]

The Gladiators received the *Flygvapnet* serials 231 to 285 inclusive.

The Winter War

Relations between Sweden and Finland, and especially between their air forces, were excellent, and frequent exchanges between aviators and squadron visits had cemented that bond. Of course there was much natural sympathy for their neighbour when the Russians brutally invaded, the feeling also being who would be next on Stalin's agenda, reinforced when he absorbed Estonia, Latvia and Lithuania. Public donations were received to aid the Finns and with the money raised there was sufficient to purchase both a small number of Gladiator fighters and a few licence-built Hawker Hart bombers.

Following talks between Major Hugo Beckhammar and the Finnish Commander-in-Chief, Marshal Baron Carl Gustaf Emil Mannerheim at Helsinki, the decision to assist was taken on 15 December, with aircraft ready to operate from 10 January 1940. They were to support the Swedish and Norwegian volunteers on the ground in the general area bounded by Uleåborg (Oulu) – Hossa – Kärkjävi and the base selected was Kemi with the frozen Lake Olkkajärvi, 9 miles (15km) north of Rovaniemi, as advance base 'Oskar'. The unit flew up on 10 January as planned.

F = *Flottielje* (Wing) 19, commanded by *Kapten* Åke Sönderburg, and with *Kapten* Björn Bjuggren as Executive Officer, fielded twelve Gladiators (with eleven pilots), which represented a big investment for them as this was about 33 per cent of the *Flygvapnet's* existing fighter strength at the time. These Gladiators saw action against the Soviet Air Force from January 1940 for a period of sixty-two days, flying on no fewer than sixty of them despite icy conditions, which on occasions rendered their guns inoperational, aiding Finland on the northern front. A few were fitted with ski landing gear and some had under-wing ordnance racks capable of carrying eight small bombs.[31] The Gladiators featured the 'Skull and Crossbones' pirate symbol on either side of their fuselages with yellow aircraft letters on their rudders.

The F19's first taste of battle occurred on 12 January when nine Gladiators flew from Kemi to 'Oskar' from where four of them escorted the four Harts on a bombing attack against Soviet forces west of Märkjärvi before attacking a Soviet air base nearby and claiming to have destroyed three Polikarpov I-15s but three of the four Harts were also lost. The Gladiators were dispersed to both 'Oskar' and a second advance base, 'Ulrik', at Uleåborg with a third, 'Svea' near Posio, as a reconnaissance base. Two more Soviet fighters were brought down on 17 January. A second SB bomber was brought down over Oulu on 1 February and a large TB-3 four-engined bomber was forced to crash-land on 10 March. Three of the Gladiators were lost, serial 274 in air combat on 23 January, when Second Lieutenant John Sjoquist was killed; a second crashed near Uleaborg on 20 February while a third was lost on a test flight on 10 March when Engineer-Lieutenant Ake Hildinger was killed, these latter two were serials 284 and 285

With the end of the war on 13 March the unit ceased operations and was inspected by Marshal Mannerheim on 25 March, in recognition for their aid before they returned home to Sweden.[32]

Swedish service

The Gladiators were originally assigned to *Flygflottij 8* and *Flygflottilj 10* (in addition to *Flygflottilj 19*). Although they were deemed already obsolete when delivered, the Gladiators served for a long period with the F20 *Kadettskola* (Air Cadet School) at Uppsala, north of Stockholm, as a training aircraft for solo and formation training. Their strength peaked in 1938 when there were fifty-one Swedish Gladiators in service at Barkarby and forty-nine in 1939 but by 1940 just three remained there while thirty were based at Fårösund/Säve. This figure remained fairly constant with thirty-two machines at Bråvalla in 1941; eleven at Barkaby and fifteen at Bulltofta/Barkåkra in 1942; one less in 1943 and one less in 1944. By 1945 the total in service had shrunk to thirteen and only one remained flying by 1946.

In the event a large number of Swedish Gladiators were lost in accidents, thus serials – 234, 235, 236, 237, 239, 241, 242, 244, 245, 246, 247, 248, 250, 251, 252, 253, 259, 260, 264, 267, 268, 269, 270, 271, 272, 274, 276, 280, 284 and 285 all ended their days violently. Others were retired due to their age and lack of spare parts, including 266 in 1942; 243 in 1944; 237, 255, 257, 258, 261, 262, 275, 277 and 279 in 1945; 240, 249, 254, 263, 273 and 283 in 1946; of the final six, 231, 232, 233, 256 and 265 were retired in 1947, while only 278 has been preserved for posterity.

Survivors

1. Shuttleworth Collection, near Biggleswade, Bedfordshire. (Mark I Serial L8032 – G-AMRK still flying.)
2. Fighter Collection at Imperial War Museum, Duxford, Cambridgeshire. (Serial N5903 – flown as G-CBHO.)
3. Gloucestershire Aviation Collection 1998/Jet Age Museum, Staverton (serial N5914 – Former Norwegian No. 263). Mk.II, incorporating parts from serials N5697 and N5698.
4. RAF Museum, Hendon, London (Mk.I – Serial K8042). In No. 87 Squadron colours. Also forward fuselage of serial N5628.
5. Swedish Air Force Museum, Malmen, Linköping, Sweden. (Swedish serial Fv278.)
6. Royal Norwegian Air Force Museum, Bødo (serial N5641.) Former No. 263 Squadron aircraft.
7. Armed Forces Museum, Oslo (serial N5643).
8. Malta War Museum, Fort St Elmo, Valletta, Malta GC (serial N5520, 'Faith') – fuselage only.
9. Fleet Air Arm Museum, Yeovilton, Somerset (serial N5518).
10. Retro Track and Air, Cambridge (serial N5719).A large number of Gladiators have been recovered from various lakes in Norway, where they were abandoned in 1940 and have been pretty well preserved. No doubt many of these will eventually appear on exhibition. Included in the finds are serials N5628, N5632, N5638, N5647, N5693, N5704, N5905 and N5907.

Chapter Eight

Hawker Audax

The substitution of wood covered with fabric held together by wire-bracing that had endured from the Great War era and that had dominated military aircraft construction throughout the 1920s, was finally ended by the British Hawker aircraft designer Sydney Camm and Managing Director Fred Sigrist with the Warren-truss tubular metal methodology revolution. This much simplified aircraft production and resulted in a far more durable product, less prone to the elements and also made maintenance far easier. Coupled with an in-line engine, which resulted in a pleasing and streamlined profile, the RAF biplane aircraft of this era, among the last of their kind, combined durability with elegance, even if they did not advance either speed, payload or range very much over what had gone before.

The family of two-seater light bombers and single-seater fighters that Hawker subsequently produced in the early 1930s was a large one with variants corresponding to the various specialist needs of the time, and from 1929, with the Hawker Hart, a steady flow followed with the Audax (Army Co-Operation and Training); Nisr (radial-engined export variant); Hind (Day Bomber) and its South African derivative, the Hartebeest (Ground-Attack); Hector (Army Co-Operation); Hardy (Counter-Insurgency), Demon(two-seater fighter); the Fury (single-seater fighter); the Nimrod (Naval shipborne); and Osprey (Naval).

It was Air Ministry specification 7/31 in particular, with the emphasis on Army Co-Operation duties (that in 1931 were mainly, if naively, envisaged as the virtually unopposed Imperial policing of the Empire), that triggered Hawker's response, which was the submission of the Hart K1438 as a suggested prototype. This aircraft did not entail a great deal of innovation from the original design, merely involving the addition of a hook or hoop mechanism between the undercarriage spreaders for message retrieval (the container being slung a wire between two poles and 'snatched' by a low-flying approach path), the extension of the engine exhaust manifolds aft to avoid the glare of the flames obscuring the pilot's vision and the additional of suitable life-saving equipment, compasses and similar kit, in case of stranding in remote areas.

The Air Ministry, strapped for cash under Winston Churchill's extension of notorious and baleful 'Ten-Year' ruling,[1] which his equally myopic successors at the Treasury gleefully upheld year-upon-year as a means of debilitating re-armament, were happy to maintain the continuity that such almost identical products ensured, and accepted the Hawker design. They placed an initial order for forty machines, assigning to her the official name of Audax, which is Latin for audacious. She was expected to replace the Armstrong Whitworth Atlas and the Westland Wapiti in this role.

The first aircraft from this order, K1995, made its maiden flight on 29 December 1931, and began equipping RAF squadrons from the following year initially with No. 4 Squadron in February 1931.

The basic design was that of a single-engined, single-bay biplane, of all-metal, fabric-clad, construction. The two-man crew comprised the pilot and an observer/rear gunner. The power plant was the 525hp (391kW) 5-cyliner, in-line, Rolls-Royce Kestrel 1B engine with Arthur Rowledge's pressurized cooling system. Some later models used the alternate 620hp (462.33kW) Kestrel X. The wingspan was 37ft 3in (11.35 m), the overall length was 29ft 7in (9.02m) and the height was 10ft 5in (3.17m). It had a wing area of 348ft² (32.33m²). Weights were 3,251lb (1,475kg) empty, and 4,381lb (1,987kg) fully laden. The defensive armament was a solitary, fixed, synchronized, forward-firing .303in (0.769cm) Vickers Mk.II or Mk.V machine-gun, with 600 rpg; and a single, scarf-ring mounted, flexible .303in Lewis gun with five 97-round drums, in the observer's cockpit. Her modest offensive payload was a maximum of eight 20lb (9.07 kg) bombs on under-wing racks, or, as a training machine, four 20lb (9.07kg) practice bombs carried on under-wing racks, or two 112lb (50.80kg) supply containers similarly mounted. They could also be fitted with a ventrally mounted pendant arm under the wing tips with a socket for carrying a Holt magnesium flare well clear of the outer inflammable fabric of the wing. This spectacular pyrotechnic device, triggered electronically, was used as a night-landing aid. It had a maximum speed of 172mph (275km/h), and a service ceiling of 26,400ft (8,047m), the fuel capacity was 350 gallons, giving a range of 430miles (692km), an endurance of 3.5 hours, and a stall speed of 55mph (88.5 km/h).

Later production models had the tail-skid, inherited from the Hind, replaced by a tail-wheel.

The serial number ranges were:

K1995 to K2034 (40 aircraft).
K3055 to K3145 (91 aircraft), under contract 190684/32, were delivered between June and September 1933.
K3679 to K3721 (43 aircraft).
K4381 to K4406 (26 aircraft), sub-contracted by Gloster.
K4838 to K4862 (25 aircraft); (India) sub-type, sub-contracted by Gloster. This was a tropicalized variant with a larger radiator and extra equipment for dealing with the conditions in the Indian sub-continent.
K5120 to K5176 (57 aircraft), sub-contracted by AVRO.
K5201 to K5256 (56 aircraft), sub-contracted by Bristol.
K5561 to K5603 (43 aircraft), sub-contracted by Westland.
K7307 to K7366 (60 aircraft), sub-contracted by AVRO.
K7469 to K7553 (85 aircraft), sub-contacted by Bristol.
K8311 to K8335 (25 aircraft), sub-contracted by AVRO.

In addition thirty Audax were either converted, or completed as, Hawker Hart (Special) aircraft (serials K4407 to K4436 inclusive). These were tropicalized variants with desert equipment and the de-rated Kestrel X power plant for use by the RAF in the Middle East.

Of the total of those constructed, including prototypes, 'specials' and foreign sub-types, by 1937, sub-contractors AV Roe & Company (AVRO) had built 142, Bristol built 141, Gloster built 51 and Westland built 43. An additional 34 were built for Iraq and 57 for Persia/Iran, plus a further 10 were produced in Iran itself. Front-line service with the RAF at home was brief, because the Westland Lysander began to replace them as Army Co-Operation machines as early as 1937/38 after which the Audax became mainly a training aircraft.

Most Audax aircraft were initially sent to bomber squadrons of the RAF, serving with: No. 2 Squadron; No 4 Squadron; No. 5 Squadron, which used them as makeshift single-seat fighters until replaced by Curtiss P-36 Mohawks in 1942; No. 13 Squadron; No. 16 Squadron; No. 24 Squadron; No. 26 Squadron; No. 28 Squadron, at Kohal, India until replaced by the Westland Lysander in 1942; No. 52 Squadron in Iraq between July 1941 and January 1942, the aircraft themselves being flown by pilots from No. 31 Squadron on local reconnaissance flights; No. 77 Squadron; No. 112 Squadron still had the Audax on its establishment in 1939; No. 146 Squadron in India and Burma, also utilizing them briefly as single-seater fighters until 1942, until replaced by Curtiss Mohawks; No. 173 Squadron in Egypt until 1942; No. 208 Army Co-Operation Squadron was flying with the Audax as late as March 1938; No. 211 Squadron, twelve machines, June to November 1937; No. 226 Army Co-Operation Squadron 1937–39; No. 237 (Rhodesian) Squadron in Kenya seeing action in the Sudan and Eritrea in 1941, when the Hardy replaced her; and No. 267 Squadron in Egypt as local communications and transport machines until 1942.

Later the majority went to Flying Training Squadrons (FTS), serving with: No. 2 FTS, No. 3 FTS, No. 4 FTS at Habbaniya, Iraq, No. 5 FTS, No. 6 FTS, No. 7 FTS, No. 8 FTS, No. 9 FTS, No. 10 FTS and No. 11 FTS and No. 18 Elementary and Reserve Flying Training School in 1938.

Four Audax aircraft served with the Royal Navy's Fleet Air Arm, being transferred from the RAF. They joined No. 780 Conversion Course Squadron from May 1941 and served through into 1942, being allocated the Navy serials 50, 51, 52 and 53. The final Navy Audax (serial K4395) was not struck off charge until January 1945.

The Audax also served with the RAF College, and at the Royal Aircraft Establishment (RAE), Farnborough. Peacetime losses to accidents and mishaps were heavy, a total of ninety-two Audax being lost between 27 October 1932 and 4 January 1938. Among the squadrons losses were heaviest in No. 2 and No. 26, each losing eight machines apiece in that period; while No. 4 lost five aircraft, one of them along with a No. 2 Squadron aircraft in a collision over South Wanborough, Hampshire, on 28 May 1937; No. 13 lost four and Nos. 77, 208 and 285 Squadrons lost two apiece and No. 16 Squadron just one machine.

Heavier were the accident rates from the Flying Training Schools, as might be expected. Both No. 2 and No. 4 FTS lost nine aircraft each in this time period, with the former losing two aircraft on 12 October 1937 and another pair on 29 November 1937 near Pwlheli, while the latter squadron also lost two in a collision at Abu Sueir on 5 June 1936; No. 3 and No. 9 FTS lost eight apiece, No.11 FTS, wrote off seven Audax while Nos 5, 6 and 8 FTS lost six each, No. 10 four and No. 7 just one.

By the outbreak of war in 1939 around 400 RAF Audax were still serviceable.

Their later duties included acting as towing vehicles for the General Aircraft GAL.48 Hotspur glider.

In the Middle East the Audax saw the briefest of operations at the onset of the East African campaign. No 237 (Rhodesian) Squadron, based at Nairobi, Kenya, with a mix of Hawker Audax, Hart and Hardy biplanes, had been formed on 22 April 1940 when No. 1 Squadron, Southern Rhodesian Air Force was re-designated. When war with Italy appeared imminent the squadron moved up to the forward landing strip of Gordons Tree on the border of Italian-occupied Ethiopia and Eritrea. By September all the Audax aircraft had been used up when the unit moved into the Anglo-Egyptian Sudan.

The defence of Habbaniya in Iraq in 1941

On 1 April 1941, the pro-Nazi Iraqi politician Rashid Ali, aided and abetted by four similarly minded Iraqi Generals ('the Golden Square'), staged a *coup d'état* and overthrew the pro-British Government. They called on assistance from Hitler and the Vichy-French in Syria and assembled a force of 9,000 of their own troops with fifty artillery pieces and many armoured cars, and, by 1 May, had besieged the RAF airbase at Habbaniya. The insisted that all flights cease immediately prior to its evacuation.

The British Air Officer Commanding, Air Vice-Marshal Herbert George Smart, despite having only 2,500 mixed defenders, rejected all these demands and, while awaiting reinforcement, resolutely took the fight to the enemy. From a rag-bag mixture of aircraft at his disposal he assembled an *ad hoc* air group, which was named the Habbaniya Air Striking Force.

The units that made up this force comprised the following: 'A' Squadron under Wing Commander Glynn Silyn-Roberts, situated on the Main Field with ten Hawker Audax; 'B' Squadron, led by Squadron-Leader Anthony Greville Dudgeon, at Main Field, with a solitary Bristol Blenheim, twenty-six Airspeed Oxfords, eight Fairey Gordons and four Gloster Gladiators; 'C' Squadron commanded by Wing Commander Christopher William Mitchell 'Larry' Ling DFC, based at Polo Field with ten Hawker Audax; 'D' Squadron led by Wing Commander John Gosset Hawtrey, based at Main Field, with an additional ten Hawker Audax; and a Fighter Flight under Flight Lieutenant Robert Seayears 'Bob' May, at Polo Field, with nine Gloster Gladiators. Known Audax at 4 SFTS at this time were K3099, K7502, K7542, K7544, K7512, K3111, K5235, K7514, K7528, K7539, K3124.

Determined to take the initiative, Smart began bombing attacks on the Iraq army positions at 0500 on 2 May. Although the Audax only normally carried a maximum of eight small 20lb bombs, the RAF mechanics managed to customise twelve of them to accommodate a pair of more useful 250lb (113kg) bombs and with these they joined in the general air raids that quickly inflicted damage on the enemy artillery and armour, so much so that, within a day, the Iraqis started pulling their forces out, effectively ending the immediate danger.

To rectify this humiliation, and aid their new ally, the Luftwaffe flew in fourteen Messerschmitt Bf.110 twin-engined fighters of the 4.ZG.76 and fifteen Heinkel He.111 bombers of the 4./KG.4, from airfields near Athens on 11 May. These aircraft, designated as *Fliegerfüher Irak,* under *Oberst* Werner Junck, transited via Vichy-French airfields in Syria, which made them very welcome, to Mosul, and from there they soon began operating, but with remarkably little effect and lost twenty-one of their number in the process. Meanwhile British relief columns were landed and started on their way and, by 17 May, the air base was relieved. Fighting continued for several more weeks but eventually Rashid Ali and his cronies fled via Iran to Berlin and the pro-British Government was re-installed.

Burma

No. 5 Squadron was based at Risalpur, India, close to the Khyber Pass on frontier policing duties in February 1941, and replaced its Hawker Harts with the Hawker Audax, on the 18th of that month, and its official operational status was changed from Light Bomber Squadron to Fighter Squadron! It continued employing the Audax in this capacity through to September 1942. When, in December 1941, the Japanese invaded Malaya and Burma, the squadron moved to Dum Dum on 11 December, where it was supposed to act as fighter defence for the port of Calcutta (now Kolkata), in West Bengal. Presumably the British higher authorities thought that if the Imperial Japanese Navy attacked, then Japanese Zero pilots would be defeated by dying of laughter! As quickly as possible in the chaos of the British retreats and defeats at Singapore and Mandalay, the unit began receiving Curtiss Mohawk IV fighters as replacements, although the last Audax remained on strength until late September.

In a similar manner, No. 28 Squadron, another long-established Indian-based unit on Internal Security duties was based at Kohat, on the North-West Frontier carrying the unit code 'US'. In December 1941 their role was changed to that of Army Co-operation, Burma, and remained in place until 28 January 1942 when they moved forward to Lashio, Shan State, in north-eastern Burma, but by this time the Audax had been mainly replaced with the Westland Lysander II.

Foreign operators

Canada

The Royal Canadian Air Force utilized a batch of five Audax to replace the old Armstrong Whitworth Atlas as instructional airframes only until they were withdrawn from service in 1943.

Egypt

The Egyptian Air Force used thirty-four surplus RAF Audax aircraft of a 750hp (560kW) Armstrong Siddeley Panther VIA radial-engined variant supplied under the Anglo-Egyptian Treaty of 1936. These machines (also known as the Avro 674) served with Nos. 1 and 2 General-Purpose Squadrons. They conducted coastal patrols at the behest of the British but did not engage in any combat missions. The future Chief-of-Staff the Egyptian Air Force, Group Captain Adel Amin Hafez, learned to fly as a pilot in the RAF in an Audax aircraft.

India

All three main Indian Air Force squadrons, No. 1, No. 2 and No. 3 Squadrons flew the Hawker Audax (India) variant, from batches delivered from 1941 onward. No. 1 Squadron converted from the Hawker Hart to the Audax at Ambala from June 1940 onward; No. 2 Squadron converted to the Audax in September 1941 and utilized them for several months until they were replaced by Westland Lysanders; and No.3 Squadron formed at Peshawar with the Audax on 1 October 1941, later employing their aircraft as target tugs with No. 1 Service Flying Training School (SFTS) at Ambala between November 1941 and June 1942, including serial numbers K3088 and K3102.

In addition No. 4 Coastal Defence Flight (CDF) had five Audax on establishment in December 1941, K4845, K4847, K4851, K4142 and K5569. With the Japanese invasion of Burma this unit was deployed forward to Moulmein airfield with a small detachment that included two Audax arriving on 2 January. The very next day the Japanese 77 *Hiko Sentai* operating from Lampang, with nine Nakajima Ki-27 Nate fighters, attacked the airfield and in strafing attacks immediately destroyed four of the aircraft, including both Audax.

Later in 1942 those Audax aircraft based at Digboi airfield in north-east Assam, doubled up as makeshift fighters in 1942, so desperate had the situation become. No. 1 Squadron employed them for coastal patrol work and also training, and circumstances forced them to fly them in their original Army Co-Operation profile between September 1943 and January 1944. Meanwhile No. 3 Squadron flew local patrols over the North-West Frontier helping suppress the ever-antagonistic Madda Khel tribesmen in Waziristan from October 1941 until September 1943. In May 1943 the insurgents of the Pir of Pagaro's Hur, in the Scind, who had long been fermenting insurrection, wrecked the *Lahore Express* on the 16th and in the retaliatory action against further attacks, No. 3 Squadron deployed its Audax aircraft, strafing and dropping incendiary bombs, to destroy PML-F Hur base camps. Wartime losses included one Audax on 1 June 1940 while on North-West Frontier Patrol (NWFP), two more, from No. 3 Coastal Reconnaissance Squadron (CRS) were lost to accidents on 1 January 1942 and 1 March 1942 respectively. On 1 April 1942, two Audax from the SFTS at Ambala collided and were written off. The final combat loss was incurred on 30 July 1942, when serial K4856 of 3 CRS, flown by Pilot Officer Zal Beram Sanjana, with Air-Gunner Sergeant Jayakumar Arya, was lost while carrying out a TAC sortie over Dara Adam Khel in north-eastern Khyber Province during the Hur operation.

No. 2 Squadron again briefly deployed the Audax between June and August 1942, operating K4838, K4843, K4848, K4852, K4856, K4857, K4858, K5571, K5572, K5575 and K5579 in that period. This unit still had two Audax, serials K5561 and K5327, on its establishment at Kohat as late as November 1943.

Iraq
The Iraqi Air Force ordered thirty-four of the Hawker Nisr in 1936. They were equipped with the 620hp (462.33kW) Bristol Pegasus IIM radial engine. They used them against the British at Habbaniya in May 1941.

Persia/Iran
Known as the Hawker Nisr the Pratt & Whitney Hornet radial-engined variant served with the Afghan Air Force from 1934 onward. The country changed its name from Persia to Iran on 22 March 1935, at which date there were twenty-nine Audax aircraft with the Hornet engine and another twenty-eight with the Pegasus engine on strength, a total of fifty-seven Nisr aircraft having been delivered directly from the UK, while an additional ten were constructed locally by the newly constructed 'Shahbaz' Iranian Aircraft Factory at Doshan Teppeh, south-east of Tehran. This plant produced five home-built Nisr aircraft in 1938 and a completed a further five in April/May 1939. Serial numbers allocated for the whole Nisr fleet were 401–461 inclusive.

At this period all Iranian regiments were composed of a mixture of aircraft types, with the Audax predominating.

By the summer of 1939 expansion saw 1 Regiment at Qila Murgha with twenty-six Audax on strength, 2 Regiment at Tabriz with ten Audax, 3 Regiment at Mashad with seven Audax and 4 Regiment at Ahvaz with ten Audax on establishment. In addition the Flying Training School at Mehrabad had a further eight operational Audax.

The Iranian variants saw action against the RAF and Soviet forces from August 1941. When, after the Shah refused to expel Nazi officials from the country, and fearing sabotage of the vital oil wells, the Allies, under Lieutenant-General Edward Pellew Quinan, GOC 10 Army, attacked in Operation Y on the 25th. No. 261 Squadron RAF attacked and destroyed the Audax at Ahvaz air base, and on the 26th destroyed another in the air. With the ceasefire many Audax were destroyed but in the aftermath at least two of them were operated by the British Flight Training School at Doshanteppeh.

Later the Americans helped re-establish the Iranian air force but even in December 1943, the Regiment at Tehran still had ten Audax on strength, the Fighter Training School, also at Tehran, had fifteen in use while another eleven Audax were at the Aircraft Park and Maintenance Unit (MU). Indeed the Audax still featured on Iranian Air Force returns into the 1950s, when 1 and 2 Reconnaissance Regiments between them still had seven Audax on their strengths and the Pilot Training School another four machines.

Malaya
The Straits Settlement Volunteer Air Force (SSVAF) flew the Hawker Audax (Singapore) variant, which was powered by the Kestrel V engine, which produced 695hp (520kW) at 3,000 rpm. This unit had been formed on 25 March 1936 and was based at Seletar with eight Audax, one of which was K5142, as well as two Hawker Harts and two Avro Tutors.[2] In November 1938 six of the Audax made a formation flight from Singapore to Mergui airfield, Rangoon and back again.

These eight Audax took no part in the fighting of 1941, having been sent, along with the Harts, to Southern Rhodesia on the eve of the East African campaign.

Rhodesia
The Southern Rhodesian Air Force received a batch of eight Audax aircraft formerly with the Straits Settlement Volunteer Air Force at Singapore, in 1940, along with two Hawker Harts from the same source, to supplement six Hawker Harts that had been received in April 1937. Based near Salisbury (now Harare) they subsequently served in the East African theatre of war.

South Africa
The South African Air Force widely employed the Audax as a training machine and some seventy-eight machines were received from RAF stocks in total from 1940 onward.

Preserved aircraft

Only a single Audax is thought to have survived. This is the former serial number K5600, built under AM contract 406498 by Westland under sub-contract, and placed on charge on 5 March 1937. It served with No. 226 Army Co-Operation Squadron and then with 2 School, Army Co-Operation before joining 10 Maintenance Unit (MU) on 8 June 1939. Its final service was with 10 School, Technical Training, at Kirkham, Liverpool from 26 September 1940. Recovered in 2003 and restored by Aero-Vintage (UK) it is fully airworthy and has the civilian registration G-BVVI, being now part of the Historical Aircraft Collection.

Chapter Nine

Hawker Fury

This beautiful and delicate little biplane fighter is best known for being the first RAF fighter to exceed 200mph (320km/h) in level flight. She was a contemporary of the same company's equally stylish Hawker Hart light bomber, which with its many derivatives had an even great longevity. Both came from the inspired design team that Hawker assembled at Kingston-on-Thames, south-west London, under Sydney Camm[1] and this dainty and elegant aircraft with sensitive controls that responded beautifully to the pilot's touch, illustrated his style of clean, simple lines that were to result in the Hawker Hurricane monoplane a few years later.

The Air Ministry had, in the late 1920s, set out their requirement for a new naval fighter[2] that would be faster and quicker climbing than contemporary machines for maritime work, the task of intercepting enemy bombers approaching the fleet in pre-radar days requiring a high rate of climb, with range being a secondary factor. Under Air Ministry Specification F.21/26 Hawker's answer had been the Interceptor Fighter. This aircraft was powered by the Jupiter IV engine and made her maiden flight in 1929. She was tested at Martlesham Heath and then very quickly, the design was modified to meet the new N.20/27 specification and she was re-engined with the 450hp (330.97kW) Mercury radial. This gave her a best speed of 218mph (350km/h) at 10,500ft 3200.4m) with a laden weight of 3,178lb. The wingspan was 30ft (9.144m), overall length 23ft 8.25in (7.2199m).

The earlier Hawker design, the Hoopoe, had been abandoned, and the resulting second machine, this time developed from the Interceptor, emerged as the Hornet, in line with the existing company naming policy of alliteration, but its initial power plant now became the 420hp (313.32 kW) Rolls-Royce F.XIC, a 12-cylinder, in-line, liquid-cooled engine, which was enclosed with a smooth streamlined cowling finely tapered to enhance the plane's aerodynamics, giving it a unique profile. With that power plant it achieved speeds of 207mph (331.13 km/h) at the Aeroplane and Armament Experimental Establishment (A&AEE) at Martlesham Heath airfield in Suffolk. This compared very favourably with the Bristol Bulldog, which was just 174mph (280.03km/h), while even the Hart itself was capable of 184mph (296.12 km/h). Even so, it was immediately modified to take the 480hp (358kW) Rolls-Royce F.XIS and F.XIIS water-cooled engines, featuring the unique pressurized cooling system. The latter power plant produced a top speed of 214mph (344.4 km/h) at 10,000ft (3048.0m) with a fully laden weight of 3,490lb (1583.03kg), while increasing the overall length to 26ft 2.25in (8.1343m).

The maiden flight of the Hornet (J9682) took place at Brooklands airfield, near Weybridge, Surrey, in March 1929 piloted by Chief Test Pilot George Bulman and this was followed by the first public display of the Hornet, which was in London, at the Olympia Aero Show in 1929. The Hornet was tested most successfully with first the F.XIA and then the F.XIS engine with a motor compressor and results exceeded Air Ministry requirements. Its climb rate was close to 2,400ft/m (730 m/min), which would achieve its primary task. Its main competitor was the Fairey Firefly II, but this was rejected, being mainly of wooden construction when the Air Ministry had demanded all-metal, and it lacked the superb handling qualities of the Hornet, although it was marginally faster. The Hornet was equally favoured over the later Belgian-inspired Fairey *Fantôme*. Thus the RAF awarded Hawker's a small contract for three prototype aircraft to their new 13/30 Specification and these became serials K1926, K1927 and K1928, the first making its maiden flight in July 1930 powered by a 525hp (391.65kW) Kestrel IB, with which it achieved 202mph (325.81km/h) at 10,800ft (3291.8m). The two later prototypes utilized the 550 hp (410.3kW) Kestrel IIS engine instead.

This was at the height of the depression, money was extremely tight and there was no obvious enemy in sight[3] and the bargaining process was protracted. The slower Bulldog was more generally adopted despite being a less efficient weapon of war and was attractive to the politicians only because it was much cheaper (a scenario that has become very familiar again in Britain's defence systems today). Thus the Fury's initial production order, when it came in 1930, was tiny by later standards, just twenty-one machines, although more followed. One would have thought the name Hornet was an 'aggressive' enough title for a fighter aircraft, but the Air Ministry rejected it as not being 'ferocious' enough and substituted their own choice, Fury. The availability of the new V-12 engine, with the centrifugal compressor and pressurized cooling system, which was named the Kestrel, also restricted output. Their rivals, Gloster favoured the Mercury radial and this was also to feature in the Fury story.

The first flight of the Fury I was again conducted by Bulman from Brookland on 25 March 1931. Meanwhile, three special variants appeared, the 'Intermediate' Fury (G-ABSE) a private venture (P.V.), which Hawker used to test the IVS Kestrel and the Goshawk engines; the 'High Speed' Fury, an official prototype (K3586) with tapered wing form, and featuring the pared-down 'vee' interplane struts. It was intended to test the advanced design features for Hawker's own proposed response to the Air Ministry F.7/30 Specification for a four-gun fighter, the Hawker P.V.3. As such it became the test bed for the 695hp (511.17kW) Goshawk III with the heavy steam condenser equipment and the PV112 engines. The P.V.3 itself first flew on 15 June 1934. It had a wingspan of 34ft (7.3152 m), a laden weight of 4,760lb (2159.09kg) and achieved a top speed of 224mph (360.49 km/h) at 14,000ft (4267.2m). This power plant was later substituted by the 705hp (518.53kW) Goshawk B.41, which reduced all-up weight to 4,550lb (2,063.845kg) and thus pushed speed up to 232mph (373.7km/h) at 15,500ft (4,724.4m), but it was destined to lose out to the Gloster Gladiator. However, based on Air Ministry Specification 6/35 with the 639hp (477kW) Kestrel VI engine with semi-evaporated cooling, it attained a top speed of 229.91 mph (379km/h).

The 'Intermediate' Fury had also featured a variety of engine types, starting life with the Kestrel IIS, and having semi-enclosed streamlined wheel pants with Messier oleo struts fitted. This was followed in 1932 by a Kestrel IVS for supercharger testing and in October 1933 the Kestrel VI was trialled, followed in May 1935 by the Goshawk II and the following August the enhanced Kestrel VI ('Special') was tested in its turn. All these tests helped formed the basis of the Fury II prototype.

This aircraft had a swept-back top wing with a span of 29ft 6.25in (8.9779m) and first flew on 3 May 1933 with the 600hp (441.3kW) Kestrel S, which gave it a maximum speed of 245mph (394.29km/h) at 10,000ft (3048.00m). This aircraft was then re-configured to take the 695hp (518.47kW) Goshawk III, with straight leading edges to the top wing and 'N' struts. The airframe incorporated the newly introduced tubular steel and aluminium constructions for the fuselage and 'dumb-bell' wing spars. Ailerons were installed on the top plane only. This produced a best speed of 238mph (383.02 km/h) at 16,000ft (4,876.8m), with a fully laden weight of 3,708lb (1,681.8kg). Following these experiments the aircraft was converted into a Fury-II and in September 1934 assigned to No. 43 Squadron. However, in 1936 it was again pulled out of squadron service to be used as a trials aircraft for the Rolls-Royce Merlin at their plant.

Also, in October 1933, Camm briefly had a design plan for a 'Fury Monoplane'. The concept, and it was nothing more than that, was a four-gun fighter with enclosed cockpit and retractable undercarriage, but it was soon abandoned and was soon replaced by what was to eventually emerge as the Hurricane.

Eighty-four production models powered by the IIS Kestrel engine were built by Hawker and many were sub-contracted to General Aircraft Ltd (GAL) and in total 117 Fury-Is were produced. They first joined No. 43 Squadron at RAF Tangmere, West Sussex, in May 1931. This unit familiarized itself with the Fury and became the 'Red Arrows' of their day, mounting stunning aerobatic performances up and down the country to much acclaim. The Fury, despite its small numbers, thus became quite familiar to the British public. No. 25 Squadron replaced its Armstrong Whitworth Siskin 3a aircraft with the Fury and quickly demonstrated its versatility, winning the Phillip Sassoon Fighting Area Trophy in 1933 with a record score of 99.9 per cent. They also introduced the concept of 'tied-together' aerobatics, having three machines connected in *vic*-formation by a bungee-cord, which then took-off, carried out their aerial routine and then landed with the cord intact. At the Empire Aerial Days at London's Hendon airfield between 1933 and 1935 this proved a great attraction and was only achieved with great skill and the high degree of responsiveness of the Fury herself. They also won the speed contest at the 1934 Zurich International and represented the RAF at the Canadian Centennial in Toronto, Ontario, the same year.

The Fury-II, which first flew on 20 August 1935, was a single-seater biplane fighter with an overall length of 27ft 9in (8.15m), a wingspan of 30ft (9.14m) and a height of 10ft 2in (3.10m). The wing area was 251.98ft^2 (23.41m^2). The empty weight was 2,734lb (1,240kg), and the loaded weight was 3,609lb (1,637kg). It was powered by a single 690hp (515kW) Rolls-Royce Kestrel IV V12 engine with composite cooling, improved fuel and oil systems, a more streamlined airframe and modified and reduced wheel spats. This gave a maximum speed of 223mph (360km/h) at an altitude of 16,500ft (5030m). The service ceiling was 29,500ft (8,990m), with a rate of climb of 2,600ft/m (13.2 m/s) and the range was 270 miles (435km). The wing loading was 14.4 lb/ft^2 (21.5 kg/m^2). It was armed with a pair of 0.303 in (7.7mm) Vickers Mk IV synchronized machine-guns, which replaced the earlier models Mk III, with 600 rpg.

The fuselage was of all-metal construction forward and composite construction aft the cockpit, with straight canvas-covered wings with rounded tips and with the upper slightly staggered forward. The undercarriage was fixed with a traverse bar connecting the wheels, and featured a prominent rearward angled skid instead of a tail wheel. A total of 112 Fury-IIs were produced, eighty-nine by General Aircraft Ltd (GAL) at Hanwell, West London, who received an order in 1936.

The Fury-Is were allocated serials K2899 to K2908 inclusive and K3730 to K3742 inclusive, while the Fury-IIs had serials K7263 to K7285 inclusive and K8218 to K8306 inclusive.

Fury-IIs replaced the Fury-I with Nos. 1, 25 and 43 Squadrons from the autumn of 1936 to March 1937 and the same year equipped the newly re-formed No. 73 at Mildenhall, Suffolk, and No. 87 at Tangmere, Sussex, both on 15 March, where they replaced the Siskin, and, in October, No. 41 Squadron newly returned from Aden, where they replaced the two-seater Hawker Demon. Their time with these last three squadrons was brief as they soon re-equipped with the Gloster Gladiator. The Fury was also serving with the Advanced Training Flight at Cranwell in 1933 and with No. 5 Flying Training School in 1938.

Hawker touted the Fury widely on the continent, and several variants appeared down the years to meet their demands, while the shortage of availability of the Kestrel led to trying out several alternative power plants like the 650hp (485kW) Hispano-Suiza 12N and 12X engine in Spain, the 9-cyliner Pratt & Whitney for Persia (Iran), the 710hp (529.66kW) Lorraine Petrel HFRS for Yugoslavia, while Norway's requirements were for a test example powered by the Armstrong Siddeley Panther IIIA, a 14-cylinder radial, but no orders resulted. The Rolls-Royce Goshawk was a development of the Kestrel with a steam condensation cooling system, but this increased weight and was detrimental to the Fury's outstanding performance.

The elegant Fury served with the following RAF Squadrons: No. 43 Squadron at RAF Tangmere, Sussex, from May 1931 to January 1939; No.1 from February 1932 to November 1938; No. 25 Squadron from February 1932 to October 1937; No. 73 Squadron from March 1937 to July 1937; No.87 Squadron from March 1937 to June 1937; and No. 41 Squadron from October 1937 to January 1939. It also served with No. 3 Flying Training School (FTS) at Cranwell, Lincolnshire, where it continued to be employed as a trainer well into the war.

Foreign service

Norway

The *Haerens Flyvevesen* took delivery of a single experimental Fury (serial number 401), which was powered by a 500hp (373kW) Armstrong-Siddeley Panther IIIA engine with two concentric Townsend rings. This engine shifted the aircraft's centre of gravity (cg) forward, tending to affect performance in the air and making it prone to 'nose-ins' on the ground. The engine also gave it an overall length of 25ft 10.5in (7.8867m), a fully laden weight of 3,500lb (1,587.53kg) and a top speed of 201.5mph (323.48 km/h) at 16,400 ft (4,998.7m) and it first flew on 5 August 1932. Armament consisted of two 7.7mm Spandau machine-guns.

This machine was delivered to Norway in 1933. Had it had been successful the plan was to licence-build this variant at the *Kjeller Flyfabrikk* (Norwegian Army Factory at Kjeller, Skedsimo, north of Oslo), but, in the event it was not selected and instead the Gloster Gladiator was chosen. In 1936 the machine was disposed of.

Persia (Iran)

The decision had been made in January 1932 for the Persian air force to be brought up to date and Captain Elis Nordquist, a Swedish officer, was brought in to advise how best to do this. Among the first results of his work was that, in January 1933, the Persian Government authorized Contract No. 100118/33 for Hawker to supply the *Havayi Niru-ye-ye Iran-e Shahanshahiy* with sixteen Furies. They differed considerably from the RAF model having the 750hp (559.5kW) Pratt & Whitney Hornet S2B1-G radial engine, which drove a three-bladed Hamilton Hydromatic airscrew. The first of this variant were delivered in July 1933 and they received the serial numbers 201–216 inclusive. Meanwhile, extensive testing at Brookland's in the latter months of 1933 had revealed several problems with the American engine, and in November the Persian authorities decided that future orders would be powered instead by a British power plant.

This resulted in changes to the next order, which followed in May 1934 with Contract No. 366843/34 for a further twelve machines. This differed in that the Fury was powered by the 645hp (481.17 kW) Bristol Mercury VI S2 radial (which had been trial tested on serial number 203 at Brooklands in September 1934) with special cowlings and it achieved a top speed of 215mph (346.01 km/h) at 16,500ft (5,029.2m). This engine gave them an overall length of 24ft 6.25in (7.4739m). In the event only eight of the twelve were eventually delivered to Persia from between November 1934 and January 1935[4] and these were allocated the serial numbers 217–224 inclusive. These were deemed superior in performance, so much so that at least two of the earlier batch, 203 and 208, were returned to Hawker to exchange their Pratt & Whitney engines with the Mercury, the first flying with the new power plant on 25 September 1934.

Persia became Iran in 1935 by which time it was training its own pilots at the new College. The United States Minister to Iran, Cornelius Van Hermert Engert reported observing a formation of ten Hawker Fury fighters during the *Coup D'état Day Parade* fly-past over Teheran in November 1937.[5] Seven months later there were fifteen Furies with the 1st Air Regiment at Qila Murgha, while the Flying Training School at Mehrabad had three more and by November 1939, the Fury strength reached a peak with twenty-one at Qila Murgha, four at Mashad, three at Mehrabad with two more undergoing routine refits.

The Iranian Furies were the last to be employed on combat duties, as they were still being flown on border patrol duties as late as 1942/43 and there is an unconfirmed report that one even lingered on as late as 1949.

Portugal

Three examples of the Fury-I were delivered by Hawker to the *Aeronáutica Militar* in 1934. They were allocated to the *Grupo Independente de Aviao de Proteco e Combate* (Independent Escort and Fighter Group) at Tancos Air Base, Vila Nova da Barquinha, north-east of Lisbon, from 1934.

One Portuguese Fury was destroyed during the Spanish Civil War. This aircraft may possibly have been part of the small *Missão Militar Portuguesa de Observçãoem Espanhha* (Military Observation Mission in Span) under *Capitáo de Aeronáutica* António Dias Leite with three pilots.[6]

South Africa

Fury-II's equipped with Kestrel VI engines were supplied to the South African Air Force prior to the outbreak of war, seven being acquired in 1935 and these were delivered in September the following year. They received the South African Air Force (SAAF) serials 200–206 inclusive and were initially allocated to the Central Flying School (CFS) which moved from Zwartkop Airfield to Kimberley. At the beginning of 1939 the Furies were re-assigned being split between 2 Fighter-Bomber Squadron based at Waterkloof Air Station, Pretoria, and 4 Fighter-Bomber Squadron at Durban.

When on 31 August 1939, 1 Transvaal Air Squadron at Waterkloof Air Station with Hawker Hartebeest aircraft, was re-designated as 1 (Fighter-Bomber) Squadron under Major Noel Gray Niblock-Stuart, they were re-equipped with six Hawker Furies and four Hawker Hurricane-Is and trained on their new machines until May 1940. The Fury also served alongside the Hartebeest with 41 Squadron for a short period in 1941.

In August 1940 six further Fury aircraft, ex-RAF, reached South Africa, and they were followed by further batches between October 1940 and January 1941, totalling sixteen in all. With No. 43 Squadron some Fury aircraft took part in the 'Air Commando' tours of the country, and even flew mock air combats with the captured Fiat CR.42.

Another unit, 8 Squadron SAAF, did not form until February 1942 and received the Hawker Fury from 43 Squadron RAF. They never served in combat and were disbanded after only seven months on 24 August 1942.

Spain

Three examples of the Fury, which first flew on 7 April 1936, were delivered on 11 July 1936 by Hawkers to the *l'Aviacion Militar de la República Española* in June

1936, equipped with the 612hp (457kW) Hispano Suiza 12Xbrs engine. They had a maximum speed of 234mph (377k/h) at 13,400ft (4,084.3m). These machines also were equipped with a special cantilever undercarriage with the wheels internally sprung by Dowty, but were delivered lacking machine-guns. They were allocated the serials 4-1, 4-2 and 4-3. Originally the armament was to be the Vickers Mk III and then the 12.7mm Vickers C, but the Spanish authorities examined the possibility of fitting them with the 13.2mm Hotchkiss-en-Cie, which the French had originally designed as a heavy anti-aircraft gun, and which several navies, including the Japanese, used in that capacity. As each stripped-down gun weighed in at a hefty 83lb (37.5kg), it is difficult to think this would have been a good move for the delicate little Fury! In the event they carried neither weapon. The outbreak of the Civil War resulted in an arms embargo by the League of Nations (to which only Great Britain and France actually adhered to in practice) and the Spanish were thus forced to pillage any suitable weapon from other demolished warplanes and fit them before the three aircraft could join the conflict, most received two 13.2mm Hispano machine-guns. This same embargo also marked the end of the planned licence-building of fifty more Furies in Spain itself and the two sides had to look to Italy and the Soviet Union for alternatives.

Both the Republican and the Nationalist combatants flew the Fury during the Civil War, frequently utilizing them for dive-bombing attacks. During the Republican's attempts to halt the Nationalist Army of Lieutenant Colonel Juan Yagüe's advance on Madrid fierce battles were fought at Badajoz, Trujillo and Talavera de la Reina. During these the Republican air force was engaged with Andrés Garcia La Calle leading a mixed force of fighters. On 31 August 1936 in the Talavera de la Reina-Oropesa area of Toledo, La Calle in a Fury in company with two Nieuport 52s, destroyed two Fiat 32s of the Nationalist air force. On 3 September again La Calle was flying the Fury along with Loire 46 and Dewoitine D37s in heavy air fighting and scored further victories, which set him on the way to being one of the Nationalist air aces.

One was written off in the defence of Madrid in November 1936, and later the second was also wrecked when the synchronizing mechanism for the machine-guns malfunctioned and it shot away its own propeller. Parts from both crashed machines were collected and re-built as one 'new' and flyable Fury, which duly received the serial 4-4. The third machine (4-3) ran out of fuel over Nationalist lines and made a forced landing whereupon it was taken over and restored for active duty with Franco's forces, although its subsequent fate remains obscure.

Yugoslavia

The export model of the Fury-I for the Yugoslav Government featured the 745hp (555.77kW) Kestrel XVI piston engine, giving a top speed of 252mph (405.55km/h) at 16,000ft (4,084.3m), the best speed of any of the type. It had a reduced wing of 250ft^2 (23.226m^2) and was fitted with a low-drag radiator and a cantilever undercarriage with internally sprung wheels. Most carried two extra machine-guns under the wing. An initially batch of six Fury-Is was produced to this format by Hawker and were delivered to the *Jugoslovensko kraljevsko Ratno vazduhoplovstvo Pomorska avjacja* (JKRV – Royal

Yugoslavian Air Force) in 1932. A second batch, this time of Fury-IIs, powered by the Hispano-Suiza 12NB radial, which gave them a top speed of 222mph (357.27 km/h) at 15,100ft (4,602.5m), and armed with two twin 7.7mm Spandau machine-guns, was delivered between 1936 and 1937. A larger batch of forty more was licence-built in Yugoslavia, twenty-four by *Fabrika Autobusa i Specijanih Vozila a.d, (Ikarus)* and sixteen by *Fabrika Aeroplane i Hidroavioa (Zmaj)*, both located at Zemun, Belgrade.

On 6 April 1941 the Fury was serving with 5. *Lovacki puk* (Fighter Wing), commanded by *Potpukovnik* (Lieutenant-Colonel) Leonid Badjak, with the 35 and 36 *Lovacka grupa* (Squadron) at Medosevac, Niš, Nišava District, in southern Serbia.

War service

East Africa

South Africa's 1 Squadron flew their six Furies over from Pretoria to the port of Durban where they were crated up and, on 26 May 1940, shipped to Mombasa aboard the freighter *Takliwa*. They arrived at Mombasa, Kenya, in East Africa on 1 June and were re-assembled. Their pilots, who had been sent north to Egypt earlier, returned and were united with the aircraft and the unit moved forward to support the British liberation of Abyssinia. They moved up to the forward air strips of Wajir and Buna in north-eastern Kenya close to the Abyssinian border, in July, with three machines assigned to each field, as point defence fighters.

The Furies were soon in action, for, on 3 August, an Italian Caprion Ca.133 of 8ª *Squadriglia*, 25⁰ *Gruppo*, made a reconnaissance penetration over Wajir. The three Furies were ordered to intercept, but one (serial 206) failed to get off the ground. However, the other pair, Flight Lieutenant Robert Blake in 203 and Flight Lieutenant Patrick Rushmere in 205, did get away and managed to quickly get into attacking positions seven miles out. They met the intruder head on and quickly shot it down in flames with the loss of the entire crew. This neat little victory was marred the following day when two Furies were involved in a collision above the Nanyuki airstrip, Lakipia, during a training exercise, both 203 and 204 being destroyed, although both pilots survived.

A revenge attack was mounted against Wajir on 6 August when two Ca.133s from 9ª *Squadriglia*, 25° *Gruppo*, bombed the field. Two Furies from No. 1 Squadron intercepted and claimed to have hit both Italian machines, without damage to themselves.

Nine fresh Hawker Furies were on the establishment of 2 Squadron, which was formed from 1 Squadron on 30 September 1940, and twelve were on strength by January 1941 including serials 211, 212, 213 and 214. They were part of a very mixed group that, for a while, included both Hurricanes and Gladiators and the Fury aircraft were principally employed in the army co-operation role with 1 Bomber Brigade and even undertook the ground-attack role in the subsequent drive north. However, it was in the interceptor role that they first saw action. On the 19/20 October three Ca.133s attacked Garissa airfield, in east Kenya, and a pair of Furies ('F' Detachment – Lieutenant Hendriks Johannes Piet Burger and Lieutenant Marthinus Christo Wiese) scrambled away and shot one of the bombers down. The delicate little Fury was finding operating conditions here rather trying. To gain a height of 20,000ft took twenty minutes, while their engine coolant sometimes boiled at 3,000ft.[7]

A fortunate near-miss took place over Archer's Post, north of Isiolo, Eastern Province, on 31 October when a pair of SAAF Junkers Ju.86s carrying General Jan Christian Smuts, the Prime Minister of South Africa, General Sir Hesperus Pierre van Ryneveld, Chief of the General Staff and founder of the SAAF, Major General Alan Cunningham, commander of the British forces in East Africa and Major General Alfred Reade Godwin-Austen, commander of 2 African Division in the attack on Italian Somaliland, were intercepted by a trio of Furies from 'D' detachment, 2 Squadron, under Captain Jack Meaker. Before recognition was finally made one Fury, piloted by Lieutenant Douglas Dolley Pannell, opened fire on the leading bomber, but luckily for the subsequent campaign and indeed, all concerned, his aim was off and no harm was done.

By April 1941 the work of the Fury was done and 2 Squadron dispensed with them to 70 Operational Training Unit (OTU) at Nakuru.

Yugoslavia

When Germany invaded on 6 April 1941 in Operation *Marita*, Hitler's angry response to the anti-German change of the Yugoslavian Government, the 35. *Grupa*, 5. *Lovacki puk*, commanded by Major Vasa Zifvanovic was at Kosancic, Leskovac, with fifteen Hawker Fury-IIs on its establishment. The Squadron, whose main mission was the fighter defence of Nis itself, had two *Lovacka eskadrila* (Flights), 109 commanded by *Kapetan* (Captain) Pavle Goldner and 110 *eskadrila* commanded by *Kapetan* Oyo Sep. Although hostilities only formally commenced on the 6th, for several weeks the Furies had been attempting to catch high-flying Luftwaffe reconnaissance machines busy surveying the area in preparation for the land assault, but they were powerless to prevent it, lacking both speed, height, and early-warning.

The 5. *Lovacki puk*'s other unit, 36. *Grup*, commanded by *Major* Drago Brezovsek, and also having a strength of fifteen Fury-IIs, was at Rezanovacka Kosa, Kumanovo. The two *eskadrila* were 111, commanded by *Kapetan* Vojislav Popovic, and 112, commanded by *Kapetan* Konstantin Jermakov. They had the air defence of the city of Skopje as their main mission. All units were on high alert and prepared for action with men sitting strapped-in and ready to go at first light; a two-plane early patrol toward Kratovo had already taken off. Even so the Luftwaffe's opening attack, when it came, proved overwhelming. Approximately thirty Messerschmitt Bf.109 single-engined fighters and Bf.110 twin-engined fighters from the II/*Zestörergeschwader* 26 (II/*ZG 26*) and the *Lehrgeschwader* 2 (*LG.2*) suddenly appeared putting into action *Untemehmen Strafgericht* (Operation Retribution) the opening air attacks that paved the way for the ground invasion.

Just a single Fury was destroyed by the initial strafing attack, but as the 111. *eskadrila* desperately attempted to claw their way upward they were massacred by the modern German fighters who had the advantage of height, speed, armament and combat experience. The companions of 112. *eskadrila* did manage to gain a little altitude, but it availed them nothing. In a brief encounter, which lasted between 0611 and 0620, eleven Fury fighters had either been destroyed outright, including the two commanding officers, or had been badly damaged and crash-landed. Almost half their strength had therefore been wiped out in the opening minutes of the battle. *Leutnant* Friedrich Geißhardt of the *Stab LG.2* alone claimed to have destroyed four Fury fighters and *Oberleutnant* Erwin Clausen of *3./LG 2* three in this action. In return the *II/ZG 26* lost just two Bf. 110 aircraft along with one from *1/LG2*. On two occasions Fury fighters were seen to ram their opponents after running out of ammunition. Just two Furies survived from 36. *grupa* and these were sent to Stubol air strip, near Dolni Stubol, Macedonia, to reinforced 35. *grupa* but one crashed *en route* and the only survivor was destroyed by strafing Bf.110s two days later.

The 35. *grupa* had evaded detection at Kosancic, and the Bf.109's instead destroyed sixteen Breguet XIX reconnaissance aircraft at neighbouring Sorlince mistaking them for their intended prey. Five of the 11. *eskadrila* Furies attempted to overhaul the enemy as they withdrew but, perhaps fortunately for them, failed to do so and returned to base. To avoid a return visit the unit shifted base to Bojnik field. From there six 109. *Eskadrila* machines attempted to intercept a large group of Heinkel He.111s but could not catch them. The Furies were plagued with jamming machine-guns throughout this period, but as they could not get close enough to use them this proved irrelevant. It was more important on 8 April when they were sent to strafe advancing *Panzer* columns at Bela Palanka, but poor weather hampered this mission and with the tanks closing in on their bases all the flyable Furies pulled out to Kraljevo next day, two of them being brought down by 'friendly fire' from their own (understandably) jittery ground troops who considered that everything that flew was German, which, increasingly, it was.

The Fury numbers continued to be steadily decreased; several damaged machines were put to the torch to prevent them falling into enemy hands when the *grup* was forced to shift base again on the 10 April, moving to Preljina, Cacak, where they refuelled and then straffed the advancing enemy at Cuprija, Morava, and flew on to Sarajevo. By now just eight Fury aircraft remained operational with 35. *Grupa* and these were yet again forced to move base to Niksic, Montenegro, on 13 April. On the way they were jumped by twelve Fiat CR.41s and another Fury was destroyed. Four days later Yugoslavia surrendered unconditionally and the unit was ordered to cease combat operations with immediate effect. Several of the seven surviving Fury aircraft that were damaged were destroyed by their own ground crew but two in flyable condition were captured intact when Italian forces occupied the airfield. These two aircraft were later taken to Guidonia Montecelio, near Rome, where the *Regia Aeronautica's Centro Sperimentale di Volo* was located. They were given the codes '43' and '53' and put through a series of test flights. It is thought that after this their captors utilized them both as fighter trainers.[8]

Iran

Fears that the Shah, Mohammed Reza Pahlavi, who had ousted the pro-British Qajar Dynasty earlier, was pro-Nazi and that he was encouraging the clandestine infiltration of Germans into the oil-rich nation prompted the British and Soviet Governments to take pre-emptive action and between 25 August and 17 September military forces from both nations moved in and crushed Iranian resistance in Operation *Countenance*. There were several spirited actions by land, sea and air, with RAF Hawker Hurricanes and Gloster Gladiators from No. 261 Squadron predominating during Operation Y, the air strikes when five or six Hawker Audax were destroyed.[9] The Iranian flyers were outclassed, particularly at the battle for Gīlān-e-Gharb, Kermanshah Province, on the Iraqi border, when in aerial fighting six Iranian fighters were destroyed. Iran's position was clearly hopeless and on 30 August the Shah called for an end to armed resistance and for the invasion to be no longer opposed by force. However, this was ignored by some Iranians and among those who determined to resist to the last were pilots of the Qaleh Morqhi 1st Air Regiment, near Teheran itself.[10]

As Soviet armoured columns approached the capital two Fury fighters, piloted by Wing Commander Shishtari and Captain Vassiq, took off and made strafing attacks on the tanks. When all their ammunition had been expended these two escaped to try and reach the airfield at Zanjan in north-west Iran determined to join thirteen aircraft of 2 Air Regiment who already fled there, and carry on the fight.[11] On 17 September they were intercepted by five Polikarpov I-16 fighters over the Caspian Sea, Vassiq being shot down and Shishtari eventually running out of fuel and crashing in a forest.[12]

Reza Pahlavi was deposed and the Crown Prince Mohammad became the new Shah. The Iranian air force was reduced to border patrolling and by December 1943 there were eleven active Fury fighters based at Teheran, with a further four others idle at the nearby Aircraft Park and Maintenance Unit, while the Flying Training School had just a single Fury on its strength. By the end of the war the majority of the Fury complement had been reduced to trainers and hacks.

Preserved aircraft

1. At the Aero Vintage and Historic Aircraft Collection (HAC) facility is a Mk I Fury (serial number K5674 (G-CBZP)), which carriers the Hawker number 41H/67550. The history of this aircraft is that it was delivered to 2 ASU on 20 November 1935 and passed to the establishment of No. 43 Squadron at RAF Tangmere on 2 June 1936. It was flown by Flying Officer (later Air Chief Marshal Sir) Frederick Rosier commanding 'B' Flight between December 1936 and January 1939. It carried the name Queen of North and South. Retired after a final flight on 22 February 1939, it was stored successively at 5 Maintenance Unit (MU) and 47MU before being shipped to South Africa on 5 August 1940 aboard the *Clan Mathieso*, arriving on 20 October. Allocated the SAAF Serial 215, it went to No. 13 Squadron (renumbered as No. 43 Squadron) at Swartkop Air Base, Centurion. In March 1942 a forced landing through lack of fuel saw the machine damaged and retired from service and scrapped at No. 2 Air Depot, Kimberley. Retrotec commenced restoration work when the aircraft was returned to the UK in 1992 and it was on display at IWM Duxford, Cambridgeshire in 2011 before being flown again from Goodwood on 30 July 2012. It is the only one of its kind and is based at Hangar 3 at Duxford.

Chapter Ten

Heinkel He.50

Although under the terms of the Treaty of Versailles, which went into effect in 1920, Germany had been forbidden to construct military aircraft, and the German Flying Corps was disbanded, the nations aeronautical companies soon found ways to evade that ruling, stretching civilian aircraft to the limits,[1] developing racing aircraft, seaplanes and manufacturing aircraft in pieces for assembly overseas, and finally building for overseas customers. Long before the Third Reich came into being Germany's aviation industry was in the van of developments, and, aided by secret Soviet facilities at Lipezk, the *Reichswehr* High Command were able to hone warplane tactics to a high degree.

One leading company was that of Ernst Heinkel, who specialized in seaplane development and whose Warnemünde products broke many inter-war records and were highly rated in the international field. As early as 1923 he had been given secret instructions by a certain *Major* Kurt Student[2] to build a wheeled biplane capable of military reconnaissance work; this turned out to be the Heinkel HD 17, and was followed by the HD 21, and all the while he successfully fooled the Allied Control Commission's inspectors time after time. The Heinkel company also developed catapult-launched maritime aircraft in the He.38 and He.60, and this attracted attention from the other side of the globe where the Imperial Japanese Navy was expanding its naval air arm, in particular the dive-bomber concept, in order to mitigate its inferiority in battleship strength vis-à-vis the United States.

In 1931 the Imperial Japanese Navy, which had already placed earlier orders with the company, gave a contract to the Ernst Heinkel *FlugzegWerke* (Aircraft Manufacturing Company) for a two-seater dive-bomber with a bomb-load capacity of up to 550lb (250kg). The aircraft was to be fully stressed for launching via catapult and also to be employed either with wheels from carriers or land bases, or with floats as a seaplane bomber.

The Heinkel He.50 was an equi-span, two-bay, biplane dive-bomber, of mixed construction, with a rectangular-section fuselage of welded steel tubes, which provided a strong core strength, outside of which wood formers and stringers created an oval outer layer that was fabric-covered. The forward section of the fuselage had a light alloy covering up to the engine housing. The wings were conventional, of wood composition, fabric covered. They were equal size, barely staggered, and as befitted her role, had ailerons on all four panels.

The initial prototype, the He.50aW (*Werke No.* 406, civilian registration D-ISIH, later TH+HJ) was built as a floatplane in the summer of 1931. The aircraft was equipped with twin floats and had a 390hp (291 kW) Junkers L5m six-cylinder, inline water-cooled engine. This power plant proved insufficient for the specification. When damaged in a hard landing this machine was abandoned.

The second prototype, the He.50aL (*Werke No.* 408, later He.50 V-1) was built as a carrier/land-based dive-bomber, with wheels. The engine selected was the 490hp (365kW) Siemens Jupiter VI 9-cylinder, single-row, radial, (derived from the Gnome-Rhône/Bristol). This machine was re-designated as the He.50 V1 (V = *Versuchsflugzeuge* – Experimental aircraft) and was assessed by the *Reichswehr* (German Defence Ministry) in 1932. Dive-bombing tests were carried out at Breitling, close to Warnemunde, with 1,000lb (453kg) concrete blocks being dropped on moored targets.

This machine was followed by another prototype, He.50 V-2 (D-2471), which was evaluated at the RDL *ErprobungsStelle* at Staaken, west Berlin, and at Lipezk (L103), north of Voronesh, Russia and, when that establishment closed, at the *Deutsche Verkehrsfliegerschule* (DVS – German Commercial Flying School) from May 1933. Of those built that were designated as the He.50b, some were taken for evaluation and training by the German authorities, D-IDUI going to the A/B 82 *Flugzeugführerschule* (FFs – Fighter Flying School) at Quakenbrück, (Air Landing Ground B109) in Lower Saxony; D-IKTE going to A/B 52 FFs at Halberstadt, in Saxony-Anhalt; D-ILIO being sent to the *Jagdgeschw* (Fight School) at Schleissheim with the DVS; and three, D-IFEA, D-ILFI and D-IDSE, ended up at the RDL No. 1 *Jagdgeschw* at Werneuchen, north-east of Berlin.

The fourth machine of the prototype group, became the Heinkel He.66, which followed the same general arrangement, all being powered by the 600hp (373 kW) *Brandenburgishce MotorWerke* (*Bramo* –Brandenburg Engine Works) 322B (Siemens SAM 22B) radial engine. This latter machine was purchased by the Imperial Japanese Navy and ultimately was developed into the Aichi D1A, Type 96 Carrier Bomber,[3] which the Allies much later on were to allocate the code-name 'Susie'.

Meanwhile, following the evaluation of the He.50 V1, the *Reichswehr* had placed orders for three further development machines and two of these three RLM aircraft were used to equip a *Reichsverkehrsministerium* (RLM – Reich Air Ministry) *Fleigstab* (Staff Flight), which conducted dive-bombing tests at the Rechlin proving ground on 2 and 3 February 1932. Different specimen bomb racks were fitted for these tests and then the two aircraft were flown across to Jüterbog (Altes Lager) airfield, Brandenburg. Here another one hundred dives were undertaken with a make-over as a single-seater, and with the 600hp (441kW) SAM 22b, which gave her a speed of 185mph (297.7km/h) in a power dive; she was not considered ideal, but *was* available.

A production run of these aircraft to equip their new planned dive-bomber units was approved and, as the He.50A-1, twenty-five were ordered in 1933 and a further thirty-five on 1 January 1934. Some of the civilian registrations are as follows:- D-2471, D-IBYY, D-ICYS, D-IDAG, D-IDAO, D-IDDY, D-IDEA, D-IDOA, D-IDOI, D-IDRE, D-IDSE, D-IDSH, D-IDUI, D-IDYY, D-IEJA, D-IFEA, D-IFUY, D-ILIO, D-ILNI, D-IGLU, D-IHXO, D-IKIE, D-IKTE, D-ILAY, D-ILFI, D-ILIO, D-ILNI, D-IMAA, D-IMMA, D-IMOE, D-INAO, D-INAY, D-INOX, D-IODA, D-IQVR, D-IRAM, D-ISIH, D-ITNK, D-ITNY, D-ITQE, D-IUKI, D-IVIY and D-IVYI.

The plan was to fully equip by 30 September, but to meet these numbers the sixty total was still deemed insufficient. By this period the Weimar Republic had been swept aside by the *Nationalsozialistische Deutsche Arbeiterpartei* (National Socialist German Workers Party – NSDAP (Nazi) party and under their charismatic and nationalist leader, war production began to gear up rapidly. The new *Reichsluftfahrtministerium* (Reich Air Ministry – RLM) under Hermann Göring proceeded as quickly as it could to expand all air arms, although still secretly. On 1 October 1933 the formation of the first dive-bomber units was announced, with specialist dive-bomber training being carried out by the *Jagdgeschwader* 132. By 30 September 1935, the requirements list for new machines included fifty-one He.50 dive-bombers. When Ernst Udet, a dive-bomber advocate, took over the *Technisches Amt* (Supply Department) he wound things up a notch more. By 1935 the He.50As were joining their operational units, the *Sturzkampfgeschwader Schwerin*, later I/St.G. 162 and eventually, by 1938, nine Luftwaffe squadrons.

The He.50A had an overall length of 31.ft 6in (9.6m), a wingspan of 37ft 8.25 in (11m), a height of 14ft 9.75 in (4.5m) and had a wing area of 374.59ft^2 (34.8m^2). Her weight was 3,528lb (1,600kg) empty and 5,778lb (2,620kg) fully laden. She was powered by a single 650hp (485kW) nine-cylinder Bramo 322B (SAM 22B) radial engine, which gave her a top speed of 146mph (235 km/h) at sea level and a cruising speed of 118mph (190 km/h). She had a range of 373 miles (600km) at 110 mph (177 km/h). Her service ceiling was 20,998 ft (6,400m) with a rate of climb of 820 ft/min (250 m/min). She was armed with a single 0.312in (7.92mm) MG-15 flexible machine-gun in the observer's rear seat; with an alternative fixed forward-firing MG-17 machine-gun in dive-bombing mode, and could carry a single 551lb (250kg) bomb.

As we have seen the consensus was that the Heinkel He.50 dive-bomber was satisfactory enough to proceed with until better machines arrived and a variant, the He.50L followed, with twenty-five being built by Heinkel and thirty-five more constructed by the *Bayersiche FlugzeugWerke AG (BFW)* at Augsburg.[4] Training of dive-bomber pilots was carried out by the *Fliegergruppe* (Air Wing) Döberitz formed in April 1934. Later that summer twelve He.50s joined *Fliegergruppe* Schwerin (where they replaced the Arado Ar65 and Heinkel He.51 fighter types employed up to that date) and they were joined by two dozen more He.50s in 1935. The first military test came with Hitler's International gamble of re-militarizing the Rhineland on 7 March 1936. For this operation, largely a bluff that was not called, the *Stukagruppe* 165 at Kitzingen, flew two *Staffeln* of He.50s up to Frankfurt/Main airport and the third *Staffel* to Mannheim, in case the French attacked.

By 1937 the He.50 was serving with the *Stab* and I./*Sturzkampfgruppe* 162 *Immelmann*, at Schwerin, and the II./162 at Lübeck-Blankensee; and the I./*Sturzkampfgruppe* 165 at Wertheim.

The He.50A was always regarded as a stop-gap dive-bomber until heavier types were developed, and they were steadily replaced, firstly by the Henschel Hs.123 and then the ultimate Stuka, the Junkers Ju.87. The majority of the He.50As in German hands were then relegated to the dive-bomber trainer mission, in which role it continued until the end of 1943.

Experiments with aircraft carrier construction

Exceptions to this duty were the three He.50s (D-ISH – TH + HJ; D-ITNY – TH + HK; and D-ITQE – TH + HJ) utilized from April 1937 onward for the catapult trials at the Travemünde experimental facility on the Baltic coast, in connection with the construction of the *Graf Zeppelin*, Germany's first, but never completed, aircraft carrier. The *Oberbefehaber de Luftwaffe* (*ObdL* – Supreme Command of the Luftwaffe) announced that the selected aircraft, had she ever have become operational, would include nine Junkers Ju.87C dive-bombers, specially converted for naval usage, but to test the launching techniques and how they would affect the 'navalized' Stuka, the He.50 was used. She was an ideal choice, having originally been specifically built stressed for catapult launching and hooked arrestor-wire landings for carrier operations. More, the German Naval Attaché in Japan had inspected the carrier *Akagi* at Sasebo in 1935, prior to her rebuilding,[5] when she was operating the Aichi D1A as part of her air complement, and passed on his observations to the design team.

The initial *Trägerflugzeug* (carrier-borne aircraft) trials programme was initiated on March 1938 utilizing the He.50s as well as Arado Ar.195s, Arado Ar.197s and Avia Bk.534s. Simulated carrier launchings and landings were carried out, but it was the actual catapult testings that involved the He.50.[6] These trials took place aboard a 60-ft long barge, with a pneumatic catapult mounted aboard, in the estuary of the Trave River. Initial tests were not satisfactory but for landings a *Deutsche Maschinenfabrik* (DEMAG) electro-mechanical apparatus was put in place. For power-assisted launching two *Deutsche Werke* compressed air-driven telescoping catapults were designed. With a length of 75ft (23m) they were able to accelerate an 11,000lb (5,000kg) Stuka dive-bomber to a speed of 181mph (130km/h). A complex loading system was involved in the planned operations. There were two sets of rails, which were tracked to the two hangar lifts, one located amidships and one forward on the flight deck. The aircraft were loaded from their hangars by cranes, which positioned them onto collapsible launching trolleys. Once emplaced, the combined unit was taken up on the lifts and wheeled along the rails to the launch point. They would then be fired off by compressed air and this would propel the slide inside the track – well over the bow of the flight deck. The aircraft would detach and become airborne while the trolley itself would stay locked inside the slide path aperture, only detaching on manual release of the towing cables. The detached trolleys were then pushed onto recovery platforms; these would convey them down to 'B' deck, where they could be rolled back into the upper hangar and re-used via another rail track.

It was estimated that one aircraft could be launched every thirty seconds. The number of aircraft able to form a combat strike was eighteen, after which there would have been an embarrassing hiatus of almost an hour while the catapult air reservoirs replenished. Despite the complexity of the system, normal 'rolling' take-offs would only have been performed in emergencies while the catapults were 'down'. The system would have allowed simultaneous launch and recovery if deemed essential, and obviated the necessity of carriers turning out of formation and losing anti-aircraft or anti-submarine protection while doing so, to launch a strike.

Foreign service

The He.50 in Chinese service – fact or elaborate myth?

With the increasing seriousness of the Japanese incursions into China during the 1930s, the *Kuomingtang* Government is widely reported as placing orders with Heinkel for their own variant, after a visit by a Chinese delegation on an arms-buying mission. This version was said to have been designated as the He 66aCH. They had the 480hp (358kW) Siemens Jupiter VIIF radial engine and twelve were built, but, so great was the need for the expansion of the Luftwaffe, that these twelve aircraft were taken over by the Germans, who utilized them as the He.50B.

This was not the end of the matter, for according to many books, a further Chinese order was reputed to have followed in 1934, this time for a He.66bCh, which allegedly had the *Bramo* 322B engine installed with a NACA engine cowling. When these were finally released for export, it is said, they were crated up and shipped from Hamburg to Hong Kong, arriving there in January 1936.[7] Here they remained in storage for more than a year, only finally joining the Chinese Air Force at Peking (now Beijing) in July 1937. The reasons for any such delay was not too hard to seek, as one observer recalled, '… the Japanese spared no effort in trying to prevent German armament sales to China, so it took a long time until the order could finally be fulfilled.'[8] In fact the Japanese Intelligence services mounted a continuous watch on ships offloading cargoes at Hong Kong, which they regarded as '…a loophole…' for the Chinese to arm themselves. Strict monitoring was done and much anti-British Press propaganda was generated by the release of such information. So much pressure was put on the British authorities that they even resorted to informing the Japanese themselves of such armament shipments.[9]

By the time any such crated aircraft would have been released from the Bund, conveyed to Peking (now Beijing) and assembled eighteen months would have elapsed. On assembly their tails were said to have been painted bright yellow to avoid confusion with the Aichi D1A1, not surprisingly as they were to all intents and purposes, identical machines. In the event they were stated to have been employed in their true role for only, '…two months of undistinguished service'.[10] Other reports state that these aircraft carried large, yellow identification panels on their wings and fuselages. This would certainly have made them visible, and, as so, good targets for marauding Japanese fighters! It is much more likely that these yellow markings indicated their role as trainers, which is how they spent almost all their service life in China.

However, the distinguished aviation scholar and historian, Lennart Andersson, is totally dismissive of the whole story. In his detailed history of the Chinese Air Force, which he researched over a great number of years,[11] he failed to find any evidence of any such shipments reaching China and concluded the whole body of material on the He.50 in Chinese service was '...pure fiction'. It may well be that these 'He.50s' may have been confused with the Henschel Hs.123s, which certainly *did* reach China by sea, were used briefly and then relegated to training.

Japan

Although not strictly the same aircraft the dive-bomber that resulted from Heinkel's early collaboration with the He.66, was so similar that they could be termed 'sisters' rather than cousins. The Aichi Tokei Denki *Kabushiki Kaisha* (KK – Stock Corporation) at Nagoya took delivery of the prototype and their designer Tokukhiro Goake worked on it to adapt it for IJN service. A much-strengthened undercarriage was deemed necessary for carrier operations and the power plant was changed, with the 580hp (433kW) Nakajima Kotobuki Kai-1 radial engine being mounted in all except the final forty-four D1A1s. These later machines were, instead, equipped with the 640hp (477kW) Kotobuki 3 fitted with a Townend Ring.

A further improvement was the fitting of the 730hp (544kW) Hikari-1, 9-cylinder radial, with a NACA cowling and this variant became the D1A2. Some 162 D1A1s were built between 1934 and 1937, and 428 of the D1A2 were produced between 1936 and 1940. They saw much combat service in China, serving aboard the aircraft carriers *Akagi*, *Kaga* and *Ryūjō*, and with the 12, 13, 14 and 15 *Kokutai* ashore. In addition the Japanese puppet state of Manchukuo (the former Manchuria) had a small air complement and two D1A1s (coded M407 and M408) were trialled by them in 1937, but not, finally, adopted for service.

By the outbreak of the Pacific war in December 1941, the majority of these machines had been relegated to dive-bomber training duties, although sixty-eight remained in service on second-line duties until as late as July 1942.

Spain

It is reported that a solitary He.50 was briefly evaluated in Spain during the Spanish Civil War. Usually reported as a He.50G,[12] of which two were registered (D-IGLU and D-INAO) she was part of *Versuchtjagdstaffel 88* (VJ/88 – Experimental Fighter Squadron), which included a diverse selection of types including some Henschel Hs.123s and the Heinkel He.112. This unit was shipped out to Cadiz and established at Tablada airfield in December 1936. She operated until 1 April 1937 and was then turned over to the Spanish Nationalist. It is not thought that this machine was used on any combat mission.

War service

China

As we have seen the twelve aircraft of the first batch built by Heinkel for China, were retained in Germany, as the Luftwaffe had '...confiscated the Chinese order'.[13] They later turned up, via training schools, seeing combat on the Baltic Front in 1944, where Jupiter engines were also employed by other Estonian-manned aircraft. Whether a second batch was ever ordered, and whether, if they were, they ever got delivered and used, is also very debateable.

Estonia

When the Soviet Night Harassment units proved so successful, the Luftwaffe was moved to emulate them and all manner of older aircraft were reclaimed from back areas and training schools to take join the new *Nachtschlacht* units. The He.50A was a natural choice for such missions and from the summer of 1943 onward served in this role with the NSGr. 11.

Formed under the *Flieger-Ergäanzungsgruppe Estland (Erg.Fl.Gr. Estonia)* at Pskov-West airfield, on the Pskov Oblast, Russia, just east of the River Velikaya,[14] from the *Seeaufklärungsgruppe* 127 (*SAGr.* – Maritime Reconnaissance) on 18 October 1943, this unit, commanded by Tallin-born *Oberleutnant* Gerhard Buschmann, comprised the former *Stab* (Staff), 1. and 2. *Staffeln* from that unit, which became the *Stab, 1.* and 2. *Nachtschlachtgruppe 11 (Estnisch* – Estonian) with the unit symbol 3W+ painted over the original Luftwaffe indication letters, while still leaving the individual aircraft figures behind the *Balkenkreuz* (+) intact.[15] Losses steadily reduced this number to sixteen machines in September and to fifteen in October.

They operated under *3 Fliegerdivision*, whose *Kommandeure* was *Generalmajor* Sigismund Freiherr von Falkenstein, on the Kurland Front, being composed wholly of Estonian volunteer airmen, accompanied by a small Luftwaffe liaison cadre, and generally flew in support of the Estonian-manned 20 *Estnische Freiwilligdivision* (Estonian Volunteer Division) initially fighting around Lake Peipus with night harassment missions on clear weather nights moving from Pskov-West to Jõhvi (Jõhvi or Jewe), on the main coastal road between Oru and Amula, 32 miles (50km) west of Narva Bay, from 1 November before moving to Idritsa airfield, on the Pskov Oblast near the Latvian border, and losing a He.50 in a crash-landing in thick fog there on the 14th. Bad weather prevailed throughout this period and another He. 50 was damaged on landing on 27 November. At this time the *Stab*, 1./ and 2./ *Staffeln* had twenty-six He 50s on establishment. They continued operating from here over Christmas and into the New Year as and when conditions permitted.

On 4 February 1944 the unit was ordered to fall back to Rahkla on the main road east of Rakvere, Wesenberg, north-eastern Estonia, but only remained there briefly before deploying to Jõhvi (Jewe), airfield in Ida-Viru County, Estonia, about 32 miles (50km) back from the Soviet border.

During the Battle of Narva, when repeated Soviet offensives mounted regardless of loss and cost, were thrown back time-and-time again over a period of six months, the unit alternately flew from here and Rahkla, sorties being flown over the Narva and Tartu (Dorpat) area. In the latter part of June 1944 the Estonian *öölahingulennukite üsus* (Night fighting aircraft) flew their 3,000th combat mission. Lieutenant Albert Vaart alone was credited with 224 sorties. Most remained loyal to fighting for their adopted cause and their homeland, with the Soviet advance some had their resolve weakened, and some Estonian flyers sought refuge across the Baltic. To cite just one example, on 1 September 1944, a 3./NSGr He.50, (3W + NO) crash-landed at Alva, in Gotland, Sweden, seeking sanctuary, after flying from Liepāja, Latvia. Both aircrew survived and the aircraft was sold for scrap.

By 1 August some twenty-two He.50s remained on strength, all with the *Stab* or 1./ *Staffel*. Rahkla and Jõhvi had to be abandoned in the rout and September found the 1./NSGr 11 at Poltsamaa in central Estonia and down to just seventeen He.50s. When the Soviet tanks overran Estonia on 14 September the unit retreated back through Latvia into the Kurland (Courland) pocket with their backs to the Baltic. After a brief transit via Blome, northern Latvia on 18 September and Smitten between 18 September 1944 and 24 September 1944, by 22 September they had a temporary respite at Liepaja (Libau-North), Latvia, before again moving on to the Mazeikiai (Maschaiken), on 29 September where they remained until 1 October with a total establishment strength of thirty-nine aircraft of all types and still sub-ordinated to 3 *Fliegerdivision*.

The unit was finally disbanded on 7 October 1944 despite the vehement pleas of their pilots to carry on as a fighting unit. This was stated to be mainly due to the lack of spare parts to keep them flying making their continued usage impossible. Others have argued that with the number of Estonian-manned aircraft that had deserted (five to seven are the figures commonly put forward), the *Wehrmacht* did not wish to risk this trickle becoming a flood. Whatever the truth, the unit was wound up and the 1,200 personnel associated with it dispersed among German air and land commands.[16]

Chapter Eleven

Heinkel He.59

The *Reichsmarine* produced a specification in 1930 for a military seaplane but, under the existing restrictions that barred the production of warplanes, it was ordered as a civilian aircraft. The natural choice for the manufacturer of such an aircraft was the Heinkel AG at Warmünde, that had long specialized in such types and Heinkel was an old, and very experienced, hand at evading the Allied Commission official restrictions by this time.

The design brief was for a torpedo-bomber and maritime reconnaissance aircraft, capable of operating with equal efficiency as a twin-float seaplane or from land bases with a wheeled undercarriage. In the event she was pressed into service also as a troop transport, an air-sea rescue aircraft and a training machine.

Designer *Ing.* Reinhold Mewes[1] came up with an outline design the same year. His concept was for a fairly hefty, twin-engined biplane.

The He.59a was the first prototype (*Werke No.* 378, civilian registration D-ARAR, named '*Silbermöwe*' ('Herring Gull')), and was built as a seaplane with prototype metal floats. However, as the V-1, she did not finally take to the air until January 1932. She went to the RDL research station at Travemünde.

The He.59b seaplane was the second prototype (V-2) and she, oddly enough, led the way, making her maiden flight at Warmünde in September 1931. This machine (*Werke. No.* 379), civilian registration D-ABIF, named '*Raubmöwe*' (literally 'Robber Gull' – the Skua), was later transferred to the secret test site at Lipetsk, in the Soviet Union for trials, returning to Travemünde when that unit closed down. A second He.59b (*Werke No* 442, civilian registration D-AKIV), christened '*Seemöwe*' (Seagull), also went to the *Erprobungstelle* (*E-Stelle* – Testing Grounds) at Tavemünde.

Detailed evaluation and testing followed with the He.59A, of which fourteen were built for evaluation and testing in 1932. One aircraft (civilian registration D-AGYP) went afloat for sea trials aboard the *Sperber* (Catapult Ship) *Krischan* (800 tons), which had a deck aft capable of carrying two small seaplanes or one large one, which were hoisted aboard by her 12-ton gantry.[2] The results of such trials brought about a re-design with the front of the aircraft altered to accommodate a single 7.92mm MG-15 machine-gun in an open position, the addition of a dorsal open mounting likewise equipped, and with glazed panels in the ventral step. These changes produced the He.59B-1 (subsequently re-designated as the B-0), which was a batch of sixteen pre-production machines.

These were the first of three main variants and were built as the He.59B-2, being themselves a further upgraded version of the B-1 and featuring a glazed bomb-aimers position, encased in an all-metal nose. Three MG-15s were now mounted with the addition of a ventral position.

The He.59B-3 was specifically built as a reconnaissance aircraft. Extra bunkerage was obtained by fitting extra fuel tanks in the after-fuselage spaces, and one of the machine-guns was removed to accommodate them.

The He.59C-1 was originally planned as an even more pared down version of the B-3, with no defensive armament whatsoever. This aircraft, built by Arado (*Werke No.* 530), civilian registration D-AKYH, named '*Lachmöwe*' ('Black-headed Gull') also went to the *E-Stelle* at Travemünde. In the event this proved impractical in wartime and she was subsequently put into service as an air ambulance and as a training machine. This was followed by a dedicated *Seenotdienst* (air-sea rescue) machine with not just the defensive armament but the bomb-aiming equipment and all other offensive payload totally eradicated, better ventral vision achieved by fitting glazed nose-panelling, and with medical equipment, six inflatable dinghies and a folding ladder carried. As such she was designated the He.59C-2. A further refinement of this machine was the He.59D-1, which combined both the training and air-sea rescue roles. Forward visibility was further improved by the adoption of a round nose section.

The He.59E-1 was built at Arado to train torpedo-bomber aircrew in the mechanics of height, alignment and dropping techniques and the associated equipment this specialized art required, but was otherwise the equivalent of the D-1. Similarly, in order to familiarize aircrew with the skills required in maritime reconnaissance and aerial photography, an unarmed variant with three aerial cameras emplaced was designed. For this specialized training, a total of six of these He.59E-2s were built by Arado. Finally, airborne navigation techniques and equipment grew more sophisticated, and the He.59N appeared. All of these were *conversions* from existing He.59D-1s and not fresh construction, the work being done by the *Walther Bachmann Flugzeugbau*, Ribnitz, with extra radio and direction-finding apparatus fitted to familiarize aircrew in the latest manifestations of marine navigation.[3] This completed the small, but diverse, He.59 family.

Large and ungainly, somewhat underpowered, and with pathetic defensive armament, she nonetheless proved able to survive and adapt and gave sterling service for almost a decade. Her virtues were that she was simple to fly and to operate, with few vices, was capable of adaptation and operated in a wide range of climates and situations.

The He.59B-2 had a crew of four, consisting of pilot, radio-operator, bomb aimer and gunner.

It was of composite construction, with a large, box-shaped fuselage with no saving graces, but sturdily built of steel framing skinned with fabric. For strength, the after-section was encased in metal sheeting, as was the whole tail section. The wings were of wood construction, being a two-beam framing with the front panels of plywood, and the main surface areas fabric-covered. Her twin floats each contained in the undersides a 198 Imperial gallon (900-litre) fuel tank, which were in addition to the main internal bunkerage, to give a maximum capacity of 593.91 Imperial gallons (2,700 litres.) Additionally, it was possible to replace her bomb load with further tanks, which would bring her maximum capacity to 703.9 Imperial gallons (3,200 litres.) Normal range was 585 miles (942km), with a maximum ferry range with the extra tanks of 950 miles (1,530km).

The He.59B-2 variant had a wingspan of 77ft 9in (23.70m), an overall length of 57ft 1in (17.40m) and a height of 23ft 3.5in (7.10m). Her wing area was 1,649 ft^2 (153.2m^2). She had an empty weight of 11,023lb (5,010kg), an operating weight of 19,841.6lb (9,000kg) and a fully laden weight of 20,026lb (9,119kg). She was powered by two 660 hp (492kW) *Bayerische Motoren Werke AG* (BMW) VI 6.0 VI ZU, twelve-cylinder, water-cooled V12 engines each driving a Cuatripala propeller. Against the trend for amphibious aircraft of the day, rather than mounting these engines high, above the upper wings, the Mewes design positioned her two engines in nacelles mounted between the upper and lower wings. Each engine drove a fixed-pitch, four-bladed propeller. This gave the He.59 a maximum speed of 137mph (221 km/h) at sea level, with a cruising speed of 115mph (185 km/h). She had a service ceiling of 11,480ft (3,500m), with a laborious climb to 3,300ft (1,000m) of 4.7 minutes. Her defensive armament comprised three 0.312in (7.92mm) *Rheinmetall-Borsig* MG-15 flexible machine-guns, which were carried in the nose, and in both dorsal and ventral positions in the rear fuselage. Her offensive armament naturally varied according to the mission type; as a torpedo-bomber she could carry a single 1,764lb (800kg) torpedo; as a patrol bomber she could carry two 1,100lb (551kg) bombs or four 551lb (250kg) bombs; as an anti-submarine or patrol bomber she could tote up twenty 110lb (50kg) bombs or, alternately, depth-charges, while as a minelayer she could accommodate four magnetic mines of 1,002lb (500kg) payload.

It was not until 1933 that the He.59 was ordered into production with batches being built both by Heinkel and under licence, by Arado *FlugzeugWerke,* at Warmünde. Those built by the parent company include the three prototypes, one HD59a (*Werke No.* 378, civilian registration D-2214, and later D-ARAR); and two HD59bs (*Werke No.* 379, civilian registration D-2215, later D-ABIF and *Werke No.* 442, civilian registration D-2622, later D-AKIV), and production He59Cs (*Werkes Nos* 528 to 543 and 836 to 840); and He59Ds (*Werkes Nos.* 1510–1529), for a total of forty-four aircraft. Arado constructed a total of 122 aircraft, including He59D (*Werkes No.* 931, civilian registration D-APUH) two He.59E (*Werkes Nos* 2863 and 2871). Among reported (but not all confirmed) *Werkes Nos* for the remainder are 931, 933, 935, 960, 1309 to 1332, 1514, 1522, 1628, 1725 to 1726, 1819 to 1831, 1834, 1839–1855, 1898, 1974 to 1996, 2584, 2595 to 2604, 2610, 2758, 2787, 2792 to 2798, 2827, 2862, 2864 to 2870, 2872 to 2874 and 2995.[4]

In the 30 September 1935 expansion programme provision for twenty-one He.59s (described as 'General Purpose') was included. By 1938, with the Coastal Air Force Command being abolished and replaced by the *General der Luftwaffe beim Oberkommando der Kriegsmarine (Ob. D.M.)* the Aircraft Procurement Programme of 1 July 1937 called for no fewer than 105 He.59s to be ready by March 1939.

A total of 142 were built of all types in three main variants.

Civilian registrations include: D-ABAZ, D-ABIF, D-ABOF, D-ABUI, D-ADAI, D-ADIU, D-ADOD, D-ADXU, D-AFFA, D-AFFE, D-AFFK, D-AGOR, D-AGOS,

D-AGUI, D-AGUV, D-AGYP, D-AHAN, D-AHDC, D-AHET, D-AKAR, D-AKIV, D-AKOS, D-AKYH, D-ALOV, D-ALOZ, D-ALVD, D-AMEZ, D-ANEL, D-ANFL, D-ANYL, D-APIE, D-APUH, D-APYZ, D-AQEV, D-A1UV, D-ARAN, D-ARAR, D-AROO, D-ARYX, D-ASAM, D-ASOD, D-ASOO, D-ATOI, D-ATYP, D-ATYR, D-AVEQ, D-AXYA, D-AZEX, D-AZOK, D-AZOX, D-AZOF, D-AZOK, D-AZUK and D-AZOX.

Some military codes include: DA + MG, DA + MI, TH + HM, TH + HN, TH + HO, TV + AZ, TV + HM, TV + HZ, TW + HA, TW + HB, TW + HD, TW + HE, TW + HF, TW + HG, TW + HH, TW + HI, TW + HJ, TW + HJ, TW + HL, TW + HM, TW + HN, TW + HO.

Names include: *Lachmöwe* (D-AKYH), *Raubmöwe* (D-ABIF) and *Seemöwe* (D-AKIV).

Introduced into the Luftwaffe in 1935, she was not finally retired from service until 1944.

Air-Sea rescue

The infant Luftwaffe in the Baltic pioneered and refined air-sea rescue work and the He.59 was to be the main workhorse in the early years and on into the war itself.[5] In the spring of 1935 the task of organizing the swift and efficient recovery of downed aircrews off Germany's coasts was assigned to the *Luftkreis-Kommando VI (See)* (Regional Air Command VI, Naval) at Kiel by means of an *ad hoc* flotilla of small and ancient boats, and Lieutenant-Colonel Konrad Goltz, a supply officer with that unit, was nominated for the responsibility. Goltz divided the North Sea Baltic up into rescue zones and in 1938, when war with Great Britain loomed at the time of the Munich Conference, initiated a programme of aerial units.

No fewer than fourteen He.59s were initially acquired and a contract was placed with Walter, Bachman and Ribitz, Mecklenburg, to gut and re-equip these machines to full *Luftwalfen-inspektion des Sanitätswesens* (Luftwaffe Medical Inspectorate) standards. This work was carried out with typical German thoroughness and included the fitting of first aid equipment, artificial respiration machines and electrically heated sleeping bags, hypothermia being an obvious hazard in such cases. The fuselage had a floor hatch cut into the floor, with a collapsible ladder to reach down to the surface of the water and a internal hoist was built in to retrieve injured and inert aircrew up into the hull from the sea. Additionally, these He.59s were equipped with lockers with life-belts, signal flares, respirators, and lamps for night missions. A large forward-looking searchlight was mounted in a ventral position in the nose of the aircraft. Thus transformed, the old He.59 was the best, indeed just about the only, ASR aircraft in the world's air forces, and was to remain so throughout the war, the Allies merely copying them much later and, until that time, relying only on the barest of minimum aids for their ditched aircrews. By the time war came a year later, active units included the *Seefligerhorst Nordeney* and in 1937 the *3./KüFlGr.106* at Hoernum on the island of Sylt. During the war Air-Sea Rescue (ASR or *Seenot*) units that utilized the He.59 included *Seenotflugkdo 1, 2, 3, 4, 5, Seenotflugkommando 2,* and *Seenotstaffel 2* and *11.*

War service

Initial wartime missions against Great Britain were mine-laying sorties and torpedo-bomber attacks on coastal convoys off Harwich and the approaches to the Thames Estuary. The He.59 was in service with most of the Luftwaffe's *Küstenfliegergruppes* (Coastal Reconnaissance Groups), *3./Kü.Fl.Gr.106* (coded M2+) led by *Gruppenkommandeure Oberleutnant* Hermann Jordan, at Borkum, then at Rantum, Hörnum on Sylt Island, List and finally Bad Zwishenahn near Oldenburg; *3./Kü.Fl.Gr.406* (coded K6+) under *Oberleutnant* Wolfgang von Wild, at List; *3./KüFl.Gr.506* (coded S4+) under *Major* Henrich Minner at Pillau and then Norderney Island; *1./Kü.Fl.Gr 707* at Kiel-Holtenau and *3./Kü.Fl.Gr.706* (coded 6I+ and 8L+ respectively) under *Gruppenkommandeure Oberleutnant* Hermann Edert, at the *Seefliegerhorst* (Seaplane base) at Dievenow, in Poland, and then Norderney Island and *2./Kü.Fl.Gr.906* (coded 8L+) under *Oberleutnant* Hermann Lessing respectively at Rantum, List, Bad Zwishenahn and Grossenbrode. Between them these units had the majority of the still operational He.59s but all were scheduled for early conversion to other types.

Minelaying

The He.59's box-like fuselage was able to accommodate magnetic mines. When the limited stocks of magnetic mines came to be used, the Germans had expected the British to be taken by surprise and slow to react. In fact, the British had experimented with magnetic mines as early as the Great War, and although they had not developed huge numbers, had all the expertise on hand to counter such weapons, once their constructional and operational details could be ascertained. The German type was different to the British and actual hands-on information was the basic requirement. The dropping of such mines by parachute soon gave the British the insight they required.

The war was barely a week old when, on the 10 September 1939, the freighter *Magdepur* (8,641 GRT) was sunk in low water off Orfordness. Despite intensive minesweeping in the area, no mines were located, but shortly afterward a second merchant ship was badly damaged by a detonation in the same area. Her hull was not pierced but her engines were wrecked by the blast. This indicated a non-contact type of mine.

On the night of 22/23 November further laying took place and an observer at a British coastal artillery battery on the south Essex coast near Shoeburyness, reported a German seaplane dropping what he described as a long, cylindrical object, likened to '...a sailor's kitbag...', by means of a parachute on the foreshore. The mine landed in the glutinous mudflats for which the lower Thames is notorious and the failsafe device that was supposed to destroy it in such an event failed to operate. A naval officer and a photographer ventured out, took photographs and the following day Lieutenant-

Commander John Garnault Delahaize Ouvry and Chief Petty Officer Charles Edward Baldwin, part of a five-man team from the Mines Department of HMS *Vernon,* the Royal Navy torpedo and mining establishment at Portsmouth, at enormous risk to themselves, carefully rendered the double detonator device harmless and took it back to base.[6] Here its secrets were revealed, it was a ground mine, so could not be 'swept' by having any mooring wires cut like a conventional contact mine, and it was magnetically operated.[7]

Countermeasures (*degaussing* cables wrapped around each vessel to reduce the magnetic effect of the ship's field, and the 'LL-sweep' to harmlessly denote them in suspected laid areas), were commenced, which eventually overcame this 'secret weapon' and kept it within reasonable bounds, but while the Germans were aware that this weapon was both dangerous to shipping and invulnerable to elimination, they also knew that laying them from the air had comprised the weapon. Nonetheless they continued to lay them in increased numbers from the air as well as from submarines and five ships were sunk in the Thames estuary alone in October.[8]

On the night of 6/7 December 1939, the *3./KflGr.106, 3./506* and *3./906* machines again sortied and dropped a total of twenty-seven magnetic mines in the estuaries of the Humber and Thames rivers and in the Downs off Deal, Kent, all well-used coastal shipping routes. In retaliation, on 12 December, RAF Bomber Command sent eight Armstrong-Whitworth Whitley bombers to attack the seaplane bases at Borkum and Sylt, but they achieved little or nothing.

Air-sea rescue – the first missions

Almost the first aircrews that had reason to thank the *Seenotdienst* ASR He.59s for their rescue were not German but British. On 18 December 1939 a force of twenty-four RAF Vickers Wellington bombers from Nos. 9, 37 and 149 Squadrons were sent to attack the German fleet off Heligoland and Wilhelmshaven. Not for the last time these big bombers failed to score a single hit but they were intercepted by German fighters and suffered a very heavy defeat and, for the loss of just one fighter plane, twelve bombers, half the British force were shot down, No. 37 Squadron alone losing five out of six aircraft, while a further three crash-landed and were written off after reaching the UK. The ditched heavy bombers were all over the Bight and the He.59s had a very busy day picking the surviving British aircrew from the wreckage and saving the lives of twenty of them. The RAF itself had absolutely no way to rescue its own men in this way.[9]

Torpedo woes

With regard to the airborne torpedo, although the Heinkel He.115 was overdue to replace these veterans in active service, the continued frailty of the German 1,600lb (725.74kg) LT F5 torpedo[10] ensured that the He.115s could not be deployed. The LT F5 was the German version of the Norwegian torpedoes *Horten-T* type, designed by Louis Victor Robert Schwarzkopf of the *Berliner Maschinenbau A.G.,* which had a 2,187-yard

(2,000m) range, a maximum speed of 33 knots (38mph) and a 441lb (200kg) Hexanite explosive warhead. This was manufactured by the *Kriegsmarine* (German Navy) under a licence obtained in 1933, and the version developed by the *Seeluftsreitkrafte* (the naval air division) featured a maximum speed increased to 40 knots (46mph), with a 551lb (250kg) Hexanite warhead.[11] The German flyers affectionately dubbed this torpedo *ato* (from atem – air torpedo) and it was probably a reasonable weapon for the comparatively sheltered waters of the Baltic where it had been developed at the Norwegian Navy's Horten Naval Base in Vestifiord; this weapon was found to be unsuitable for the North Sea and Atlantic combat zones.

The LT F5 torpedo soon proved a very temperamental beast and therefore required a dangerously slow approach at low altitude when making a drop, otherwise it would malfunction; steering and the failure of the detonators on impact being the most commonly cited reasons, and, for the He.115B, that approach speed was below their stalling speed!

Even so, the He.59B herself had problems employing this aerial torpedo, for their Siemens *Elektrischer Träger* (ETC – electrically operated carrier) bomb racks were not rated to carry such a heavy piece of ordnance. Also, the ventral machine-gun position under the chin of the He.59B interfered with the launching process. Both matters were duly adjusted with the removal of the chin weapon and the reinforcing of the racks to the required standard. Less simple to manage was the production of the torpedo itself; this had a very low priority at the time (thanks in part to Göring's total disinterest in any weapon pertaining to maritime warfare) and only 135 torpedoes were in stock and available as late as March 1940.

Until the LT F5 could be toughened up, and a new and more reliable steering mechanism fitted, the He. 59 carried out the missions and, from October 1939 onward, they were the principal offensive aircraft against the British coastal convoys. On 7 November three He.59s made an attack on two British destroyers off Lowestoft, Suffolk, but only one aircraft managed to release her torpedo, and that missed completely. Their one and only success, however, was the sinking of the British minesweeping trawler *Active* (185 GRT) off Rattray Head on 18 December 1939. The vessel's commander, Captain David Sutherland, later told reporters, 'An aerial torpedo landed in the water beside us and hit under the waterline.' Four of her crew were killed.

This lack of a reliable torpedo was felt acutely during the invasion of Norway in April 1940, where the bulk of the aerial opposition to the Royal Navy up to the time of the Anglo-French evacuation in June, had, perforce, been carried out by dive- and conventional altitude bombing, was keenly felt. Included in the original German dispositions for this occupation was *Kampfgeschwader z.b.V 108* (*z.b.V = zu besonderen Verwendung* – for special purposes) established at Fuhlsbüttel, Hamburg, and commanded by *Kommodore Oberst* Ernst-August Roth who was appointed as *Transportchef See* (Sea Transport Chief) as early as March 1940, although the aircraft were not actually moved to their operational airfields until 8 April just prior to launching *Unternehmen Weserübung* ('Weser Exercise' the codename for the invasion of Denmark and Norway on 9 April), in order to maintain secrecy. This force was established especially for the operation with aircraft supplied from various existing *K. Fl Gruppen*[12] and included the *I. Gruppe/Kampfgeschwader z.b.V 108*, commanded by *Gruppenkommandeur Major* Hermann Lessing, whose 1./108 and 2./108 *Staffeln* were equipped with the He.59, from Norderney Island; *II. Gruppe/K.G.z.b.V 108* commanded by *Gruppenkommandeur Major* Herbert Kaiser, whose 4./108 and 7./108 *Staffeln* both had the He.59 on their establishment, from List on Sylt Island; and *III./K.G.z.b.V 108*, commanded by *Gruppenkommander Oberst* Otto-Lutz Förster, with their 5./108 and 6./108 *Staffeln* both equipped with the He.59. In total the unit contained twenty-two He.59s. Later, as the German occupation proceeded, other units moved up. In May the *1./Kü.Fl.Gr 706* moved to Trondheim and in August the 5. *Seenotstaffel* was established for ASR work with the He.59 headquartered at Sola, Bergen, which had detachments at Trondheim, Tromsø, Hammerfest and Kirkenes. Further south the I/706 with the He.59 was based at Thisted, at the north-west tip of Denmark, on the Thisted Breding.[13]

Meanwhile, earlier and far to the south, the He.59 had found other, surprising, missions of great moment. During the invasion of the Low Countries in May 1940, a series of surprise attacks paved the way for conventional forces to quickly overwhelm the small neutral nations. One such was the Netherlands, and as early as March it had been planned to seize the vital Willems Bridge over the Maas River in the heart of the city of Rotterdam, by *coup de main*. For this purpose the 3./108 *Staffel* had been withheld from the Norway force and, on 14 March, had been re-organized as the *Sonderstaffel Schwilden* (Special Squadron Schwilden) commanded by *Hauptmann* (Captain) Horst Schwilden, and transferred to the authority of *Kommandeur Generalleutant* (Lieutenant-General) Kurt Student's 7. *Fliegerdivision* for special adaptation and training.

On the morning of 10 May the force of twelve He.59s from the *Schwilben Staffel* were loaded with 120 special force troops from *11./Infanterie-Regiment 16,* commanded by *Oberleutnant* Hermann-Albert Schrader, and twenty-two sappers from *2 Kompanie Pionier-Bataillon,* at *Zwishenahner See*, a large lake in Ammerland. The He.59 proved quite capable of carrying thirteen fully equipped soldiers in addition to her four-man aircrew. They made an audacious flight and on reaching the target zone, separated into two six-plane approach groups, making their final approach from both east and west along the river, in order to split the defenders' fire. Both groups landed under fire, taking many hits, alighting on the Maas where their assault force quickly seized both the Willems Bridge and the nearby railway bridge, the Leeuwen Bridge and the Jan-Kuiten Bridge, all of which they held under fierce counter-attacks until the Dutch surrendered on the 14th.

During the subsequent Dutch counter-attacks and fierce fighting four He.59s (*Werke Nos* 1830, 1995, 2593 and 2599) were destroyed or rendered beyond repair. Every one of the surviving eight machines, which managed to take off, still under heavy fire, received damage of some sort but were subsequently repaired and returned to the *Höhere Fliegerausubildungskommando 2*. The *Schwilden Staffeln* itself was disbanded on 12 May and these eight machines returned to service with training units while their aircrew were returned to the *3./K.G.z.b.V 108*.

Seenot under fire

The value of the *Seenot* He.59s was now proven beyond dispute and. in an early wartime re-organization, Goltz, now a *Generalmajor*, was appointed a chief of the newly established *Der Inspektion des Seenotdienstes* (Air-Sea Rescue Inspectorate). Further advances had been made already; the Luftwaffe had developed a green marker dye to spread over the surface of the water as a visual locator. A system of Sea Rescue Floats was originated by September 1940, equipped with bunks, blankets, signal flares, dry clothing, food and water, the essentials to keep aircrew alive until help reached them. They were used by the ditched airmen of both sides with equal thankfulness. Every Luftwaffe fighter aircraft was fitted with an inflatable rubber dinghy in readiness for the attack on England, at the insistence of Adolf Galland, a leading ace. The British doggedly stuck to their 'Mae West' life jackets and that was it.

During the summer of 1940, totally unarmed He.59s, painted white, with prominent Red Cross markings, operated in the English Channel, the outer Thames Estuary and off the Essex coast in the air-sea rescue role, saving the lives of both German and British aircrew who had ditched in the sea.[14] Despite being the major sea-power of the day the British had little or no ASR aircraft to do what the German *Seenot* He.59s were doing very efficiently and effectively.

The British refused to distinguish between the *Kriegsmarine*- and Luftwaffe-operated He.59 missions and those of the *Seenotdienst*, a suspicion that became a conviction when one of the latter was shot down on 11 July and the pilot's log was found to have British convoy positions noted down. The Germans insisted that rules were being followed, that Articles 3, 6 and 17 of the 1929 Geneva Convention covered their units work.[15] With regard to the disputed logbook they argued, reasonably enough, that the British convoys was where their attacking aircraft had been shot down so that they had to note their locations in order to make the start of their searches. It cut no ice at all. When Winston Churchill heard of this practice he immediately ordered that they all be shot down without fail, and this was subsequently done. On 13 July the Air Ministry Bulletin 1254 declared without any reservation, that this was to be the case.

The first victim of this new attitude was originally a He.59.D, one of a batch built by Arado, but converted to the He.59N profile by the Walther Bachmann *Flugzeugbau* at Ribnitz and delivered on 26 April. This aircraft (*Werke No.* 1994, D-ASAM) from 3./ *Seenotflugkommando* based at Norderney, was shot down by the three Spitfires of Blue Section of No. 74 Squadron. She crash-landed eight miles off Hartlepool, and her crew, one of whom was badly injured, were rescued by a British ship. Despite protests that this action had violated Article 9 of the 1929 Geneva Agreement relating to Red Cross work in war these attacks continued. The wreck of the aircraft was later brought to shore and examined to see if it had any armament or minelaying equipment, which, in both cases, proved not to be case. To give some legitimacy to this action to shocked neutral nations like the USA, it was later declared that they were legitimate targets because they were active Luftwaffe aircraft; further excuses fed to the British press by the Ministry of Information (!), who were happy to glorify such action, were that the He.59Cs captured, were found to have had long-range radios aboard, which, it was claimed, were used to report British convoys![16] Reported Enigma signals traffic was deciphered by the WAAF-operated 'Y' service operators in Kent, from which it was claimed that Berlin was ordering, via *Luftflotte 3*, that the ASR aircraft report any British convoys that were observed during their missions.[17] Misinformation continued and a totally unfounded story was circulated stating they were secretly landing agents ashore in readiness for the invasion. (That the Germans were allegedly using *white*-painted aircraft to carry out such missions *at night*, although obviously absurd, apparently did not arouse any incredulity among the British press or the BBC to whom it was being fed, or, *if* it did, they loyally overcame such scruples.)

The He.59s continued their work but were soon under the cosh. On 9 July another He.59 (*Werke No.* 1726, coded D-ASUO) was attacked by a Spitfire from No. 54 Squadron and had to crash-land on the Goodwin Sands, in the English Channel, off Deal, Kent. This aircraft, with the machine-gun bullet holes in its tail and after fuselage, was also brought ashore and placed on exhibition. All four crew members became PoWs. Next, on 11 July, a *1./Seenotflugkdo* He.59, (*Werke No.* 1846, coded D-AGIO) was engaged by a British destroyer and then shot down by an Avro Anson aircraft from No. 217 Squadron. The four aircrew took to their dinghy and were captured off the Channel Islands to become PoWs. On 20 July an He.59C-2 (*Werke No.* 0838, coded D-AKAR) from *1. SeenotflugKdo* was searching for three fighter pilots from the 3./JG.27 known to have bailed out of their aircraft off Cherbourg, when three British fighters from No. 601 Squadron pounced, forcing her crew to abandoned her south of Selsey Bill, Dorset; the crew were all killed. Then yet another of the 3. *SeenotflugKommando*'s He.59s (*Werke No.* 1989, coded D-AROO) was lost on 27 July, when six Hurricanes from No. 615 found an easy kill and shot her into the Channel north-east of Dover, killing four crew members aboard instantly and wounding a fifth, who was rescued. On 28 July, another He.59N from this unfortunate unit (*Werke No.* 1851, coded D-ASUC), was thoroughly shot to pieces by a No. 111 Squadron fighter ten miles west of Boulogne. The pilot managed to make a crash-landing but the aircraft exploded on contact and two of the crew had been killed outright while the other three were badly wounded. When a He.59N from *1. SeenotflugKdo*, piloted by Colonel Otto Dreyer, the *Gruppenkommander*, made a sea landing in order to assist this aircraft, she was promptly shot up by another No.111 fighter, wounding two of her crew. The Heinkel He.59N was so badly damaged she was written off.[18]

After the loss of so many defenceless He.59s to RAF attacks, the Germans repainted the survivors in normal sea camouflage colours and continued using them in this role, and also continued to save British as well as German aircrew, without discrimination, but with defensive armament.[19] There is even a claim that one He.59, under attack, managed to shoot down a Hawker Hurricane fighter in retaliation. Soon though, they had to be given their own fighter escort for each mission. Their size and vulnerability eventually led to them being replaced by the Dornier Do.18 and Dornier Do.24 in these rescue missions.

Torpedo developments

Although this increasingly ceased to involve the He.59 as the year went on, with regard to the torpedo-armed units as a whole, as more of them became operational that summer, the number of attacks increased. In one attack against convoy OA 203 in the Moray Firth, Scotland, carried out on 23 August, two freighters, the 5,035 GRT *Llanishen* and the 6,680 GRT *Makalla* were claimed sunk. However, this increased activity, rewarded or not, expended 130 torpedoes and inevitably led, as the supply position had not been rectified, to a return to the shortages of the spring. Indeed the situation became dire and at one time only thirty-eight LT F5s were on hand!

This grave shortage came about when the Germans were still (officially) preparing for Operation *Seelöwe* (Sealion), the invasion of England, during which the seaplane units were expected to help cope with the Royal Navy acting against the lumbering German invasion fleet. To oversee this *General-der-Flieger* Joachim Coeler was appointed in command of *Fliegerkorps 9*. Coeler was perfect for the job having a long association with maritime aviation dating back to the Great War and his most recent appointments had been commanding *Führer de Luftstreitkräfte* (*FdLuft* – Commander, Naval Air Force) and then *FdLuftWest* (*FdLuftWest* – Commander, Naval Air Force West) from the end of June 1939 to 28 April 1940. A tiny part of his force included *Kü.Fl.Gr.106* under *Oberstleutnant* Hans Jordan, with two *Seenot* He.59s on its strength.[20]

The *1./706* had formed with the He.59 at Kiel-Holtenau under *Gruppenkommandeur* Hermann Lessing, on I January 1940 and, after being based briefly at Copenhagen moved to *Seefleigerhorst Aalborg*, using Limfjord until the Jutland, north Denmark, base had the barest facilities, and, at times when the sea iced up here, operated from Thisted. Not until late in 1940 did the unit convert to the He.115.

Later the He.59 was used more for short-range reconnaissance work between 1940 and 1941, with units working in such diverse locations as from the river Gironde, in France, flying patrols over the Bay of Biscay; from the northern wastes with the *Küstenfliegergruppe Stavanger*, Norway; on the River Bug and from Odessa and Nikolayev on the Black Sea with *Seenotstaffel 8*; in the central Mediterranean with *Seenotstaffel 4*; one He.59 *Seenot* machine working with the *Kommando 1./JG 54* under *Staffelkapitän Oberleutnant* Hans Götz, from the Vuoksi River at Priozerk (Käkisalmi) flying sorties over north-western Lake Ladoga near the besieged city of Leningrad; and from the placed waters of Lake Konstanze on the Swiss-German border.[21] Her dotage was spent as a transport and training aircraft, and these proved her ultimate missions until retirement in 1944.

Foreign service

Finland

In May 1943, two HE.59Ds were leased to the *Ilmavoimat* (Finnish Air Force) and these were later joined by a second pair. The Finns used them in the maritime rescue role in August. At least one of these machines wore Finnish national markings. They operated during the summer months when the upper Baltic was ice-free, but both machines were written off in August 1944.

Spain

In mid-1936 the *Legion Kondor* group *Aufklärungsstaffel 88* (*AS./88* – Maritime Reconnaissance Squadron 88) operated the He.59B-2, including D-AFFK listed as a He.59E (*Werke No.* 2606) from the *Seeflieger Gruppe* AS/88 during the Civil War. Two He-59s arrived in Spain aboard the German freighters *Kamerun* (5,042 GRT) and *Wigbert* (3,648 GRT) in August 1936 from Hamburg via Lisbon, Portugal, and began operating from Struts base at Cadiz and from Melilla before moving across to Pollensa, on the island of Mallorca, in July 1937 to continue operations. The group undertook offensive coastal patrolling off the east coast of Spain, and making several clandestine torpedo strikes during their blockade of enemy harbours. There were never more than seven He-59s (or I-59s as the Spanish designated them) operating at any one time, but due to losses and accidents a total of eighteen different aircraft were deployed in total.[22] The unit's weapon of choice was either bombs or the LT F5 torpedo, but the latter was still a very unreliable weapon, and was to remain so for some time further. Many bombing attacks were carried but the first attack with the torpedo occurred on 30 January 1937, when a He.59 piloted by Werner Klümper carried out a torpedo attack against the 1,253-GRT mail ship *Dolphin*, this being the first attack made by an aerial torpedo since the Great War. However, the torpedo failed to release as his ground crew had omitted to connect the electrical contact to the torpedo release lock![23] Klümper had no choice but to return to base and load up with two 551lb (250kg) bombs for a second attack. Two direct hits were scored with these weapons and the *Dolphin* was set on fire. To save the ship her captain ran her aground on the beach at Nerja, Malaga.

This was but the first of many failures by the He.59s of AS./88 to make effective aerial torpedo strikes. The He-59's only recorded torpedo attack success was on the night of 21 June 1938, when a torpedo dropped by *Hauptmann* Martin Harlinghausen, the *Kommandeur*, scored a hit on the British steamer *Thorpeness* (4,700 GRT), which was offshore and approaching the mole at Valencia harbour with a cargo of grain. When she sank near the harbour mouth, the Nationalists claimed she had hit a mine, but she went down in such deep water that this was an obvious lie. The unit also conducted coastal reconnaissance missions. British Intelligence reports stated that these units '...had failed to show any results...', but the Germans themselves considered that, '... operations against the Red Navy and Red Merchant Marine in the Mediterranean waters' had been entirely successful. The Spanish nicknamed them '*Zapatones*' ('Big Shoes') because of the enormous size of their twin floats.

The unit ceased operations in the spring of 1939, at which time six had survived, three of which returned to Germany, while the remaining trio were later handed over to the *Aeronautica Miltiar* and *Aeronautica Naval* units of Franco's forces. They formed the *Hydra 52* unit, still at Pollensa, and took part in numerous air-sea rescue missions during World War II, saving the lives of British, Italian and German air crews whose aircraft had been forced to ditch in the Western Mediterranean. In 1946 all three were largely worn out and were ultimately grounded through lack of spare parts. They were all subsequently scrapped that same year.

Chapter Twelve

Henschel Hs.123

In 1934 the decision was taken that Germany required a dive-bomber to support the army's land operations. The planning called for a two-step approach, the principal aim of the first orders being to initiate aircraft that could be produced quickly. The design for these machines was to be of as an advanced a type as possible, but, conversely, had to be produced quickly to meet deadlines. Thus the new aircraft was to be a biplane until more advanced monoplane types in the pipeline could be readied. In reality the plane was viewed as a stop-gap machine between the existing Heinkel He.50s, which were already recognized as inadequate for all-out dive-bombing, and the arrival of the 'heavy' monoplane dive-bomber, which both Heinkel and Junkers were busy experimenting with.

The two main contenders for the new aircraft were Fieseler and Henschel *FlugzeugWerke A.G.* Both companies utilized the 725hp (541kW) BMW 132A-3, 9-cylinder, air-cooled radial engine to power their initial prototype machines, but there the similarities abruptly ended. The Fieseler offering, the Fi.98 biplane, proved little or no advance on what had gone before, with a mass of wires and strut bracings to support the wing cellule. The Fieseler just didn't 'look right' and her performance during trials re-emphasized the old adage, that if it didn't look right it wouldn't fly right, and nor did she. In stark contrast the Henschel design was of a clean and ground-breaking appearance. Instead of a maze of wire rigging, most of her loading was taken by a pair of hefty, outwardly canted, struts. She had the wide-chord NACA-type engine cowling and presented a much more workmanlike appearance. Right from the start the Henschel outclassed and out-performed its rival and it was clear that Oskar Robert Henschel and his construction team, under *Dipl. Ing.* Friedrich Nicolaus, had created a little gem of a plane.

The first *Versuchsflugzeug* (V-1 – Prototype 1) machine (*Werke No.* 265, V-1, civil registration D-ILUA) powered by a 725hp BMW 132A 9-cylinder radial engine[1] driving a three-bladed propeller, made her maiden flight without any armament aboard, at Johannisthal, Berlin, on 8 May 1935. On 8 May the same year she was exhibited to the Luftwaffe top brass, including Ernst Udet, at Johannisthal airfield near the capital, prior to being transferred to the Test Centre at Rechlin. It was here that the gun armament of two MG-17s along with their associated synchronising equipment and 500rpg (rounds per gun), were installed in the upper segment of the engine cowling.[2]

Henschel produced further prototypes, each designed to test out different engine types, propeller fittings, armament fits, and a variant with an enclosed cockpit in 1935, two of which were also subsequently rebuilt in different configurations for further trials. Details of these subsequent prototypes are as follows:

The V-2 (*Werke No.* 266; apparently, she was never allocated any civilian registration letters), appeared in May 1935 and began flight-testing in the following month, among the test pilots being a certain Major Robert Ritter von Greim, later, as a *Generalfeldmarschall* (Field Marshal) destined to be the last commander of the Luftwaffe. She was fitted with a 770hp Wright Cyclone GR-1820-F 52 engine, with a narrow, short-chord cowling featuring eighteen valve fairings. This engine drove a three-bladed, adjustable-pitch, propeller. She went to the *Erkprobungsbeginn dei de E-Stelle* at Rechlin in June 1936 to be assessed, but she was subsequently damaged in a ground-loop at Schönefeld Field, Berlin, in August. Reliance on any foreign-built equipment was deemed unwise so, on re-building in early 1937, at a cost of RM 12,458, she was altered to become the V-8 and, in this guise, featured a 725hp BMW 132A-3 driving a three-bladed propeller. She then received the civilian registration D-IUPO and was allocated to the RLM's *Luftzeugamt* (Office of Aviation Equipment) in Kölleda, Thuringia, north of Weimar. While with the *E-Stelle in Erprobung* she was allocated the new *Werke No.* 670, which has caused confusion ever since!

The V-3 (*Werke No.* 267, D-IKOU) also arrived in May 1935 and was also sent to Rechlin where she was tested between July 1935 and August 1936. She had the same power plant but driving a two-bladed, variable-pitch, propeller. In May 1936 she was personally flown by *Oberst* Ernst Udet. She was used as the test aircraft for a new type of flexible fuel tank designed to expand to fill available space inside the aircraft instead of a fixed dimension metal tank, and thus offer a greater range of design options. This was to become part of the Ju.87's make-up. Also tested was the *So 1 II-Würfe* under-wing bomb-release apparatus and also trialled was the *Revi IIIb* reflex sight and the *Kronprinz AG spornrad* (tail-wheel) in place of a skid.[3]

After damage in an accident and repairs, the aircraft returned to Rechlin where, on 1 April 1937, it crashed while pulling out of a dive, killing *Flugzeughbau GmbH* test pilot Heinz Wulf.

The V-4 (*Werke No.* 266, D-IZXY) was not completed until April 1936, even though it had the same engine installed, due to being chosen by the RLM as the lead aircraft for the A-0 pre-production batch. After the acceptance tests at Schönefeld she went to Rechlin in September 1936 and was used for various bomb container trials. Under the *So II* package, she had a range of ten vertically mounted *Elvemag 5C 10* bomb tubes,[4] in two banks of five, each tube containing an *Sprengbombe-Cylindrisch* 10 (*S.C.*10) 25lb (12kg) fragmentation bomb, with small steel pellets impeded in concrete, inserted into her fuselage. Testing tended to show that such small weapons, delivered vertically, were capable of accurate delivery onto a target but that the ground access to re-load these tubes on such a small aircraft was very restricted and not practical for any rapid re-arming turn-around in the field and *Tech-amt* shelved the whole project (although they were to later be subject to widespread use during the war in modified form). Instead, the *So III* package was chosen, with a simpler under-lower-wing rack carrying two 110lb (50kg) bombs adopted.

The V-5 (*Werke No.* 796, D-INRA) had the 830hp (619kW) BMW 132G engine driving a three-bladed propeller when first completed in March 1936, being the sixteenth A-1 production aircraft.[5] The machine was then due to be equipped with the 830hp (619 kW) BMW 132G radial, but, once again, before this could be implemented this change was dropped and she then appeared at the 4th International Aviation Meeting at Dübendorf, Switzerland, flown by test pilot Othmar Schürfeld, with the 910hp (678.58 kW) BMW 132J, fitted with the *Zusatzeinspritzung (Methyl-Alkohol)* liquid cooling unit, in July 1937. This necessitated structural alterations to accommodate the bigger fitments. This power plant drove a three-bladed Junkers (licensed Hamilton) adjustable-pitch metal propeller with a 19.68in (50cm) spinner. Another planned feature, an enclosed cockpit, also failed to materialize.

This much-altered aeroplane subsequently featured yet a third engine in October 1937, the 960hp (716kW) BMW 132K V109W (*Werke No.* 55053), with the engine, beneath a long-chord cowling and driving a Junkers-Hamilton *Verstellorpeller* three-bladed propeller. This version first flew on 23 October and later joined a Luftwaffe *Staffel*, but the engine failed in service and once more required a replacement. Further testing at Rechlin followed before, on 12 January 1939, she was finally returned to Luftwaffe charge.

The V-6 (*Werke No.* 797, D-IHDI) was the seventeenth A-1, fitted with a fully enclosed cockpit, which had a sliding hood. She featured an extra pair of machine-guns emplaced beneath the lower wings. The pilot was provided with an armoured headrest and this entailed building up the fuselage immediately aft of the cockpit into a turtleback to attain the necessary height. Both the sliding hood and the armour were incorporated into the A-1. She was trialled with the 910hp (678.5kW) BMW 132J engine and then with the 960hp (716kW) BMW 132K radial, driving a three-bladed, adjustable-pitch *Vereingite Deutsche MetallWerke* (VDM) hollow-bore propeller.[6] She was scheduled to become the prototype of a proposed C-1 variant, but in the end this was not proceeded with.

The V-7 (*Werke No.* 985, D-IUPO), another from the A-1 batch, was originally scheduled to appear in July 1937. Due to additional requirements, which included an enlarged main internal fuel tank, required so that the auxiliary tank could be done away with and replaced by a mounting for a 551lb (250kg) bomb, she was not completed until September, and even then did not have her intended power plant, which was having teething problems. A temporary main driver, the BMW 132K V100 radial engine (*Werke No.* 55054) was not delivered until 26 October and the V-7 first flew the following month. However, it was not until June 1938 that the designed engine, the BMW 132 K V110 was fitted and testing commenced at Rechlin with test pilot Hanna Reitsch. This continued through to 5 September when the aircraft was handed over.

Two of these prototypes were tragically destroyed within a period of three weeks while undergoing testing at Rechlin. Due to the demanding nature of the designed mission, both disintegrated while attempting to recover after performing high-speed dives and shedding their upper wings in the process. These structural weaknesses led to a strengthening of the centre-section struts in the fourth prototype, the V-4. This appeared to solve the problem and subsequent near-vertical dives and their recovery proceeded without any further tragedies. This fourth prototype therefore provided the basis for all subsequent production but with a modified power plant.

In June 1935 a pre-production batch of sixteen Hs.123 A-0s (*Werke Nos.* 628 to 635; and 788 to 795 inclusive) were ordered based on the V-4, the first of which was ready to fly in July 1936 and the last of the batch took to the air that same December.

These A-0s were followed by the A-1 (built by both Henschel and A0), which featured armour protection and a windshield for the pilot, and B-1 of all-metal construction, of which Henschel (three-digit *Werke Nos.*) built 100 in five batches,[7] for a total of 240 aircraft, which, with the prototypes and A-0 variants, resulted in 265 aircraft[8] (one prototype being rebuilt and allocated another *Werke No.* as recorded above).

The V-5 and V-6 prototypes and one A-1 (*Werke No.* 788) utilized the BMW 132J V 55 engine for dive-bombing tests. Another A-1 (*Werke No.* 789) experimentally used the BMW 132J 55 engine (*Werke No.* 55042). The *Sturzflugerprobung* at Rechlin also used two other aircraft (*Werkes Nos.* 819 and 2247) at Rechlin up until 16 January 1937. They were fitted with the *Revi 3b* bomb sight and later adopted the *Revi C/12 A* gun sight.[9] Another A-1 (*Werke No.* 958) was retained by Henschel for experiments with the all-metal ailerons, which were later fitted to the B-1 series. By 11 January 1938, 223 Hs.123s had been received and by 25 June a total of 255 had been delivered of a total of 262 including the prototypes.[10]

She first entered service in the summer of 1936 and, against all odds and predictions, was fated to continue serving until late 1944. The initial production A-1s joined the 1./162 *Immelmann*. The Hs.123 was combat-tested, as were so many of the fledgling Luftwaffe's new aircraft, in the Spanish Civil War. The superiority of the Junkers Ju.87 ensured that the Hs.123 was not to last long as the Luftwaffe's principal dive-bomber and after only a short period, production was stopped.

The Henschel Hs.123A-1 was a single-engined, single-seat, open cockpit, biplane dive-bomber and close-support aircraft. She was of sesqui-plane plan form and was principally of dural sheet construction, with fabric-skinned wings and tail components, while the B-1 was an all-metal machine. She was fitted with a fixed landing gear. As was usual at this period some aircraft were fitted with the *FuG VII* radio equipment with a stub aerial mast atop the upper wing and aft attachment atop the tail, while most were, initially anyway, not so equipped.

A total of 261 Hs.123s were produced, including six prototypes (one given two *Werke Nos.*) and the sixteen pre-production models. The Henschel company built 139 of them at their Johannisthal and Schönefeld, Berlin, plants, seven prototypes, 103 production models for the RLM and twelve for China[11] and a further 140 were sub-contracted to *AGO-FlugzeugWerke* at Oschersleben, Börde, north-west of Leipzig who completed 129 of them. The last Hs.123 rolled off the line in October 1938.

The Hs.123A-1 had an overall length of 27ft 4in (8.33m), a height of 10ft 6.33 in (3.21m) and an upper wing area of 3,940 sq ft (0.36604 sq. m) The total wing area was 267.482ft^2 (24.85m^2).

She was powered by the 880hp (656.03kW) BMW 132Dc 9-cylinder radial engine with a NACA cowling, which drove a two-bladed, variable-pitch, metal propeller. She had a maximum speed of 212mph (341km/h) at 3,936ft (1,200m), a cruising speed of 196mph (315km/h) at 6,560 ft (2,000m), with a climb rate of 1,640ft/min (500m per/min) and a ceiling of 29,350ft (900m). Her internal fuel capacity was 59.4 Imperial gallons (270 litres) and she could carry an external aluminium fuel tank of 34.34 Imperial gallons (130 litres) capacity, which could be jettisoned in an emergency. Other than the Heinkel He.51, the Hs.123 was the first to carry such a tank.[12] Her normal range was 534 miles (859km). The weights were 3,131lb (1,420kg) empty, with a maximum take-off weight of 4,795lb (2,175kg).

The armament consisted of two 0.312in (7.92mm) MG-17, fixed, forward-firing machine-guns in the upper noses with 500rpg magazines. She had an external gun sight mounted just before the small windshield. Her offensive armament was steadily developed as time went on. Initially she had five hard-points with a ventral fuselage main ordnance capability of a single 551lb (250kg) bomb carried under the central fuselage on a swing crutch, which threw the bomb forward and outward between the undercarriage, and two inboard, under-wing fitments rated to 441lb (200kg) each, and two outboard under-wing hard points of 110lb (50kg) each. Alternative bomb loads were one 551lb bomb and four 110lb (50kg) bombs; four 110lb (50kg) SC-50 bombs, or, later, two containers each holding 92 × 4.4lb (2kg) fragmentation bombs, or an alternative fitment of two under-wing pods each housing a 20mm MG FF cannon.

The *I.St.G. 162* received D-ILRO, D-IPFY, D-IYLU, D-IZHO, D-IGMH, D-IHFY, D-IKLY and D-IKSW and on 1 April was re-designated as the *IV.(St)/L.G.* at Schwerin, Mecklenburg-Vorpommern, moving to nearby Barth in July; D-IKHA, an A-0 (*Werke No. 788*) went to the *E-Stelle* at Rechlin; while D-IJOM, an A-1, went to *Hansa Lufbild* for aerial photography operations. Among other units the Hs.123 equipped the *3./Fliegergruppen 10* and *50* in 1938; A/B *Schule 71* (A-1); the *7./St.G. 165 Immelmann* (A-1); the *II./SG.1* (A-1); the *SchG.1*; (A-1 and B-1); and the *4./SchG.2* (B-1). Other civilian registrations included D-ILVA, D-ILVY (*Werke No.* 2331); D-ILXL (*Werke No.* 2259), D-1OJI (*Werke No.* 2317), D-IPNC, an A-1 (later carrying WL-IPNC) and D-IYQU (*Werke No.* 2319).

The *II./St.G. 162* was formed at Lübeck-Blankensee on 1 April 1936, and later that year converted to the Hs.123 through to March 1937, when it helped in the formation of the *III./St.G. 165*. On 1 April 1937 *II./St.G.162* was re-designated as the *I./St.G.167*. The unit carried out intensive training duties for a year before re-equipping with the Ju.87. The *St.G. 165* was formed at Kitzingen of 1 April 1937, with the Hs. 123 and moved to Schweinfurt, Bavaria, where it re-equipped with the Ju.87. The *I./St.G. 165* began re-equipping with the Hs.123 in March 1937, converting to the Ju.87 in September. The *II./St.G. 165* formed on 1 April 1937 with the Hs.123 instead of the planned Heinkel He.70s, but began conversion to the Ju.87 in August 1938. The *III./St.G.165* likewise formed with the thirty-four Hs.123s at Fürstenfeldbruck, shifting based to Wertheim on 1 October, where it began re-equipping with the Ju.87.

At the time of the Munich Crisis *Fliegergruppe 10* was created at Tutow, Demmin, on 1 August 1938 with the Hs.123As drawn from all manner of units. A crash familiarization course followed in case of war and in September the unit moved to

Brieg, Silesia (now Brzeg). Once the Sudetenland was occupied and digested into the Reich, these machines all dispersed back to their units once more, many of them re-forming as the *I./St.G. 160* at Insterburg, East Prussia, in November where they converted to the Ju.87. Similarly *Fliegergruppe 50* was hastily assembled for Munich on 1 August 1938, at Lechfeld, Bavaria, and equipped with the Hs.123, moving to Grottkau, Silesia, on 20 September. These aircraft gave air cover for the troops moving into the Sudetenland working from Paulsgrund, Ratibor (now Racibórz). At the end of the crisis the Hs.123s were used to form the *II./St.G.163* on 1 November at Bad Langenslza, Thuringia, and then at Breslau-Schöngarten where they converted to the Ju.87. Another Munich emergency unit, *Fliegergruppe 20* was at Tutow where, on 1 November, it was re-designated as *II.(Sch.)/LG.2* and began re-equipping with the Hs.123. In a similar fashion *Fliegergruppe 30* was demobilized to Straubing in Lower Bavaria, and re-equipped with the Hs.123 and supported the occupation of the ceded Czech territories. On 1 November 1938 it was based at Barth and was re-designated as the new *I./St.G.162.*

The *II.(Schlacht)/L.G.2* (coded L2 +) was destined to become the most famous of all Hs.123 units. On formation at Tutow, on 1 November 1938, with aircraft from the disbursed *Fliegergruppen 20* and *40,* and containing a battle-hardened *cadre* of Spanish intervention veterans, this unit was one of the most professional in the Luftwaffe. Conversion to the Hs.123 followed, and, in turn, they were scheduled to move on to the Ju.87.

For, despite outstanding work achieved in Spain, realistic exercises held in 1938 convinced the *Führungsstab* (Command Staff) that biplanes had no future role in war for the Luftwaffe and the Hs.123 was largely withdrawn and replaced by the Junkers Ju.87 Stuka. The two constructors, AGO and Henschel, received orders that all jigs, models and production tooling for this type were to be scrapped forthwith. Moreover the *Schlachtfliegerguppen* (Close Support Groups) were also abandoned in the aftermath of the Czechslovakian crisis. The sole remaining unit, *Schlacht 10,*[13] was absorbed into the *Lehrgeschwader 2* becoming *II (Schlacht)/LG 2*, and by 1 September 1939, remained the only surviving operational HS.123A-1 unit, the bulk of the remainder passing to the training cadres.[14]

So successful was she to subsequently prove in the ground-attack profile that in 1943 calls were made to renew production afresh, but by then all the jigs had already been destroyed long ago and, by 1944, there were insufficient spare parts to keep her operational but a few remained operational, working with training units, until the German surrender in May 1945.

Luftwaffe wartime operations

Poland

The *II.(Schlacht)/LG 2* on the outbreak of war was commanded by *Major* Georg Spielvogel, and had a strength of forty Hs.123s. The unit was initially moved up to its pre-war station at Alt-Siedel, Oppeln, Silesia, and then to Alt-Rosenburg only some 15km from the Polish border. They were assigned close air support for the *1.* and *4. Panzer Divisions*. The Hs.123's service in Poland in September 1939 proved outstanding and here her efficiency and success in the field came as a real eye-opener to those who, just a year before, had declared her 'finished'. She was far from that and, in the hands of people like Adolf Galland, who flew the Hs.123 in combat between 1 September and 1 October as *Staka* of the *5. Staffel*, duly earning himself the *Ritterekreuz des Eisemen Kreuzes* (Knights Cross of the Iron Cross) in the process, she really established her reputation. They flew very low-level strafing missions with only 110lb (50kg) wings below the wings and caused mayhem and havoc, particularly in the Polish cavalry units.

Early missions were flown against Polish troop concentrations at Przystajn, north of Łódź and Panki, south of Łódź,[15] Four Hs.123s were lost this day; *Leutnant der Reserve* Josef Wöhrl, *Feldwebel* Kurt Zeltner and *Oberleutnant* Troha Egon made forced landings and survived, while *Uffz* Arthur Kracht was shot down at Kłobuck and became a PoW. Their next target was a Polish armoured train at Popów railway station, south-east of Kalisz, and later they made two further attacks, during which they lost *Feldwebel* Neszerie at Noldau east of Wroclaw. This intense schedule became the pattern for the Hs.123s in the days that followed.

On 5 September they headed northward, moving base firstly to Witkowice and then to Wolbórz working from a makeshift airstrip, on the route to Łódź from where they destroyed a huge Polish troop column on 8 September. They then contributed to the great encirclement battle of Radom from 9 September onward. On 9 September, while make a reconnaissance near Okecie, Warsaw, in the unit's Fieseler Fi.156 spotter plane, and seeking new targets for his unit, Spielvogel's aircraft was hit by ground fire from German sources and crashed near Wolbórz, killing both himself and *Oberfeldwebel* Anton Szigorra. On 13 September, following Spielvogel's death, Major Wolfgang Neudoerffer, another former Condor Legion man and at that time an officer at the RLM *Führer-Reserve*, who was filling in time on temporary duty to the *Luftkriegscchule* (LKS – Luftwaffe Cadet College) at Wildpark-Werder, Berlin, was appointed *Gruppen Kommandeur* in Spielvogel's place to temporarily deal with the unit's administration.[16] Meanwhile, the day-to-day combat duties of the *II (Schlacht) LG 2* on the battlefield, were dissolved upon the *Staka* (*Staffelkapitan*) of *4. Staffel*, *Hauptmann* Otto Albert Bernhard Weiß.[17] Up to 17 September the unit flew repeated missions against the disintegrating Polish Army at Poznan, culminating in the trapping and destruction of the armies on the Bzura river. Their final sorties were made on 25 September against targets in Warsaw itself, which had been turned into a fortified camp. At one point the unit was even visited by the top-ranking Nazi hierarchy, Adolf Hitler himself, accompanied by *Feldmarschall* Hermann Göring, Heinrich Himmler and their retinues, in recognition of their outstanding work.

Of course, the Hs.123 did not get things all its own way in Poland, as any cursory glance at even the incomplete returns of the Luftwaffe's *Generalquartiermeister* (Quartermaster-General) held at the Imperial War Museum, Duxford, will indicate. On 1 September they lost *Unteroffizier* (*Uffz.* – Corporal) Jürgen Kracht to anti-aircraft fire at Klobuck, he being made a PoW, and on 3 September *Leutnant* Siegried Panten's 4. *Staffel* machine was damaged in a landing accident at Alt-Roskenberg. Polish AA artillery was the main danger, and *Oberleutnant* Friedrich Lampe of the 6. *Staffel* was shot down over Slawno on 7 September. Three further accidents followed, *Leutnant* F N U Rasch of 4. *Staffel* writing off his aircraft (*Werke No.* 3226) on 9 September while landing at Wolborz; another HS.123 (*Werke No.* 2251) was pranged at Mazowszany on 13 September and on 27 September *Uffz.* Herbert Dieterle of 6. *Staffel*, totally obliterated his aircraft (*Werke No.* 2432) in a crash-landing at the same airfield.

During the attack on the fortress of Modlin, near Warsaw itself, on 26 September, continuous Stuka attacks were launched against it to break the final resistance. The principal anti-aircraft defence fell upon the 8 Motorized AA Battery, commanded by *Kapitan* Józef Płodowski, which had four 40mm Bofors guns, each as a semi-independent platoon. This unit was charged not only with the AA defence of Modlin itself but also the nearby Vistual (Wisla) bridges. On the 26th this battery claimed to have destroyed two Junkers Ju.87s, one from the *1./StG 1* and another badly damaged, with 70 per cent hits, which became a write-off. The battery's 'eye' was in.

The following day, the 27th, the air attacks continued and joining the Stukas were eleven Hs.123s of the *II (Schlacht)/LG2*. The first attack arrived over Modlin at 0832 and continued until 0917. One Hs.123 was hit by flak, this being a unit of the 4. *Staffel*, piloted by *Uffz.* Josef Harmeling, which was so badly damaged that she had to make an inverted crash-landing close to Wierszów (Wiersze). His aircraft (*Werke No.* 2269) had 45 per cent damage. The second attack was made by five Hs.123s between 1410 and 1454, and a near miss flak burst brought down another 4. *Staffel* aircraft, that of *Uffz.* Karl Henz (*Werke No.* 816), which was totally destroyed. *Kapitan* Płodowski, who was with the *IV.* Platoon gun at the time, and its battery commander, Reserve Officer *Podporucznik* (ppor. – Second-Lieutenant) Tadeusz Jaegereman, were both interviewed later and recorded the incident clearly. The *Kapitan* instructed Tadeusz to hold his fire until the leading aircraft was within 1,093 yards (1,000m). Henze dived almost straight down the battery's gun barrel, even so the first three shells missed this nil-deflection target, but the following bursts were true and the shells blew the Herschel's tail clean off. Henze baled out by parachute and landed within 164 feet (50m) of the battery and was instantly taken prisoner by Polish troops. Płodowski interrogated him instantly. Henze told them he was a 24-year-old Bavarian, flying from Grójec, and that his commander had expressly forbidden him to make any dive-bombing attacks on the AA battery, but that, after the two losses earlier (he said that an Henschel Hs.126 light reconnaissance plane of the *1.(H)/31*, operating out of Preussisch-Krawam, had also been shot down) Henze had wanted to prove that these troublesome guns *could* be silenced![18]

Modlin itself surrendered the following day and the Polish campaign was effectively over. The high pilot loss rate, almost 25 per cent, did not detract from the fine work achieved and ensured a prolonging of the HS.123's survival for another campaign.

Belgium and France 1940

Having won another stay of execution by its work in Poland, the *II. /LG 2* was steadily built up to a strength of forty-nine Hs.123s over the winter of 1939–1940 at Braunschweig (Brunswick) and then Mönchengladbach, Düsseldorf, close to the border of Holland and was thus ready when the German *Blitzkrieg* was launched against the complaisant West on 10 May 1940. Again they proved most effective on the field of battle. The effect that they had on troops unused to air attacks had the immediate effect of halting the disposal of Hs.123s and their retention in the front line listings when the next series of invasions of western European countries was being readied. They were assigned the close-support mission for the German 6 *Armee*, which was tasked with forming the German right hook, crossing the River Meuse and heading for the English Channel after negating the Allies static defence system of forts and canals.

Their first major mission was supporting the German *Sturmabteilung Koch* para- and glider teams for their audacious assault on the Eben-Emael fortress and the vital bridges across the Albert Canal. They moved to Kaarst airfield, Neuss, and flew sorties that smashed Dutch attempts to relieve the besieged fortress complex. Mission duly accomplished; the unit was switched to supporting the subsequent fast-moving land operations in the west. On 11 May the Hs.123s took on the biplanes of the Belgian Air Force, strafing Janeffe airfield, near Liege, and claiming seven but destroying five out of nine Fairey Fox IIIs of *10 Goetsenhoven Jeneffe IIIe Corps d'Armlée 5/III/1 Escadrille* they caught on the ground, these being 114, 115, 162, 163 and 168. They subsequently also attacked St Trond, losing one Hs.123 to AA fire and two more fell to French and British fighter attacks on 12 and 13 May. On 14 May RAF Hurricanes of Nos. 242 and 607 Squadrons shot down two more, but their pilots survived, and a third fell to flak, but in return one No. 242 Hurricane was destroyed by a team attack by a pair of Hs.123s. The unit moved briefly to Duras (St Trond-Brustem) landing strip 1.5 miles (2.4 km) north-west of St Trond, supporting 6 *Armee* until Brussels fell.

By 22 May 1940, the *II./LG 2*, under *Hauptmann* Otto Albert Weiß, was based at a captured Belgian airfield 3.7 miles (6km) north of Cambrai. The German *Panzergruppen* under General Paul Ludwig Ewald von Kleist, led by the ever-impetuous *Generaloberest* Heinz Wilhelm Guerdian ('Der Schnelle Heinz' -'Fast Heinz') had already plunged full-tilt on ahead westward through the disintegrating French armies while their supporting infantry were slow to catch up and were still lagging to the east of the town. This left an awkward gap before they did so, and the French seized the moment to launch a counter-attack into it by their 7 Army, with a column of fifty tanks and 150 trucks attempting to sever the head of the German advance from its tail by meeting up with a similar British thrust from Arras.

The approaching French armour was sighted by a Heinkel He.46 light spotter plane heading toward them and made an urgent message drop on the airfield warning them of the danger. Weiß himself immediately took off with a section of four more Hs.123s and within four minutes sighted the French armoured column that had penetrated across the *Canal de la Sensee* unopposed. Weiß carried out an initial strafing run at the head of the column and then radioed in his sighting report back to *Gruppe*

Kommandoposten (Command Post), ordering his entire force into the air including the Bf.109s of the I./JG 21 sharing the same field. While waiting for the rest of his aircraft to join them Weiß directed his accompanying quartet into attacks on the leading elements of the column crippling a dozen enemy tanks.

The surviving French pressed on and the leading tanks were also engaged by two batteries of the Luftwaffe's *I/Flak-Regiment 33* with their 88mm cannon firing and between them they managed to stop the French assault dead destroying a total of forty French tanks.[19]

Next day, during the battle of Arras, another heavy tank attack, this time by the British, was also smashed. They then moved to St Pol and for the next week were fully engaged in harrying the fleeing Allies back to the Channel coast. With the bulk of the British armies evacuated back to England from Dunkirk, the main land fighting swept south and the unit moved to Puisieux, south of Arras. Here, the German offensive overwhelmed the remaining Allied armies south of the Somme, which were quickly broken. By 17 June the unit's pell-mell progress saw them striking at their furthermost point at Dijon from the Auxerre airfield, Burgundy. One victim of this otherwise overwhelmingly successful campaign was *Leutnant* Siegfried Panten of 4. *Staffel*. He had survived the Polish battles, but, on 5 June, his fate caught up with him in the form of the Morane-Saulnier MS.406 French fighters of the *Armée de l'Air's Groupe de Chasse I/6* from Marignane. In a brief encounter at 1030 that morning his Hs.123 (L2+BM) was hit by *Sous-Lieutenant* (Sub-Lieutenant) Alaine Janis and crash-landed just north of Hallu, to the south of Chaulnes, on the Somme in Picardy, northern France. Panten was seriously injured and died of wounds, being buried close by to his aircraft, which he had managed to get down in remarkably good condition.

In recognition of the role the unit had played in the victory of 1940 the *Kommandeur* and all three *Staffelkaptäns* were awarded the *Ritterkreuz des Eisernen Kreuzes*. On 22 June the unit was then withdrawn to its home base of Waagum, Braunschweig. Here, instead of converting to the Junkers Ju.87 as expected, the unit was instead provided with the Messerschmitt Bf.109E-4B fitted with a single 551lb (250kg) bomb. Conversion of the pilots in the use of this faster machine was conducted at Böblingen and adapting from the relatively tame and simple to fly Hs.123 proved challenging, and about 20 per cent of the existing pilots 'washed out'. Those not rejected got their new mounts and joined in the Battle of Britain and its aftermath. It remained a Bf.109 unit through to March 1941, when its strength was expanded in readiness for the planned assault on the Soviet Union with three extra *Staffeln*, two of which re-introduced the Hs.123 back into the fold once more to ensure the expertise of the veterans was not wasted. Slow in comparison to the Bf.109E as they undeniably were, their accuracy for ground-support was equally not to be denied. But before *Barbarossa* began, a move south into the Balkans suddenly presented itself.

The Balkans 1941

As we have seen, once France surrendered, the Hs.123 was thought, yet again, to have had her day, and had been to Germany to re-equip as a Bf.109 outfit, but this was never fully done and when Hitler invaded Yugoslavia in the spring of 1941, the little biplane was again among the leading Luftwaffe attackers that smashed that country within a few weeks. She served with the *II (Schlacht)/LG. 2* throughout and in that rugged terrain, again demonstrated her flexibility and endurance. Her former *Kommandeur*, *Major* Otto Weiß, had undergone *Generalstab* training at the *Luftkriegsakademie* (Air Warfare School) at Gatow, Berlin, between 15 October 1940 and 15 February 1941, when he had been appointed to the *Ia op/Jagdfliegerführer 2*, but, with the sudden decision put into force *Wirkung* (Operation) *Marita*, part of their *Balkanfeldzug* (Balkan Campaign) with Yugoslavia now as an enemy instead of an ally, and the need for experienced leaders, he was hastily re-assigned back to lead his old unit once more on 26 May and was to remain with them until 13 January 1942 when they were re-designated as *I./Schlachtgeschwader 1*, remaining until 22 April.

On 5 April 1941, operating directly under *General der Flieger* Wolfram Freiherr von Richthofen's famous *Fliegerkorps VIII*, the Hs.123s were based in Bulgaria, with the thirty-two (twenty operational) Hs123As of *10./LG 21* stationed at Wraździebna airfield at Sofia. As soon as the invasion commenced they sortied against Rezanovacka Kosa airfield, but found most of the birds had flown. However, they destroyed a single Hawker Fury fighter and other small aircraft. They then flew close-support to the German *12 Armee* at Stracin, Kratovo, losing one aircraft, and subsequently carried out attacks on Skopje airfield, Macedona, on 6 April, and the next day visited Kumanovo airfield in the same manner and also attacked ground forces at Gradsko, Vardar, Shtip (Stip) and Veles (Велес) all in Macedonia and airfields at Lodi, Amfikleia, Greece. The Germans speedily advanced through Yugoslavia and smashed the Greek and British armies in Greece, with the Hs.123s supporting the *Fallschirmjäge-Rgt. 2* in crossing the Corinth Canal on 26 April. By May the unit was working from Molaoi, far south of Athens itself before being pulled out in readiness to take up their new positions ready for a new enemy.

The *II.(Schlacht)/L.G.2.* was ordered to a new assignment, moving up in stages to the north of Warsaw and so, in stark contrast to the warm sunshine and blazing heat of Greece the Hs.123s quickly found themselves back in Poland again, being based at Praszniki (Przasnysz or Prsschinitz), close to the border with Soviet-occupied Lithuania.

The Soviet Union 1941

Yet again, her previous successes ensured that the Hs.123 took part in Hitler's final showdown with Stalin. Initially she was employed on the northern sector of that thousand-mile front. On 22 June the *Gruppe* had twenty-two Hs.123s on establishment, seventeen of which were operational, having been in continuous combat for several weeks followed by the swift move north. After the overwhelming successes of opening air assaults, they were switched to supporting the *Panzerguruppe 3* on the Central Front in the drive that took Minsk by the end of the month, switching airstrips almost daily working out of Sudauen, East Prussia (now Suwalki, Poland), Berźniki, Reicki, Sloboda in the Ukraine, and on across the Dnieper River toward Smolensk.

A Hs.123B-1 fell at Grodno, Ukraine, on 24 June, and others were damaged in enemy night attacks on Repicki on the night of 3–4 July, while another aircraft was shot down by intense AA fire at Bosheikovo on 6 July. These casualties reduced the numbers of operational Hs.123s to a mere fourteen machines.

On 3 August another switch took place and the *II. Gruppe* found themselves working the Dno, Pskov Oblast, front near Lake Ilmen helping the *16. Armee*, and the thrust to Chudovo and Lyuban from Novgorod, Veliky, north of Lake Ilmen, working from Spasskaya airfield. By September the Hs.123s were flying sorties from Lyuban just south of Leningrad and over Lake Ladoga before being hurried south to participate in the assault on Moscow itself being engaged at Bryansk by October and moving in support of *9. Armee* via Belyy Dvor, Belarus, and Moshna, Belarus, and the heavy fighting for Kalinin in support of the surrounded *1. Panze* where they again won high praise.

As the weather worsened the attacks slowed, hesitated and faltered toward the end of November. Again with the massive Soviet counter-offensive in December huge gaps were torn in the Axis lines and every available aircraft was required to try and stem the onrush. Meanwhile, *Staffelkaptäne Majors* Georg Dörffel (5), Werner Dörnbrack (4), Alfred Druschel (6) and Bruno Meyer (10) had all received the *Ritterekreuz des Eisenen*. In all these operations the Hs.123s earned fame once more and their continuous 'shuttle' sorties were instrumental both in protecting their base airfield and in blunting the enemy spearheads. They saw the onset of the worst Russian winter in years and the Hs.123's open cockpits did not prove conducive for blizzard-like conditions. In recognition of all they had achieved Otto Weiß received the Oak Leaves to his Knight's Cross. The Hs.123s were pulled back to Werl, North Rhine-Westphalia, and here they formed the core of the *Schlachtgeschwader 1 (SG.1)*. During the course of operations in the Soviet Union during 1941 a total of fifteen Hs.123s were lost these being *Werke Nos*. 631, 820, 938, 940, 943, 966, 979, 2254, 2277, 2322, 2358, 2429, 2347, 2425 and 2514.

Despite these losses the Hs.123 proved herself a real asset, one of her most enduring features being the ability to maintain a high degree of operational readiness. *Ad hoc*, in-the-field modifications included removal of the wheel spats when operating from mired air strips, extra armour plate being added to mitigate the enormous amount of ground fire encountered over Russia, adding extra machine-guns, slinging 20mm cannon beneath the lower wings, incorporating specialized 'cold-start' apparatus to deal with temperatures that plummeted to minus 30^0 and lower, while dust filters were soon to be required when the mud and snow turned to wind-blown sand on the southern sectors of the front line.

1942–44

In January 1942 the unit was re-designated as *Schlachtgeschwader 1* (*SchlG.1* – 1 Ground Attack Wing) back at Werl, Dortmund. After prolonged revitalization and refitting the new unit reported ready for combat again at the end of April and moved forward to its new base of Grammatikovo, south of Bourgas, Bulgaria, on the Black Sea coast, on 2 May.

The *I./Schl.G.1* had a total of eighteen Hs.123s on establishment in March 1942 while at Dugino, Vyazma. The Hs.123s were all concentrated into *II. Gruppe*, which had formed at Lippstadt, North Rhine-Westphalia, on 13 January, the new *8./Staffel* absorbing all of *10. (Schlacht) /L.G.2*'s Henschels. However, they only flew the Hs.123 until April, when they returned home to convert to the Bf.109E-7 and again passed on these Henschels to *7.Staffel*.

The new unit's first mission was to support ground forces in the eastern Crimea until 18 May when they started flying sorties over the Izyum Salient, the Hs.123 contributing 259 sorties before moving to support the drive on Stalingrad that summer. On 18 June *Major* (later *Oberstleutnant*) Hubertus Hitschhold, took over as *Kommodore*, a position he held for the next year. On 29 June a severe blow was dealt to *7. Staffel* when they lost three of their number at Shchigry, north-east of Kursk in one day. On 1 August there were twenty Hs.123s ready for operations, which were to support what was fondly imagined to be the final moves on Stalingrad. During the battle *Staffelkapitän* Josef Menapace was wounded over the city and the grinding battle had reduced the Hs.123 numbers to a mere eleven machines by 1 December, necessitating the introduction of the Bf.109 to keep their operational strength up to the mark. The year's operations had cost a total of just five Hs.123s.

With the Soviet counter-attack at Stalingrad in November 1942, the unit, initially flying from threatened Morosovskaya airfield on the west bank of the Don River, was once more forced into a succession of base moves as they fell back westward under the onslaught. Losses in the first eight months of 1942 were severe, the *7./Staffel* losing *Werke Nos.* 855, 858, 939, 2248, 2271, 2285, 2332, 2333, 2344, 2426, 2431; *8./Staffel* losing *Werke Nos.* 632, 794, 832, 969, 971, 2256, 2274, 2284, 2302 and 2345; while *I./Staffel* lost 2270, 2291, 2336 and 2434 and *II//Staffel* lost 223 for a total of twenty-six aircraft. Fortunately only three pilots were killed, *Leutnant* Rolf von Zahradnícek to AA fire close to Okovokovo on 7 February, and Hans Stenkamp and *Uffz.* Heinrich Klein in a collision at Schtschigry, Kursk Oblast, on 29 June.

While the bulk of the unit exchanged their Bf.109s for Fw.190s the *7. Staffel* remained an Hs.123 outfit and continued flying the biplane. Between January 1943 and June that year missions were concentrated on Kuban bridgehead, which was under constant assault, and in an Soviet air attack on their base field at Anapa, on the north coast of the Black Sea, on 19 April, two Hs.123s were lost and by July just sixteen Henschels remained on strength.

With the launching of the ill-fated Operation *Zitadelle,* to pinch out the Kursk salient, in July, operations moved to the north but at the end of the month the *Gruppe* was at Rogan airfield, Kharkov, where another Hs.123A was lost to enemy fighters. Here *Hauptmann* Josef Menapace, *Kommandeur 7. Staffel* from 20 August, earned himself a formidable reputation in tacking the Soviet T-34s ,chalking up an impressive tally flying his Hs.123 named in honour of his friend as 'Rolf von Zahradnícek'. Before he was killed in action by flak fire over Strakholessye in the Pripet (Pripyet) Marshes on 6 October 1943, Josef had clocked up 723 combat missions and shot down two Soviet fighters, earning himself the *Ritterkreuz des Eisemen Kreuzes* in the process.[20]

In order to keep the unit going Hs.123s were called in from training schools, any auxiliary duties and even, it is said, from salvage yards. Even so, it proved barely possible to find sufficient flyable Hs.123s but such was their popularity and considered value at the front that *Generaloberst* Wolfram von Richthofen, *Kommandeur* of *Luftflotte 4* demanded to know whether the Hs.123 production lines could be re-started, but with all the jigs and tools scrapped in 1940, the cost of re-tooling was just too prohibitive to start again from scratch.

The Kursk battle in July 1943 was to be the last throw of the Reich and was defeated so totally that from then on in it was eighteen months of steady retreat, with the Hs.123s being thrown in like pebbles against the Red tide sweeping irresistibly westward. On 18 October the *II./Schl.G.1* was re-designated as the *II./S.G.2* forming at Kiev-*Sud*, Ukraine, and immediately moved to Kirovograd in the Ukraine. The Hs.123s were utilized by the *6. Staffel* up to December and then transferred to *4.Staffel*. There were nine Hs.123s remaining by 1 November after heavy fighting working out of Karankut airfield in central Crimea to cover the planned evacuation. In the end they had to be pulled back to Kirovograd once more.

By the end of January 1944, there were just thirteen Hs.123s remaining on the establishment of *4. Staffel*, nine with the *Staffel*, three under repair plus one unassigned aircraft. These few were not enough to remain a viable front-line outfit and *4. Staffel* was ordered to convert to the Focke Wulf Fw.190 there and then. Thus, on 4 May these were distributed to reserve duties. *6. Staffel* still reported four Hs.123s on strength on 29 September, based at Seregélyes, Fejér, Hungary, south of Budapest, but her day was done, save for lowly duties like glider tug, supply droppers and such. The Hs.123 thus saw out the war in which it had led for so long, working in the background. None have survived.

Foreign service

Austria
The Austrian Government, concerned at events across its border, decided to increase its air defences by building up the *Österreichisches Luftstreitkräfte* (Austrian Air Force) but, ironically, it was to German aircraft manufacturers that they turned. A small delegation, led by *Generaloberst* Alexander Löhr, and with *Hauptmann* Johann Schalk, of *2. Fliegerregiment* at Graz, as chief test pilot, was sent to tour the Reich's leading aircraft factories in search of suitable machines to order. Among the requirements was one for a dive-bomber and naturally Schalk flew the Junkers Ju.87. However, in order to have a fair comparison, and because he visited the Henschel works to view the Hs.126 reconnaissance aircraft, he also tried out the Hs.123. After flight-testing D-INVI, Schalk's report was far from enthusiastic. He sought a Stuka, a dive-bomber but he did not consider the Hs.123 to be one. Her bomb load was puny compared to the Junkers, her biplane construction was outdated and these facts overrode the Henschel's greater manoeuvrability in his view. The Hs.123, Schalk considered, was more a *Grabenkamp* (trench warfare) machine. In this he was to be proven totally

correct. The Austrians ordered the Ju.87 to meet their needs and plans. Unfortunately for them the former waif from the Vienna streets, Adolf Hitler, had other plans for his former compatriots and the *Anschluss* made nonsense of any such orders.[21]

China

As related below, twelve Hs.123s, originally ordered by Portugal but never paid for, were offered to the visiting Chinese Purchasing delegation in 1937. The RLM offered the Chinese a package that also included all the equipment and spare parts, for a price of *Reichsmark* 2,017.000.00, or RM 168, 133.33 apiece. Negotiations were conducted in China by the *Deutsche Handelsgesellschaft für industrielle Produkte* (HAPRO – German Trade Company for Industrial Products) and they drew up the contract on 3 November. The Chinese accepted this deal on 22 November at Henschel's Schönefeld plant in Berlin.[22] The package included the sea transportation from Bremen, but due to Japanese diplomatic opposition, the planned shipment sailing from Bremen of 26 November, was delayed for a month.

Once the behind-the-scenes machinations between the German and Japanese Governments had been smoothed over the shipment went ahead. Each machine was dismantled and crated and a thirteen-man team, headed up by Heinkel Test Pilot (and Luftwaffe Reserve Officer) Alexander von Winterfelat, who also acted as the representative of the *Reichsverband de deutschen Luftfahrt-Industrie* (RDLI – Association of the German Aviation Industry), and which also included specialists like Herr Bernhard Bauske, responsible for the aircraft's engines and hydraulics, and Walter Neff, responsible for the aircraft's electrical equipment, radios and machine-gun armaments, were assembled to accompany the aircraft, and oversee their subsequent re-assembly and testing in China. After protected negotiations with the Japanese and Italians, eight machines were loaded aboard the ship, which sailed via Venice for the voyage out to Hong Kong, but the German party sailed in a faster passenger vessel and consequently arrived in Hong Kong several days earlier than their charges.

The original plan called for the Hs.123s to be re-assembled at the RAF's Kai Tek airfield, but continued Japanese pressure on Great Britain thwarted this and the eight aircraft remained crated and were transported north to Hankau (Hankow), Wuhan, by rail.[23] Between mid-January and mid-February 1938 both crated aircraft and the German team assembled at the heavily camouflaged, wooden assembly hangar, along with an assigned interpreter, Mr Wang, two cooks and a chauffeur and commenced work. Once each Hs.123 was put together it was test-flown by von Winterfelat. Meanwhile, a second batch of four further Hs.123s arrived in April by the same torturous route and was also assembled. Concurrently, the training of the assigned (and as it turned out, quite inexperienced) Chinese pilots and ground crews got underway. This resulted in accidents, which further delayed the programme, one Hs.123 having its upper wing destroyed when it ran into the assembly hangar for example, and another was beset by technical difficulties. However, it was the Chinese pilots' attitudes that proved the biggest hazard; they were not used to formation flying, nor had they ever used airborne radios before. All the Hs.123s, given the Chinese serial numbers 1501 to 1512, were readied by April 1938, and had been flight-tested by mid-May, but the aircrew training continued beyond that.

By June 1938 nine of the Hs.123s, serials 1501 to 1509, freshly painted in Chinese colours and markings, were assigned to No. 15 Squadron, with the other three held in reserve or for spares. The German delegation then left for their return journey, again via Hong Kong, but before they could embark once more, von Detlof Winterfeldt, Bauske and Neffe were recalled by the Chinese authorities who remained unsatisfied, and had to fly back to Hankow onboard the Lufthansa subsidiary airline Eurasia's Junkers Ju.52/3m. After a few days the problems were resolved and the German team returned to the Reich in August 1938, whereupon von Winterefeldt submitted two reports on his mission.[24]

The Chinese 15 Squadron flew their Hs.123s on combat operations from August 1938 until the spring of 1939. They initially employed them as dive-bombers, flying three missions against Japanese warships on the River Yangtze-Kiang, dropping a total of forty-eight 110lb (50kg) bombs, and claiming to have damaged at least one Japanese destroyer. Several aircraft were lost to anti-aircraft fire and to accidents and by mid-1939 the surviving Hs.123s were relegated to the role of training machines with No. 6 Fighter Squadron.[25]

Portugal

The Portuguese *Aeronáutica Militar* (Army Air Force) and *Avação Naval* (Navy Air Force) sought to modernize their equipment and President Antonio Salazar's one-party state naturally turned to friendly right-wing nations, Italy and Germany, for assistance. A *Missão Militar* was despatched to both countries with a view to examination and purchase, the air side being headed up by a First World War fighter ace, Major António de Sousa Maya, then in command of the *Grupo Independente de Aviação de Protecção e Combate* (Independent Escort and Fighter Group) from Tancos Military airfield north of Lisbon. The choice for a ground-attack aircraft finally came down to three machines, the Hs.123, the Italian *Breda Meccanica Bresciana* (Breda) Ba.65 ground attack aircraft manufactured at Brescia, Lombardy, and the Polish *Polskie Zaklady Lotnicze* (P.Z.L) P.23 *Kara* (Carp) light attack bomber built at Mielec. Although both her rivals were monoplanes, with enclosed cockpits and all the refinements, and seemingly the favourites, the Hs. 123, after testing, was the preferred option. The P.23 was tough enough but unable to carry out dive-bombing attacks to the degree required; the Ba.65 lacked manoeuvrability and both were rejected.

Negotiations were accordingly opened with the Henschel *FlugzeugWerket AG*, which resulted in an order for twelve Hs.123A-1s. These machines were duly built but in 1937 it became apparent that the purchase was not going to be made. The reason for this volte face was political rather than practical, as Salazar had been impressed by Mussolini's intervention in Spain (which had been on a far greater scale than Germany's) and wished to maintain close links with his fellow despot. He therefore ordered the Breda to be delivered instead of the Hs.123 and that was that!

The Henschel aircraft had been under the jurisdiction of the *Reichsluftfahrtministium* (RLM), pending the expected transfer, and their future remained doubtful. However, this impasse happily coincided with a visit by yet another group of visitors, this time being the Chinese Purchase-Commission at the behest of the Kuomintang Government who were desperate to acquire some modern aircraft from any source to oppose the increasing incursion into their territory by the Japanese. The delegation, having visited the Henschel establishment and expressed an interest in the Hs.123, and the RLM quickly offered to make these intended Portuguese machines available to them instead, although whether they revealed their origins is not clear.

Spain

Two Hs.123s were crated up and shipped to Cadiz, Spain, aboard the freighter *Wigbert* for use by the Condor Legion in September 1936 under Operation *Feuerzauber (Magic Fire)*. The following month they were joined by a third machine. They were assembled at Tablada, Seville, receiving the codings 24•1, 24•2 and 24•3, and their pilots were *Leutnant* Heinrich 'Rubio' Brücker, *Uffz.* Emil Rückert and *Uffz.* August Wilmsen. They formed the *Patrulla de bombardeo en picado* (Dive-Bomber Patrol) based at Jarez de la Frontera just north of Cadiz and were commanded by *Versuchs Jagdgruppe 88* (*VJ/88* – 'Experimental Fighter Squadron'). These three were joined by a further trio, which arrived early in March 1937, and were coded 24•4, 24•5 and 24•6. Two additional pilots came with them, *Feldwebel* (Sergeant) Fritz Hillmann and *Uffz.* Hermann Beurer.

It was here, according to Adolf Galland who later flew her in Poland, that the Hs.123 pilots discovered that the BMW engine developed a loud whine at around 1,800rpm, the effect of which, when they made their runs at a height of around 30 ft (9m), was more than sufficient to unnerve enemy troops and horses! The technique was used with some success later in Poland with apparently satisfactory results where it became known as the '*akustische Kopfwelle*' ('sonic headache'). They also established a real rapport with the ground troops and, even though at this stage they had no direct radio contact with them, managed to provide them with the almost immediate air support that they required and established a firm precedent. This method of attack was also dangerous, which was quickly proven by the loss of Rückert's Hs.123 on 25 March 1937, to ground fire, the pilot being killed. On 1 April 1936 the pilots and ground team numbered thirteen, to which two civilians, Henschel representatives, Werner Busch and Walter Krone, were added. The group then became *Stuka/88* and moved to Vitoria, Madrid. On 22 May a second Hs.123 fell victim to ground fire at Ochandiano (Otxandio) in the Basque region of northern Spain, while a third, flown by *Uffz.* Wilmsen, was lost attacking Republican troops at Cinturón de Hierro, part of Bilbao's 'Iron Ring' fortifications, on 11 June 1937, and again the pilot died.

The only two survivors, 24•3 and 24•5, of the six Hs.123s used by the Condor Legion, were handed over to Franco's Air Force in August 1937 and assigned to the *5-G-17* and used in the south of the country.

Another eleven Hs.123s were sold to the *Aviation Nacional Adquirio* (Spanish Nationalist Air Force) in August 1938 and arrived in 1939. These were assigned the codings 24●7 to 24●18 inclusive, and served in the *Gruppo 24 Aviacion del Tercio* but saw no combat action. The Spanish called the HS.123 *Angelito* (Little Angel). Two of these machines were subsequently lost in accidents, 24●17 crashing on 3 October 1939 while serving with the *Escuadrilla de Bombardeo en Picada de la 2 Region Aeria*; and 24●13 crashing on 5 December 1941.

During the war on the Eastern front, the Spanish volunteer pilots of *La Escuadrilla Azul* (The Blue Squadron) as the *15 Spanische Staffel/VIII. Fliegerkorps* of JG.27 was named, were reputed to have 'managed' some Hs.123s 'in collaboration' with their Luftwaffe colleagues in the winter of 1941/42 and flown some combat missions with them. Although this tale is widely repeated, the actual numbers of serviceable, open-cockpit Hs.123s before Leningrad or Moscow, able to operate in those terrible conditions, let alone have aircraft to spare, makes it barely credible, but, if it really did occur, then it can only have been for the barest minimum of sorties.[26]

After the Civil War finished the Spanish Nationalist air force kept the Hs.123 in service for many years, indeed the very last one (an A-0 at that!) suffered a crash in 1952 and was finally written off in 1953. The Hs.123 remained to the end, one tough and robust little bird.

Chapter Thirteen

Nakajima E8N 'Dave'

The Imperial Japanese Navy was grossly under-estimated by the West prior to the outbreak of war in the Pacific in December 1941. The Japanese were constructing the most powerful battleships in the world, the *Yamato, Musashi* and *Shinano*.[1] These monsters (for their day) with displacements of 67,000 tons compared to the 35,000-tonners then still being built in Great Britain and the United States, were armed with nine 18.1-inch guns against the 16-inch of the US ships and even smaller 14-inch adopted by the British. Also the Japanese had built and were building classes of heavy cruisers and fleet destroyers at least a decade ahead of their Western counterparts and had armed them with the so-called 'Long Lance' torpedoes[2] which outranged all Western types and left no wakes, but especially with regard their Navy Air Arm. The Japanese had developed long-range, twin-engined, land-based torpedo- and altitude-bombers like the Mitsubishi G3M 'Nell' and Mitsubishi G4M 'Betty', which had operational ranges far in excess of anything available to the Allied navies, while their carrier-borne Mitsubishi Type O, 'Zeke' or 'Zero' fighters, Aichi D3A1/2 'Val' dive-bombers and Nakajima B5N 'Kate' torpedo-/level bomber (an exception to the rule in that she could perform both functions, but equally efficiently as demonstrated in the Pearl Harbor attack) were all of the topmost standard, and, more importantly, numerous and trained to achieve a high degree of accuracy. In the same way their shipborne reconnaissance floatplanes were of an equally high calibre and, pre-war, the most useful of the types then in service, although even then destined to soon be replaced by more superior types, was the Nakajima E8N.

The IJN relied heavily on these aircraft, which were carried by their battleships and heavy cruisers, to a far greater extent than did the Allied fleets. Although they had ten operational and several auxiliary aircraft-carriers available when they went to war (although Allied 'experts' only credited them with six), their policy was to cram these ships full of attack aircraft and fighters, and they left the scouting for the enemy fleet mainly to the ship-carried and catapult-launched seaplanes, all of which had excellent ranges. The IJN even designed and constructed some of their big cruisers (*Chikuma* and *Tone*), or later in the war, converted (battleships *Hyuga* and *Ise*, twenty-two, heavy cruiser *Mogami*, eleven) many of their big ships to carry large numbers of these aircraft. By contrast, the Royal Navy, due to Government economic restrictions and the attitude of disinterest and neglect by the RAF that controlled them pre-war, was forced to employ multi-purpose aircraft. Examples of this policy were the TSR, of which the Fairey Swordfish and Albacore described in these pages are typical, which had to carry out the functions of torpedo-bomber, reconnaissance and spotter duties in one airframe; or the absurdity of the Blackburn Skua concept. With this aircraft, the

RAF (who had control of all Fleet Air Arm aircraft from 1917 to 1939) imposed the dual roles of fighter and dive-bomber on the design, which were diametrically opposite requirements, despite the fact that the Royal Navy specifically requested priority for the latter as the predominant one required. Invariably this policy resulted in 'Jack-of-all-Trades' aircraft not very good at any of the roles assigned compared to dedicated types. Thus the Royal Navy Fairey Fulmar fighter was a two-man aircraft expected to equal the performance of the single-seater interceptors of the IJN and USN. The Americans went the other way for, although their ships could carry more planes than their Japanese equivalents, and many, many more than the Royal Navy vessels of the same type and tonnage, they split the roles of scout and dive-bomber into separate squadrons, even though, as in the case of the Douglas SBD Dauntless, both were using the same aircraft type. Their aircraft were as good, or in some cases, better than their Japanese opposite numbers, although they lacked range, and far superior to British maritime types, but the duplication of effort was wasteful.

The standard shipborne scout floatplane featured by the IJN in December 1941, was the Nakajima E8N. She was a single-engined, two-seater catapult-launched biplane with a large central main-float and two outriggers carried under the lower wings to port and starboard. This machine had been specifically designed and developed as a replacement for the Nakajima E4N Type 90-2-2. The wings, which were slightly more raked back than its predecessor, were slightly lengthened but with a reduced chord resulting in a smaller area, while the E4N's dorsal fin was done away with and the vertical tail surface was enhanced in height.

No fewer than seven prototypes were built, the first being completed in March 1934, and they were tested in direct competition against the Aichi E8A1 and the Kawanishi E8K1, which were both monoplanes. However, eventually Nakajima's biplane emerged as the preferred option due to its superior manoeuvrability and ruggedness. The IJN granted Nakajima a production contract in October 1935 and the new type was designated the Navy Type 95 Reconnaissance Seaplane Model 1.[3]

The E8N1 was equipped with the 580hp (433kW) Nakajima Kotobuki 2 *Kai* 1, radial engine in a prominent NCA cowl. She was of composite build, an all-metal framing covered with fabric with an open cockpit.

The aircraft's details were a length of 28ft 11in (8.81m), a span of 36ft (10.98m), and a height of 12ft 7in (3.84m). The wing area was 285.14 square/ft (26.5 square metres). The empty weight came out at 2,904lb (1,320kg), while the maximum take-off weight was 4,180lb (1,900kg). The wing loading was 14.7lb/ft squared (71.7kg/m squared).

The subsequent model, the E8N2, received a more powerful 630hp (480kW) *Kai* 2 nine-cylinder air-cooled radial driving a two-bladed propeller. This gave her a cruising speed of 115mph (186km/h) and a maximum speed of 186mph (301km/h). The range was 558 miles (904km) and the service ceiling was 23,845ft (7,270m). The climb rate was 9,845 ft (3,000m) in six-and-a-half minutes. The E8N2 was armed with two .303in (7.7mm) machine-guns, one fixed forward-firing and the other flexible rear-firing, and could carry a pair of 66lb (30kg) bombs.

At the time the E8N joined the fleet the Sino-Japanese Incident was in full swing and this little aircraft was immediately put to good use. Not only did she carry out numerous reconnaissance missions, but also acted as an artillery spotter and, on occasions, attacked what would today be termed 'targets of opportunity' as an improvised dive-bomber. Losses against Chinese fighter opposition proved surprisingly small.

In total 755 E8Ns were built either by Nakajima Hikoki K K, Koizumi (seven prototypes and a 700-machine production run between 1934 and 1940) or sub-contracted out to Kawanishi Kokuki K/ K, Konan (48 machines between 1938 and 1940), with final production ending in 1940. It was employed extensively in the fleet, being carried aboard all the battleships, sixteen cruisers and five seaplane tenders as follows: battleships *Fūso*, *Haruna*, *Hyūga*, *Ise*, *Kirishima*, *Kongō*, *Mutsu*, *Nagato* and *Yamashiro*; heavy cruisers, *Aoba*, *Ashigara*, *Atago*, *Chokai*, *Haguro*, *Kako*, *Kashima*, *Kumano*, *Maya*, *Mikuma*, *Mogami*, *Myōkō*, *Nachi*, *Suzuya*, *Takao* and *Tone*; light cruiser *Katori*, and seaplane tenders *Chiyoda*, *Kamoi*, *Kiyokawa Maru*, *Sagara Maru* and *Sanuki Maru*.

The E8N was involved from the very start in the Pacific War, when the *Kido Butai*'s six carriers approached Pearl Harbor on the morning of 7 December, the accompanying heavy cruisers *Chikuma* and *Tone* both launched their floatplanes to carry out patrols to the south to prevent any surprise attacks from that area by random US forces, and the battleships *Hiei* and *Kirishima* also launched their 'Dave's at 0500 to conduct anti-submarine patrols ahead of the force. This left the carrier free to concentrate all available aircraft for the two main strikes.

Their best war work was at the Battle of the Java Sea on 27 February 1942, when a mixed Allied cruiser and destroyer force of American, British and Dutch ships was defeated by a similar Japanese squadron, including the heavy cruisers *Haguro* and *Nachi*, which inflicted heavy losses on them, sinking the light cruisers *De Ruyter* and *Java* and destroyers *Electra*, *Jupiter* and *Kortenaer*, and damaged the heavy cruisers *Exeter* and *Houston*, without any loss to themselves. This was partly due to the fact that the Allied cruisers which still nominally carried catapult aircraft were mainly without them, while the Japanese heavy cruisers deployed theirs to very good effect and were able to watch and plot the Allies every move and take counter-action. From the very first sighting on the ships' radar at dawn, through the first intercepted sighting report at 0935, and all through the battle, the Japanese floatplanes remorselessly stalked the Allied ships.

Similarly, the E8Ns proved invaluable in locating and pinpointing the fleeing surviving ships, as on 1 March when the heavy cruisers *Ashigara*, *Haguro*, *Myoko* and *Nachi* all launched their floatplanes to find and locate the *Exeter* with her two destroyer escorts *Encounter* and *Pope*, and sank them all. Likewise heavy cruisers *Chikuma* and *Tone*'s E8Ns located the tanker *Pecos* and destroyers *Edsall* and *Pilsbury*, which were all subsequently sunk, and the heavy cruiser *Maya*'s floatplane located the destroyer *Stronghold*, which was also duly despatched three miles south of Bali on 2 March, along with several merchant vessels crammed with civilian and military refugees. Thus the next day the heavy cruiser *Maya* launched two E8Ns, which located the tanker

Francol, the depot ship *Anking*, the Dutch *Tjisaroea* and two minesweepers south-east of Tjilatjap, Java, all of which were sunk along with the Australian sloop *Yarra*, which valiantly attempted to defend them on her own.

During the Guadalcanal campaign in October 1942, both the battleships *Hiei* and *Kirishima*, and on a separate occasion, the heavy cruisers *Atago* and *Takao*, used their onboard E8Ns to drop magnesium flares to illuminate the target area prior to their night bombardments of Henderson Field.

The heavy cruisers *Maya* and *Nachi* under Vice-Admiral Boshirō Hosogaya, also utilized their B5Ns during the confused and unsatisfactory action off the Komandorski Islands in the Aleutians on 27 March 1943,[4] when they badly damaged the American heavy cruiser *Salt Lake City* and destroyers *Bailey* and *Coghlan*. The *Maya*'s No. 1 catapult plane was an early casualty, however, being badly damaged and set ablaze by her opening gun salvo and she had to be ditched. Similarly, *Salt Lake City*'s spotter was also destroyed by a direct hit. The vulnerability of these seaplanes during gun actions was always their weakness.

Later in the war, when the Allies adopted a simple 'coding' of names for Japanese aircraft, the E8N received the application 'Dave', but by this time, the autumn of 1942, she was in the process of being relegated to secondary duties and was steadily being replaced by monoplane types like the Aichi E13A1 Type 0 and the Mitsubishi F1M2. However, the E8N continued to serve as a seaplane trainer, a communications aircraft and for liaison work.

Foreign service

Uniquely, this Japanese aircraft was utilized by the German Navy. Early in 1941 Vice-Admiral Paul Wenneker, the German Naval Attaché in Tokyo, authorized the purchase of a E8N and she was loaded aboard the *Kriegsmarine* supply ship *Münsterland*. This vessel met the German *Hilfskreuzer* (Auxiliary Cruiser) HSK-1 (Auxiliary Cruiser) *Orion*[5] at Maug Island in the northern Marianas group on 1 February 1941. She was painted up with British roundels and the identification serial L5196[6] as part of the subterfuge and it was hoped this would fool any British merchant ship unfamiliar with aircraft types. This was the sole known example of a German warship utilizing a Japanese float plane.

The Japanese developed a strong alliance with the Thai (Siamese) Government, which aided and abetted the Japanese in their invasions of both Malaya and Burma in 1941–42. Before the war this liaison was strong and in 1938, when the Thais were building up their armed forces with purchases of foreign aircraft, the Royal Thai Navy placed an order for eighteen E8N1s. These were delivered by sea during 1940 and were re-classified as the BRN-1 but apparently did not take part in the brief and bitter little war between the Thais and the Vichy-French that erupted at that time. They served with the Thai Sea Squadron between 1940 and 1945, mainly at RNAB Sattahip from 1943 where they worked with Curtiss Hawk IIIs and Hawk 75Ns. In 1945 they suffered their first combat casualties.

The British Army had driven the Japanese Army out of Burma with heavy casualties in 1944–45 and were organizing themselves to do the same in Malaya and Singapore. As part of the preparatory work in readiness for the planned liberation invasion, the British East Indies Fleet mounted a minesweeping operation off the Phukut between 24 and 27 July 1945. Force 63, comprising the battleship *Nelson*, the escort carriers *Ameer* and *Empress*, heavy cruiser *Sussex* and destroyers, *Paladin*, *Racehorse*, *Raider* and *Rotherham*, provided cover for a flotilla of fleet minesweepers and, as part of that protection, the Fleet Air Arm Grumman F6F Hellcats of the two escort carriers made pre-emptive fighter sweeps over known Japanese air bases on the Kraa Isthmus, flying 150 sorties in the period. This was Operation *Livery*. The Hellcats of No.809 Squadron from *Ameer* attacked Chalong Bay and Sungei Patani and reported that they had destroyed eight Japanese aircraft. In fact, some of these were Thai machines and they included one BRN-1 totally destroyed and two others badly damaged by strafing and written off. The other fifteen BRN-1s survived the war and served on for a while post-war until lack of spare parts made them ineffective.[7]

Chapter Fourteen

Polikarpov I-15 *Chaika* and Variants

Many of the biplanes examined in these pages consisted of a mere handful of aircraft, 'penny packets' most of them, especially those of the democracies. But the Polikarpov was a different case indeed and many thousands of them were built in the years before the Soviet Union became involved with Hitler and Mussolini's regimes and their respective leaders' towering ambitions. The Soviet Union had a vast armaments industry, driven by the dictator Josef Stalin, a psychotic megalomaniac responsible for the death of millions of his own innocent subjects. It was estimated that four-fifths of senior Soviet air leaders were ultimately eliminated in this way prior to the war. Nickoli Nikolaevich Polikarpov had been the doyen of Soviet fighter design before the war, and his team had been responsible for forty different aircraft types since he had joined the *Voenno-vozdushnaya Flota* (Military Air Fleet). He designed his first fighter aircraft, the IL-400 and a succession of biplanes followed but such dedication was no guarantee of immunity in the surreal insane lunacy of Soviet Russia and, in 1930 Polikarpov, by then, with Dimitry Pavlovich Grigoroviich, the leading designer at the *Tsentral'nyi konstruktorskii byuro* (TsKB – Central Design Bureau), was incarcerated with his team under political detention and sentence of death at Butyrika prison in Moscow. With his sentence commuted to life imprisonment he was placed under OGPU (*Obyedinyonnoye Gosudarst Vennoye Politcheskoye Upraveiye* – Joint State Political Directorate or Secret Police) supervision at Factory No. 39, *im Menzhinskii* the 'Special Design Bureau'. Allocated to Factory No. 36, he introduced a new fighter, the I-5 in 1934, and was assigned as Chief Designer at No. 36 Factory. With those of his team who had also survived he formed the Polikarpov Brigade and from 1938 he developed this aircraft into the I-153 of 1939. The subsequent excellent performance of these aircraft probably saved him from a firing squad during the massive purges and liquidations of the armed forces from 1935 onward.

The I-15 was a modification of the I-5, which was still under development at the time by Andrei Tupolev. Slowness of progress led the designer to prepare two alternative designs, the I-14A and the I-14B, which were both biplanes, in the hope one would be a success, and both of these were subsequently put into production. Polikarpov, on his release from confinement in August 1932, had been put in charge of the original I-5 plan and through this typically Soviet labyrinth, he developed it into the I-15 forever associated with his name and the *Voenno-vozdushmniye Sily* (VVS – Soviet Air Force).

The single-seater *Chaika* (Seagull) took her name from the form of her upper wing and was first flown by test pilot Valery Pavlovich Chkalov[1] in October 1933. The design followed the I-5 closely but, as the TsKB-3, the 'gull-wing' configuration came about from the inner section of the upper wing halves, formed from welded steel tubing instead of being wooden, and were shaped down at a 60 degree angle to connect with the forward fuselage either side of the cockpit. The fuselage was of composite construction forward, with steel and duralumin, while the rear was fabric covered. The wings were of wooden, single bay, construction and their bracing was minimalist with the two interplane struts being of a sloping shape. The horizontal tail surface was braced with struts instead of being cantilever, while she retained the fixed and static tail-skid rear landing gear but the main undercarriage was cantilever with disc brakes to the wheels.

The power plant was a single 750hp (559kW) SGR-1820-F3 Wright Cyclone M25V radial engine, which drove a two-bladed metal propeller, whose pitch could be adjusted on the ground. Initial testing was followed by two months further of ground and air trials and the outcome of all was adjudged to be most satisfactory. The requirement to build up the *Voyenno-Vozdushnye Sily* (VVS, Military Air Forces – the Soviet Air Force) was deemed paramount and orders were placed for large-scale production, even though no deal had been struck to licence-build the Cyclone engine. In order to get the building underway a compromise power plant, the 480hp (358kW) Shvetsov 9-cylinder, single-row piston M-22 engine was fitted, this being the Bristol Jupiter VI, sub-licensed from Gnome-Rhône, which was enclosed in a narrow-chord Townend ring cowl. It also drove a two-bladed metal prop which had adjustable blades. This was commonly used on Soviet aircraft from the late 1920s and stocks were adequate until the R1820 became fully available. The performance was not outstanding with this engine but after 404 machines had been built with it installed the superior R1820 gave much improved results, and the I-15 under stringent State testing conditions outperformed all other Soviet fighter aircraft, being agile and fast, she could also match the climb rate of the best of the overseas fighter aircraft she was compared to.

She had an overall length of 20ft (6.1m), a height of 7ft 2-39/64 in (2.20m), a wing span of 31ft 11.9in (9.75m) and a wing area of 235.74 ft^2 (23.55m^2). The empty weight was 2231lb (1012 kg); while the maximum loaded weight came out at 3,119lb (1,415kg). The maximum speed with the R1820 was 199mph (320.26 km/h), with a climb rate of 3,280ft (1,000m) in 1 minute 6 seconds (7.60m/s) and 16,400ft (4,998.72m) in six minutes, with a service ceiling of 24,669ft (7519m). The I-15's internal fuel capacity was 68 Imperial gallons (82 US or 310 litres), which gave her a range just under 300 miles (478km). Offensive armament was either four 0.3in (7.62mm) *Pulemet Vozdushny* (PV-1- aerial, air-cooled) fixed, forward-firing, nose-mounted, machine-guns with 650 rpg, and a rate of fire of 750rpm. The pilot aimed through a long OP-1 telescopic gun sight, which passed through a circular aperture in the clear windscreen. There were also two under-wing hard-points for either two 44lb (20kg) bombs or four 22lb (10kg) bombs for six *Reaktivny Snaryad* (Unguided) RS-82 rockets.[2]

Production was concentrated at *Gorkovsky Avtomobilny Zavod* (GAZ – Gorky Automobile Factory, *Zavod* = factory) No. 1 and GAZ No. 39 in Moscow, and continued until late in 1935 and resumed in January 1937 once results from Spain had been analysed. The aircraft were soon swelling the ranks of the *Istrebitezny Aviatsionnyi*

Polk (IAP – Fighter Aviation Regiment) in large numbers and were exported following favourable reports.

Although designed and initially produced as a pure interceptor during her long career the I-15 was employed in the ground-attack/fighter-bomber/close support role and performed all these missions well. On 21 November 1935 the world altitude record was taken by famed test pilot Vladimir Konstantinovich Kokkinaki in a modified TsKB-3, which attained a height of 47,818ft (14,575m).

Some 1,020 I-15s were built and stayed in combat service for a full decade (1935–1944).

The I-15*bis* data differed in its most obvious appearance by abandoning the gull-wing indentation in the inner upper wing form and substituting more conventional flat wings, which were wider, and incorporated the Clark YH flat-bottomed aerofoil,[3] resulting in greater wing area and maximized lift with strength. Also, many senior technical officers were of the opinion that this layout was detrimental to both the pilot's lateral vision, crucial in dog-fighting, and that it adversely affected the directional stability of the aircraft. She also differed in the following respects from the original model – by having an increased wingspan to 33ft 5.5in (10.198m) and a wing area of 242.2ft² (22.501m²). The maximum speed was increased to 230mph 370km/h) at 9,845ft (3,000m). She could tote approximately 331lb (150kg) of under-wing ordnance on four under-wing hard points (outboard 55lb (25kg) AO-25 bombs each, inboard 110lb (50kg) each, giving two 110lb (25kg) *Fugasnaya Aviatsionnaya Bomba* (General-Purpose Bombs – FAB-20SV) bombs and two 55lb FAB-25 GP bomb combinations. Some had *Radio Stahntsiya Istrebitelnaya* (Fighter Radio System –RSI) equipment fitted. A total of 2,696 of the *bis* were built.

There was also the DIT-2, a two-seater trainer version with dual controls built, based on the *bis*, but lacking the armoured seat and machine-gun armament. Only two prototypes were eventually built at *Zavod*-1 in 1939. The addition of the second seat changed the centre of gravity (cg) of the aircraft dramatically, and also increased the weight despite the stripping out of combat equipment. This tended to make the DIT-2 prototypes prone to spin, hardly conducive to pilot training, and the type was not proceeded with.

The I-153*ter* was an attempt to improve the combat performance of the I-15 and I-15*bis* after the first combat reports from the Spanish Civil War had been analysed. The Polikarpov team was by now under Aleksei Ya Shcherbakov, with Artem Iranovich Mikoyan and Mikhail Iosifovich Gurvich. The decision was taken to revert to the original I-15 'Gull' formed upper wing while at the same time retaining the Clark YH aerofoil. The monoplane I-16 was operational but the VVS policy favoured a mix of types from their experience (the Italian Air Force was similarly disposed at this same period and mixing it with the CR.32 had convinced Polikarpov the biplane was still a viable option). Damage in the field when operating from primitive air strips in the wilds of central Spain also convinced him that the fuselage and appendages needed 'beefing up' but to improve performance in the air the new machine was to incorporate a retractable undercarriage, designed by Dmitry Lyudvigovich Tomashevitch, to lessen the drag effect, but it was manually operated as a weight-limitation factor. The wheels were wider. She had a NACA-style cowling and exhaust pipe collector fitted, also navigation lights, while a certain percentage were equipped with radios. Likewise, the armament was changed, and she carried four of the 0.3in (7.62mm) *Shpitalny-Komaritski Aviatsionny Skorostrelny* (Rapid-Fire Aerial Machine Guns – ShKAS) fixed, forward-firing, nose-mounted machine-guns ShKAS PV-1) machine-guns with an improved rate of fire of 1,000rpm.

Once again the designed power plant, the 860hp (633.67kW) Shvetsov M-62 air-cooled, 9-cylinder radial engine equipped with twin superchargers was not available and so early prototype 95001, and successors, had a temporary fit of the 750hp (560kW) M-25V. The maiden flight was in August 1938 and was not an unqualified success during the *Nauchno-issledovatel'skij Institut* (NII – Scientific Test Institute) trials that followed, the wings lacking rigidity, vibration problems with the ailerons and tail unit, but, nevertheless despite frequent failures, including another machine which came apart in mid-air while diving at 310mph (498.9 km/h) production was maintained. The second prototype, 96005, was flight-tested at Baku, Azerbaijan, and a programme of 454 flights was carried out. Faults remained however, although between June and September of the following year, the I-153*ter* managed to pass the State test procedures. The maximum speed attained by the M-25V powered version was 264mph (424km/h) which was a large improvement over her predecessor. The ceiling was pushed to 28,500ft (8,700m). The M-62 engine was finally fitted that same summer, and great hopes for a much-improved performance were displayed when this machine came to be flight-tested on 16 June. At an altitude of 15,100ft (4,600m) this aircraft reached 275mph (443km/h) and while this was marginally better, much more had been hoped for. However, as before, production continued to be pressed forward, the perceived inadequacies being overridden by the need for numbers and continued output. This shortfall had largely been self-imposed by the political 'cleansing' but Stalin brooked no excuses and all such programmes were driven forward relentlessly by those who remained for fear of a similar fate.[4] Thus GAZ-1 cranked up to four-dozen I-153s a week in 1939 and delivered 1,011 machines that year. This output rose to 2,362 in 1940 and tailed off to just sixty-four produced in 1941.

Although it was clear that Polikarpov's optimism was misplaced, and that hopes that his old design could not just be continually improved was becoming obvious, a further attempt was made to do just that. A pair of trial machines (96012 and 96039) were fitted with the 1,100hp (820kW) Shvetsov M-63 power plant (which was termed the '1940 standard'), but even this failed to mitigate the fact that this biplane concept had reached its limits. Despite this, and Polikarpov's abrupt dismissal from the project and his subsequent abject fall from being the Soviet Union's 'Fighter King', more I-153s were produced than any other variant, some 3,437 entering service over the following three years before production ceased in 1941. Polikarpov made one final effort to square the circle and this was to result in the I-190 but the tide of aviation history just could not be reversed, and the biplane was phased out as a front-line fighter by the VVS, a process that the Luftwaffe enormously accelerated in June of that year.

On acceptance the VVS re-designated the I-153*ter* as the I-153. Her length was 20ft 3in (6.17m), wingspan 32ft 9.5in (10m) and height 9ft 2.25in (2.80m). She had a total wing area of 238.3 ft² (22.14m²), while her weights came out at 3,201 lb (1,452kg) empty and 4,221lb (1,960 kg) laden and 6,652lb (2,110kg) maximum. With the designed M-62 driving an AV-1 variable-pitch propeller she achieved 280mph (444km/h) at an altitude of 15,100ft (4,600m). The range was 292 miles (470km) but fifty specially adapted machines for the land-based air arm of the *Voenno-Morskoj Flot SSR (VMF)* (Military Maritime Fleet of the USSR – the Soviet Navy or 'Red Fleet'), featured enlarged internal fuel tanks as well as external drop tanks, a combination that doubled their effective reach. The I-153's normal combat ceiling was 25,105ft (10,700m), with a climb rate of 2.985 ft/min (15m/s). Armament was normally four fixed, forward-firing 0.3in (7.62mm) ShKAS machine-guns with 650rpg.

Again the I-153 airframe was constructed of chromium-molybdenum steel, which was covered in duralumin forward up to the pilot's cockpit, and with fabric to the rear of that point, with wooden wings fabric clad, and duralumin tail surfaces skinned with fabric. Later, shortage of essential metal brought on by the vast expansion of all arms of military aviation, brought about the concept of the I-153 *Univirsal'nyy Derevo* (UD – All-wood) in which the after-part of the fuselage would have been constructed with a wooden monocoque instead of the steel framework. The idea worked but was never implemented. Instead of a skid the I-153 had a solid rubber non-rotating, tail wheel worked by the rudder movement. The retracting undercarriage was manually operated via a hand-operated wheel in the cockpit and folded rearward through 90⁰ into the root of the wing.

The stresses of combat operations revealed a large number of defects in the I-153. Although it was their Japanese opponents that earned the reputation of being 'fire-traps' and burning easily, in encounters over Mongolia in 1939 the I-153, although it established a good reputation, revealed that the absence of a fire-wall between the pilot and the fuel tank situated just in front of his cockpit was a deadly omission. Any damage to the engine invariably caused a blaze which, fanned by the retractable undercarriage wheel wells, quickly spread aft resulting in death or injury. An incident of this type occurred on 27 August 1939 when the senior military representative test pilot of the GAZ-1, Bela Ignatevich Arady (a Hungarian by birth) was flight-testing an I-153. No combat was involved but the aircraft's engine suddenly ignited at 1,000m above the airfield. Arady turned off the ignition and brought the fighter safely down and then extinguished the blaze. It was recorded by his boss that this was not the first time Arady had experienced such a fire in the I-153 and his face had been badly burnt.[5]

Other engine problems included the failure of the supercharger, which resulted in the M-62 only having a service life of between sixty to eighty hours. Many other problems could be traced back to GAZ-1 and the poor quality of the materials used for joints and other specialised parts. The vibration problems of the frontal metal fittings of the wing framing, which sometimes came apart in the air, continued, and the ailerons and upper wings continued to have vibration problems, sometimes terminal. Exhaust pipes came loose in the air, fuel and oil pipes leaked, motor blocks cracked. This was all indicative of shoddy workmanship.

Because so many I-153s were completed, she was frequently used as an aerial test-bed for all manner of innovations and the variants were many and varied. Perhaps the most spectacular were the ramjet experiments. One I-153 was utilized as a test machine for the *Dopolnityelnyi Motor* (supplementary engine), the DM-4 ramjet. Experiments with subsonic ramjets to boost fighter performance had been proposed by Igor Alekseyvich Merkulov of the Design Bureau in 1939 and such engines had been developed through the DM-1 to the DM-2 by June 1940. The more powerful DM-4 had been bench tested and the basis was that the propulsive ducts burnt the same gasoline fuel as the aircraft's own engine, being fed by an auxiliary pump, driven by the same engine, around the double-skinned jet pipe throat and nozzle to cool the inner wall. While still in liquid form, this fuel was sprayed into the interior duct and ignited electrically. The resulting flame extended beyond the rear of the parent aircraft, which meant replacing the after fabric covering by flush-riveted aluminium sheeting.

On 3 October 1940 two of these large boosters, each having a 1ft 7.75in (500mm) diameter, a length of 78in (1.98m) and a weight of 66lb (30kg), were slung beneath both of the lower outer wings of I-153 (serial 6024) and flight-trialled by test pilot I A Loginov. The firing sequence was approximately ten seconds, but could, in theory, be longer. The DM-4 provided the I-153 with a 31.7mph (51 km/h) spurt, pushing her speed up from 241.7 mph (389 km/h) to 273.4mph (440km/h). Fuel consumption similarly soared and that, coupled with the associated problems on manoeuvrability and drag, resulted in the tests being abandoned in December after seventy-four test flights.

Many experiments were conducted on various improvements to the armament. Following trials with the 0.5in (12.7mm) TKB-10 (the *Berezin Syncronni* – Berezin Synchronized – BS) gas-operated machine-gun, this resulted in a production run of 150 of the I-153BS which, due to shortages in production, mounted just one of these weapons in her fuselage and two ShKAS in the wings. With the effectiveness of the cannon-armed fighter the I-153's machine-guns appeared puny in comparison and trials were done with a pair of 0.787in (20mm) *Shpitalnyi-Vladinirov*[6] *Aviatsionnyi Krupnokalibernyi* (ShVAK – Shpitalnyi-Vladinirov large-calibre aerial cannon) on the I-153P (P= *Pushechnyy*). This proved unsatisfactory for although hitting power was improved weight increased and affected performance, while the pilot's windshield tended to become obscured during firing, hardly an aid to accuracy. There were also complications in the production of the cannon itself; it required its own specialized cartridge cases and this led to supply complications. It was abandoned during the course of the war for simpler options. Additionally, some 400 aircraft were adapted later to carry the 3.2in (82mm) *Reaktivny Snaryad* (Rocket-powered – RS) RS-82, an unguided rocket on RO rail launchers slung under the lower wing. Some were fitted with gun cameras.

With the eclipse from front-line interception role, the I-153 was increasingly used as a ground-attack and harassment aircraft. The I-153*Sh* and I-153*USh* variants reflected this shift, with the addition of under-wing provision for ShKAS machine-guns in pods and 5.5lb (2.5kg) sub-munitions, the *Protivitahnkovaya Avia-Bomba* (PTAB – armour-piercing aerial bomblets) for use against the German *Panzers*. They were capable of penetrating up to 60–70mm of tank armour.

The work of aeronautical scientist Aleksei Ya Schyerbakov into pressurized aircraft cabins for high-altitude operations, resulted in his 'minimum leak' type being tested on the I-153V (V = *Vysotnoi* – Height). This led to the development of the I-153V-TKGK (*TKGK* = *Turbokompressor Geremetichyeskoi Kabine* (turbo-charged, hermetically sealed cabin) High-Altitude Air Defence interceptor. This variant achieved a maximum speed of 300mph (492km/h) and could operate to a service ceiling of 33,793ft (10,200m). However, only twenty-six of this variant were finally built.[7]

In total, 3,459 of this variant were built.

Pre-WWII Soviet use

Spain

I-15s with Soviet 'volunteer' pilots first began arriving in Spain to fight for Republican forces on 13 October 1936 and quickly proved popular, subsequently equipping several Spanish units. They were all young pilot graduates eager to prove themselves but sadly lacking in experience. Early in May 1937 a second batch of these volunteers arrived in Spain from Baku, and all travelled on fake passports and adopted Spanish pseudonyms upon arrival. Stalin was eager to aid any resistance to the further spread of Fascism and supplied many warplanes despite the 'Non-Intervention' agreements that he, along with Hitler and Mussolini, had signed but ignored.

The first I-15s arrived in Spain in two deliveries, twenty-five at Cartagena on 28 October 1936 and fifteen at Bilbao on 1 November. They formed a fighter group with three ten-plane squadrons and first went into action on 4 November claiming to have destroyed two CR.32s and two Junkers Ju.52 transports without loss to themselves. The Soviet contribution was initially successful, but as more modern German and Italian types arrived the balance swung against them again. One successful innovation was the formation by Anatol Serov and Mikhail Yakushin of an I-15 night-fighter unit, the *Patrulla de Caza Nocturna* under *Teniente* Walter Katz. There was also the *Escuadrilla de Veuzo Noctumo*, which was used to defend Madrid against attack. The I-15s were fitted with elongated exhaust pipes led back along the fuselage, which had exhaust collection ring flame dampers and landing lights.

Over the period of intervention (Operation X as the Soviet authorities termed it) 116 Poplikarpovs were sent to Spain and a further 287 were built under licence there. In total 220 I-15s were destroyed. Of this total 91 were shot down in air-to-air combat, 27 were destroyed on the ground at their airfields, 9 were lost to anti-aircraft fire, 87 were written off in accidents and 6 force-landed in enemy territory and were captured. Soviet pilots flying the I-15 were 63 in 1936 but just 41 in 1937 when they were replaced as being too slow. Three Soviet I-15 pilots were killed in 1936 and three more in 1937 when training of Spanish pilots took precedence.

It was not only Russians who flew the I-15s in Spain, many other nationalities, drawn by either adventure, money or political persuasion, arrived to serve one side or the other. They were known as the *Brigadistas Internacionales* (International Brigade). One former American Army Air Corps and United Air Lines pilot, Albert John Baumler, volunteered for the Republican cause and was assigned to the *Escuadrilla Kosakov*, which was flying I-15s. On 16 March 1937 he shot down a Fiat CR.32 and four days later nailed a second. On 17 April he added to his tally by claiming a Heinkel He.51, with a second as a 'probable' before he was transferred to the *1 Escuadrilla de Moscas* flying I-16s. When the I-15*bis* arrived in 1938 the Spanish pilots dubbed them the 'Super Chato'.

The Spanish themselves set up 1, 2, 3 and 4 *Escuadrilla de Chatos* under *Grupo de Chatos* 26, led by *Capitán* Vicente Castillo Monzó, which initially acquitted themselves well. Several Spanish I-15 aces came to the fore, one being *Capitán* Jose Falco San Martin who initially flew as a *Sargento* (Sergeant) and then as a *Teniente* (Lieutenant) with the short-lived 5 *Escuadrilla de Chatos* in March 1938 before transferring to the 3 *Escuadrilla* under *Capitán* Juan Comas Borrás. Between 10 July and 2 November San Martin had confirmed kills of three Heinkel He.59s and a CR.32 and had thirteen victories to his tally by the end of the war, all achieved in the I-15 and including no less than four Bf.109s.

Toward the end of the war 26 *Grupo* were operating from Sisones and then Manises just before the final Nationalist victory.

Soviet and Republic of China Air Force against Japan

The Republic of China Air Force (ROCAF) was not officially formed until 1936 under the auspices of *Generalissimo* Chiang Kai-Shek and his wife. On establishment it consisted of 9 Bomber and Pursuit (Fighter) Groups and four Independent Squadrons, all equipped with a variety of imported aircraft. On 18 July 1937, for example, a batch of thirty I-15s arrived from Russia to be incorporated into the Chinese Air Force, being handed over at Lanzhou, Gansu.

Following the signing of the Sino-Soviet Non-Aggression Pact (*Zhōng-sū Hù Bù Qīnfàn Tiáoyué*) on 21 August 1937, the Soviet Union sent military aid to the Chinese fighting the Japanese, and this included the Soviet Volunteer Group under General Dair Asanovich Asanov. In October 1937 some 450 pilots and ground crews assembled at Alma-Ata (now Almaty), in Kazahkstan and moved to China, and the force included 155 fighter aircraft, half of which were operated by the Chinese themselves and half by Russian 'volunteer' pilots. The Pursuit (Fighter) forces were commanded by *Kombrig* (Brigadier-General) Pavel Vasilievich Rychagov who had served in the same capacity in Spain,[8] and they flew at various times from airfields at the then Chinese Capital, Nanking (now Nanjing), Jiangsu Province, Hankow (now Hanakou) Hubei Province, Chungking (now Chongqing) central China, with the main base at Lanchow (now Lánzhou), Gansu Province in northern China. By September 1938 there were 133 I-15 and I-15*bis* fighters on strength. In November 1938, for example, 5 Air Group comprised 17, 28 and 29 Pursuit Squadrons, each with ten I-15s on hand. On 18 July 1939 a fresh Pursuit Group arrived at Langchow with thirty Ia-15*bis*.

Battles were intermittent, with intense action being followed by long pauses according to the situation, which was complicated by the fact that the Soviets accused the Chinese, after heavy losses, of leaving all the air fighting to their men, while the Chinese Government kept back reserves with one eye on the simultaneous civil war with the Communists. In intense air battles over Chunking in July 1939 there were several losses as, for example, on 11 July when the commander of the I-15s, Zheng Shaoyu in serial no. 2310, had his aircraft badly shot up, but survived, while his wingman, Liang Tiancheng in 2307, was shot down.

In January 1940 32 Pursuit Squadron went to Chengtu (now Chengdu) in Sichuan Province, and traded in their I-15s for the I-15*bis* and the 29 Squadron similarly re-equipped at Peishiyi airfield (now Baishiyi), Chengtu, with eleven I-15*bis* and likewise 25 Squadron at Langchow, Gansu Province, in July and 7 Squadron. On 16 December the new 11 Pursuit Squadron was set up at Chengtu with 41, 42, 43 and 44 Squadrons with fresh graduate pilots and had four brand-new I-153 *Chaiki* as well as twenty I-15*bis* among a mix of types. While this was going on the Chinese were forced to fight alone and suffered heavy losses. These included the commander of 3 Air Group, Major Lin Zuo, who crashed while testing an I-15, which had just been overhauled. Further accidents included the death, on 3 March 1939, of two pilots of 22 Squadron at Kunming, Yunan Province, both Lieutenants Liu Kai and Mei Erdang being killed in a collision between their I-15s, and six days later an identical accident at Liánshán, Liaoning, between two I-15s, killed another two pilots. Further accidents with the I-15 killed five more Chinese pilots between 4 January and 4 October.

By June 1940 the Chinese 4 Air Group had three Pursuit Squadrons of I-15*bis* each with nine machines on its strength, some of them taken from other groups in order to defend Chengtu and Chunking and intercept Japanese bombers working from Hankow during that summer offensive. Then, in September, the Japanese Navy introduced the Mitsubishi A6M Type O fighter to China, which in several fierce encounters, totally destroyed the Chinese fighter force culminating on 13 September when in under half an hour the Zero shot down twenty-seven I-15*bis* fighters from 21, 22, 24 and 28 Pursuit Squadrons above Chunking. On 26 October this sorry tale was repeated at Chengtu airfield when further I-15*bis* from 28 and 32 Pursuit Squadrons were destroyed. The Chinese were again forced to ask the Soviets for help and placed three new orders for aircraft. Included among them were ninety-three I-153s with deliveries commencing in November 1940. Just how the I-153 was thought capable of dealing with the Zero is unclear but 5 Air Group with 17, 26 and 29 Pursuit Squadrons received twenty-six *Chaiki* (four of which they promptly wrote off in accidents at Chengtu, and the rest were destroyed in the air battles of 14 March); 3 Air Group at Kumul (now Hami), Xinjang Province, received seventeen in February 1941 and every one was destroyed by the Zero on 14 March. This massacre saw the loss of several commanding officers, including Huang Xinhua, Ceng Zeliu and Zhou Lingxiu of 5 Air Group while 17 Squadron was totally annihilated and 3 Air Group was reduced to just five serviceable machines. 4 Air Group received twenty, which all went to 7, 8, 21, 23 and 28 Pursuit Squadrons.

Seventeen survivors from 5 Air Group were ordered to seek sanctuary at Nanzheng, Shaanxi Province, but were caught on the ground at Tianshu, Gansu Province, while refuelling and were wiped out, their commander Lü Enlung being stripped of his command for carelessness. On 26 May 29 Pursuit Squadron suffered exactly the same fate, when eighteen I-153s were intercepted and the two leaders, Commander Yu Pingxiang and Zhang Senyi, were shot down while all the rest, under Tang Zhouli, were caught on the ground refuelling and all sixteen destroyed. Only 4 Air Group survived by virtue of the fact that it was still re-equipping at Shunangliu (now Shuangliu) Sichuan Province. In further battles in July and August 1941, 21 Squadron lost several more commanders, including Captain Ou Yangdeng and Lieutenant Gao Chunchou, while 29 Squadron lost Tang Zhouli, Wang Chongshi and Huang Rongfa on 11 August.

During their time in China the Soviet pilots lost over two hundred of their number in battle, until the signing of the Soviet-Japanese Non-Aggression Pact (*Nisso Fukashin Joyaku*) on 13 April 1941, after which they were progressively withdrawn, although many of their aircraft and associated equipment were handed over to the Chinese. They were eventually replaced by the mercenary pilots of the American Volunteer Group (AVG) under former Army Air Corps officer, Claire Chennault. Chinese operations with the I-153, not surprisingly, tailed off after these disasters, although 17 Squadron under Liu Qingguang, with eleven machines, was deployed to Kunming, Yunnan Province, in January 1942. They moved up to Laxu, in Burma, later but did not become engaged as the Japanese drove the British out of the country, other than some ground-attack sorties. They were withdrawn to Chengtu in July.

The Nomonhan Incident (Khalhin Gol River Battle)

Khalhin Gol, Outer Mongolia, a river that ran along the border of the Japanese puppet state, Manchukuo and Soviet Mongolia, saw fierce fighting between 11 May 1939 and August 1939. The Soviets operated the 70 IAP, commanded by Major Vyacheslav Mikhaylovich Zabaluev, as part of 57 Special Corps, and in mid- May this unit's strength included fourteen I-15bis but by 20 May only nine remained operational. To replace losses, which totalled thirteen by the end of the month, and a further thirty-one by the end of June, on 23 May thirty-five I-15bis of the 22 IAP were transferred east, being joined by further batches, totalling forty I-15bis being sent out as reinforcements in July 1939. Here they duelled against the Japanese Kawasaki Ki-10 ('Perry') and the Nakajima Ki-27 ('Nate').[9] The I-15bis came off worst in these encounters; in July yet a further sixteen I-15 types were destroyed, and they were soon switched to ground-attack missions. As operations scaled down losses fell, in August five I-15bis and eleven I-153s were lost in combat and by the time operations ceased on 16 September, nine more I-153s had been destroyed.[10] It was estimated that the Soviets lost sixty I-15bis in combat and five more in accidents and sixteen I-153s in combat and six in accidents. By contrast the Japanese Army Air Force lost one Ki-10 and sixty-two Ki-

27s in combat and thirty-four Ki-27s written off after battle damage. The British Air Ministry Intelligence Reports on these actions concluded that the Japanese aircraft had suffered '...considerable losses... in these air battles'.[11] This type of analysis did much to increase the complaisance of the British with regard to Japanese air power prior to the disasters of Malaya, Singapore and Burma that followed.

Against Finland

Among the Soviet fighter units employed was the 13 *Avio Escadrille* of 61 *Avio* Brigade of the Red Banner Baltic Fleet Air Force, fitted with ski undercarriages. The Finns claimed that a total of twelve I-15*bis* were shot down in aerial dogfights during the 'Winter War' to which they allocated serials in the VH-1 to VH-11 range. These included serial 4616, which belonged to the 152 IAP, which made a forced landing on ice at Lake Oulunjäriv, central Finland, on 24 December 1939. The Finns restored her to working condition and assigned her the numeral VH-11.

Other foreign users

Finland

When the Soviet Union invaded Finland they had an overwhelmingly superior air force of 700 fighters and 800 bombers to deploy against a mere handful of *Flygvapnet* (Finnish Air Force) machines. The *Hävittäjälenolaivue* (fighter squadrons) were hastily reinforced by purchases from abroad and undeterred by the odds, manage to inflict very heavy casualties on the Russians.[12] During the 'Winter War' the Finns claimed a kill ratio in their favour of more than three-to-one.

The fighting was not always one-sided and as many as twenty Soviet pilots who later became aces in World War II cut their teeth in the I-15 and I-15*bis* in this brief conflict, and also in the I-153 during the post-June 1941 struggle also. One example was *Starshiy Leytenant* Piotr Kozachenko, a veteran from the Soviet volunteer pilots that fought in China in 1937. His first combat missions were flown with the 38 IAP but, on 1 February 1940, he was tasked with setting up a brand new *Eskadrilya* for the 25 IAP equipped with the I-153. On 2 February a trio of I-153s from this new unit, aided by ten I-16s, duelled with ten Finnish Fokker D.XX1 fighters above Rauha, Kozachenko being credited with the destruction of one Fokker, that flown by Danish volunteer pilot *Luutnantti* (Lieutenant) Fritz Rasmussen of LLv24.

In total the VVS-RKKA (*Raboche-Krest'yanskaya Krasnaya* – Workers and Peasants Red Army) lost seven I-15s in air-to-air combats, fifteen more were shot down by Finnish AA fire, while a further fifty-one I-15s failed to return and were assumed destroyed from various causes.[13]

Finns captured eight of these fighters during their wars with the Soviets, and those that were restored were given the serials VH-101, and VH-12 to VH-18 inclusive. Three more were captured during the so-called 'Continuation War' when Finland fought a 'parallel' war against the Soviets alongside the Germans; they were allotted the serials VH-19 to VH-21 inclusive. These VH serials were changed to IH serials from

4 June 1942 onward. The Finns also purchased a further eleven I-153s from captured German stocks on 18 November 1942, but, after being taken over at Wien (Vienna) airfield on 7 December, only ten were delivered and three were damaged *en route* and were delayed, one more being obtained as late as 27 August 1943. Those operated by the Finns were all re-armed with four 0.303in (7.70mm) Browning M.39 water-cooled machine-guns and a BBC.AAK-1 gun sight replaced the PAK-1.a reflector sight. These were later re-allocated the serials IT-22 to IT-31 inclusive.

Two Polikarpovs were allocated to *Lentolaivue* (*LLv*) 29 (29 Squadron) as fighter-trainers and the others joined LLv34 until that unit itself was disbanded, whereupon these machines joined the *Taydennyslentolaivue 35* (T-LeLv-35). During the course of the war IH-1 and IH-4 were retired in late 1942, IH-2 crashed at Kymi, and IH-3 was damaged at Vesivehmaa. The final pair capable of flight made their last trips on 12 March 1945, when they were put into storage.

Germany

During the opening phases of Operation *Barbarossa* many Soviet front-line airfields were overrun and intact aircraft captured including many I-15s.

WWII use

Approximately one thousand I-15s and variants were still in service when the German invasion began in June 1941 and many were destroyed in the opening hours sitting in neat rows on their runways. They were organized in regiments, each one consisting of four squadrons with fifteen aircraft as establishment strength plus a staff unit of three, for an official establishment total of sixty-three machines. However, the difference between the official establishment strength and the true operational strength was often stark. To take just one example, the 62 Fighter Air Brigade contained the 8, 9 and 32 IAP and their complements in June 1941 were the I-153 – establishment 72, operational 2; I-15*bis* – establishment 35, operational 4; I-15 – establishment 29, operational 8.

The nominal strengths of some fighter units, including independent squadrons at the time of the German invasion, where they are actually listed and known, are high, and mainly comprise I-153s with a sprinkling of earlier types, but these figures should be taken as very approximate indeed and they do not include frequent cases where units were equipped with mixtures of I-16s, I-153s and/or I-15*bis*, but their returns do not differentiate with numbers for each type. Many Soviet fighter aircraft were destroyed by the Luftwaffe sitting on the ground, or captured intact after the airfields were overrun, but not always because they were surprised but because they were inoperational for various reasons and unable to take off. Generally speaking the further from the front-line they were based the more likely the biplanes were to have survived the initial Luftwaffe onslaughts of the first month of operations.

The 265 *ShAP* used the I-15*bis* on the Leningrad front in 1941. Aces still emerged from the ranks of I-153 pilots. *Kapitan* Alexi Stepanovich Khlobystov of the 153 IAP at Leningrad claimed two Junkers Ju.87 Stuka dive-bombers, one each in June and July 1941. Naval Major[14] Aleksandr Gerasimovich Baturin with the 71 IAP-

KBF (*Krasnoznamyonnyy Baltiyskiy Flot* – Red-Banner Baltic Fleet) operating out of Lagsberg, Tallin, Estonia, shot down a Junkers Ju.88 bomber on 21 August, while trying to protect Soviet troop convoys evacuating the area, and he added a Bf.109 over Yam (Kingisepp) on 21 September and claimed a Ju.87 six days later. However, they were clearly outclassed as fighters and were frequently in subsidiary roles. There were some successes as interceptors but more often they were used as ground-attack aircraft with a few excellent results. The 72 SAP at Vayenga (now Severomorsk-1), Murmansk, was co-operating with the VVS-SF (*Severnyy Flot* – Northern Fleet) and 14 Army, charged with protecting the vital port and supply port and naval bases of Arkhangelsk and Murmansk and the Kola peninsula, and had seventeen I-153s and twenty-eight I-15*bis* on its strength on the outbreak of hostilities but their biggest contribution to halting the German advance in the far north was the destruction of a vital bridge in Petsamo at the end of September 1941 when twenty-eight Polikarpovs were used as dive-bombers.

Even as late as spring 1943 the I-153 was claiming victims. Polkovnik Dimitrii Yermakov with the 286 IAP flew missions with the biplane between May 1942 and April 1943, destroying a Bf.109 on 22 October and another on 14 January. Finally, by November 1943, all of Polikarpov's biplane veterans were removed from front-line units.

Preserved aircraft

1. This machine is the former serial No. 6316 and was used by 2 Aviation Fighter Squadron, Northern Navy. It was restored in Russia during 1998 and performed flying shows in New Zealand. It is part of the Museum of Aerospace Paris and stored at Le Bourget.
2, 3 and 4. Three I-153s were retrieved and restored between 1991 and 1999 under the direction of Sir Tim Wallis to become part of Alpine Deer Group's, Alpine Fighter Collection at Wanaka, Otago, South Island, New Zealand. The original M-62 radial engines being deemed beyond repair these machines were fitted with the AZsh-62IR geared radial and in this configuration all three flew again at the 'Warbirds over Wanaka' display in 2000. One I-153 (registration ZK-JKMI) remains at Wanaka at the time of writing; One I-153 (serial 7027, registration ZK-JKM), went to *Fondacion Infantes de Orleans* at Sabadell, Spain; One (registration ZK-JKNI) was reported going to Training Services Inc, at Virginia Beach, Va. and also at the Jerry Yagen Fighter Factory, (serial 6316, registration N153P). One was also reported under restoration at the Imperial War Museum site at Duxford, Cambridge.

Chapter Fifteen

Polikarpov Po-2 (U-2)

Known to the Soviets as the *Kukuruznik* (Maize) or 'crop duster' this simple, undemanding little biplane was indeed nothing more or less than an agricultural aerial sprayer in appearance, but appearances in this case, were very deceptive. She was to be produced in huge numbers, some sources claiming as many as 40,000 in total; whatever the truth of that assertion, she was built in the tens of thousands and remained in full production for the incredible time span of 1928 to 1953, and even beyond if re-builds are included.

Despite her docile appearance she was originated as a military aircraft, albeit as a basic trainer to replace the British-originated Avro 504 *Avrushka* U-1 (U= Utility). In the monolithic Soviet state that the USSR had become under Vladimir Ilyich (Ulyanov) Lenin and then Stalin, little differentiation was made in the usage of any asset and as the successive Five Year Plans ground on, she was to prove equally at home over the vast prairie-like cereal fields of the Ukraine as she was with the *Voenno-vozdushnaya Flota* (VVF -Military Air Fleet). Utility she looked and utility she acted being the most versatile of aircraft in both peace and war. She was thus designated as the Polikarpov U-2 and it was not until 1944, well after Nikolai Polikarpov had died, that this title was changed to Po-2 in commemoration of its designer, and to fit in with the new Soviet system.

Intended as an *Uchebny-Samolot* (Primary Trainer) with the emphasis on introducing a uniform training syllabus nationwide, and to do so with the maximum simplicity and lowest cost, the U-2 as it first appeared perfectly matched these criteria in the last two categories. She was indeed 'basic' with ease of construction, maintenance and repair as primary factors; the overall impression of this wooden aircraft was of a plain, solid box-structured fuselage assembly, with planks of thick-corded, wings that consisted merely of four thick-sectioned rectangular slab-like square-ended panels with no saving grace or style. The ailerons, elevators and rudder utilized the same block approach. It flew as it looked and Polikarpov had to go back to the drawing board at Factory No. 25 to completely re-design the concept to make it a viable project.

The caterpillar still did not re-emerge as a butterfly at the end of this process, but the result was a marked improvement and, more usefully, it fulfilled its design function. Her longitudinal stability was notable, and, essentially for the training role, she was a difficult machine to put into a spin. The fuselage remained much the same but now the wings were of single-bay construction, with round tips, being forward staggered with 'N' struts. The whole tail area was re-built emerging much heightened and with a large rudder and big elevators. An uncompromisingly sturdy cross-axle landing gear of 'A' form with slightly splayed and unshielded tyres ensured that cadet pilots' 'heavy' landings would be catered for (and later proved most valuable when operating in the most primitive of terrains like fields, forest clearings, the snow-covered steppes or primitive roadways).

Remaining of wood construction, this two-seater biplane carried an instructor and trainee in tandem in two separate open cockpits. She had an overall length of 26ft 10in (8.17m), a wingspan of 37ft 5in (11.40m), a height of 10ft 2in (3.10m) and a wing area of 357ft² (33.2m²). Her unladen weight was a mere 1,698lb (770kg) and laden was 2,271lb (1,030kg), with a maximum take-off weight of 2,976lb (1,350kg). The initial power plant for this unassuming little aircraft was the 99hp (74kW) five-cylinder Shvetsov M-11 radial but production models were pulled along by the 125hp (93kW) D-5 variant gave her a maximum speed flat out of 94mph (152 km/h), with a cruising speed of 68mph (110 km/h) and she had a range of 391 miles (630km). Her rate of climb was 546 ft/min (2.78m/s). When it came to arming her she carried a single, ring-mounted, 0.303in (7.62mm) ShKAS machine-gun carried in the after bay. It was not until 1941 that tests were made to see how the U-2 handled with a light bomb load and she regularly operated with six 110lb (50kg) bombs, three apiece under each lower wing, although like everything else about her, her range of loadings was enormous.

The maiden flight of the first prototype, the U-2TPK, took place on 7 January 1928 with Mikhail Mikhaylovich Gromov as her pilot.[1] A small prototype run of machines were tested to satisfaction and GAZ-23, at Leningrad, was selected as the construction plant which commenced tooling up in 1929 and similar Soviet plants, including the Red Aviator factory at Moscow, continued to churn out the U-2 and Po-2 for the next two decades only ceasing in 1949. By June 1941 more than 13,000 U-2s had been built and they went on building them.

The wartime construction figures for the Po-2 were:[2]

Plant	Location	1941	1942	1943	1944	1945
387	Kazan	1235	2225	2733	3045	2155
464	Moscow-Dolgoprodny	0	0	71	736	557
471	Shumerlya	0	0	53	657	427
494	Kozlovka	0	18	270	695	427
Total:		1235	2243	3127	5133	3566 = 11,738

The Soviet official output was later to be joined by many foreign plants while a Polish variant, the CSS-13, was still being produced in 1959! Tens of thousands of Stalin's 'Young Eagles' cut their teeth on this pedestrian aircraft over the next few decades. The average tyro undertook fifty to sixty thirty-minute flights with an instructor. This was followed by solo flights, take-offs and landings ('circuits and bumps') before moving on to more challenging types like the R-5. Attrition was high but production matched it.

Her versatility ensured longevity, and her diverse duties over the first decade of her life were legion, she acted not only as a trainer but as a crop-duster, VIP transport, regimental 'hack' and air ambulance for remote regions of the vast USSR. A large number of specialist variants appeared to fulfil these diverse needs.

The U-2A (with two-sub types, the U-2AP/U-2AO (AP – *Aeropyl* (Aerial Duster), OP – *Aeroopylitel* (Aerial Pollinator)) was a single-seater, which appeared in 1930 as a crop-dusting aircraft and, as such, it featured a 551lb (250kg) hopper built into the rear fuselage. This required considerable alterations; the front cockpit was moved forward by 9.75in (0.25m), the fuel tank was re-located to the upper wing and that had its central section increased in depth to accommodate it, the rear wing struts were reinforced and moved forward, while the whole of the rear cockpit, with dashboard and dual-controls, were removed. This enabled both the tank and dispenser to be inbuilt in their place. Sub-types included capacity for aerial seeding and fluid dispensing. In order for her to operate in all-weather conditions on farm fields, she had a special reinforced double landing gear arrangement with a second rim welded to the original assembly, which gave a total width of 9.84in (25cm). The empty weight was 1,446.23lb (656kg), and loaded weight was 2,204.62lb (1,000kg), with a wing loading of 47.14 lb/ft^2 (30.2kg/m^2). The take-off distance was 394.7 ft (120m) and landing distance was 328.08 ft (100m) with a range of 124.27 miles (200km) and a ceiling of 9,842.5 ft (3,000m). This proved to be the most successful civilian version of the U-2 and 1,235 were constructed between 1930 and 1940.[3] It formed the basis of many other adaptations. After a pause in production during World War II, it continued to be built in numbers in this form again from 1944 onward when it was fitted with a 115hp (86kW) M-11K engine. By the time production finally ceased around 9,000 aircraft had been built.

The U-2SP (SP – *Spetsnaz* – Special Purpose) was one such modification from the *Aeropyl*, which appeared in 1934. The chemical tank and dispenser equipment were totally removed and two single-seat cockpits were installed, but with only the pilot's cockpit being fitted with controls. One or two passengers could be transported, or light cargo loads carried in combinations, and it found use as a local liaison machine. The changes altered performance; maximum speed increased by 4.9 mph (8 km/h), take-off distance by 65.6 ft (20m) and range by 217.4 miles (350km). The flight endurance increased by 2.5 hours and the ceiling increased by 984.25 ft (300m.) A total of 861 were built up to 1939.

The *Sanitamyi Samolyet* (Ambulance Plane) version of the U-2 first appeared in 1934 and was designated as the U-2S1, with a later sub-type, the U-2SS. A medical compartment was built into the after-fuselage, which could accommodate a doctor or nurse, with a hinged roof section for a stretcher case. Windows were built into later models.

A courier version appeared in 1934 and had a five-year production life. This aircraft, the U-25P, had the upper fuselage radically altered in order to accommodate a third open cockpit. With this extra space it could be used as a mail plane or a small passenger aircraft for short hops and was employed as such by *Aeroflot* and smaller operators. Altogether 861 of this variant were built, and their obvious value meant that during the war they were in demand as liaison aircraft by the army. Derived with the same objective as this type was the U-SPL, which had an enclosed rear cabin that replaced the open cockpit. Later a side door was added on the port side of the cabin and this sub-type became the Po-2L.

There were also experimental aircraft and adaptations that often vanished as quickly as they appeared. The U-2G (G – *Gorzhanu*) was a one-off experimental machine of 1934 that had all the controls linked to the central column to test a concept of Nikolaj Gorzhanu. The U-2KL saw a pair of aircraft that had a bulged canopy built over the rear canopy, and they first flew in 1932. A one-off aircraft, the U-2LPL, where the pilot operated the machine in a prone position was a research aircraft that appeared in 1935. The fitting of a caterpillar-tracked landing gear was experimented with in 1937. The work was conducted by N A Chechubalin, working with BRIZe a division of the *Glavnoe Upravienie Severnogo Morskogo pub* (Chief Directorate of the Northern Sea Route – GLASVSEVMORPUT or GUSMP) who had been involved in the aerial survey of the Soviet Arctic. In order to operate light aircraft on the morass of thawed-out tundra such tracking was considered useful to spread the load. Experiments with this equipment were conducted at the Krasnoyarsk Air Depot in northern central Siberia. However, the tracking gear itself added weight, as did the reinforced supporting gear. Experiments were conducted with a U-2 so fitted, and also with a heavier R-5 (No. 403) but they were not successful. The experiment was later repeated in 1947.

Experiments to achieve a lower, smoother profile for interceptors continued until 1939.[4] The first of several floatplane variants, the U-2M (*Morskoy* – Marine) or MU-2 (*Morskoy Uchebnyi* – Marine Instructional) designed by Sergei Aleksandrovich Kocherigin, later head of the *Tsentral'nyi Konstruktorskii byuro* (TsKB – Central Design Bureau) appeared in 1931 and underwent testing by Igor Vyacheslavovich Chetverikov of the Dimitry Pavlovich Grigorvch *Opytno Konstruktorskoe Byuro* (OKB – Experimental Design Bureau) the same year. She had the conventional layout of a large central float with two wingtip stabilizing floats, but it did not prove satisfactory adaptation, although Chetverikov gained valuable knowledge that helped in his subsequent flying boat designs including the MDR-6 (Che-2). In 1935 a research machine was produced, the Polikarpov E-23 (E – *Eksperimenial* (Experimental); 23 because it was built at Factory No. 23 at Leningrad), which was used to evaluate the practicality of inverted flight.

In an effort to upgrade the basic trainer model N G Mikhelson and A I Morshchikhin inserted a 200hp (149kW) M-48 engine into the same profile. This was the Polikarpov U-3, but although on paper it should have produced a superior product, in fact it did not. Nor was a trial fitting of the Siemens Sh.14 engine considered pursuing further. Another of N G Mikhelson's efforts to boost the U-2 saw the U-4, which was essentially a pared-down original with a more slender fuselage profile and other alterations. Again, it did not achieve very much in the way of improvement and only a limited production resulted. The same designer also made a second adaptation of the Po-2 to operate as a floatplane, this time specifically with the immediate aim of attaining the seaplane altitude record in 1937. For this a 710hp (529kW) Wright R-1820-F3 Cyclone radial engine was fitted and several aircraft were built. On yet another trial machine the Rudlicki 'V-Tail' was experimented with in 1934 by Eugene Filatov. Invented by the Odessa-born aviation scientist Jerzy Stanislav Rudlicki, while working in Poland in 1930, this idea combined the two tail control surfaces of conventional aircraft, rudder and elevators, into one integral system, which was vee-shaped and had moveable rear sections known as 'ruddervators'. It was also known as the 'Butterfly Tail'.[5]

Yet another highly specialized role in such a vast nation as the USSR was that of Geographic Aerial Survey work and aerial photography. Once the war was over expansion work to the east was extended and the Po-2P photographic variant appeared.

From reconnaissance to bomber

The military continued to use the U-2 as a primary trainer up to and after the German invasion, but, once the enemy was at their throats the Soviets soon found myriad other uses for this modest little aircraft. Acting as a liaison aircraft, carrying vital despatches and orders between military commanders across the vast and quickly-changing front line, casualty evacuation aircraft, with dual litters held in nacelles under the lower wings and impromptu light transport were added to her repertoire. And it was not only the men-folk who were provoked into defending what was now (for the period of the war anyway) Stalin's 'Holy Mother Russia' from the Axis threat, but dedicated daughters of the revolution as well.

One of the most celebrated of Soviet female pilots was Second Lieutenant Anna Timofeyeva-Yegorova and she cut her teeth on the Polikarpov. She later commanded the 805 Ground Attack Regiment and she flew over two hundred combat missions. One of sixteen children she had learned to fly at an early age in Moscow and became an instructor herself. On the outbreak of war in June 1941 she had volunteered for combat duty and soon found herself as a U-2 pilot flying reconnaissance missions over the front line, interspersed with communications duties, for the next two years during which she was once shot down in flames by a Luftwaffe fighter aircraft, and, although she had no parachute, somehow survived, retrieved important documents from the burning wreckage and delivered them by hand to the front. After this she was deemed worthy enough to retrain on the Ilyushin Il-2 *Shturmovik* ground attack plane and became an expert in this dangerous field of aviation.

The origins of the U-2 as a bombing platform, unlikely as it would have seemed pre-war, appear to have been in September 1941. The Black Sea port of Odessa was under siege from Romanian and elements of the German 11 *Armee*, as the Axis armies surged ever eastward and held out for seventy-three days. The fighting was intense and the Germans brought up a force of 426 pieces of heavy artillery to pound the defences. For lack of much else, civilian U-2s of the Civil Air Fleet Detachment were pressed in to the aid of the Independent Aviation Detachment, commanded by V A Sedlyarevich. They were assigned aerial reconnaissance and gun-locating missions, their job being to pinpoint the artillery positions when they fired and report back to the commander of the fortress defence for counter-battery fire to be laid down. The use of these machines was really a last-gasp stop-gap but it was to have unforeseen consequences.

One U-2 pilot, *Komsomal* Pyotr Serge Bevz who had carried out several such sorties, flying between ten to twelve hours each day, asked his commander whether he might take bombs on his next mission. His request was granted and, on 3 September, Bevz first located and then bombed an artillery site, the first ever recorded such attack by a U-2. Bevz's success was confirmed and he was permitted to organize further such missions and was killed carrying out another bombing raid on 13 September.[6] His dedication led to him being awarded a posthumous Order of the Red Banner. But it did more; it led to the formation of the first military U-2 units.

The first Night Bomber Air Wings were formed with U-2s that winter. These machines and their military pilots were rushed into use, there was ample stocks of the type to hand, and they became perfectly adapted to front-line action. These hastily organized U-2 units participated in their first combat missions in the defence of Moscow in January 1942.[7] The makeshift bomber's potential was realized; it was cheap, easy to fly, already in mass production, made from readily sourced and abundant ample materials, wood and fabric, and best of all, utterly expendable. For the hard-pressed Stalin and his VVS-RKK minions, it was an ideal option.

The U-2's designer, Nikolay Polikarpov, whose earlier star was rapidly setting, also saw the possibilities and set about designing a professional combat variant of his little work-horse. The result was the U-2Lsh (*Lsh* – *Lyokhki Shturmovik* – Light Ground Attack) and U-2VOM-1 (*Voyenno Ognyemyot Mashina* – Aerial Flamethrower, which appeared in 1941 with an ROK (POKC) ventrally shackled beneath the aircraft's fuselage) variants, both existing aircraft and new construction being featured to carry out the ground-attack mission. The lower wing was beefed up and equipped with ventral light bomb carriers, capable of toting a maximum bomb load of 264lb (120kg) made up of combinations of small ordnance, either explosive, incendiary or flare. The solitary 0.303in (7.62mm) ShKAS scarf-ring mounted machine-gun remained the solitary defensive weapon, with the old *Degtyaryov Aviatsionny* (DA – Airborne Degtyaryov – after Vasily Degtyaryov, first director of Soviet armament directorate) machine-gun of the same calibre, sometimes mounted as an alternative. The Soviet troops lauded these aircraft as the *Kukuruznik* (corn-cutter) as they mowed down the enemy! Later the U-2LNB appeared (LNB – *Lyokhki Nochi Bombardirovshchik* – Light Night Bomber), which was able to carry a heavier payload in order to accommodate flares or a searchlight. It had a muffler on the engine exhaust. Both types benefitted by the addition of a more lethal load of four 3.2in (82mm) *Reaktivny Snaryad* (RS-82) rockets, which packed a better offensive punch. Polikarpov himself was alleged to have quipped that the militarized U-2 could, '…fly up to a window and look over the sill to see if the enemy was inside!'[8] Before the adoption by the world's military of helicopters in the post-war years, the U-2 was probably the closest one could actually get to such a concept.

The survival of such a vulnerable flying machine was of little or no consequence to the occupants of the Kremlin, but for practical wartime operations it was deemed an ideal weapon for nocturnal usage. Its flimsy construction left little radar echo, while the U-2's low altitude operating height aided this immunity from detection. The very fragility of the U-2's construction was sometimes to her advantage in that bullets and even cannon shells passed right through the fuselage, and (provided they did not hit the pilot, the fuel tank or the engine) might not cause fatal damage, even if, cosmetically, damaged U-2s sometimes resembled sieves on their return to base.

Their low speed, at first glance seemingly an insurmountable problem for her own protection, actually helped in her survival for the Bf.109s and Bf.110s sent to obliterate her had stalling speeds roughly the same as the U-2's best cruising speed, with the result that the attackers closed too fast, and were only able to bring their powerful guns to bear for the briefest of times before overshooting. Even the unsophisticated engine with which she was fitted was turned into an asset. Noisy and laboured, harsh and clattering, the uncowled and unsynchronized Shvetsov radial made nights hideous with their racket. To the *Wehrmacht* squaddie shivering in his slit trench and attempting to get a few hours much-needed sleep, that sound was both unwelcome and frustrating. The psychological effect such attacks had on the victims, was out of all proportion to the effort required by even a small number of, seemingly immune, U-2s. The Germans equated the noise of the U-2 with that of a sewing-machine and dubbed her *Nähmaschine* accordingly. With jarred nerves (would she drop a bomb or not? If so, would I be under it?) the term night-harassment came into the vocabulary of the Axis troopers. So successful was this subtle form of warfare in eroding the morale of the ground troops subjected to it, that the Luftwaffe soon saw fit to emulate it and before long were creating their own *Nachtschlacht* units. By contrast, when the U-2 suddenly shut off her nerve-jangling motor and went into an almost silent glide attack, another fear was transmitted by the very quietness of her approach before she jettisoned her ordnance over her target of choice.

588 Regiment

With women determined to do their bit in the front line of aviation, the egalitarian aspect of this contribution was therefore invoked by the Communist Party and constituted a powerful propaganda angle for Stalin, and, like the slogan 'The Great Patriotic War' from a man who had murdered millions of his own subjects and would go on doing so, was an obvious manifestation of someone desperate to rally the whole nation to a common cause. Prominent among such honest patriots was Marina Raskova, already famous for her pre-war aerial accomplishments, in one of which she had set a world record for non-stop flight between Moscow and Komsomolsk, Amur, in 1938. In 1942 three VVS Regiments were established with all-female contingents and one of these was the 588 Night Bomber Regiment. The unit was set up at Engels, close to Stalingrad on the Volga River, and U-2s formerly used as trainers were drafted in to equip them in their new task. They undertook their first combat operation on 8 June 1942, targeting the HQ of a German division, one U-2 failing to return. Forty women, half pilots, half navigators, all of them flying without parachutes,[9] were assigned at any one time. In combat they operated in threes, with two aircraft zigzagging and acting as lures for the enemy searchlights and flak and while they were thus diverted, the third of the trio would locate and attack the target, before taking the place of one of the decoys and repeating the process. Back at base the majority of engineers and mechanics were female as were the armourers responsible for keeping the U-2 fully bombed-up. This latter job was no sinecure either, for once the Regiment got into its stride up to ten sorties a night could be mounted, the record being eighteen in a single night!

Their initial offensive armament was, essentially, meagre, explosive grenades dropped from the navigator's cockpit, light bombs, and the physical damage they could inflict upon the enemy was negligible. However, the mental damage was rather more effective and, as 'nuisance' raiders, their contribution was considered most effective.

The origin of the German name of *Nachthexen* (Night Witches) for these women U-2 pilots came about by the frequent use of glide attacks by this unit. The rustle sound, being the noise of the wind in the U-2's wires and struts as she approached over the heads of the targets, descending at half the speed of a parachutist, was likened to the noise of a besom broom in use and this, coupled with the fact that the pilots were female, led to the epitaph being applied, much to the resentment of the women pilots themselves it should be said. They were patriots, not 'witches' they insisted, but the name stuck and (much like Kaiser Wilhelm branding the British Army in 1914 as a '…contemptible little army' being later adopted by the soldiers themselves as 'The Old Contemptibles'), the name 'Night Witches' was to become worn with pride in later years.[10]

Among the famous female pilots, some of whom were still alive well into their nineties, was Nadezhda Popova, who was awarded the Hero of the Soviet Union, with a Gold Star, the Order of Lenin and the Order of the Red Star, who died at the age of 91 in July 2013. She had joined 588 Regiment at the age of nineteen having already been trained at a flying club and then employed as a flight instructor. She survived being shot down on at least three occasions. Other notable women pilots included Yevdokiya Bershanskaya, the Regiment's commander, Flight Commanders Tat'yana Makarova and Yevgeniya Zhigulenko. Among those with high mission totals were Irina Sebroava (1,008); Natalya Meklin (908), Polina Gelman (860); Rufina Gasheva (848) and Vera Bjelik (813).[11]

During the five successive battles on the Taman Peninsula, separating the Crimea from the Kuban, between February and October 1943, the 588 made such an effective contribution that it was re-named as 46 Taman Guards Night Bomber Aviation Regiment; being nominated as a Guards unit signalling that the Regiment had been deemed worthy of the highest honour. This honour extended to the pilots themselves; when Raskova was killed in a crash in 1943, her cremated ashes were interred in the walls of the Kremlin. She was one of thirty-one female aircrew killed flying the U-2/Po-2 during the war.

War programme variants

Other military duties that the U-2 was found most useful for included reconnaissance and artillery observation, carrying out tactical *Razvedka* (reconnaissance). To vastly improve upon the original example of Sedlyarevich's unit, a purpose-built variant, the U-2NAK, appeared, in which the observer's cabin was fully equipped with Army-type radios to transfer this vital information. The aircraft thus equipped concentrated their observations on '…defence lines, artillery firing positions, headquarters, supply installations and reserve positions'. This *Razvedka* data was immediately, '…passed to the staff which controlled the air assets and, if combat was under way, to all lower headquarters through regiment by clear text radio transmission'.[12]

Nor was the original function of the U-2, pilot training, omitted, indeed the vast wartime expansion of the VVS necessitated an equal increase in numbers of air school machines. An improved variant, the U-2UT (UT – *uchebno-trenirovochnyi* – primary trainer) was introduced from 1941 and featured the 115hp (86kW) Shvetsov M-11D engine. Production was limited due to more modern training aircraft receiving priority for this power-plant.

To ferry military and political VIPs around the thousand-mile long front, and to afford these officers and *commissars* some degree of protection against the elements during these flights, a whole slew of covered accommodation adaptations, the so-called *Limuzin* (limousine) variant, appeared during the war. These 'Limo' conversions featured various degrees of relative opulence from a range of different designers, three in 1943 alone. There was the U-2 *Limuzin* from L N Marjin, U-2 *Limuzin* VG from V G Grigoriev, the U-2L from Aram Nazarovich Rafaelants and the L Zusman U-2 *Limuzin*.

This trend continued on culminating in the war years with the Po-2LS (*Limuzin Sviaznoj* – Communications Limousine) of April 1945. In this latter aircraft designer Mikhail Markelovich Kulik took extra liberties with the original design. The lower wing was reduced in length by 3.28ft (1m), producing a wing area of 339.06 ft² (31.5m²) and the aircraft had her ailerons removed and full-span slotted flaps inserted in their place, which could be lowered to a maximum of 45⁰. In addition, both sets of wings were fitted with fixed, leading-edge duralumin slats, 0.0315in (0.8mm) thick extending from just outboard the line of the upper fuselage to just before the curvature of the wingtip. The tailplane was made adjustable and flap-linked. The overall canopy was aerodynamically shaped for pilot and two passengers and was of shaped Plexiglas, with access via a door on the port side. Because a fuselage spar had to be sliced through for this egress a strengthened door frame took its place. The radically altered appearance was matched by a low landing speed of just 45km/h for gentle touch-downs at an approach angle of 12⁰. Good though this variant was, it did not proceed to production. Post-war the ultimate conversion was the Po-2L *Pasazhir* (Passenger) of 1948.

Also used for army unit liaison work, inter-battle zone links and internal military flights of which there proved ever-increasing demand, as well as night bombing and a dozen other uses, some nine thousand machines of the U-2VS (*Voiskovaya Seriya* – General Purpose) variant were introduced in 1941 and continued to be produced to the end of the war. She was later re-designated as the PO-2VS. From 1943 the Po-2ShS (*Shtab* – Staff) appeared with the rear fuselage widened to accommodate a fully enclosed cabin capable of enclosing the pilot and up to three passengers.

The evacuation of war zone wounded also featured of course and a modification of the pre-war ambulance was designed by A Ya Scherbakov, and designated as the Po-2S1. There were two other sub-types; the S2 was powered by the M-11D engine. Meanwhile, the S3/4 was equipped with two cylindrical container pods atop each lower-wing to carry stretchers. In addition to the pilot there was a seat in the rear fuselage for a nursing attendant with medical equipment. In 1941 designer Georgi Ivanovich Bakshaev had adapted the U-2 with two ventrally mounted wing-fairings for stretchers, which became the S3 – also known as the Po2SKF. One novel concept that the Communists introduced in a large scale during the war was the aerial broadcasting of propaganda to enemy troops. It was designed to play on fears and was used as yet another method of eroding morale and encouraging defeatism and desertion among cut-off units. In 1944 this had progressed far enough for the specially-adapted Po-2GN (GN – '*Golos s Nebo*' – Voice from the Sky) to appear as a limited variant in its own right, with a loudspeaker system inbuilt to blast out announcements.

A few floatplane variants re-appeared in 1944, they being the Po-2P, which had specially designed *Tsentralniy Aero Girdrodinamcheskiy Institut* (TsAGI – Central Aerohyrodynamic Institute) or CHAI-10 floats. This, the MU-3, was trialled between July and September 1944 but not adopted.

The Po-2 on the offensive

In May 1944, the Soviets were making advances and preparing for the big offensive against the German central front, Operation *Bagration*. As part of these diversionary offensives, the Po-2 units, including the Womans Bomber Regiment, were ordered to bomb targets in Donets basin. That month in excess of 1,200 such sorties were carried out by the what was now officially the Po-2. They used flare bombs to mark targets and incendiary bombs. Prominent in these attacks was Marina Chegeva.

By January the Soviets were ready for the final offensive towards Berlin itself. A big attack was launched on 16 January 1945, the troops pushing off all along the line two hours before dawn. But already the German defenders had been softened up by repeated night attacks conducted by no fewer than 209 Po-2 aircraft that been flying strikes against pre-targeted troop positions, command posts and communications centres.[13]

By the end of the war Po-2 aircraft had flown over 24,000 combat sorties, during which they had delivered an estimated 3,000 tons of bombs and 26,000 incendiaries upon the heads of the enemy. No fewer than twenty-three women pilots earned or partially earned their Orders of the Red banner flying this little machine. It was an outstanding record for an aircraft considered neither combat fit nor capable of warlike operations a few years earlier. She had been obsolescent in 1941; she emerged a heroine in 1945. Her peacetime operations duly resumed but, remarkably, her fighting days were still far from over!

Aeroflot

The national airline, *Aeroflot –Rossiyskye Avialini* (Russian Air Fleet) used the Po-2 for crop-dusting, aero-medical services and mail delivery as well as a training aircraft, and during World War II was instrumental in training 20,907 Po-2 and Li-2 pilots. From 1944 they used Po-2S (*Santarny* – Sanitary or Ambulance) conversions for mail flights and, although official Po-2 production ceased in 1949, for another decade individual aircraft were constructed in Aeroflot machine works.

OSOAVIAKhIM and DOSAAF

In 1927 the *Obshchestvo Sodeisevija Oborone Aviatsichnonnio-khmicheskomu Stroitelstvu SSR* (OSOAVIAKhIM – Union of Societies of Assistance to Defence and Aviation Chemical Construction of the USSR) was set up in order to create a powerful civilian reserve force for the armed services. All types of sporting activity were encouraged in order to hone a second-tier of skills and aptitudes by the young people on the new Soviet state so that, in the event of war, they would be already fully fit and ready. Among the many aptitudes encouraged were parachuting, gliding and basic flying and for these a large number of U-2s were operated by the organization. The war of 1941–45 appeared to fully justify this preparation and it was continued. In 1951 the organization was streamlined and modified and became the *Dobrovol'noe Obshchestvo Sodeĭstvĭĭa Aviatsii* (Volunteer Society for Co-operation with Army, Aviation and Fleet – DOSAAF) at which time just a few Po-2 aircraft still remained. This new organization remained in force until 1991.

BashNeft
A specialized variant, the Po-SPL *Limuzin*, appeared in 1933 for service survey work surrounding the exploration of new oil fields in southern Russia and with the subsequent *Bashineft Ekhimkonbinat* (*BashNeft* – Bashkir Petrochemical Integrated Enterprise) based at Ufa (Bashkir), Bashkortostan on the Volga. An ambulance version, the Po-SP (Paramedic) was also utilized by this vast oil and gas concern, which was established in 1935. The Limo variant aircraft were used in the exploration work that followed and in the construction of the oil pipelines being used to convey executives, engineers and workers and the Paramedic variant evacuated injured personnel along the rugged territory being explored and the route of the oil pipelines.

Foreign use
Albania
The *Forcat Ushtarake Ajore Shgipetare* (*FASh* – Albanian People's Army) took delivery of seventy-eight Po-2s between 1951 and 1965, and some continued to operate in a civilian role as late as 1985.

Bulgaria
The *Bulgarska Narodna Armiya* (BNA – Bulgarian People's Army) received ten Po-2s between late 1949 and 1950, and they were based at Dolna Mitropolija Air Base with the 1 (initial Training) *Escadrila* of the People's Air School. They were also used as liaison aircraft. They later received some Polish-built CSS-13s between late 1949 and 1969. One of these, built in 1950 (LZ-K19) is on exhibition at the Bulgarian Air Force Museum at Krumovo, Plovdiv, southern Bulgaria.

They were also used by civilian operators.

China, People's Republic
The *Zhōngguó Rénmin Jiĕfàngjūn* (PLAAF – People's Liberation Army Air Force) operated the Po-2 between 1949 and 1968. It is uncertain precisely how many were used, but at least two survive today and are on exhibition at Chinese museums at Datangshan and Xiaotangshan, Beijing.

Czechoslovakia
The *Československé Vojenské Letectvo* (Czechoslovakian Air Force) operated the Po-2 under the designation General Logistics System (GLS) K-62 (K = *Kuryrni* – Courier) between 1945 and 1957.

The civilian operator Slov-Air also flew them.

Finland
The Finnish Air Force used four Po-2s that were captured during the 'Continuation War' of 1941 onward. The Finnish pilots christened them as the *Hermosaha* ('Nerve Saw').These machines were as follows:

1. VU-2, which went to *LentoLaivue 30* (*Le.Lv30* – Flying Squadron 30) on 29 June 1942, and which crashed and was written off on 31 May 1943.
2. (Also) VU-2, which was a closed-cabin U-2NG, and which served with *HävittäLentoLaivue* (*HLe.Lv 28* – Fighter Squadron 28) from 4 February 1944 until 17 July 1944 when it was written off.
3. VU-3, which served with *TukiLentoLaivue 12* (*TLe.Lv 12* – Reconnaissance Squadron 12), from 7 March 1944 until 1945.
4. VU-4, which also served with *TLe.Lv 12*, from 8 March 1944 until she was transferred to *HLe.Lv 32* (Fighter Squadron 32) on 3 June 1944; she was damaged beyond repair on 23 June 1944.

France
The Free-French Air Force used the Po-2 with their *Le Groupe de Chasse* Regiment, *Normandie-Niemen* unit on the Eastern Front as General Charles de Gaulle was eager for his flyers to be seen to be actively engaged on *all* fronts in World War II. Accordingly, late in 1942, fourteen French pilots, along with supporting technicians, commanded by Major Jean Louis Tulsane, were despatched from the Middle East to Severny-Ivanovo Training Air Base north-east of Moscow. As part of their equipment four Polikarpov U-2s were made available to them and training took place with these machines from 1 to 18 December. Once this was satisfactorily completed, the four aircraft were retained and used by the French as courier and liaison machines.

Germany
Starting with those captured in Spain during the Civil War and shipped back to the *Erprobungsstelle* (*E-Stelle* or Testing Site) at Lärz airfield, at Rechlin, under *Oberst* (Colonel) Edgar Petersen, for routine examination. From June 1941 many hundreds (the precise number is impossible to verify) of Po-2s were captured, relatively intact through lack of fuel or spares, or only lightly damaged when airfields were abandoned with the advance of the Panzers. Most of these *Beute-Flugeuge* (captured aircraft) were assembled and burned or scrapped as they had nothing to teach the Luftwaffe. A few were retained and turned against their former owners, being utilized by such clandestine 'Special Operations' *Reichkommandos* like Grand Admiral Wilhelm Franz

Canaris's *Sonderverband Brandenburg* unit, and similar, dropping spies and operatives behind Soviet lines, and others were put to use by Germany's allies.

East Germany
In East Germany two Polikarpov Po-2s were operated by the *Kasernierte Volkspolizei-Luft* (KVP – Air Arm of the State Police) from 1950. Later they were retired to the *Gesellschaft für Sport und Tegnik* (GST – Sport and Technical Association) who used them as glider-tugs and parachute dropping aircraft until as late as 1968.

Hungary
The *Magyarország Rendőrsége* (National Police) rather than the Hungarian Air Force, operated twenty-four Po-2s and ex-Polish CSS-13s between 1948 and 1958. From 1954 some Po-2s operated on agricultural duties until replaced in 1960 by more modern types.

Later, the *Magyar Sport Iroda* (Hungarian Sport Bureau) operated the Po-2 as a glider tug and parachute dropper prior to the 1956 uprising, three in Dunakeszi, Pest, and one in Kispostag, Fetér. Some lingered on until as late as 1968 when all save two were destroyed. This pair still exist, one of them in flying condition.

Laos
The Government of Laos took delivery of ten Po-2s from the Soviets in 1960 in the wake of the *coup d'etat* of Colonel Kong Le in August. They were utilized as liaison and light transport aircraft. Backed by the North Vietnamese Army the communist *Pathet Lao* (Lao Nation) finally took control of the country in December 1975, it becoming the *Sathalanalat Paxathiptai Paxaxon Lao* (Lao People's Democratic Republic) including a few surviving Po-2 aircraft.

Latvia
Following the German liberation of Latvia in 1941, the Soviets re-organized the surviving pro-communist Latvian pilots, living in the USSR and on 15 March 1943, the Latvian Bomber Aviation Regiment was formed. Consisting of three squadrons, plus reserves, it main function was night bombing and harassment missions and was commanded by Major Karlis A Kirss. It was initially equipped with the Polikarpov Po-2 aircraft. From 28 September, 1943, the *Latyshskiy Bombadirovshchik Aviacionyj Polk* (BAP – Latvian Bomber Aviation Regiment) was attached to the 242 Night Bomber Aviation Division part of the 6 Air Army supporting the North-West Front. In January 1944 the Latvian Regiment was moved to 313 Night Bomber Aviation Division, under 15 Air Army. The unit distinguished itself in the fall of Rēzekne, Latgalia, in eastern Latvia, and was re-designated as the 1 Rezeknes Latvian Night Bomber Aviation Regiment and in April 1945 became part of 284 Night Bomber Aviation Division.[14]

Mongolia
The aviation detachment of the *Mongol Ardyn Armi (Tsereg)* (MPRA – Mongolian People's Revolutionary Army) acquired twenty U-2A/Po-2s at intervals between 1932

and 1963. The first U-2As arrived in 1932 in the wake of the anti-communist rebellion of that year, which was harshly put down. In the aftermath there was a delivery batch of fourteen U-2As and R-1 (DH-9) and a total of twenty-three pilots were trained in the Soviet Union. They served the *Bŭgd Nairamdakh Mongol Ard Uls* (BNMAU – Mongolian People's Republic), which became, in effect, a vassal state of the USSR, although still claimed by China as part of their territory.

The state airline, *Mongolyn Irgenii Agaaryn Teever* (MIAT – Mongolian Civil Air Transportation), based at Ulaan Baatar, also took delivery of a single Po-2 in 1946 and used her as a mail-delivery aeroplane for many years; she even featured on a state postage stamp of the period.

North Korea
Starting in August 1947, the Soviet Union had already delivered substantial numbers of Po-2s to the Communist-dominated northern half of Korea, which they had 'liberated' in August 1945, and of these, a total of eighteen remained in service with the so-called *Chosŏn Minjujuŭi Inmin Konghwaguk Hanja* (Democratic People's Republic of Korea Air Force or DPRKAF) in July 1950 when the Northern armies made a totally unprovoked and violent invasion of the democratic south. The United Nations, for one of the very few occasions in its long existence, stood up to communist aggression and rallied to the defence and a bitter struggle ensued.

The first use of the Po-2 was on 28 November 1950, when a lone 'night nuisance' raider made an attack on Pyongyang airfield, then in UN hands. Such raids took place intermittently whenever the moon allowed night operations against bases at Suwon and Inchon. A large raid was made on the night of 16/17 June 1951, when fifteen Po-2s, aided by other types, bombed the southern capital, Seoul and destroyed five million gallons of aviation fuel, a result that was considered a real success for the North Koreans for such a modest outlay.

The NATO allies even gave her the compliment of assigning yet another warplane codename for the Po-2, for, despite her antiquity, to them she became the 'Mule'. The name allocated may well have been an ironic or sarcastic epithet but the Americans who so named her forgot one thing, mules can kick!

The Russians were very much involved behind the scenes, as puppet-masters, although they worked through the Chinese, and Stalin did not want an outright confrontation. Towards the end in early October 1953, the North Koreans leader wanted to escalate air attacks, and sent General Nam Il, the KPA Chief-of-Staff, to the CPVAF's headquarters at Adong, to press the Chinese on those lines. But the Chinese air force, represented by Nei Fengzhi, refused, as, with permission from Beijing, he was only permitted to allow the North Koreans to continue flying the Po-2s at night to 'heckle' the UN forces. Thus the Po-2 remained the only communist aircraft that the UN troops had to contend with to the end.[15] They proved elusive enough to cause headaches, however, and the aircraft was to uniquely inflict upon the US the very last deadly strike from an airborne source, yet another fact added to the many chalked up by this aircraft. In Korea the enemy used them as night-harassment units in the same way, and the American troops were just as troubled by them, dubbing such Po-2 visitations as 'Bed Check Charlie' as they always appeared just as their victims were nodding off.

This event took place in 1953, just three months prior to the cease-fire[16] American troops were emplaced on the island of Cho-do, a small chunk of rock in the estuary of the River Taedong in the Yellow Sea off the west coast of North Korea to the north of the South Korean capital, Seoul. As aerial protection against the North Korean and Communist Chinese MiGs and other Soviet-supplied aircraft, the United Nations forces had occupied several such outposts and installed radar warning, radio interception listening stations and other strategic facilities on them. They were frequently attacked by the Reds, and just a few months before four North Korean Po-2s, a legacy to them from the Soviet 'liberation' of their territory in 1945, had bombed the Cho-on radar arrays, killing four of their own citizens and wounding two Americans. The island, just above the 38th Parallel, was protected by regular patrols of Lockheed F-94 Starfire, radar-equipped, all-weather jet fighters over the area, and by a single battery ('Able') of the 933rd Anti-Aircraft Artillery (Automatic Weapons) Battalion.[17] The 933rd was a Mobile (i.e. Towed) unit and 'A' Battery was emplaced atop Cho-do.

Despite these precautions on the night of 15 April, at least one enemy confirmed as a biplane, and almost certainly a Po-2,[18] flew in 'low and too slow' from the bases across the water and she failed to show up amid the ground clutter on the airborne radar scopes of the F-94s. The little wooden-and-fabric biplane penetrated the island's own radar defences in a manner that a modern 'stealth' bomber would be proud of. According to one survivor of the attack, Albert Villanueva, the first he knew of the bombing was a tremendous rush of air pressure and he blacked out. When he came to he found he had been badly injured, and that two of his companions, Privates First Class Herbert Tucker and William Walsh, had been killed by the same explosion and their gun mounting was destroyed.

These two US Army privates may have had the melancholy fate of being the last to be killed by enemy air attack, but the US Air Force was to take even heavier losses from this frail little relic. On the night of 17 June 1951 Suwon Air Base (K-13) two Po-2s had made a (pre-announced), return attack and had hit and destroyed one North American F-86 Sabre parked there, while eight others from the 335 Squadron USAF, had been badly damaged by the resulting fires as ammunition 'cooked off'. [Po-2 -9, USAF – 0.]

The Americans tried everything to nail the Po-2s during their incursions; the North American F-86 Sabre was a day fighter and too fast, attempts were made with North American F-82 Twin Mustangs, North American T-6 'Mosquitoes' and even a heavily armed Douglas B-26C Invader, and this later recorded the first success by shooting down a Po-2 on the night of 23 June 1951. Another fell to the guns of a US Marine Corps Douglas F3D-2 Skyknight of VMF(N)-513 flown by Lieutenant Joseph Corvi and Sergeant Dan George on the night of 10 December 1952. This was the first ever occasion that radar tracking and lock-on without any visual contact had resulted in a confirmed kill, and the same team claimed a 'probable' later that night. [Po-2 – 0, USAF and USMC – 2.]

Meanwhile the Lockheed F-94 Starfire's earlier efforts at interception had been restricted following an incident on 3 May when Second Lieutenant Stanton Granville Wilcox and radar operator Irwin Louis Goldberg's F-94, (serial 50-887) from 319 Fighter Interception Squadron (FIS) had been homed onto 'Charlie' by Chodo's radar. The Starfire closed to within firing range and signalled 'Splash' to indicate they had achieved a kill but all further communication abruptly terminated. It was assumed that they had either flown into the wreckage of their target or had throttled back to 110mph (180 km/h) during the attack, stalled and crashed in to the sea. As a precaution following this incident the F-94 was stopped from flying at speeds under 160mph (257.50 km/h) or flying below an altitude of 2,000ft (609.60m). [Po-2 – 1, USAF- O.]

The Po-2 attacks continued, and indeed even grew bolder. Cho-do was hit almost every night, while, on 15 June, nine North Korean night intruders made a bold attack on the mansion residence of South Korean President Syngman Rhee near the Capitol building in Seoul, dropping three 100lb (45.35kg) thermal bombs, one of which landed 1,000ft (304.80m) away, and wounding seven people. They repeated the raid in even greater strength the following night and also set a fuel dump ablaze at Inchon.

It was not until the US Navy tried their hand with F4U-5N Chance-Vought Corsair propeller-driven night-fighters that the Po-2 started taking losses. On the night of 30 June, Navy Lieutenant Guy Pierre Bordelon, on loan from the carrier *Princeton* (CV-37) destroyed two Yak-18s guided by ground radar controllers and repeated the feat the following night, shooting down two more and on 16 July nailed a fifth. He also got two Silver Stars and an 'Ace' status; the magazine *Life* reported that Bordelon was '…the first man to become an ace by getting there last with the least'.[19] [US Navy -3 – Po-2 -0.] In total just seven Po-2s were destroyed by UN forces during the course of the active war. About ten Po-2s are thought to have survived the war, being gradually withdrawn from active service due to lack of spare parts until by the 1960s all had gone.

Poland

The *Lotnoctwo Wojskowe i Obrony Powietrznej* (Polish Air and Defence Forces) used Soviet supplied Po-2s in training units and in squadrons as liaison machines. Many of these Po-2s were used in military operations, using their airborne machine-guns and hand grenades against the *Ukraińska Powstáncza Armia* (UPA – Ukrainian Insurgent Army), an ethnic minority that murdered many thousands of Poles in the Bieszczady mountain region from March 1944 onward. Several Po-2s were shot down by the UPA but were destroyed by their aircrews to prevent them falling into their hands. Following the murder of a Polish General, Operation *Wisla* (Vistula) was launched, which was the forcible removal of the entire Ukrainian population but sporadic fighting continued until as late as 1947.

The official civil airline, *Polskie Linie Lotncze Lot* (LOT Polish Airlines), operated five Po-2s in 1945–46. It also operated twenty licence-built CSS-13s for aerial crop dusting and spraying and also for forestry work, between 1953 and 1956.

The *Aeroklub Polski* (Polish Aero Club) used the Po-2 as a training aircraft, as glider tugs and as a delivery vehicle for sky divers.

The *Marynarki Wojennej* (Polish Navy) also employed the Po-2 as did the *Wojskach Ochrony Pogranicza* (WOP – Polish Border Protection Forces.)

Poland was the only Soviet satellite nation to manufacture the Po-2 under licence. In 1948 an agreement was entered into between Moscow and the *Centraine Studium Samoltów* (CSS – Central Aircraft Studies) at the *Instytut Lotnctwa* (Institute of Aviation) in Warsaw, under the Director, Stanislaus Lassoty. The designer put in charge of the project was Tadeusz Soltyk, and the Polish variant differed in a number of ways. They were link-equipped, dual-controls, a bomb bay, and a sighting window built into the lower starboard wing. They also had Polish flight instruments and the improved 125hp (92kW) 5-cylinder M11D radial engine. The new aircraft was designated as the CSS-13. Building was commenced at PZL Mielec that same year and the prototype was delivered to the Institute of Aviation. During trials it was found to be satisfactory and full production was authorized at PZL Mielec in 1949 and continued until 1950, when 180 aircraft had been delivered. In 1952 production was re-started, but at WSK Okecie, Warsaw, and continued until 1956, by which time a further 380 machines had been completed. They gave good service and the last one was not de-commissioned until 1978.

The *Lotnicze Pogotowie Ratunkowe* (LPR – Polish Air Ambulance Service) used some Po-2s and later the specially-designed, home-built CSS-SI3 (S for *Sanitarny* – Sanitary). This latter was a 'medivac' variant designed by Tadeusz Sultyka in 1953, of which a total of fifty-nine were completed. They were gradually replaced by the Yak-12S. Examples of these served in the same capacity in the Czech Republic and in Hungary.

Romania
The *Aeronautica Regala Romania* (Royal Romanian Air Force) received a few captured Po-2s toward the end of 1941. After the communist take-over it became the *República Socialista de Romania Aeriene* (People's Republic of Romania Air Force) and in 1949 a further forty-five Po-2s were supplied from the USSR and they began operating them from April 1950. Some remained in service until as late as 1977.

Turkey
The *Turk Hava Kurumu* (THK – Turkish Air League) obtained two U-2s as a gift from the Soviet Government on the Tenth Anniversary of the Republic in 1933.

Tyva Republic
The tiny *Respublika Tyva* (Tannu-Tuva) between Siberia and Mongolia has existed as a separate state since 1921. It was swallowed up by Stalin in 1944 but during its brief existence it had established its own independent army comprising a cavalry regiment and a War Department, and a single three-seater U-2SP was obtained from the Soviet Union circa 1937. A spare M-11 engine and other reserve equipment were requested for this machine for delivery in January and February 1940. A second aircraft, a basic U-2 trainer, was ordered on 25 November 1939 through the *Technoeksport* (Techno-

export) organization, a division of the Soviet *Народный комиссариат внешней торговли СССР* (People's Commissariat of Foreign Trade) in Moscow, also for delivery in 1940. It is thought these were taken back into Soviet service after the country was absorbed back into the Soviet state.

Yugoslavia

The *Jugoslav Ratno Vazduhoplovstvo* (JRV – Socialist Federal Republic Air Force) received a total of eighty-seven Po-2s between 1944 and 1947 and a further thirty-seven post-war before President Josip Broz Tito's rupture with Stalin in 1948. Many served on until as late 1962.

They served in the following units: *Vazduhoplovni Transportni puk 1* (1 Transport Aviation Regiment) from 1944 to 1948; *Vazduhoplovni Školski puk 1* (1 Training Aviation Regiment) from 1945 to 1952; *Vazduhoplovni Školski puk 2* (2 Training Aviation Regiment) from 1946 to 1948; *Vazduhoplovni Noći Bombarderski puk 184* (184 Light Night Bomber Aviation Regiment) between 1948 and 1952; *Eskarila za Izviđanje* (Liaison Squadron) of 1, 3, 5 and 7 Military Districts between 1952 and 1959; and *Eskarila za Izviđanje za Avijacijska Korpus 3* (Liaison Squadron of 3 Aviation Corps between 1950 and 1956.[20]

Progressively from the mid-1950s they began to be phased out of military service into civilian usage and many went to the *Vazdohoplovni Savez Jugoslavije* (Aviation Association of Yugoslavia) as glider-tugs and utility aircraft.

Preserved aircraft

1. Serial No. 8-0571, at the Museum of Polish Arms, Volobzeg.
2. Serial No. 0434, registration SP- at the National Museum of Agriculture and Agri-Food Industry, S Zreniawa.
3. Civil Registration SP-BHA at the Kbely Aviation Museum, Kbely, Czech Republic.
4. Hungarian Aviation Museum, Szolnok, Hungary.
5. The Shuttleworth Collection, near Biggleswade, Bedfordshire has G-BSSY fully restored to airworthiness first flying on 10 January 2011.
6. At Tushino airfield, Moscow, another fully flying Po-2 is owned by the Federation of Amateur Aviators of Russia.
7. The *Koroski Aeroklub* based at Mislinska Dobrava, Slovenj Gradee, in Slovenia has another airworthy Po-2.
8. In Hungary, the Goldtime Foundation flies with passengers from the Hungarian Museum of Transportation at Budaöras airfield. It was restored to a flying condition by Károly Császár, head executive of the Kaposvár branch of the foundation and the Farkashegy workshop in 1984. She first flew in Switzerland the following year and in 1986, flying at the Budaörs air show, Császár died at the controls while airborne and, incredibly, the aircraft landed itself with very little damage and she still flies.
9. One Po-2 is on display at the Szolnok Museum of Military Aviation, Hungary.
10. Another fully restored Po-2 is held by the Military Aviation Museum, Virginia Beach, Va.

Chapter Sixteen

Supermarine Walrus I and II (and Seagull V)

Reginald Joseph Mitchell, CBE, FRAeS, (1895–1937) will, of course, will always be associated with the Supermarine Spitfire design. It is all the more remarkable then that another of his offspring was the outstandingly ugly Supermarine Walrus. No two aircraft could be of greater contrast but both were born around the same period and both served throughout World War II and beyond. It is hard to believe that such a diversity of aerodynamics existed side by side and from the same originator, but they did. Of course working for Supermarine Aviation at Woolston, Southampton from 1917 (and as their Chief Designer from 1919), a firm that specialized in seaplane designs, and continuing on that theme later as Chief Engineer from 1920 and Technical Director seven years later, maritime aircraft was his forte. When Supermarine was acquired by the larger Vickers organization in 1928, he was retained due to his acknowledged expertise in that field. Overall, Mitchell was responsible for no fewer than twenty-four types of notable aircraft, including the Sea King seaplane and carrier-based fighter of 1921 to meet RAF specification N6/22, and which became the record-breaking Sea Lion in 1922, and civilian transport seaplane known as the Sea Eagle in 1923, both amphibians. Mitchell was also responsible for a cutting-edge series of racing seaplanes, the ill-fated S.4 of 1925; the record-breaking S.5 of 1927 and, of course, the record-breaking Supermarine S.6B, which carried off the Schneider Trophy in 1931 and subsequently set the world air speed record.[1] This beautiful design later morphed into the Spitfire, despite the RAF's obsession with the heavy bomber and its then-held belief (shared in political circles and motivated by cost) that '...the bomber would always get through'. The Supermarine Company's Seagull II might be said to be the starting point for the Walrus. This amphibian progressed into the Seagull III and these nine wooden construction machines were under consideration to be carried aboard the Australian Navy's seaplane carrier HMAS *Albatross*. She had originally been built in 1928 but had been paid off into reserve due to lack of suitable aircraft in 1933. However, it was deemed desirable by the Royal Australian Air Force (RAAF), for a more robust design to be employed in the Air-Sea Rescue/ Reconnaissance roles as they would be required to withstand repeated shocks and strains from being catapulted from a ship in a fully operationally loaded condition. The RAAF were at that time responsible for the design and manning of Navy aircraft and servicing personnel, much like the RAF controlled all aspects of the Royal Navy's aircraft in the inter-war period, while the Royal Australian Navy (RAN) provided the observer and telegraphist/air gunner. A metal-construction aircraft was deemed essential and, as the RAF initially distanced itself from the project, the RAAF went ahead in issuing its own specification to several British aviation companies and ended up in direct consultation with Supermarine, which already had the speculative private venture Seagull V underway. Only after this *fait accompli* did the RAF subsequently express any interest in the type.

The principal advantage of being a catapult-launched aircraft rather than the existing Seagull III, was that the carrying ship did not have to stop in order to lower the machine into the water for her to taxi into the air; indeed they could be launched in conditions that might preclude the Seagull III getting airborne at all. The problem remained for recoveries of course. The Seagull V had the same size wings as the Seagull II, but the numbers of struts were reduced from twelve to eight, with the engine borne on the inner four. This followed a prolonged period of hydrodynamic testing of scale mock-ups in the Vickers Aircraft water tank at St. Albans.

Supermarine allocated their Type 228 designation to this concept, initiated as a private venture, and, as a largely hand-built, prototype to what was to become the first Walrus, and the Type 236 designation and the Type 307 for the 2/35 specification, which led to the eventual production run series of the Walrus I and Type 315 for the Mk II while the Seagull V was the Type 320.

The prototype Seagull V (serial K4797, the former N-1 and later N-2, which became the Walrus), was commenced in 1930 but did not first take to the air until 21 June 1933 a very leisurely rate of construction typical of those straightened times. She had a 'single-stepped' aluminium hull, with stainless steel used for hard-working fixtures. Wooden construction was initially rejected for Australian usage due to its decomposition in the tropics. She was flown by Captain Joseph 'Mutt' Summers, Vickers Group Chief Test Pilot in Southampton Water. Just five days after her maiden flight Summers demonstrated her in London, flying her from Hendon during the Society of British Aircraft Constructors Show when she publically carried out an impressive loop in front of the assembled throng, an event which, it is said, even left Mitchell himself speechless!

She was powered by the Bristol Pegasus IIL.2P engine, a rear-propeller fitted 'pusher-type' engine of 625 hp (460 kW). This engine nacelle was positioned behind the cockpit between the upper and lower wings, and was later to be angled off-centre to port by 3 degrees to offset the thrust of the four-bladed wooden propeller which impinged on just one side of the fin, giving a continued 'yaw'. This engine had individual exhaust stubs, lacking a collector ring, and the noise generated gave her a distinctive, and far from subtle, pulse. This led to one test pilot (Alex Henshaw) commenting that the Walrus was, '...the noisiest, coldest and most uncomfortable...' aircraft he had ever flown! There was very little resemblance to the preceding Seagull III other than the name. As designed, the Seagull V was the first amphibian in the world capable of being launched by catapult with a full military load. Among the many features incorporated in this unique design was the ability to fold the wings while aboard ship in order to accommodate her in a hangar, the stowage width being 17ft 11in (5.5m) maximum. She also had flaps on the lower wings to aid this process. The wings had a slight rear sweep back, and were of composite design, fabric covering over wooden ribs and stainless-steel sparring. The upper set encompassed two fuel tanks. When folded for stowage aboard ships the width was reduced to 17ft 5in (5.33 m). She had a high-set tail plane, reinforced on 'N' struts. The rear wheel was of solid aluminium, and it was possible to couple this to the taxiing rudder, while being disconnected during take-offs or landings. The initial undercarriage proved to be too inflexible in practice and this had to be adjusted. This undercarriage retracted fully into recesses in the lower wing.

Australia had twenty-four Seagull Vs (Type 223) ordered as direct purchases from Supermarine under their 6/34 specification, dated 27 August 1934. They allocated them the serial numbers A2-1 to A2-24. The first machine, A2-1, made her maiden flight on 25 June 1934 and after considerable delay due to production bottlenecks, the final delivery, A2-24, did not make her maiden flight until 28 April 1937. These Australian machines were completed at the same time as the second batch of Walrus Is (serial numbers K8338 – K8345).

In the fleet, a great deal of effort was devoted between the wars to building suitable hangar spaces aboard British battleships and cruisers but these fragile fire hazards were ever regarded with some considerable distaste by many naval officers. The larger *County* Class heavy cruisers were large enough to accommodate box-like hangar structures to house them, while the *Town* Class light cruisers had hangars built into their design, totally altering the traditional classic British cruiser profile. I can find no evidence that the monitor *Terror* ever carried a Walrus at one stage of her career as alleged by some, although as shore bombardment was her sole remit she may have worked in conjunction with them. In the event by 1943 most of these costly conversion no longer seemed relevant as amphibians were generally withdrawn when carrier aircraft predominated. It was a biplane at a time when the United States and Japanese Navies, unencumbered by Treasury restrictions and RAF neglect, were developing monoplane amphibians for the same task. The lower wings of the Seagull V, and the resulting Walrus, were fixed in the shoulder position, and had a stabilizer float under each, the Walrus floats being rather larger than the Seagull V. The radial engine was housed in a nacelle slung from the upper wing, and drove a four-bladed propeller. She was normally armed with a pair of Vickers .303-in (7.7mm) 'K' gas-operated machine-guns in either two bow positions or dorsal positions amidships, where they were mounted on a Scarff Ring dating back to World War I. They could carry a bomb or depth-charge load to a maximum of 760lb (345kg) mounted under the lower wings.

Another unique feature of this aircraft was that the control column was not fixed but was capable of being plugged into either of two floor-level sockets, one for the pilot position on the port side and one to starboard, reserved for the co-pilot if the nose gun was unmanned. Frequently, it appears, just the port control column would be utilized in flight and when control was transferred the column was just unplugged and passed across to be re-plugged. Being an amphibian the aircraft carried inflatables, two canvas sea-anchors, mooring cables, mooring lights, fog bells, towing hooks and cables and boat-hooks.

To launch, the catapult was trained out with the Walrus in place at the rear end; the three-sections were then extended. With full power on the Pegasus a charge of 7lb of cordite was fired, which gave an initial thrust. Then one was in the hands of the almighty! Retrieval was rather more complicated, if no less hairy. The Walrus could land in a swell of up to seven feet but of course the flatter the water the better. The Walrus had to be craned back aboard her parent ship and for this the equipment also included lifting-tackle stowed above the engine in a compartment in the upper wing. In anything but the calmest of seas this procedure was no sinecure. The usual practice was for the parent vessel to make a curving approach to try and create a calm zone of flat water. The Walrus would land in this and power across to the ship, which would have the crane ready. A light cable or rope was then lowered down to the crew member atop the wing and he would hook it on to the sling. A stouter cable was then lowered down and shackled on. The aircraft was then lifted out of the water and lowered back onto the catapult. This required patience and skill, especially in any sort of a seaway. Once safely down in position half a dozen small block-and-tackles were secured to the cradle, which locked her safely on. The total flight and servicing team aboard comprised the pilot, navigator and radio operator, with a rigger airframe, engine mechanic, radio mechanic, armourer, a naval rating trained in parachute packing, and a writer for admin. A complete spare Pegasus engine was carried aboard, housed in a tin inserted into a wooden crate to keep it dry for regular refits.

The Walrus was a tough aircraft, despite her ungainly appearance. She had to be to withstand the pressure of frequent catapult launches. One account asserts that she was fully capable of aerobatics, and that she could be 'looped and bunted', at least until the water accumulated in her bilges started moving around, which could cause undesirable effects. Wing loading was 11.8lb/ft (57.6 kg/m), with a power/mass of 0.094 hp/lb (0.16 kW/kg).

The trial aircraft underwent prolonged Marine Aircraft Experimental Establishment (MAEE) testing at the Felixstowe, Suffolk, facility. She was briefly embarked aboard the battle-cruiser *Repulse* and battleship *Valiant* for tests. Sea trials commenced in February 1934 aboard the carrier *Courageous* where she was flown by Lieutenant-Commander Caspar John (a later First Sea Lord). Testing continued with No. 702 Catapult Flight and from the battleship *Nelson* at Portland Harbour, Dorset, and at the Royal Aircraft Establishment, Farnborough, Hants, where she was first shot off with a full war load piloted by Flight Lieutenant Sydney Richard Umbee. Despite all this the Air Ministry remained unimpressed and aloof, a typically snooty letter being received from them stating that, '.....we do not envisage any role for an aircraft of this type with H. M. forces'. Serving RAF officers with little or no experience of fleet work, were equally sneering claiming that such an aircraft would be destroyed in seconds by fighter aircraft – although how they were to reach her in the mid-Atlantic or Pacific oceans where battleships and cruisers on Trade Protection would normally operated, apparently never occurred to their land-locked minds. Casper John was instructed by his then superior, Rear-Admiral Maitland W S Boucher, DSO, to fly the machine at Calshot in 1934. Further testing followed at Gibraltar, Sheerness and underway recovery in the choppy waters of the Kyle of Bute in Scotland, which resulted in some modifications and alterations to improve handling in all weathers. A feature added was a warning horn that the undercarriage was down after the machine somersaulted while landing in such a condition with Admiral Sir Roger Backhouse, C-in-C Home Fleet, aboard – he survived and so did the redoubtable amphibian.

The Australians ordered two dozen of these machines in August 1934, under their Specification 6/34, also powered by the 775hp Bristol Pegasus IIM2. It had a crew of three, and was armed with a solitary Vickers 'K' 0.303-in (7.7mm) machine-gun in the pointed bow and another in the dorsal open cockpit. The Seagull Vs had a gross weight of 6,847lb (3,106kg), a wingspan of 46ft (14.02m) and an overall length of 38ft (11.6m) on the chassis. The first of these Australian aircraft were ordered straight from the drawing board as the Seagull V A2 and the first flew on 25 June 1935. They were flown by RAAF aircrew but operated aboard RAN warships under a special arrangement similar to that which existed in Great Britain at the time, but which was to be phased out just before the war. Ironically the seaplane carrier HMAS *Albatross* had been laid up at Garden Island base through lack of operating funds. In 1936 a catapult was fitted to her and she was re-commissioned to conduct trials with a Seagull V aircraft, before returning to reserve status. Thus she was never used to fly the new Supermarine amphibian aircraft *operationally* with the RAN, as she was once more laid up and then sold.

The first two aircraft (carrying Australian serials A2-1 and A2-2) instead were allocated to the heavy cruiser HMAS *Australia* on 9 September 1935 and later to the new light cruiser HMAS *Sydney*, both of which happened to be in British waters at the time. The old *Albatross* was then transferred to the Royal Navy as part-payment for the cruiser *Hobart*. On her final voyage from Sydney Harbour she was given a commemorative escort of Seagull Vs under Squadron Leader Cyril Beresford Wincott, RAF. On reaching the UK the *Albatross* commissioned at Devonport on 6 October 1938 for trials with one of her cranes removed, but almost immediately, on 30 November, was placed into reserve. With the international situation darkening again, she was re-commissioned in June 1939 with six Walrus aircraft from No. 710 NAS and allocated for deployment at war station Freetown, Sierra Leone, to provide air surveillance duties which the RAF lacked any resources to do. Her Walrus were initially deployed to search for surface raiders during the hunting down of the German Pocket Battleships and armed surface raiders, but later anti-submarine patrolling predominated when the U-boats moved south. Between July and August she conducted harbour and sea trials. From 25 August 1939, she became fully operational, but, because of the lamentable state of the Navy, and British defences, at this time, she had no catapult installed. She embarked six Walrus I aircraft of No. 710 Squadron, and sailed for Freetown in September, where she was employed as a Static Base Ship for reconnaissance and trade defence duties, with her aircraft searching for German blockade runners and armed merchant cruisers (the HK ships). During this time she was at Bathurst, Gambia and visited the Dakar French Navy Base in December, but it was not until 1940 that she once more had a catapult re-installed to launch her Walrus aircraft!

At this period the RAN had two heavy cruisers, *Australia* and *Canberra*, and was in the process of adding three brand-new light cruisers, which had originally been built, or were building, in the United Kingdom for the Royal Navy, *Apollo*, *Amphion* and

Phaeton (all of the 'Modified-*Leander*' Class). They were taken over by the RAN and renamed as *Hobart, Perth* and *Sydney*. The Seagull Vs were operated by No. 9 Squadron and No. 101 Fleet Co-Operation Flight, which later became No. 5 Squadron and on 1 January became No. 9 (Fleet Co-Operation) Squadron. *Hobart* and *Sydney* received their aircraft in 1939. A further thirty-seven Walrus aircraft that were built for the Royal Navy were also taken over by the Australians and delivered in batches between 1939 and 1944. As well as on board the cruiser fleet, these Walrus served with Nos. 5, 9 and 10 Squadrons RAAF. The Australians nicknamed this strangely configured and far-from-beautiful aircraft 'The Pusser's Duck' (and a Duck's Head with Naval Crown still remains as the official badge for 9 Squadron RAAF to the present day).[2]

These machines were assembled to completion and then test flown from Eastleigh airfield and on Southampton Water for approximately half-hour periods before being dismantled again, inspected and crated up for trans-shipment to Australia with the engines boxed separately. They were once more re-assembled at RAAF No. 1 Aircraft Depot, at Laverton, Victoria State. Many joined No. 101 (Fleet Co-Operation) Flight at Point Cook air base, which provided training for the type. From April 1936 this unit was re-designated as No. 5 (Fleet Co-Operation) Squadron and based at Richmond. The Squadron's role was to provide aircraft and personnel for ships of the RAN, and it had a secondary mission of carrying out air surveys for the Australian Government. Typical of these latter missions was one conducted by a team comprising Pilot Jim Alexander in A2-4/VH-ALB, with Flight Sergeant Norman Kerr and Wireless Operator Leading Aircraftsman (LAC) David George Barnes, from Darwin in the Northern Territory in which they worked with noted anthropologist Dr Donald Thompson. They initially mapped the Aboriginal tribal boundaries in the Amhem Land region and subsequent missions included survey work of the Northern coastline in conjunction with the survey ship HMAS *Moresby*, working also from Millingimby Mission Station.[3]

Meanwhile, the original machine was finally purchased by the Air Ministry in January 1935, re-equipped with the 680hp (510kW) Bristol IIM2 Pegasus, an improved version of which became the standard power plant and which gave her a maximum speed of a stately 135mph (215km/h) at an altitude of 4,750ft (1,450m). She had a range of about 600 miles (965km) and a service ceiling of 18,500ft (5,650m). The bow became rounded and fitted with two mooring bollards with two 'squarish' observation windows on either side of the fuselage. In this new configuration the Walrus (K5772) first flew on 16 March 1936. The Mark I was therefore taken into Royal Navy service as the new standard Amphibian Boat Reconnaissance (ABR) machine for catapult launchings. This aircraft, piloted by Lieutenant Douglas Charles Vincent Pelly, later crashed in Gibraltar harbour, fortunately without casualties. Later this machine was retrieved and was subsequently repaired. Hoped for orders from Japan never materialized (the Imperial Japanese Navy had far superior types of their own under development at this time), and the Civil War in Spain dashed hopes for orders from that Government also.

The British Specification 2/35 called for the Fleet Air Arm to equip with the Seagull V as a Fleet General Reconnaissance Amphibian and renamed her as the Walrus I. An initial order was placed in 1935 under Specification 2/35 and contract No. 391700/35/C.4 1(c), for twelve machines, named Walrus in celebration of a rather incongruous appearance (Henshaw again, '…it reminded me of a large iron dustbin filled with empty soup-tins…'). They were allocated serial numbers K5772 to K5783 inclusive. Further orders followed. Under Specification 37/36, contract 472708/35 (ex-391700/35) a further eight machines were ordered, receiving serials K8338 to K8345 inclusive. Twenty-eight more Walrus I aircraft were contracted for under 472708/35, with serial number allocations K8537 to K8564 inclusive, one of which was loaned to the RAAF for the light cruiser *Sydney* on 26 April 1940. The largest contract for the Mk I, under Spec 37/36, was placed on 10 July 1936, when no fewer than 168 were ordered from Woolston under 534422/36. These received the inclusive serials L2169 to L2336 and included machines destined for the RAF, the RAAF and the RNZAF. This order was followed, as the peace faded away and war loomed, by a further Woolston order under contract B974377/39, for fifty further Walrus, and they were serialled as P5646 to P5720 inclusive, the first flying on 28 September 1939. Finally, Vickers received contract No B21120/39 for fifteen more machines, and these had the serial numbers R6543 to R6557 inclusive. In all, Supermarine produced 281 of these Mk I aircraft (four of which were not finally delivered as they had been destroyed by enemy bombing while under construction). Modifications included changing the hinging of the lower wing trailing edges from a downward fold of 180 degrees to that of a 90-degree upward fold. The original model had an external oil cooler but this was found to be superfluous and was done away with.

The late 1930s was a time of considerable expansion of the British armed forces after two decades of neglect by a succession of Governments. It was, as always with the UK, too little and far too late, but at least work was started. However, it was found that twenty years of rundown had left the infrastructure at a low ebb and priorities crowded in on each other in quick succession. On the air side the Fleet Air Arm had been totally neglected and, from being the leading maritime air power in 1918 the British maritime air strength had fallen to a very poor third twenty years later. The need for fighters for home defence took priority of course and decisions had to be made for less glamorous additions like the Walrus. An Air Ministry Memo of 1938 spelt out the dilemma.

The FAA programme calls for production of twenty Walrus (Amphibian) a/c a month ASAP and 90 Albacore (TSR) a month in 12 or 15 months time. The present rate of delivery of Walrus is three a month, and Albacore not yet fully in production, but urgent steps have been taken to accelerate this and also to provide a secondary source of supply of each type. A total production of twelve Walrus a month will be achieved in nine months time, and it is hoped that this will be raised to twenty a month, if required, in about sixteen months time. With regards Albacore, it will not be possible to provide full requirement without creation of new capacity.

In 1939, due to the big orders for the Spitfire, the Walrus production was concentrated on Saunders-Rowe (SARO) at Cowes on the Isle of Wight. All the jigs and tools were transferred over, although the SARO aircraft were built with wooden hulls. Vickers-Supermarine built 285 Mk I Walrus with metal hulls. SARO completed a total of 461, broken down as 270 Mk I machines and 191 Mk IIs. This gave a total of 746.

The resulting shift of production across the Solent from Woolston to Saunders-Roe Ltd (SARO) eased the Walrus situation. The first batch of ten Walrus Is from this source was under contract B21120/39, and they had serials R6582 to R6591 allocated to them, the first flying in May 1940. This was followed by contract B43393/39 for the Mk II Walrus, with the serial range W2670–W2729, which began to be delivered from 12 January 1940 onward. One of these machines, W2705, went to the heavy cruiser HMAS *Australia* in October 1942, while another, W2707 was delivered to the RNZAF as late as January 1943. Mk IIs were also ordered from Vickers-Supermarine, no fewer than 150 of this type being contracted for under B67952/39, and arriving from June 1941 onward. Many of these went to the RAF ASR units, while W2740 was allocated to the RNZAF as their L59 in November 1944.

SARO produced 270 Mk Is, (of which six were not finally delivered) making a total of 551 Mk Is, plus two more built for the Argentine Government in 1939. They were joined later by a further six post-war and two were embarked aboard the light cruiser *La Argentina* and were still active in 1958 – surely the longest-serving Walrus aircraft of all. Another nation, similarly hostile to Great Britain although ostensibly neutral, was the Irish Republic. The Irish Air Corps operated three Mk Is including N18, N19 and N20, which it obtained from RAF stocks (serials L2301, L2302 and L2030 from a batch of 160 (L2169–2336) built for the Fleet Air Arm by Supermarine Aviation Works (Vickers) Ltd and used as fishery and patrol machines by No. 1 Coastal Patrol Squadron, Irish Air Corps from Baldonnel Airfield, Dublin. The three had short careers; N19 crashed at Baldonnel on 18 September 1940 and the hull was damaged. The wings were fitted to N18, which had lain idle since it had also force-landed in the sea off Ballytrent, Co. Wexford, during delivery by Lieutenants Higgins and Quinlan. N18 was absconded on 1 September 1941 by four Irishmen who wanted to join the Luftwaffe and fight the British. They headed for Cherbourg in German-occupied France, but the aircraft was forced down by RAF Spitfires at RAF St Eval, Cornwall. The Irishmen and their aircraft were duly returned to Ireland unharmed. The third of the trio, N20, also crashed, on 3 September 1942, and was written off. The single survivor, N18, soldiered on, being assigned to the General Purpose Flight in 1944 and finally withdrawn from service on 8 August 1945. She was purchased by Aer Lingus Teo, becoming their EI-ACC. She was later bought by Wing Commander Rod Kellet, DSO, DFC, RAF, of No. 615 (County of Surrey) Squadron, Royal Auxiliary Air Force, in March 1947, being re-registered as G-AIZG and used as a hack at their base of Biggin Hill airfield, Greater London. She was sold for scrap at Thame, Oxfordshire, two years later. The wreck was rescued at a cost of £5 by the Historic Aircraft Preservation Society and restored as a static display at the Fleet Air Arm Museum, Yeovilton, Somerset, between 1963 and 1966.

The Turkish Government ordered six Seagull Vs for which they made outright purchase deal with the company, and these half-dozen were powered by the Pegasus engine. These replaced or reinforced their existing fleet of Supermarine Southampton flying boats (the Supermarine Type 221, later designated as the Scapa and the Type 227, which became the Stranraer- Type 304). All six arrived in 1938.

The dimensions of this type were a span of 45ft 10in (13.97m) and an overall length of 37ft 2in (11.35m) or 37ft 7 in (11.45m) on chassis, a height of 15ft 3 in (4.65m) with a wing area of 610 ft² (56.67m²). Maximum speed for these machines was 135mph (217 km/h) at 4,750ft (1,448m). The climb rate was a leisurely 1,050 ft/min (5.3m/s) with 12.5 minutes to an altitude of 10,000ft (5,639m) with a ceiling of 17,090 ft (2,210m). Weights were 4,900lb (2,233kg) empty; 7,200lb (3,266 kg) gross. The range was circa 600 miles (966km). Notable facts, often overlooked, were that the Walrus was the first British aircraft to enter squadron service with a fully retractable main undercarriage. It was also the first to have a completely glazed cockpit.

When the waves kicked up while taxiing and hit the hot 680hp (510kW) Bristol Pegasus engine the resulting steam cloud was often quite spectacular, earning her one of her many epithets, this one from Admiral Sir James Somerville, 'The Steam Pigeon'; other names included 'Ugly Duckling' (after an aviation magazine had described her as '…looking like a pregnant duck waddling down the runway…') and 'Flying Gas Ring' but generally she became known in the services simply under the fondly derogative name of 'Shagbat' for obvious visual reasons being in equal measure 'coarse, abundant and unkempt' (OED).

The light cruiser *Leander* was also transferred to the RNZN and carried a Walrus for a period. This was L2222, which was to have a very chequered history. She was assembled at Hobsonville in March 1938 joining *Leander* with No. 720 Flight. While aboard she conducted a series of Pacific Island aerial surveys later that same year. The loss of her catapult cradle forced her to operate from the sea only during periods of calm weather, but she surveyed Christmas Island on 24 November and later became part of No. 700 Squadron. She was not finally landed back ashore at Brisbane until 5 April 1942.

One of the first ships equipped with the Walrus was the light cruiser *Achilles* and she served in the Pacific pre-war and later was transferred to the Royal New Zealand Navy. At the time of the mysterious disappearance of the American woman aviator Amelia Earhart in her Lockheed 10-E Electra aircraft near Howard Island in the Pacific on 2 July 1937, the *Achilles* was steaming northward to the east of the Phoenix Islands and reported scrambled and unclear radio signals. However, the US authorities did not make any request for *Achilles* to join in the search, especially of Gardner Island, due, it was thought, to Roosevelt's obsession with possessing the nearby Canton Islands, ownership of which both the USA and Great Britain were in dispute over at the time, although they had been claimed for Great Britain since the early 19th-century.[4]

Wartime service

In the Royal Navy the Mk I joined the Catapult Flights and Squadrons of the British Battle Fleet and many cruisers, where they were utilized for gunfire spotting, target towing for AA practice (dangerous work for the target itself was rarely hit – hence the famous signal from towing plane to warship, 'I am pulling this bloody thing, not pushing it!'), and reconnaissance. By the outbreak of war there were 162 Walrus commissioned into the fleet and flying from shore bases. During the war years the Walrus was embarked as a catapult-launched aircraft on the following HM ships – the battleships *Anson, Barham, Duke of York, Howe, King George V, Malaya, Prince of Wales, Queen Elizabeth, Resolution, Rodney, Valiant* and *Warspite*; the battle-cruisers *Renown* and *Repulse*; the heavy cruisers *Berwick, Cornwall, Cumberland, Devonshire, Dorsetshire, Exeter, Kent, London, Norfolk, Shropshire, Suffolk, Sussex* and *York*, and the light cruisers *Ajax, Belfast, Bermuda, Birmingham, Ceylon, Edinburgh, Effingham, Fiji, Gambia, Glasgow, Gloucester, Jamaica, Kenya, Liverpool, Manchester, Mauritius, Newcastle, Newfoundland, Nigeria, Sheffield, Southampton, Trinidad* and *Uganda*.

The original Walrus I embarked aboard *Exeter* was K8542 originally delivered to the School of Naval Co-operation on 30 December 1936. She joined the *Exeter* on 1 March 1937 with No. 718 Squadron. By 28 June 1940 she had been loaned to the Australians and was serving aboard the light cruiser *Sydney* as replacement for A2-21, which had been damaged at Mersa Matruh. In September 1939 a solitary Walrus was embarked aboard the carrier *Ark Royal* with No. 820 NAS. During Operation *DX* off Norway in April/May 1940, *Ark Royal* had embarked five Walrus amphibians from No. 701 NAS, which embarked on June 7. On 12 May the carrier *Glorious* embarked six Walrus of No. 701 NAS and on 18 May flew them all ashore at Harstad where they remained throughout the campaign on a wide variety of duties.

On 31 October 1939 the first Walrus casualty of the war was L2261 (F9C) of No. 711 Squadron, piloted by Lieutenant S M Bird, with Lieutenant Cecil Henry Edward Osmaston and Leading-Airman William Henry Brown. She was working from the heavy cruiser *Sussex* in the Atlantic when lost.[5]

No. 701 Naval Air Squadron was formed on 24 May 1939 from No. 701 (Catapult) Flight FAA (itself the former No. 444 (Fleet Reconnaissance) Flight FAA) at Kalafrana, Malta. The unit returned to home waters and took part in the Norwegian campaign of 1940. Six Walrus aircraft were transported aboard the carrier *Glorious* off Greenock at 1300 on 12 May 1940 and transported ashore on 18 May to support operations at Harstad, northern Norway, under the command of Commander Robert Syme Denholm Armour, RN. These six machines were fully employed during the ill-fated Narvik campaign, flying anti-submarine patrols, escorting convoys, ferrying British and French high-ranking officials and officers to and fro and conducting communications operations, essential in northern Norway where roads were few and the mountainous terrain was difficult for any type of land operation. Amphibians were ideal for this type of warfare. In total, these Walrus aircraft carried out 250 sorties of various types and they continued in action until the very end in Norway. An attack by five Walrus with Hawker Hurricane fighter escort was mounted in the vicinity of Norfold on 6 June.

In fact the very last aircraft to take off from the carrier *Glorious* was a No. 701 Walrus, which had landed aboard with top secret communications at 0100 on 8 June. This Walrus departed at 0207 and later the *Glorious* ran into the German battle-cruisers

Gneisenau and *Scharnhorst* and she, and her accompanying destroyers, *Acasta* and *Ardent*, were all sunk by them with very few survivors.

Their final operation was a bombing attack by five Walrus on German troop positions and installations at Solfolla, north of Bodø on 6 June, following which the five survivors were re-embarked aboard the carrier *Ark Royal* for return to the United Kingdom when the Allies pulled out of Norway. No. 701 returned to the Mediterranean again and became attached to No. 201 Group, RAF, during Operation *Husky,* the invasion of Sicily, in July 1943. Later the squadron was based near Reykjavik, Iceland and was again re-embarked aboard the carrier *Argus* in October 1940.

On 18 May 1940, the Walrus from the heavy cruiser *Devonshire*, operating off Norway, was intercepted and shot down by a German He.111 bomber from the Luftwaffe's 1(F)/122, at Malangsfjord, Rysraumer. The pilot, Lieutenant Ronald William Benson Dare, was killed and Midshipman Anthony David Corkhill was wounded, but rescued, as was Leading Airman William Henry Hill, who later died later of his wounds.

Another casualty was a Walrus based at Sandbanks Royal Motor Yacht Club (HMS *Daedalus II*) on air-sea rescue service with Nos. 764 and 765 Squadrons, FAA, and crewed by Lieutenant Michael Covernton Hoskins and Lieutenant Thomas Essery Rose-Richards. This aircraft was shot into the sea by the Luftwaffe, south of Anvil Point, Swanage, on 7 October 1940.

Early highly secret trials took place with a pair of Walrus based at Lee-on-Sea, on the Solent, with experimental air-to-surface (ASV) radar sets. By 1942 the Type ASV Mk II radar had been added to their repertoire, the battleship *King George V* using one as late as November 1944. By this time the majority in service were employed in either the training role as a support aircraft, including 'Admirals Barges', distributed among twenty-nine second-line Fleet Air Arm Squadrons. The Royal Air Force also operated significant numbers of the Walrus in an air-sea rescue (ASR) profile, with the amphibian featuring on the establishment of twelve squadrons, and seeing service in the United Kingdom, the Mediterranean and the Indian Ocean area with South-East Asia Command (SEAC). The first such unit to receive the Walrus for this mission was No. 276 Squadron at Harrowbeer, Devon, and they operated the Walrus over the Channel between January 1942 and November 1945. More than a thousand Allied airmen were rescued after being forced to ditch at sea, mainly from RAF Bomber Command and the United States 8th Air Force, No. 277 Squadron being credited with a total of 598 such rescues alone.

While Seagull Vs were embarked in regular units of the Royal Australian Navy they were also flown from the requisitioned Armed Merchant Cruisers *Manoora* and *Westralia* for the first part of their career where they operated in the southern oceans. For a time one operated in company with the minesweeping sloop and survey vessel, *Warrego*. Three of these machines were damaged while flying with Royal Navy aircrew, A2-9, A2-21 and A2-24. The RAN also acquired thirty-seven former Royal Navy Walrus of both Marks, between 1939 and 1944. Among their operators was 71 Wing in the Admiralty Islands, Pacific. The Royal Canadian Navy also received the Walrus during the war having one Mk I and four Mk IIs transferred to it between 1939 and 1944, and, post-war, in 1946, took delivery of three more, a solitary Mk I and two Mk IIs. Similarly, the Royal New Zealand Air Force took delivery of nine Mk I Walrus and one Mk II in the 1943–44 period for use as training aircraft. The Walrus II, with her wood-composite hull and rubber-tyre tail-wheel, first appeared as re-builds of Mk Is by Supermarine but with hulls by SARO at Beaumaris on Anglesey. They were re-designated as X1045 and X1046 respectively and the first one flew on 2 May 1940. The former went to No. 754 Squadron and the latter to No. 700 Squadron.

These wooden-hulled aircraft utilized less-limited metal alloy resources, at a premium with the huge expansion of RAF Bomber Command, and had the bonus that they were deemed to have been more popular with their aircrews. Orders duly followed, with sixty-five being contracted for under B43393/39, and receiving serials in the range X9460 to X9558 inclusive. Deliveries of this batch commenced in March 1942, many of them being allocated to the Australians, one going to the heavy cruiser *Australia* in November of that year, and another to the AMC *Westralia*, while another (X9512) went to New Zealand. The RAF received the bulk of the rest. These were followed by a further thirty-five Mk IIs (serials X9559 to X9593 inclusive) under contract B43393/39, the first of which was delivered from July 1942 onward, mainly to the RAF's ASR units. Cowes also received two subsequent Mk II contracts before production was phased out, with fifty machines ordered under contract B119490/40 (serial Nos. Z1755–Z1823 inclusive) with deliveries commencing from September 1942; and 100 more under contract B19490/39, with serials HD837–HD936, being delivered from November 1942. These latter saw the end of the range and many of them survived into post-war usage before being scrapped between 1946 and 1947.

In total SARO built 190 of this type (one of which was destroyed at Cowes by Luftwaffe bombs). By the time they arrived the battleship and cruiser-carried catapult plane was starting its decline with the arrival of the first escort carrier, HMS *Audacity* in 1941. Several escort carriers did, in fact, carry the Walrus for periods, during the Operation *Dracula* strikes against Rangoon and the Tenasserim Coast the *Khedive* had one Walrus ASR as a detachment of No. 1700 NAS aboard, in April/May 1945, and during the same period *Empress* had another from the same unit during Operation *Bishop* airstrikes on the Nicobar and Andaman Islands. As ASR machines the British Pacific Fleet found them useful and the fleet carrier *Victorious* also had two Walrus aircraft on her establishment for that purpose as late as August 1945 and the strikes on the Japanese home islands.

In total, SARO built 490 of the 746 Walrus aircraft when production finally ceased in January 1944. The Walrus served with No. 700 Squadron, which was formed at Royal Naval Air Station Hatson, Orkney Islands (HMS *Sparrowhawk*) on 21 January 1940 by the amalgamation of all the 700 series Catapult Flights totalling forty machines. This Squadron survived until March 1944 before being disbanded. The Walrus also served with Nos. 701, 711, 712 and 714 Squadrons of the Royal Navy and also with Nos. 269, 275, 276, 277, 278, 281 and 282 RAF Squadrons based in Great Britain, and with Nos. 283, 284, 292 and 294 Squadrons RAF in the Middle East.

There were frequent silly accidents. On 16 August 1938, Walrus I L2177 of No. 711 Flight in the Mediterranean landed at Kalafrana, Malta, without a hatch being properly secured. The aircraft rapidly filled with water and sank. She was later salvaged by No. 102 MU and on 23 September 1940 joined the Australian light cruiser *Sydney* from Aboukir to replace the damaged K8542. She also served aboard the light cruiser *Glasgow* with No. 700 Squadron until that ship was badly damaged by torpedo bombers while at anchor in Suda Bay Crete, following which she returned to the *Sydney* on 1 March 1941.[6]

On Friday 23 December 1938, a Walrus from 714 Flight embarked aboard the light cruiser *Manchester* was landing close to Cochin Harbour, Ernakulam, Tavancore State, when it struck some telephone wires stretched across the backwaters of the harbour and crashed in the water, which was very shallow at this spot. The aircraft's nose broke off and was destroyed, and the pilot, Sub-Lieutenant (A) John Frederick Repington Collis, RN, and co-pilot, acting Sub-Lieutenant Peter Noble Boxer, RN, were both killed and Lieutenant Francis Myrddin Griffiths, RN, escaped with just a slight injury (*The Times*, 'British Seaplane Crash in India').

War service

One of the earliest Walrus casualties was K8556, of No. 754 Squadron, which crashed near Southampton in November 1939 killing two of the crew.

When France and the Low Countries threw in the towel in June 1940, the British Isles were closely besieged and the English Channel became the front line. German *Schnell-boots* (known to the Royal Navy as E-boats, as larger versions of our own MTB/MGBs) proved an increasing menace to coastal convoys operating from their bases in occupied France. Among the many defensive measures considered and trialled during this difficult period was the mounting of a 20mm Oerlikon cannon in the nose of a Walrus. However, this proved a step too far and was never adopted.

Off Dakar, Senegal, in West Africa and the Free French attempt to coerce the pro-German Vichy French forces to change sides in Operation *Menace*. This mission totally failed after two days of indecisive operations. One Walrus aircraft, L2247 piloted by Flight Lieutenant George John Isaih Clarke, RAAF, with Lieutenant Commander William Gove Fogarty, RAN and Petty Officer Telegraphist Colin Kenneth Bunnett embarked aboard the heavy cruiser *Australia*, spotting for the British battleships *Barham* and *Resolution* while bombarding Vichy forts, was intercepted by three French Curtiss Hawk 75A fighters, which shot her into the sea. Two of her crew were seen to have baled out successfully but all were killed.

Walrus K8542 from HMAS *Sydney* was employed as the spotter aircraft for a bombardment of the Italian air base at Makri Yalo, Rhodes, on 4 September 1940 by the light cruisers *Orion* and *Sydney* and destroyers *Dainty* and *Ilex*. This aircraft was later badly damaged in an accident at Mersa Matruh while operating ashore from RNAS *Aboukir* and taken into 103 MU being replaced by L2177.

A detachment from No. 700 Squadron was set up at Lews Castle, Stornoway, Isle of Lewis, and operated six Walrus aircraft from the slipway at Cuddy Point in the castle grounds (HMS *Mentor*). Two Walrus aircraft were lost here in an accident on 14 October 1940.

On 18 November 1940, a Walrus from the heavy cruiser *Devonshire* bombed Italian positions in Italian Somaliland during the Battle of Spartivento on 27 November 1940. As well as the battleship *Ramillies* and the battle-cruiser *Renown*, the British squadron had the heavy cruiser *Berwick* and four *Town* Class cruisers, *Sheffield, Manchester, Southampton* and *Newcastle* in line to oppose two Italian battleships and six heavy cruisers. Two of the *Towns* attempted to fly off their Walrus aircraft during the course of the action but, once more the speed with which the action developed and the wind conditions prevented any being launched before the gun duelling with the enemy commenced. The aircraft were on fixed, cross-deck type and not rotating catapults and this meant that the ship itself would have had to be turned, which was impracticable with a surface action impending. The *Sheffield* launched her aircraft prior to the action, but was not able to recover it until after the battle had ended for obvious reasons. The Walrus was retrieved, most efficiently, within six minutes.

In one of the rare occasions that the Walrus was used in her fleet bombardment 'spotter' role the light cruiser *Sheffield* launched her Walrus (K2228) off Genoa on 9 February 1941, Operation *Result*. Force 'H', under the command of Vice-Admiral Sir James Somerville, and comprising the battleship *Malaya*, the battle-cruiser *Renown* and the *Sheffield*, then conducted a ninety-minute bombardment of harbour installations and the port area. However, the observation was an all-round failure. The Italian battleship *Caio Duilio* was in dry-dock repairing the damage she had received at the earlier attack on Taranto, but the Walrus observers failed to spot her there and reported no Italian battleships present. Thus she escaped being targeted. Four Italian merchant ships were sunk and another eighteen damaged to varying degrees, the lighthouse was destroyed and the oil terminal was set ablaze. In fact most of the 15-inch gun salvoes landed in the water rather than on target and although it was good propaganda, little real damage was done other than yet another dent to Mussolini's pride.

A Walrus I, L2231, briefly joined the battleship *King George V* in 1941 but had been landed ashore at Arbroath in June 1941, after the *Bismarck* battle, and was involved in an accident with Lieutenant Thomas James Arthur RNVR as pilot that month.[7]

In the eastern Mediterranean in March 1941, the Italian fleet received another drubbing from the British Mediterranean Fleet at the Battle of Cape Matapan when three heavy cruisers and two destroyers were sunk without any British losses. The light cruiser *Gloucester* used her Walrus during the opening phases of the battle for scouting. The battleship *Barham* embarked L2293, a Walrus I that had previously served with Nos. 764 and 765 Squadrons at Lee-on-Solent and Sandbanks, but she was not aboard when the ship was torpedoed and sunk, also in the Eastern Mediterranean later that year, having been transferred to HMAS *Perth* on 5 June 1941. This machine briefly embarked aboard the heavy cruiser *Canberra* in exchange for L2322 but only until 27 November when she returned to the QANTAS Rose Bay depot until 17 December when she was damaged after a bad landing caused by engine failure. This machine briefly embarked aboard the heavy cruiser *Canberra* in place of L2322. On 27 November, however, she was damaged during a rough landing caused by engine failure and had to be returned to the QANTAS depot at Rose Bay for repairs, which lasted until 17 December. When repairs were complete she was re-embarked and continued operations. On 24 December she was again sent ashore to be refitted. On completion she joined HMAS *Westralia* on 27 August 1942 but again only briefly and was ashore at Rathmines again in September and never saw service afloat again.

The *Canberra* was served by a range of Walrus machines, having A2-22 replaced on 25 December 1940 with L2293, from the Far East Communications Flight, at Seletar, Singapore, which had been shipped to Australia aboard the freighter *Mangola* along with L2318. Both were badly damaged by heavy seas on 15 January 1941 and had to be landed at Colombo, Ceylon, for repairs, but these proved too extensive and they were scrapped. Between 15 January and 23 October 1941 the L2321 was carried, also, on 2 March 1941 *Canberra* embarked Walrus L2322, formerly aboard the *Westralia*. This aircraft was damaged several times by both weather and accidents. Finally, off Freemantle, she was wrecked by the blast from the ship's 4-inch AA guns during a practice sub-calibre shoot, while sitting with her wings spread on her catapult. She was landed ashore for repairs on 25 October 1941 and replaced by L2293. The L2327, first delivered to the FAA back on 24 May 1939, was also briefly embarked before transferring to HMAS *Australia* in January 1942. Likewise, W2768, a Walrus I delivered originally on 13 January 1942 to Lee-on-Solent, was transferred to Australia on 1 May 1942 at Rose Bay, NSW, with No. 9 Squadron. She embarked aboard *Canberra* on 15 May but was ashore again within the month to have ASV equipment fitted, after which she joined the *Australia* on 1 July 1942. *Canberra*'s final Walrus I was P5715, which had first flown on 19 April 1940 and gone into storage. She was transferred to the Australians on 1 May 1942 and assembled at Rathmine and then flew to RAAF Amberley, Queensland. She embarked aboard *Canberra* on 15 June 1942 and went down with that vessel when she was sunk by Japanese cruisers in the ghastly defeat of the Battle of Savo Island on 9 August.

At 0015 on 1 March 1942 HMAS *Perth* was sunk by Japanese surface forces off St Nicols Point, north-west Java in the aftermath of the Battle of Java Sea. Going down with her was her Walrus, which had been embarked in November 1941, ex-HMAS *Manoora* and HMAS *Canberra*, and its crew of five including fitters, only Flying Officer Allen Vernon 'Jock' McDonough and one other survived as POWs.

The heavy cruiser *Australia* also saw a large turn-over of Walrus aircraft during her war career.

A Walrus I, W2768, was embarked on 1 July 1942, to replace one that had only been aboard since 8 June but had been landed at Archerfield, but W2768 herself which was lost in an accident on 6 October. A Walrus I, W2705 built in March 1941 was transferred to No 9 Squadron RAAF on 15 April 1942 and embarked aboard *Australia* on 11 October. However, she was disembarked on 23 November, and was finally scrapped in 1948. Her replacement was to have been W2707 from the same batch, but she was never embarked and instead went to the RNZAF. X9516 took her place embarking on 24 November until another Walrus I, X9520 built in May 1942 and transferred to the RAAF in November, joined the *Australia* on 11 January 1943 when X9516 went ashore again. But the new machine only lasted one week, and on 18 January was disembarked at Townville for No. 9 Squadron. With them she crashed twice and was scrapped in May 1944. W2755, originally delivered to Lee-on-Sea in August 1941, was transferred to the RAAF on 1 May 1942 and joined the *Manoura* on the 26th. She was damaged by fire and repaired at QANTAS Rose Bay facility and joined the *Australia* from Townville on 19 January 1943. She was twice damaged in accidents and finally disembarked on 27 June 1943. Meantime X9513, which had been built in June 1942 and transferred to the RAAF in October, serving aboard the *Westralia* in November and December 1942, was embarked aboard *Australia* off Dunk Island on 8 April, replacing W2755. She was eventually transferred to No. 5CU and based at Horn Island on air-sea rescue work, being scrapped in May 1945. A Walrus II, received by the RAAF in April 1943, was collected from No. 9 Squadron at Bowen and embarked aboard *Australia* on 24 June. On 19 October she was damaged while being hoisted aboard after a mission and in December was disembarked to No. 9 Squadron once more, being returned to the Royal Navy in October 1945 aboard the maintenance carrier *Perseus* and later was embarked aboard the light fleet carrier *Vengeance*, where she was irreparably damaged by a Ford truck moving engines on the flight deck. On 17 April 1944, the *Australia* took aboard the HD812, a Walrus II built by SARO in February 1943, but she was flown ashore at Momote Island, Papua, New Guinea, just ten days later. She survived the war and was scrapped in 1948. The last Walrus II to serve aboard this heavy cruiser was HD860, built by SARO in May 1943 and transferred to the RAAF in September. She joined *Australia* on 19 December 1943. When the *Australia* had her catapult removed during a refit in March 1944, this Walrus remained being lowered into the water and hoisted out when required but this arrangement only remained in place until 2 April when she made her last flight. She went to *Warrego* for ASR work off Papua where she was christened 'Rescue Angel' by her crew. These details are included just to show the enormous attrition rate that the Walrus aircraft suffered, although actual loss through enemy action was comparatively rare.

Harking back to their work aboard the seaplane carrier *Albatross* earlier in the war, she had continued her deployment at Freetown and conducted frequent anti-submarine patrols from January 1940 through to May, when with the French capitulation and the adoption of Vichy-French collaboration policies, coupled with the earlier loss of the aircraft carriers *Courageous* and *Glorious,* her role became more important. In June she worked with the heavy cruiser *Devonshire* and continued to be Freetown-based on patrol and anti-submarine duties patrolling the West African trade routes.

A notable rescue mission by Walrus aircraft based on *Albatross* at this time occurred when on 14 January, the former Blue Star Line passenger vessel, the 7,472GRT *Eumaeus*, was torpedoed twice and then shelled 118 times and finally sunk by the Italian submarine *Commandante Cappellini* (Lieutenant Commander Salvatore Todaro) some

118 miles west of Cape Sierra Leone. Twenty-three of her complement and passengers were killed and sixty-eight left abandoned in shark-infested waters. Walrus P5667 of No. 710 Squadron located the enemy submarine and dropped two bombs, which exploded close alongside and caused internal damage. The crippled submarine left and received sanctuary from fellow Fascist dictator Franco's forces at La Ruz, Grand Canaria, finally being repaired sufficiently to reach her base at Bordeaux, France, safely. Meanwhile the Walrus, although only having sufficient fuel to return to base, landed on the sea in a position about 120 miles west of Freetown, in order to aid survivors. Lieutenant Cheesman gave aid to men in the water, and then swam for two empty lifeboats drifting nearby for them to reach safety. Eventually the trawler *Spaniard* came out from Freetown and towed the Walrus back to base. For their humanitarian work Lieutenant Vernon Beauclerk George Cheeman, Royal Marines, was awarded the MBE, Sub-Lieutenant Walter Claude Broadburn a Mention in Despatches (MID) and Chief Petty Officer Donald William Dale was awarded the British Empire Medal (BEM). Cheesman was later drafted to the heavy cruiser *Cornwall* as her Walrus pilot, only to be sunk in the Indian Ocean by Japanese Navy dive-bombers in April 1942; he survived after many hours in the sea and went on to a distinguished career in the Fleet Air Arm.

By February 1941 the tired old engines of the *Albatross* required refitting. She sailed for the Simonstown Navy Base, South Africa, for emergency repairs, which enabled her to continue on until the autumn. But her state required a more comprehensive refit and in November she sailed to the port of Mobile, Alabama, in the United States to be refitted under Lend-Lease, and this lasted until March 1942.

The *Albatross* emerged in April and, after trials, sailed back to Freetown once more. Meantime the Japanese had been running riot in the Indian Ocean and she was transferred to the East Indies Station in May 1942. She therefore sailed on 3 May as part of the escort for troop convoy WS18, along with the light cruiser *Gambia* and destroyer *Tetcott*, from Freetown to the Cape of Good Hope. The *Albatross* was detached and rejoined the convoy later with the cruiser *Frobisher* and later the battleship *Resolution*, finally leaving it on 30 May for trade defence duties in the Indian Ocean. Japanese long-range submarines had been sinking Allied merchant ships in the Mozambique Channel with impunity and Operation *Throat* was launched in a belated attempt to stop their work. *Albatross*, along with two Eastern Fleet destroyers, *Foxhound* and *Griffin*, were deployed to the base of Ile Mayote, north-west of Madagascar for her Walrus aircraft to work alongside four Catalina PBY seaplanes and patrol the area. It was a case of shutting the stable door because the bulk of these submarines had withdrawn from the area, and the operation was quickly abandoned once this became apparent. However, German U-boats took over and were extremely active in the approaches to the Gulf of Aden and then later, off the Cape where they sank eleven ships.

Back in the Far East No. 1430 Flight based in Hong Kong had two Walrus aircraft on its strength in December 1941, L2259 and L2819, and these were overwhelmed in the fall of the colony on 25 December.

Although under Operation *Ironclad* earlier, the principal Vichy-French bases had been occupied by the British to cease their co-operation with the Japanese, it was decided that the rest of that large island should also be occupied and, under Operation *Streamline*, the carriers *Illustrious* and the *Albatross* were assigned as air cover units for Force 'M' a powerful Royal Navy force comprising the monitor *Erebus*, light cruisers *Birmingham, Caradoc, Dauntless* and *Gambia*, minelayer *Manxman* and twelve destroyers formed to carry out this operation. The *Gambia's* Walrus patrolled off Diego Suarez on the 10th as the invasion commenced, and *Albatross* supplied others. Between November 1942 and July 1943 *Albatross* refitted extensively at Durban and then Bombay and then returned to the UK arriving at Devonport in September, disembarking her Walrus complement and being converted into a repair ship.

The heavy cruiser *Exeter* had been equipped with two Walrus aircraft pre-war, K8341 and K8343, the former of which later transferred to her sister ship, *York*. From the spring of 1938 this first pair was replaced by two more Walrus machines, K8556 and K8560, and the latter she carried into the war along with K8557. The light cruiser *Ajax* had a Fairey Seafox embarked. Her sister ship HMNZS *Achilles* and she were equipped with the Walrus in April 1936 (K5774), which served for two years returning to the UK with her in 1938. Her replacement, K5783, was lost in 300 fathoms off Aitutaki on 15 July 1939, after falling from the recovery crane. A third Walrus from No.720 Squadron took her place, L2241, which embarked on *Achilles* in 1938. This machine, in turn, capsized and sank while taxiing on take-off in the Indian Ocean near Aden on 1 April 1939 and never reached New Zealand. Apparently a replacement was due to be shipped out to Panama for her to collect but she never made it there and she therefore went into the battle with no aircraft at all embarked. The Walrus aircraft aboard the heavy cruiser *Exeter* during this battle was damaged by the *Admiral Graf Spee* and had to be ditched before she could be launched on 13 December. At 0623 an 11-inch shell, not a direct hit but one that fell short of the *Exeter*, sent many splinters inboard, which completely wrecked the Walrus then being prepared for launching. Her fuel system was punctured and avgas leaked out across her decks and the aircraft was promptly ditched. The two light cruisers fired a total of 2,065 6-inch shells of which between 90 and 95 scored hits, a success rate of just under 5 per cent. Had the *Achilles* had her Walrus embarked and had *Ajax's* Fairey Seafox not been rendered ineffective through faulty R/T communications this hit rate would probably have been far higher; but in truth 6-inch shells made little impression on *Graf Spee's* armoured hide. The *Achilles* finally received her replacement aircraft (NZ152 ex-L2236 from No 712 Squadron) in 1941. The *Ajax* subsequently received Walrus L2243 but this aircraft was involved in a collision with Seagull V A2-17 at Candia, Crete on 12 January 1941 and replaced her aboard the Australian light cruiser *Perth* on the 12th of that month, returning to the Royal Navy on 7 April. She was sent into storage on 30 December 1943.

On 4 November 1939 the Australian light cruiser *Hobart* exchanged her A2-23 for former Royal Navy No.715 Flight Walrus I L2171 from Singapore and later that month this aircraft conducted a photo-mosaic of Bombay (Mumbai), India. She remained aboard until 6 June when she, in turn, was landed ashore at RAF Khormaksar, Aden and replaced by L2321. The former returned to Seletar, Singapore in April 1941 and later served with No. 788 Squadron at Mombasa.

Italy entered the war on the side of Germany on 10 June 1940 and the Walrus soon saw action against them. On 6 June the Australian light cruiser *Hobart* embarked Walrus L2321 from Khormaksar, Aden. On 19 June Walrus L2321 from the *Hobart,* flown by Flight Lieutenant Thomas Davies, *dive-bombed* (!) the Italian wireless station ashore on Centre Peak Island, north-west of Al Hudaydah, Aden, in the southern part of the Red Sea. The aircraft was catapulted in position 15 degrees 33'N, 41 degrees 26'E and the attack was made at 0604. Four 112lb bombs were dropped on W/T huts, one being destroyed and the other damaged. Four 20lb bombs were dropped on a concrete pier but although direct hits were obtained, little damage was observed. On completion, the aircraft proceeded to Kamaran Island, off the coast of Yemen, where she refuelled and returned to Aden.[8] On 20 June the same aircraft conducted anti-submarine patrols and two days later made a coastal reconnaissance flight from Ras-el-Bir to The Brothers. She was also dispatched to assist in the hunt for the Italian submarine *Evangelista Torricelli* sunk off Perim Island on 22 June by the destroyers *Kandahar* and *Kingston*, but took no part in its destruction. The Walrus had been damaged by the blast of the ships anti-aircraft guns during an Italian air raid and plans were made to land her at Obstruction Pier for repairs when the ship next docked at Aden. The aircraft was still able to operate and between 24 and 30 June carried out further anti-submarine patrolling. The Walrus was disembarked overnight ashore at Berbera, British Somaliland, on occasions. Here the tiny British garrison was in retreat from superior Italian forces so it was a risky business. On 8 August, at 0317, three Italian CR.42 fighters made an audacious strafing attack on the airfield there and destroyed one Gloster Gladiator fighter and damaged another. It was thought aboard *Hobart*, that these attackers had come from Zeila, the Italian HQ, and the Walrus was catapulted off to make a bombing raid there in the hope of catching the enemy on the ground while refuelling. However, on arrival over the target no enemy fighters were seen at Zeila. A pair of 112lb bombs was released from 800 feet, which unfortunately fell some forty yards short of the Italian Residency. The Walrus circled the town three times at an altitude of just 250 feet, repaying them in kind by machine-gunning the Residency and several Italian machine-gun posts before returning safely to *Hobart* at 0700.[9] The final duty for this Walrus was to make a reconnaissance of the Berbera plain while the British evacuated. She was duly disembarked at Aden, as planned, but strong winds damaged her wingtips while secured at Obstruction Pier and she had to be sent to Khormaksar for them to be repaired. By 30 August she had resumed anti-submarine patrols.

Her adventures were far from over and, on 5 September, while *Hobart* was escorting a convoy, she was attacked five times by Japanese high-level bombers. They failed to score any hits, as usual, but the ship's Walrus, sitting on her catapult, was damaged by the blast of her own anti-aircraft guns. Fourteen mainplane ribs were damaged as was one of her tailplane ribs, and every rib in her rudder was distorted. After stripping the machine down she was flown to Khormaksar to have these all replaced, which work was completed on 7 September. The Walrus flew patrols from Khormaksar until 12 October when she re-embarked. She continued patrols in the Red Sea and Indian

Ocean area through to December, hunting enemy armed merchant raiders. Eventually *Hobart* returned home and on 28 December L2321 was disembarked to RAAF Pearce and was then re-embarked aboard the heavy cruiser HMAS *Canberra* on 15 January 1941 when she returned to Colombo. She was eventually returned to the Fleet Air Arm on 23 October. She spent time at RNAS Puttlam, Ceylon, and finished her days at RNAS Gan, Addu Atoll, in 1943/44.

Meanwhile, on 29 November 1940 the Walrus (NZ151 ex-L2222) on loan from the Fleet Air Arm since June 1938, and embarked aboard the light cruiser *Leander,* carried out an attack on Banda Abula, in Italian Somaliland. This machine later served with the Seaplane Training Flight RNZAF as Z4, at Hobsonville between November 1944 and June 1945 and was returned to the Royal Navy in September 1945.[10]

Among the five confirmed enemy submarines that were destroyed by the action of Walrus aircraft during the war was the Vichy-French *Poncelet* (Q-141). Under the command of Lieutenant Pierre Henri Septimes Bertrand De Saussine De Pont Gault, she supported the pro-Nazi forces in resisting the Free French under General Charles de Gaulle who were seeking to liberate Gabon and Libreville, and she attacked a troop convoy fifty miles south-west of Gabon, hitting the sloop *Milford* with a torpedo. The missile failed to detonate and she was in turn bombed by Walrus L23268 of No. 700 Squadron from the heavy cruiser *Devonshire* and subsequently attacked with depth-charges by the *Milford,* being so damaged that she was forced to surface and surrender. This submarine was subsequently scuttled off the Gulf of Guinea on 9 November, her commander going down with his ship. The Walrus crew, Sub-Lieutenant Anthony David Corkhill, Midshipman (A) Peter Henry Parsons and Naval Airman Andrew Evans, all received gallantry awards for this mission.

On 23 May 1941, Walrus L2184 of No. 700 Squadron, aboard the heavy cruiser *Norfolk,* was damaged on her catapult by shellfire from the German naval squadron comprising the battleship *Bismarck* and heavy cruiser *Prinz Eugen.*

The heavy cruiser *London* had Walrus R6543 of No. 700 Squadron embarked and, on 3 October 1941, they were escorting a convoy of war supplies to the Soviet Union when a submarine was sighted. No friendly units had been reported in the area and the Walrus, crewed by Sub-Lieutenants David James Chaplin and Oliver Murphy Cairns, with Leading Airman H W Barrett, attacked, dropping depth-charges, but to no avail. It was later revealed that their target had been a Soviet submarine well out of position and she survived.

Off Malaya when the battleship *Prince of Wales* along with the battle-cruiser *Repulse,* were attacked and sunk by Japanese Navy torpedo-bombers, the Walrus of No. 700 Squadron, with Petty Officers William Thomas J Crozier and Stephen Damerell, along with Telegraphist Air Gunner (TAG) Mervyn F A Rose as crew, embarked aboard the *Repulse* had earlier located the Japanese invasion barges and, on return, had been an impotent witness to the destruction of the two British capital ships. She later ran out of fuel and landed at sea. The destroyer *Stronghold* had to be sent out from Singapore and found her 60 miles out and towed her back to the dockyard on 10 December. She later joined the Anti-Submarine unit based at Seletar on 18 December.

The repaired heavy cruiser *Exeter* had a Walrus of No 700 Squadron embarked on 13 January, while based in Java with the British, American and Dutch cruiser squadron in 1942. On 30 January during a Japanese air attack on the ship, this machine was hit in both wings and rendered inoperational. She was dumped ashore for repairs at the port of Batavia before *Exeter* sailed on her final battle missions and this Walrus survived the Japanese invasion reaching Colombo, Ceylon, aboard a coaster that ran the gauntlet and arrived safely on 4 March.

The Royal New Zealand Navy was formed in October 1941. Both the New Zealand-manned light cruisers *Achilles* and *Leander* were based at Auckland and worked with Australian and American cruisers in escorting convoys in the south Pacific area while the Japanese tide swept toward that area. But both vessels had the Walrus aircraft and all facilities landed ashore and replaced by extra anti-aircraft weapons at this time.

The Soviet Union became another unlikely recipient of the Walrus, when P5706 was lent to them under the terms of Lend-Lease in 1942, taking passage to Murmansk as deck cargo aboard the freighter *Ocean Freedom*. She was later damaged in an accident and transferred to the 16 Air Transport Detachment and was never returned to the UK.

Also in 1942 the final confirmed enemy submarine sinking was scored by Walrus W2709 belonging to No. 700 (Levant) Squadron, crewed by Lieutenant Dennis John Cook, Sub-Lieutenant Peter Alan Jordan and Leading Airman P Garrett-Reed, which attacked a U-boat east of Cyprus in the eastern Mediterranean. The submarine, which turned out to be the Italian *Ondina*, which had been implicated in the sinking of the neutral Turkish vessel *Refah* with the loss of 160 lives, was damaged and subsequently finished off by the South African sloop *Protea* and trawler *Southern Maid*.

In addition to the predations of enemy action, accidents kept occurring with the Walrus, one of the most tragic being that which befell the *Australia*'s Walrus, L2327, of No. 9 Squadron, piloted by Flight Lieutenant Edward James Rowan, near the Santa Cruz Island, Solomons, on 19 February 1942, as recorded by Midshipman Dacre Henry Deudraeth Smyth aboard her at the time, and cited in the book of her life.[11]

Shortly before noon, and after circling until we were ready to pick him up, the Walrus came down to land on the 'slick'. Owing to some as yet unknown cause, he came in too close to the ship and crashed into the ship's port quarter just above the water line, breaking up and bursting into flames immediately. The second whaler as crash boat was immediately lowered and the first whaler was also sent away as a lifeboat. A motor surf boat from *Chicago* reached the spot where the aircraft had sunk first and succeeded in saving the observer, Sub Lt Robert Joseph Jackson, and the air gunner. Flying Officer E.J. Rowan RAAF, the pilot, was not seen. While the boats were away, an air alarm was received and the ship went to 'Repeal Aircraft' stations. Both whalers were hoisted at 1220, the two survivors having been transferred from *Chicago*'s boat. Fortunately no enemy aircraft were sighted.

An official ANZAC naval enquiry on 26 March came to the conclusion that the waist safety belt failed to prevent Rowan's head striking the instrument panel and knocking him unconscious, causing the resulting collision and his inability to escape the sinking aircraft.

A particularly nasty incident took place with X9559, a Walrus II that had served briefly aboard the battleship *Howe* between 13 October and December 1942 before being handed over to Australia on 19 January 1944. She joined No. 5 CU on 11 June and just two days later she rescued the two-man aircrew from an RAAF Vultee Vengeance dive-bomber, which had come down in the sea in Princess Charlotte Bay, Queensland. She was involved in a minor accident but was exchanged for L2322 with No. 8 CU on 15 August with an aircrew from Bowen. On 25 October 1944, she was dispatched to conduct a reconnaissance of the New Guinea coast near Wewak, and had an Australian Bristol Beaufort as fighter escort for the mission. Captain Evetson of 1 Air Liaison was embarked, and his mission was to see what Japanese opposition remained on Karaka Island (Paris Island), in the Kairiru Strait off Cape Kerewop. Watched by the Beaufort aircrew, the Walrus landed in the sea close to the island and two men, Pilot Officer Walter Burford Bernie and Captain Morris Glen Evetson AIF, lowered the dinghy and paddled ashore. On the way in they met a native in a canoe and asked him whether there were any Japanese left on the island. They were told there were none, but this was a lie and a trap. On landing, they were shot from ambush, wounded and taken prisoner. The Japanese then paddled out to the aircraft where they shot and wounded the pilot, before setting the Walrus on fire and destroying it totally. Warrant Officer Joseph Merrick Tomors Brown RAAF died a few days later from sickness and wounds. This incident was later the subject of a Japanese War Crimes Trial.

In August 1944 a Walrus was reported as serving aboard the escort carrier *Stalker* off Malacca, while a Walrus I, W3085, formerly embarked aboard the light cruiser *Gambia*, piloted by Royal Australian Air Force Pilot Officer Bruce Ada, took part in the last rescue operation of World War II on 10 August 1945. Along with two other Australian ASR specialists, Ada had been transferred to the British Pacific Fleet during the Okinawa campaign and the final drive on Japan. They had embarked aboard the carrier *Illustrious* and, at the vast Manus anchorage, Ada had transferred to the carrier *Victorious*. She had two Walrus aircraft aboard, which she christened 'Darby' and 'Joan' and Ada flew 'Darby', W3085. On that day a New Zealand fighter pilot with the FAA, Pilot Officer Derick Morton, had been forced to ditch and his companions had sent out a 'Mayday' signal and Ada was dispatched *post-haste* to the rescue. While still *en route* to the scene, however, an American submarine, the *Petro*, had surfaced and rescued Morton. When 'Darby' arrived the US submarine commander, never having seen such a weird and wonderful aircraft in all his life, immediately submerged, thinking that it was so odd it just had to be Japanese. Consequently Ada patrolled up and down searching for Morton until he was dangerously low on fuel and on his return to the fleet, he was, in turn, forced to ditch though an engine fire. Ada and his crew were rescued but W3085 was beyond help and was shelled by a couple of British destroyers and put under.[12]

Just about the last operational Fleet Air Arm Walrus II was still serving at Eastleigh as late as 9 September 1947.

Some sources state that a total of 744 Walrus aircraft were completed. William Green gave this number, which he broke down as 287 built by Supermarine and 453 by SARO, reduced by four aircraft that were destroyed in German bombing attacks prior to delivery.[13] Bruce Robertson also gives this as the final total, but gives a different breakdown, 278 built by Supermarine and 462 by SARO.[14] Owen Thetford has a totally conflicting total, citing 746 completed, with 285 built by Supermarine and 461 by SARO.[15] Other sources state that a total of 746 Walrus aircraft were completed, 555 Mk I and 191 Mk II.

As numbers of carrier-borne aircraft dramatically increased in the period 1942–45, the need for such machines rapidly faded away and despite all the enormous effort put into battleship and cruiser designs to accommodate them in the pre-war and early war years, their hangars, complicated equipment and highly vulnerable (and much disliked) fuel storage facilities had all been done away with by the end of the war and the space utilized as cinemas, extra AA guns and similar equipment. The same applied to the few surviving Australian ships; by 1944 Walrus aircraft no longer featured on RAN cruisers and No. 9 Squadron was disbanded.

A former No. 701 Squadron Walrus, W3012, based at Beirut, Lebanon, with Lieutenant Reginald David Pursall, RN, Flight Lieutenant Henry Withy, RAF and Flight Lieutenant P Garrett-Reed, RAF, were detached to the Sea rescue Flight at Hal Far airfield, Malta. In a rescue carried out just five miles off the coast of Sicily on 20 March 1943, she was attacked by a Bf.109, but escaped with just a damaged float. Not deterred by this narrow escape, on 18 April 1943 this aircraft and team saved four Vickers Wellington bomber crew adrift between the Italian garrison islands of Lampedusa and Pantellaria, and landed them at St Paul's Bay, Malta.

The Walrus for air-sea rescue work began to be phased out from 1944 onward, being largely replaced by the Sea Otter. No. 269 Squadron still flew Walrus aircraft from RAF Davidstowe Moor, near Camelford, Cornwall, between January and March 1944. However, uses continued to be found for this aircraft and No. 624 Squadron re-commissioned at Grottaglie, Italy in December 1944, under the command of Squadron Leader Gerald Michael Gallagher, being employed as 'mine-spotters' in the Adriatic off the coasts of Italy and Greece. These Mk I Walrus aircraft were also operated from Falonara, Foggia, Hassani, Littorio, Rosignano, Sedes, Treviso and Hal Far, Malta. One even made an 'unauthorized' landing on the Grand Canal in Venice! The Squadron was finally disbanded in November 1945. One would have thought that the Walrus was sufficiently unique a bird not to be attacked by one's own forces, but nothing can deter Americans in full 'gung-ho' mode. On 20 April 1944, at Cutella, Italy, squadrons of Australian Kittyhawks and Mustangs were lined up and were being refuelled when they were strafed repeatedly by four Republican P-47 Thunderbolt fighter-bombers. Several fighters were burnt out and among the casualties was an ASR Walrus, whose pilot was killed in the attack.

Post-war the Egyptian Navy took delivery of a Mk II Walrus, W3016 (as N3016), in September 1945.

The London branch of the Niels Ronald Bugge, Tonsberg, whaling company, Hector Whaling, under the United Whalers Ltd, London, flag purchased three Walrus-Is post-war and used them as route spotters during the 1946/47 Antarctic whaling season operating from the 1946-built fish factory ship *Balaena*, which had a war-surplus catapult fitted for the purpose. The three were fitted with covered dinghies, tents, immersion suits, emergency rations, and signalling equipment. They were overhauled and refitted by SARO and named as *Boojom* (G-AHFM), *Moby Dick* and *Snark* in a ceremony at East Cowes, but the Americans refused permission for them to use any American homing radio system. They were in the charge of John Grierson.[16] They ended their days on a dump at Cowes, Isle of Wight, in 1949. Similarly another whaling outfit, the Netherlands Whaling Company, the last such Dutch-based organization, embarked the Walrus for similar purposes, but these were never actually used on operations. This company later adopted helicopters for the job but ceased trading in 1964.

Walrus HD874 of No. 9 Squadron was put into storage between 1943 and 1947 before being renovated by QANTAS, her wooden hull being replaced by the steel hull of A2-20 held in store there since 1946. Work was done by Rathmines Maintenance Squadron and the composite aircraft became the RAAF Antarctic Flight's *Snow Goose* in October. Under the auspices of the Department for External Affairs she saw service from Heard Island with the Australian Antarctic Research Expedition but only made a single flight before being damaged in a storm on 21 December 1947 with winds gusting above 120mph.[17] She was stripped and abandoned but was recovered by the Department of Transport vessel *Cape Pillar* thirty-three years later taken to Point Cook and restored from 2001 onward.[18]

Eric McIlree, an Australian entrepreneur, acquired four aircraft, VH-BGP, the former Seagull V A2-3, and VH-ALB and VH-BLP, both ex-RAF Walrus, plus X9519, which never received any civilian registration. They operated for Amphibious Airways, a company he set up to transport workers between New Guinea and New Britain and operated from Rabaul for a period along with some old Avro Ansons in charter and air ambulance work. The company was involved in several accidents and ceased trading in 1954. All McIlree's Seagull and Walrus aircraft were burnt at Camden in order to save hangar space, although some parts survived and were sold to Squadron Leader Peter Gibbes MVO, DFC, AFC, RAAF to help in the restoration of A2-4.

The final Walrus to serve actively in the Royal Navy lingered until 1956, this being P5656 originally ordered under the 1939 contract B974377/39 from Vickers-Supermarine Woolston. She ended her days incongruously about as far from the sea as she could be being scrapped at Birmingham in 1956.

Survivors

1. Walrus L2301, ex-Irish N18, is at the Fleet Air Arm Museum, Yeovilton, Somerset. Served with Irish Air Corps and sold post-war until abandoned at Haddenham airfield. It was recovered in 1963 by the Historic Aircraft Society and presented to the Fleet Air Arm Museum who restored her between 1964 and 1966 for exhibition.
2. A Seagull V is at the RAF Museum, Hendon, London. It is a 1934-built aircraft sent to No. 101 Flight RAAF in 1936 and flew from the light cruiser *Sydney* and

No. 9 Squadron until 1946. Post-war, it had a succession of civilian owners until acquired by the RAF Museum in 1973 and restored at RAF Henlow, Beds, for display at Hendon since 1979.

3. Supermarine Seagull Mk V A2-4/VH-ALB, HD874, is at the RAAF Museum, Point Cook, Victoria, Australia.

4. W2718 (G-RNLI) is at Vintage Fabrics, Audley End Airfield, Saffron Walden, Essex. This is mainly a fuselage that was once made into a caravan, with other parts from the same aircraft, including pieces of wings, plus new-build material, and was partly restored at Great Yarmouth by Dick Melton, former head engineer at the Charles Church Collection, Popham, Hampshire. She is still currently under restoration.

Chapter Seventeen

Vickers Vildebeest and Vincent

T he contrast between the RAF's equipment provided by the British Government for the defence of Malaya and Singapore and the opposing Imperial Japanese Navy Air Force's aircraft committed to their conquest could not have been starker. Nothing illustrated the self-congratulatory complacency of the colonial rulers and their political masters in Whitehall more than the disparity of these aerial forces. Nor could the difference in priorities have been clearer. While Churchill was obsessed with bombing German cities into dust and supplying the Soviet Union with modern aircraft[1] the British Empire in the Far East was to be defended with Brewster Buffalo fighter aircraft (which, when flown against the Japanese Mitsubishi Zero amounted to legalized and authorized suicide – not my words but those of a US Marine Corps fighter pilot at the Battle of Midway); while to attack the Japanese invasion fleet offshore an unwieldy and already long-obsolete RAF torpedo-bomber was sent on missions doomed to failure, while sleek, long-range and superbly trained Japanese Navy land-based aircraft summarily dealt with the battleship *Prince of Wales* and battle-cruiser *Repulse,* with minimal loss. The total bankruptcy of British defence planning between the wars was typified by this British military machine, the Vickers Vildebeest.

The origins of this aircraft date back to Air Ministry Specification 24/25, which originally requested a high-altitude bomber as a successor to the Hawker Horsley. How this requirement morphed into totally the opposite type of plane, a low-level torpedo-bomber and army co-operation aircraft, was a complex story but that is how it transpired. Air Ministry Specification 23/25 of the same date had called for a day bomber, reconnaissance aircraft and torpedo-bomber, for which the Gloster Goring, Handley Page HP 34 Hare, Hawker Harrier and Westland Witch all became unsuccessful contenders while Vickers product was selected for the role instead.

The Vickers company, which had achieved fame through their Vimy bomber, one of which had made the very first transatlantic aerial crossing with the British aviators Captain John Alcock and Lieutenant Arthur Whitten Brown in June 1919,[2] submitted their design, the Type 132 in June 1926, which resulted in a Air Ministry contract for a single experimental machine.

The airframe was constructed at Vickers Weybridge, Surrey, plant and was completed early in 1928. The maiden flight took place from nearby Brooklands in April of that year. It was a large biplane machine, with open, stepped-down aft, cockpits and of parallel and equal rectangular wing form, with wires and struts lacking any grace and resembling an up-scaled Vendace or Vixen. The airframe was of all-metal construction with fabric covering and it had a crew of two. Its power plant was initially to have been the supercharged Bristol Orion engine built around the Jupiter VI with supercharging by James Edwin Ellor at the RAE. This was still under development, and, although it was trialled once in a Gloster Gamecock, cooling and distortion problems caused the Air Ministry to shelve it in the end. While it was still a contender, however, the Jupiter VI was intended as an interim power plant. On 17 November the Air Ministry loaned Vickers a 460hp geared Jupiter VIII engine but this too had overheating and vibration problems and its successor, the Jupiter X1F, fitted to the first prototype as the Type 194, Series III, proved little or no better, and nor was the Series IV with the same power plant as the Type 209.

A second prototype was built as a private venture by Vickers and appeared in 1930. This was the Type 204, and this was powered by yet another alternate engine, the air-cooled Armstrong-Siddeley Panther IIA. She went to the Air Ministry as the Series IV. Yet again it suffered from over-heating difficulties, which lessened the aircraft's already poor performance. This second prototype should have been converted to a Series VII specification as the Type 217, but this was never done.

Finally, in January 1931, the problem was partially solved with the introduction of the 580hp Bristol Jupiter VIII radial engine, which was originally the Cosmos Jupiter designed by Roy Fedden of Cosmos Engineering, a company absorbed by the Bristol Company post-war after bankruptcy and which was developed by them and Fedden through several marks and introduced the first mechanically driven supercharger. The Mark VIII was also the first to be fitted with reduction gearing and developed 440hp (330kW). The Vickers design had two main rivals for the original specification shortlisted by the Air Ministry, the Blackburn Beagle and the Handley Page HP 34 Hare, but in the end trials conducted on 14 September 1928 at Martlesham Heath, Suffolk, went against the Beagle and the Vildebeest prevailed.[3]

Thus the Vildebeest, and the General Purpose Bomber variant developed from her, the Vickers Vincent, were the preferred Air Ministry choices. The initial Air Ministry production order was placed for a total of nine aircraft in 1931, her role being finalized as a torpedo-bomber/army co-operation aircraft. Engines problems continued, despite this, and the Jupiter was developed through the Mercury to the Pegasus, which became the final choice of power plant for later batches of the Vildebeest.

As the Type 244 the first production aircraft made her maiden flight in September 1932 fitted with the Bristol Pegasus IM3 engine, which developed 660hp (448kW). The standard details for the Vildebeest 1 were a crew of two, an armament of one single .303 (7.7mm) Vickers fixed forward-firing machine-gun shooting through the propeller arc, and one .303 (7.7mm) flexible rearward-firing Scarff-ring mounted Lewis gun. The wingspan was 49ft (14.94m), the overall length was 36ft 8in (11.18m) and it had a height of 14ft 8in (4.47m). The wing area was 728sq/ft (67.6sq/m). The empty weight was 4,229lb (1918.24kg) and fully laden 8,100lb (3674.89kg). The maximum speed was 140mph (225.31 km/h) with a climb rate of 630ft/min (3.20m/s). The service ceiling was 19,000ft (5,791.20m) and its range was 1,250 miles, with a 1,100lb (500kg) bomb load of a single 18-in (457mm) torpedo, held at an angle on a crutch between the two legs of the ungainly, spatted, landing gear beneath the fuselage. A total of twenty-two of this type were produced up to 1933, all going to the RAF. One aircraft was fitted with the Jupiter XFBM engine as the Type 214 for testing and when this power plant was re-designated as the Pegasus 1M3 and lubricated with a mineral-based engine lubricant, in 1934, it became the Type 263. The improved 635hp (474kW) Pegasus IIM3 engine was fitted in the Type 258 variant, of which thirty were constructed for the RAF, joining squadron service in 1935 as the Mark II.

Vincent

In 1931 Vickers had designed a general purpose adaptation of the Vildebeest as a private venture, which it hoped would replace both the existing Westland Wapiti Army Support aircraft and the Fairey IIIF type then in service. An existing Vildebeest I was so adapted to this design in the period 1932/33. The modifications simply effected, the torpedo-mounting gear was removed and a long-range auxiliary fuel tank was fitted in its place. Provision was made for a third crew member and extra survival and navigation equipment was carried including collapsible long-range radio masts, ground radios, message retrieval hooks, pyrotechnics, personnel sleeping bags etc. To allow for the extra weight, the Bristol Pegasus IIM3 radial, developing 660hp (490kW) was mounted. Trials and evaluation flights were made in Africa and the Middle East and, when these proved satisfactory, the Air Ministry Specification 16/24 was initiated for further conversions and limited production of the new Type 266, named the Vickers Vincent. Over a three-year period, between 1934 and 1936 a total of 197 Vincent aircraft were either converted from Vildebeest Is or built from scratch. The ability of the Vincent to take off in under 400 yards made it the ideal colonial policing aircraft for the more primitive regions of the Empire.

When the first Vincent went into squadron service it was with No. 84 Squadron at Shaibah, Iraq, in December 1934 and within three years this variant was standard equipment with six squadrons in the region, and six more at home, Nos. 5, 8, where it replaced the Fairey IIIF at Khormaksar, Aden, in February 1935 and still retained eight on its strength in September 1939. The Vincent served as the main workhorse pre-war with No. 45 Squadron, where from 1935 it operated alongside Hawker Hart and Fairey Gordon light bombers in Iraq and Palestine, No. 55 Squadron in Iraq between 1937 and March 1939 when it was replaced by the Bristol Blenheim, No. 84 Squadron which operated a mixed Vildebeest and Vincent strength from Shaibah, Iraq between December 1934 and February 1939 when it began to receive the Blenheim, No. 207 Squadron where it replaced the Fairey Gordon in 1935 and worked mainly in the Sudan, No. 223 Squadron, briefly between February 1937 and June 1938, being based at Nairobi, Kenya, and No. 244 Squadron which was equipped with them from 1 November 1940 at Shaibah airfield when it was re-established from 'A' Flight, seeing combat action against the rebellious Iraqi Army in May 1941 and also in Persia (Iran) from August of the same year, and not withdrawing the final Vincent until as late as January 1943. The odd Vincent served with Nos. 5, 27, 31 and 47 Squadrons but not as part of their principal aircraft complement.

The Vildebeest variants all had the same wingspan, height, maximum ceiling, armament and bomb capacity as the Mark I. A variation was the Vildebeest II. This was the prototype equipped with the Jupiter XF engine. This variant featured a different tailplane and the ventral fin was omitted. Thirty of this mark were ordered in December 1933 and completed between 21 July and 22 December 1934. There was also the Vildebeest III, which had the 635hp (474kW) Bristol Pegasus IIM3 power plant, and was a three-seater variant (pilot, navigator and observer – experience having seemingly proven the need for more precise over-water orientation) of which 162 were built for the RAF in four batches between 4 February 1935 and 28 August 1936, but fifty-one of these became Vickers Vincent GP bombers, while 111 were completed as torpedo-bombers. She had an empty weight of 4,773lb (2,170kg) and a gross weight of 8,501lb (3,864kg). The maximum speed was 143mph (230km/h) and the climb rate and range were as the Mark I. The two-man Vildebeest IV first introduced the 825hp (615kW) Bristol Perseus VIII sleeve-valve, 9-cylinder radial engine, which was for the first time fitted in a NACA cowling.[4] This power plant drove a three-bladed propeller and increased speed to a maximum of 156mph (251 km/h) and the climb rate was 840 ft/min (4.3 metres per second). But yet again overheating made this power plant largely unsuitable for tropical deployment. Nonetheless some of the older Vildebeest were re-equipped with this engine. The overall length was 37ft 8in (11.481m) and weight came out at 4,724lb (2,142.77kg) empty and the gross weight was as the Mark III. The range was extended to 1,625 miles (2615.2km). As the main purpose of the aircraft was Far Eastern defence, only eighteen of this variant were finally produced in two batches between March and November 1937, as their service was strictly limited to UK-based conditions.

As a torpedo aircraft the first service test Vildebeest were operational from October 1932, when one joined No. 100 Squadron, based at RAF Donibristle, Scotland, and was later joined by ten of the second tranche, which eventually replaced the Horsley. The following year this squadron was re-deployed to Seletar, Singapore. One aircraft, K2929, a Mark II, fitted for target-towing, was destroyed when the engine failed and it crash-landed on 28 September 1937.[5] No. 100 Squadron was joined by No. 36 Squadron, similarly re-equipped and fitted with wooden two-bladed rather than metal three-bladed propellers. Two further squadrons were based at home airfields, one Vildebeest being assigned to No. 22, which had re-formed on 1 May 1934 at Dalgety Bay, Donibristle, Fife (later RNAS HMS *Merlin*) followed by a full re-equipping shortly afterward. The following year, after Mussolini's brutal invasion of Abyssinia, they were rushed out to Malta as part of Britain's reaction, but when strong reaction was replaced by the weak League of Nations sanctions (which totally failed to work), they returned home again. The Vildebeest were also assigned to No. 42 Squadron when it was reformed from 'B' Flight of 22 Squadron at Donibristle on 14 December 1936 and they later moved to Bircham Newton, Norfolk. No. 273 was also equipped with six Vildebeest (supplemented by four Fairey Seals) when it re-formed at China Bay, Ceylon, on 1 August 1939. Their duties were largely restricted to coastal patrols and towing drogues for anti-aircraft gunners and air-to-air gunnery target practice for which duty they were fitted with standard winches for drogues, and similar duties. They were replaced by Fairey Fulmar aircraft as late as March 1942 but these proved almost equally as futile a defence when they met the Mitsubishi Zeros from Admiral Chūichi Nagumo's five big aircraft carriers there a month later.[6] Meanwhile, No. 7 Squadron acted as a trials unit while No. 1430 Detatched Flight based at Hong Kong flew the type having K2818, K2924 and K6370 on its strength at Kai Tak in December 1941.Three of the first Vildebeests went to 'A' Flight, based at Gosport for torpedo-dropping trials, another was tested out for night operations and yet another as a general purpose bomber. One early batch and three second batch machines were utilized for experimental work.

The Vildebeest military serials included the ranges K2810 to K3822 for the Mark I, K2916 to K2945 for the Mark II, K4156 to K4155, K6369 to K6414 and K8078 to K8087 while the Vincent military serials included the ranges K4105 to K4188, K4656 to K4750 and K6326 to K6368.

Overseas orders

In June 1930 the original prototype was fitted with the 595hp (448kW) Hispano-Suiza 12-lbr, 12-cylinder water-cooled V-12 in-line engine, which gave her a quite different appearance, and she was equipped with a pair of Supermarine seaplane floats as the Type 216. Her details were listed at the time as an overall length of 40ft (12.192m), a height of 16ft 3ins (4.953m), a wing span of 49ft (14.935m), a wing area of 728sq ft (67.7 sq/m). She had a 'bare' weight of 5,100lb (2,313.32kg), with a gross weight of 9,100lb (4,127.69kg). Wing loading was 12.5lb sq ft (61.2kg) and apower loading of 15.3lb hp (6.95kg CV). Her performance figures were given in a contemporary edition of *Flight* magazine as follows:

Altitude ft (m)	Max mph (km/h)	Climb (minutes)
3,280 (1,000)	127.5 (205)	6.5
4,920 (1,500)	124.0 (200)	11.0
6,560 (2,000)	120.0 (193)	17.0
9,840 (3,000)	107.0 (172)	43.0

The initial rate of climb was 600 ft/min (3.05 m/sec), the absolute ceiling was 11,000ft (3,350m), while cruising speed at 6,560 ft (2,000m) was 106 mph (170km/h) and fuel consumption was 206 lb/hr (94 kg/hr). It was pointed out that the aircraft could configured either as a seaplane or a landplane and that a variety of engines (sic) could be fitted to suit customers' preferences.

In September 1931, the Vildebeest II venture, with British civilian registration G-ABGE, was flown from Woolston with floats and a dummy torpedo in place for a tour of the Baltic States in the hope of clinching some sales in that turbulent region.

Piloted by Captain Henri Charles Blard RAFRO, she visited Riga, Latvia, and was inspected by military officers, and also Estonia, but no sales resulted.

More successfully, the following year the Government of Spain was impressed enough with the Vildebeest to place an order to build some under licence by the recently established *Constructciones Aeronáuticas SA* (CASA), at Getafa, and two prototypes with interchangeable float or wheel undercarriages were constructed and conducted trials at Weybridge. Both were bought by Spain and a contract signed for twenty-five more, making a total of twenty-seven being delivered. These were the Type 245, utilized by both the Spanish Republican Air Force, the wheeled version and also by the Spanish Navy for coastal patrol work, with codes ranging from T-3 to T-27, and two of the latter were fitted with these floats as torpedo-bombers with the *Grupo 73*, being coded T-16 and T-17. Almost all these machines were destroyed or scrapped by 1945 but one wheeled and one float version survived into the post-war era. CASA had fitted the bulk of these aircraft with the same Hispano-Suiza HS 600 inline engine, which gave her a different profile to her British counterparts. Also she carried two Vickers machine-guns mounted in the engine cowling as well as the single Lewis gun aft. A few received alternate experimental power plants.

During the Spanish Civil War, which broke out between the Republicans and the Nationalists under General Franciso Franco in 1936, many of the Vildebeests stayed loyal to the Republic and many were destroyed, one being the first victim of Joaquin Garcia-Morato, a well-known Nationalist ace pilot.

In 1935 the Government of New Zealand authorized a large programme of coastal defence aircraft, and purchased twelve Mark III Vildebeest, of the three-seater Type 277. These were demonstrated to the New Zealand High Commissioner at Weybridge by Matt Summers on 31 January 1935 prior to the initial eight shipping out aboard the transport ships in batches, the first reaching Auckland on 20 April and being assembled at Hobsonville. These were joined by other batches which comprised the following Mark III Type 277 Vildebeest:

Transport	NZ Serial	Ultimate fate
Rangitata	NZ101	No. 2 Flight Training Squadron. Crashed on landing at Woodbourne 7 August 1940.
Rangitata	NZ102	Scrapped Ohakea 14 June 1944, Now restored at Wigram Museum.
Rangitata	NZ103	Badly damaged in force landing Canal Reserve, Christchurch 6 February 1940. Withdrawn.
Rangitata	NZ104	Crashed in Lake Ellesmere 9 June 1939 during bombing practice. Not repaired.
New Zealand Star	NZ105	Scrapped 4 June 1944, parts in storage RNZAF Museum Wigram.
New Zealand Star	NZ106	Crashed Ashburton 24 March 1938. Not rebuilt.
New Zealand Star	NZ107	Scrapped 4 June 1944.
Waipawa	NZ108	Force-landing in Woodbourne River 23 May 1940. Scrapped.

Two further aircraft arrived in 1937, NZ109, which became an instruction aircraft at Rongotai on 27 September 1940, and NZ110, which crashed at Wigram during a night flying exercise on 11 May 1939, burning out and being totally destroyed and all the crew, Pilot Officers William Dawson, Reginald McCrorie and LAC George West died of their injuries. In 1940 the last pair of the first assignment arrived, NZ111 which served with No. 2 FTS and was scrapped at Ohakea on 4 June 1944 and NZ112, which crashed in the sea while flying from Woodbourne with No. 2 FTS on 23 June 1941. Yet further replacement Mark III Type 267s followed them, being the former K4612 (NZ113), which was scrapped at Hobsonville on 27 August 1941; K4598 (NZ114) which stalled and crashed into the sea from 250 feet off Muriwai on 25 February 1942 during training exercises; K4952 (NZ115) and K4592 (NZ116) both of which collided and crashed into the sea during a training exercise on 17 September 1941.

These were unique in that they had folding wings and long-range drop tanks. A further four of the standard Type 267 torpedo-bomber variant were also acquired by the RNZAF, these being K6401 (NZ119) scrapped at Te Rapa 24 June 1943, K6397 (NZ120), scrapped 29 January 1942, K6396 (NZ132) scrapped at Ohakea on 10 March 1944 and K6395 (NZ133), scrapped Hobsonville 15 January 1942, along with a single Mark II converted to the same configuration, K4187 (NZ117), which stalled and crashed on a golf course near Nelson while serving with No. 2 (GR) Squadron on 9 April 1941, killing all crew members, Flight Lieutenant Lionel Squire, Corporal Ernest Johnson and AC1 Lindo Thomson. Five more Mark II, Type 267s were obtained in 1940, these being the former K4593 (NZ128) scrapped at Ohakea 28 April 1943, K4595 (NZ130) wrecked in storm at Nelson February 1944, K4589 (NZ131) scrapped at Ohakea 14 July 1944, K4597 (NZ134) scrapped at Ohakea 10 March 1944 and K2821, converted to a Mk III and scrapped on 27 August 1941 at Hobsonville. A further twelve of the Type 286, two-seater Vildebeest IVs also went to New Zealand. They were powered by the 825hp (615kW) Bristol Perseus, diverted from an eighteen-aircraft batch ordered by the RAF. These were also used for photo mapping and other associated governmental duties and were: K6410 (NZ121) damaged in a storm at Hobsonville 21 August 1942 and never repaired; K6413 (NZ122) which went on a mission in the Tasman Sea on anti-submarine patrol on 30 October 1942 with the loss of the entire crew, Flying Officers Charles Gunn, Stanley Bromley and Robert Dent; K6414 (NZ123), scrapped at Rongotai in May 1943; K8080 (NZ124), which crashed in a storm at Waipapakauri on 12 March 1942 and was never repaired; K8081 (NZ125) a former No. 42 Squadron machine, crashed on take-off from Waipapakauri on 12 February 1942 with loss of AC1 David Sutton and injury to Sergeant John Joseph Worden and AC2 K Curtis; K8083 (NZ126) scrapped at Te Rapa on 26 June 1944; K8086 (NZ127) scrapped at Rongotai 9 July 1943; K8079 (NZ129), K8078 (NZ136) and K8084 (NZ138) all three of which were destroyed in a fierce storm at Waipapakauri on 26 August 1942; K6409 (NZ137) scrapped at Rongotai 24 June 1943; and K8085 (NZ139), which was scrapped for spares at Hobsonville 15 January 1942 without seeing service. The Vildebeest subsequently served with eight Royal New Zealand Air Force units, Nos. 4, 5, 6, 7, 8, 22, 30 and 42 Squadrons.

To her aircrews the Vildebeest was known as 'The Pig', which gives some indication of her merits or otherwise.

War service

The Vildebeest was clearly obsolete long before the outbreak of the Second World War in September 1939, and was scheduled to be replaced by the Bristol Beaufort, but 101 of them were, incredibly, still in front-line service. While the two home-based squadrons briefly used them, No. 22 from Thorney Island, West Sussex and No. 42 off the East Coast, they were only suitable for anti-submarine patrolling at best. The Bristol Beaufort finally re-equipped these two units in February and April 1940 respectively, but those languishing in Singapore and other Far Eastern bases with Nos. 36, 100 and 273 Squadrons never ever received modern aircraft and, scandalously, were forced to go to war with the Japanese in December 1941 still flying their antiques. The results were predictable dreadful.

About eighty-four Vincents also continued serving in front-line units at this time. They were deployed on combat duty during the East African Campaign, and also operated coastal reconnaissance and anti-submarine patrols from Aden in the Red Sea. Vildebeest aircraft bombed Italian army columns near Djibouti with an escort of Gloster Gladiators. On the night of 12/13 June 1940 five Vincents from No. 5 Squadron, under Wing Commander John Francis Tifnel 'Ginger' Barratt DSO, DFC, raided Macaaca airfield at Assab, Eritrea, while later, when an Italian Savoia-Marchetti Sm81 made a forced landing 150 miles east of Aden, the same officer led three Vincents in a mission to take it as prize, in which he was eventually successful. During October the Vincents of this squadron flew 115 sorties against dissident tribesmen in Aden, emboldened by the Italian victory in British Somaliland, but the following month they were removed from the squadron inventory, their mission completed.

Internet claims that a Vincent had attacked the Italian submarine *Galileo Galilei* and forced her to surrender, are complete and utter nonsense, however, for she was in fact damaged by the Royal Navy armed trawler *Moonstone* twice on 18 and 19 June 1940 and surrendered to the British destroyer *Kandahar*, who towed her to port intact. No aircraft were involved.[7]

No. 8 Squadron was based in Aden with twelve Vincents and had been involved in the withdrawal from British Somaliland, after which they were involved in evicting the Italians from Eritrea and the Battle of Keren in 1941. No. 8 Squadron later returned to Aden, and operated Vincents up to April 1942. No. 244 continued to operate its Vincents up to November of 1942. No. 47 Squadron was based in the Sudan throughout the war and operated against Italian forces in East Africa.

Vincents from No 244 Squadron based at Sarjah also took part in helping the British Army squash the abortive Iraqi uprising by Rashid Ali supported by the Nazis, which took place in 1941. For a time they were besieged by the Iraq army at Habbaniyah where one was captured and reputedly flown by the rebels. Amazingly Vincents continued to serve with the RAF in this theatre in January 1943 and even after that date found employment in subsidiary duties for another year after that.

Between 1940 and 1941 twenty-seven further Vildebeest aircraft were transferred from surplus RAF stock to the Royal New Zealand Air Force. Sixty-two more were also acquired during this period. No provision was ever made for the RNZAF aircraft to carry torpedoes on combat duties. Their main duties in the early period of the war continued to be scouting and reconnaissance in the southern Pacific, looking for German armed merchant raiders and later they were based at Fiji in December 1941 as the Japanese swept over the region. They were also employed as pilot trainers. The same applied to the sixty-two Vincents also transferred to New Zealand.

Continuous reports, still repeated by modern 'experts' on the Internet, even today, claim that the Vildebeests attacked a Japanese cruiser off Kota Bharu on 8 December. This would be the light cruiser *Sendai*, which, with the destroyers *Ayanami*, *Isonami*, *Shikinami* and *Uranami*, was part of the escort for Lieutenant General Tomoyoki Yamashita's 25 Army. They only reported a bombing attack by Lockheed Hudson light bombers, however and the ships suffered no damage whatsoever. While acting as a light bomber aircraft, eleven Vildebeest, accompanied by three Fairey Albacores, attacked vital road bridges.

On 10 December two No. 36 Squadron Vildebeests, K4169 and K6402, were involved in a collision while preparing for a night take-off by six of their aircraft and three Lockheed Hudsons of No. 8 Squadron at 0200 from Seletar to attack Japanese ships reported off Beserah by jittery defending Indian troops. One of the aircraft was engaged in loading its bombs at the end of the duty runway and when taking off had not observed the second machine, which was then taking off itself. In the resulting inferno all their crews, including Airmen John Christie Miller, Sidney Walter Morris and Squadron Leader Graham Felix Witney of K4161, were killed except Flying Officer Kenneth Ernest Langley, who was very badly injured and died in hospital on the 15th. The remaining four Vildebeests duly attacked some small boats seen off the coast, without any apparent effect.

On 26 January 1942, the Japanese made a landing at Endau on the east coast of Malaya, only 150 miles from Singapore. Twelve Vildebeest aircraft, three from No. 36 and nine from No. 100 Squadron, each reportedly armed with 500lb (1,100kg) armour-piercing bombs, and led by Squadron Leader Ian Terence Byathan Rowland, were dispatched against the invasion fleet, which again included the *Sendai*, and were given an escort of six Brewster Buffalo fighters. The lumbering bombers had been ordered to carry out a dive-bombing attack on the ships but found the Japanese Nakajima Ki-27 'Nate' fighters (inevitably, but incongruously as they were entirely dissimilar in every way, identified as Mitsubishi Type O , or Zeros!) waiting for them. Five of the twelve Vildebeests were lost and no damage was inflicted on the Japanese. Later that same day a second strike was made by seven Vildebeest from No, 36 Squadron and seven from No. 100 Squadron, armed with 250kg bombs (550kg) along with three Fairy Albacores, the force commanded by Squadron Leader Richard Frederic Cyprian Markham, and the massacre was even greater. The fighter escorts, seven Hawker Hurricanes and four Brewster Buffaloes, were late taking off and missed the rendezvous and Japanese Army Nakajima Ki-27 fighters massacred six of the eight Vildebeests and two of the three Albacore were lost and both British Squadron Leaders were among those killed. Despite claims of numerous hits during both raids, of the two Japanese transports,

Kanbera Maru suffered only slight damage and just eight casualties among her crew, while *Kansai Maru* was even less damaged and both continued about their business.

One of the last raids the Vildebeest participated in during the defence of Malaya, took place on 23 January, when twelve machines, staging through Kluang, made a night bombing attack with 250lb (550kg) bombs on Japanese aircraft based at Kuantan airfield. The next night nine Vildebeests, six of No. 100 Squadron, made a similar attack on the vital Singapore to Segnant railway bridge at Labis, which they claimed to have destroyed while on the 25th nine Vildebeests from No. 36 Squadron and three from No. 36 Squadron struck Japanese positions at Batu Pahat.

The thirteen surviving Vildebeests were withdrawn to Kemajoran, Java, on the last day of January 1942. A month later, what remained of the combined Vildebeest aircraft, a total of nine along with a single Albacore, under the command of Squadron Leader John Trevor Wilkins, were based at Tjilkampek (Cikampek) western Java. There were no torpedoes for them to use against the Japanese landing forces, only bombs. On 28 February these flew three hundred miles to Madioen, in eastern Java, and were refuelled. Then eight Vildebeests and one Albacore, with an escort of fifteen Allied fighter aircraft, made a similarly futile bombing attack on a Japanese invasion force off Rembang on 28 February. They claimed to have sunk eight ships, but in truth only damaged two transports, *Johore Maru* and *Tokushima Maru*, while the light cruiser *Kinu* was slightly damaged by near-misses, shrapnel from which killed three crew members. In return the Vildebeest took yet further casualties including yet another Commanding Officer, Squadron Leader Wilkins, whose mount, K6377, was damaged by a Japanese fighter, crash-landed and was a write off.

Only two Vildebeests remained with No. 36 Squadron after this episode and they shifted bases first to Andir and then to Tjikembar and on to Tasikmalaja. From there three of them bombed Kalidjati on 4 March. The two remaining operational aircraft were ordered to try and reach Burma on 6 March, but both were lost over Sumatra.

Meanwhile, No. 273 Squadron based in Ceylon (now Sri Lanka) continued to operate Vildebeests until March 1942 when they were officially replaced by Fairey Fulmar fighters, although one or two were still actually airborne and puttering around when the Japanese carrier force raided the area a month later.

Incredibly, a new unit was formed with Vildebeest aircraft as late as February 1942. This was No. 6 Squadron, RNZAF, which was established at Milson and equipped with Vildebeest and Hind aircraft. The squadron survived in this form until October 1942 when it was disbanded. With the tardy arrival of Lend-Lease Consolidated Catalina PBY seaplanes, the unit was reformed once more at Fiji in May 1943 along with No. 5 Squadron RNZAF, which itself had been established in November 1941 with equally antique Vickers Vincent bombers and Short Singapore flying boats. The rest of the Vildebeest/Vincent contingent of the RNZAF continued to serve in subsidiary and training roles, about 50 per cent of them being gradually written off in accidents. These are the inevitable by-products of wartime training of course but using such obsolete equipment surely increased the already high risks. Typical of these unfortunate incidents was one recorded on 12 February 1942 by a Vildebeest of No. 7 Squadron,

(NZ125, the former RAF K8081 transferred in October 1940). She took off with a three-man crew from Waipapakauri but stalled when only some twenty feet from the ground, crashing and bursting into flames. The aircraft was a total write-off and unfortunately AC1 David Sutton was killed while Sergeant John Joseph Worden and AC2 K Curtis were both injured.

By the end of 1943 most of these New Zealand Vildebeests were retired and scrapped, whole batches were simply buried at the end of the war, a fact that, ironically, served to preserve a few for future generations.

Survivors

1. A composite Vildebeest/Vincent airframe is under restoration at the Royal New Zealand Air Force Museum, Wigram, near Christchurch. The bulk of the re-build is from a Mark II Vildebeest (NZ102) and there are also elements of Vildebeest NZ105 and Vincent NZ355 and NZ357 in the mix. NZ102 arrived at Auckland in March 1935 aboard the freighter *Rangitata* and was assembled at Hobsonville, joining the Bomber Reconnaissance Flight from 1937 onward. She transferred to No. 2 Flying Training School at Woodbourne then at the end of 1940 went to Whenuapai, finally being scrapped by the Production Engineering company at Marton. She was recovered here in 1972 by the Museum of Transport and Technology, and MOTAT exchanged her for de Havilland Mosquito wings in 1986.

2. A private venture by Don Subritzky at his farm in Dairy Flat, north of Auckland. As the RAF's K6357, this Vincent had served with No. 55 Squadron in Iraq between 1937 and 1939. It was one of several purchased by the New Zealand Government just before the war and was shipped to Auckland on the freighter *Gamaria* on 17 July 1939. She was re-assembled at No. 1 Aircraft Depot, Hobsonville, and joined a Territorial Squadron, becoming NZ311 and serving with eleven others of the type. The unit was renamed as Auckland (General Reconnaissance) Squadron on the outbreak of the Second World War and conducted maritime reconnaissance duties. Later she was transferred to Ohakea Air Gunners' and Observers' School and later went to Whenuapai and then in 1941 Nelson and Omaka with No. 2 (GR) Squadron. She ended her operational days as a target tug with No. 1 (Bomber) Operational Training Unit at Ohakea towing target drogues, being retired on 4 November 1944. Her remnants were buried at Marton, Manawatu, from which she was finally retrieved in 1970. Both the fuselage and wings survived this transition and the subsequent search by MOTAT for the Air Force Museum project components, and when they had had their fill she was purchased by the current owner but there is insufficient storage space to fully assembly her.

3. One of the Spanish Vildebeest airframes is thought to have survived.

Notes

Chapter 1

1. Pavel Beneš, Miroslav Hajn, Jaroslav Koch and Vaclav Malý.
2. Czechoslovakia herself was given no say in this carve up. Jan Masaryk, the Czech Ambassador to London, asked for a seat at the meeting to decide his nation's fate and was briskly dismissed. 'If you have sacrificed my nation to preserve the peace of the world, I will be the first to applaud you,' he told Prime Minister Neville Chamberlain and the preening Lord Halifax British Foreign Minister. 'But if not, gentlemen, God help your souls!' – Wheeler-Bennett, John W. 1948. *Munich: Prologue to Tragedy*, London: Macmillan.
3. A derivative of duralumin – an alloy first discovered by German physicist Alfred Wilm; patented by the *Duerener MetallWerke AG* plant in October 1909 and championed by Hugo Junkers for aircraft construction.
4. Vičko, Peter Boris and Vičko, Ryan Peter 2005. *The Soviet Union's Role in the Slovak National Uprising – The Talský Affair: Incompetent, Traitor or Pawn?*
5. Bilý, Miroslav and Vraný, Jiří 2008. *Avia B-534: Czechoslovak Fighter, 3rd and 4th Version (Model File)* , Prague: MBI.

Chapter 2

1. Sueter, Murray Fraser 1928. *Airmen or Noahs – Fair Play for our Airmen: the Great 'Neon' Myth Exposed*, London: Pitman & Sons.
2. Till, Geoffrey 1979. *Air Power and the Royal Navy 1914–1945; a Historical Survey*, London: Jane's.
3. Joubert de La Ferte, Philip 1960. *Birds and Fishes: the Story of Costal Command*, London: Hutchinsons.
4. Also known at that time as The Great West Aerodrome, and what is today London Heathrow.
5. A famous racing driver on the Brooklands Circuit and a Schneider Trophy contender, Staniland was to die in 1942 testing the Fairey Firefly.
6. Although float-equipped Sharks did serve with the Royal Canadian Navy until 1943/44 and had their floats replaced with wheels to provide training for flight deck handling parties. Five of these were embarked, one each aboard five Royal Navy escort carriers, *Patroller, Puncher, Ranee, Reaper* and *Thane*, at Esquimalt RCN base to provide such practice training during their voyage to the East Coast, whereupon they were unceremoniously dumped overboard, having ended their usefulness!
7. A more flattering explanation for the nickname was opined by famed Swordfish pilot Charles Lamb, this being that she was so-termed because she continued to be able to cope with more, and an ever-diverse, range of ordnance during her long career. See Lamb, Charles 1977. *To War in a Stringbag*, London: Cassell.
8. Among the FAA units based here were No. 788 Fleet Requirement Unit, a detachment equipped with Swordfish, Skua, Walrus and Fulmar-IIs, No. 796 Eastern Fleet TBR Pool, a detachment from Royal Navy Air Section, Port Reitz (HMS *Kipanga*) equipped with Swordfish, Albacore and Walrus aircraft, which operated between 22 June 1941 and 22 November 1943. Port Reitz itself, just north of Mombasa, was a major storage and distribution centre, and among the Swordfish-equipped units that passed through there were No. 796 Squadron, the Eastern Fleet Torpedo, Spotter and Reconnaissance Pool; No. 810 Squadron disembarked from the carrier *Illustrious* in May and August 1942; No. 814 Squadron disembarked from the carrier *Hermes* in October 1941; No. 824 Squadron disembarked from the carrier *Eagle* in April 1941; No. 827 Squadron disembarked from the carrier *Formidable* in April to May 1942 and No. 829 Squadron detached

from RNAS *Tanga* (HMS *Kilele*) in August 1942. Port Reitz is nowadays Kenya's Moi International Airport.

9. The squadron's Swordfish are credited with sinking a U-boat on 19 July by the Fleet Air Arm Museum, but absolutely no German or Italian submarine was sunk that day by any Allied action.

10. The squadron veterans, having passed through Machrihanish so many times, dubbed the base 'Clapham Junction'.

11. Among Slater's 'innovations' was insisting that his teams aboard the MAC-ships signed Ships' Articles in the traditional manner, thus sub-coordinating themselves to the vessel's Master, duly receiving the traditional one shilling (5p) per month and a bottle of beer per day! They wore the silver Merchant Navy lapel badges on their uniforms.

12. Today this is Glasgow Airport.

13. They did not find it, for, although British claims still persist in insisting that the Fairey Fulmars and Hawker Hurricanes destroyed thirty-six Japanese aircraft, the truth has been long known that total Japanese losses were seven aircraft against the British loss of twenty-five. See Smith, Peter Charles Horstead 1999. *Aichi D3A1/2 Val.* , Ramsbury: The Crowood Press.

14. Charles Lamb, the pilot of the last Swordfish to land aboard the carrier before she was hit, states she was the first British naval loss of World War II but this is untrue, the submarine *Oxley* had been sunk by the British submarine *Triton* in error off the coast of Norway on 10 September.

15. For the full account of this convoy see – Smith, Peter Charles Horstead 1994. *Arctic Victory: The Story of Convoy PQ18*, Stourbridge: Crécy Books.

16. Somerville, Admiral of the Fleet Sir James 1996. *The Somerville Papers*, edited by Michael Simpson, Aldershot: Scolar Press for Navy Records Society.

17. *Fido* was the American Mk.24 ASW Acoustic Homing Torpedo, produced by Western Electric and introduced in March 1943 which was a 680lb (308.44kg) torpedo of 19in 48.26 cm) diameter, 84in (213.36cm) in length with a 92lb 41.73kg) high-explosive (HE) warhead. The homing system comprised four piezoelectric hydrophones operating at 24kHz sending signals to a vacuum tube processing system with proportional steering. They could be dropped at heights from 200 to 300ft (60.96m to 91.44m) at a aircraft speed of 138mph (222 km/h). Once in the water they performed an immediate search circle around a 150ft (45.72m) diameter and a depth of 50ft (15.24m). Upon target detection the acoustic homer took over. They were made available to the Royal Navy and the Admiralty christened them *Oscar*. This was one of the first instances of their (rather unfortunate) usage by British aircraft. They were eventually credited with sinking six U-boats.

18. Due to a fire in the dockyard, this work was never completed and she was later to serve as the French carrier *Dixmude* operating Douglas SBD Dauntless dive-bombers against the Viet-Minh in French Indo-China in 1945–47.

19. *Campania* earned post-war fame as the floating Festival of Britain ship, touring British ports in 1951 before she was disposed of.

20. There are endless arguments about the cause of this accident and who was culpable, the American constructors or the British operators. At the time Churchill ordered it all to be hushed up and the dead were buried in mass graves, which naturally not only caused intense grief and hurt to the relatives, both then and since, but has fuelled the usual conspiracy theorists in both the UK and USA to ever greater speculation as the years go by without official explanation. This lack of transparency, seventy-three years since the tragic the event took place, is inexplicable.

21. Thomas, Andrew 1998. *Light Blue Stringbags: The Fairey Swordfish in RAF Service*, article in *Air Enthusiast*, Issue No. 78, November/December, Stamford: Key Publishing.

22. Group-Captain Thomas Quintus Horner to the author, see Smith, Peter Charles Horstead 2011. *Critical Combat: The Royal Navy's Mediterranean Campaign in 1940*, Barnsley: Pen & Sword Maritime.

23. The ancient *Argus* was being used as a training carrier.

24. In the event *Dunkerque* was eventually repaired and, like *Strasbourg*, managed to escape to join the Vichy Fleet at Toulon on 19 February 1942.

25. Commander John Bruce Murray to the Author on 23 May 1979. His full account of both attacks is contained in – Smith, Peter Charles Horstead 2011. *Critical Combat: The Royal Navy's Mediterranean Campaign in 1940,* Barnsley: Pen & Sword Maritime.

26. Historians continually claim the Royal Navy upper echelons were not air-minded at this period, yet they had six brand-new carriers building, more than any other nation and Pound and Cunningham, always belittled for their lack of air-mindedness, fought hard, and eventually got, command of the Fleet Air Arm from the indifferent control of the RAF, and were the driving forces behind this attack.

27. Cunningham of Hyndhope, Admiral of the Fleet Sir Andrew Browne 1951. *A Sailors Odyssey:* London: Hutchinsons.

28. See Schofield, Brian Betham, CB, CBE. 1973. *The Attack on Taranto,* London: Ian Allan, and Smithers, A.J. 1995. *Taranto 1940 – A Glorious Episode*, London: Leo Cooper.

29. Ciano, Count Galeazzo, 1947. *Ciano's Diary 1939–1943.* Edited by Malcolm Muggeridge, London: William Heinemann Ltd.

30. They had been operating in company with *Sheffield* for some time and had made many dummy attacks on her, so she should have been most familiar. She had two sloping funnels, the *Bismarck* had a single upright funnel with a cap; *Sheffield* had triple turrets, *Bismarck* dual; and there were numerous other quite outstanding differences, quite apart from their respective sizes. Nonetheless, as Captain Russell Grenfell observed, '…they went down expecting to see an enemy, and such is the power of suggestion that it was as an enemy that most of them saw her'. Grenfell, Captain Russell, 1953. *The Bismarck Episode*, London: Faber & Faber. In the event *Sheffield* held her fire and managed to avoid the torpedoes aimed at her. She was also able to report that many of the magnetic pistols fitted to the torpedoes had detonated prematurely on hitting the water. This enabled matters to be rectified for the second strike and contact pistols were substituted.

31. See Smith, Peter Charles Horstead 1995. *Eagle's War: The War Diary of an Aircraft Carrier,* Stoubridge: Crécy Books.

32. Cunningham of Hyndhope, Admiral of the Fleet Sir Andrew Browne, 1951. *A Sailors Odyssey,* London: Hutchinsons.

33. Eventual disposals were V4685, V4688 to No 815 NAS; V4689 to No. 789 NAS, to SAAF Wingfield, Cape Town, and eventually to the A&AEE at Boscombe Down for searchlight and radar experiments and then the Telecommunications Flying Unit (TFU) and later the Radar Research Flying Unit (RRFU), at RAF Defford, Worcestershire; V4692 to No. 810 NAS, HMS *Grebe*, RNAS Dekheila, and then crashed aboard the escort carrier *Hunter;* V4693 to No. 789 NAS at SAAF Wingfield, Cape Town, and was written off on 6 December 1944; V4694 to No. 810 NAS surviving several crashes at RNAS Machrihanish and two aboard the carrier *Argus* before being finally written off aboard the escort carrier *Vindex.*

Chapter 3

1. *Report on dive bombing,* RAE South Farnborough, dated October 1940 (AIR 14, 181/ IIH/241/3/406; Inst/3005/AAH/93, AIR 2/3176; *Notes on Dive Bombing and on the German Ju.88 Bombing Aircraft,* Air Ministry, dated February 1941 (AIR 14 181/IIH/241/3/406) and *Memo* dated 14 December 1940, AIR 14 181/IIH/241/3/406.

2. Many sources incorrectly cite the number as 802, counting the two prototypes as extra, but they were, in fact, *included* in, and *not* extra to, the original serial number batch of 100 machines, as listed above.

3. Brown, Captain Eric, with Green, William, and Swanborough, Gordon, (editors), 1987. *Wings of the Navy: Flying Allied Carrier Aircraft of World War Two,* Shrewsbury: Airlife Publishing Ltd.

4. As the Japanese army moved steadily down the western coast of Malaya, their frequent amphibious landings in the rear of Commonwealth forces caused confusion and despair among the defenders. All the major units of the Japanese Navy were off the eastern coast, but innumerable local Malaysian small craft were 'hidden' by their panic-stricken owners, found by the Japanese, and pressed into service as impromptu troop carriers. There being little or no British naval presence at Singapore, they operated with relative immunity, it being almost impossible to tell if they were friend or foe.

5. Shores, Christopher, Cull, Brian and Izawa, Yasuho, 1992. *Bloody Shambles: Vol. 1 & 2*, London: Grub Street.
6. Rated as torpedo boats but actually, at 1,290 tons, small destroyers.
7. The unit, part of the *1. Jagdgeswader 77*, later became the *6/JG.5* when it was re-designated in January 1942.
8. Somerville, Admiral of the Fleet Sir James, 1996. *The Somerville Papers*, edited by Michael Simpson, Aldershot: Scholar Press for Navy Records Society.
9. On 5 March 1942 Grand Admiral Erich Raeder broke the news to Adolf Hitler that the Japanese were planning to establish bases on Madagascar. On 27 March the *Kriegsmarine* requested the Japanese go-ahead with their operations, while also sending their own submarines and supply ships to the area. Japan had been planning since 18 December 1941, to launch their 'Divine Dragon' Operation No. 2, which involved using Type 'A' (*Kai 1*) midget submarines (*Sensuikan*), two of each being towed to the target area by long-range conventional submarines *I-10, I-16, I-18, I-20, I-27, I-28* and *I-30* from Penang, under Captain Ishizaki Noboru; in a similar attack to that conducted at Pearl Harbor on 7 December. Additionally the auxiliary cruisers and supply ships *Aikoku Maru* and *Hokoku Maru* were to be despatched.

Chapter 4

1. Hence CR – C for *Caccia* or Fighter and R for Rosatelli.
2. So-termed after the James Warren and Willoughby Monzoni bridge bracings, which were of equilateral triangular form, which carried both compression and tension most economically, the best-known example being the Manhattan Bridge in New York City. The same principle, and terminology, had been subsequently applied to biplane bracings with the alternating diagonal truss of the interplane struts.
3. These pilots adopted *nom de guerres* for their period of service to further the farce, famous Italian ace *Sergente Maresciallo* Guido Carestiato, for example, used the name 'Efisio Ciarotti'.
4. The Nationalist Government was backed by the Soviet Union, which also sent aircraft and 'volunteer' pilots, along with socialist and anarchist groups from various nations. Britain and France adopted the usual appeasement policies of 'Non-Intervention' and the Nyon Patrols, which totally failed to prevent arms getting through to both sides
5. Their sister unit, 159ª *Squadriglia*, flew the Breda 65 A80 in this period.
6. 168ª and 169ª *Squadriglia* did not fly the CR.32 in this period.
7. Ciano, Count Galeazzo, 1947. *Ciano's Diary 1939–1943*, London: William Heinemann.
8. The annexing of Austria into Germany.
9. Invention of Fenenc (Franz) Gebauer, an Austrian living in Hungary, which fired 500-round belts of 7.92 x 57mm *Mauser* cartridges via fixed twin-barrelled guns driven from the aircraft engine's crank-shaft.

Chapter 5

1. Despite assertions by self-proclaimed 'experts' on American websites there seems no evidence that the CR.42 ever served in the Spanish Civil War.
2. AS = *Africa Settentrionale* – North Africa – units equipped with sand filters for desert operations.
3. Famously, on 25 December 1940, a 72ª *Squadriglia* CR.42 dropped a canister over Hal Far airfield with a cartoon of Christmas greetings '...to the boys at Hal Far and Kalafrana'.
4. Smith, Peter Charles Horstead, 2006. *Skua! The Royal Navy's Dive-Bomber*, Barnsley: Pen & Sword Aviation.
5. Woodroofe, Thomas, 1947. *In Good Company*, London: Faber.
6. Smith, Peter Charles Horstead, 2012. *Pedestal: the Convoy that Saved Malta*, 8th edition, Manchester: Crécy Naval.
7. The 'official' Battle of Britain was, in fact, just about over by the time the Italians arrived, the accepted end termination date being 29 October 1940.
8. To make a good impression on their German allies the Fiats were re-painted in an exotic scheme of pale green and light blue, while their pilots were kitted out in special new and equally sartorially outstanding uniforms – neither kept out the cold!

9. Compounded by the fact that on this same day, back in Italy, the Royal Navy's Fleet Air Arm sank three Italian battleships in their 'secure' fleet base at Taranto!

10. See Cattaneo, Gianni, 1971. *The Fiat CR.42*: Windsor: Profile Publications; for a very Italian-orientated account of these operations see – Haining, Peter, 2005. *The Chianti Raiders: The Extraordinary Story of the Italian Air Force in the Battle of Britain*, London: Robson Books.

11. The Italians, themselves in equal measure fearful, envious and in awe of the Germans, had been warning the Belgians, with whom they had previously many close ties, about an impending German invasion ever since the previous November.

12. One other CR.42 had already been written off in March due to an accident.

13. A fourth CR.42 had to be abandoned *en route* by rail, at Ingelmunster, West Flanders. Thus, right up to the last moment possible Italy was supplying the enemy of her German partner with military aircraft.

14. Cull, Brian, Lander, Bruce and Weiss, Heinrich, 1999. *Twelve Days in May*, London: Grub Street.

15. Baudru, Rémi, 1998. *Le Fiat 42 Du Bretagne*, Paris: *Le Fana De L'Aviation*, Issue 338, January 1998.

16. LW= *LuftWaffe*

17. Beale, Nick, 2001. *Ghost Bombers: The Moonlight War of NSG9*, London: Classic Publications.

18. The British aircrew reported this plane had 'blown up' and that it fell in blazing pieces into the lake, but, in truth, Gressler was back flying operations again within weeks.

19. Peršen, Lovro, 2015. *Hunting Tito: A History of Nachschlachtgruppe 7* in World War II, London.

20. Both the Soviet Air Force and the United States Army Air Corps were more successful in bombing Szeged later in the war, while NATO bombed it in 2007!

21. Incorrectly identified as Polikarpov I-17s, of which only a few prototypes were ever built and which never entered service.

22. Punka, George, Kozlik, Victor and Sarhidai, Gyula, 1996. *Hungarian Eagles: The Hungarian Air Forces 1920–1945*, London: Hikoki Publications; Skuiski, Przemyslaw, 2006. *Fiat CR.42 Falco*, London: Mushroom Model Publications.

Chapter 6

1. Top speeds were – Fox – 195mph (361km/h), Gamecock – 154mph (249km/h) and Siskin 156mph (251km/h).

2. See, for example, an American magazine carried a story that 'Like the big guns of a battleship, all of which can be fired by one man, all six of the new fighters machine-guns may be fired by the pilot,' and similar – 'New Fighting Plane Carries Six Guns', *Popular Science Monthly*, June 1931 edition, New York, NY.

3. Their ground crew, which somehow kept the old machines flying, were Sergeants Max Quinton and Mort Kieley, LACs Jock Thom, Les Fitzpatrick, Ted Bainbridge and Ken Carrera and ACs Harry Saddler and Oswald Henry, Griffiths RAFVR.

4. Serial nos. K5273, K5286, K5299, K5316, K7793 and K7884.

5. The Italians records make no mention of this incident.

6. Allegedly a playful and disparaging pun on the English word 'cutlass'?

Chapter 7

1. RAF Mark Is were retro-fitted with the Fairey-Reed from March 1938 onward but soon afterward the Hawker Hurricane and Supermarine Spitfire began to arrive in the squadrons.

2. Brownings were in limited supply as they were allocated to the Hurricanes and Spitfires. Experiments were still being made well into the war, for example serial K8042 was placed under the control of the Controller of Research and Development (CRD) at Boscombe Down on 22 September 1941. An extra pair of -.303 (and .7mm) machine-guns were fitted under the top wing, to give a total of six, each having 425rpg. See Mason, Tim, 2010, *The Secret Years: Flight Testing at Boscombe Down, 1939–1945*. Manchester: Hikoki.

3. Named after Paul Kollsman, a German-born California *émigré* truck driver who became a multi-millionaire on the strength of it. See du Feu, A. N., 1968, *Evolution of Modern Altimeter*, article in *Flight International*, 26 December 1968 edition, London.

4. The Royal Navy finally wrestled control of the seagoing naval aircraft back from the Air Ministry after a twenty-year battle, but very late and when war came mixed crews were still commonplace, even at sea. The difference between the British fleet's aircraft, and those of Japan and the United States, where the sailors controlled all aspects of the aircraft they had to fight with, could not have been starker. Monoplanes had been requested, the Blackburn Skua for dive-bombing (with only a very limited fighter capability), and the Fairey Fulmar, a cumbersome two-seater developed from a bomber design under specification P.4/34. Neither was expected to stand up to modern shore-based types of fighter aircraft, but that is exactly what both did face when war came and both were found wanting as pure fighter machines.

5. The Dowty-Rotol group at Steverton, Gloucester, had been formed from the Rolls-Royce and Bristol propeller manufacturers and their variable-pitch propellers later served with the Spitfire, Hurricane and Defiant in the Battle of Britain.

6. Winton (Pratt), John, 1986, *Carrier Glorious: The Life and Death of an Aircraft Carrier*, London: Leo Cooper.

7. In the Mediterranean, on just one day, the Italians sent 126 bombers against the fleet, dropping 514 bombs and failed to score a single hit and this was repeated time and time again. See Smith, Peter Charles Horstead, 2011, *Critical Conflict: The Royal Navy's Mediterranean Campaign in 1940*. Barnsley: Pen & Sword Maritime.

8. Smith, Peter Charles Horstead, 1995, *Eagle's War: The War Diary of an Aircraft Carrier*. Stourbridge: Crécy Books.

9. This information all from Crick, Darren and Cowan, Brendan, *ADF-Serials, Australian & New Zealand Military Aircraft Serials & History – RAAF Gloster Gladiator,* November 2013. Integrity Technical Solutions.

10. This was because of foggy conditions in the area but it did not prevent the Fox aircraft taking off at 0420 for Jeneffe.

11. Louie, D. Y., 1998, *Chinese Air Force Gladiators in Action*, article in *Small Air Forces Observer, Vol 22, No. 4. December 1998*. Carmel, CA. Small Air Force Clearinghouse (SAFCG).

12. Stalin employed 810,000 troops, 1,500 tanks and 3,000 military aircraft in an attempt to crush Finland. By contrast Finnish fighter aircraft strength *peaked* at 166 aircraft, of which only 128 were operational fighters, on 15 March 1940.

13. American aircraft manufacturers used similar methods at this same time to by-pass USA neutrality laws when supplying the British, by pushing the aircraft across the Canadian border instead of flying them over as operational units. The German authorities, although sympathetic to the Finns, as reluctant allies of the Soviets, had already delayed the passage of Italian Fiat G.50 monoplane fighters destined for *LeLv 26*. As a consequence the promised G-50s did not finally arrive until March.

14. Keskinen, Kalevi and Stenman, Kari, 1998, *Finnish Air Force 1939–1945*. Carrolton. Squadron/ Signal Publications, also Luukkanen, Eino, and Salo, Mauno A. (Translator) 1992, *Fighter Over Finland: The Memoirs of a Fighter Pilot (Wings of War)*. New York: Time Life Education.

15. Kössler, Karl, *Die Deutschen Gladiatoreon*. Article in *Model Magazin*, July 1980 Issue.

16. Most of these never got into battle and survived the debacle and returned to RAF service, K7961, K7988, K7989, K7984, K7990, K8033 being returned to No. 107 MU in June and K7932 to No. 1413 (Met) Flight later the same month.

17. Carr, John, 2012, *On Spartan Wings: The Royal Hellenic Air Force in World War Two*. Barnsley: Pen & Sword Aviation.

18. They would have received the serials 27 to 30 inclusive.

19. They would have received the serials 57 to 60 inclusive.

20. Brūvelis, Edvīns, 2012, *Latvijas Aviācijas Vēsture 1919–1940, (Latvian Aviation History 1919–1940)*. Riga: Riga House.

21. Irbitis, Karlis, 1986, *Of Struggle and Flight: The History of Latvian Aviation*. Stittsville, Ont: Canada's Wings.

22. Shores, Christopher, with Foreman, John, Ehrengarde, Christian-Jacques, Weiss, Heinrich and Olsen, Bjørn, 1992, *Fledgling Eagles: Complete Account of Air Operations during the "Phoney War" and Norwegian Campaign*. London: Grub Street.

23. The Treaty of 1373 signed by King Edward III of England and Queen Eleanor of Portugal , and ratified at Windsor and confirmed at Aljubarrota in 1386, pledging 'perpetual friendship', established this.

24. These fears were very well-founded, both Germany and Great Britain had contingency plans to occupy these islands; Germany as an advance base for her Atlantic campaign and Britain as a substitute base in case Hitler and France seized Gibraltar. President Franklin Delano Roosevelt also had his eye on the Azores as an advanced American outpost should Germany conquer the UK, declaring on 14 August 1941, that the Azores, the Canary Islands and the Cape Verde Islands, were America's 'eastern frontier' in a speech made aboard the British battleship *Prince of Wales* during the 'Atlantic Charter' meeting with British Premier Winston Churchill.

25. Belcarz, Bartiomej and Peczkowski, Robert, 1996, *Gloster Gladiator, Monografie Lotnicze No. 24*. Gdańsk: Adam Jarski- A J Press.

26. Becker, Dave, 1992, *On Wings of Eagles: South African Military Aviation History*: Durban. Walker-Ramus.

27. Shoeman, Michael, 2002, *Springbok Fighter Victory: East Africa. Vol 1 1940–1941*. African Aviation Series No. 11. Nelspruit, RSA: Freeworld Publications CC.

28. Baker, Edgar Charles Richard, 1992, *Ace of Aces- M St. J Pattle: Top Scoring Allied Fighter Pilot of World War II*. Benoni, RSA: Ashanti Publishing.

29. NOHAB were a locomotive building company, at Trollhätten, north of Göteborg, who branched out into building Bristol Aero's Jupiter engines under licence in 1930.

30. 120 Republican EP-106 (Seversky P-35 export variants) had been ordered as the J9, but, in the event, only sixty were ever received the other half of this order being diverted by the US Government to the United States Army Air Corps.

31. F19 was a component of Major Hugo Beckhammar's Swedish Volunteer Unit, which also had a bomber squadron with four Hart (B4) aircraft, a transport squadron with two Junkers F.13 aircraft and a Raab-Kazenstein 26 (Sk.10) trainer as a liaison machine.

32. Keskinen, Kalevi, Stenman, Kari & Niska, Klaus, 1974, *Suomen Ilmavoimien Lentokoneet 1939–72 (Finnish Air Force Aircraft 1939–72)*. Helsinki: Tietoteos.

Chapter 8
1. Churchill, when Chancellor of the Exchequer, had, in June 1928, proposed to the Committee of Imperial Defence (CID) that the 1919 ruling that envisaged no major war for ten years, reasonable enough in 1919, should be self-perpetuating, which meant by the ambulatory nature of this decision the time to re-arm fully receded day-by-day into infinity. By the time it was finally rescinded in 1933, insufficient time was left to re-arm against the Axis powers who had been doing so for years. Many of Mr Churchill's problems when he re-entered office in the dark days of 1940, can thus seen to have been self-inflicted. Of course, with the politicians 'selective memory' this fact was conveniently overlooked at the time and has been glossed over ever since.

2. SSVAF member Mowbray Garden, quoted in Shores, Christopher and Cull, Brian, with Izawa, Yasuho, 1992, *Bloody Shambles. Volume One – The Drift to War to the Fall of Singapore*. London: Grub Street.

Chapter 9
1. The Hawker team was outstanding and included Leslie Appleton, Roy Chaplin, Stuart Davies, and Frederick Page among others.

2. The Air Ministry was responsible for all aspects of naval aircraft in Britain between the wars, unlike Japan and the United States navies who designed their own. Consequently, the Fleet Air Arm became very much a neglected and 'Cinderella' force as the RAF, naturally, concentrated on their own needs first. This malign legacy resulted in an inferiority that lasted well into World War II.

3. Fascist Italy had not yet set out to conquer Abyssinia, Hitler had not yet come to power in Germany, Japan was still, nominally, a friendly power and France, the most powerful continental nation, was going through a period of internal turmoil.

4. The four Fury fighters that were cancelled had four Hawker Audax light bombers ordered in their place.
5. Engert, Jane, 2006, *Tales from the Embassy: the Extraordinary World of C. Van H Engert*. Cirencester: Heritage Books.
6. Viera, Rui Aballe, 2011, *Taking the Tigers Pulse: Portuguese Military Missions in Spain, Between Vigilance and Co-Operation (1934–1939)*. Lisbon: Faculty of Social and Human Sciences, New University of Lisbon.
7. Shoeman, Michael, 2002, *Springbok Fighter Victory: East Africa, Vol 1 1940–1941*. Mpumallanga, RSA: Freeworld Publications CC.
8. Napier, Sid, 1998, *The Yugoslav Furies; Small Air Forces Observer, Vol. 22, No.4*. Carmel, CA: Small Air Force Clearinghouse (SAFCH).
9. The irony of aircraft built in Bristol and Weybridge being shipped thousands of miles to Iran to destroy each other cannot have been lost on some!
10. Stewart, Richard Anthony, 1988, *Sunrise at Abadan: the British and Soviet Invasion of Iran 1941*. Westport, Ct.: Praeger.
11. Babaie, Mehdi, 2005, *Tankhe Nirooy-e Havai-3 Iran (The History of the Iranian Air Force)*. Tehran: Novin Press.
12. Cooper, Tom and Bishop, Farra, 2006, *Iran-Iraq War in the Air: 1980–1988. Chapter 2 – The Shah's Eagles*. Atglen, PA: Shiffer Military History.

Chapter 10

1. The modifying *Pariser Verhandlungen* (Paris Negotiations) of May 1926, contained a concession that permitted the Germans to build aircraft '… conforming to the aeronautical performance of current types of fighter aircraft' which proved a big enough loophole for them to drive a whole Air Force through.
2. Later, as a Luftwaffe General, to command the *Fallschimjäger* (Paratroop) forces in World War II.
3. The IJN used the term 'Carrier Bomber' as an euphemism for dive-bomber to keep the expansion of this arm of their fleet as secret as possible.
4. Later re-designated as the Messerschmitt AG.
5. The Japanese were most helpful, supplying the German naval architect Wilhelm Hadeler, who would design the first German carrier, with more than 100 blueprints of the *Akagi*, plus some of the brand-new *Sōryū* then still under construction.
6. Griehl, Manfried, 2012, *Typenkompass Heinkel*. Stuttgart: Motorbuch GmbH.
7. Hotte, Christian, *Chinese He66*, article in *Small Aircraft Observer* (SAFO), Vol. 22, N.4/1996.
8. Louie, D Y, *He66 and Hs123A1 in Chinese Service*, article in *Small Aircraft Observer*, SAFO, Vl. 20, No.3 1996.
9. The German Naval Attaché in Tokyo, *Kapitän zur See* Joachim Lietzmann, reported to Berlin in October 1937 that he had been frequently quizzed on German armament shipments to China, to which he had informed the Japanese that, while orders pre-dating the conflict which were still outstanding had to be fulfilled, further shipments had been stopped '…for a fairly long time'. From November 1937 the Germans also supplied detailed lists after Admiral Wilhelm Canaris at the *Abwehr* (Military Intelligence) and the *Oberkommando der Wehrmacht* (OKW – Supreme Command of Armed Forces) had double-checked Japanese claims, supplying cargo details of no less than thirteen German ships cargoes being vetted. Krug, Hans-Joachim, Hirama, Yōichi, Sander-Nagashima, Berthold Johannes and Nestlé, Axel, *Reluctant Allies: German-Japanese Naval Relations in World War II*. Annapolis.MD. Naval Institute Press.
10. Berlab, Stefan, 2005, '…for China's Benefit.' The Evolution and Devolution of German Influence on Chinese Military Affairs, 1919–1938, Doctoral Dissertation. Brisbane: Queensland University of Technology, School of Humanities and Human Services.
11. *A History of Chinese Aviation: Encylopedia of Aircraft and Aviation in China until 1949*, 2008: Taipei, Taipei. AHS of ROC.
12. Including *World Air Forces – Historical Listings*.
13. Corum, James, 1997, *The Luftwaffe- Creating the Operational Air War 1918–1941*. Lawrence, Ks: Kansas University Press.

14. Some sources state the unit formed at Pärnu (Pärnu or Pernau) Idritsa.

15. A *3./ Staffel* was raised later, on 27 December 1943, but these used the Arado Ar.66. From February 1944 the Fokker CV-E began arriving to supplement both types. On 18 September 1944 the units strength was recorded as 17 He.50, 13 Ar.66C and 7 Fokker CV-E. By August the 2./ *Staffel* had wholly converted to the C V-E with only the *Stab* (2 He.50) and the 1./ *Staffel* (20 He.50) remaining with the Heinkel.

16. It has also been recorded that the official disbandment took place at Heiligenbeil, East Prussia. Four veteran Estonian pilots from this unit survived to attend a meeting at the Finnish Air Museum as guests of the Finnish Air Society in 2007, they being Hendrik Arro, Kaljo Alaküla, Valdo Raag and Feliks Prodo.

Chapter 11

1. Mewes was later to earn fame as the designer of the Fieseler Fi.156 *Storch* (Stork) liaison aircraft.

2. The He.59 was considered too large for this work and never served afloat again. The *Krischan* herself was shortly afterward re-named as the *Bernhard von Tschirschky*, and was later to be bombed and sunk at Hamburg in 1944.

3. Sternkiker, Edwin, 2010, *Doppeldecker und Strahlbomber über Ribnitz: die Walther Bachmann Aircraft 1939–45* (*Biplane and Jet Bombers over Ribnizi: Walther Bachmann Aircraft 1934–45*). Rostock: Redieck & Schade.

4. See Koos, Volker, 2003, *Ernst Heinkel Flugzeug Werke 1933–1945,* (*Typenbucher Deutsche Luftfahrt* series). Bonn: Heel Verlag GmbH; Koos, Volker, Ernst Heinkel, 2007, *Vom Doppeldecker zum Strahltrieb Werke.* Bielefeld: Delius Klasing Vlg GmbH; Roba, Jean-Louis, Ledet, Michel, Cony, Christophe and Neulen, Hans Werner, 2008, *Les hydravions allemands de la Deuxième Guerre mondiale:* Volume 1. Les Farges: Editions Lela Presse.

5. Kühn, Volkmar, 1978, *Der Seenotdienst der Deutschen Luftwaffe: Der dramatische Einsatz einer Handvoll Männer für Freund und Feind:* Stuttgart: Motorbuch Verlag.

6. Cowie, Captain John Stewart RN, 1948, *Mines, Minelayers and Minelaying.* Oxford: Oxford University Press and Turner, John Frayn, 1955, *Service most Silent: the Navy's Fight against Enemy Mines.* London: Harrap.

7. The German type was detonated by change of magnetism in the vertical field, which required the passage overhead of a ship built in the northern hemisphere, having its north magnetic pole downwards.

8. Roskill, Captain Stephen Wentworth, 1954, *The War at Sea, 1939–1945, Volume 1 – The Defensive.* London: Her Majesty's Stationery Office.

9. Hess, Carl, 1955, *The Air-Sea Rescue Service of the Luftwaffe in World War II.* German Monograph Series. Montgomery, Al: Air University, Maxwell-Gunter Air Force Base.

10. The failure rate for LT L5 aerial launchings by He.59 and He.115s during trials in 1939 was an incredible 49 per cent and these failure rates were probably higher under actual combat conditions.

11. Hexanite was an explosive that had been developed for the Kaiser's Navy before the Great War as an alternative, and more powerful, torpedo warhead than TNT.

12. The *3./106 Staffel* had converted from the He.59 to the He. 115 at Großenbode, Schleswig-Holstein, and transferred eleven He.59s across; likewise the *1./907 Staffel*, a mixed aircraft unit, which also passed over its He.59s; and the *3./906 Staffel* similarly passed on its He.59s while converting to the He. 115.

13. After the initial invasion operation had concluded, the *Kampfgeschwader z.b.V* 108 was disbanded and aircraft were re-assigned to their units. On 15 June the *Kampfguruppe z. b.V* was formed, which included the *1./Staffel* equipped with seaplanes.

14. It was estimated that approximately two hundred British and German pilots were rescued from the sea in the 1940 air fighting, the greater proportion of them (approximately 170) German. Throughout the whole war it was estimated that a total of 11,561 airmen were saved by the German *Seenot* flyers, 7,746 German and 3, 815 Allied owing their lives to them. See Dierich, Wolfgang, 1995, *Die Verbaende de Luftwaffe 1939–1945: Gliederungen und Kurzchroniken, eine Dokumentation.* Stuttgart: Motorbuch Verlag.

15. Article 3 stated that '… the belligerent who remains in possession of the field of battle shall take measures to search for the wounded.' Article 6 itemised the fact that, 'Mobile' ambulance formations should, '…be protected and respected by the belligerents,' while Article 17 stated that 'Vehicles, equipped for sanitary evacuation, travelling singly or in convoy, shall be treated as mobile sanitary formations…' See *Convention of Geneva of 27 July, 1929, for the Amelioration of the Condition of the Wounded and Sick of Armies in the Field*, contained in Bevans, Charles (editor), 1968, *Treaties and Other International Agreements, Vol. 2, Multilateral*. Washington DC: Library of Congress.

16. The He.59s carried a *FuG/V aU* (*FunkGeräte V* – wireless device Mk V) Receiver/Transmitter for aircraft which operated in the 3.0 to 10.0 MHz, 35–750 KHz range for aircraft-to-base communication.

17. The fact that *all* aircraft had to have radios; that to effect prompt and efficient rescue missions they had to be directed to the right areas with the minimum of delay by this means; that British convoys could quite clearly be seen by anyone with high-powered binoculars in the Dover Straits during the hours of daylight; and that the Germans had the *Freya* radar system emplaced at Cap Griz Nes which carefully tracked the ships by night and day; that the Luftwaffe from their bases in France had ample high-speed reconnaissance machines to fulfil such missions quite easily at little risk to themselves, all counted as nothing.

18. Such incidents were very far from isolated, see De Zayas, Alfred-Maurice M, 1979, *Die Wehrmacht-Untersohnungstelle*. Munich: Universitas/Langen Muller, published in English as *The Wehrmacht War Crimes Bureau, 1939–1945*. 1989: Lincoln, NE. University of Nebraska Press. If, as is frequently said, that it is always the victors who write the history of wars, then there are unbiased examples here a-plenty to demonstrate that indeed may be the case.

19. *Air-Sea Rescue Operations in Europe during World War II: Historical Perspectives on a Footnote in International Law*. 1979: Air Force Review.

20. One feels that more than *two* He.59s might have been required had it come it! Perhaps fortunately for tens of thousands of *Wehrmacht* troopers, their barges never did have to face the Royal Navy in the English Channel, or, had they got ashore, the mustard-gas that was being prepared for them there. That mustard gas *was* indeed to be used had the Germans managed to get ashore, see Shirer, William Lawrence 1962, *The Rise and Fall of the Third Reich: A History of Nazi Germany*. London: Secker & Warburg. Very soon *Seelöwe* was called off; the *Führer*, whose land-orientated head and heart was never in it, was already looking eastward.

21. For a fuller account of these diverse operations see – Thompson, Adam, 2013, *Küstenflieger: The Operational History of the German Coastal Air Service, 1935–1944*. Stroud: Fonthill Media.

22. López, Rafael Permuy, and O'Donnell, Cesar, 2010, *Seaplanes of the Condor Legion: The Story of AS./88 Squadron in the Spanish Civil War 1936–1939*. Atglen, Pen: Schiffer Publishing.

23. Excellent eyewitness statements of these attacks are contained in Thiele, Harold, 2004, *Luftwaffe Aerial Torpedo Aircraft and Operations in World War II*, Crowborough: Hikoki Publications.

Chapter 12
1. This was a licence-built Pratt & Whitney Hornet.
2. The *So I-17* package – *Sorte* (Type) I-17. An alternative armament package with an additional pair of *Fabrica Militar de Braço de Prata* (Braço de Prata Arms Factory, Lisbon – or FMP) machine-pistols with 100 rpg, was also trialled, but was not considered effective.
3. Kronprinz AG, located at Solingen-Ohling, had produced a flexible tail-wheel of small dimensions 11.41 in × (290mm) × 4.33 in (110mm). See – Sengfelder, Günther, *German Aircraft Landing Gear: A Detailed Study of German World War II Combat Aircraft*. 1993: Atglen, Pen. Schiffer Publishing Inc.
4. *L.Dv 169- Entwurf einer Beschreibung und Bedienungsvorshrift des Bombenabwurfgerätes Elvemag 5C 10/IX. Fl. No. 50 250; L Dv162* (Draft Description and Operating Instructions of Bombing Device Elvemag 5C 10/IX.
5. The original plan to fit her with a 610hp (454.87kW) Junkers Jumo 210 C, in-line engine had been abandoned.

6. Later used on the Messerschmitt Bf.109 and Focke-Wulf Fw.190 fighter and Dornier Do.217 and Heinkel He.177 bomber aircraft.

7. 260 and 265 to 267 inclusive; 631, 632 and 670; 788–797 inclusive; 818 to 865 inclusive; 936 to 979 inclusive; and AO (four digit *Werke Nos.*) built 140 in three batches – 2248 to 2358 inclusive; 2424 to 2436 inclusive; and 2729 to 2738 inclusive.

8. *Bundesarchiv Militärchiv* (BA/MA), Freiburg im Bresgau, RL 3/2617.

9. Originated by the *Optishe Anstalt Oigee* company of Berlin, this *Reflexvisier* (Reflector Sight) was developed into the standard Luftwaffe gun sight. See – *Hauptmann* Wolf Graf von Baudissen, *Generalstab, L.Dv.108 Entwurf einer Beschreibung und Bedienungsworchfrift fur das Reflexvisier REVI/C/12A. Der Recihminster der Lufthard und Oberbefhishaber der Luftwaffe.*

10. *Reichsluftfahrtministerium Technnisches Amt* ('C-amt') LC III 1a and *Flugzeugbestanende* (Aircraft Files) dated 1 May 1940.

11. *Henschel Jahresbericht* (Henschel Annual Report 1939).

12. Again reports on internet sites run by self-proclaimed 'experts', claiming that these tanks were fitted with 'igniters' appear unfounded. Examination of the manufacturers servicing manual for the Hs.123's *Zusatzbehälter* (Auxiliary Tank) reveals absolutely no mention of an Igniter (*Zünder*) whatsoever.

13. This unit had originated on 1 July 1938 as *Fliegergruppe 40.*

14. *Lehrgeschwader* – literally – Demonstration Wing – were mixed-group Wings whose *raison d'etre* was the testing of new aircraft/ordnance/tactics. In the case of the *LG. 2* the ground-attack mission was to be combat-tested in the *II Gruppe*. In practice these LG units went to war as mixed-unit combat wings and their versatility ensured they continued to be used thus for a considerable time.

15. According to the journalist Cajus Bekker, the ordnance delivered consisted of *Flambos* – incendiary bombs with impact fuses) – see Bekker, Cajus, *Angriffshöhe 4000 – Einkriegstagebuch der Deutschen.* 1968: Oldenburg. Verlag Gerhard Stalling, published in English as *The Luftwaffe War Diaries*, 1968: London. Macdonald Publishing.

16. de Zeng IV, Henry Lawrence and Stanley, Douglas G, *Dive Bomber & Ground Attack Units of the Luftwaffe 1933–1945, A Reference Source, Vol. 1.* 2009:Hersham. Classic/Ian Allan.

17. Neudoerffer relinquished his duties on 1 December having been shifted again in October, to perform a similar role with the *III./KG 4*, once the fighting in Poland was over. and on the same date Weiß formerly assumed control as *Kommandeur* until 15 October 1940, during which he received the *Ritterkreuze* and promotion to Major. *Hauptmann* Egon Thiem then took over until 26 May 1941.

18. Wawrzyński, Miroslalwl, *Kalendarium działań baterii plot.nr. 8 obronie Modlina we wrześniu* (*The Diary of A/A Battery No. 8 in Defence of Modlin in September 1939) Militaria I Fakkty 5.* 2001: Warsaw. Militaria I Fakkty; and Emmerling, Marius, *Luftwaffe nad Polską 1939, Cz. III Stukaflieger.* 2006: Gdynia. Wydawmoctwo Armagedon. I am grateful to Mr Mirek Wawrzuński Pruszków for making these records available to me with permission to use them here.

19. Brütting, Georg, *Das waren die Deutschen Stuka-Asse 1939–1945.* 1995: Stuttgart. Motorbuch Verlag; and *Die Wehrmachtberichte 1939–1945 Band 1, 1 September 1939 bis 31 Dezember 1941* (*The Wehrmacht Reports 1939–1945, Volume 1, 1 September 1939 to 31 December 1941)* , 1985: München. Deutscher Taschenbuch Verlag GmbH & Co. KG.

20. Obermaier, Ernst, *Die Ritterkreuzträger der Luftwaffe: Band II – Stuka- und Schlachtflieger 1939–1945.* 1976: Mainz. Verlag Dieter Hoffmann.

21. Both Löhr and Schalk went on to have successful careers with the Luftwaffe, the latter earning himself the *Ritterkreuz* flying Messerschmitt Bf.110's with *Zestörergeschwader 2* during the war.

22. *Auftrag Ost: 12 Stück Hs.123A mit Ersatzteilen, RM 2,017.600.*

23. Their original destination was to have been the No. 1 Aircraft Fabrication Factory at Henguyang, Hunan.

24. *Die Abwicklung des Auftrages Ost* (The handling of the Eastern Order) and *Die Grundausbildung einer Staffel Henschel Hs 123A in China* (The basic training of the Heinkel Hs.123A Squadron in China.

25. This section is principally based on articles by Rudolf Höfling, viz – *Le Henschel Hs 123A en Chine*, which appeared in the French *Air Magazine No. 23, Decembre/Janvier 2005*, and *Bombowiec nurkujący Henschel Hs 123 A-1 w Chinach*, which appeared in Polish magazine *Militaria I Fakty, wv 2/2005*. I am grateful for his permission to use them thus and for Miroslaw Wawrzyński for supplying them and their translation.

26. Fernández-Coppel, Jorge, *La Escuadrilla Azul: Los Pilots Españoles en la Luftwaffe* (*The Blue Squadron: Spanish pilots in the Luftwaffe*), 2006: Madrid. La Esfera de Los Libros S.L.; Fitzsimmons, Bernard, *Illustrated Encyclopedia of 20ᵗʰ Century Weapons and Warfare*, 1967: New York. Columbia House; Frank, Joseph, *The Axis Air Forces: Flying in Support of the Luftwaffe*, 2012: Santa Barbara, Cal. Praeger.

Chapter 13

1. The latter was converted, while building, into the world's largest aircraft-carrier in the aftermath of the Midway battle, but this proved a waste of resources as she was sunk by a combination of American submarine torpedoes and poor damage control, on her maiden voyage without ever launching any aircraft. She would have probably offered great resistance in her original battleship form.

2. This name was never used by the Japanese themselves but was an American post-war application which has since become 'established' in many quarters. It was thought to have originated with the US naval historian Samuel Eliot Morison. The Japanese termed them the Type 93 *Sanso Gyorai* (Oxygen Torpedo) a reference to their propulsion and they had a maximum range of 40km (approximately twenty-five miles), normal range of 20km (around twelve miles), a speed of 52 knots and carried a 1,100lb (550kg) warhead. They were totally incapable of being carried by any aircraft of that time, although on today's western Internet sites they are frequently cited as having been so!

3. Francillon, René Jaquet 1970, *Japanese Aircraft of the Pacific War*. London: Putnam.

4. This is the correct local date due to International Date Line.

5. *Orion* (ex-*Kumark*) was the first of the Armed Merchant Raiders to be converted for attacking isolated Allied merchant vessels at sea. She was known to the Germans as *Schiff-39* and to the Royal Navy ships hunting her as Raider 'A'. She sank six ships by direct action and others in minefields she laid and was never intercepted. She was finally sunk by Soviet action in the Baltic while evacuating civilians with heavy loss of life in 1945. The *Münsterland* later became a blockade-runner and attempted to reach Germany with a cargo of latex in 1944. She was shelled, driven ashore and abandoned off Cap Blanc Nez on 21 January 1944.

6. This serial belonged to a Fairey Battle bomber shot down over France in 1940.

7. The Japanese responded with Kamikaze attacks using Army Mitsubishi Ki-51 'Sonia' light bombers for suicide attacks against the British ships. The heavy cruiser *Sussex* was hit by one which disintegrated against her hull without doing any damage whatsoever – this is still incorrectly recorded at the Fleet Air Arm Museum, Yeovilton as an attack by a Aichi D3A 'Val' – and another Sonia which attacked the escort carrier *Ameer* was destroyed by her AA gunners, crashing harmlessly into the sea some 500 yards out. One minesweeper, the *Vestal*, was also hit, and so badly damaged she had to be sunk, while another, *Squirrel*, was sunk by mines.

Chapter 14

1. Chkalov was fated to be killed in December 1938 testing another of Polikarpov's designs, the I-180. Also killed testing this aircraft was test pilot Tomas Suzi, while Athansios G Proshakov had to bail out to avoid the same fate as the other two.

2. Léonard, Herbet, 2004, *Les chasseurs Polikarpov*. Rennes: Editions Larivière.

3. Invented by US Army Aviator and innovator, Colonel Virginius Evans Clark at McCook Field, Moraine, Ohio, in 1922.

4. Yefim, Gordon and Dexter, Keith, 1999, *Polikarpov Biplane Fighter Variants. Wings of Fame, Volume 17*. London: Aerospace Publishing; and Maslov, Mikhail A, 2005, *Polikarpov I-153, Wydawnictwo Militaria 222*. Warsaw: Wydawnictwo Militaria.

5. Demin, Anatolii, (translated by George M Mellinger), 2011, *Soviet Fighters in the Sky of China*: Moscow: *Aviatsiia I Kosmonavtika*, January 2011.

6. Boris Shpitalnyi and Semyon Vladinirov the guns designers.

7. The first I-190 prototype, which turned out to be the final Polikarpov fighter design, which first flew on 30 December 1939. This machine had an enclosed cockpit, utilized the 1,100hp (820kW) Tumanskii M-88V radial with an elongated cowling, and a propeller spinner. With this she attained a top speed of 279mph (450km/h) and an altitude of 40,682 ft (12.400m). She carried a powerful offensive armament of two ShVAK cannon and four ShKAS machine-guns, never went beyond the experimental stage, but the second prototype took the pressurised cabin and turbo-charger for her M-90 engine driving a ducted spinner, combination on from the I-153N-TKGK and finally terminated in the end of the series, the I-195 which was to have been further strengthened, but which, with the crash of the I-190 on 13 February 1941, and continually over-heating problems, was abandoned before completion.

8. Rychagov, an acknowledged ace with six victories, later was promoted and briefly commanded the VVS RKKA. Having seen examples of bad workmanship in his various combat positions, including the Winter War in Finland, and while in his cups, he criticised Soviet aircraft in front of Stalin, who commented, 'You really should not have said that!' He was summarily arrested as part of the still on-going purges, along with many other Spanish veterans, and he and his wife were brutally tortured by the NKVD before, on 28 October 1941, being executed. Dzoga, I M and Kuznetcov, Nikolai Ivanovich 1983, *The First Heroes of the Soviet Union*. Irkutsk.

9. Despite many claims on websites to the contrary, the Mitsubishi A5M ('Claude') was *not* involved in this incident.

10. Kondratyev, Vladimir P. 2002, *Khalkhin-Gol. Voyna v Vozdukhe*. Moscow: *Techika-Molodezhi* 'Aviation' Series.

11. Air Intelligence Division Weekly Summary, 4 December 1940. Contained in AIR22/73, National Archives, Kew, London.

12. A famous Finnish quote of the time was, 'So many, many Russians, where are we going to bury them all!'

13. Maslov, Mikhail A. 2010, *Poplikarpov I-15, I-16 and I-153 Aces (Aircraft of the Aces Series)*: Oxford. Osprey Publishing.

14. Soviet naval aviators uniquely, retained the Red Army-style rankings at this period.

Chapter 15

1. Gromov was to become one of the greatest of Soviet aviators, breaking several records in the 1930s, becoming a Hero of the Soviet Union and later founder of the Gromov Flight Research Institute at Zhukovsky, south-east of Moscow, with one of the longest runways in the world. Being the first to fly the U-2 might therefore, now be viewed as a good omen for her future.

2. Byushgens, Georgy Sergeevich, 1994, *Samoletostroenie v. SSSR (Aircraft Constructed in the USSR, 1917–1945, Vol, 1*. Moscow: TsAGI Publishing Department.

3. Shavrov, Vadim Borisovich, 1994, *Istoria Konstrukisii v Samoletov SSR (History of aircraft construction in the USSR)*. Moscow: Mashinostroene.

4. The Germans were working on the same lines and eventually produced the Henschel Hs.132, which was nearing completion when captured by the Red Army. Post-war another German development, the DFS-346, was also taken back to Russia where, as the Samolyot 346 in 1946 further testing continued. Post-war the British Gloster Meteor F.8 (*Prone*) and the American Lockheed EP-80 and Northrop XP-79 also sought similar solutions.

5. The concept never caught on for aircraft, although the American Beechcraft did produce the *Bonanza* in 1947 which featured it. It was ahead of its time for today modern Unmanned Combat Air Vehicles (UCAV), or 'Combat Drones' now use it, and its inverted alternative, with great success.

6. Izmaylov, Aleksander Aleksetvich (Editor), 1968, *Ayiatfiya I Kosmonavtika SSR (Aviation and Astronautics in the USSR)*. Moscow: Military Press.

7. Izmaylov, *op cit*.

8. *New York Times,* 14 July 2013 edition.
9. Parachutes *were* allocated from 1944 onward, but flying such low altitudes, their effectiveness was small, the women themselves stating that their best uses were for comfortable seats and in lieu of armour protection from ground fire!
10. More books have been written about this unit than any other WWII Soviet military regiment, and among the large number are – Myles, Bruce, 1990, *Night Witches: The Amazing Story of Russia's Women Pilots in World War II.* Chicago, IL: Academy Chicago Publishers; Noggle, Annie, 2002, *A Dance with Death: Soviet Airwomen in World War II.* College Station, Tx: Texas A & M University Press; Strebe, Amy Goodpaster, 2008, *Flying for Her Country: The American and Soviet Women Military Pilots of World War II.* Washington DC: Potomac Books; Pennington, Reina, 2002, *Wings Women and War – Soviet Airwomen in World War II Combat.* Lawrence, Ks: University of Kansas Press. There is even a film by Boris Yeltsin and D Matt Geller's Timedale Entertainment Company, written by Gregory Alan Howard, of which a trailer already exists.
11. At this period of history, the Germans utilized skilled women pilots like Hanna Reitsch and Melitta Schiller as test pilots; the British had many women pilots who worked as ferry pilots taking warplanes from the factory to the serving squadrons, the Americans had their WASPs, but none of these employed them as full combatants in fighting units, while the Japanese would never have entertained any such notions for their women.
12. Whiting, Richard R, 'Soviet Air-Ground Co-ordination 1941–1945', in Cooling, Benjamin Franklin (Editor), 1990, *Case Studies in the Development of Close Air Support* Washington DC: Office of Air Force History.
13. Izmaylov, *op cit.*
14. The Luftwaffe also created a Latvian air unit, which later became the *Luftwaffen-Legion Lattland* with volunteer Latvian pilots, but these flew the Arado Ar.66 and NOT Po-2.
15. Fengzhi, Nei, 1989, *Zhanchang: Jhangjun de Yaglan* (*Battlefields: The Cradle of Generals*). Beijing: People's Liberation Army Press.
16. That cease fire is still in place – there has never been an 'official' end to North Korea's unprovoked aggression.
17. Futrell, Robert Frank 1961, *The United States Air Force in Korea 1950–1953.* New York: Duell, Sloane & Pearce.
18. The North Koreans also used Yak-18 and Lavochkin La-11s for these missions, but both were monoplanes.
19. Anon, 'Navy finally gets an Ace', *Life*, issue dated 27 July 1953, pp.21–23.
20. Dimitrijević, Bojan, 2006, *Jugoslovensko Ratno Vasduhoplovstvo 1942–1992* (*Yugoslav Air Force 1942–1992.* Belgrade: *Uiverzitet u Beogradu* (Institute for Modern History, Belgrade).

Chapter 16
1. Mitchell, Gordon, 2006, *R. J. Mitchell: Schooldays to Spitfire.* London: Tempus Publishing.
2. Pusser, Royal Navy slang for Purser (the old name for the Supply or Logistics Officer aboard warships who purchased everything – it gradually became associated with the Navy itself. In the Royal Navy the battleship *Anson* called her Walrus 'The Pussers Spitfire' – a backhanded dig at Mitchell's two extreme designs!)
3. Nicholl, Commander George William Robert, OBE 1966, *The Supermarine Walrus.* London: Foulis.
4. The British survey sloop *Wellington* and the American minelayer/seaplane tender *Avocet*, had reportedly exchanged gunfire on this issue a few weeks earlier during their nations respective Solar Eclipse Expeditions, and relations were strained. See Anon. 1938, HMS *Wellington* 1935–1937. Auckland: Wilson & Horton.
5. One source claims that she was surprised by three Messerschmitt Bf.109 fighters and destroyed with her entire crew. This would indeed have been a surprise as she was working in the South Atlantic at this time many thousands of miles beyond the remotest range of any Bf.109 aircraft!
6. When the *Sydney* was much later sunk with all hands by the German disguised raider *Kormoran* some 150 miles south-west of Carnarvon, Western Australia on 19 November, this Walrus went down with her.

7. Repaired she later was transferred to the RAN and re-assembled at the QANTAS facility at Rose Bay, NSW, by No. 1 Transport and Movements Office, Sydney from 19 January 1944, serving with 8 CU from 7 May but was badly damaged when her undercarriage collapsed landing at 'Mercantile' – the code name for Momote Strip, Admiralty Islands, on 17 June and she was written off.

8. Operational Record Book, RAAF Detachment HMAS *Hobart*.

9. ORB RAAF Detachment HMAS *Hobart*.

10. L2222 was restored at RAAF Rathmines and joined No 9 Squadron until returning to RNZAF service on 10 June 1942 when she and W2707 were loaded aboard the freighter *Rimutaka*, at Garden Island Dockyard to exchange with A2-5 and A2-12 then serving aboard *Achilles* and *Leander*. By November she had become part of the Seaplane Training Flight at Hobsonville before being stored at Woodbourne in June 1945 and then returned to the British Pacific Fleet on 7 September. W2707 which was transferred with her, joined the Seaplane Training Flight of the RNZAF and was lost when she crashed in the upper Waitemata Harbour, Hobsonville, on 10 October 1944. While taking off her port float and wing tip were damaged by a large wave and as she settled back onto the water the port wing again submerged. The Walrus sank by the head off Chelsea Wharf seven fathoms down, both Flying Officer John Marshall and Flying Officer William Morrison being drowned, although LAC L.E. Whitefield RNZAF scrambled clear and survived.

11. HMAS *Australia*, M Alan Payne.

12. Ada later transferred to the light carrier *Venerable* and was at the liberation of Hong Kong where his new Walrus was involved in another rescue mission, that of a ditched FAA Avenger crew.

13. Green, William, *Warplanes of the Second World War, Volume 5.*

14. *Serials 1878–1987.*

15. Thetford, Owen and Gray, Peter, *Encyclopaedia of World Aircraft.* 1970 London: Putnam.

16. *Flight* magazine, 25 July 1946 issue.

17. Some sources state this event took place on 5 January 1948.

18. As a Walrus Mk II, HD874 would have had a wooden hull. The aircraft taken to Heard Island had a metal hull. It is suspected, but not proved, that the aircraft was re-hulled by QANTAS with the spare hull from A2-20 (qv), which Qantas was reported as holding as a spare hull in 1946. Other hulls that might have been available included those from A2-1 and A2-5, both of which had been converted to components in 1945.

Chapter 17

1. In 1942 Mark II Hurricanes were shipped to Russia in convoys and the Royal Navy was forced to protect them with Mark I Sea Hurricanes of lower performance – such was the state of Britain's shambolic defences even at this stage of the war.

2. This unique achievement is almost unknown in Great Britain today, but pre-dated Charles Lindberg's much-hyped solo crossing by almost eight years.

3. Wildebeest is Dutch for 'Wild Cattle', (also known as Gnu), a Boer name who also applied the term Vildebeest. As it was Vickers policy at the time to name their aircraft with letters beginning with 'V', the Afrikaans spelling was adopted after consultation with Sir Pierre Van Ryneveld, a Vickers consultant from South Africa, which was then part of the British Empire, although it was often misspelt in contemporary documents as Vildebeeste or Vildebeast.

4. NACA was the National Advisory Committee for Aeronautics, a US Federal Agency concerned with improving all aspects of aviation development. The streamline cowling significantly enhanced engine performance from 1927 onward and was widely adopted world-wide.

5. White, Arthur, 1994, *Hornet's Nest: A History of 100 Squadron 1917–1994*, Square One Publications.

6. Despite the fact that the Japanese and the Americans reported them as 'Spitfires' at the time *and* for many decades afterward!

7. She was later commissioned by the British as HMS *X-2* , later becoming HMS *P-711.*

Index